Luxury Home Plans

MW00782348

GARLINGHOUSE

Library of Congress No.: 98-75667/ISBN: 0-938708-85-6
Covers & Interior Layouts by Debra Novitch

— Publisher: James D. McNair III —
Editorial Staff: Debra Cochran, Sue Barile

Submit all Canadian plan orders to:
The Garlinghouse Company
60 Baffin Place, Unit #5
Waterloo, Ontario N2V 1Z7

Canadians Order only: 1-800-561-4169
Fax#: 1-800-719-3291
Customer Service#: 1-519-746-4169

Distinguished Styling

A home designed for today's lifestyle. Formal areas are located to either side of the foyer. A decor ceiling accents the elegant dining room. Bay windows allow for natural illumination and further enhance the living and dining rooms. An open layout between the kitchen and the breakfast area provides an open, airy atmosphere to this spacious family living area. Amenities abound in the kitchen. A center work island/snack bar, a walk-in pantry and ample storage and workspace have been included. The family room includes a cozy fireplace and flows easily from the breakfast room. The grand master suite is crowned by a vaulted ceiling and includes a compartmented, luxurious bath. No materials list is available for this plan. The photographed home may have been modified to suit individual tastes.

PLAN NO. 24566

Total living area	2,641 sq. ft
First floor	1,377 sq. ft.
Second floor	1,264 sq. ft.
Basement	1,316 sq. ft.
Garage	673 sq. ft.
Bedrooms	three
Bathrooms	2 full, 1 half
Foundation	basement, slab or crawl space

Photography by Susan Gilmore

Design by The Garlinghouse Company

PRICE CODE E

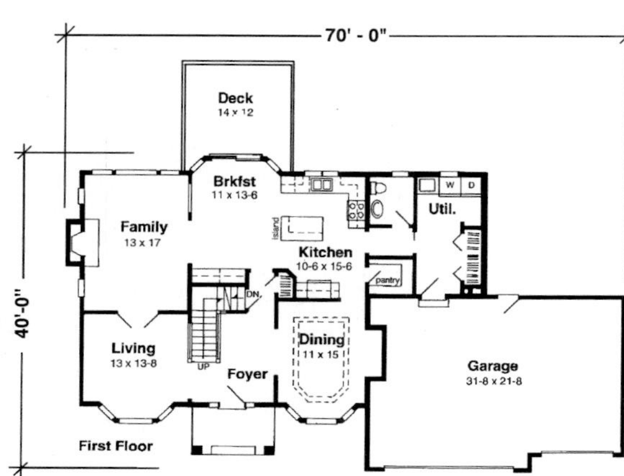
70' - 0"
40'-0"
Deck
14 x 12
Brkfst
11 x 13-6
Family
13 x 17
Util.
Kitchen
10-6 x 15-6
Living
13 x 13-8
Dining
11 x 15
Foyer
Garage
31-8 x 21-8
First Floor

No. 24566

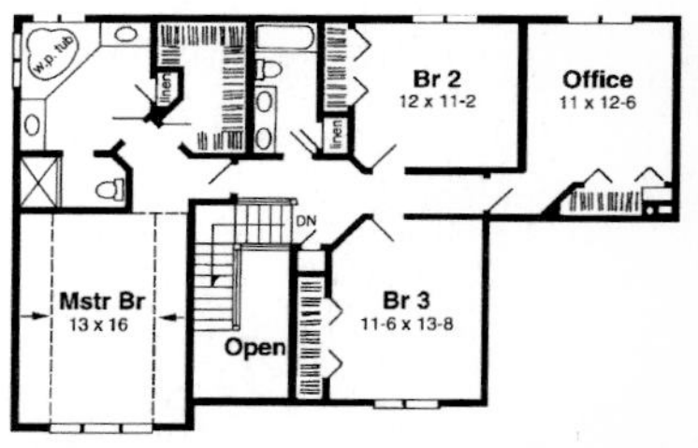
Br 2
12 x 11-2
Office
11 x 12-6
Mstr Br
13 x 16
Br 3
11-6 x 13-8
Open
Second Floor

CLASSIC EUROPEAN STYLE

PLAN NO. 97716

Total living area	4,589 sq. ft
First floor	3,392 sq. ft.
Second floor	1,197 sq. ft.
Basement	3,392 sq. ft.
Bedrooms	four
Bathrooms	3 full, 2 half
Foundation	basement

Photography by Ron & Donna Kolb — Exposures Unlimited

Tim Burks — Builder

Design by Studer Residential Design

PRICE CODE F

The cozy hearth room promotes intimate family gatherings.

The gracious exterior of this exciting classic European style home is accentuated by dual boxed windows, dramatically curved stairs and a glassed entry decorated with tall columns. A grand foyer greets guests as they arrive, showcasing the exquisite dining room, and Great room. Colonial columns are repeated at the entry of the Great room and a magnificent window treatment, including French doors introduces the expansive terrace. The master bedroom suite showcases a tray ceiling and fireplace. The double-sided fireplace serves the bedroom and dressing area creating a majestic setting for the whirlpool tub. Completing the grandness of this room is a discreetly placed oversized shower and his-n-her vanities. Encouraging family interaction this creatively arranged kitchen, breakfast room and angled French doors provides access to the terrace and allows light to flow through the open space. The cozy hearth room with fireplace and furniture alcove promotes intimate family gatherings. Split-stairs lead to a second floor gallery/balcony and three spacious bedrooms. No materials list is available for this plan. The photographed home may have been modified to suit individual tastes.

The library is reminisent of an era of classic workmanship illustrated with crown molding, built-in shelves and cabinets.

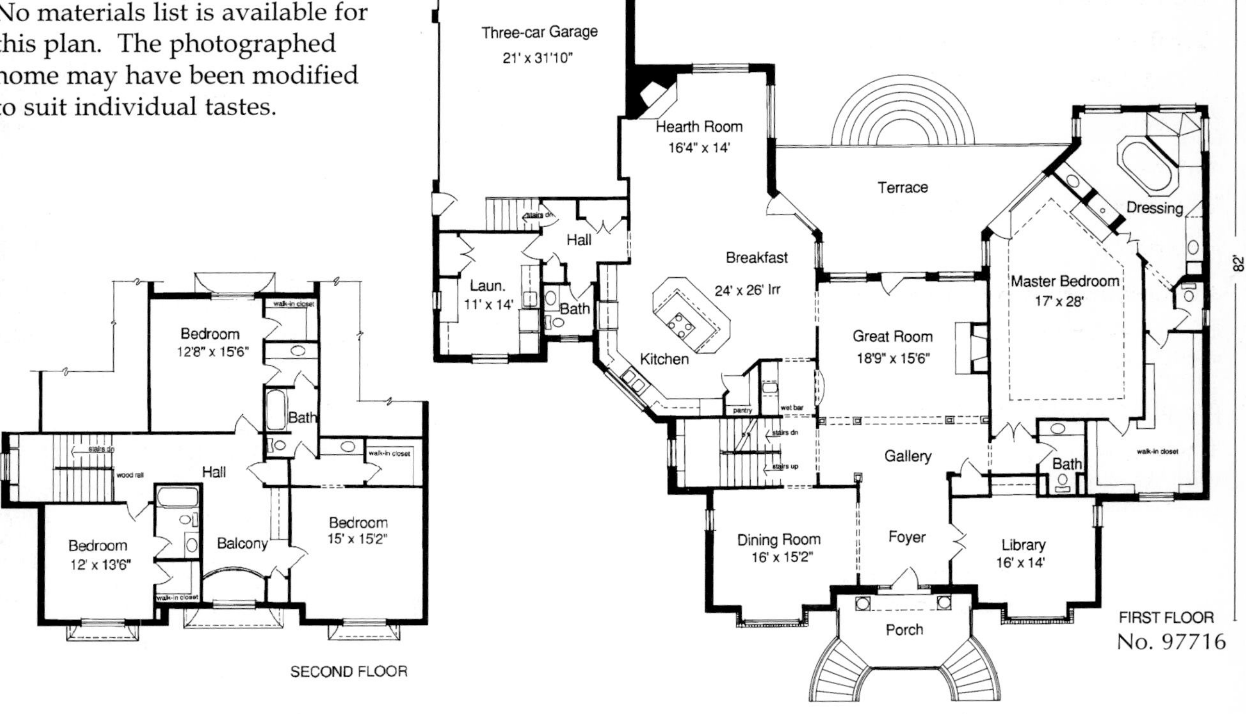

Three-car Garage
21' x 31'10"
Hearth Room
16'4" x 14'
Terrace
Dressing
Hall
Breakfast
24' x 26' Irr
Laun.
11' x 14'
Bath
Kitchen
Great Room
18'9" x 15'6"
Master Bedroom
17' x 28'
Gallery
Bath
walk-in closet
Dining Room
16' x 15'2"
Foyer
Library
16' x 14'
Porch
82'
87'
FIRST FLOOR
Bedroom
12'8" x 15'6"
Bath
Hall
Bedroom
12' x 13'6"
Balcony
Bedroom
15' x 15'2"
SECOND FLOOR

No. 97716

Your Master Bath will feel like a private spa with high ceiling, dual vanity and Roman tub.

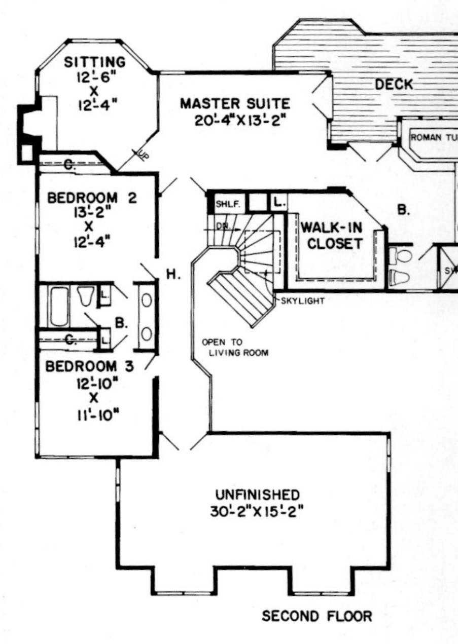
SITTING
12'-6" X 12'-4"
MASTER SUITE
20'-4"X13'-2"
DECK
ROMAN TUB
BEDROOM 2
13'-2" X 12'-4"
SHLF.
L.
WALK-IN CLOSET
B.
H.
B.
SKYLIGHT
OPEN TO LIVING ROOM
BEDROOM 3
12'-10" X 11'-10"
UNFINISHED
30'-2"X15'-2"
SECOND FLOOR

PATIOS FOR INDOOR/OUTDOOR LIVING

With a special television room plus a family room and an upstairs sitting room, there's plenty of opportunity for everyone in the family to enjoy personal activities and pursuits. The well-designed kitchen adjoins the formal dining room and also has its own dining nook with lots of windows for sunny family breakfasts and lunches. Both the living room and family room open onto patios for indoor/outdoor entertaining. The second floor sitting room, complete with a fireplace and warm hearth, adjoins the spacious master suite with its six-piece bath complete with Roman tub and oversized, walk-in closet. Two smaller bedrooms flank a walk-through bath to complete the second floor of this roomy, family home. The photographed home may have been modified to suit individual tastes. Rear elevation shown.

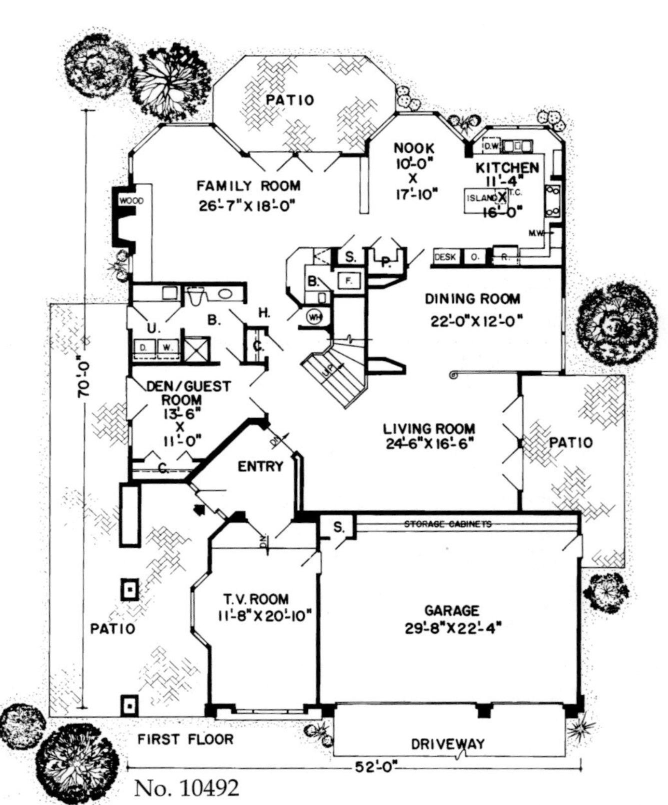
PATIO
NOOK
10'-0" X 17'-10"
KITCHEN
11'-4" X 16'-0"
ISLAND
FAMILY ROOM
26'-7"X18'-0"
WOOD
DESK
DINING ROOM
22'-0"X12'-0"
U.
B.
H.
DEN/GUEST ROOM
13'-6" X 11'-0"
LIVING ROOM
24'-6"X16'-6"
PATIO
ENTRY
70'-0"
S.
STORAGE CABINETS
T.V. ROOM
11'-8"X20'-10"
GARAGE
29'-8"X22'-4"
PATIO
FIRST FLOOR
DRIVEWAY
52'-0"

No. 10492

PLAN NO. 10492

Total living area	4,441 sq. ft
First floor	2,409 sq. ft.
Second floor	2,032 sq. ft.
Garage	690 sq. ft.
Bedrooms	four
Bathrooms	3 full
Foundation	slab

Design by The Garlinghouse Company
Photography by John Ehrenclou

PRICE CODE F

The Dining Nook provides a bright and relaxing area for family meals or a quiet cup of coffee.

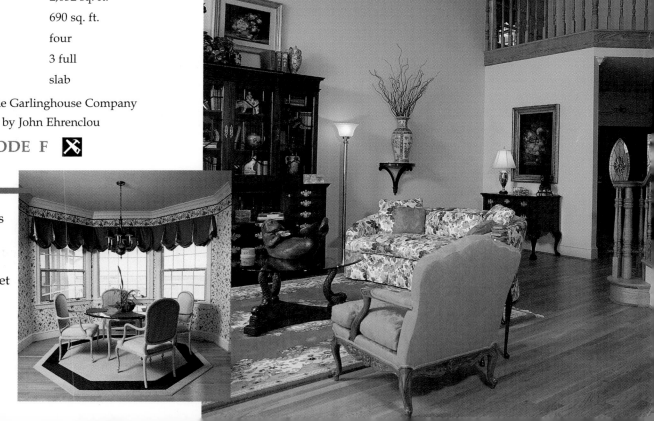

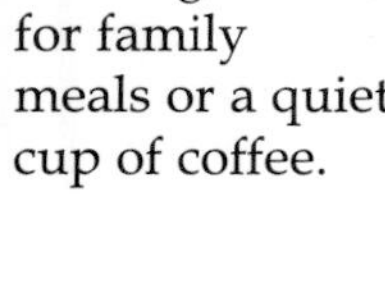

Multiple gables, a box window and easy maintenance combine to create a dramatic appearance to the two-story European classic home. Excitement abounds in the Great room beginning with a wall of windows across the rear, a sloped ceiling, and an entertainment center nestled in the corner set to one side of the columned fireplace. The kitchen offers an island with a sink that looks directly through French doors onto the patio and an oversized breakfast room. The dining room ceiling has a raised center section with molding and a furniture alcove is added for extra roominess around the table. The luxury and convenience of the first floor master bedroom suite is highlighted by his-n-her vanities, a shower and whirlpool tub. The second floor provides a private retreat for a guest suite or for a family with teenagers. A bonus room over the garage offers the option of a fourth bedroom. A balcony provides a view of the Great room and foyer. No materials list is available for this plan. The photographed home may have been modified to suit individual tastes.

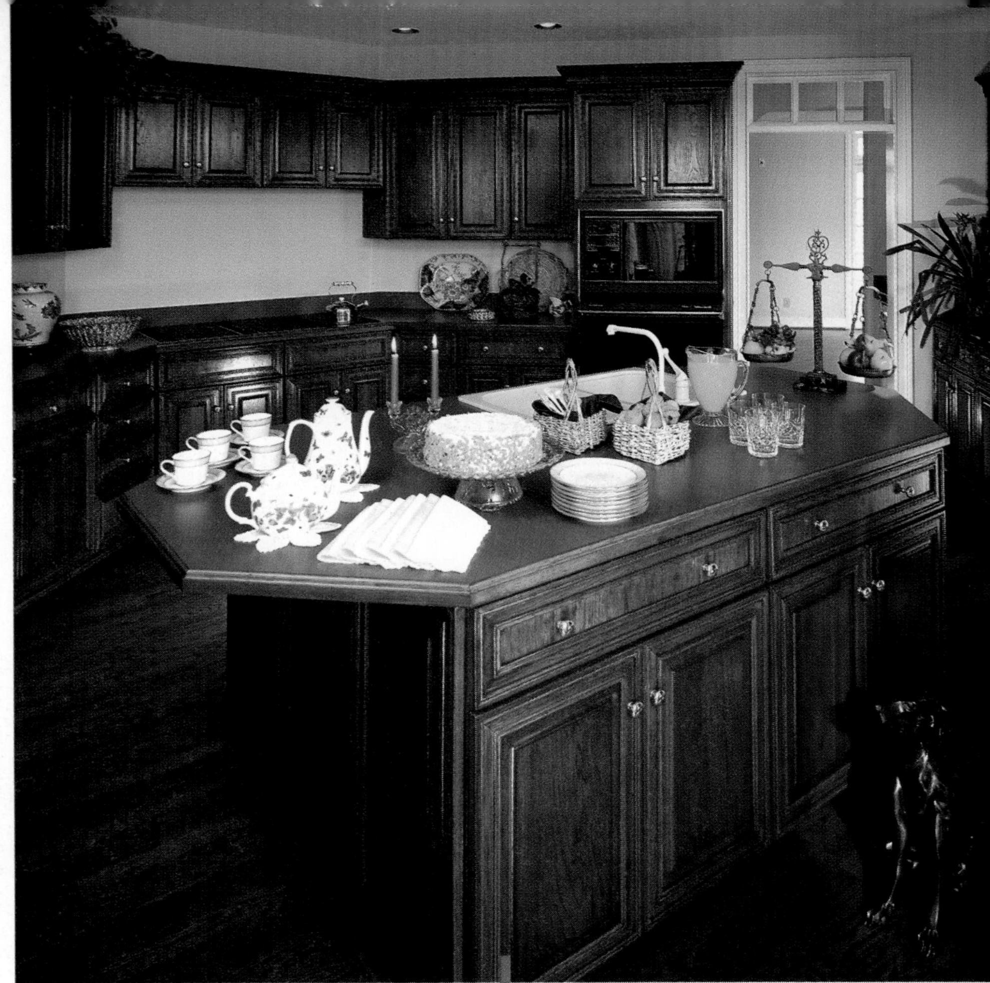

The kitchen expands into the oversized Breakfast room building a feeling of spaciousness.

An entertainment center and a spectacular fireplace are only a few of the luxuries this home provides.

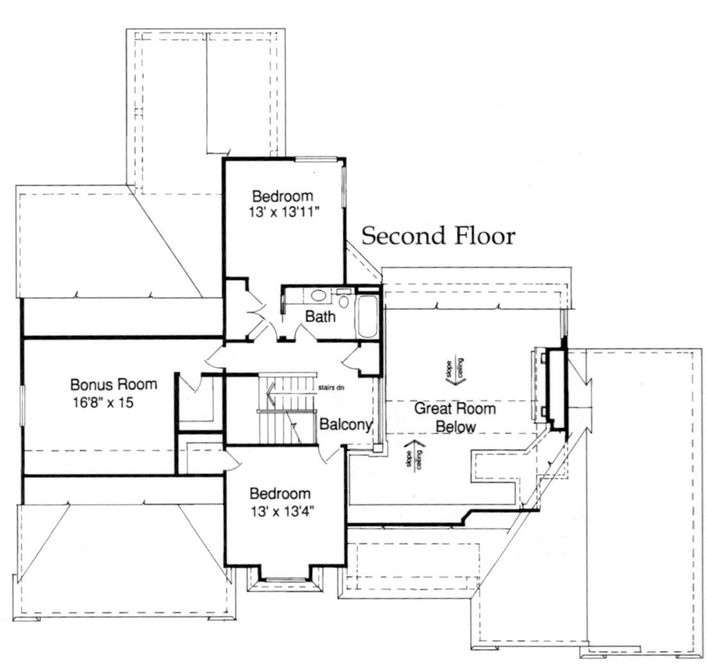
Second Floor
Bedroom
13' x 13'11"
Bath
Bonus Room
16'8" x 15
stairs dn
Balcony
Great Room
Below
slope ceiling
slope ceiling
Bedroom
13' x 13'4"

Two-Story European Classic

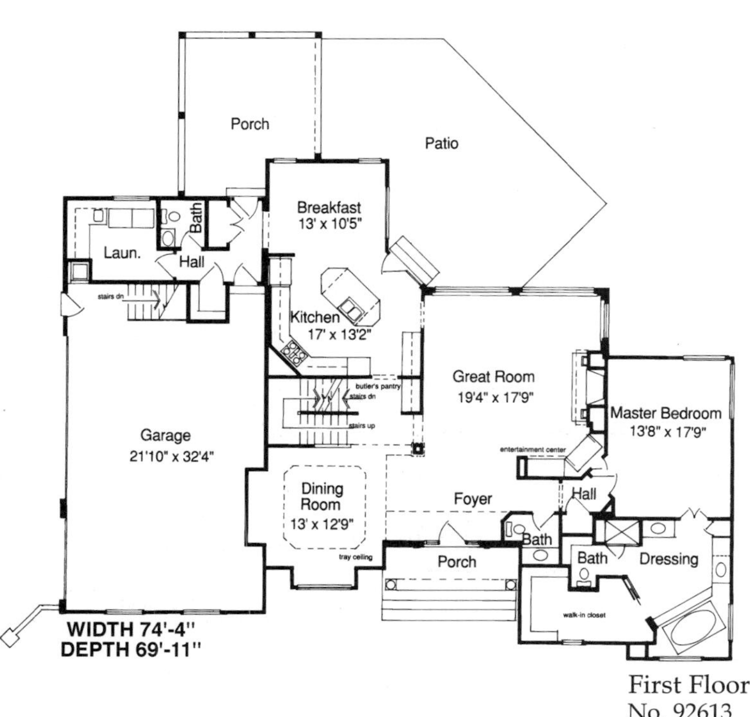

Porch
Patio
Breakfast
13' x 10'5"
Bath
Laun.
Hall
stairs dn
Kitchen
17' x 13'2"
butler's pantry
stairs dn
stairs up
Great Room
19'4" x 17'9"
Master Bedroom
13'8" x 17'9"
entertainment center
Garage
21'10" x 32'4"
Dining
Room
13' x 12'9"
tray ceiling
Foyer
Hall
Bath
Bath
Dressing
Porch
walk-in closet
WIDTH 74'-4"
DEPTH 69'-11"

First Floor
No. 92613

PLAN NO. 92613

Total living area	2,846 sq. ft
First floor	2,192 sq. ft.
Second floor	654 sq. ft.
Bonus	325 sq. ft.
Basement	1,922 sq. ft.
Garage	706 sq. ft.
Bedrooms	three
Bedrooms	2 full, 2 half
Foundation	basement

Photography by Ron & Donna Kolb — Exposures Unlimited

Design by Studer Residential Design, Inc.

PRICE CODE E

Visions of Luxury

by Debra Cochran

Home, domicile, dwelling place, abode, residence. Whatever words you use to describe it, a house is one of the biggest decisions that you will make in your life. As a successful, person you want a home that portrays you, your personality, and your family style. Your home will epitomize the status you have attained. It has been considered by many as a way of measuring your success. You're not only "moving up" in your type of home, you are moving on... to "Luxury."

Maybe, you can picture exactly what you would like in your mind's eye. It may be the interior that you think of when you are dreaming of a luxurious home. You might imagine grand, two-story foyers graced by cascading stairways, elegant formal areas and magnificent private living spaces. Perhaps after a stressful day the thought of a master suite with a spectacular private bath, sitting area, volume ceiling treatments and embers glowing in the romantic fireplace comes to mind. Or as an accomplished chef, dreams of that perfect gourmet kitchen equipped with work islands, expansive counter space and state of the art appliances are the visions that go running through your mind.

But why buy a stock blueprint book when looking for homes in this range? Why not go straight to an architect? Most people either have definite ideas of what they are looking for in a home or don't have any idea where to start. You may have more means to invest than ever before in a home. Yet, you want to plan and budget intelligently. You have just found a perfect place to start. Stock blueprints save time and money. You may find the perfect home, or it would be, with a few modifications. That old adage, "Time is money" always proves true. Just think of the time that is saved by starting with a home plan and an idea, instead of just with an idea.

Within the pages of this book you will find a wide range of homes in all sizes and styles. These are opulent, palatial homes that live sumptuously. Whether you are thumbing through to "just get ideas", looking for specific features or interested in decorating techniques, you have made an important first step. Posh to magnificent showplace, stately elegance to the dramatic, let's take a look at what makes a luxurious home. Perhaps you are interested in a traditional, a classical or a European home. Perhaps spaciousness is what gives you a luxurious feeling. Each member of the family having their own private living space; this is what you think of when you are visualizing a luxurious home. However, whatever style or size you decide on, you will want a balance between the formal and informal living spaces. The importance of each living space should not be minimized. Your dinner parties will be spectacular with an air of sophistication in your tastefully elegant dining room. Yet, the indulgence of your master suite should pamper you with complete relaxation and become your haven away from the stresses of everyday. So the extravagant crystal chandelier in the formal dining room is as important as the whirlpool tub and twin basins of the master bath.

Now is the perfect time to be looking for your new home. Today's designers are on the cutting edge with innovative designs taking into consideration lifestyle, an assortment of styles, tastes and site locations. You have worked hard to achieve this level of success in your professional life. You have always gone to the experts for advice in their specialties. The Garlinghouse Company has developed a network of experts to help you in your search for a new home design. Our collection of home plans has been created by award winning architects and designers. You will find prime designs for every building site and every lifestyle. Thumb through the following pages. The perfect home that you have been envisioning may be just a few pages away.

before you build...

FREQUENTLY

Can I make changes to the plans?

Your builder can make simple non-structural changes. The Garlinghouse Company Design Staff can make significant structural changes after the purchase of the erasable, reproducible vellum. Or if you prefer, you may have the changes done locally after the purchase of an erasable reproducible vellum. For details see page 251.

What do I get with my plans?

Exterior Elevations
Foundation Plan
Typical Wall Section
Cabinet details (most plans)
Fireplace details (if available)
Information necessary to construct Roof
Typical Cross Section
Detailed Floor Plans
Stair Information (if available)

Will these plans meet my local building codes?

All plans are drawn to conform to one or more of the industry's national building standards. However, your plan may need to be modified to meet your local code.

What benefit is there in buying stock blueprints as opposed to starting from scratch with an architect?

First of all you save in time. You start out with a drawn "idea" of what you want and can customize the home from that point. Second, you save money; in fact in many instances you can save thousands of dollars.

ASKED QUESTIONS

you should read!

What does the materials list Include?

A materials list will include quantities, dimensions and specifications of major materials needed to build your home and are available for most plans at a modest additional charge. You will get faster, more accurate bids and avoid paying for unused materials and waste. Due to differences in regional requirements electrical, plumbing and heating/air conditioning equipment specifications are not designed specifically for each plan.

GARLINGHOUSE PLAN SERVICE
TOPEKA, KANSAS
10340

How can I find out if I can afford to build a home?

The Garlinghouse Company offers Zip-Quote just for this purpose. By purchasing Zip-Quote you can find out the building cost for your new home without waiting for a contractor to compile the bids. We offer Zip-Quote in two options, Itemized Zip-Quote and Bottom Line Zip-Quote. For a detailed explanation of this product please see order page 252 at the back of the book.

This two story brick home features the old fashioned look of turn-of-the-century homes mixed with a contemporary floor plan. The bright two story foyer is framed by an elegant dining room to the left and a study, for after hours work, on the right. The generous, island kitchen opens into a breakfast area surrounded by glass and perfect for reading the morning paper. The enticing master suite features a sitting area that makes the perfect get-away. Upstairs you'll enjoy a dramatic view of both the foyer and the family room below. No materials list is available for this plan. The photographed home may have been modified to suit individual tastes. This plan is not to be built within a 75 mile radius of Cedar Rapids, IA.

"Get away from it all" in your private Master bedroom with Sitting area.

Surrounded by light, the island kitchen and eating area have a warm atmosphere.

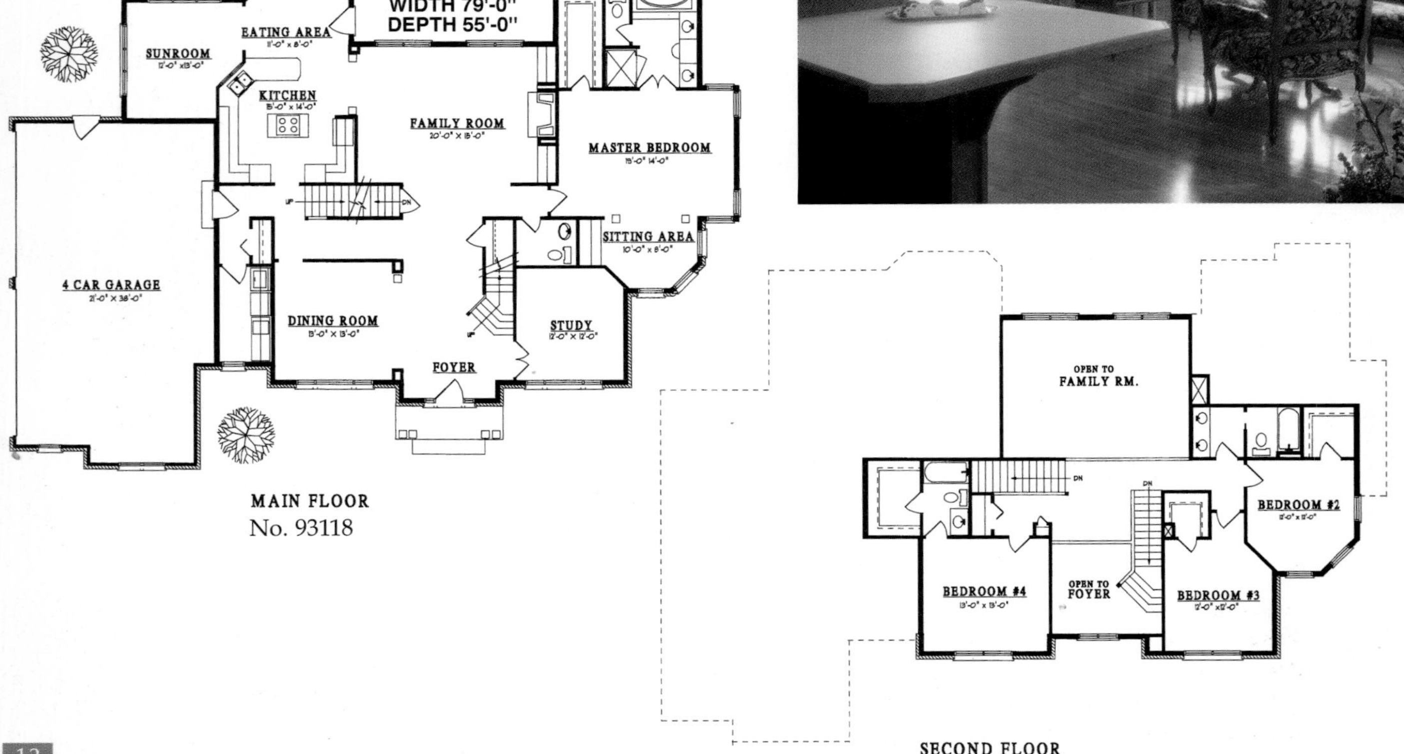
WIDTH 79'-0"
DEPTH 55'-0"
EATING AREA
SUNROOM
KITCHEN
FAMILY ROOM
MASTER BEDROOM
SITTING AREA
4 CAR GARAGE
DINING ROOM
STUDY
FOYER
OPEN TO FAMILY RM.
BEDROOM #2
BEDROOM #4
OPEN TO FOYER
BEDROOM #3

MAIN FLOOR
No. 93118

SECOND FLOOR

TURN-OF-THE-CENTURY APPEAL

PLAN NO. 93118

Total living area	3,397 sq. ft
Main floor	2,385 sq. ft.
Second floor	1,012 sq. ft.
Basement	2,385 sq. ft.
Garage	846 sq. ft.
Bedrooms	four
Bathrooms	3 full, 1 half
Foundation	basement

Photography Supplied by
Ahmann Design, Inc.
Sattler Home Builders — Builder
Design by Ahmann Design, Inc.

PRICE CODE F 

High ceilings, built-ins and a cozy fireplace provide the backdrop for a warm gathering place.

Cathedral ceilings and a balcony overlooking the formal dining room lend drama to this stately home.

Here's a stately home that's a treasure chest of popular features, including a sunken Great room, a spectacular breakfast nook, and a bridge-like balcony on the second floor. The luxurious, first floor master suite is a marvel, with two huge walk-in closets, a five-piece bath, and a sitting room with bay window. The second and third bedrooms each have a walk-in closet and private bath. The Great room features a bar, fireplace, and built-in cabinets for TV and stereo, all crowned by a sloping, beamed ceiling. Both the dining room and the foyer have cathedral ceilings and are overlooked by the second floor balcony. A fully equipped kitchen enjoys a sweeping view of the patio and opens to the stunning nook. All in all, this is a fabulous and impressive home. The photographed home may have been modified to suit individual tastes.

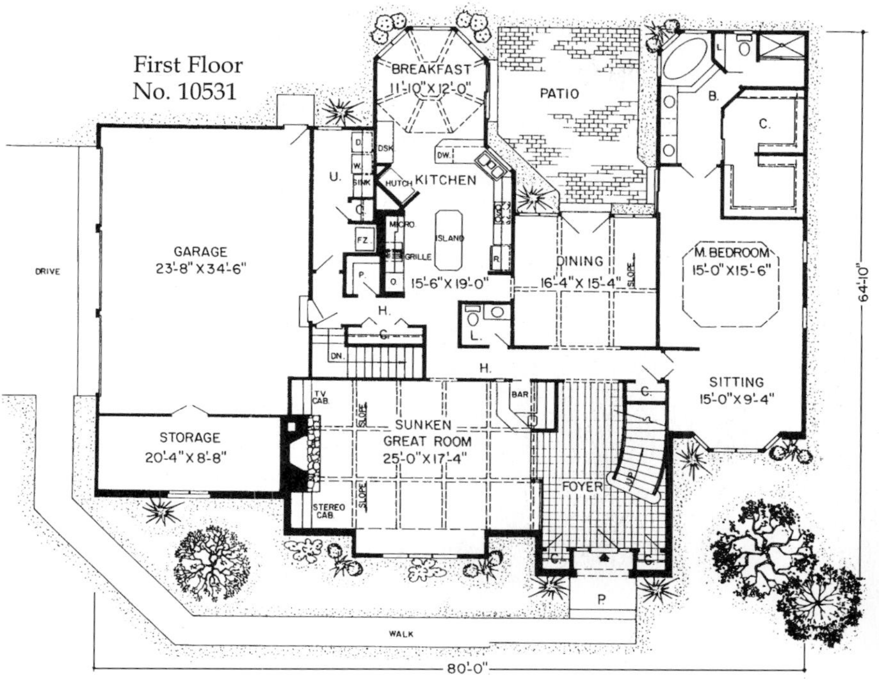
First Floor
No. 10531
BREAKFAST
11'-10"X12'-0"
PATIO
KITCHEN
HUTCH
DSK
DW.
U.
GARAGE
23'-8"X34'-6"
DRIVE
MICRO
ISLAND
FZ.
GRILLE
15'-6"X19'-0"
DINING
16'-4"X15'-4"
M.BEDROOM
15'-0"X15'-6"
B.
C.
H.
L.
DN.
SITTING
15'-0"X9'-4"
TV CAB
BAR
SUNKEN
GREAT ROOM
25'-0"X17'-4"
STORAGE
20'-4"X8'-8"
STEREO CAB
FOYER
SLOPE
WALK
80'-0"
64'-10"

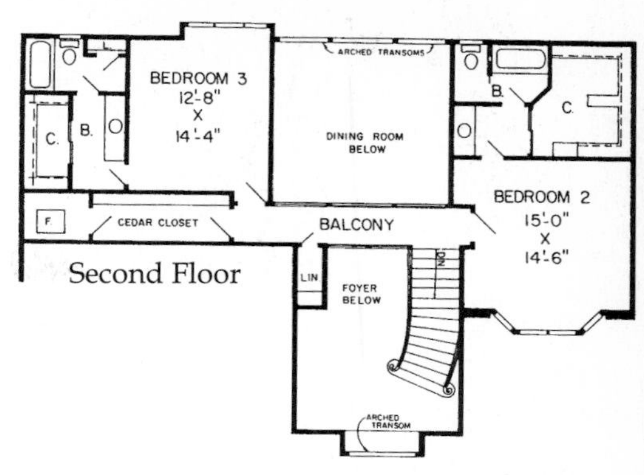
BEDROOM 3
12'-8"
X
14'-4"
ARCHED TRANSOMS
DINING ROOM
BELOW
C.
B.
CEDAR CLOSET
BALCONY
BEDROOM 2
15'-0"
X
14'-6"
Second Floor
LIN
FOYER
BELOW
ARCHED
TRANSOM

OUTSTANDING DESIGN

PLAN NO. 10531

Total living area	3,576 sq. ft
First floor	2,579 sq. ft.
Second floor	997 sq. ft.
Basement	2,579 sq. ft.
Garage & Storage	1,001 sq. ft.
Bedrooms	three
Bathrooms	3 full, 1 half
Foundation	basement

Photography by John Ehrenclou

Design by The Garlinghouse Company

PRICE CODE F 

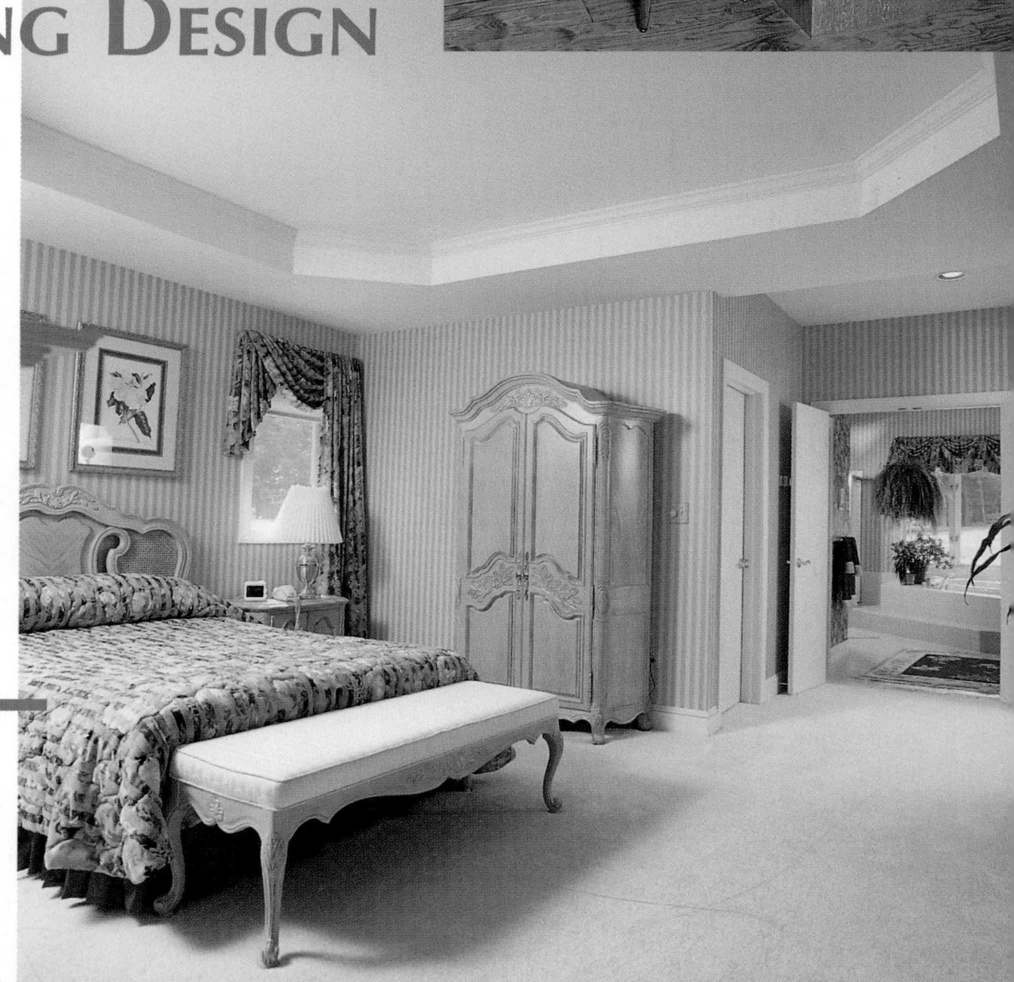

A private retreat awaits you in the first floor master suite which includes two huge walk-in closets, a five-piece bath, and a sitting room with a bay window.

Gracious living is the rule in this brick masterpiece designed with an eye toward elegant entertaining. Window walls and French doors link the in-ground pool and surrounding brick patio with the interior living spaces. The wetbar, acomplete with wine storage provides a convenient space for a large buffet in the family room. Built-in bookcases in the living room, family room, and skylit second floor library can house even the largest collections. Separated from living areas by halls or a bridge, every bedroom is a quiet retreat, with its own dressing room and adjoining bath. The photographed home may have been modified to suit individual tastes.

Magnificent glass doors usher you into this grand foyer.

An eye for detail is evident in every aspect of this home.

PLAN NO. 10666

Total living area	4,562 sq. ft
First floor	3,625 sq. ft.
Second floor	937 sq. ft.
Garage	636 sq. ft.
Bedrooms	five
Bathrooms	4 full, 1 half
Foundation	basement, slab or crawl space

Photography by John Ehrenclou

Design by The Garlinghouse Company

PRICE CODE F 

Arches Dominate Stately Facade

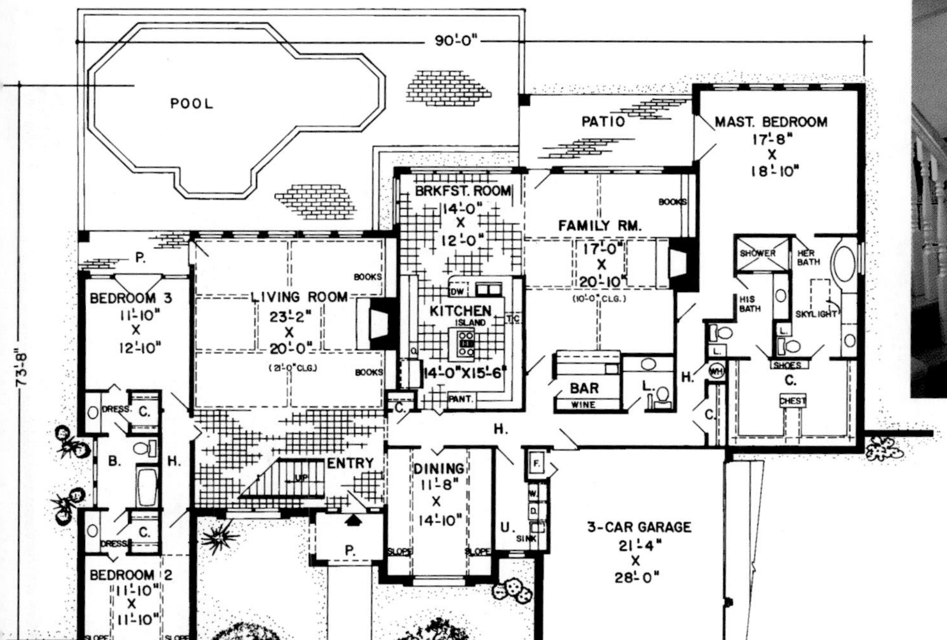

FIRST FLOOR

No. 10666

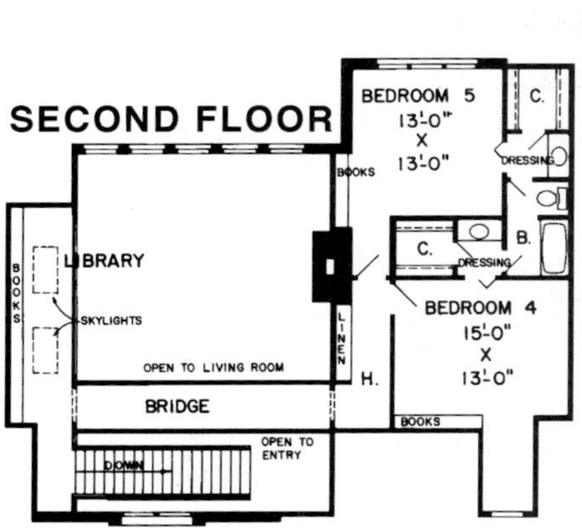

SECOND FLOOR

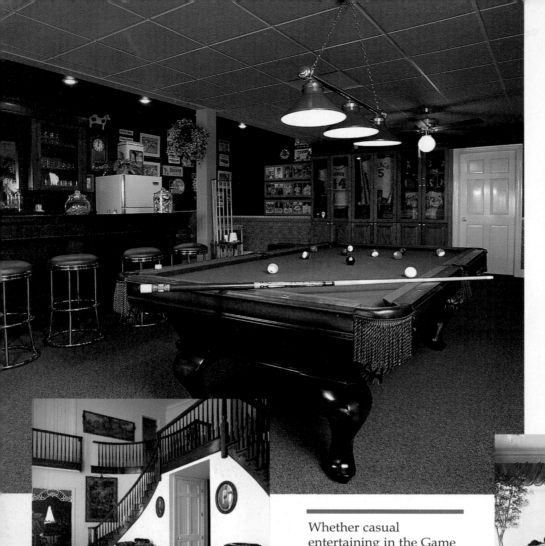

Imagine living in the graceful elegance of this sprawling, Georgian beauty. From the impressive columned facade to the two-story drama of the receiving hall, this home has style! Flanked by the formal living and dining rooms, the receiving hall leads straight back to a sun-filled, fireplaced gathering room surrounded by an outdoor terrace. The open kitchen and breakfast room combination features a cooktop island and extra-large storage pantry. Walk up the curving staircases of the receiving hall to four spacious bedrooms, each adjoining a bath. The master suite enjoys the toasty warmth of a fireplace, a garden tub, a built-in vanity and double sinks. The photographed home may have been modified to suit individual tastes.

Whether casual entertaining in the Game room or formal attire in the Parlor, your guests will feel like royalty in every corner of this spectacular home.

Georgian Drama at its Best

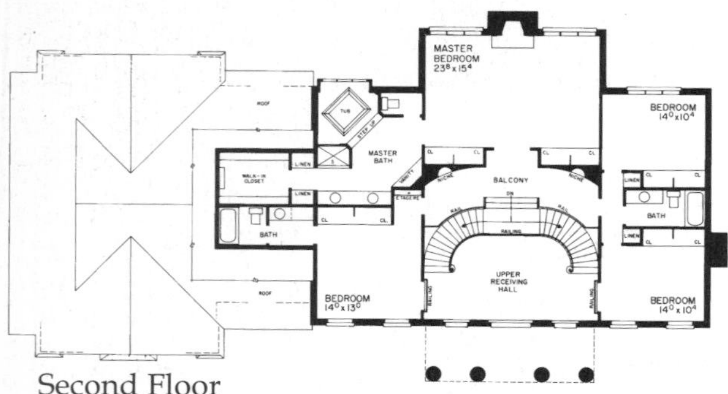
MASTER BEDROOM
BEDROOM
MASTER BATH
BALCONY
UPPER RECEIVING HALL
BATH
BEDROOM
BEDROOM
Second Floor

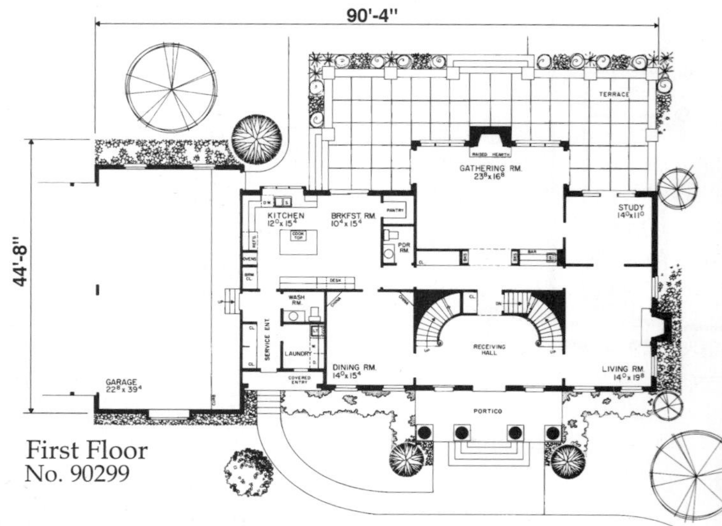
90'-4"
44'-8"
TERRACE
GATHERING RM.
KITCHEN
BRKFST RM.
STUDY
RECEIVING HALL
DINING RM.
LIVING RM.
GARAGE
PORTICO
LAUNDRY
SERVICE ENT.
First Floor
No. 90299

PLAN NO. 92623

Total living area	2,653 sq. ft
First floor	1,365 sq. ft.
Second floor	1,288 sq. ft.
Basement	1,217 sq. ft.
Garage	491 sq. ft.
Bedroom	four
Bathrooms	2 full, 1 half
Foundation	basement

Photography Supplied by Studer Residential Design, Inc.

Design by Studer Residential Design, Inc.

PRICE CODE E

Classic beauty and character define the lines of this home.

The classic good looks of this two-story home are accentuated by an arch-topped window over the entrance and the use of brick trim and dental molding across the front. The tray ceiling in the formal living room and the dining room and the corner columns pulls these two rooms into a unit. The stairs are located with access directly into the kitchen. Windows located on either side of the corner sink flood the counter with natural light. The sunken family room with a fireplace brings a warm feeling to this private area of the house. A luxurious bedroom suite with a sloped ceiling is the highlight of this four bedroom second floor. A balcony overlooking the foyer, a plant shelf, an arched window, a skylight, and a laundry chute are extra features that help to make this a home unsurpassed in style and value. No materials list is available for this plan. The photographed home may have been modified to suit individual tastes.

The luxurious master suite is secluded on the first floor. Elegant touches include a library, morning room with built-ins, a bar with wine storage, and a sun porch with French doors leading into the dining room. The living room and foyer rise to the second floor which is comprised of three large bedrooms and two well-placed baths. The photographed home may have been modified to suit individual tastes.

An open Foyer leads to a two-story Living Room with a fireplace.

Relax in the whirlpool tub in the luxurious Master Suite.

PLAN NO. 10534

Total living area	3,440 sq. ft
First floor	2,486 sq. ft.
Second floor	954 sq. ft.
Basement	2,486 sq. ft.
Garage	576 sq. ft.
Bedrooms	four
Bathrooms	3 full, 1 half
Foundation	basement, slab or crawl space

Photography by John Ehrenclou

Design by The Garlinghouse Company

PRICE CODE F 

Private Court with Hot Tub

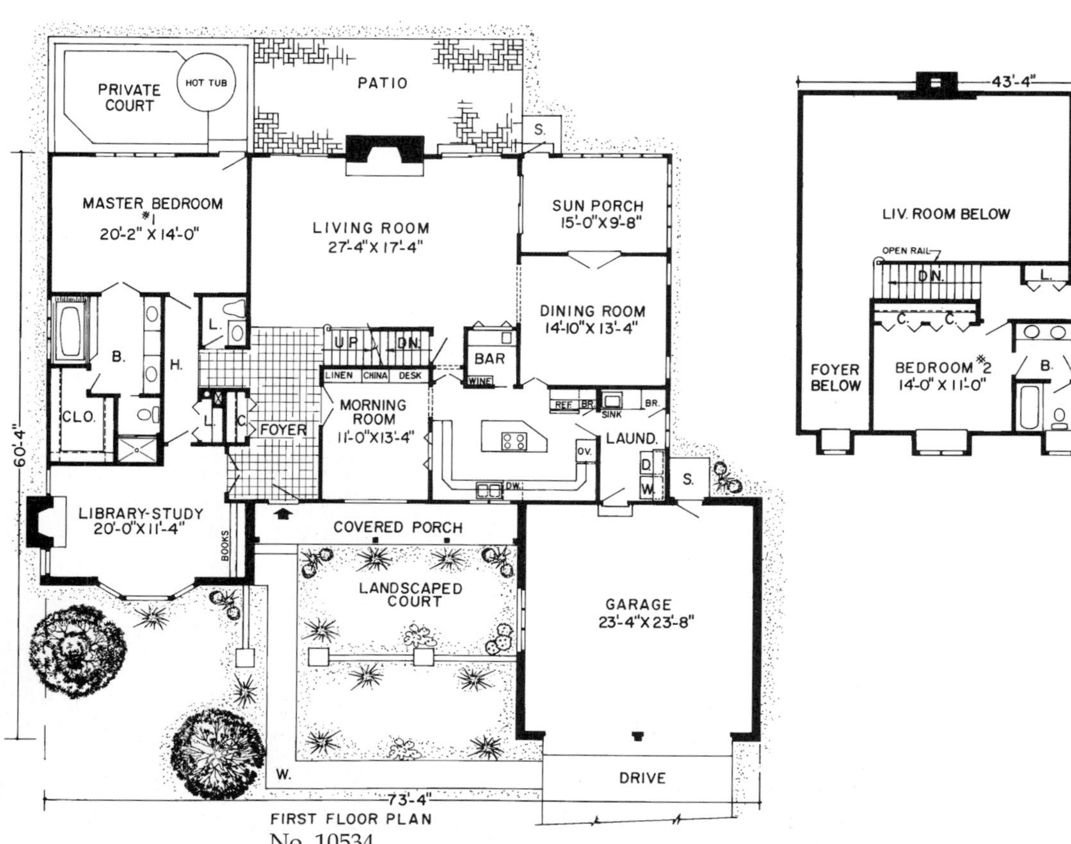
PRIVATE COURT
HOT TUB
PATIO
S.
MASTER BEDROOM #1
20'-2" X 14'-0"
LIVING ROOM
27'-4" X 17'-4"
SUN PORCH
15'-0" X 9'-8"
DINING ROOM
14'-10" X 13'-4"
B.
H.
L.
UP
DN.
BAR
LINEN
CHINA
DESK
WINE
CLO.
C.
FOYER
MORNING ROOM
11'-0" X 13'-4"
REF
BR.
SINK
BR.
LAUND.
OV.
DW.
D
W
S.
LIBRARY-STUDY
20'-0" X 11'-4"
BOOKS
COVERED PORCH
LANDSCAPED COURT
GARAGE
23'-4" X 23'-8"
60'-4"
W.
DRIVE
73'-4"
FIRST FLOOR PLAN
No. 10534
43'-4"
LIV. ROOM BELOW
BEDROOM #4
14'-10" X 13'-4"
OPEN RAIL
DN.
L.
C.
B.
C.
36'-0"
FOYER BELOW
BEDROOM #2
14'-0" X 11'-0"
B.
BEDROOM #3
14'-2" X 11'-4"
SECOND FLOOR PLAN

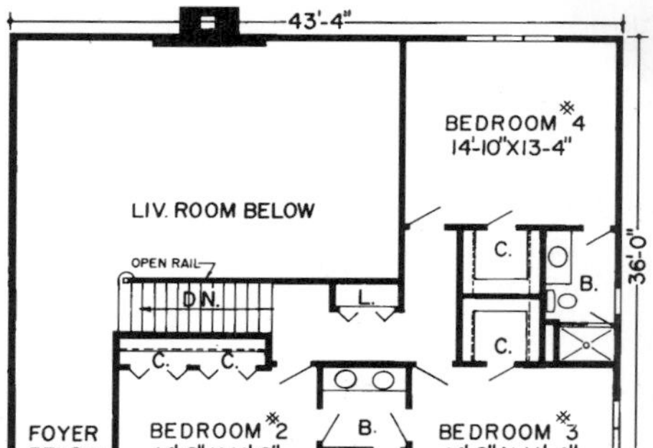

Take advantage of southern exposure and save on energy costs in this beautiful family Tudor. Heat is stored in the floor of the sun room, adjoining the living and breakfast rooms. When the sun goes down, close the French doors and light a fire in the massive fireplace. State-of-the-art energy saving is not the only modern convenience in this house. You'll love the balcony overlooking the soaring two-story foyer and living room. In addition to providing great views, the balcony links the upstairs bedrooms. You're sure to enjoy the island kitchen, centrally located between formal and informal dining rooms. And, you'll never want to leave the luxurious master suite, with its double vanity and step-up whirlpool. The photographed home may have been modified to suit individual tastes.

PLAN NO. 20071

Total living area	3,169 sq. ft
First floor	2,186 sq. ft.
Second floor	983 sq. ft.
Basement	2,186 sq. ft.
Garage	704 sq. ft.
Bedrooms	four
Bathrooms	2 full, 1 half 1 three-quarter
Foundation	basement

Design by The Garlinghouse Company

PRICE CODE E 

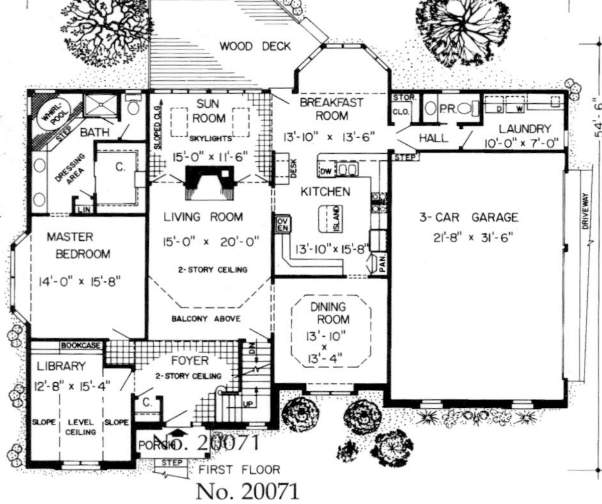

67'-0"
WOOD DECK
54'-6"
WHIRLPOOL
STEP
BATH
DRESSING AREA
C.
LIN
SLOPED CLG.
SUN ROOM
SKYLIGHTS
15'-0" x 11'-6"
BREAKFAST ROOM
13'-10" x 13'-6"
STOR.
CLO.
PR.
HALL
LAUNDRY
10'-0" x 7'-0"
STEP
DESK
KITCHEN
ISLAND
OVEN
13'-10" x 15'-8"
PAN
3-CAR GARAGE
21'-8" x 31'-6"
DRIVEWAY
MASTER BEDROOM
14'-0" x 15'-8"
LIVING ROOM
15'-0" x 20'-0"
2-STORY CEILING
BALCONY ABOVE
DINING ROOM
13'-10" x 13'-4"
BOOKCASE
LIBRARY
12'-8" x 15'-4"
FOYER
2-STORY CEILING
DN
UP
C.
SLOPE
LEVEL CEILING
SLOPE
PORCH
STEP
FIRST FLOOR

No. 20071

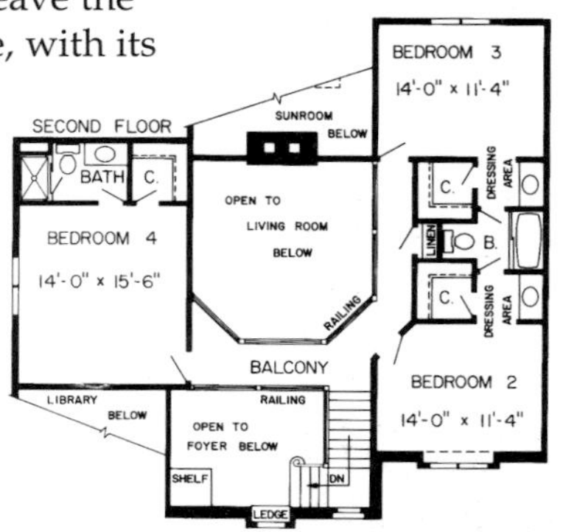

SECOND FLOOR
BATH
C.
BEDROOM 4
14'-0" x 15'-6"
SUNROOM BELOW
OPEN TO LIVING ROOM BELOW
RAILING
BEDROOM 3
14'-0" x 11'-4"
C.
DRESSING AREA
LINEN
B.
C.
DRESSING AREA
BALCONY
RAILING
BEDROOM 2
14'-0" x 11'-4"
LIBRARY BELOW
OPEN TO FOYER BELOW
SHELF
LEDGE
DN

Step up into your pampering whirlpool tub.

Beauty and character flow from every corner of this design.

UPDATED TUDOR

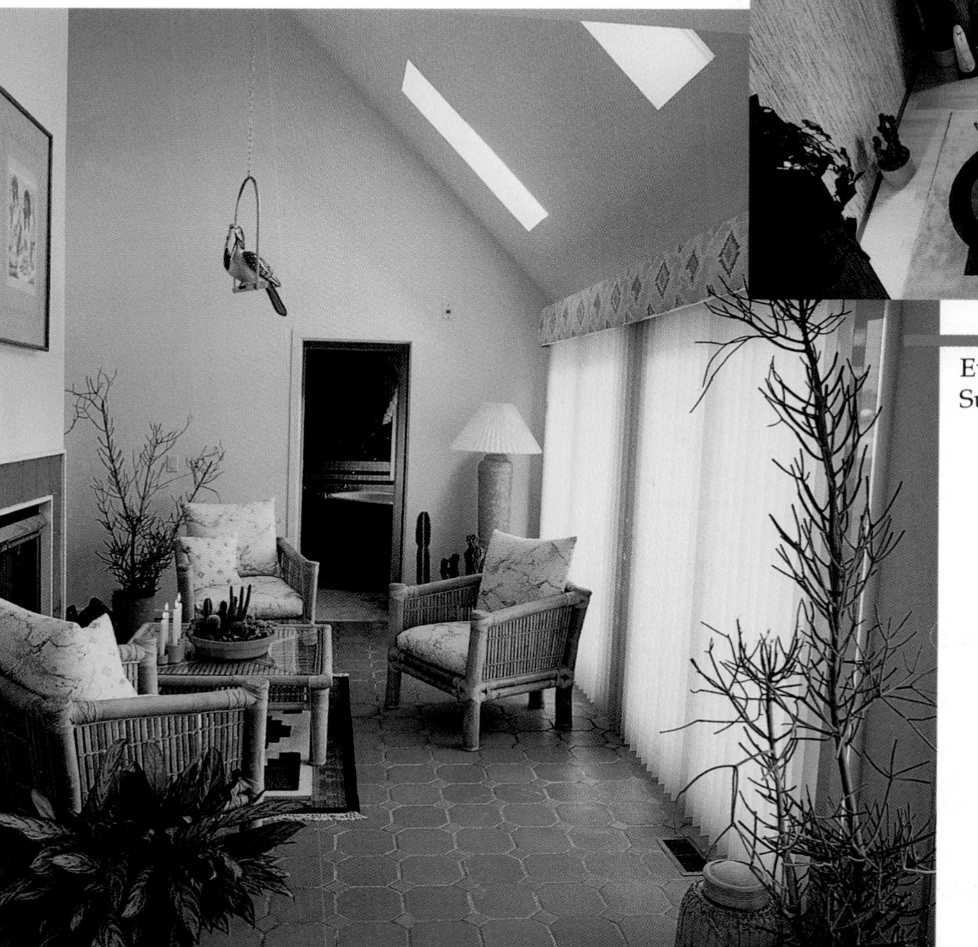

Every day will feel like Summer in this Sun Room.

Brick and stucco make for an exciting combination in this two-story design. The three-car garage entry to the rear allows for a full exterior architectural display. The grand foyer, with a lovely curved staircase, enjoins the formal step-down living and dining room. The kitchen presents a uniquely different geometric concept to allow a full two-sided view. An additional rear staircase adds ease in reaching the second floor bedrooms, game room and master suite with it's own luxurious bath and walk-in closet. The photographed home may have been modified to suit individual tastes.

Spectacular spaces define this grand home built for entertaining a crowd or simply accommodating the needs of your family.

Graceful Window Arches

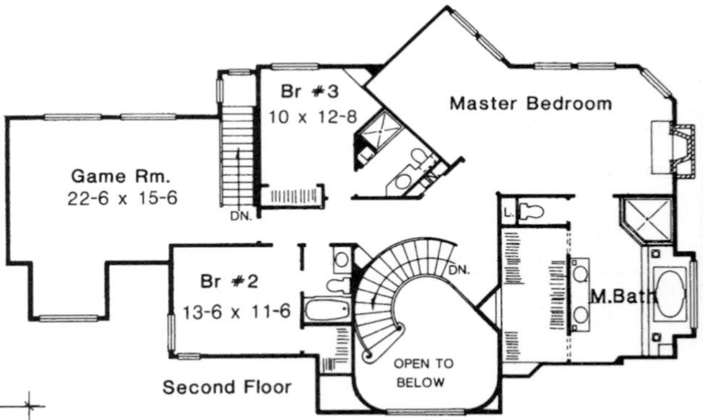

Br #3
10 x 12-8
Master Bedroom
Game Rm.
22-6 x 15-6
DN.
Br #2
13-6 x 11-6
DN.
M.Bath
OPEN TO BELOW
Second Floor

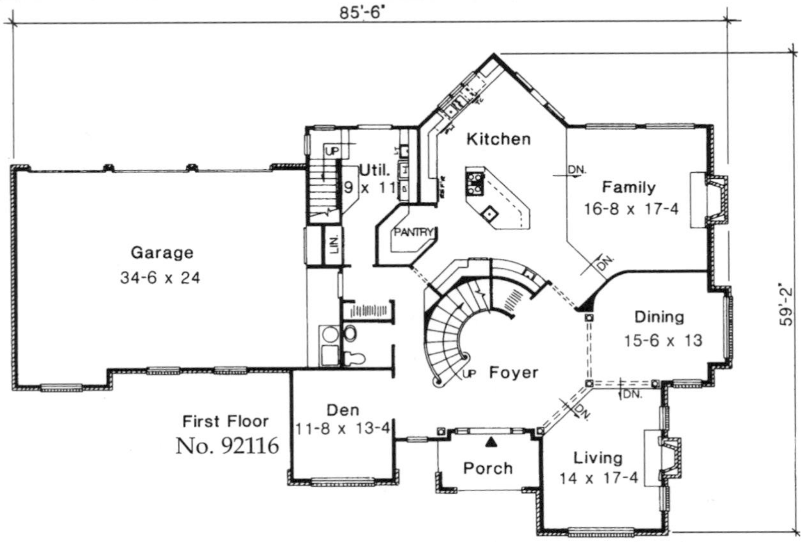

85'-6"
Kitchen
UP
Util.
9 x 11
DN.
Family
16-8 x 17-4
PANTRY
LIN.
Garage
34-6 x 24
DN.
Dining
15-6 x 13
59'-2"
UP Foyer
DN.
DN.
Den
11-8 x 13-4
Porch
Living
14 x 17-4

First Floor
No. 92116

PLAN NO. 92116

Total living area	3,992 sq. ft
First floor	2,108 sq. ft.
Second floor	1,884 sq. ft.
Bedrooms	three
Bathrooms	3 full, 1 half
Foundation	crawl space

Photography by James Reuter Jr.
Design by Northwest Home Designs

PRICE CODE F 

Lofty ceilngs and a curved staircase beckon you to the second floor.

The openness of this floor plan gives an open airy feeling to this home. The Great room truly lives up to its name. A two-story ceiling and a fireplace accent the room with grandeur. The study is enhanced by a second cozy fireplace and built in bookcases. The dining room has a built-in area for the hutch and elegant columns defining the room. The kitchen includes a peninsula counter/snack bar and an island. The nook accesses the sunroom and the rear porch. Upstairs, there are four bedrooms. The master suite is topped by a vaulted ceiling over the bedroom and includes a spacious master bath and a private deck. The guest suite includes a private bath and the secondary bedrooms have private access to a full bath. No materials list is available for this plan. The photographed home may have been modified to suit individual tastes.

A beautiful, open kitchen with a creative design is loaded with counter and cabinet space.

Wide Open Spaces

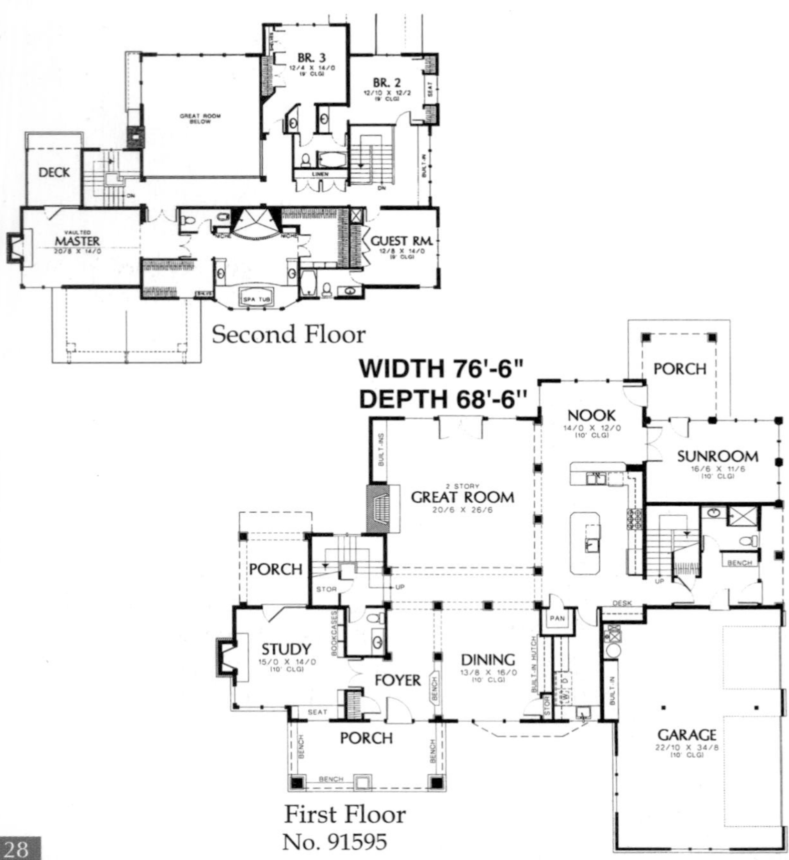

BR. 3
BR. 2
GREAT ROOM BELOW
DECK
MASTER
GUEST RM.
WIDTH 76'-6"
DEPTH 68'-6"
PORCH
NOOK
14/0 X 12/0 (10' CLG)
SUNROOM
16/6 X 11/6 (10' CLG)
2 STORY GREAT ROOM
20/6 X 26/6
PORCH
STUDY
15/0 X 14/0 (10' CLG)
FOYER
DINING
13/8 X 16/0 (10' CLG)
PORCH
GARAGE
22/10 X 34/8 (10' CLG)

Second Floor

First Floor
No. 91595

A gorgeous fireplaced Great room flows easily from the spacious kitchen, allowing the cook as well as guests free to mingle from room to room.

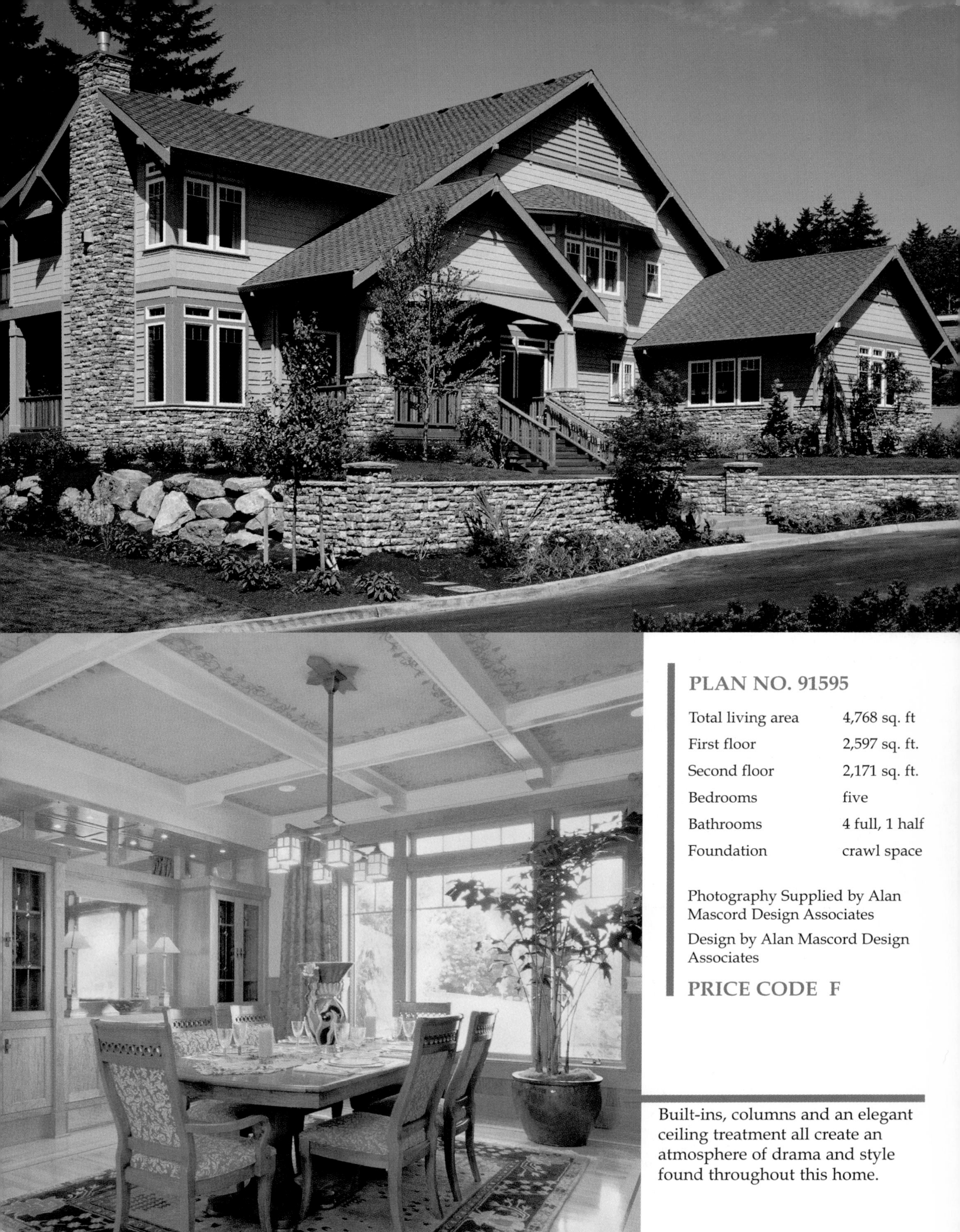

PLAN NO. 91595

Total living area	4,768 sq. ft
First floor	2,597 sq. ft.
Second floor	2,171 sq. ft.
Bedrooms	five
Bathrooms	4 full, 1 half
Foundation	crawl space

Photography Supplied by Alan Mascord Design Associates

Design by Alan Mascord Design Associates

PRICE CODE F

Built-ins, columns and an elegant ceiling treatment all create an atmosphere of drama and style found throughout this home.

Arched, multi-paned windows and an elegant brick design that looks much larger than its square footage indicates, are just a few of the features of this plan. The impressive foyer with columns features a sky-bridge above the family room. The parlor and dining rooms are designed to provide an elegant entertaining area. The island kitchen is enhanced by its convenience to both the breakfast nook and the formal dining room. The master suite with its privacy on the first floor has a first class bath and a retreat. Take notice of the library, which features a wood mantel fireplace and window seats. Upstairs, two large bedrooms also have window seats and share another bath. The photographed home may have been modified to suit individual tastes.

Impressive Foyer with Columns

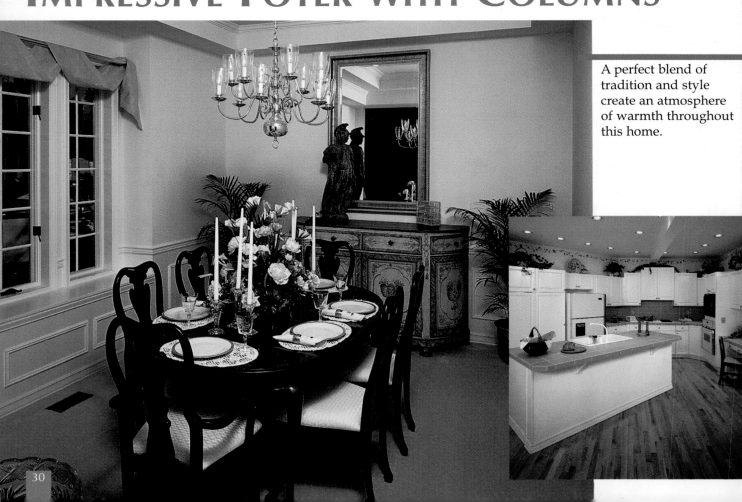

A perfect blend of tradition and style create an atmosphere of warmth throughout this home.

Creating a terrific first impression, the foyer of this home is open to the second floor.

PLAN NO. 92126

Total living area	2,898 sq. ft
First floor	2,024 sq. ft.
Second floor	874 sq. ft.
Garage	648 sq. ft.
Bedrooms	three
Bathrooms	2 full, 1 half
Foundation	crawl space

Photography by James Reuter Jr.

Design by Northwest Home Designs

PRICE CODE E

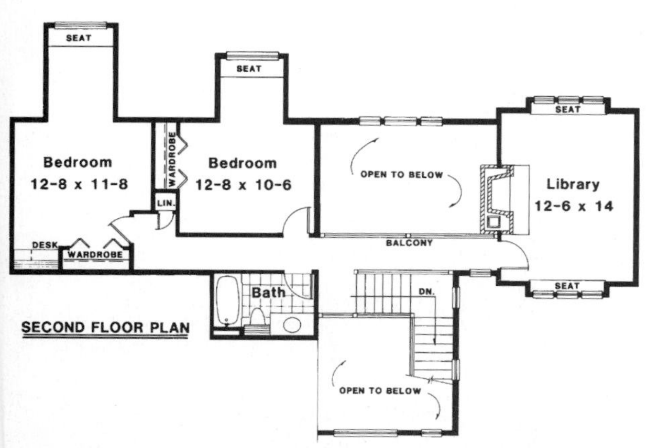
SEAT
SEAT
Bedroom
12-8 x 11-8
WARDROBE
Bedroom
12-8 x 10-6
OPEN TO BELOW
SEAT
Library
12-6 x 14
LIN.
DESK
WARDROBE
BALCONY
SEAT
Bath
DN.
OPEN TO BELOW
SECOND FLOOR PLAN

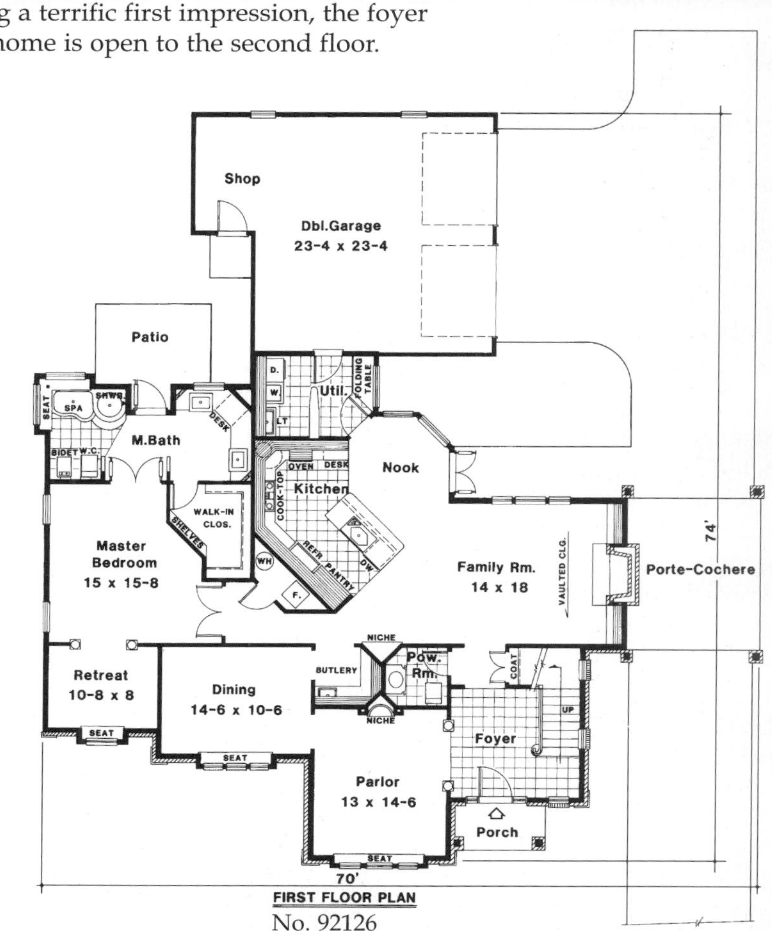
Shop
Dbl.Garage
23-4 x 23-4
Patio
SEAT
SPA
SHWR.
DESK
M.Bath
BIDET
W.C.
D.
W
LT
Util.
FOLDING TABLE
Nook
OVEN
DESK
COOK-TOP
Kitchen
WALK-IN CLOS.
SHELVES
Master
Bedroom
15 x 15-8
WH
REFR
PANTRY
DW
F.
Family Rm.
14 x 18
VAULTED CLG.
Porte-Cochere
74'
NICHE
Pow. Rm.
COAT
BUTLERY
Retreat
10-8 x 8
Dining
14-6 x 10-6
NICHE
UP
Foyer
SEAT
SEAT
Parlor
13 x 14-6
Porch
SEAT
70'
FIRST FLOOR PLAN

No. 92126

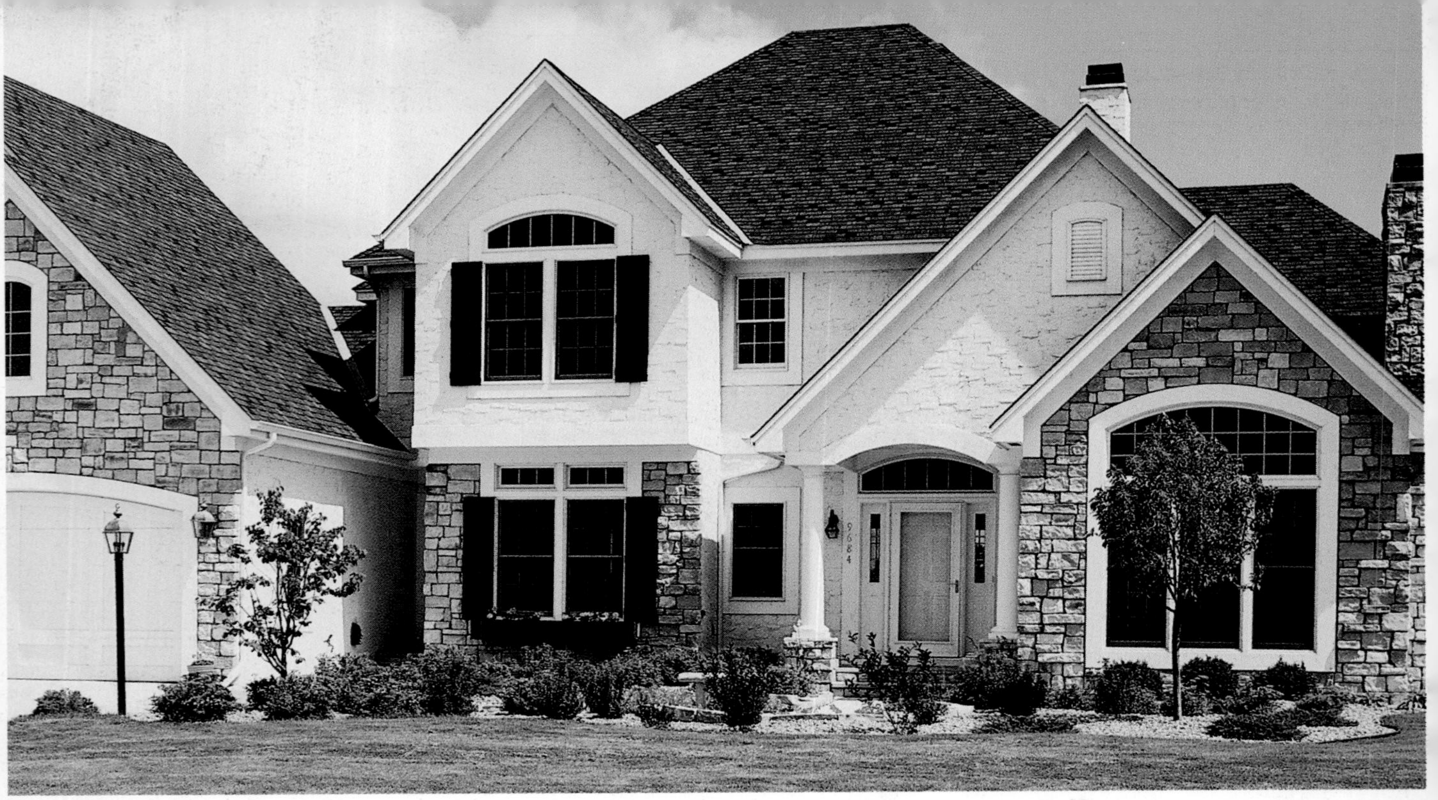

DISTINGUISHED DETAILING

Today's modern family demands a home that is functional, convenient and stylish. This home meets that criteria. A two-story foyer affords access to the formal living room, the study or the expansive family room. The living room includes a vaulted ceiling and a focal point fireplace. Pocket doors between the living room and the study give the option of privacy to thestudy. A cozy fireplace in the family room offers added warmth and ambience to the living space. A cooktop island/snack bar extends counter space in the kitchen. Other amenities include a walk-in pantry, built-in planning desk and an adjoining breakfast room. Formal dining is an elegant experience in the dining room, just across the hall from the kitchen. The second floor master suite boasts a pan vaulted ceiling, lavish private bath and an abundance of storage space. No materials list is available for this plan. The photographed home may have been modified to suit individual tastes.

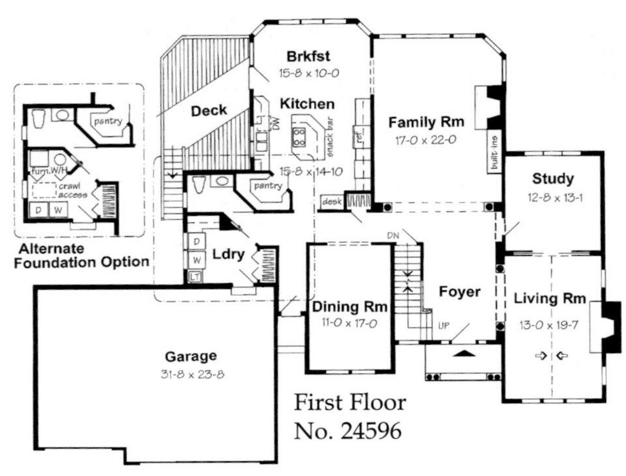
Brkfst
15-8 x 10-0
Deck
Kitchen
15-8 x 14-10
Family Rm
17-0 x 22-0
Study
12-8 x 13-1
Ldry
Foyer
Dining Rm
11-0 x 17-0
Living Rm
13-0 x 19-7
Garage
31-8 x 23-8
Alternate
Foundation Option

First Floor
No. 24596

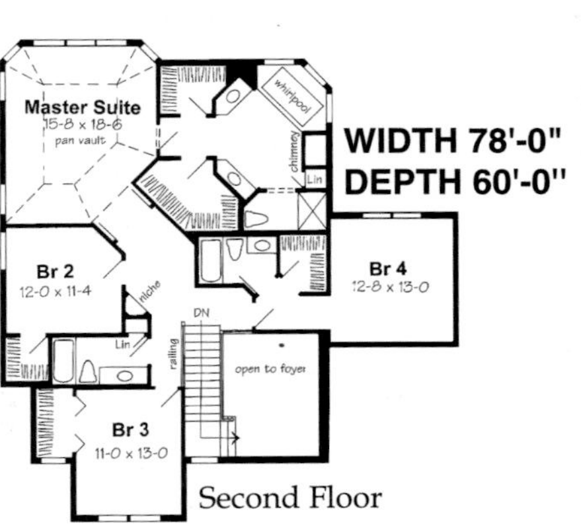
Master Suite
15-8 x 18-6
pan vault
WIDTH 78'-0"
DEPTH 60'-0"
Br 2
12-0 x 11-4
Br 4
12-8 x 13-0
Br 3
11-0 x 13-0
open to foyer

Second Floor

PLAN NO. 24596

Total living area	3,526 sq. ft
First floor	2,054 sq. ft.
Second floor	1,472 sq. ft.
Basement	2,054 sq. ft.
Garage	745 sq. ft.
Bedrooms	four
Bathrooms	3 full, 1 ha
Foundation	basement, slab or crawl spac

Photography by Susan Gilmore

Design by The Garlinghouse Company

PRICE CODE F

Refer to **Pricing Schedule D** on the order form for pricing information

Design by
The Garlinghouse Company

PLAN NO. 24653

Br 2
11-8 x 12-4
Mstr. Suite
18-4 x 13-4
linen
optional skylight
DN
railing
Br 3
11-8 x 12-5
Common
9-5 x 13-8
open to below
Bonus
11-4 x 15-8

Second Floor

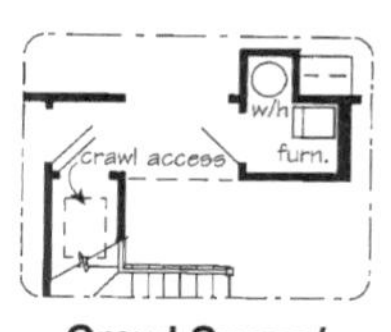

w/h
crawl access
furn.

Crawl Space/
Slab Option
No. 24653

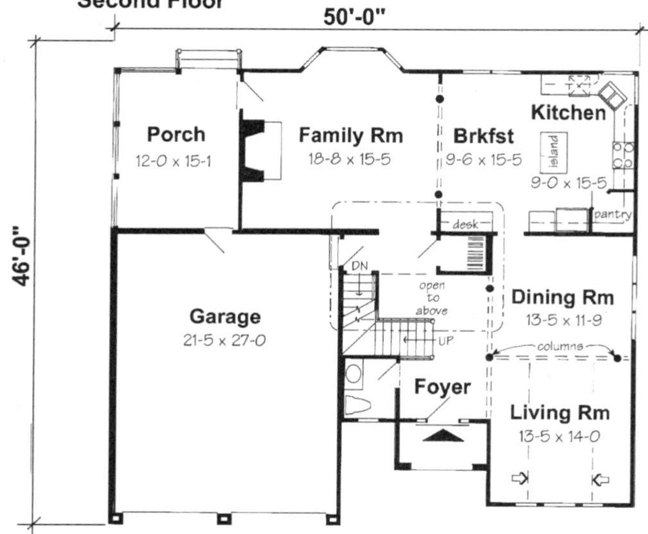

50'-0"
46'-0"
Porch
12-0 x 15-1
Family Rm
18-8 x 15-5
Brkfst
9-6 x 15-5
Kitchen
island
9-0 x 15-5
pantry
desk
DN
open to above
UP
Dining Rm
13-5 x 11-9
columns
Garage
21-5 x 27-0
Foyer
Living Rm
13-5 x 14-0

First Floor

Dignified Family Home

- This plan features:
  - — Three bedrooms
  - — Two full and one half baths
- A beautiful elevation with multi-paned windows
- A two-story Foyer
- A formal Living Room that adjoins the formal Dining Room
- A U-shaped Kitchen with an island and built-in Pantry and planning desk
- A Family Room with a fireplace
- A Master Suite with a decorative ceiling and a lavish bath
- A bonus room for future needs
- No materials list is available for this plan

FIRST FLOOR — 1,245 SQ. FT.
SECOND FLOOR — 1,333 SQ. FT.
BONUS ROOM — 192 SQ. FT.
BASEMENT — 1,245 SQ. FT.
GARAGE — 614 SQ. FT.

TOTAL LIVING AREA:
2,578 SQ. FT.

PLAN NO. 10501

Design by
The Garlinghouse Company

Refer to **Pricing Schedule F** on the order form for pricing information

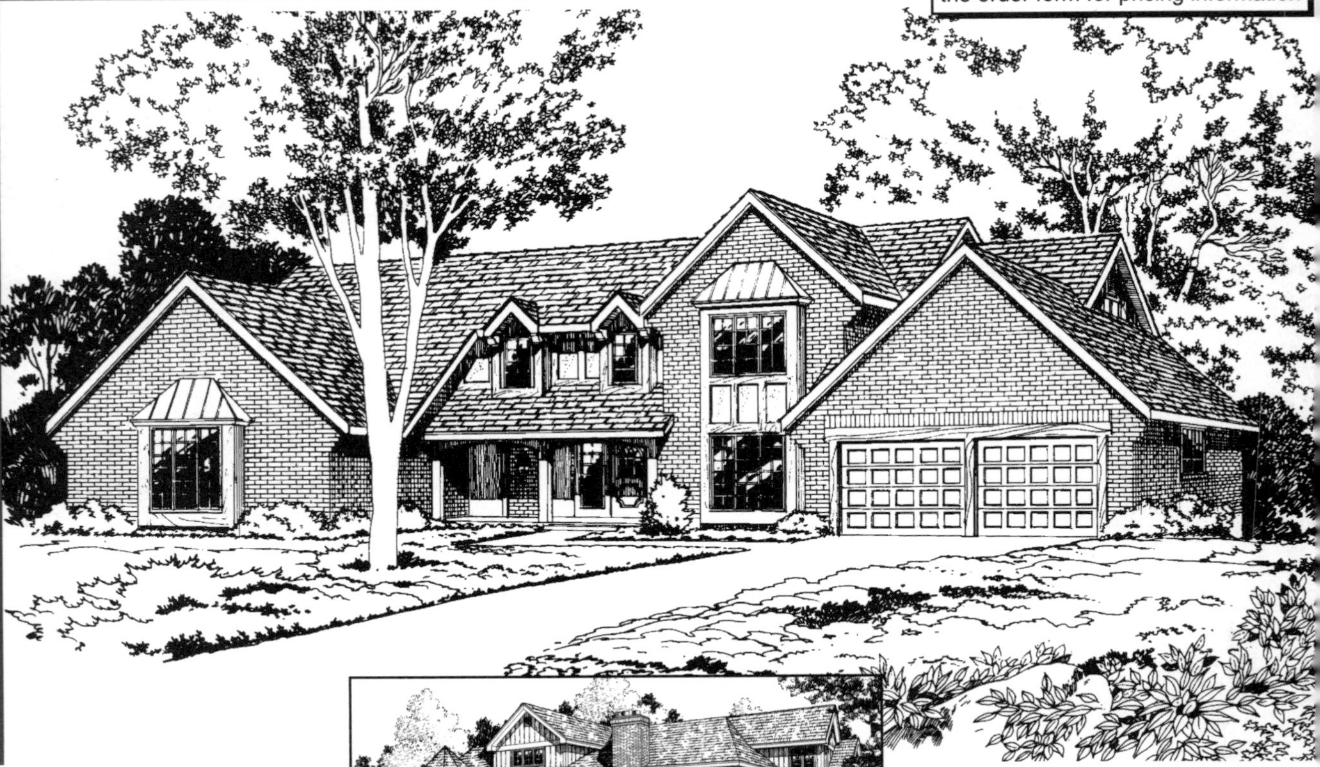

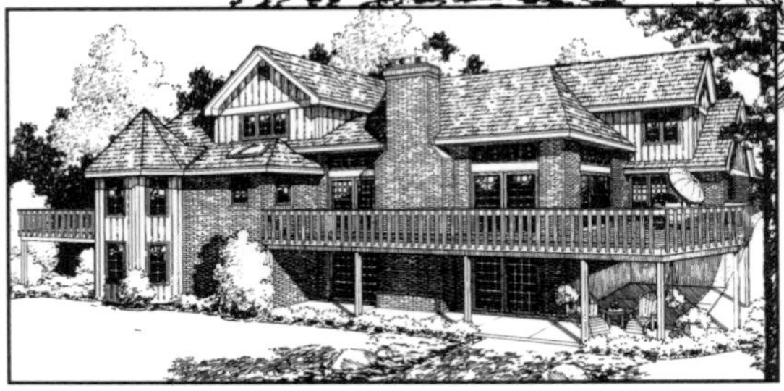

Foyer Welcomes Guests

- This plan features:
  - — Four bedrooms
  - — Two full, one three-quarter and one half baths
- A massive welcoming Foyer which steps right into the Great Room
- A Great Room enlarged by a wrap-around Deck and highlighted by a fireplace, built-in bookcases and a wetbar
- A Kitchen with a built-in desk, an octagonal Morning Room, and a central island

FIRST FLOOR — 2,419 SQ. FT.
SECOND FLOOR — 926 SQ. FT.
BASEMENT — 2,419 SQ. FT.
GARAGE — 615 SQ. FT.

TOTAL LIVING AREA:
3,345 SQ. FT.

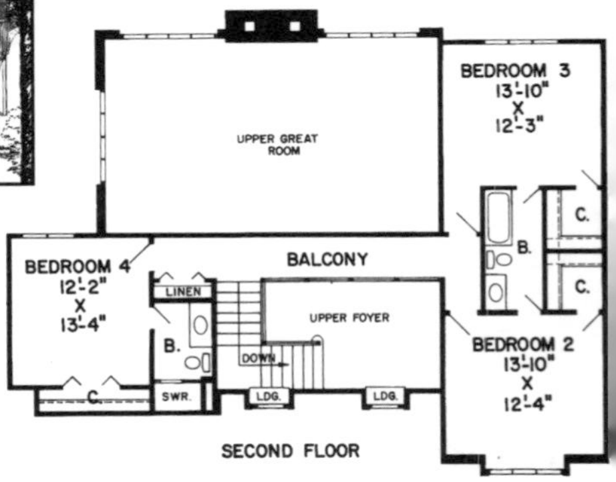

BEDROOM 3
13'-10" X 12'-3"
UPPER GREAT ROOM
BALCONY
BEDROOM 4
12'-2" X 13'-4"
LINEN
B.
C.
UPPER FOYER
DOWN
SWR.
LDG.
LDG.
BEDROOM 2
13'-10" X 12'-4"
SECOND FLOOR

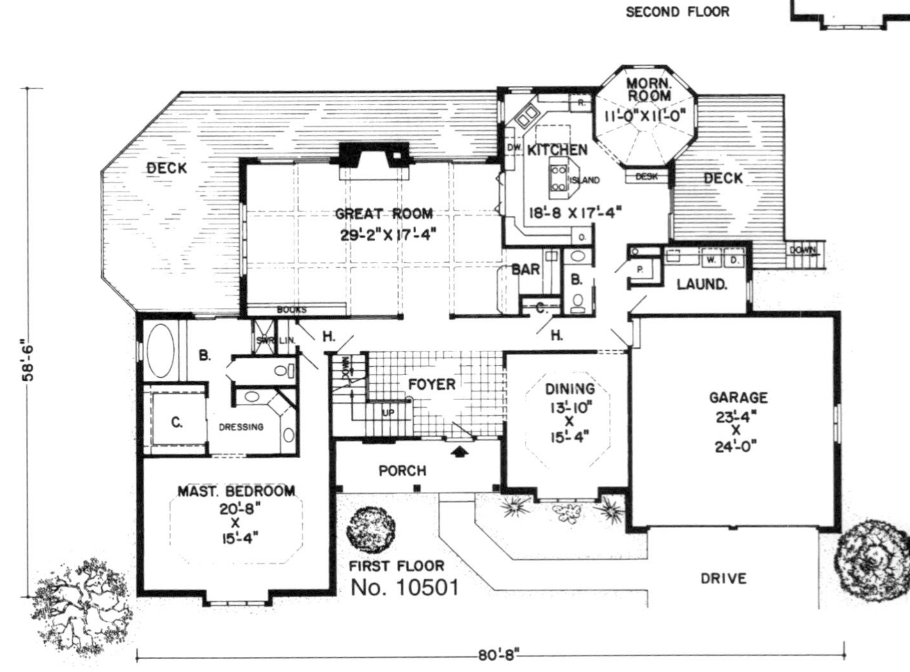

MORN. ROOM
11'-0" X 11'-0"
KITCHEN
ISLAND
18'-8 X 17'-4"
DECK
DECK
DESK
GREAT ROOM
29'-2" X 17'-4"
BAR
B.
C.
H.
H.
P.
W. D.
LAUND.
DOWN
BOOKS
B.
LIN
C.
DRESSING
FOYER
UP
DN
DINING
13'-10" X 15'-4"
GARAGE
23'-4" X 24'-0"
PORCH
MAST. BEDROOM
20'-8" X 15'-4"
FIRST FLOOR
No. 10501
DRIVE
58'-6"
80'-8"

Refer to **Pricing Schedule E** on the order form for pricing information

Design by **Rick Garner**

PLAN NO. 92576

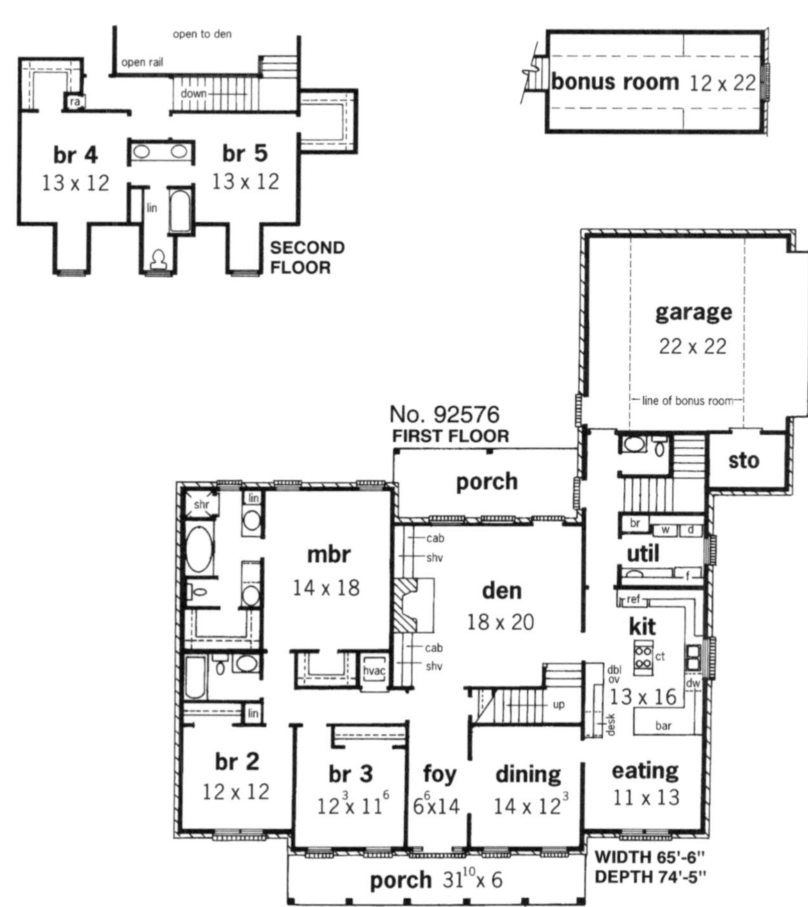

open to den
open rail
down
ra
br 4
13 x 12
br 5
13 x 12
lin
SECOND FLOOR
bonus room 12 x 22
garage
22 x 22
line of bonus room
No. 92576
FIRST FLOOR
porch
sto
shr
lin
mbr
14 x 18
cab
shv
den
18 x 20
br
w
d
util
f
ref
kit
ct
dbl ov
13 x 16
dw
hvac
up
desk
bar
lin
br 2
12 x 12
br 3
12³ x 11⁶
foy
6⁶x14
dining
14 x 12³
eating
11 x 13
porch 31¹⁰ x 6
WIDTH 65'-6"
DEPTH 74'-5"

Sophisticated Southern Styling

- This plan features:
  - — Five bedrooms
  - — Three full and one half baths
- Covered front and rear Porches expand the living space
- A Den with a large fireplace
- A cooktop island, built-in desk, and eating bar complete the Kitchen
- The Master Suite has two walk-in closets and a luxurious Bath
- Four additional Bedrooms, two on the first floor and two on the second floor
- An optional slab or crawl space foundation — please specify when ordering

FIRST FLOOR — 2,256 SQ. FT.
SECOND FLOOR — 602 SQ. FT.
BONUS ROOM— 264 SQ. FT.
GARAGE — 484 SQ. FT.

TOTAL LIVING AREA:
2,858 SQ. FT.

Design by
Corley Plan Service

Refer to **Pricing Schedule E** on the order form for pricing information

Traditional That Has It All

- This plan features:
- — Three bedrooms
- — Three full and two half baths
- A Master Suite with two closets and a private bath with separate shower, corner tub and dual vanity
- A large Dining Room with a bay window, adjacent to the Kitchen
- A formal Living Room for entertaining and a cozy Family Room with fireplace for informal relaxation
- Two upstairs Bedrooms with walk-in closets and private Baths
- A Bonus Room to allow the house to grow with your needs
- An optional basement, slab or crawl space foundation — please specify when ordering

FIRST FLOOR — 1,927 SQ. FT.
SECOND FLOOR — 832 SQ. FT.
BONUS ROOM — 624 SQ. FT.
BASEMENT — 1,674 SQ. FT.

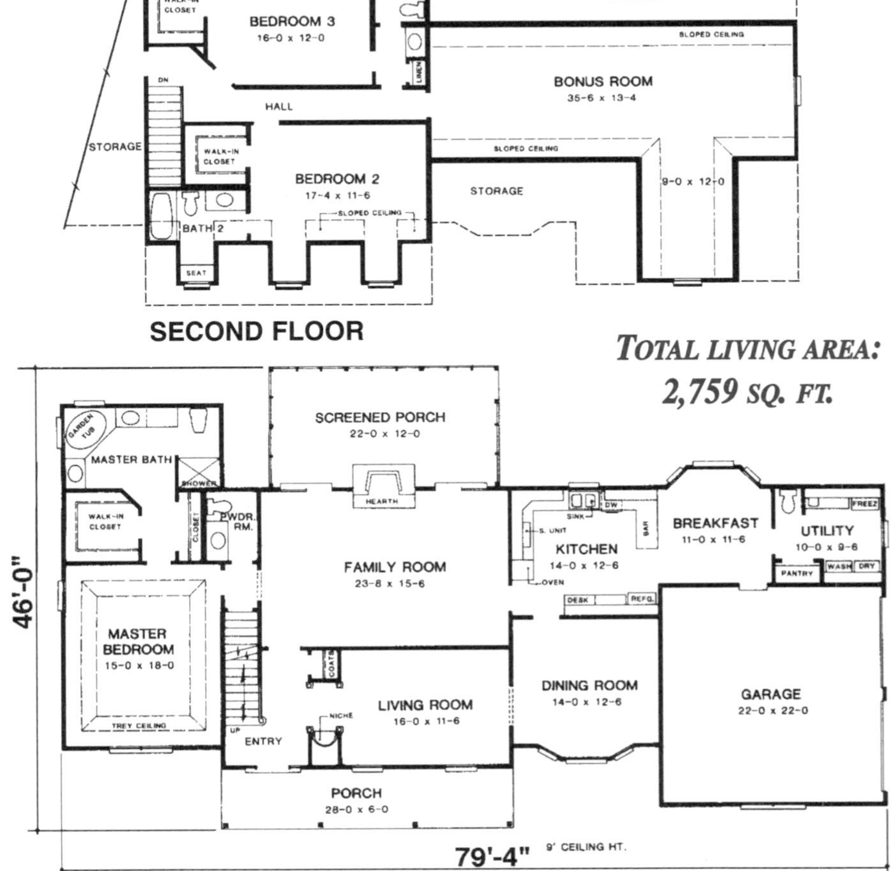

WALK-IN CLOSET
BEDROOM 3
16-0 x 12-0
BATH 3
STORAGE
SLOPED CEILING
LINEN
DN
HALL
BONUS ROOM
35-6 x 13-4
STORAGE
WALK-IN CLOSET
BEDROOM 2
17-4 x 11-6
SLOPED CEILING
STORAGE
9-0 x 12-0
BATH 2
SEAT
SECOND FLOOR
TOTAL LIVING AREA:
2,759 SQ. FT.
GARDEN TUB
MASTER BATH
SHOWER
SCREENED PORCH
22-0 x 12-0
HEARTH
WALK-IN CLOSET
CLOSET
PWDR. RM.
FAMILY ROOM
23-8 x 15-6
SINK
DW
S. UNIT
KITCHEN
14-0 x 12-6
BAR
OVEN
BREAKFAST
11-0 x 11-6
UTILITY
10-0 x 9-6
FREEZ
PANTRY
WASH
DRY
DESK
REFG.
46'-0"
MASTER BEDROOM
15-0 x 18-0
TREY CEILING
COATS
UP
ENTRY
NICHE
LIVING ROOM
16-0 x 11-6
DINING ROOM
14-0 x 12-6
GARAGE
22-0 x 22-0
PORCH
28-0 x 6-0
79'-4"
9' CEILING HT.

FIRST FLOOR
No. 90443

Refer to **Pricing Schedule F** on the order form for pricing information

Design by
Studer Residential Design, Inc.

PLAN NO. 92666

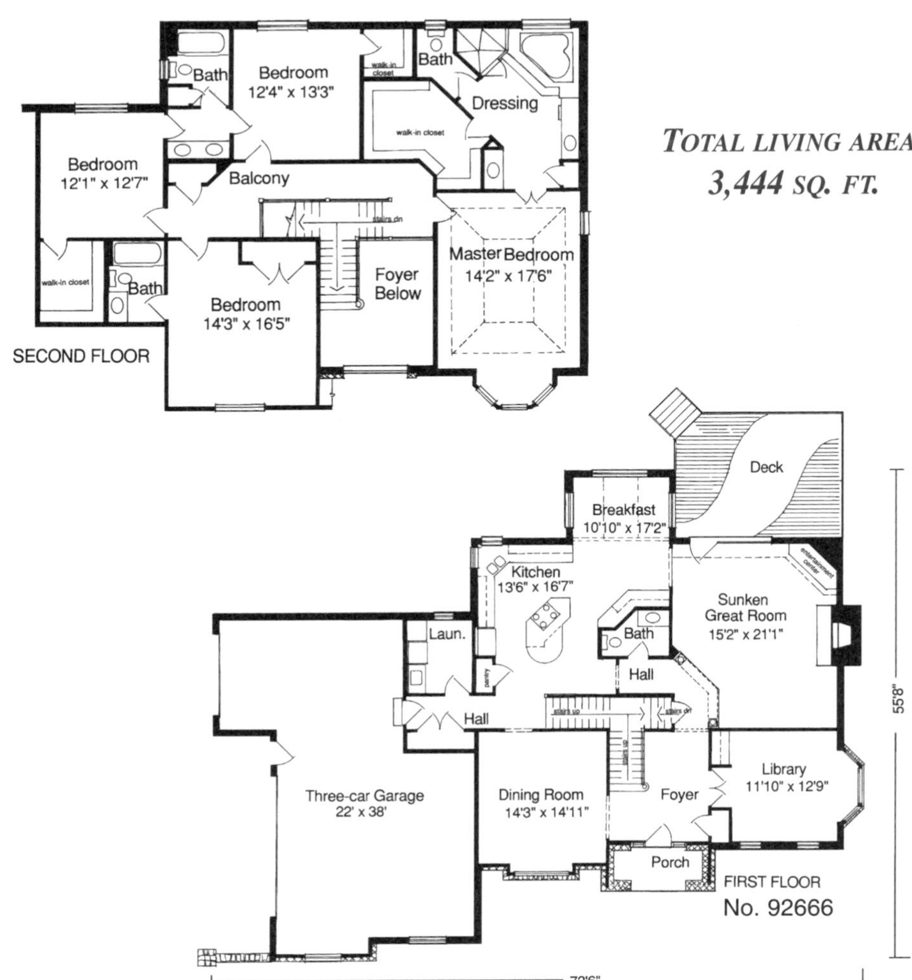

Bedroom
12'4" x 13'3"
Bath
walk-in closet
Bath
Dressing
walk-in closet
Bedroom
12'1" x 12'7"
Balcony
Master Bedroom
14'2" x 17'6"
walk-in closet
Bath
Bedroom
14'3" x 16'5"
Foyer Below
SECOND FLOOR
Deck
Breakfast
10'10" x 17'2"
Kitchen
13'6" x 16'7"
Sunken Great Room
15'2" x 21'1"
Laun.
Bath
Hall
Hall
Three-car Garage
22' x 38'
Dining Room
14'3" x 14'11"
Foyer
Library
11'10" x 12'9"
Porch
FIRST FLOOR
No. 92666
55'8"
72'6"

TOTAL LIVING AREA:
3,444 SQ. FT.

The Ultimate in Style

- This plan features:
  — Four bedrooms
  — Three full and one half baths
- A variety of exterior materials combine with a well planned interior for impeccable style
- For formal gatherings there is the Dining Room and the Library
- Family activities will be centered in the sunken Great Room and the adjacent Kitchen
- The Kitchen is open, has ample counter space and features a center island
- A deck is located in the rear for outdoor activities
- Upstairs find the Master Bedroom, which has a walk-in closet and a sumptuous Bath
- No materials list is available for this plan

FIRST FLOOR — 1,678 SQ. FT.
SECOND FLOOR — 1,766 SQ. FT.
BASEMENT — 1,639 SQ. FT.
GARAGE — 761 SQ. FT.

PLAN NO. 94995

Design by
Design Basics, Inc.

Refer to **Pricing Schedule E** on the order form for pricing information

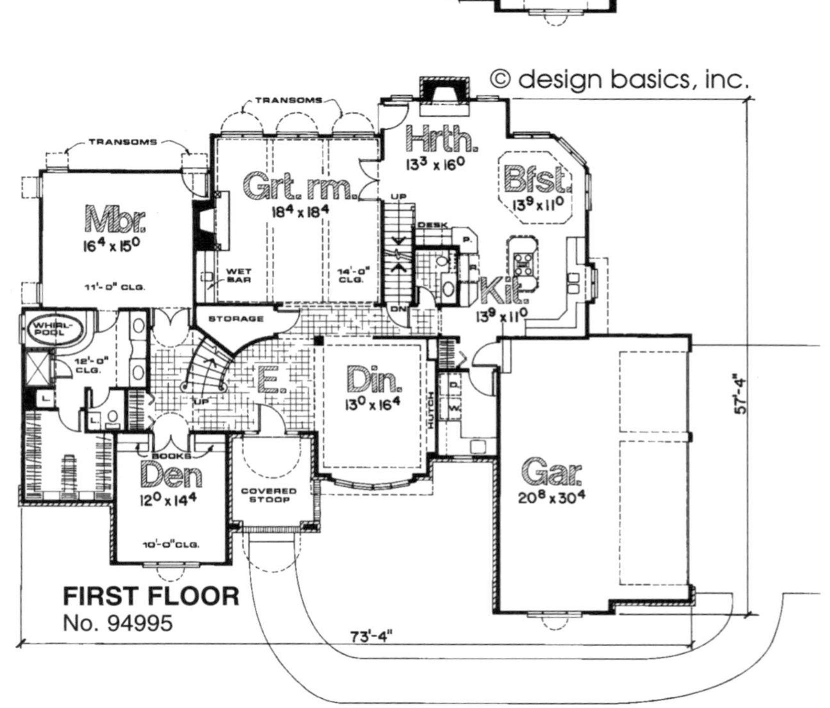

SECOND FLOOR
Br.3
13³ x 12⁰
DISPLAY
DN
OPEN TO BELOW
Br.2
12⁰ x 14⁸
10'-0" CLG.
LINEN
Br.4
13⁰ x 12⁰
© design basics, inc.
TRANSOMS
Mbr.
16⁴ x 15⁰
11'-0" CLG.
Grt. rm.
18⁴ x 18⁴
WET BAR
14'-0" CLG.
Hrth.
13³ x 16⁰
Bfst.
13⁹ x 11⁰
DESK
Kit.
13⁹ x 11⁰
STORAGE
WHIRL-POOL
12'-0" CLG.
E.
Din.
13⁰ x 16⁴
HUTCH
BOOKS
Den
12⁰ x 14⁴
10'-0" CLG.
COVERED STOOP
Gar.
20⁸ x 30⁴
57'-4"
73'-4"
FIRST FLOOR
No. 94995

Spectacular Curving Stairway

- This plan features:
- — Four bedrooms
- — Two full, one three-quarter and one half baths
- Formal entry with arched transom, is enhanced by a curved staircase
- Great Room has a cozy fireplace, a wetbar and triple arched windows
- Open Kitchen, Breakfast and Hearth Area combine efficiency and comfort for all
- Master Bedroom retreat offers a private back door, a double walk-in closet and a whirlpool Bath

FIRST FLOOR — 2,252 SQ. FT.
SECOND FLOOR — 920 SQ. FT.
BASEMENT — 2,252 SQ. FT.
GARAGE — 646 SQ. FT.

TOTAL LIVING AREA:
3,172 SQ. FT.

Four Bedroom with One Floor Convenience

Price Code: E

- This plan features:
  - — Four bedrooms
  - — Three full baths
- A distinguished brick exterior adds curb appeal
- Formal Entry/Gallery opens to large Living Room with hearth fireplace set between windows overlooking Patio and rear yard
- Efficient Kitchen with angled counters and serving bar easily serves Breakfast Room, Patio and formal Dining Room
- Corner Master Bedroom is enhanced by a vaulted ceiling and pampering bath with a large walk-in closet
- Three additional bedrooms with walk-in closets have access to full baths
- No materials list is available for this plan

MAIN FLOOR — 2,675 SQ. FT.
GARAGE — 638 SQ. FT.

TOTAL LIVING AREA:
2,675 SQ. FT.

Design by
Fillmore Design Group

PLAN NO.92275

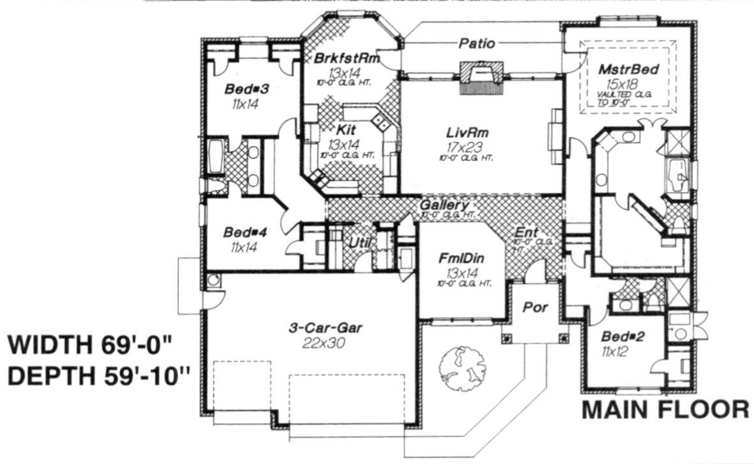
Patio
BrkfstRm
13x14
Bed#3
11x14
MstrBed
15x18
Kit
13x14
LivRm
17x23
Gallery
Bed#4
11x14
Util
Ent
FmlDin
13x14
Por
3-Car-Gar
22x30
Bed#2
11x12
WIDTH 69'-0"
DEPTH 59'-10"
MAIN FLOOR

Lavish Accommodations

Price Code: F

- This plan features:
  - — Four bedrooms
  - — Three full baths
- A central Den has a large fireplace, built-in shelves and cabinets
- Columns define the entrance to the formal Dining Room, adding a touch of elegance
- A well-thoughout Kitchen includes a walk-in Pantry and an island
- An informal Breakfast Room is directly accessible from either the Kitchen or the Den
- The Master Bedroom is enhanced by a decorative ceiling and a walk-in closet
- Four additional bedrooms, each have private access to a full bath
- An optional crawl space or slab foundation — please specify when ordering

MAIN FLOOR — 2,733 SQ. FT.
GARAGE & STORAGE — 569 SQ. FT.

TOTAL LIVING AREA:
2,733 SQ. FT.

Design by
Rick Garner

PLAN NO.92538

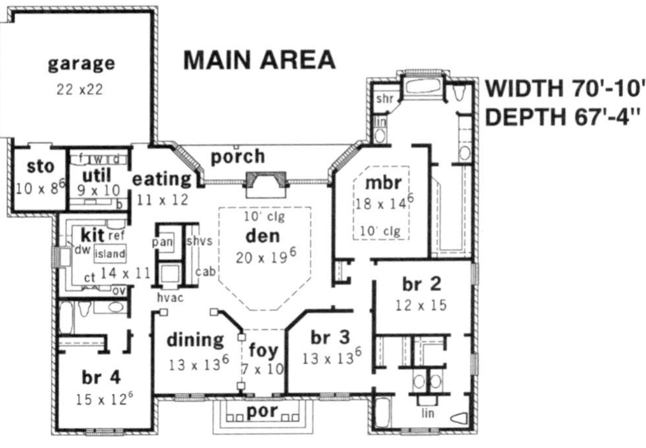
garage
22 x22
MAIN AREA
WIDTH 70'-10"
DEPTH 67'-4"
sto
10 x 8
util
9 x 10
eating
11 x 12
porch
mbr
18 x 14
den
20 x 19
kit
14 x 11
br 2
12 x 15
dining
13 x 13
foy
7 x 10
br 3
13 x 13
br 4
15 x 12
por

Design by
Chatham Home Planning, Inc.

Refer to **Pricing Schedule D** on the order form for pricing information

Family Room at Heart of the Home

- This plan features:
  - — Four bedrooms
  - — Three full baths
- The Living Room and Dining Room are to the right and left of the Foyer
- The Dining Room with French doors opens to the Kitchen
- An extended counter maximizes the work space in the Kitchen
- The Breakfast Room includes access to the Utility Room and to the secondary bedroom wing
- The Master Bedroom is equipped with a double vanity Bath, two walk-in closets and a linear closet
- A cozy fireplace and a decorative ceiling highlight the Family Room
- No materials list is available for this plan

MAIN FLOOR — 2,558 SQ. FT.
GARAGE — 549 SQ. FT.

TOTAL LIVING AREA:
2,558 SQ. FT.

WIDTH 63'-6"
DEPTH 71'-6"

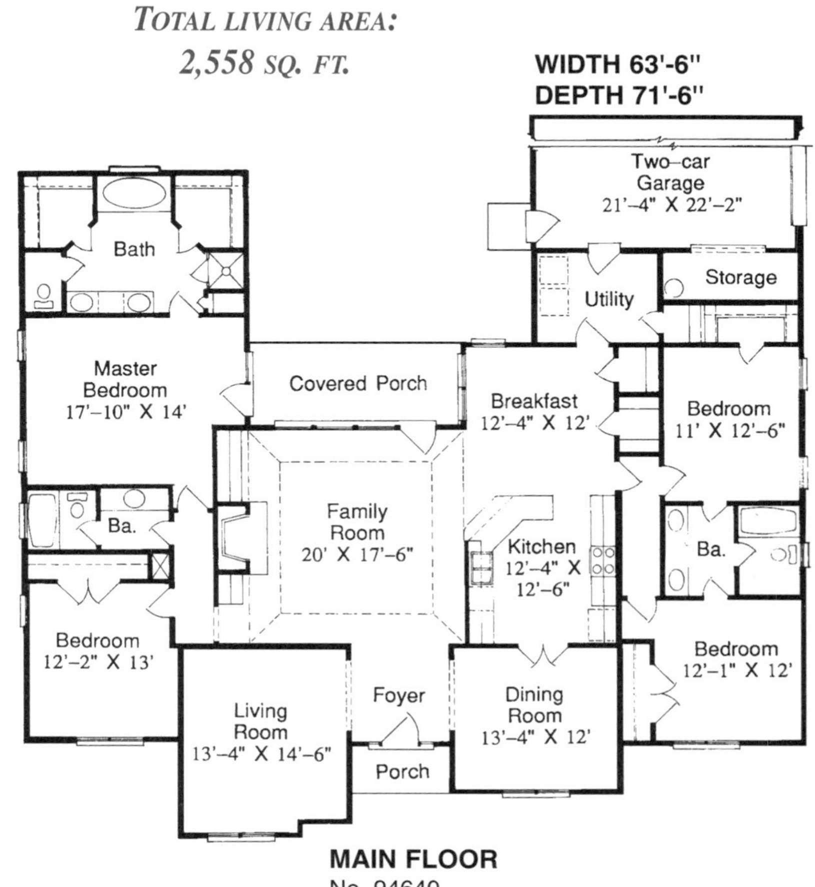
Two-car Garage
21'-4" X 22'-2"
Storage
Utility
Bath
Master Bedroom
17'-10" X 14'
Covered Porch
Breakfast
12'-4" X 12'
Bedroom
11' X 12'-6"
Ba.
Family Room
20' X 17'-6"
Kitchen
12'-4" X 12'-6"
Ba.
Bedroom
12'-2" X 13'
Foyer
Dining Room
13'-4" X 12'
Bedroom
12'-1" X 12'
Living Room
13'-4" X 14'-6"
Porch

MAIN FLOOR
No. 94640

Refer to **Pricing Schedule D** on the order form for pricing information

Design by
Frank Betz Associates, Inc.

PLAN NO. 98417

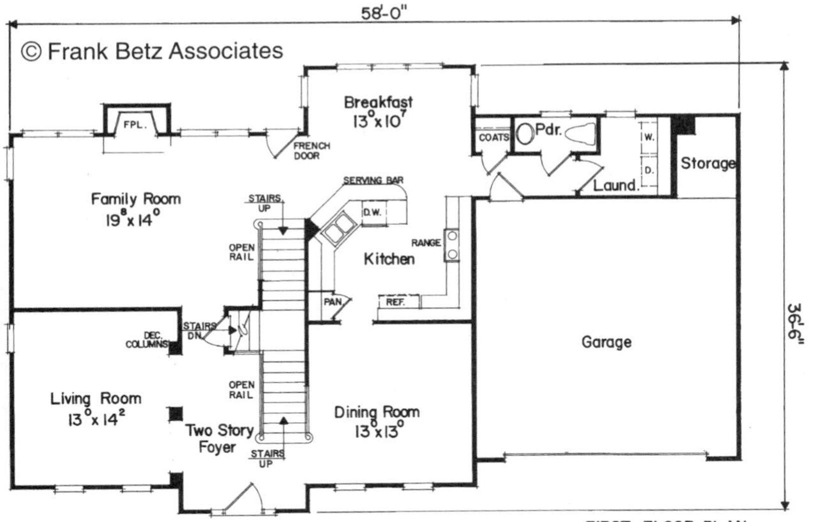

58'-0"

© Frank Betz Associates

Breakfast 13^0 x 10^7
Family Room 19^8 x 14^0
FPL.
FRENCH DOOR
COATS
Pdr.
W.
D.
Laund.
Storage
SERVING BAR
STAIRS UP
D.W.
OPEN RAIL
RANGE
Kitchen
PAN.
REF.
STAIRS DN
DEC. COLUMNS
Garage
Living Room 13^0 x 14^2
Two Story Foyer
Dining Room 13^0 x 13^0
STAIRS UP
36'-6"

FIRST FLOOR PLAN

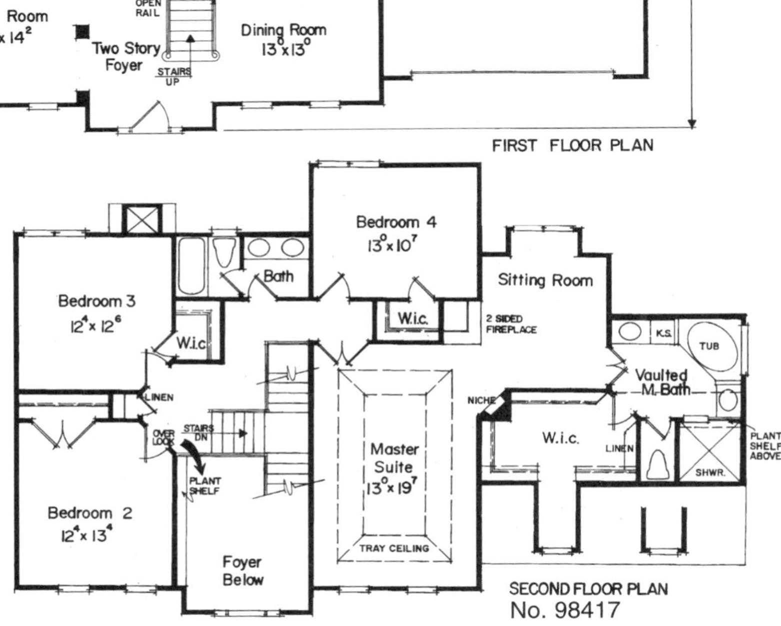

Bedroom 4
13^0 x 10^7
Bath
Bedroom 3
12^4 x 12^6
W.i.c.
W.i.c.
Sitting Room
2 SIDED FIREPLACE
K.S.
TUB
Vaulted M. Bath
LINEN
NICHE
OVER LOOK
STAIRS DN
PLANT SHELF
Master Suite
13^0 x 19^7
W.i.c.
LINEN
PLANT SHELF ABOVE
SHWR.
Bedroom 2
12^4 x 13^4
Foyer Below
TRAY CEILING
SECOND FLOOR PLAN
No. 98417

Contemporary Plan With Old World Charm

- This plan features:
  - — Four bedrooms
  - — Two full and one half baths
- The Living Room is accented by three decorative columns
- The elegant Dining Room has direct access to the Kitchen
- The Pantry and extended counter/serving bar highlight the Kitchen
- The Family Room is enhanced by a fireplace
- Master Suite has a two-sided fireplace, a Sitting Room with a bay window, and a private Bath
- An optional basement or crawl space foundation — please specify when ordering

FIRST FLOOR — 1,252 SQ. FT.
SECOND FLOOR — 1,348 SQ. FT.
BASEMENT — 1,252 SQ. FT.
GARAGE — 483 SQ. FT.

TOTAL LIVING AREA:
2,600 SQ. FT.

PLAN NO. 98539

Design by
Filmore Design Group

Refer to **Pricing Schedule F** on the order form for pricing information

An Estate of Epic Proportion

- This plan features
  - — Four bedrooms
  - — Three full and one half baths
- The grand Entry has a 20-foot ceiling and a spiral staircase
- Flanking the Entry is the Living Room with cathedral ceiling and fireplace, and the bayed formal Dining Room
- The Study has a built-in bookcase
- The Master Bedroom has a Bath and a bayed Sitting Area
- The Family Room has a wetbar and a fireplace
- An optional basement or slab foundation — please specify when ordering
- No materials list is available for this plan

FIRST FLOOR — 2,751 SQ. FT.
SECOND FLOOR — 1,185 SQ. FT.
BONUS — 343 SQ. FT.
GARAGE — 790 SQ. FT.

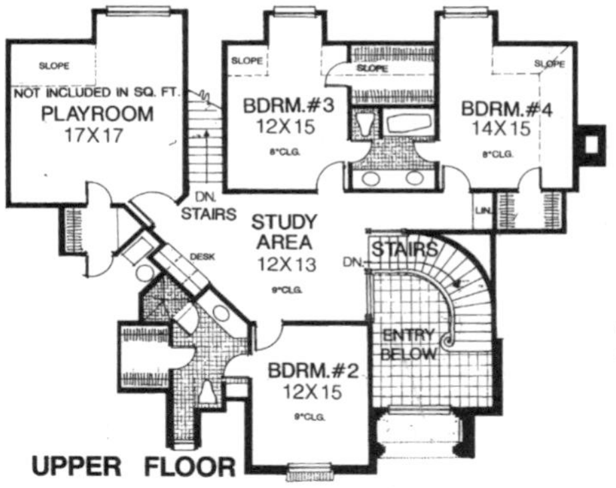

TOTAL LIVING AREA:
3,936 SQ. FT.

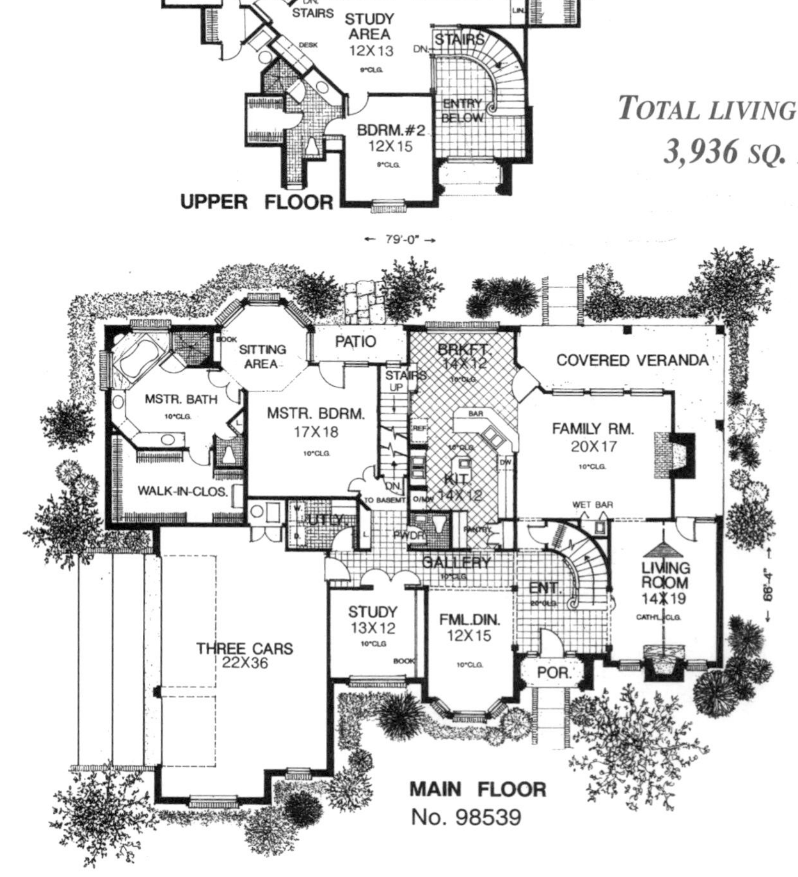

NOT INCLUDED IN SQ. FT.
PLAYROOM
17X17
BDRM.#3
12X15
BDRM.#4
14X15
DN. STAIRS
STUDY AREA
12X13
STAIRS
ENTRY BELOW
BDRM.#2
12X15
UPPER FLOOR
79'-0"
SITTING AREA
PATIO
BRKFT.
14X12
COVERED VERANDA
MSTR. BATH
MSTR. BDRM.
17X18
FAMILY RM.
20X17
KIT.
14X12
WALK-IN-CLOS.
UTIL.
PWDR.
WET BAR
GALLERY
ENT.
LIVING ROOM
14X19
STUDY
13X12
FML.DIN.
12X15
THREE CARS
22X36
POR.
66'-4"
MAIN FLOOR
No. 98539

To order your Blueprints, call 1-800-235-5700

Refer to **Pricing Schedule D** on the order form for pricing information

Design by
Ahmann Design, Inc.

PLAN NO. 99142

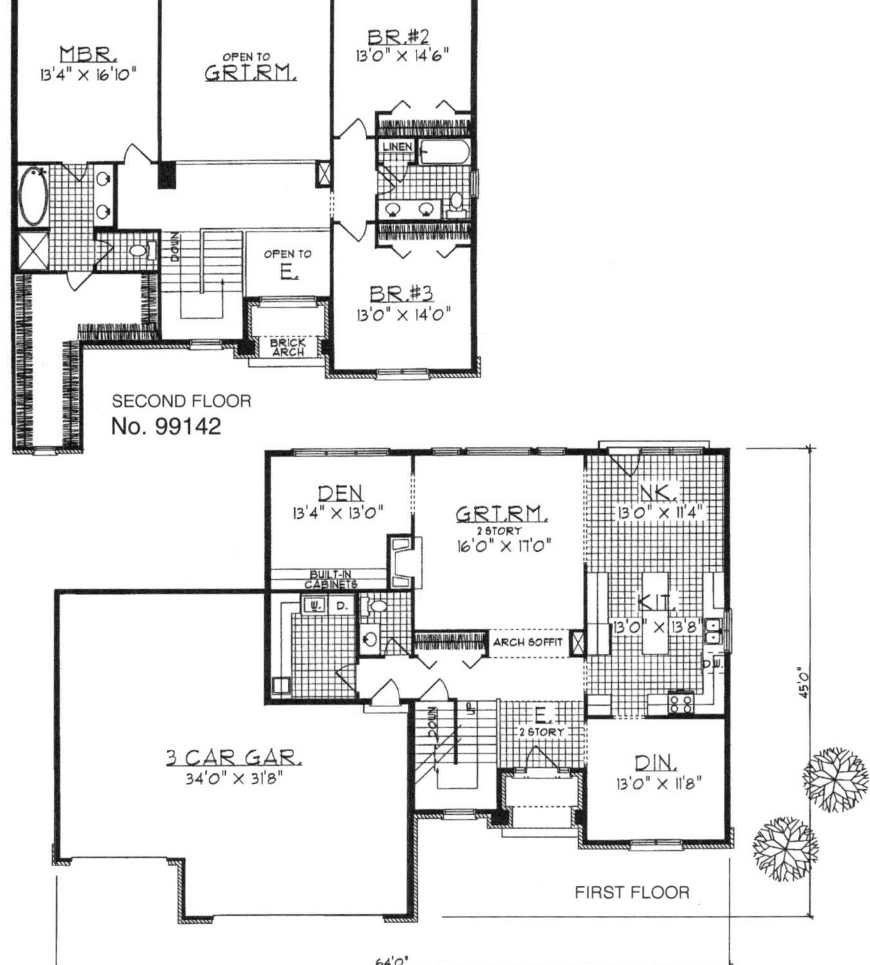

MBR.
13'4" X 16'10"
OPEN TO
GRT.RM.
BR.#2
13'0" X 14'6"
LINEN
DOWN
OPEN TO
E.
BR.#3
13'0" X 14'0"
BRICK ARCH
SECOND FLOOR
No. 99142
DEN
13'4" X 13'0"
BUILT-IN CABINETS
GRT.RM.
2 STORY
16'0" X 17'0"
NK.
13'0" X 11'4"
KIT.
13'0" X 13'8"
ARCH SOFFIT
D.
DOWN
E.
2 STORY
3 CAR GAR.
34'0" X 31'8"
DIN.
13'0" X 11'8"
45'0"
FIRST FLOOR
64'0"

Elegant Living

- This plan features:
- — Three bedrooms
- — Two full and one half baths
- The spacious Great Room has a two-story ceiling and a fireplace
- The Den features built-in cabinetry
- The formal Dining Room provides a quiet place for entertaining
- The first floor Laundry is located just off the three-car Garage
- A Nook is adjacent to the Kitchen
- The Master Suite with generous windows, also has a private Bath
- No materials list is available for this plan

FIRST FLOOR — 1,408 SQ. FT.
SECOND FLOOR — 1,184 SQ. FT.
BASEMENT — 1,408 SQ. FT.

TOTAL LIVING AREA:
2,592 SQ. FT.

To order your Blueprints, call 1-800-235-5700

PLAN NO. 99843

Design by
Donald A. Gardner Architects, Inc.

Refer to **Pricing Schedule F** on the order form for pricing information

The Great Outdoors

- This plan features:
- — Four bedrooms
- — Two full and one half baths
- Bay windows and a long, skylit, screened Porch — a haven for outdoor enthusiasts
- Vaulted ceiling in the Great Room adds vertical drama
- Contemporary Kitchen is open to the Great Room creating a spacious feeling
- Master Bedroom has a luxurious Bath complete with a bay window, corner shower and a garden tub

FIRST FLOOR — 1,907 SQ. FT.
SECOND FLOOR — 656 SQ. FT.
BONUS ROOM — 467 SQ. FT.
GARAGE & STORAGE — 580 SQ. FT.

TOTAL LIVING AREA:
2,563 SQ. FT.

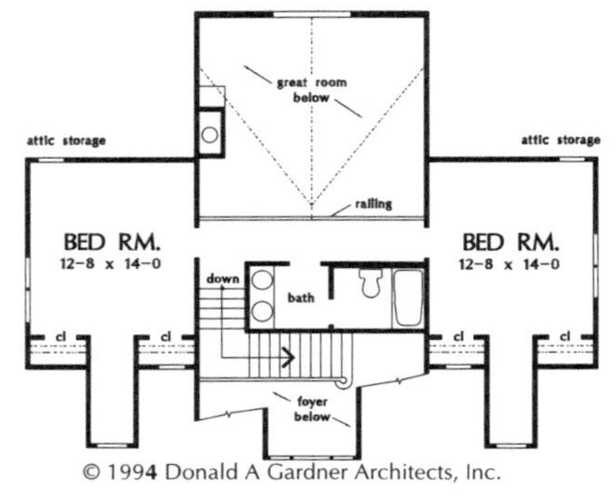

great room below
attic storage
attic storage
railing
BED RM.
12-8 x 14-0
BED RM.
12-8 x 14-0
down
bath
foyer below

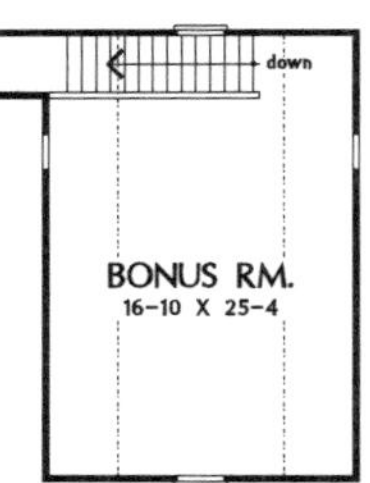

down
BONUS RM.
16-10 X 25-4

SECOND FLOOR PLAN

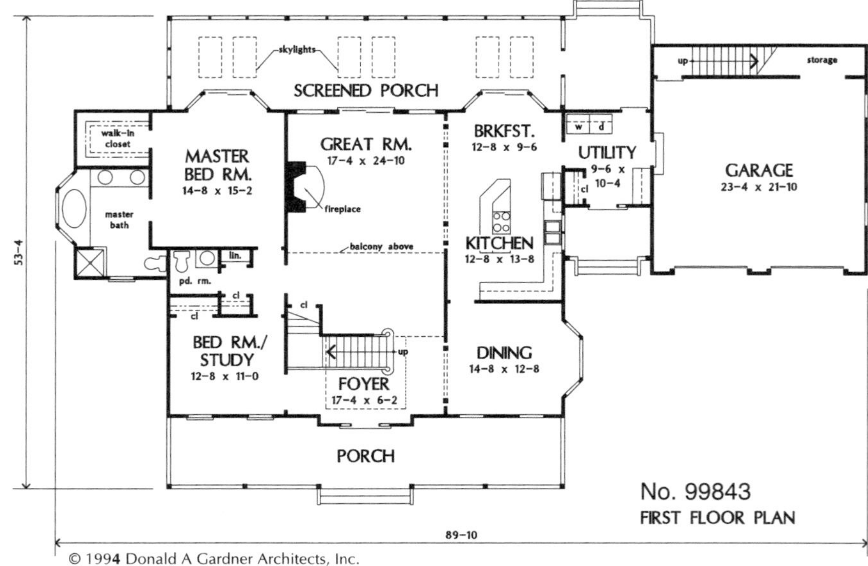

skylights
SCREENED PORCH
walk-in closet
MASTER BED RM.
14-8 x 15-2
master bath
GREAT RM.
17-4 x 24-10
fireplace
balcony above
BRKFST.
12-8 x 9-6
UTILITY
9-6 x 10-4
KITCHEN
12-8 x 13-8
up
storage
GARAGE
23-4 x 21-10
lin.
pd. rm.
BED RM./ STUDY
12-8 x 11-0
FOYER
17-4 x 6-2
up
DINING
14-8 x 12-8
PORCH
53-4
89-10

No. 99843
FIRST FLOOR PLAN

Accent on Privacy

Price Code: D

Design by Sun-Tel Designs

- This plan features:
- — Three bedrooms
- — Two full and one half baths
- Stucco exterior and arched windows create a feeling of grandeur
- Sunken Living Room has a fireplace and elegant decorative ceiling
- Sweeping views of the backyard and direct access to the rear Deck from the Family Room, Kitchen and Breakfast Nook
- Gourmet Kitchen with two pantries, full height shelving, and a large island snack bar
- Master Bedroom enjoys its privacy on the opposite side of the home from the other bedrooms
- Fabulous Master Bath with recessed tub and corner shower
- Continental Bath connects the two secondary bedrooms
- An optional basement, crawl space or slab foundation — please specify when ordering

MAIN AREA — 2,591 SQ. FT.
BASEMENT — 2,591 SQ. FT.

TOTAL LIVING AREA:
2,591 SQ. FT.

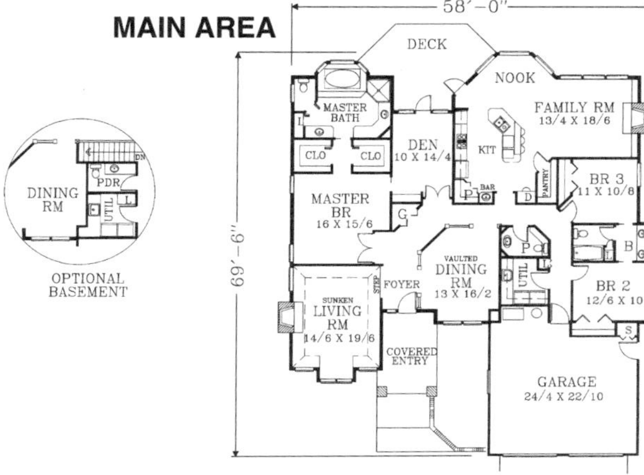
MAIN AREA
58′–0″
69′–6″
DECK
NOOK
FAMILY RM
13/4 X 18/6
MASTER BATH
CLO
CLO
DEN
10 X 14/4
KIT
BAR
PANTRY
BR 3
11 X 10/8
MASTER BR
16 X 15/6
VAULTED DINING RM
13 X 16/2
FOYER
UTIL
BR 2
12/6 X 10
SUNKEN LIVING RM
14/6 X 19/6
COVERED ENTRY
GARAGE
24/4 X 22/10
DINING RM
PDR
UTIL
OPTIONAL BASEMENT

Extra Special Luxuries

Price Code: F

Design by Donald A. Gardner Architects, Inc.

- This plan features:
- — Four bedrooms
- — Two full and one half baths
- The front door opens to a central Foyer that leads left to the formal Dining Room
- The large Great Room includes a cathedral ceiling, a fireplace, built-ins and access to an airy Sun Room
- The Kitchen has a center work island and accent columns at the entrance to the Great Room
- Indulgent Master Suite with a skylit, plush Bath and a walk-in closet
- Two additional Bedrooms share the full Bath in the hall

MAIN FLOOR — 2,602 SQ. FT.
BONUS — 399 SQ. FT.
GARAGE — 715 SQ. FT.

TOTAL LIVING AREA:
2,602 SQ. FT.

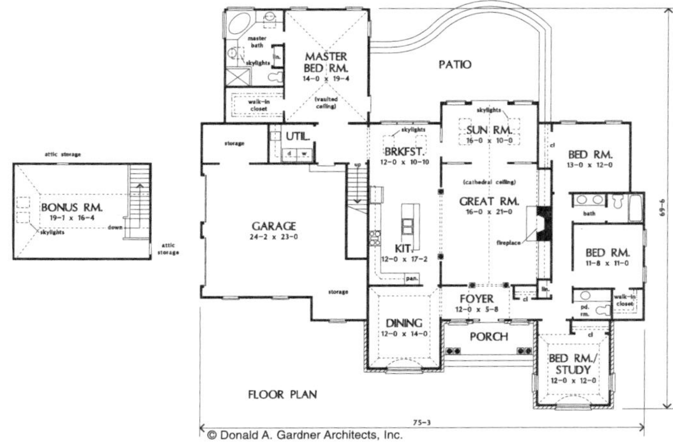
MASTER BED RM.
14-0 x 19-4
PATIO
UTIL.
SUN RM.
16-0 x 10-0
BRKFST.
12-0 x 10-10
BED RM.
13-0 x 12-0
GREAT RM.
16-0 x 21-0
BONUS RM.
19-1 x 16-4
GARAGE
24-2 x 23-0
KIT.
12-0 x 17-2
BED RM.
11-8 x 11-0
FOYER
12-0 x 5-8
DINING
12-0 x 14-0
PORCH
BED RM./ STUDY
12-0 x 12-0
FLOOR PLAN

PLAN NO. 98418

Design by
Frank Betz Associates, Inc.

Refer to **Pricing Schedule E** on the order form for pricing information

A Grand Entrance

- This plan features:
- — Five bedrooms
- — Three full baths
- The arched window above the front door provides a grand entrance
- The formal Living and Dining Rooms are only separated by a set of boxed columns
- The U-shaped Kitchen has a walk-in Pantry and a wall oven
- The Family Room has a fireplace as well as a vaulted ceiling
- Rounding our the first floor is a Den/Bedroom
- An optional basement or crawl space foundation — please specify when ordering

FIRST FLOOR — 1,424 SQ. FT.
SECOND FLOOR — 1,256 SQ. FT.
BASEMENT — 1,424 SQ. FT.
GARAGE — 494 SQ. FT.

TOTAL LIVING AREA:
2,680 SQ. FT.

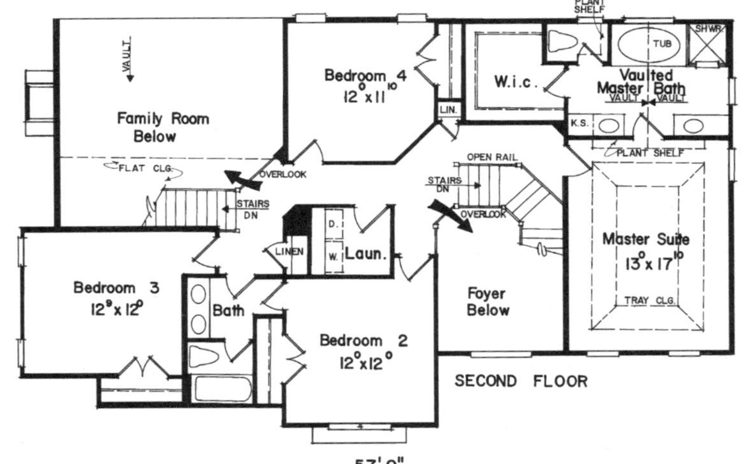
PLANT SHELF
SHWR.
TUB
VAULT
Family Room Below
Bedroom 4
$12^{0} \times 11^{10}$
W.i.c.
Vaulted Master Bath
VAULT
VAULT
LIN.
K.S.
PLANT SHELF
FLAT CLG.
OVERLOOK
OPEN RAIL
STAIRS DN
STAIRS DN
OVERLOOK
Master Suite
$13^{0} \times 17^{10}$
TRAY CLG.
D.
W.
LINEN
Laun.
Bedroom 3
$12^{9} \times 12^{0}$
Bath
Foyer Below
Bedroom 2
$12^{0} \times 12^{0}$
SECOND FLOOR

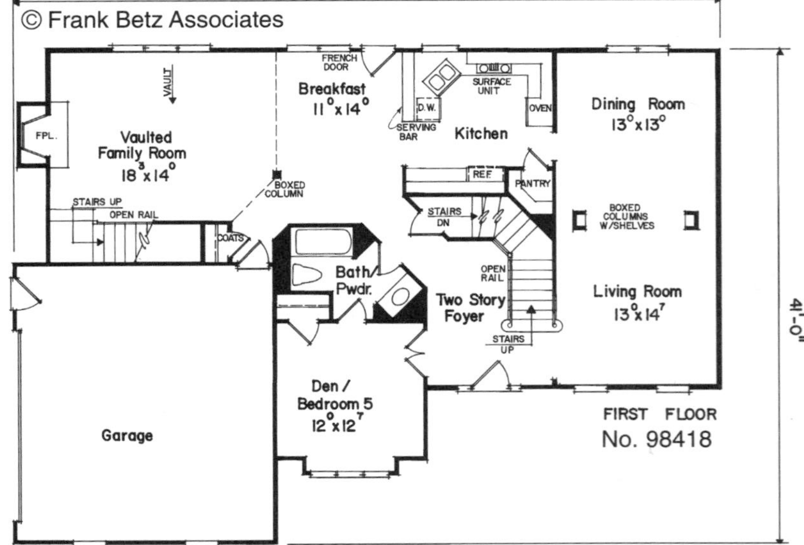
57'-0"
© Frank Betz Associates
FRENCH DOOR
VAULT
Breakfast
$11^{0} \times 14^{0}$
SURFACE UNIT
OVEN
D.W.
SERVING BAR
Kitchen
Dining Room
$13^{0} \times 13^{0}$
FPL.
Vaulted Family Room
$18^{3} \times 14^{0}$
BOXED COLUMN
REF.
PANTRY
STAIRS UP
OPEN RAIL
STAIRS DN
BOXED COLUMNS W/SHELVES
COATS
Bath/Pwdr.
OPEN RAIL
Two Story Foyer
Living Room
$13^{0} \times 14^{7}$
41'-0"
STAIRS UP
Den / Bedroom 5
$12^{0} \times 12^{7}$
Garage
FIRST FLOOR
No. 98418

Refer to **Pricing Schedule F** on the order form for pricing information

Design by
Design Basics, Inc.

PLAN NO. 99410

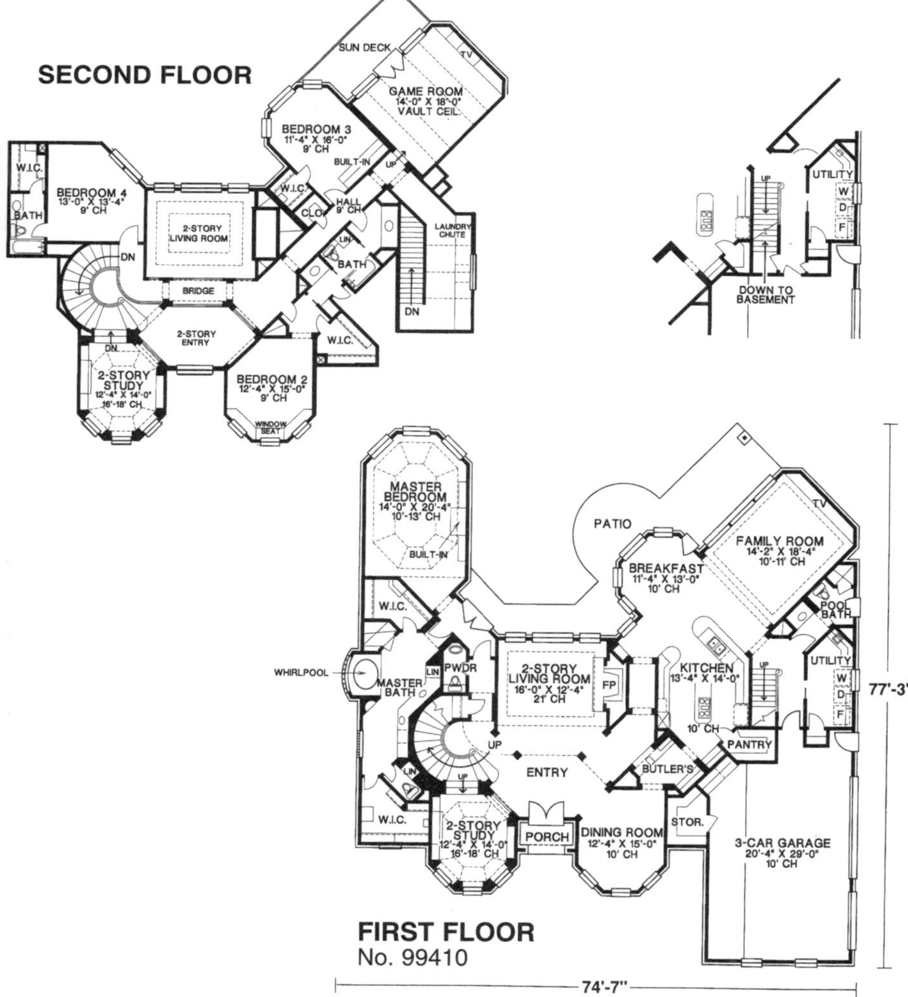
SECOND FLOOR
SUN DECK
GAME ROOM 14'-0" X 18'-0" VAULT CEIL.
TV
BEDROOM 3 11'-4" X 16'-0" 9' CH
BUILT-IN
W.I.C.
BEDROOM 4 13'-0" X 13'-4" 9' CH
BATH
2-STORY LIVING ROOM
HALL 9' CH
CLO.
LIN.
BATH
LAUNDRY CHUTE
DN
BRIDGE
2-STORY ENTRY
W.I.C.
2-STORY STUDY 12'-4" X 14'-0" 16'-18' CH.
BEDROOM 2 12'-4" X 15'-0" 9' CH
WINDOW SEAT
UTILITY
DOWN TO BASEMENT
MASTER BEDROOM 14'-0" X 20'-4" 10'-13' CH
BUILT-IN
PATIO
FAMILY ROOM 14'-2" X 18'-4" 10'-11' CH
BREAKFAST 11'-4" X 13'-0" 10' CH
POOL BATH
W.I.C.
WHIRLPOOL
MASTER BATH
PWDR
2-STORY LIVING ROOM 16'-0" X 12'-4" 21' CH
FP
KITCHEN 13'-4" X 14'-0"
10' CH
UTILITY
PANTRY
ENTRY
BUTLER'S
W.I.C.
2-STORY STUDY 12'-4" X 14'-0" 16'-18' CH
PORCH
DINING ROOM 12'-4" X 15'-0" 10' CH
STOR.
3-CAR GARAGE 20'-4" X 29'-0" 10' CH
77'-3"
74'-7"
FIRST FLOOR
No. 99410

Magnificent Presence

- This plan features:
  - — Four bedrooms
  - — Three full, one three-quarter, and one half baths
- Curved staircase leads to elevated two-story Study and the Master Suite
- Dining Room is connected to the Kitchen by a butler's Pantry
- Two-story Living Room has a fireplace and distinctive windows
- Breakfast Bay adjoins family room with built-in entertainment center
- Three Bedrooms and a Game Room on the second floor
- No materials list is available for this plan

First floor — 2,897 sq. ft.
Second floor — 1,603 sq. ft.
Basement — 2,897 sq. ft.
Garage — 793 sq. ft.

Total Living Area:
4,500 sq. ft.

PLAN NO. 98546

Design by
Filmore Design Group

Refer to **Pricing Schedule E** on the order form for pricing information

English Tudor Styling

- This plan features:
- — Four bedrooms
- — Three full and one half baths
- This Tudor styled gem has a unique mix of exterior materials
- Inside the Entry turn left to the Living Room or right into the Dining Room
- At the end of the Gallery is the Master Bedroom
- The Family Room has a sloped ceiling and a rear wall fireplace
- The Kitchen has a center island and opens to the Breakfast Area
- A skylight brightens the staircase to the second floor
- No materials list is available for this plan

FIRST FLOOR — 2,082 SQ. FT.
SECOND FLOOR — 904 SQ. FT.
BONUS — 408 SQ. FT.
GARAGE — 605 SQ. FT.

TOTAL LIVING AREA:
2,986 SQ. FT.

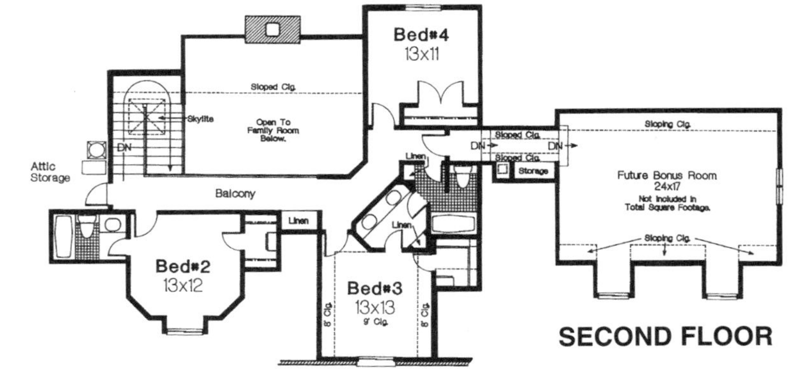

Bed#4
13x11
Sloped Clg.
Skylite
Open To Family Room Below.
DN
Attic Storage
Balcony
Linen
Bed#2
13x12
Bed#3
13x13
9' Clg.
Sloped Clg.
Storage
Sloping Clg.
Future Bonus Room
24x17
Not Included In Total Square Footage.

SECOND FLOOR

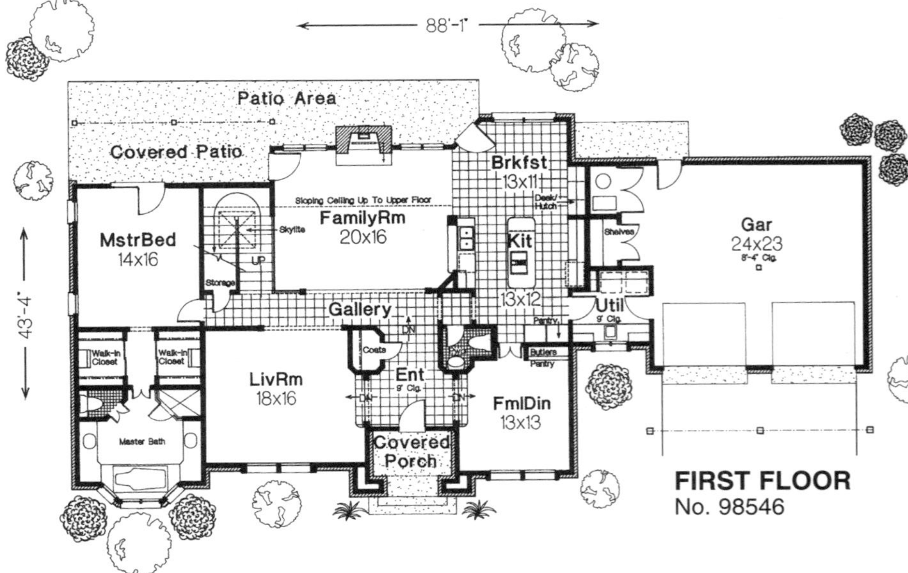

88'-1"
43'-4"
Patio Area
Covered Patio
Brkfst
13x11
Sloping Ceiling Up To Upper Floor
FamilyRm
20x16
Skylite
MstrBed
14x16
Storage
UP
Kit
13x12
Desk/Hutch
Gar
24x23
Shelves
Util
Gallery
Walk-in Closet
Walk-in Closet
Master Bath
LivRm
18x16
Coats
Ent
DN
Butlers Pantry
Pantry
FmlDin
13x13
Covered Porch

FIRST FLOOR
No. 98546

Refer to **Pricing Schedule E** on the order form for pricing information

Design by
Larry E. Belk

PLAN NO. 93041

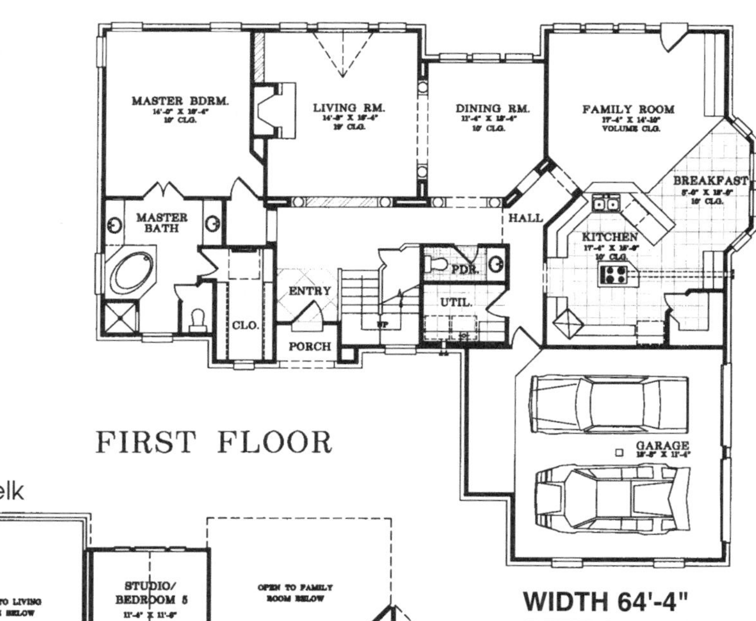

MASTER BDRM.
LIVING RM.
DINING RM.
FAMILY ROOM
BREAKFAST
MASTER BATH
HALL
KITCHEN
ENTRY
PDR.
UTIL.
CLO.
PORCH
GARAGE
FIRST FLOOR

WIDTH 64'-4"
DEPTH 53'-4"

© Larry E. Belk

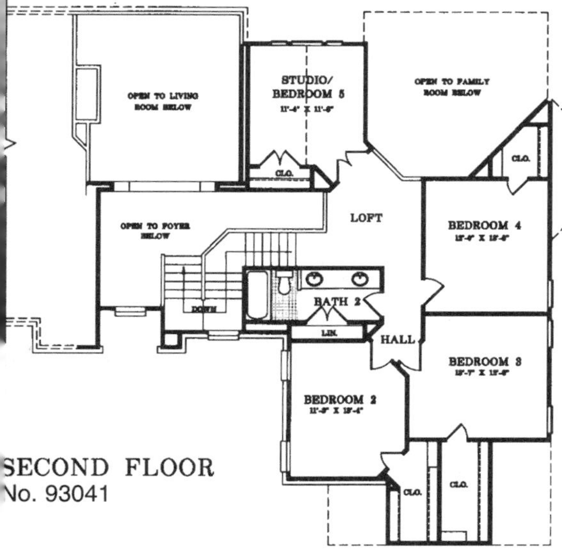

OPEN TO LIVING ROOM BELOW
STUDIO/ BEDROOM 5
OPEN TO FAMILY ROOM BELOW
CLO.
LOFT
OPEN TO FOYER BELOW
BEDROOM 4
BATH 2
LIN.
HALL
BEDROOM 3
BEDROOM 2
CLO.

SECOND FLOOR
No. 93041

Two-Story Entry Adds Grace

- This plan features:
  - — Four or five bedrooms
  - — Two full and one half baths
- All major living areas are located with views to the rear grounds
- The Kitchen, Breakfast Room and Family Room are adjacent and open to one another
- An island cooktop and double sinks, along with an abundance of storage space making the Kitchen even more convenient
- The Master Suite with an angled whirlpool tub, separate shower and his-and-her vanity
- Three additional Bedrooms located on the second floor
- No materials list is available for this plan

FIRST FLOOR — 1,974 SQ. FT.
SECOND FLOOR — 1,060 SQ. FT.
GARAGE — 531 SQ. FT.

TOTAL LIVING AREA:
3,034 SQ. FT.

PLAN NO. 99825

Design by
Donald A. Gardner Architects, Inc.

Refer to **Pricing Schedule F** on the order form for pricing information

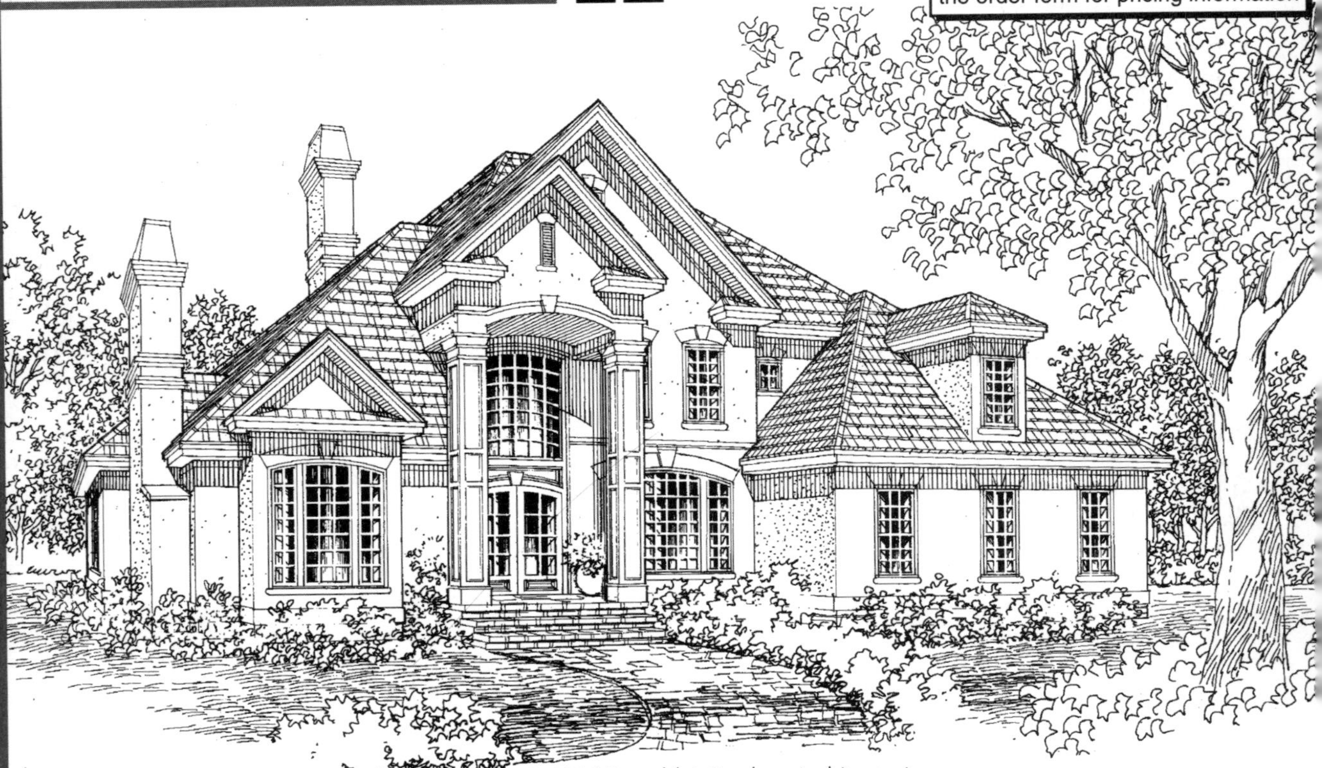

Luxuriant Living

- This plan features:
  - — Four bedrooms
  - — Three full and one half baths
- French doors, windows, and a high gabled entry make a dramatic entrance to this home
- Formal Living Room features a box bay window and a fireplace
- Large Family Room has a two-story ceiling, a fireplace and accessed the rear Patio
- Kitchen and Nook adjoin handy home Office that has a full bath
- The Master Suite features a private bath and a Sitting Area
- Upstairs find two Bedrooms each with a walk-in closet, a full Bath and a Bonus Room

First floor — 2,249 sq. ft.
Second floor — 620 sq. ft.
Bonus room — 308 sq. ft.
Garage — 642 sq. ft.

Total living area:
2,869 sq. ft.

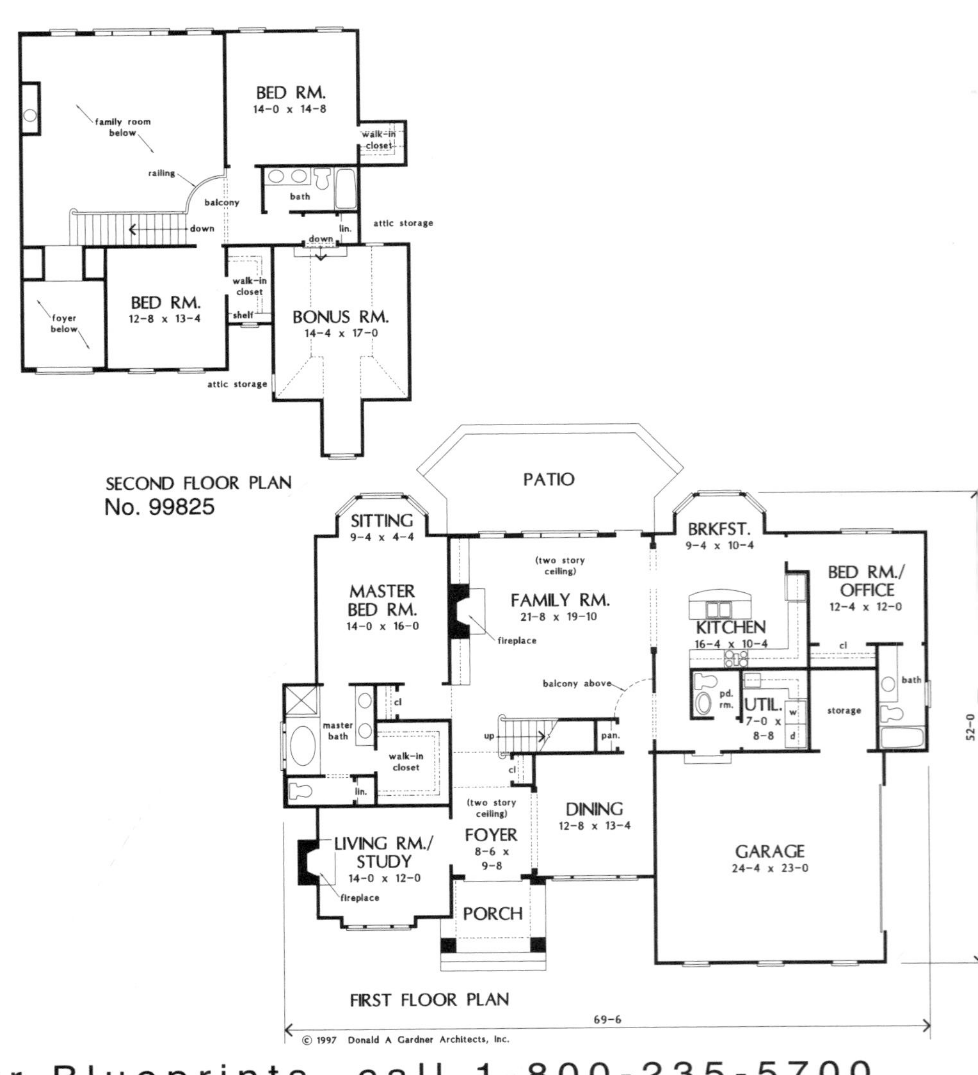

BED RM.
14-0 x 14-8
family room below
railing
balcony
walk-in closet
bath
attic storage
down
lin.
BED RM.
12-8 x 13-4
walk-in closet
shelf
BONUS RM.
14-4 x 17-0
foyer below
attic storage
SECOND FLOOR PLAN
No. 99825
PATIO
SITTING
9-4 x 4-4
MASTER BED RM.
14-0 x 16-0
(two story ceiling)
FAMILY RM.
21-8 x 19-10
fireplace
BRKFST.
9-4 x 10-4
KITCHEN
16-4 x 10-4
BED RM./ OFFICE
12-4 x 12-0
cl
bath
balcony above
pd. rm.
UTIL.
7-0 x 8-8
storage
master bath
cl
walk-in closet
up
pan.
cl
lin.
(two story ceiling)
FOYER
8-6 x 9-8
DINING
12-8 x 13-4
GARAGE
24-4 x 23-0
LIVING RM./ STUDY
14-0 x 12-0
fireplace
PORCH
52-0
FIRST FLOOR PLAN
69-6
© 1997 Donald A Gardner Architects, Inc.

Especially Unique

Price Code: E

- This plan features:
- — Four bedrooms
- — Three full and one half baths
- An arched entry and windows add a unique flair to this home
- From the 11-foot entry turn left into the Study/Media Room
- The formal Dining Room is open to the Gallery, and the Living Room
- The Family Room has a built-in entertainment center, a fireplace and access to the rear patio
- The Master Bedroom is isolated, and has a fireplace, a private bath, and a walk-in closet
- Three additional bedrooms on the opposite side of the home share two full baths
- A three-car garage
- No materials list is available for this plan

MAIN FLOOR — 2,748 SQ. FT.
GARAGE — 660 SQ. FT.

TOTAL LIVING AREA:
2,748 SQ. FT.

Design by
Fillmore Design Group

PLAN NO. 98528

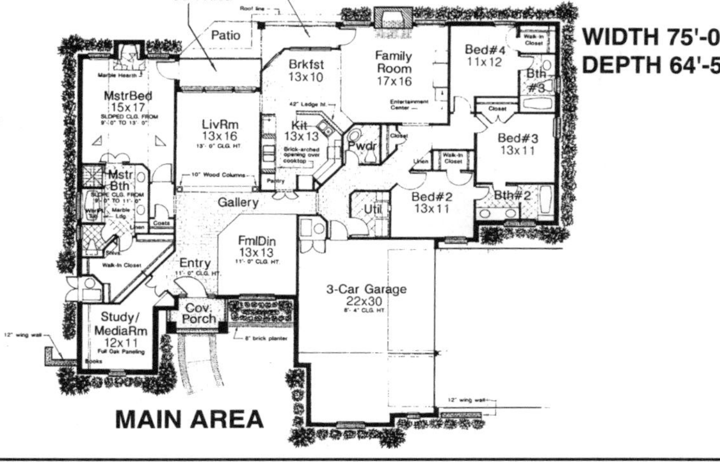

Cov. Area
Patio
Brkfst 13x10
Family Room 17x16
Bed#4 11x12
Bth #3
Bed#3 13x11
MstrBed 15x17
LivRm 13x16
Kit 13x13
Pwdr
Mstr Bth
Gallery
Util
Bed#2 13x11
Bth#2
FmlDin 13x13
Entry
3-Car Garage 22x30
Study/ MediaRm 12x11
Cov. Porch
MAIN AREA
WIDTH 75'-0"
DEPTH 64'-5"

Superior Comfort and Privacy

Price Code: E

- This plan features:
- — Four bedrooms
- — Three full baths
- A natural stone exterior with slate floors in the Foyer
- A two-way fireplace between the Living Room and Family Room
- The Breakfast Nook has a large bow window facing the terrace and pool
- Four bedrooms are grouped in one wing for privacy

MAIN FLOOR — 2,679 SQ. FT.
BASEMENT — 2,679 SQ. FT.
GARAGE — 541 SQ. FT.

TOTAL LIVING AREA:
2,679 SQ. FT.

Design by
The Garlinghouse Company

PLAN NO. 9828

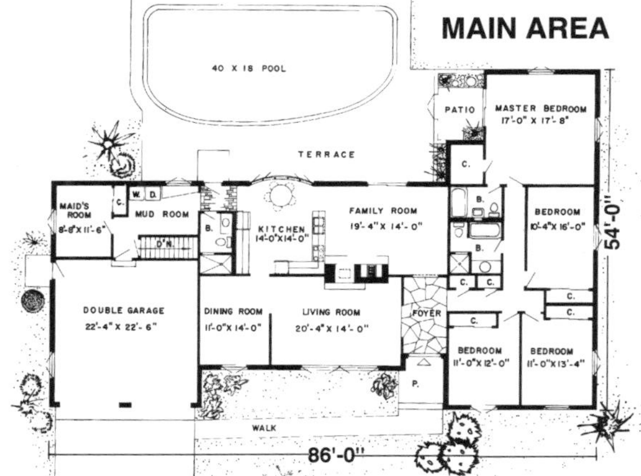

MAIN AREA
40 X 18 POOL
TERRACE
PATIO
MASTER BEDROOM 17'-0" X 17'-8"
MAID'S ROOM 8'-8" X 11'-6"
MUD ROOM
KITCHEN 14'-0" X 14'-0"
FAMILY ROOM 19'-4" X 14'-0"
BEDROOM 10'-4" X 16'-0"
DOUBLE GARAGE 22'-4" X 22'-6"
DINING ROOM 11'-0" X 14'-0"
LIVING ROOM 20'-4" X 14'-0"
FOYER
BEDROOM 11'-0" X 12'-0"
BEDROOM 11'-0" X 13'-4"
WALK
86'-0"
54'-0"

PLAN NO. 99440

Design by
Design Basics, Inc.

Refer to **Pricing Schedule F** on the order form for pricing information

Classic Home

- This plan features:
  - — Four bedrooms
  - — Three full and one half baths
- Space and light connect the entry, Gallery, Dining Room, and Living Room
- A butler's Pantry connects the Kitchen to the Dining Room
- The Master Suite encompasses a whole wing on the first floor
- Up the curved staircase find three Bedrooms all with walk-in closets
- Also upstairs is a Game Room with built-in cabinets
- No materials list is available for this plan
- An optional basement and a slab foundation — please specify when ordering

FIRST FLOOR — 2,688 SQ. FT.
SECOND FLOOR — 1,540 SQ. FT.
BASEMENT — 2,688 SQ. FT.
GARAGE — 635 SQ. FT.

TOTAL LIVING AREA:
4,228 SQ. FT.

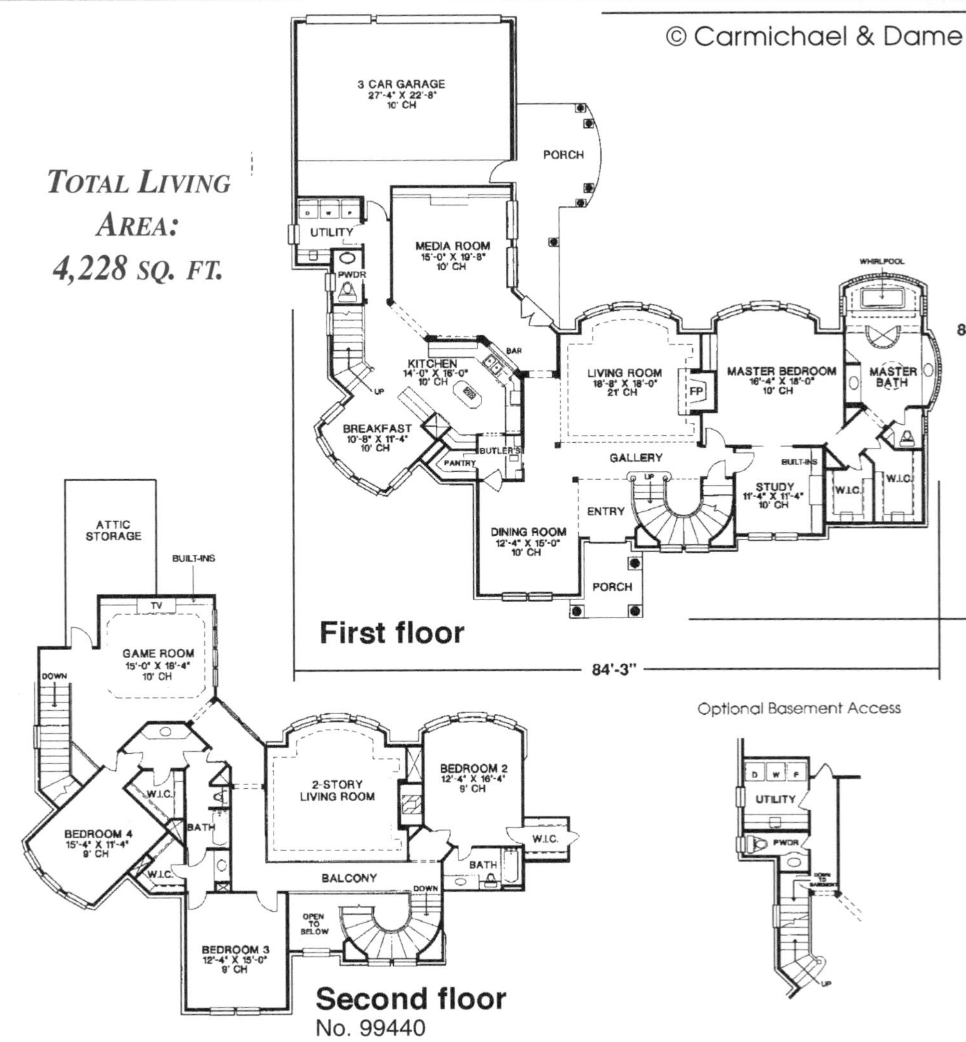

© Carmichael & Dame
3 CAR GARAGE 27'-4" X 22'-8" 10' CH
PORCH
UTILITY
PWDR
MEDIA ROOM 15'-0" X 19'-8" 10' CH
KITCHEN 14'-0" X 16'-0" 10' CH
BAR
BREAKFAST 10'-8" X 11'-4" 10' CH
PANTRY
BUTLER'S
LIVING ROOM 18'-8" X 18'-0" 21' CH
FP
MASTER BEDROOM 16'-4" X 18'-0" 10' CH
WHIRLPOOL
MASTER BATH
W.I.C.
BUILT-INS
STUDY 11'-4" X 11'-4" 10' CH
GALLERY
ENTRY
DINING ROOM 12'-4" X 15'-0" 10' CH
PORCH
80'-1
84'-3"
First floor
ATTIC STORAGE
BUILT-INS
TV
GAME ROOM 15'-0" X 18'-4" 10' CH
DOWN
2-STORY LIVING ROOM
BEDROOM 2 12'-4" X 16'-4" 9' CH
W.I.C.
BATH
BEDROOM 4 15'-4" X 11'-4" 9' CH
W.I.C.
BALCONY
OPEN TO BELOW
BEDROOM 3 12'-4" X 15'-0" 9' CH
Second floor
No. 99440
Optional Basement Access
UTILITY
PWDR
UP

Refer to **Pricing Schedule F** on the order form for pricing information

Design by
Design Basics, Inc.

PLAN NO. 99472

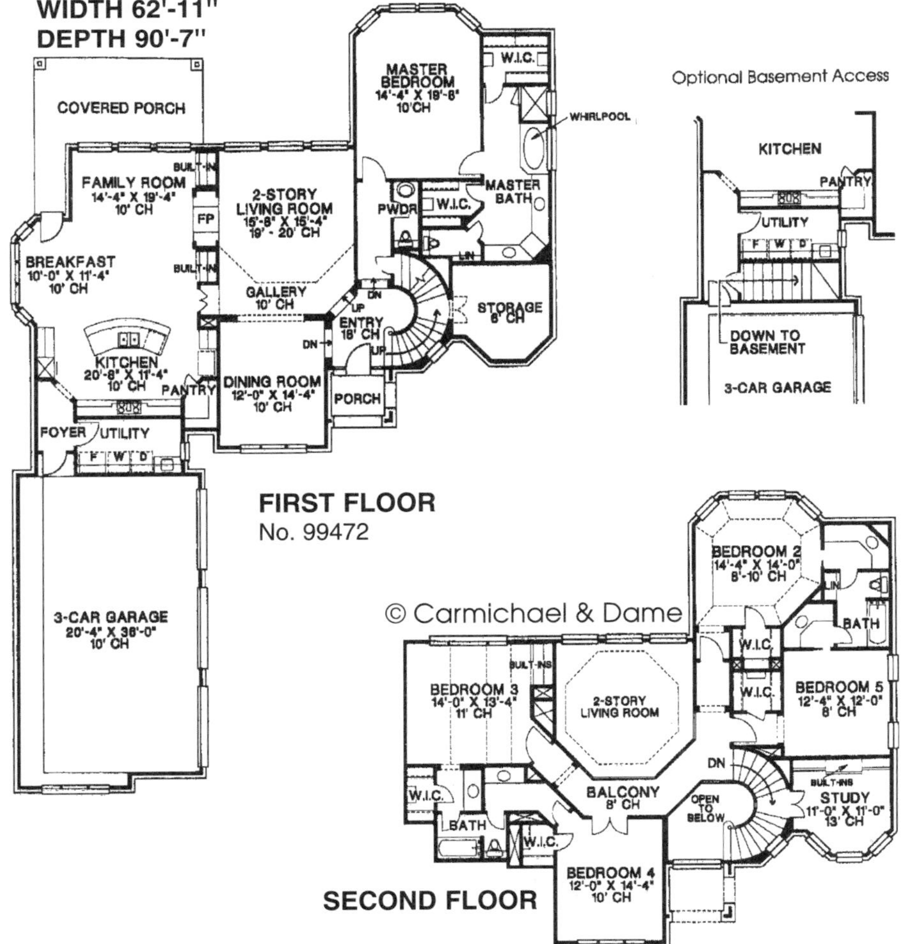

WIDTH 62'-11"
DEPTH 90'-7"
COVERED PORCH
FAMILY ROOM 14'-4" X 19'-4" 10' CH
BUILT-IN
FP
2-STORY LIVING ROOM 15'-8" X 15'-4" 19' - 20' CH
MASTER BEDROOM 14'-4" X 18'-8" 10'CH
W.I.C.
WHIRLPOOL
MASTER BATH
PWDR
W.I.C.
LIN
BREAKFAST 10'-0" X 11'-4" 10' CH
GALLERY 10' CH
ENTRY 18' CH
STORAGE 8' CH
KITCHEN 20'-8" X 11'-4" 10' CH
PANTRY
DINING ROOM 12'-0" X 14'-4" 10' CH
PORCH
FOYER
UTILITY
3-CAR GARAGE 20'-4" X 36'-0" 10' CH
FIRST FLOOR
No. 99472
Optional Basement Access
KITCHEN
PANTRY
UTILITY
DOWN TO BASEMENT
3-CAR GARAGE
© Carmichael & Dame
BEDROOM 2 14'-4" X 14'-0" 8'-10' CH
BATH
W.I.C.
BEDROOM 3 14'-0" X 13'-4" 11' CH
2-STORY LIVING ROOM
BEDROOM 5 12'-4" X 12'-0" 8' CH
BALCONY 8' CH
OPEN TO BELOW
STUDY 11'-0" X 11'-0" 13' CH
BUILT-INS
BATH
BEDROOM 4 12'-0" X 14'-4" 10' CH
SECOND FLOOR

Brick Traditional

- This plan features:
- — Five bedrooms
- — Three full and one half baths
- The stunning exterior of this home is created with brick and large windows
- Inside, the Entry soars to sixteen feet
- Both the Living and Family rooms have a rear window wall
- The Kitchen is open to the informal areas of the home
- Upstairs find four Bedrooms and a Study

FIRST FLOOR — 2,050 SQ. FT.
SECOND FLOOR — 1,467 SQ. FT.
BASEMENT — 2,050 SQ. FT.
GARAGE — 698 SQ. FT.

TOTAL LIVING AREA:
3,517 SQ. FT.

PLAN NO. 92671

Design by
Studer Residential Design, Inc.

Refer to **Pricing Schedule F** on the order form for pricing information

Two-Story Brick Colonial

- This plan features:
- — Four bedrooms
- — Three full and one half baths
- A covered front Porch and Foyer with lovely staircase greet you
- The Living Room flows freely into the Dining Room
- The Hearth Room has a 12-foot ceiling and entertainment center
- The unique Kitchen design is a cook's delight
- No materials list is available for this plan

FIRST FLOOR — 1,666 SQ. FT.
SECOND FLOOR — 1,036 SQ. FT.
MID FLOOR — 743 SQ. FT.
BASEMENT — 1,612 SQ. FT.
GARAGE — 740 SQ. FT.

TOTAL LIVING AREA:
3,445 SQ. FT.

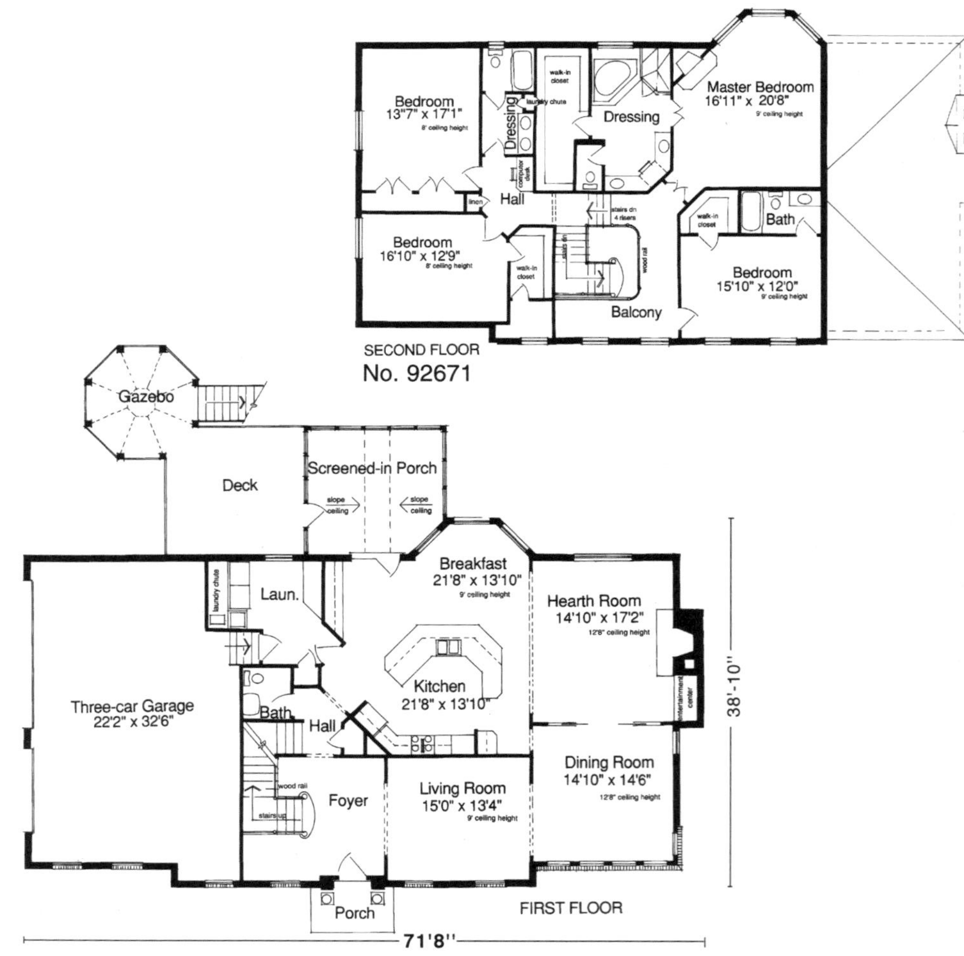

Bedroom
13'7" x 17'1"
Dressing
Dressing
Master Bedroom
16'11" x 20'8"
Hall
Bedroom
16'10" x 12'9"
Bath
Bedroom
15'10" x 12'0"
Balcony
SECOND FLOOR
No. 92671
Gazebo
Deck
Screened-in Porch
Breakfast
21'8" x 13'10"
Laun.
Hearth Room
14'10" x 17'2"
Three-car Garage
22'2" x 32'6"
Kitchen
21'8" x 13'10"
Bath
Hall
Dining Room
14'10" x 14'6"
Foyer
Living Room
15'0" x 13'4"
38'-10"
Porch
FIRST FLOOR
71'8"

To order your Blueprints, call 1-800-235-5700

Refer to **Pricing Schedule F** on the order form for pricing information

Design by
Filmore Design Group

PLAN NO. 98536

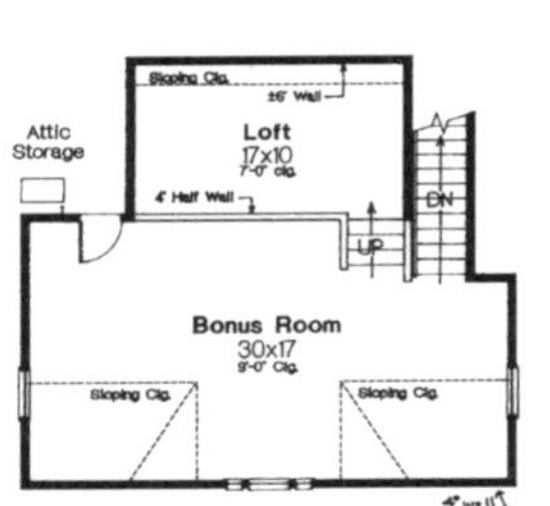

Attic Storage
Loft
17x10
Bonus Room
30x17
UP
DN

Upper Floor
Optional Bonus Room & Loft

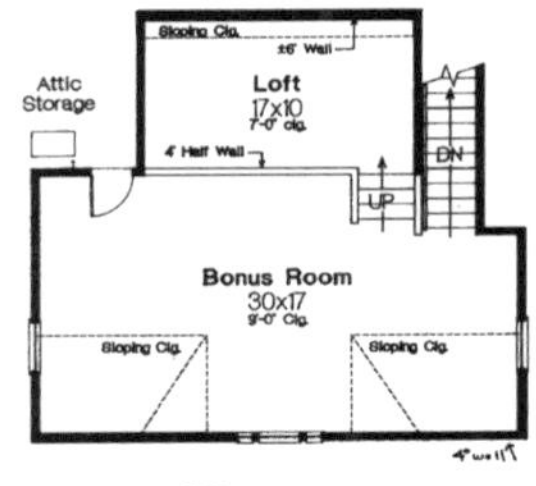

Attic Storage
Loft
17x10
Bonus Room
30x17
UP
DN

Upper Floor

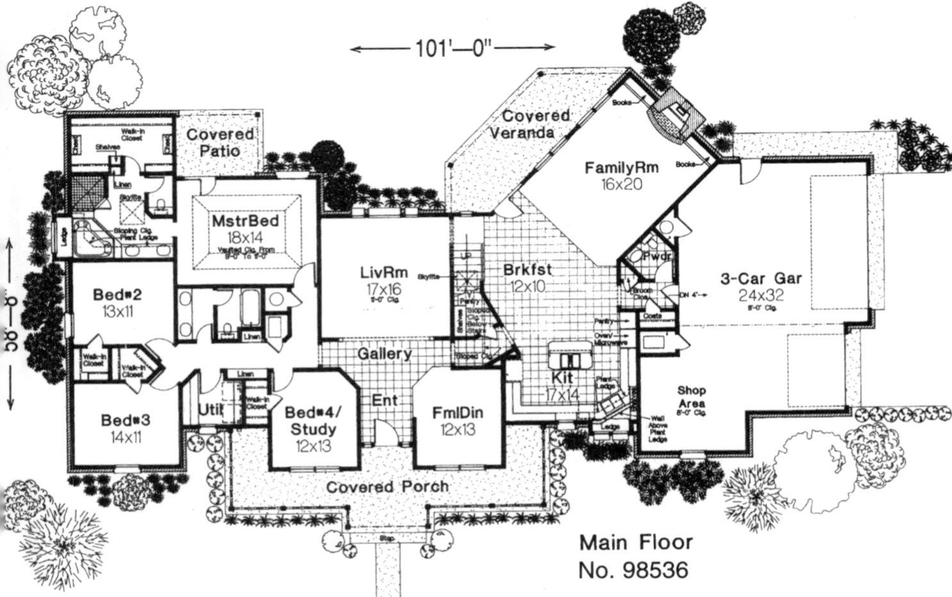

101'—0"
58'—8"
Covered Patio
Covered Veranda
MstrBed
18x14
FamilyRm
16x20
LivRm
17x16
Brkfst
12x10
3-Car Gar
24x32
Bed#2
13x11
Gallery
Kit
17x14
Shop Area
Bed#3
14x11
Util
Bed#4/ Study
12x13
Ent
FmlDin
12x13
Pwdr
Covered Porch

Main Floor
No. 98536

Country Cottage Charm

- This plan features:
- — Four bedrooms
- — Two full and one half baths
- Vaulted Master Bedroom has a private bath and large walk-in closet
- Three more Bedrooms (one possibly a Study) share a full Bath
- A loft and bonus room are above the Living Room
- Family Room has built-in book shelves and a fireplace
- An optional slab or a crawl space foundation — please specify when ordering
- No materials list is available for this plan

MAIN FLOOR — 2,787 SQ. FT.
UPPER FLOOR — 636 SQ. FT.
GARAGE — 832 SQ. FT.

TOTAL LIVING AREA:
3,423 SQ. FT.

PLAN NO. 93097

Design by
Larry E. Belk

Refer to **Pricing Schedule E** on the order form for pricing information

Just Past the Garden Gate

- This plan features:
- — Four bedrooms
- — Two full and one half baths
- The quaint exterior is reminiscent of a European cottage
- From the covered front Porch step through double doors into the Foyer with a 10-foot ceiling
- There is an arched entry from the Foyer into the Dining Room
- The Family Room and Breakfast Room are warmed by a fireplace and share a sloped ceiling
- The Living Room has French doors that open to the rear Porch
- All the bedrooms, including the Master Suite, are located in one wing
- The Kitchen is located in the rear of the home and conveniently accesses the Garage
- No materials list is available for this plan

MAIN FLOOR — 2,757 SQ. FT.
GARAGE — 484 SQ. FT.

TOTAL LIVING AREA:
2,757 SQ. FT.

MAIN FLOOR
No. 93097

GARAGE
COPYRIGHT LARRY E. BELK
UTIL
PAN
PORCH
MASTER BATH
10 FT CLG
K.S.
KITCHEN
15-4 X 13-8
10 FT CLG
42" LEDGE
LIVING ROOM
17-0 X 16-4
12 FT CLG
BEDRM 4/STUDY
13-4 X 15-0
10 FT CLG
MASTER BEDROOM
15-6 X 15-0
12 FT TRAY CLG
BRKFST ROOM
15-4 X 9-4
14 FT CLG
UP
DOWN
BATH 2
PWDR
DINING ROOM
12-4 X 14-4
12 FT CLG
ARCH
FOYER
10 FT CLG
SLOPE
FAMILY ROOM
15-4 X 14-0
14 FT CLG
BEDROOM 3
12-4 X 12-8
10 FT CLG
BEDROOM 2
12-6 X 12-8
10 FT CLG
PORCH
FP
DEPTH 68-8
WIDTH 69-6

Refer to **Pricing Schedule F** on the order form for pricing information

Design by
Frank Betz Associates, Inc.

PLAN NO. 98436

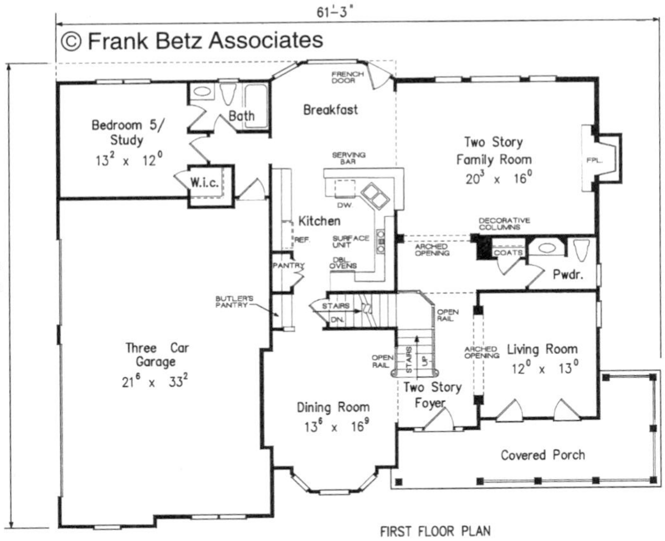

© Frank Betz Associates

FIRST FLOOR PLAN

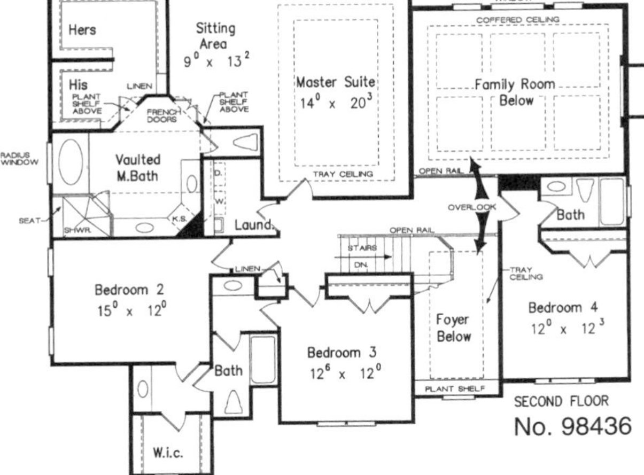

Hers
Sitting Area
9⁰ x 13²
His
Master Suite
14⁰ x 20³
Family Room Below
Vaulted M.Bath
Laund.
Bath
Bedroom 2
15⁰ x 12⁰
Bedroom 3
12⁶ x 12⁰
Foyer Below
Bedroom 4
12⁰ x 12³
Bath
W.i.c.
SECOND FLOOR
No. 98436

Home Sweet Home

- This plan features:
- — Five bedrooms
- — Four full and one half baths
- An arched opening leads into the Living Room from the two-story Foyer
- The Dining Room has a bay window that overlooks the front yard
- A fireplace warms the large Family Room
- The Breakfast Nook has a French door to the rear yard
- A double wall oven augments the Kitchen
- The second floor Master Suite has many special features
- An optional basement or crawl space foundation — please specify when ordering

FIRST FLOOR — 1,615 SQ. FT.
SECOND FLOOR — 1,763 SQ. FT.
BASEMENT — 1,615 SQ. FT.
GARAGE — 747 SQ. FT.

TOTAL LIVING AREA:
3,378 SQ. FT.

PLAN NO. 96490

Design by
Donald A. Gardner Architects, Inc.

Refer to **Pricing Schedule F** on the order form for pricing information

Stature and Dignity

- This plan features:
  - Four bedrooms
  - Three full baths
- Multiple columns and gables add appeal to traditional style
- Foyer and Great Room both have two-story ceilings and clerestory windows
- Great Room highlighted by fireplace, built-in shelves and French doors to back Porch
- Bright Breakfast bay accesses efficient Kitchen and back stairway to Bedrooms and Bonus Room

FIRST FLOOR — 2,067 SQ. FT.
SECOND FLOOR — 615 SQ. FT.
BONUS ROOM — 433 SQ. FT.
GARAGE & STORAGE — 729 SQ. FT.

TOTAL LIVING AREA:
2,682 SQ. FT.

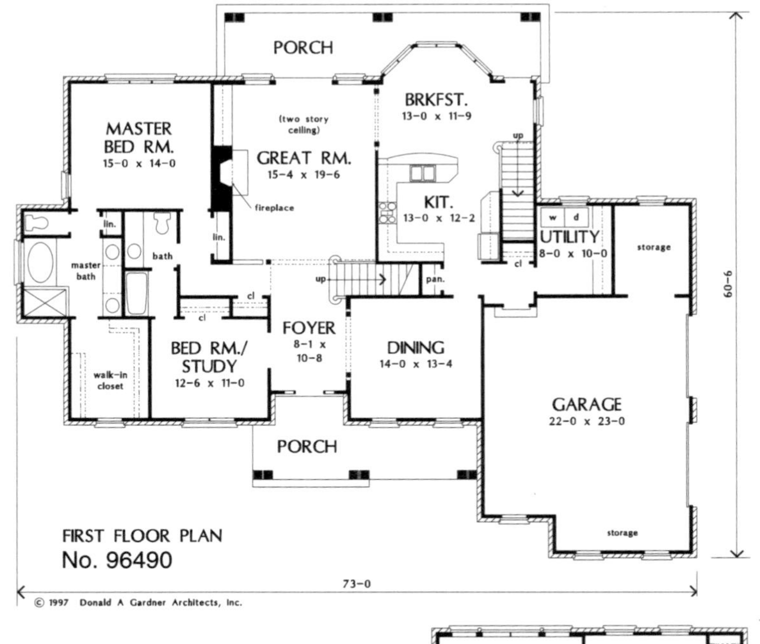

PORCH
BRKFST.
13-0 x 11-9
MASTER BED RM.
15-0 x 14-0
(two story ceiling)
GREAT RM.
15-4 x 19-6
fireplace
KIT.
13-0 x 12-2
UTILITY
8-0 x 10-0
storage
master bath
bath
lin.
cl
up
pan.
FOYER
8-1 x 10-8
BED RM./ STUDY
12-6 x 11-0
DINING
14-0 x 13-4
walk-in closet
GARAGE
22-0 x 23-0
PORCH
storage
60-6
73-0
FIRST FLOOR PLAN
No. 96490
© 1997 Donald A Gardner Architects, Inc.

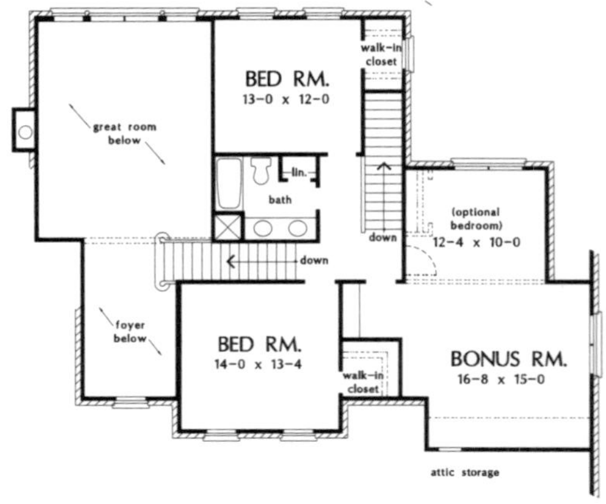

BED RM.
13-0 x 12-0
walk-in closet
great room below
bath
lin.
down
(optional bedroom)
12-4 x 10-0
foyer below
BED RM.
14-0 x 13-4
walk-in closet
BONUS RM.
16-8 x 15-0
attic storage

SECOND FLOOR PLAN

To order your Blueprints, call 1-800-235-5700

Refer to **Pricing Schedule E** on the order form for pricing information

Design by
Design Basics, Inc.

PLAN NO. 94994

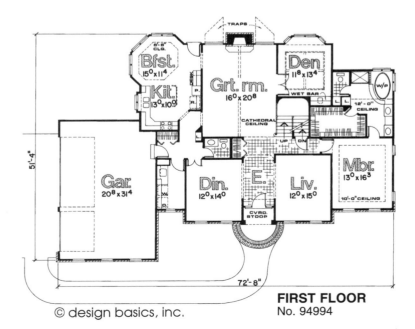

SECOND FLOOR
TRAPS
OPEN TO BELOW
DISPLAY
Br. 2
13⁰ x 12³
BOOKS
LIN.
DN
Br. 3
12⁰ x 13⁰
OPEN TO BELOW
Br. 4
12⁰ x 13⁰

TRAPS
8'-8" CLG.
Bfst.
15⁰ x 11⁴
DESK
Kit.
13⁰ x 10⁹
Grt. rm.
16⁰ x 20⁸
CATHEDRAL CEILING
Den
11⁸ x 13⁴
WET BAR
W/P
12'-0" CEILING
UP
DN
Gar.
20⁸ x 31⁴
Din.
12⁰ x 14⁰
E.
Liv.
12⁰ x 15⁰
Mbr.
13⁰ x 16³
10'-0" CEILING
CVRD. STOOP
51'-4"
72'-8"

FIRST FLOOR
No. 94994

Timeless Beauty

- This plan features:
  - — Four bedrooms
  - — Two full, two three-quarter and one half baths
- Two-story Entry hall accesses formal Dining and Living room
- Spacious Great Room with cathedral ceiling and fireplace
- Ideal Kitchen with built-in desk and Pantry
- Master Bedroom wing offers a decorative ceiling, and luxurious Dressing/Bath Area with a large walk-in closet and whirlpool tub

FIRST FLOOR — 2,063 SQ. FT.
SECOND FLOOR — 894 SQ. FT.
BASEMENT — 2,063 SQ. FT.
GARAGE — 666 SQ. FT.

TOTAL LIVING AREA:
2,957 SQ. FT.

Design by
Chatham Home Planning, Inc.

Refer to **Pricing Schedule E** on the order form for pricing information

Superb Southern Styling

- This plan features:
- — Four bedrooms
- — Three full baths
- Front Porch and dormers create a homey Southern style
- A corner fireplace enhances the Family Room
- A cooktop island and a peninsula counter add to the efficiency of the Kitchen
- Peninsula counter separates the Kitchen from the Breakfast Room
- Lavish Master Suite has a whirlpool tub
- An optional crawl space or slab foundation — please specify when ordering
- No material list is available for this plan

FIRST FLOOR — 2,135 SQ. FT.
SECOND FLOOR — 538 SQ. FT.
BONUS — 225 SQ. FT.
GARAGE — 436 SQ. FT.

TOTAL LIVING AREA:
2,673 SQ. FT.

WIDTH 62'-6"
DEPTH 70'-0"

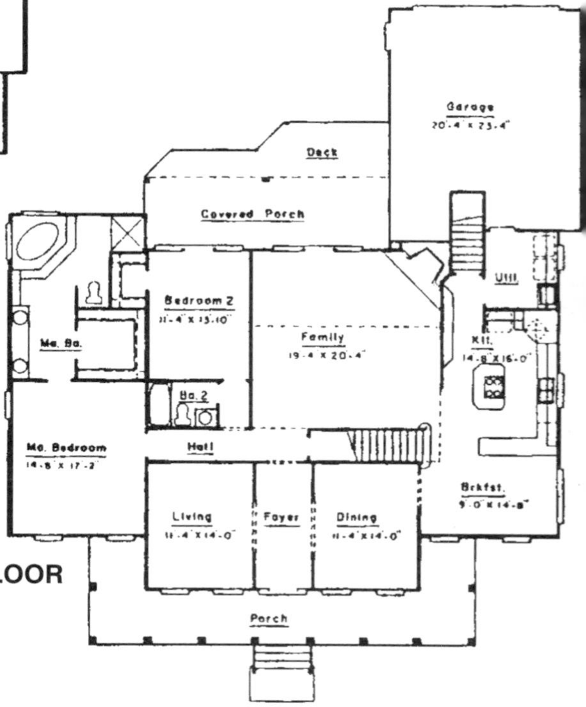

SECOND FLOOR

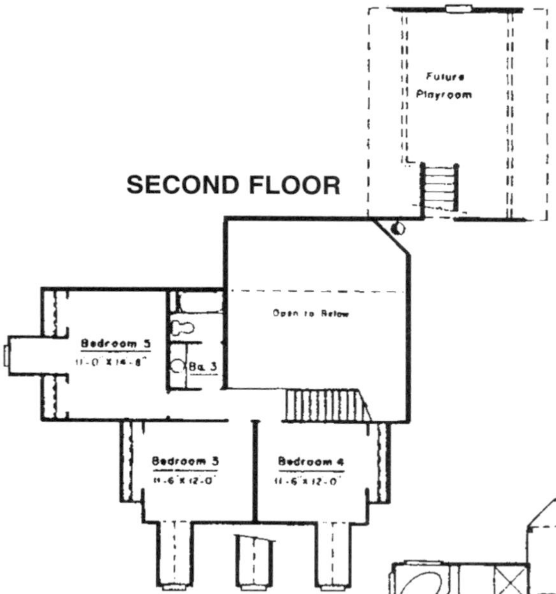

Future Playroom
Open to Below
Bedroom 5
11-0 x 14-6
Ba. 3
Bedroom 3
11-6 x 12-0
Bedroom 4
11-6 x 12-0

FIRST FLOOR
No. 94644

Garage
20-4 x 23-4
Deck
Covered Porch
Util
Bedroom 2
11-4 x 15-10
Family
19-4 x 20-4
Kit.
14-8 x 16-0
Ma. Ba.
Ba. 2
Ma. Bedroom
14-8 x 17-2
Hall
Brkfst.
9-0 x 14-8
Living
11-4 x 14-0
Foyer
Dining
11-4 x 14-0
Porch

Refer to **Pricing Schedule F** on the order form for pricing information

Design by
Donald A. Gardner Architects, Inc.

PLAN NO. 99848

© 1993 Donald A. Gardner Architects, Inc.

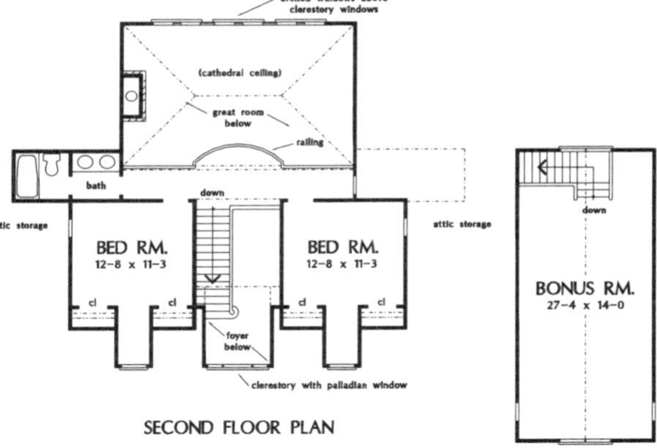

arched windows above clerestory windows
(cathedral ceiling)
great room below
railing
bath
down
attic storage
BED RM.
12-8 x 11-3
BED RM.
12-8 x 11-3
attic storage
foyer below
clerestory with palladian window
BONUS RM.
27-4 x 14-0
SECOND FLOOR PLAN

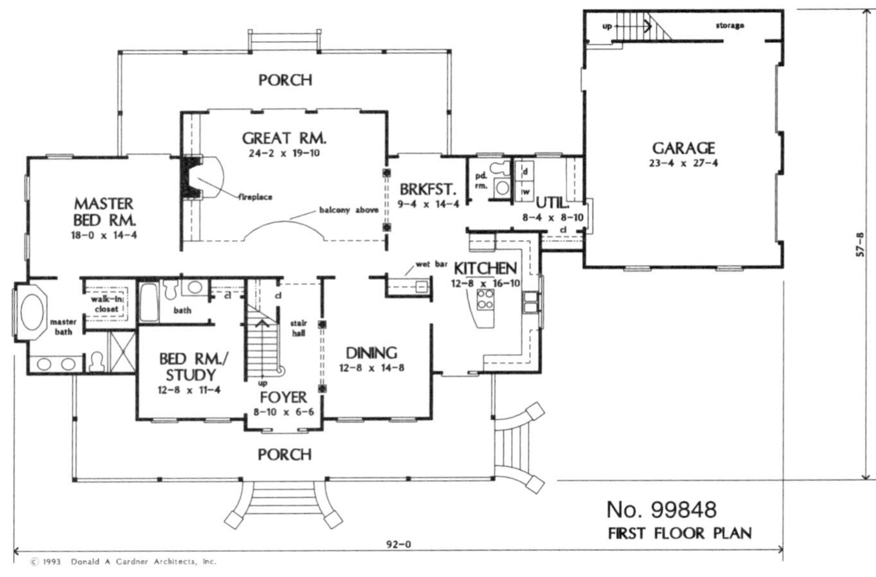

storage
PORCH
GREAT RM.
24-2 x 19-10
fireplace
balcony above
GARAGE
23-4 x 27-4
MASTER
BED RM.
18-0 x 14-4
BRKFST.
9-4 x 14-4
UTIL.
8-4 x 8-10
KITCHEN
12-8 x 16-10
wet bar
walk-in closet
master bath
bath
stair hall
BED RM./ STUDY
12-8 x 11-4
FOYER
8-10 x 6-6
DINING
12-8 x 14-8
PORCH
57-8
92-0
No. 99848
FIRST FLOOR PLAN
© 1993 Donald A. Gardner Architects, Inc.

Rambling Farmhouse

- This plan features:
  - — Four bedrooms
  - — Three full and one half baths
- Two-story Foyer with palladium window
- Great Room topped by a vaulted ceiling and highlighted by a fire-place and a balcony
- Great Room, Breakfast Room, and Master Bedroom access Porch for open circulation
- Nine-foot ceilings throughout the first floor
- Island Kitchen with direct access to formal and informal eating areas
- First floor Study/Bedroom with private full Bath

FIRST FLOOR — 2,064 SQ. FT.
SECOND FLOOR — 594 SQ. FT.
GARAGE & STORAGE — 710 SQ. FT.
BONUS ROOM — 483 SQ. FT.

TOTAL LIVING AREA:
2,658 SQ. FT.

PLAN NO. 93090

Design by
Larry E. Belk

Refer to **Pricing Schedule E** on the order form for pricing information

A European Influence

- This plan features:
- — Four bedrooms
- — Three full and one half baths
- The grand entry Porch gives way to the equally impressive two-story Foyer
- The Dining Room is separated from the Foyer by columns with arches over them
- The Living Room has a set of French doors to the rear yard
- The first floor Master Suite encompasses its own wing
- Located beyond the gourmet Kitchen is the Family Room
- Upstairs find three Bedrooms and a Gameroom, which is a great place for the kids to play
- No materials list is available for this plan
- An optional basement, slab or crawl space foundation — please specify when ordering

FIRST FLOOR — 1,919 SQ. FT.
SECOND FLOOR — 1,190 SQ. FT.
BONUS SPACE — 286 SQ. FT.
GARAGE — 561 SQ. FT.

TOTAL LIVING AREA: 3,109 SQ. FT.

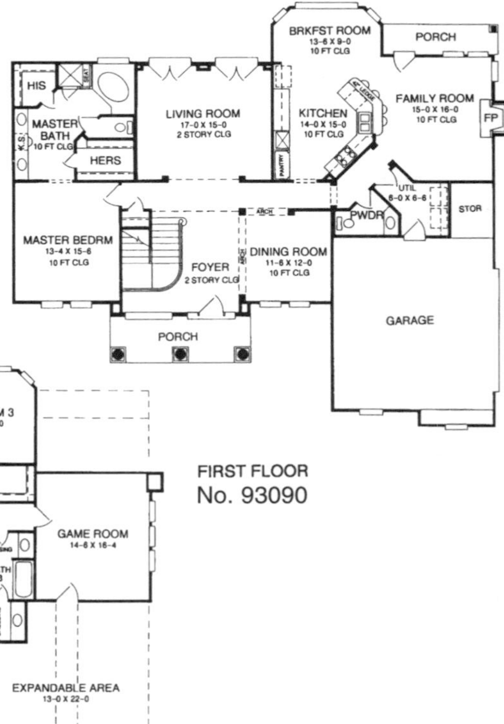
WIDTH 64–6
DEPTH 55–10
BRKFST ROOM 13–6 X 9–0 10 FT CLG
PORCH
HIS
MASTER BATH 10 FT CLG
HERS
LIVING ROOM 17–0 X 15–0 2 STORY CLG
KITCHEN 14–0 X 15–0 10 FT CLG
FAMILY ROOM 15–0 X 16–0 10 FT CLG
FP
PANTRY
UTIL 8–0 X 6–6
STOR
PWDR
MASTER BEDRM 13–4 X 15–6 10 FT CLG
FOYER 2 STORY CLG
DINING ROOM 11–6 X 12–0 10 FT CLG
GARAGE
PORCH

FIRST FLOOR
No. 93090

BEDROOM 3 13–8 X 12–0
ATTIC
OPEN TO LIVING ROOM BELOW
GAME ROOM 14–6 X 16–4
BATH 2
BATH 3
DRESSING
BEDROOM 2 13–8 X 12–0
OPEN TO FOYER BELOW
BEDROOM 4 11–6 X 12–4
EXPANDABLE AREA 13–0 X 22–0

SECOND FLOOR

Refer to **Pricing Schedule E** on the order form for pricing information

Design by
Design Basics, Inc.

PLAN NO. 99450

© design basics, inc.

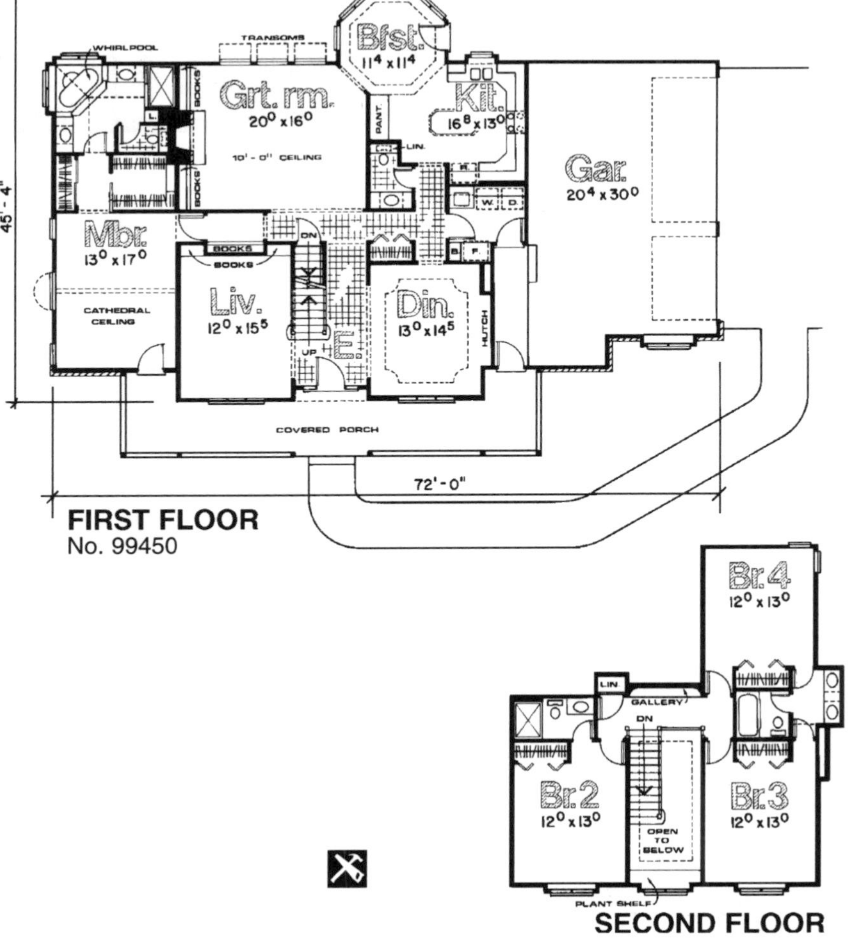

WHIRLPOOL
TRANSOMS
Bfst.
$11^4 \times 11^4$
Grt. rm.
$20^0 \times 16^0$
10'-0" CEILING
BOOKS
PANT.
Kit.
$16^8 \times 13^0$
LIN.
W. D.
Gar.
$20^4 \times 30^0$
45'-4"
Mbr.
$13^0 \times 17^0$
CATHEDRAL CEILING
BOOKS
DN
Liv.
$12^0 \times 15^5$
UP
E.
Din.
$13^0 \times 14^5$
HUTCH
COVERED PORCH
72'-0"
Br. 4
$12^0 \times 13^0$
LIN
GALLERY
DN
Br. 2
$12^0 \times 13^0$
OPEN TO BELOW
Br. 3
$12^0 \times 13^0$
PLANT SHELF

FIRST FLOOR
No. 99450

SECOND FLOOR

Fashionable Country Style

- This plan features:
  - — Four bedrooms
  - — Two full, one three quarter and one half baths
- The covered front Porch adds old fashioned appeal
- Dining Room with a decorative ceiling and a built-in hutch
- Kitchen has a center island and access to gazebo shaped Nook
- Great Room is accented by transom windows and a fireplace
- The Master Bedroom has a cathedral ceiling and a Bath with a whirlpool tub
- An optional basement or slab foundation — please specify when ordering

FIRST FLOOR — 1,881 SQ. FT.
SECOND FLOOR — 814 SQ. FT.
BASEMENT — 1,020 SQ. FT.
GARAGE — 534 SQ. FT.

TOTAL LIVING AREA:
2,695 SQ. FT.

To order your Blueprints, call 1-800-235-5700

PLAN NO. 99205

Design by
Homeplanners

Refer to **Pricing Schedule E** on the order form for pricing information

Farmhouse Feeling, Family-Style

■ This plan features:

— Four bedrooms

— Two full and two half baths

■ A sunny Breakfast Bay with easy access to the efficient Kitchen

■ A large and spacious Family Room with a fireplace and a pass-through to the Kitchen

■ Sliders that link the Family and Dining Rooms with the rear Terrace

■ A private Master Suite with his-n-her walk-in closets, dressing room with built-in vanity and convenient step-in shower

FIRST FLOOR — 1,590 SQ. FT.
SECOND FLOOR — 1,344 SQ. FT.
BASEMENT — 1,271 SQ. FT.

TOTAL LIVING AREA:
2,934 SQ. FT.

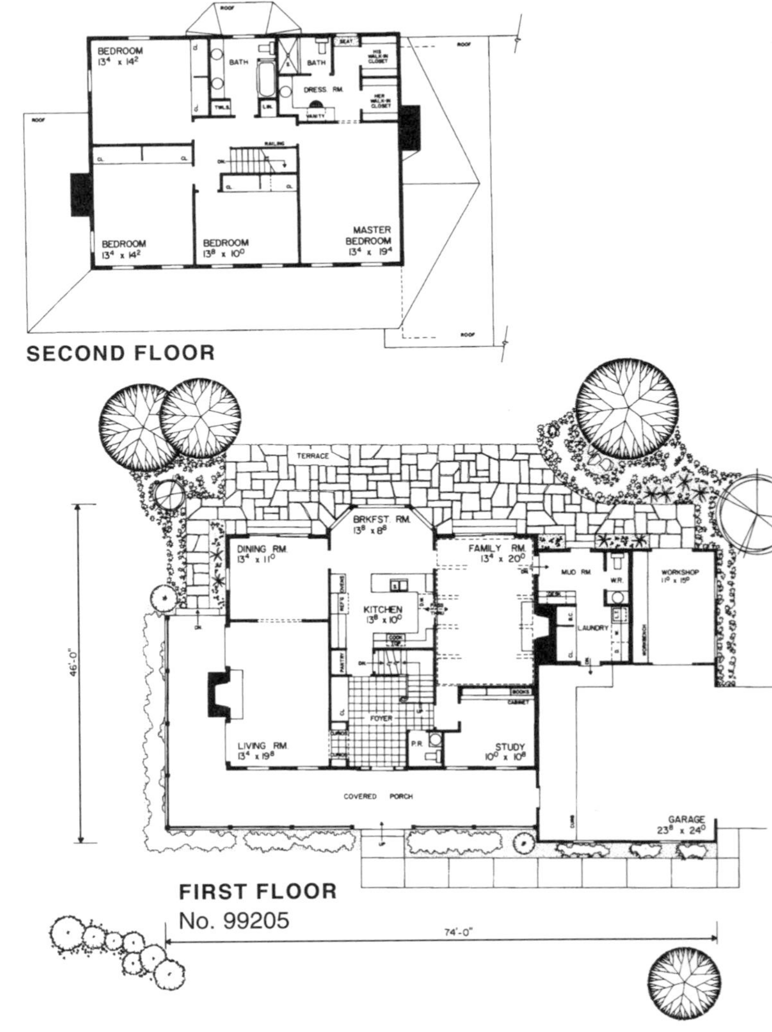
BEDROOM 13⁴ x 14²
BATH
BATH
DRESS. RM.
BEDROOM 13⁴ x 14²
BEDROOM 13⁸ x 10⁰
MASTER BEDROOM 13⁴ x 19⁴
SECOND FLOOR
TERRACE
BRKFST RM. 13⁸ x 8⁶
DINING RM. 13⁴ x 11⁰
FAMILY RM. 13⁴ x 20⁰
KITCHEN 13⁸ x 10⁰
MUD RM.
LAUNDRY
WORKSHOP
FOYER
LIVING RM. 13⁴ x 19⁸
STUDY 10⁰ x 10⁸
COVERED PORCH
GARAGE 23⁸ x 24⁰
46'-0"
74'-0"
FIRST FLOOR
No. 99205

Refer to **Pricing Schedule E** on the order form for pricing information

Design by
Studer Residential Design, Inc.

PLAN NO. 92681

Countrified Luxury

- This plan features:
  - — Three bedrooms
  - — Two full and one half baths
- A Library is located off of the Foyer and has a bay window
- The Dining Room is distinguished by a decorative ceiling treatment
- The Great Room and the Kitchen converge at the wetbar
- The dreamy L-shaped Kitchen incorporated a center island into its design
- Upstairs in the Master Bedroom find a private Sitting Area
- An oversized two-car Garage has space for storage or a Workshop
- No materials list is available for this plan

FIRST FLOOR — 1,625 SQ. FT.
SECOND FLOOR — 1,188 SQ. FT.
BASEMENT — 1,625 SQ. FT.
GARAGE — 592 SQ. FT.

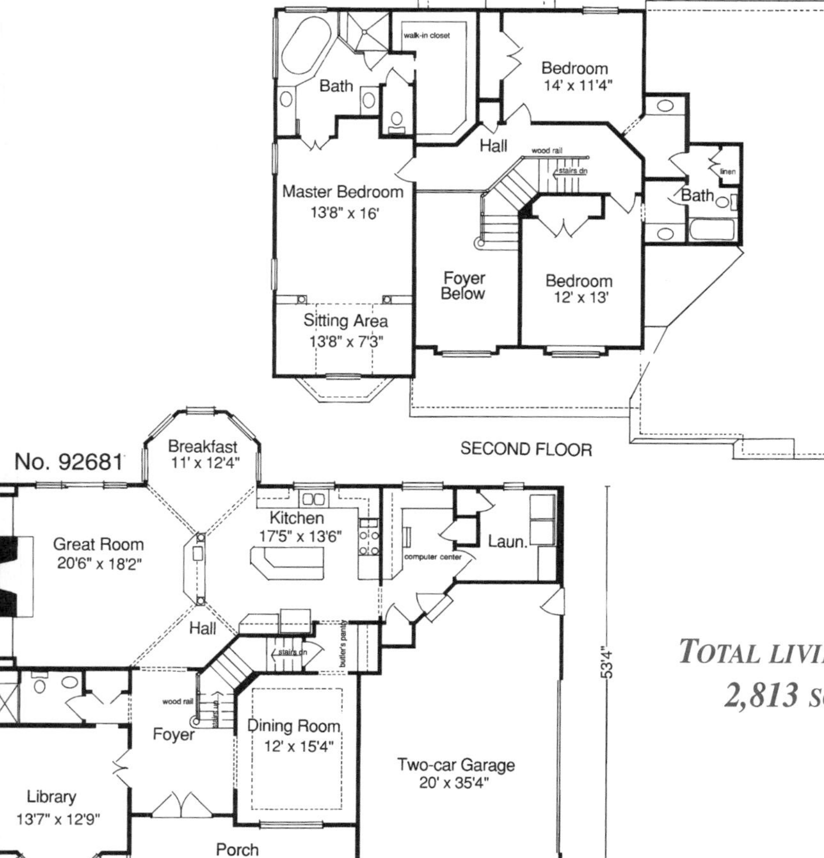

Bath
walk-in closet
Bedroom
14' x 11'4"
Hall
wood rail
stairs dn
Master Bedroom
13'8" x 16'
Bath
linen
Foyer
Below
Bedroom
12' x 13'
Sitting Area
13'8" x 7'3"
SECOND FLOOR
No. 92681
Breakfast
11' x 12'4"
Great Room
20'6" x 18'2"
Kitchen
17'5" x 13'6"
computer center
Laun.
Hall
stairs dn
butler's pantry
wood rail
Foyer
Dining Room
12' x 15'4"
Two-car Garage
20' x 35'4"
53'4"
Library
13'7" x 12'9"
Porch
FIRST FLOOR
57'7"

TOTAL LIVING AREA:
2,813 SQ. FT.

PLAN NO. 94614

Design by
Chatham Home Planning, Inc.

Refer to **Pricing Schedule D** on the order form for pricing information

Cottage Influence

- This plan features:
  - — Three or four bedrooms
  - — Three full and one half baths
- Great Room has fireplace and access to Covered Porch
- Cooktop island in Kitchen easily serves Breakfast bay and formal Dining Room
- Large Master Suite has access to Covered Porch
- Study/Guest Bedroom with private access to a full Bath
- Two second floor Bedrooms with walk-in closets
- No materials list is available for this plan
- An optional crawl space or slab foundation — please specify when ordering

FIRST FLOOR — 1,916 SQ. FT.
SECOND FLOOR — 617 SQ. FT.
GARAGE — 516 SQ. FT.

TOTAL LIVING AREA:
2,533 SQ. FT.

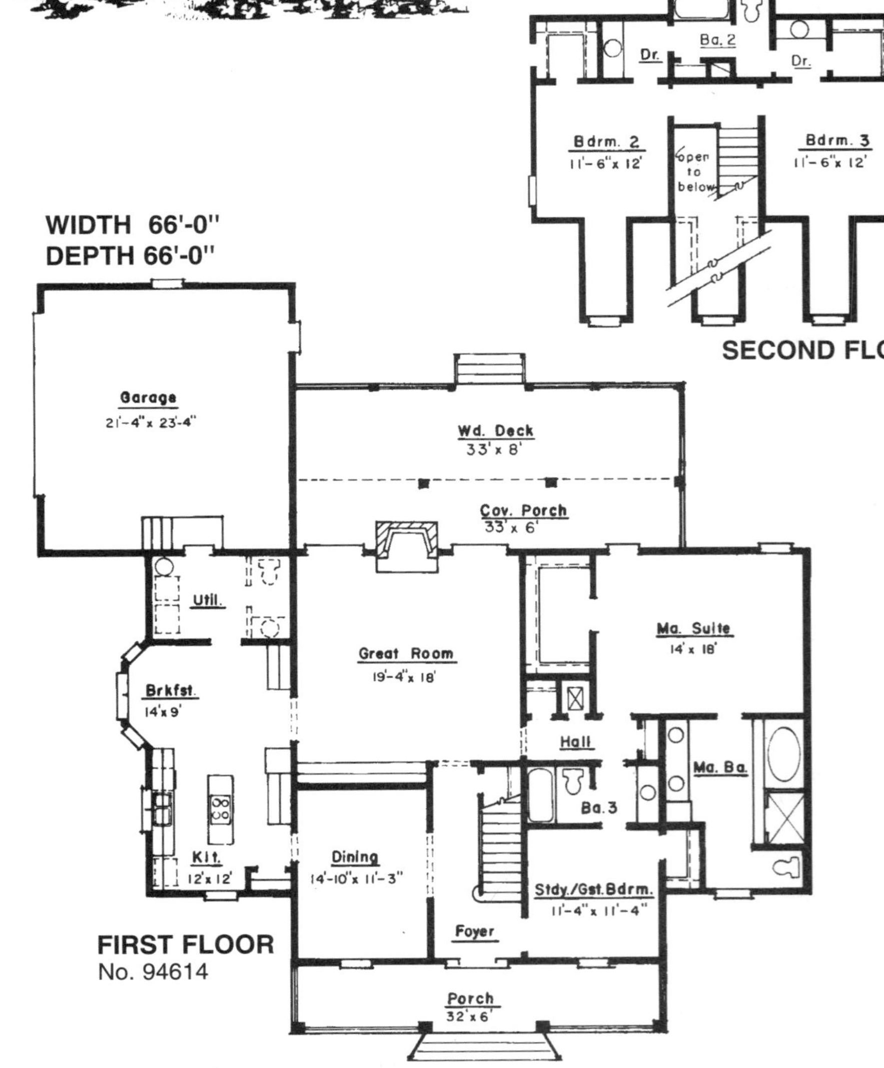

Ba. 2
Dr.
Dr.
Bdrm. 2
11'-6"x 12'
open to below
Bdrm. 3
11'-6"x 12'
SECOND FLOOR
WIDTH 66'-0"
DEPTH 66'-0"
Garage
21'-4"x 23'-4"
Wd. Deck
33'x 8'
Cov. Porch
33'x 6'
Util.
Great Room
19'-4"x 18'
Ma. Suite
14'x 18'
Brkfst.
14'x 9'
Hall
Ma. Ba.
Ba. 3
Kit.
12'x 12'
Dining
14'-10"x 11'-3"
Stdy./Gst.Bdrm.
11'-4"x 11'-4"
Foyer
Porch
32'x 6'
FIRST FLOOR
No. 94614

Refer to **Pricing Schedule F** on the order form for pricing information

Design by
Frank Betz Associates, Inc.

PLAN NO. 98437

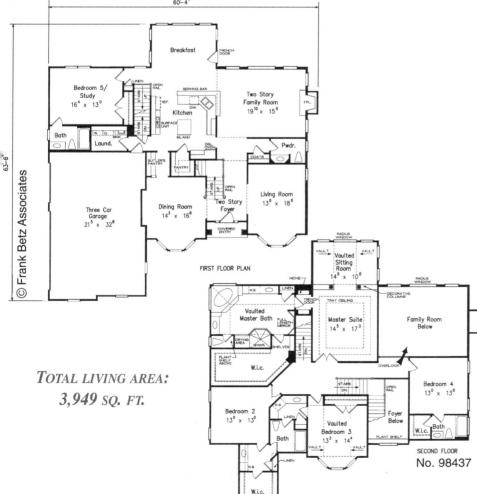

60'-4"

63'-6"

FIRST FLOOR PLAN

SECOND FLOOR

No. 98437

© Frank Betz Associates

TOTAL LIVING AREA:
3,949 SQ. FT.

Outstanding Appeal

- This plan features:
  - Five bedrooms
  - Four full and one half baths
- The Formal Dining and Living rooms are off the two-story Foyer
- A Butler's Pantry is located between the Kitchen and formal Dining Room for convenience
- An Island Kitchen with a walk-in Pantry and a peninsula counter/serving bar highlight this room
- The Breakfast room accesses the rear yard through a French door
- The second floor Master Suite is topped by a tray ceiling in the bedroom and by a vaulted ceiling above the Sitting Room and Bath
- An optional basement or crawl space foundation — please specify when ordering

FIRST FLOOR — 2,002 SQ. FT.
SECOND FLOOR — 1,947 SQ. FT.
BASEMENT — 2,002 SQ. FT.
GARAGE — 737 SQ. FT.

PLAN NO. 99424

Design by
Design Basics, Inc.

Refer to **Pricing Schedule E** on the order form for pricing information

Stately Exterior with an Open Interior

■ This plan features:

— Four bedrooms

— Two full and one half baths

■ Open Entry accented by a lovely landing staircase and access to quiet Study and formal Dining Room

■ Central Family Room with an inviting fireplace and a cathedral ceiling extending into Kitchen

■ Spacious Kitchen offers a work island/snackbar, built-in Pantry and a glass Breakfast Area

■ Secluded Master Bedroom enhanced by a large walk-in closet and lavish Bath

■ No materials list is available for this plan

FIRST FLOOR — 1,906 SQ. FT.
SECOND FLOOR — 749 SQ. FT.
BASEMENT — 1,906 SQ. FT.
GARAGE — 682 SQ. FT.

TOTAL LIVING AREA:
2,655 SQ. FT.

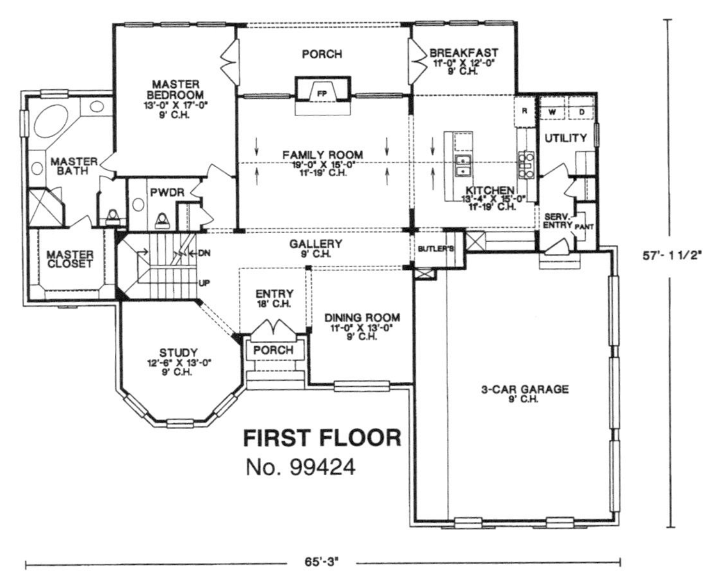
PORCH
BREAKFAST
11'-0" X 12'-0"
9' C.H.
MASTER BEDROOM
13'-0" X 17'-0"
9' C.H.
FP
FAMILY ROOM
19'-0" X 15'-0"
11'-19' C.H.
UTILITY
MASTER BATH
PWDR
KITCHEN
13'-4" X 15'-0"
11'-19' C.H.
SERV. ENTRY
PANT
MASTER CLOSET
GALLERY
9' C.H.
BUTLER'S
DN
UP
ENTRY
18' C.H.
DINING ROOM
11'-0" X 13'-0"
9' C.H.
PORCH
STUDY
12'-6" X 13'-0"
9' C.H.
3-CAR GARAGE
9' C.H.
57'- 1 1/2"
65'-3"

FIRST FLOOR
No. 99424

© Carmichael & Dame

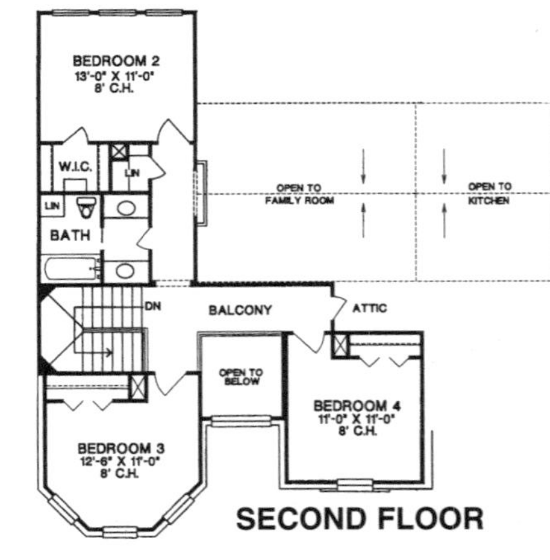
BEDROOM 2
13'-0" X 11'-0"
8' C.H.
W.I.C.
LIN
OPEN TO FAMILY ROOM
OPEN TO KITCHEN
BATH
DN
BALCONY
ATTIC
OPEN TO BELOW
BEDROOM 4
11'-0" X 11'-0"
8' C.H.
BEDROOM 3
12'-6" X 11'-0"
8' C.H.

SECOND FLOOR

To order your Blueprints, call 1-800-235-5700

Unique V-Shaped Home

Price Code: F

Design by
Landmark Designs, Inc.

PLAN NO. 99721

- This plan features:
  - — Two bedrooms
  - — Three full baths
- Bookshelves, interspersed with windows, line the long hallway that provides access to the owner's wing
- Four skylights brighten the already sunny Eating Nook in the huge country Kitchen
- A walk-in Pantry, range-top work island, built-in barbecue and a sink add to the amenities of the Kitchen
- A wide window bay and an entire wall of windows along its length illuminate the Living Room
- Master Suite with his-n-her closets, and adjacent dressing area plus a luxurious private Bath
- A Guest Suite with a private Sitting Area and full Bath
- No materials list is available for this plan

MAIN FLOOR — 3,417 SQ. FT.
GARAGE — 795 SQ. FT.

TOTAL LIVING AREA:
3,417 SQ. FT.

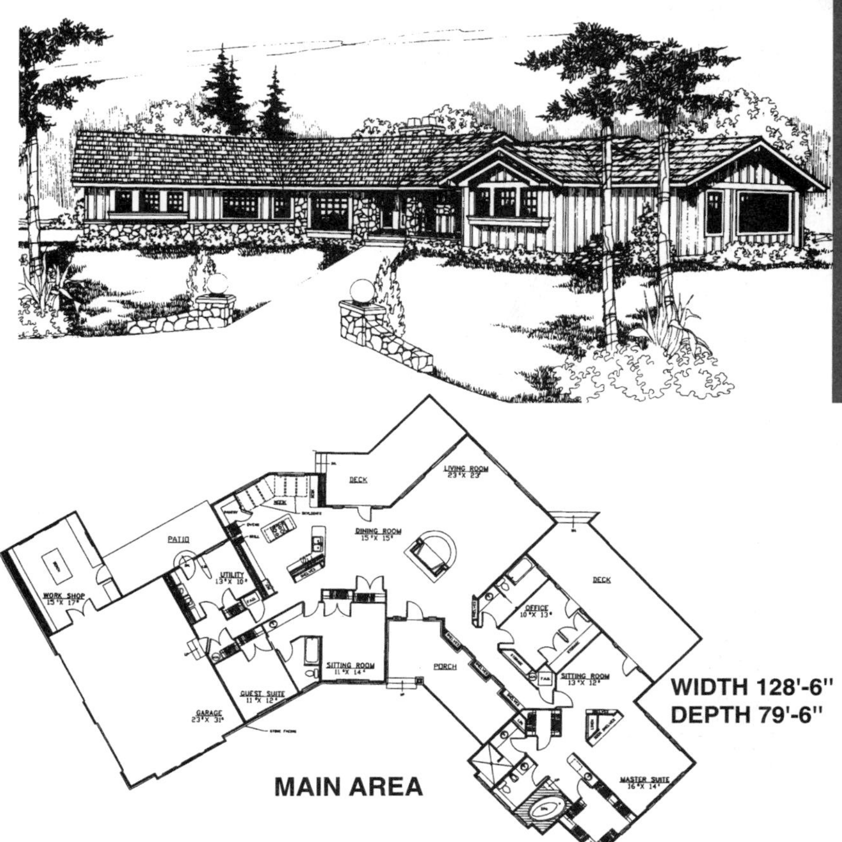

DECK
LIVING ROOM
PATIO
DINING ROOM
UTILITY
WORK SHOP
DECK
OFFICE
SITTING ROOM
PORCH
SITTING ROOM
GUEST SUITE
GARAGE
MASTER SUITE
WIDTH 128'-6"
DEPTH 79'-6"
MAIN AREA

Design by
Homeplanners

PLAN NO. 99288

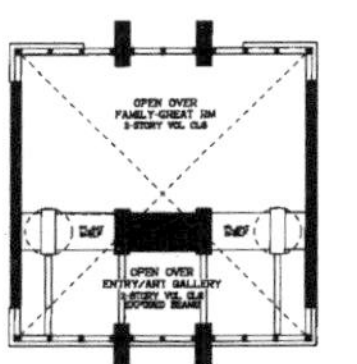

BONUS

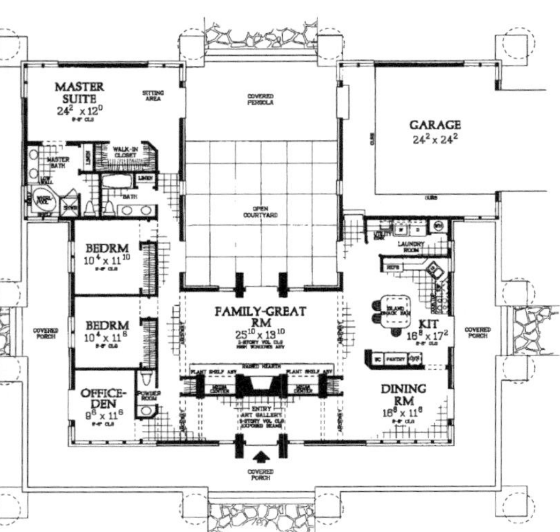

MASTER SUITE
GARAGE
BEDRM
BEDRM
FAMILY-GREAT RM
KIT
OFFICE-DEN
DINING RM

WIDTH 75'-10"
DEPTH 69'-4"

MAIN AREA

Symmetrical, Simple and Stunning

Price Code: E

- This plan features:
  - — Three bedrooms
  - — Two full and one half baths
- Deep eaves create a covered Porch on three sides
- Spacious Kitchen has an island snackbar, built-in pantry accesses Laundry/Garage entry, formal Dining Room, Courtyard and Family Room
- Private Master Suite is pampered by a Sitting Area, a walk-in closet and lavish Master Bath

MAIN FLOOR — 2,626 SQ. FT.
GARAGE — 586 SQ. FT.

TOTAL LIVING AREA:
2,626 SQ. FT.

PLAN NO. 93505

Design by
Lewis River Designs

Refer to **Pricing Schedule F** on the order form for pricing information

Luxury Living

- This plan features:
- — Four bedrooms
- — Two full and one three quarter baths
- A vaulted ceiling Foyer
- A Living Room with a vaulted ceiling and elegant fireplace
- A formal Dining Room that adjoins the Living Room, with a built-in buffet
- An island cooktop in the Kitchen with a walk-in Pantry and an open layout to the Family Room
- A vaulted ceiling in the Family Room with a corner fireplace
- A huge walk-in closet, built-in entertainment center, and a full Bath in the Master Suite

FIRST FLOOR — 2,125 SQ. FT.
SECOND FLOOR — 1,095 SQ. FT.
BASEMENT — 2,125 SQ. FT.

TOTAL LIVING AREA:
3,220 SQ. FT.

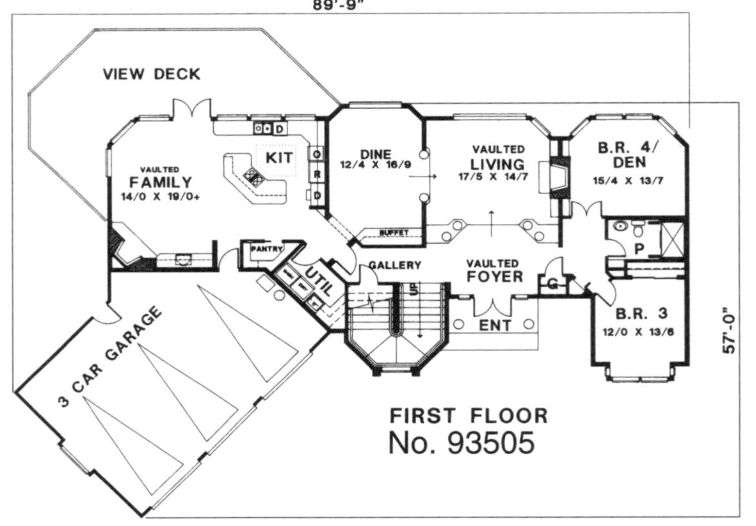

89'-9"
VIEW DECK
VAULTED FAMILY 14/0 X 19/0+
KIT
PANTRY
UTIL
DINE 12/4 X 16/9
BUFFET
VAULTED LIVING 17/5 X 14/7
B.R. 4/ DEN 15/4 X 13/7
P
GALLERY
VAULTED FOYER
ENT
B.R. 3 12/0 X 13/6
3 CAR GARAGE
57'-0"

FIRST FLOOR
No. 93505

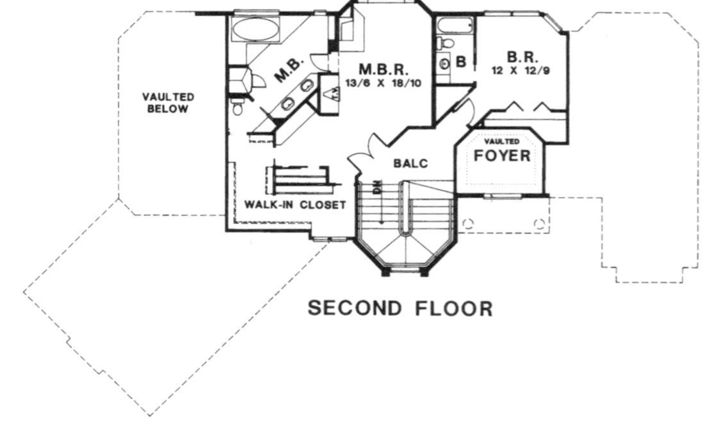

VAULTED BELOW
M.B.
M.B.R. 13/6 X 18/10
B
B.R. 12 X 12/9
BALC
VAULTED FOYER
WALK-IN CLOSET

SECOND FLOOR

Refer to **Pricing Schedule F** on the order form for pricing information

Design by
Patrick Morabito A.I.A.

PLAN NO. 93330

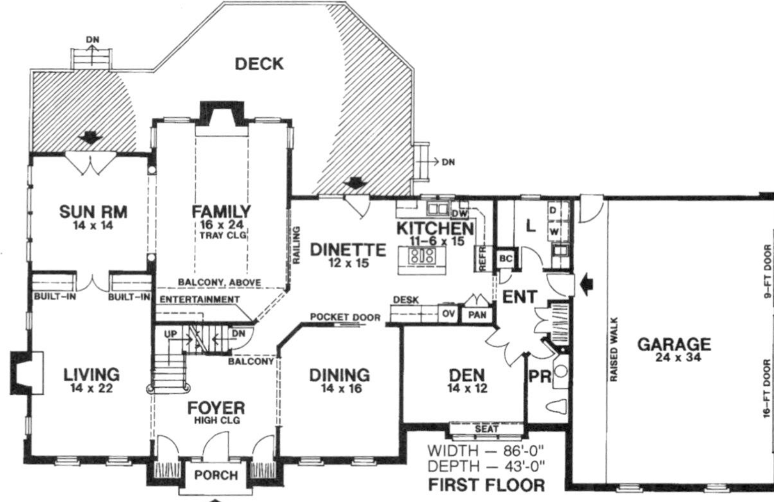

DECK
DN
SUN RM 14 x 14
FAMILY 16 x 24 TRAY CLG
DINETTE 12 x 15
KITCHEN 11-6 x 15
GARAGE 24 x 34
LIVING 14 x 22
FOYER HIGH CLG
DINING 14 x 16
DEN 14 x 12
ENT
PORCH
WIDTH — 86'-0"
DEPTH — 43'-0"
FIRST FLOOR

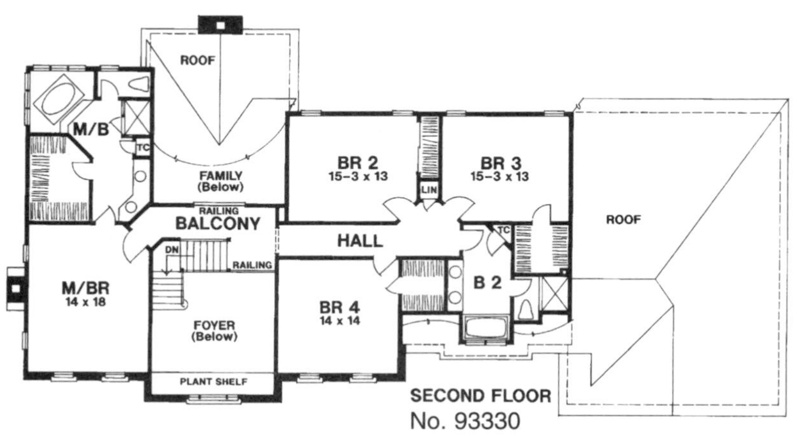

ROOF
M/B
FAMILY (Below)
BR 2 15-3 x 13
BR 3 15-3 x 13
BALCONY
HALL
M/BR 14 x 18
FOYER (Below)
BR 4 14 x 14
B 2
PLANT SHELF
SECOND FLOOR
No. 93330

A Grand Presence

- This plan features:
- — Four bedrooms
- — Two full and one half baths
- Gourmet Kitchen with a cooktop island and built-in Pantry
- Formal Living Room with a fire-place
- Pocket doors separate the formal Dining Room from the Dinette Area
- A balcony overlooks the Family Room
- Expansive Family Room with a fireplace and a built-in entertain-ment center
- A luxurious Master Bath that highlights the Master Suite
- No materials list is available for this plan

FIRST FLOOR — 2,093 SQ. FT.
SECOND FLOOR — 1,527 SQ. FT.
BASEMENT — 2,093 SQ. FT.
GARAGE — 816 SQ. FT.

TOTAL LIVING AREA:
3,620 SQ. FT.

PLAN NO. 94622

Design by
Chatham Home Planning, Inc.

Refer to **Pricing Schedule E** on the order form for pricing information

Multiple Porches Provide Added Interest

- This plan features:
  - — Four bedrooms
  - — Three full and one half baths
- Two-story central Foyer
- Spacious Great Room with large fireplace between French doors to Porch and Deck
- Country-size Kitchen with cooktop work island, walk-in Pantry and Breakfast Area
- Pampering Master Bedroom has a decorative ceiling, Sitting Area and a walk-in closet and Bath
- No materials list is available for this plan
- An optional crawl space or slab foundation — please specify when ordering

FIRST FLOOR — 2,033 SQ. FT.
SECOND FLOOR — 1,116 SQ. FT.

TOTAL LIVING AREA:
3,149 SQ. FT.

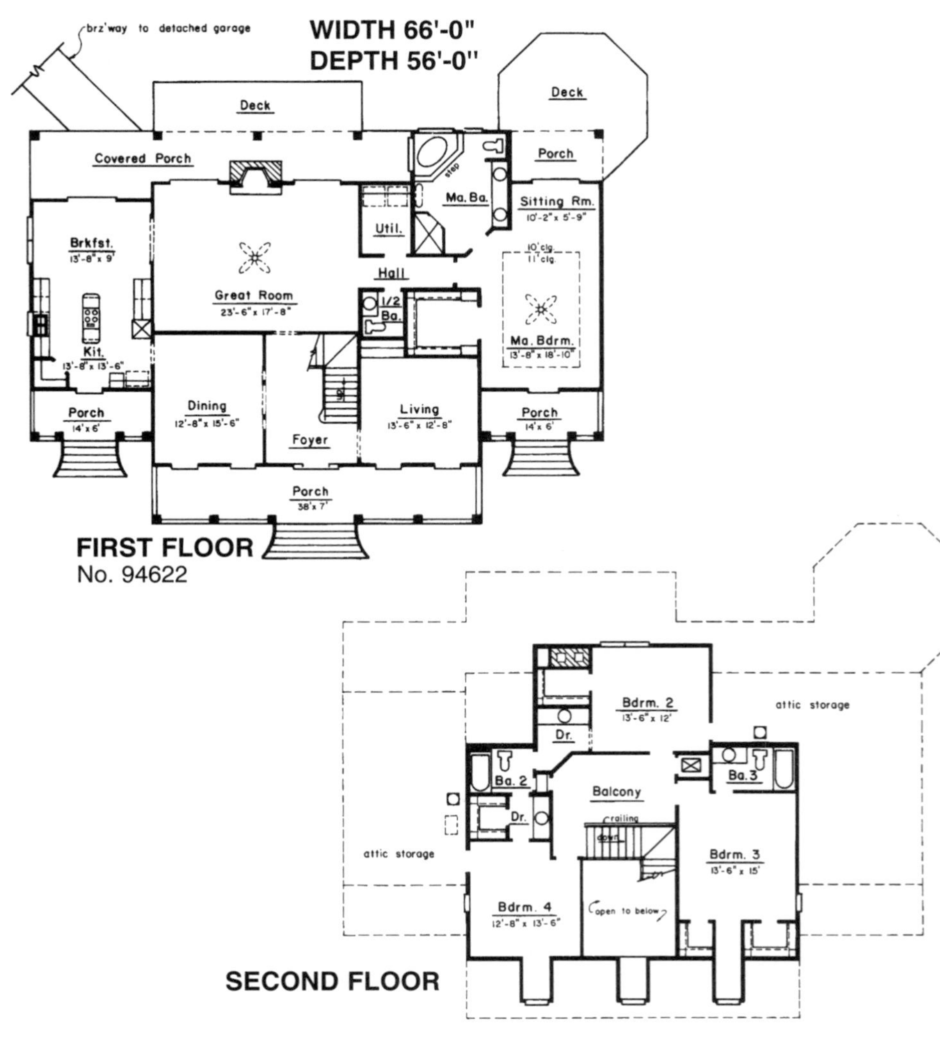
brz'way to detached garage
WIDTH 66'-0"
DEPTH 56'-0"
Deck
Deck
Covered Porch
Porch
Ma. Ba.
Sitting Rm.
10'-2" x 5'-9"
Util.
Brkfst.
13'-8" x 9'
Great Room
23'-6" x 17'-8"
Hall
1/2 Ba.
Ma. Bdrm.
13'-8" x 18'-10"
Kit.
13'-8" x 13'-6"
Porch
14' x 6'
Dining
12'-8" x 15'-6"
Foyer
Living
13'-6" x 12'-8"
Porch
14' x 6'
Porch
38' x 7'
FIRST FLOOR
No. 94622
Bdrm. 2
13'-6" x 12'
attic storage
Dr.
Ba. 2
Balcony
Ba. 3
Dr.
attic storage
Bdrm. 3
13'-6" x 15'
Bdrm. 4
12'-8" x 13'-6"
open to below
SECOND FLOOR

To order your Blueprints, call 1-800-235-5700

Refer to **Pricing Schedule E** on the order form for pricing information

Design by
Design Basics, Inc.

PLAN NO. 99400

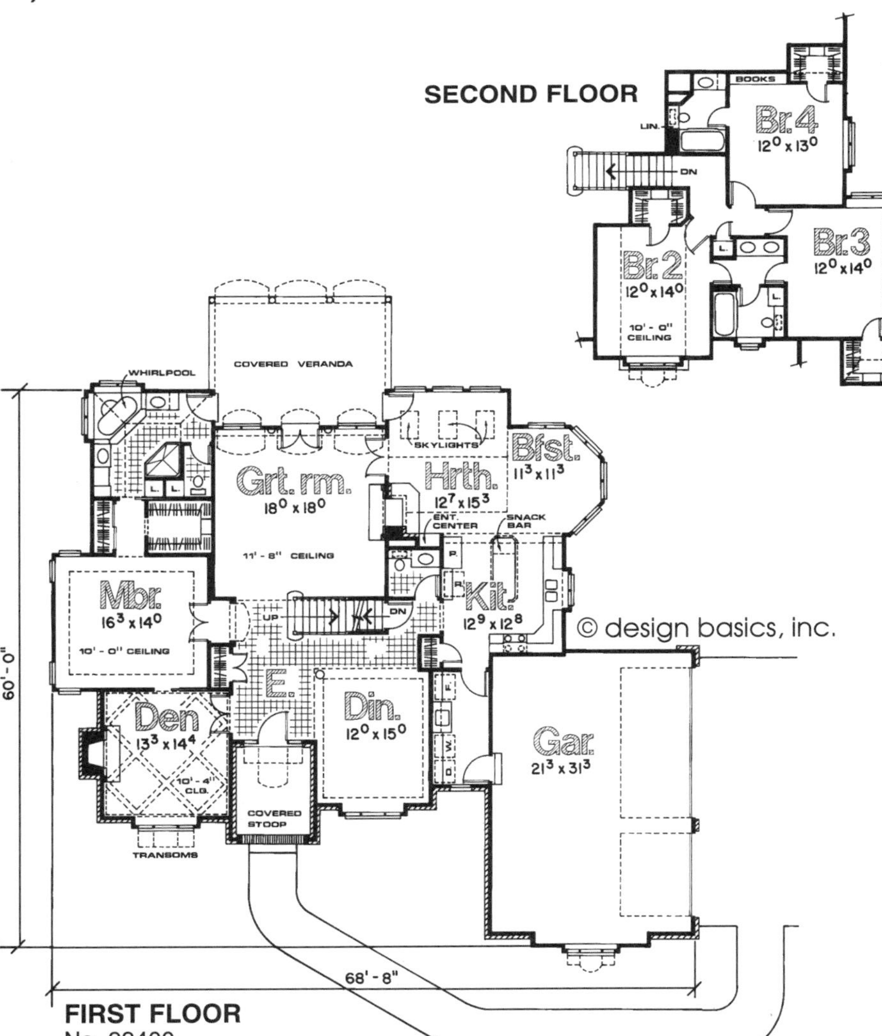

SECOND FLOOR
BOOKS
LIN.
Br. 4
12⁰ x 13⁰
DN
Br. 2
12⁰ x 14⁰
10' - 0" CEILING
Br. 3
12⁰ x 14⁰
WHIRLPOOL
COVERED VERANDA
SKYLIGHTS
Bfst.
11³ x 11³
Grt. rm.
18⁰ x 18⁰
11' - 8" CEILING
Hrth.
12⁷ x 15³
ENT. CENTER
SNACK BAR
Mbr.
16³ x 14⁰
10' - 0" CEILING
UP
DN
Kit.
12⁹ x 12⁸
© design basics, inc.
E.
Den
13³ x 14⁴
10' - 4" CLG.
Din.
12⁰ x 15⁰
Gar.
21³ x 31³
COVERED STOOP
TRANSOMS
60' - 0"
68' - 8"

FIRST FLOOR
No. 99400

Stucco, Brick and Elegant Details

- This plan features:
- — Four bedrooms
- —Three full and one half baths
- Majestic Entry opens to Den and Dining Room
- Expansive Great Room shares a see-thru fireplace with the Hearth Room
- Lovely Hearth Room enhanced by three skylights above triple arched windows
- Hub Kitchen has a work island/snack bar
- Sumptuous Master Bedroom Suite with corner windows and two closets

FIRST FLOOR — 2,084 SQ. FT.
SECOND FLOOR — 848 SQ. FT.
BASEMENT — 2,084 SQ. FT.
GARAGE — 682 SQ. FT.

TOTAL LIVING AREA:
2,932 SQ. FT.

Design by
Archival Designs

Refer to **Pricing Schedule E** on the order form for pricing information

Elegant Presence

- This plan features:
- — Four Bedrooms
- -- Two full, one three-quarter and one half baths
- There is a double door entrance into the grand Foyer
- The Living Room is to the left of the Foyer and steps up into the Dining Room
- A vaulted ceiling crowns the Family Room and the Breakfast Room
- The Master Suite is topped by a vaulted ceiling and includes a his-n-her Bath
- An optional basement or slab foundation — please specify when ordering
- No material list is available for this plan

FIRST FLOOR — 1,396 SQ. FT.
SECOND FLOOR — 1,584 SQ. FT.
BASEMENT — 1,396 SQ. FT.

TOTAL LIVING AREA:
2,980 SQ. FT

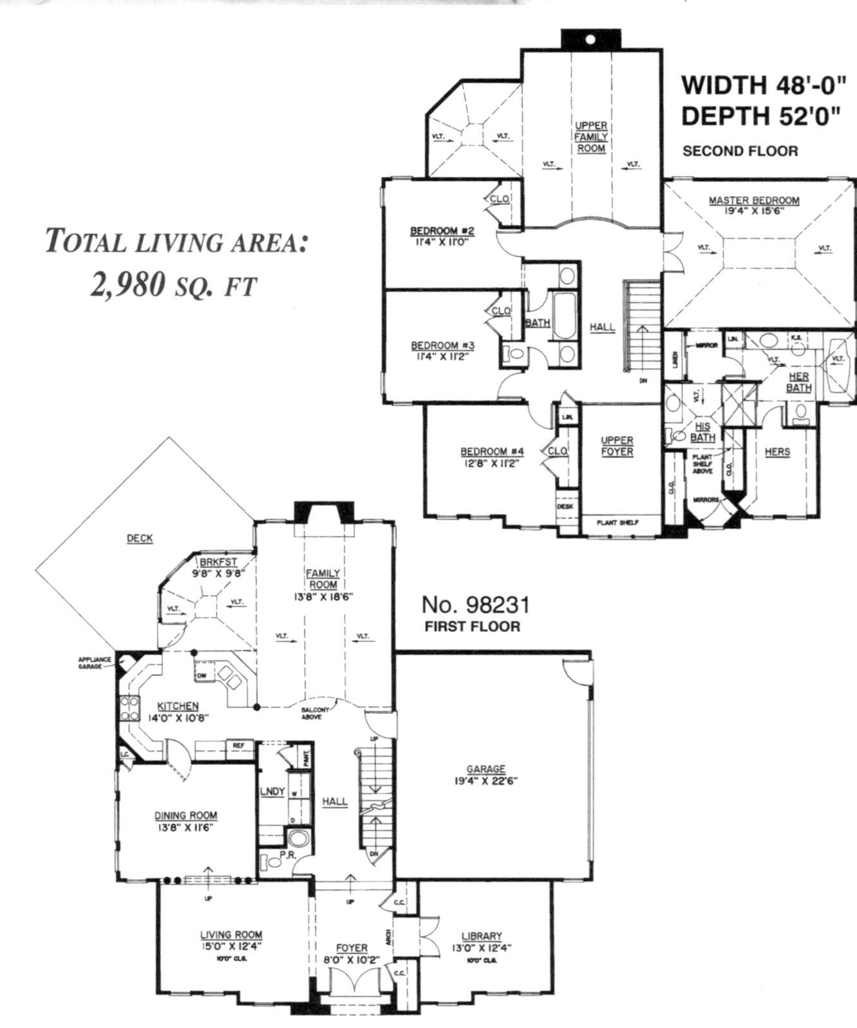
WIDTH 48'-0"
DEPTH 52'0"
SECOND FLOOR
UPPER FAMILY ROOM
MASTER BEDROOM 19'4" X 15'6"
BEDROOM #2 11'4" X 11'0"
BEDROOM #3 11'4" X 11'2"
BEDROOM #4 12'8" X 11'2"
BATH
HALL
UPPER FOYER
HER BATH
HIS BATH
HERS
No. 98231
FIRST FLOOR
DECK
BRKFST 9'8" X 9'8"
FAMILY ROOM 13'8" X 18'6"
KITCHEN 14'0" X 10'8"
GARAGE 19'4" X 22'6"
DINING ROOM 13'8" X 11'6"
LNDY
HALL
LIVING ROOM 15'0" X 12'4"
FOYER 8'0" X 10'2"
LIBRARY 13'0" X 12'4"

Refer to **Pricing Schedule E** on the order form for pricing information

Design by
Chatham Home Planning, Inc.

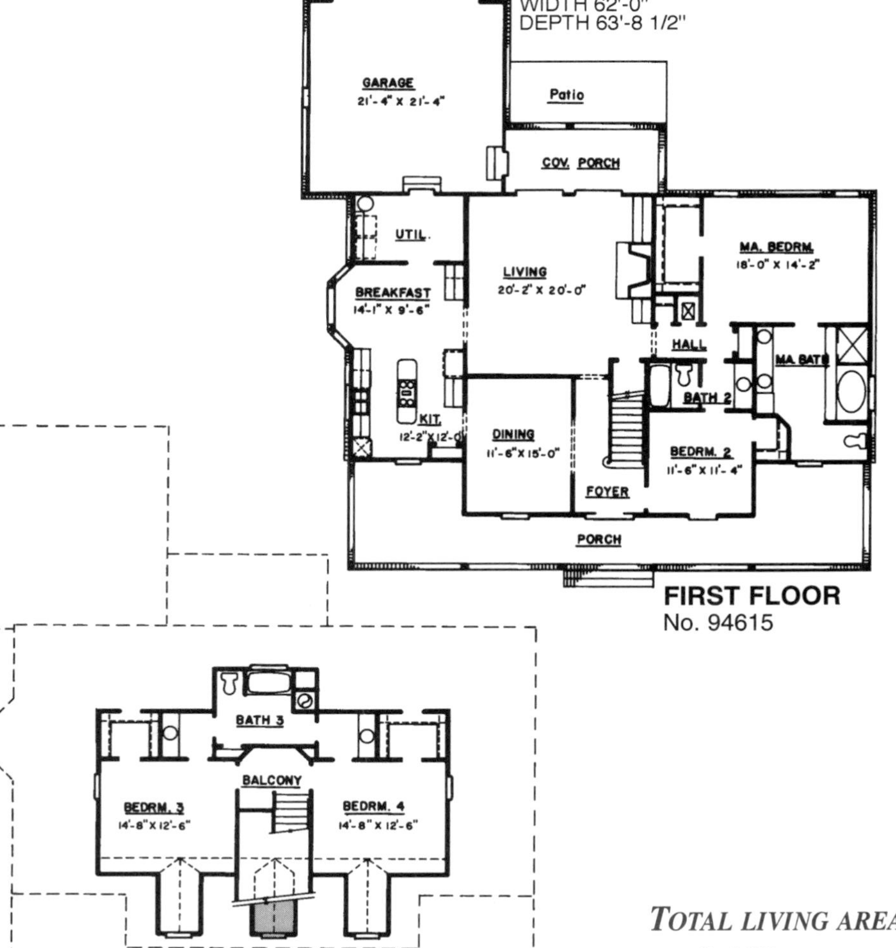

WIDTH 62'-0"
DEPTH 63'-8 1/2"
GARAGE
21'-4" X 21'-4"
Patio
COV. PORCH
UTIL.
LIVING
20'-2" X 20'-0"
MA. BEDRM.
18'-0" X 14'-2"
BREAKFAST
14'-1" X 9'-6"
HALL
MA. BATH
BATH 2
KIT.
12'-2" X 12'-0
DINING
11'-6" X 15'-0"
BEDRM. 2
11'-6" X 11'-4"
FOYER
PORCH
FIRST FLOOR
No. 94615
BATH 3
BALCONY
BEDRM. 3
14'-8" X 12'-6"
BEDRM. 4
14'-8" X 12'-6"
SECOND FLOOR

Grand Country Porch

- This plan features:
  - — Four bedrooms
  - — Three full baths
- Living Room has access to covered Porch and Patio, and a fireplace between built-in shelves
- Country Kitchen with a cooktop island and bright Breakfast Bay
- Corner Master Bedroom has a walk-in closet and private Bath
- First floor Bedroom with private access to a full Bath
- Two additional second floor Bedrooms with dormers, walk-in closets and vanities
- No materials list is available for this plan
- An optional crawl space or slab foundation — please specify when ordering

FIRST FLOOR — 1,916 SQ. FT.
SECOND FLOOR — 749 SQ. FT.
GARAGE — 479 SQ. FT.

TOTAL LIVING AREA:
2,665 SQ. FT.

PLAN NO. 94715

Design by
United Design Associates

Refer to **Pricing Schedule E** on the order form for pricing information

WIDTH 71'-10"
DEPTH 46'-0"

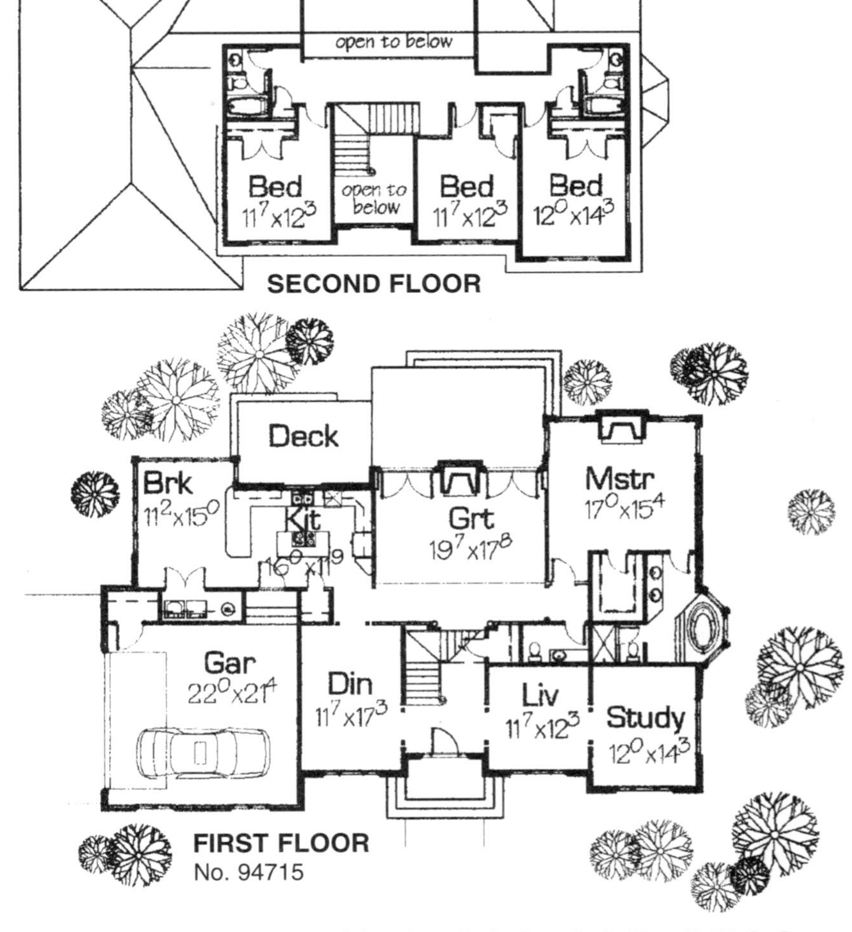

open to below
Bed 11^7x12^3
open to below
Bed 11^7x12^3
Bed 12^0x14^3
SECOND FLOOR
Deck
Brk 11^2x15^0
Kit 16^0x11^9
Grt 19^7x17^8
Mstr 17^0x15^4
Gar 22^0x21^4
Din 11^7x17^3
Liv 11^7x12^3
Study 12^0x14^3
FIRST FLOOR
No. 94715

Brick Traditional

- This plan features:
  - — Four bedrooms
  - — Three full and one half baths
- Old Southern architecture incorporates today's open floor plan
- Gracious two-story Foyer between formal Living and Dining rooms
- Comfortable Great Room with a fireplace is nestled between French doors to the rear Decks
- Hub Kitchen offers a cooktop island, an eating bar and a Breakfast Area
- Master Bedroom is enhanced by a fireplace and a plush Bath

FIRST FLOOR — 2,094 SQ. FT.
SECOND FLOOR — 918 SQ. FT.
GARAGE — 537 SQ. FT.

TOTAL LIVING AREA:
3,012 SQ. FT.

Arched Windows

Price Code: F

Design by
Studer Residential Design, Inc.

PLAN NO.92657

- This plan features:
  - — Three bedrooms
  - — Three full and one half baths
- The Foyer and Gallery are accented by the stairs that lead to the lower floor
- The impressive Master Bedroom has a walk-in closet, dressing area, and bath with a dual vanity
- Two Bedrooms on the lower floor share a full Bath
- Accented by columns, the Dining Room and Great Room are perfect for formal occasions
- An Exercise Room, Billiard Room, Media Room, and full a Bath complete the living space on the lower floor

FIRST FLOOR — 2,582 SQ. FT.
LOWER FLOOR — 1,746 SQ. FT.
BASEMENT — 871 SQ. FT.

TOTAL LIVING AREA:
4,328 SQ. FT.

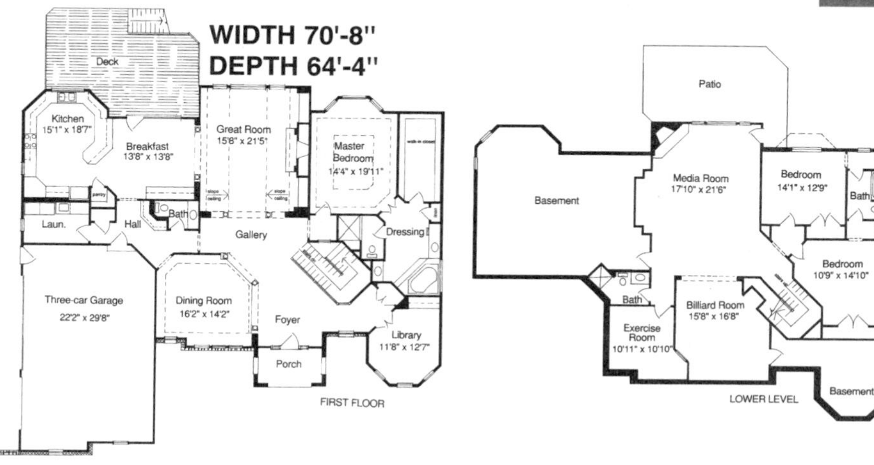
WIDTH 70'-8"
DEPTH 64'-4"
Deck
Kitchen
15'1" x 18'7"
Breakfast
13'8" x 13'8"
Great Room
15'8" x 21'5"
Master Bedroom
14'4" x 19'11"
Laun.
Hall
Bath
Gallery
Dressing
Three-car Garage
22'2" x 29'8"
Dining Room
16'2" x 14'2"
Foyer
Library
11'8" x 12'7"
Porch
FIRST FLOOR
Patio
Basement
Media Room
17'10" x 21'6"
Bedroom
14'1" x 12'9"
Bath
Bedroom
10'9" x 14'10"
Bath
Billiard Room
15'8" x 16'8"
Exercise Room
10'11" x 10'10"
Basement
LOWER LEVEL

Design by
Sater Design Group

PLAN NO.94220

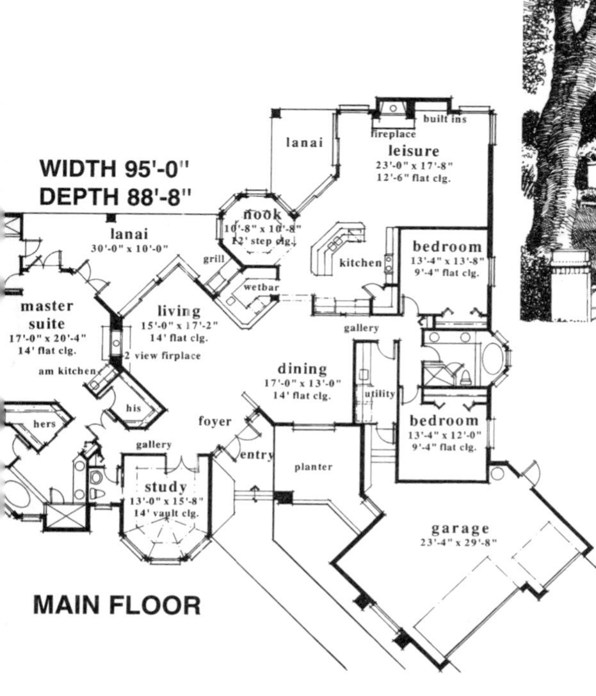
WIDTH 95'-0"
DEPTH 88'-8"
lanai
built ins
fireplace
leisure
23'-0" x 17'-8"
12'-6" flat clg.
nook
10'-8" x 10'-8"
12' step clg.
lanai
30'-0" x 10'-0"
grill
kitchen
bedroom
13'-4" x 13'-8"
9'-4" flat clg.
wetbar
master suite
17'-0" x 20'-4"
14' flat clg.
living
15'-0" x 17'-2"
14' flat clg.
2 view firplace
gallery
am kitchen
dining
17'-0" x 13'-0"
14' flat clg.
utility
his
hers
foyer
bedroom
13'-4" x 12'-0"
9'-4" flat clg.
gallery
entry
planter
study
13'-0" x 15'-8"
14' vault clg.
garage
23'-4" x 29'-8"
MAIN FLOOR

Turret Study Creates Impact

Price Code: F

- This plan features:
  - —Three bedrooms
  - —Two full, one three-quarter and one half baths
- Entry doors opening into the formal Living Room focus to the Lanai
- Wetbar easily serves the Living Room, Dining Room and Lanai
- Island Kitchen serves all informal family areas
- No materials list is available for this plan

MAIN FLOOR — 3,477 SQ. FT.
GARAGE — 771 SQ. FT.

TOTAL LIVING AREA:
3,477 SQ. FT.

Design by
Donald A. Gardner Architects, Inc.

Refer to **Pricing Schedule F** on the order form for pricing information

Stately Elegance

- This plan features:
  - — Four bedrooms
  - — Three full and one half baths
- Impressive double gable roof with front and rear palladian windows and wrap-around Porch
- Vaulted ceilings in two-story Foyer and Great Room accommodates Loft/Study area
- Spacious, first floor Master Bedroom offers a walk-in closet and luxurious Bath
- Living space expanded outdoors by wrap-around Porch and large Deck
- Upstairs, one of three Bedrooms could be a second Master Bedroom

FIRST FLOOR — 1,734 SQ. FT.
SECOND FLOOR — 958 SQ. FT.

TOTAL LIVING AREA:
2,692 SQ. FT.

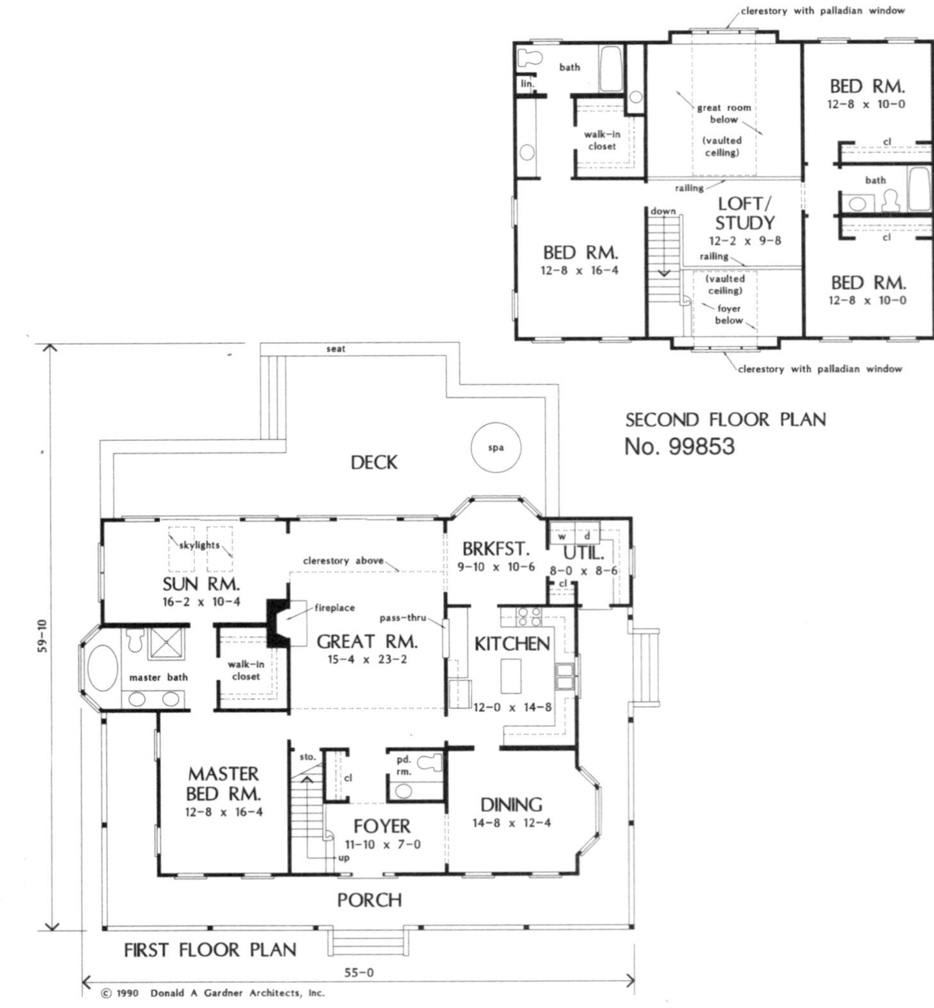
clerestory with palladian window
bath
lin.
walk-in closet
great room below
(vaulted ceiling)
BED RM.
12-8 x 10-0
cl
bath
railing
down
LOFT/ STUDY
12-2 x 9-8
railing
BED RM.
12-8 x 16-4
(vaulted ceiling)
foyer below
BED RM.
12-8 x 10-0
cl
clerestory with palladian window
seat
DECK
spa
59-10
skylights
clerestory above
SUN RM.
16-2 x 10-4
fireplace
pass-thru
BRKFST.
9-10 x 10-6
UTIL.
8-0 x 8-6
w
d
cl
master bath
walk-in closet
GREAT RM.
15-4 x 23-2
KITCHEN
12-0 x 14-8
sto.
cl
pd. rm.
MASTER BED RM.
12-8 x 16-4
FOYER
11-10 x 7-0
up
DINING
14-8 x 12-4
PORCH
55-0
© 1990 Donald A Gardner Architects, Inc.

SECOND FLOOR PLAN
No. 99853

FIRST FLOOR PLAN

Refer to **Pricing Schedule F** on the order form for pricing information

Design by
Frank Betz Associates, Inc.

PLAN NO. 98438

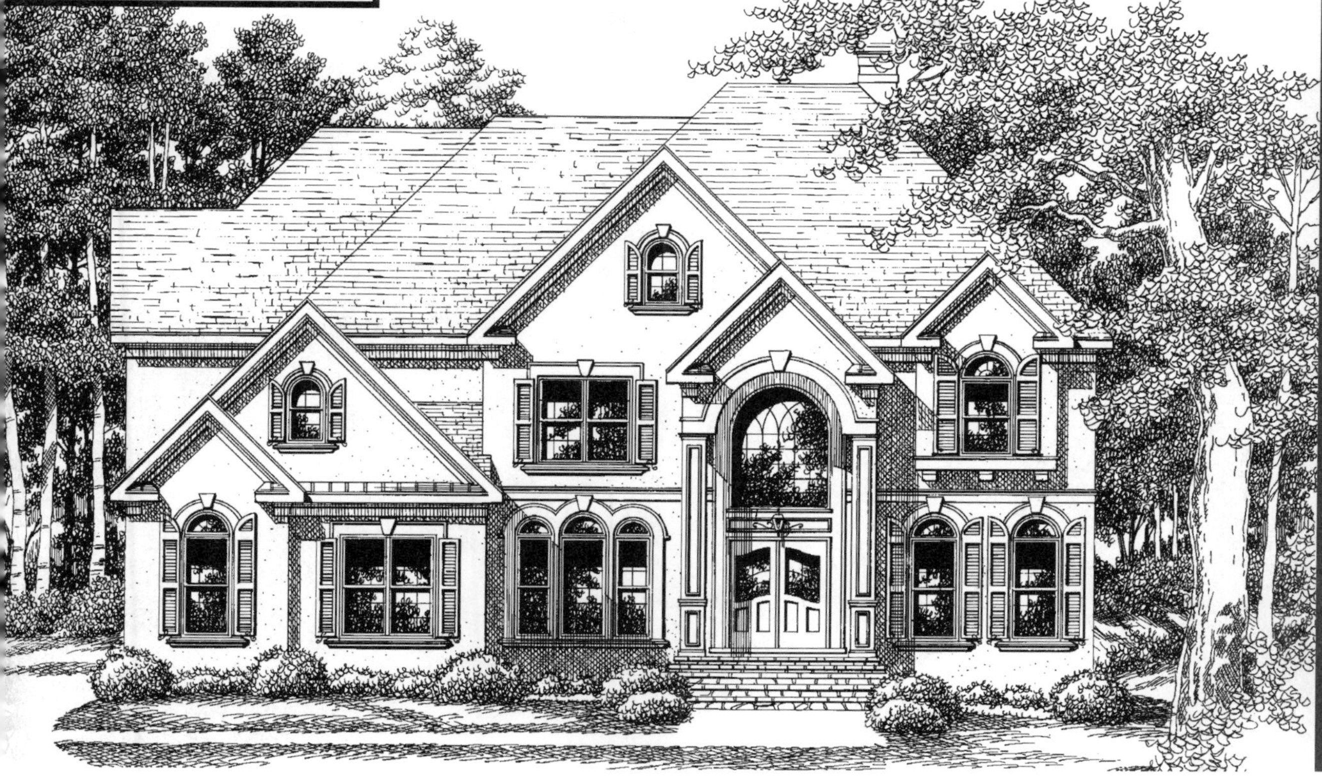

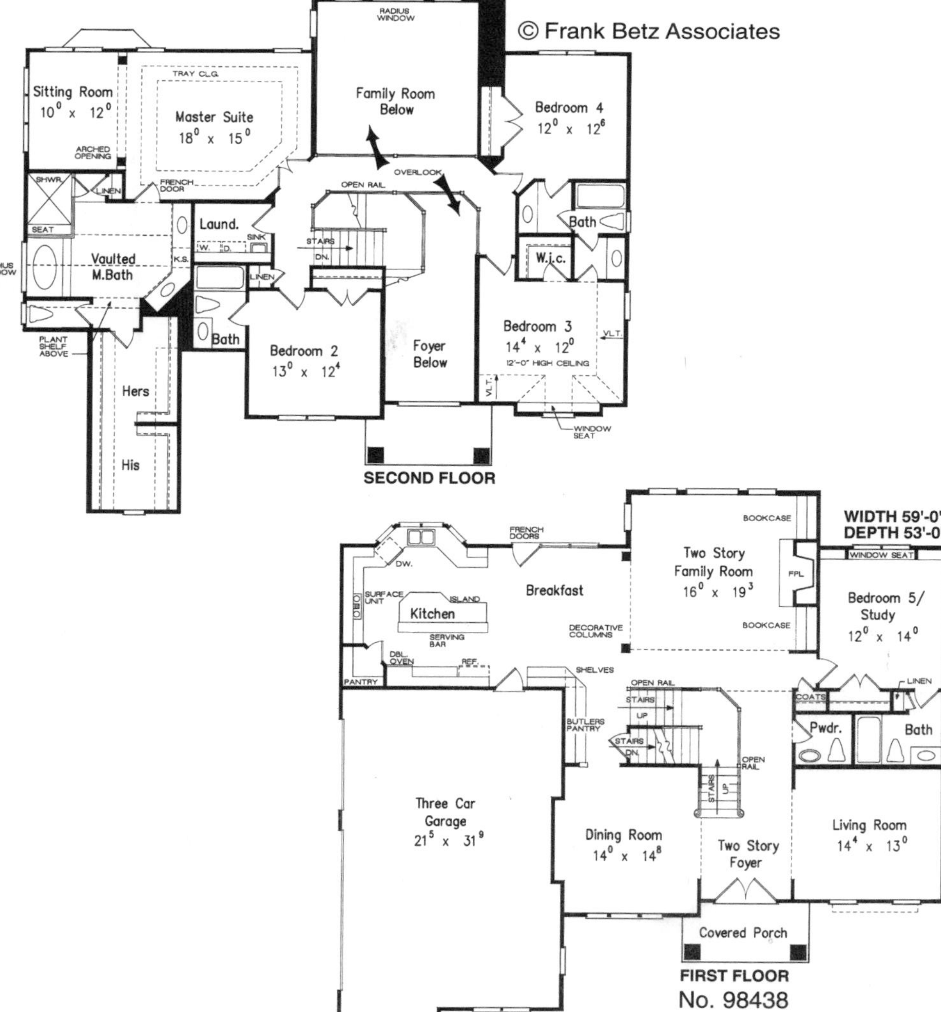

© Frank Betz Associates
Sitting Room 10⁰ x 12⁰
Master Suite 18⁰ x 15⁰
TRAY CLG.
ARCHED OPENING
FRENCH DOOR
Family Room Below
RADIUS WINDOW
Bedroom 4 12⁰ x 12⁶
OVERLOOK
OPEN RAIL
Laund.
Vaulted M.Bath
Bath
W.i.c.
Bedroom 3 14⁴ x 12⁰
12'-0" HIGH CEILING
Bedroom 2 13⁰ x 12⁴
Foyer Below
WINDOW SEAT
Hers
His
PLANT SHELF ABOVE
SECOND FLOOR
WIDTH 59'-0"
DEPTH 53'-0"
FRENCH DOORS
Breakfast
Kitchen
ISLAND
SERVING BAR
DECORATIVE COLUMNS
Two Story Family Room 16⁰ x 19³
BOOKCASE
FPL
Bedroom 5/ Study 12⁰ x 14⁰
WINDOW SEAT
PANTRY
BUTLERS PANTRY
SHELVES
OPEN RAIL
COATS
Pwdr.
Bath
Three Car Garage 21⁵ x 31⁹
Dining Room 14⁰ x 14⁸
Two Story Foyer
Living Room 14⁴ x 13⁰
Covered Porch
FIRST FLOOR
No. 98438

Windows Distinguish Design

- This plan features:
  - — Five bedrooms
  - — Four full and one half baths
- A hall through the Butler's Pantry leads the way into the Breakfast Nook
- The two-story Family Room has a fireplace with built-in bookcases on either side
- The Master Suite has a Sitting Room and a French door leading into the vaulted Master Bath
- An optional basement or a crawl space foundation — please specify when ordering

FIRST FLOOR — 1,786 SQ. FT.
SECOND FLOOR — 1,739 SQ. FT.
BASEMENT — 1,786 SQ. FT.
GARAGE — 704 SQ. FT.

TOTAL LIVING AREA:
3,525 SQ. FT.

PLAN NO. 98211

Design by
Archival Designs

Refer to **Pricing Schedule E** on the order form for pricing information

Executive Features

- This plan features:
- — Four bedrooms
- — Three full and one half baths
- His-n-her walk-in closets and a five-piece lavish Bath highlight the Master Bath
- The island Kitchen, Keeping Room and Breakfast Room create an open living space
- A fireplace accents both the Keeping Room and the two-story Grand Room
- An optional basement or crawl space foundation — please specify when ordering
- No materials list is available for this plan

FIRST FLOOR — 2,035 SQ. FT.
SECOND FLOOR — 1,028 SQ. FT.
BASEMENT — 2,035 SQ. FT.
GARAGE — 530 SQ. FT.

TOTAL LIVING AREA:
3,063 SQ. FT.

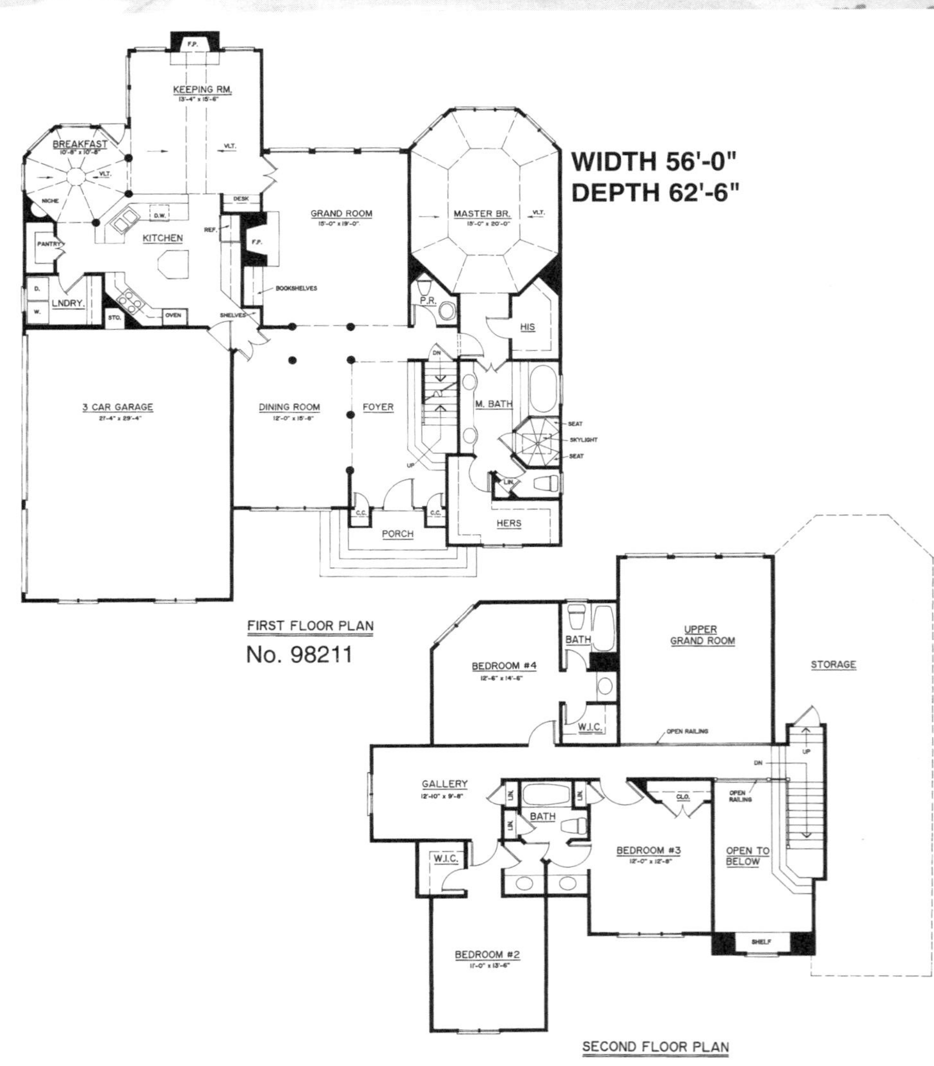
WIDTH 56'-0"
DEPTH 62'-6"
KEEPING RM.
BREAKFAST
KITCHEN
PANTRY
LNDRY.
GRAND ROOM
MASTER BR.
P.R.
HIS
M. BATH
HERS
3 CAR GARAGE
DINING ROOM
FOYER
PORCH
BOOKSHELVES
FIRST FLOOR PLAN
No. 98211
BEDROOM #4
BATH
UPPER GRAND ROOM
STORAGE
W.I.C.
GALLERY
BATH
BEDROOM #3
OPEN TO BELOW
BEDROOM #2
SECOND FLOOR PLAN

To order your Blueprints, call 1-800-235-5700

Refer to **Pricing Schedule E** on the order form for pricing information

Design by
Garrell Associates, Inc.

PLAN NO. 93604

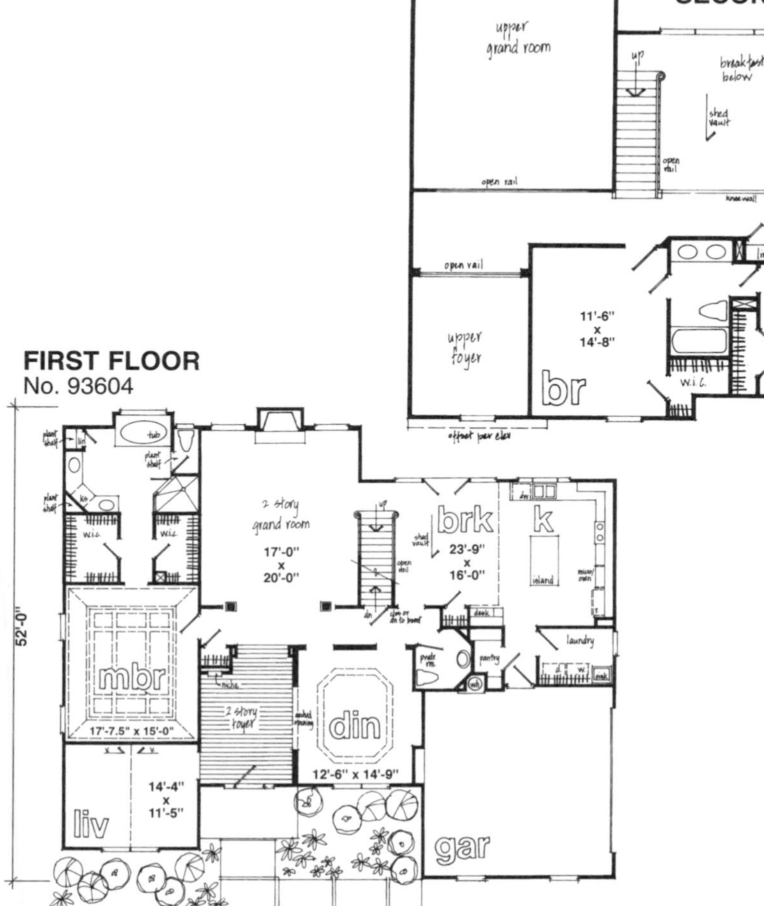

SECOND FLOOR 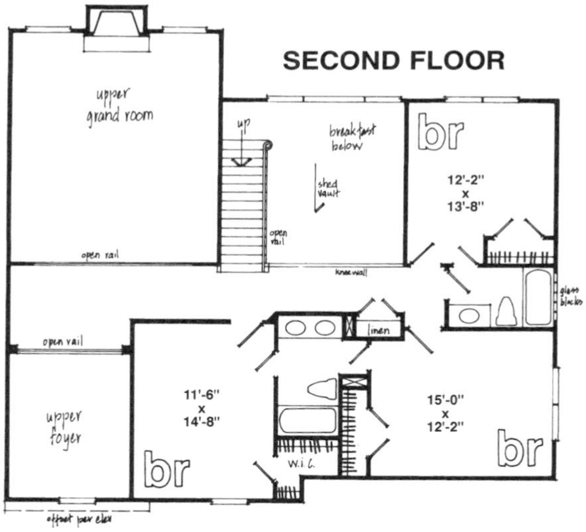
upper grand room
up
breakfast below
shed vault
open rail
br
12'-2"
x
13'-8"
linen
11'-6"
x
14'-8"
15'-0"
x
12'-2"
upper foyer
br
w.i.c.
br
FIRST FLOOR
No. 93604
2 story grand room
17'-0"
x
20'-0"
brk
23'-9"
x
16'-0"
k
island
laundry
pantry
mbr
17'-7.5" x 15'-0"
2 story foyer
din
12'-6" x 14'-9"
liv
14'-4"
x
11'-5"
gar
52'-0"
60'-0"

With Attention to Detail

- This plan features:
- — Four bedrooms
- — Three full and one half baths
- A two-story Foyer
- A formal Living Room and Dining Room perfect for entertaining
- A two-story Grand Room with a focal point fireplace
- A gourmet Kitchen with a work island, walk-in Pantry, built-in and a planning desk
- A first floor Master Suite with a decorative ceiling and a luxurious Master Bath
- No materials list is available for this plan

FIRST FLOOR — 2,115 SQ. FT.
SECOND FLOOR — 914 SQ. FT.
BASEMENT — 2,115 SQ. FT.
GARAGE — 448 SQ. FT.

TOTAL LIVING AREA:
3,029 SQ. FT.

PLAN NO. 94815

Design by
W.D. Farmer F.A.I.B.D.

Refer to **Pricing Schedule F** on
the order form for pricing information

Columns Separate Interior Spaces

- This plan features:
- — Four bedrooms
- — Three full and one half baths
- Stucco, stone, and varied windows add character to this home
- Inside the Foyer is separated from the Dining Room and Great Room by columns
- The Great Room has a two-story ceiling and a fireplace with built-ins between it
- Located in a quiet spot the Study is a fine retreat
- The U-shaped Kitchen has a center island
- The bay shaped Breakfast Area is perfect for casual meals
- The warm Keeping Room has a vaulted ceiling
- The Master Bedroom is on the first floor and features a quiet Sitting Area

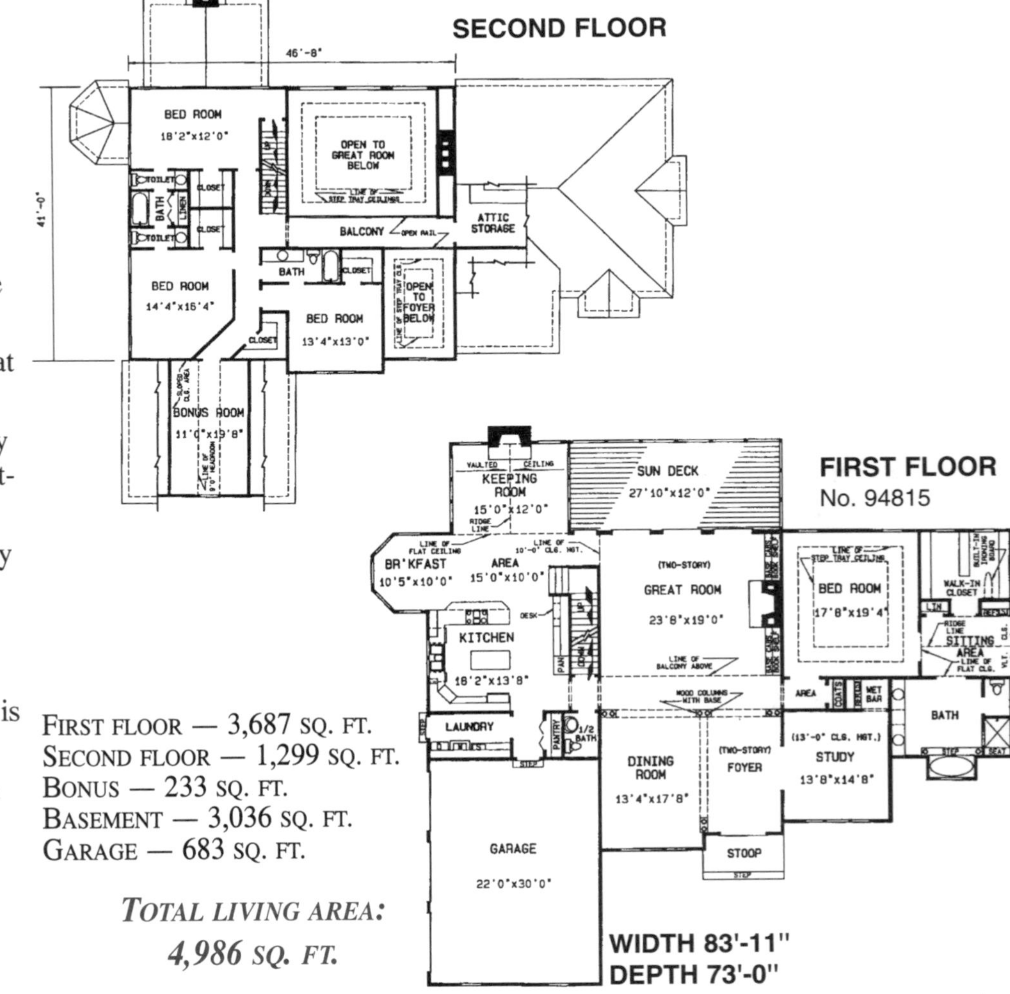
SECOND FLOOR
46'-8"
41'-0"
BED ROOM
18'2"x12'0"
OPEN TO GREAT ROOM BELOW
TOILET
BATH
LINEN
CLOSET
BALCONY
OPEN RAIL
ATTIC STORAGE
BED ROOM
14'4"x15'4"
BATH
BED ROOM
13'4"x13'0"
OPEN TO FOYER BELOW
BONUS ROOM
11'0"x19'8"
FIRST FLOOR
No. 94815
KEEPING ROOM
15'0"x12'0"
SUN DECK
27'10"x12'0"
BR'KFAST
10'5"x10'0"
AREA
15'0"x10'0"
(TWO-STORY)
GREAT ROOM
23'8"x19'0"
BED ROOM
17'8"x19'4"
WALK-IN CLOSET
SITTING AREA
KITCHEN
18'2"x13'8"
DESK
PANTRY
LAUNDRY
1/2 BATH
DINING ROOM
13'4"x17'8"
(TWO-STORY)
FOYER
(13'-0" CLG. HGT.)
STUDY
13'8"x14'8"
BATH
GARAGE
22'0"x30'0"
STOOP
WIDTH 83'-11"
DEPTH 73'-0"

FIRST FLOOR — 3,687 SQ. FT.
SECOND FLOOR — 1,299 SQ. FT.
BONUS — 233 SQ. FT.
BASEMENT — 3,036 SQ. FT.
GARAGE — 683 SQ. FT.

TOTAL LIVING AREA:
***4,986** SQ. FT.*

Refer to **Pricing Schedule F** on the order form for pricing information

Design by
Filmore Design Group

PLAN NO. 92219

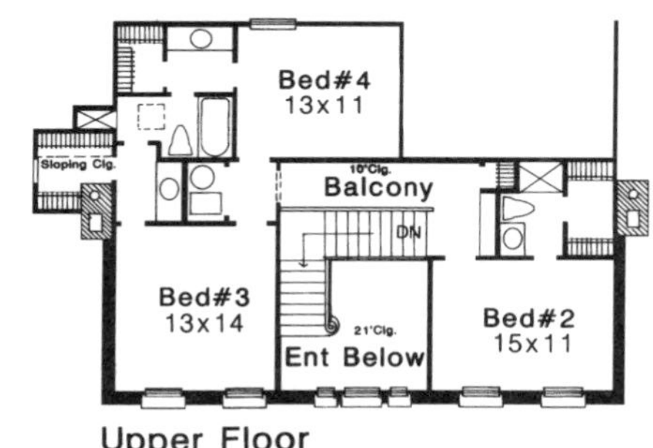

Bed#4
13x11
Sloping Clg.
10'Clg.
Balcony
DN
Bed#3
13x14
21'Clg.
Ent Below
Bed#2
15x11

Upper Floor

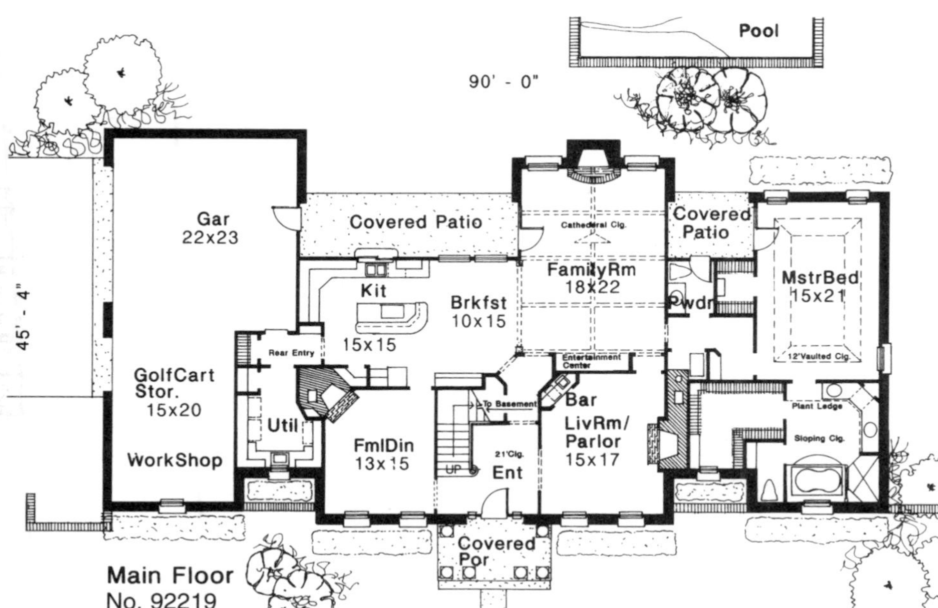

Pool
90' - 0"
45' - 4"
Gar
22x23
Covered Patio
Cathedral Clg.
Covered Patio
FamilyRm
18x22
MstrBed
15x21
Kit
Brkfst
10x15
Pwdr
15x15
Rear Entry
Entertainment Center
12'Vaulted Clg.
GolfCart Stor.
15x20
Util
Bar
To Basement
LivRm/ Parlor
15x17
Plant Ledge
Sloping Clg.
FmlDin
13x15
21'Clg.
Ent
UP
WorkShop
Covered Por

Main Floor
No. 92219

Columned Entrance

- This plan features:
- — Four bedrooms
- — Two full, one three-quarter and one half baths
- Entry hall with a graceful landing staircase
- Fireplaces highlight both the Living Room/Parlor and formal Dining Room
- The Kitchen has an island cooktop, built-in pantry and is open to Breakfast Area
- Cathedral ceiling crowns expansive Family Room
- Lavish Master Bedroom wing
- No materials list is available for this plan

MAIN FLOOR — 2,432 SQ. FT.
UPPER FLOOR — 903 SQ. FT.
BASEMENT — 2,432 SQ. FT.
GARAGE — 742 SQ. FT.

TOTAL LIVING AREA:
3,335 SQ. FT.

PLAN NO. 98563

Design by
Filmore Design Group

Refer to **Pricing Schedule F** on the order form for pricing information

Lavish Appointments

- This plan features:
- — Four bedrooms
- — Four full and one half baths
- Glassed two-story entry
- The staircase to the second floor accents the marble entry hall
- A sloped ceiling and a fireplace enhance the Living Room
- The Dining Room has a rear wall of windows
- The Kitchen has a center island with a cooktop
- The Study has a fireplace
- The lavish Master Bedroom includes a Sitting Area and an Exercise Area
- No materials list is available for this plan

MAIN FLOOR — 3,145 SQ. FT.
UPPER FLOOR — 1,181 SQ. FT.
GARAGE — 792 SQ. FT.

TOTAL LIVING AREA:
4,326 SQ. FT.

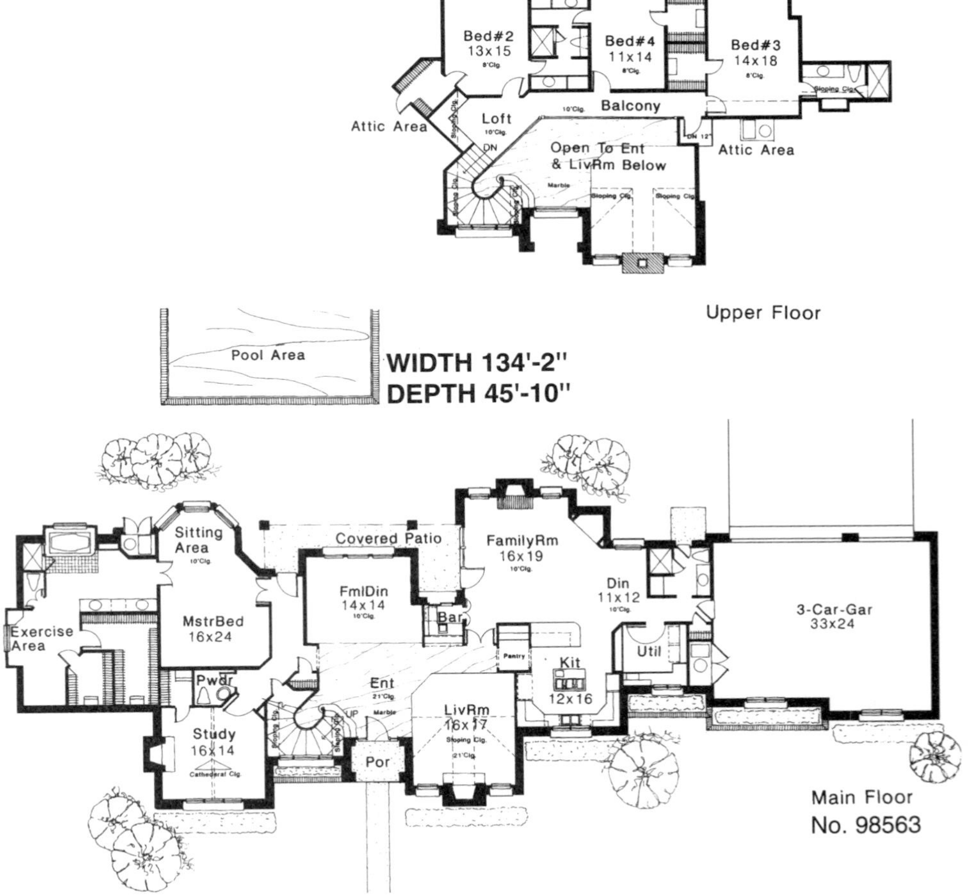
Bed#2
13x15
Bed#4
11x14
Bed#3
14x18
Attic Area
Loft
Balcony
Open To Ent & LivRm Below
Attic Area
Upper Floor
Pool Area
WIDTH 134'-2"
DEPTH 45'-10"
Sitting Area
Covered Patio
FamilyRm
16x19
FmlDin
14x14
Din
11x12
3-Car-Gar
33x24
Exercise Area
MstrBed
16x24
Bar
Pantry
Kit
12x16
Util
Pwdr
Ent
LivRm
16x17
Study
16x14
Por
Main Floor
No. 98563

To order your Blueprints, call 1-800-235-5700

Refer to **Pricing Schedule E** on the order form for pricing information

Design by **Homeplanners**

PLAN NO. 99270

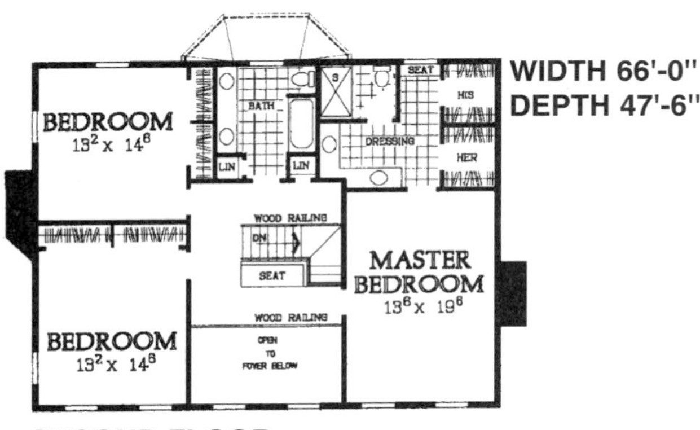
WIDTH 66'-0"
DEPTH 47'-6"
BEDROOM
13² x 14⁸
BEDROOM
13² x 14⁸
MASTER BEDROOM
13⁶ x 19⁶
BATH
DRESSING
SEAT
HIS
HER
LIN
LIN
WOOD RAILING
DN
SEAT
WOOD RAILING
OPEN TO FOYER BELOW
SECOND FLOOR

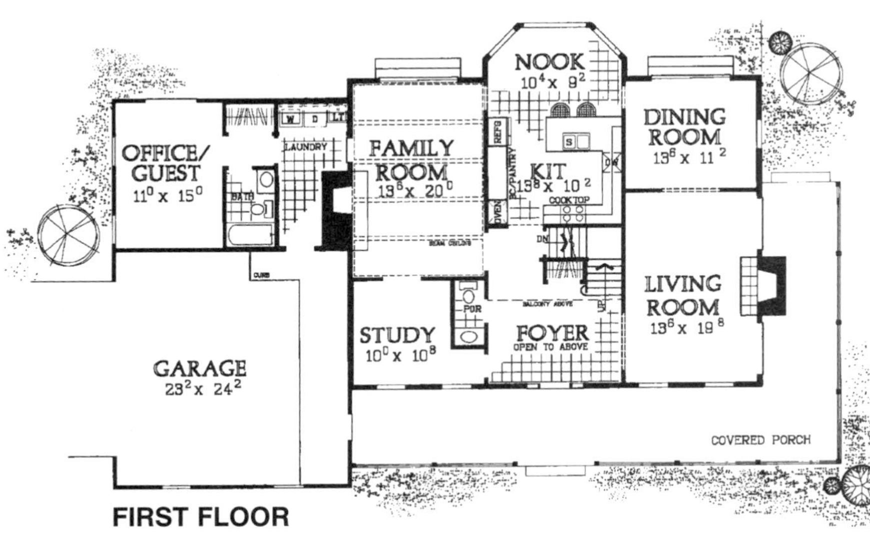
NOOK
10⁴ x 9²
OFFICE/ GUEST
11⁰ x 15⁰
LAUNDRY
BATH
FAMILY ROOM
13⁶ x 20⁰
KIT
15⁸ x 10²
COOKTOP
PANTRY
REFG
OVEN
DINING ROOM
13⁶ x 11²
LIVING ROOM
13⁶ x 19⁸
STUDY
10⁰ x 10⁸
PDR
FOYER
OPEN TO ABOVE
GARAGE
23² x 24²
COVERED PORCH
FIRST FLOOR
No. 99270

In-Home Office Space

- This plan features:
- — Three or four bedrooms
- — Three full and one half baths
- Friendly front Porch adds country charm to practical design
- Open Foyer with lovely landing staircase, flanked by Study and Living Room
- Hub Kitchen with built-in Pantry, peninsula eating bar, eating Nook and adjoining Dining Room
- Comfortable Family Room with beamed ceiling, large fireplace and access to rear yard, Laundry and Office/Guest space
- Corner Master Bedroom with Dressing Area and his-n-her walk-in closets

FIRST FLOOR — 1,762 SQ. FT.
SECOND FLOOR — 1,311 SQ. FT.
GARAGE — 561 SQ. FT.

TOTAL LIVING AREA:
3,073 SQ. FT.

PLAN NO.91501

Design by
Alan Mascord Design Associates

Sprawling Sun-Catcher

Price Code: E

- This plan features:
- — Three bedrooms
- — Two full and one half baths
- A central foyer opens to every area of the house
- A fabulous Master Suite with a garden spa, double vanity and a room-size walk-in closet
- The cozy Den has French doors to the rear patio
- Columns separate the Living Room with fireplace from the octagonal Dining Room
- An island Kitchen with twin ovens and a peninsula counter
- An Eating Nook area is open to the Kitchen
- The informal Family Room has a cozy fireplace

MAIN FLOOR — 3,160 SQ. FT.

TOTAL LIVING AREA:
3,160 SQ. FT.

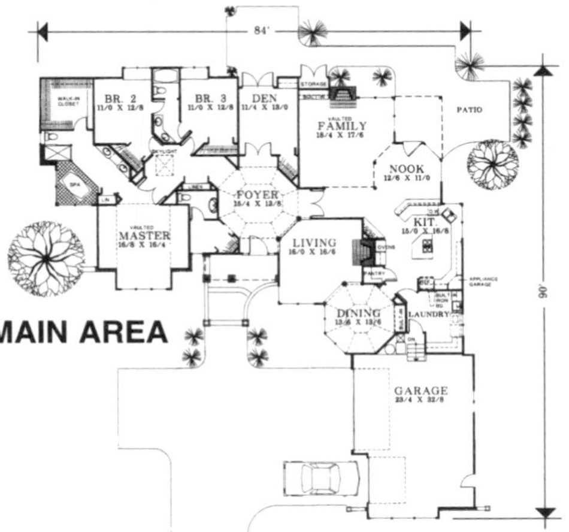

84'
BR. 2
BR. 3
DEN
FAMILY
PATIO
NOOK
FOYER
KIT
MASTER
LIVING
DINING
LAUNDRY
GARAGE
90'
MAIN AREA

PLAN NO.92209

Design by
Fillmore Design Group

Multiple Roof Lines Add to Charm

Price Code: F

- This plan features:
- — Four bedrooms
- — Three full baths
- Entry opens to Gallery, formal Dining and Living rooms with decorative ceilings
- Spacious Kitchen with a work island opens to Dining alcove, Family Room and Patio beyond
- Comfortable Family Room offers vaulted ceiling above fireplace and a wetbar
- Corner Master Suite is enhanced by a vaulted ceiling, double vanity bath and huge walk-in closet
- Three additional bedrooms with walk-in closets have access to full baths
- No materials list is available for this plan

MAIN FLOOR — 3,292 SQ. FT.
GARAGE — 670 SQ. FT.

TOTAL LIVING AREA:
3,292 SQ. FT.

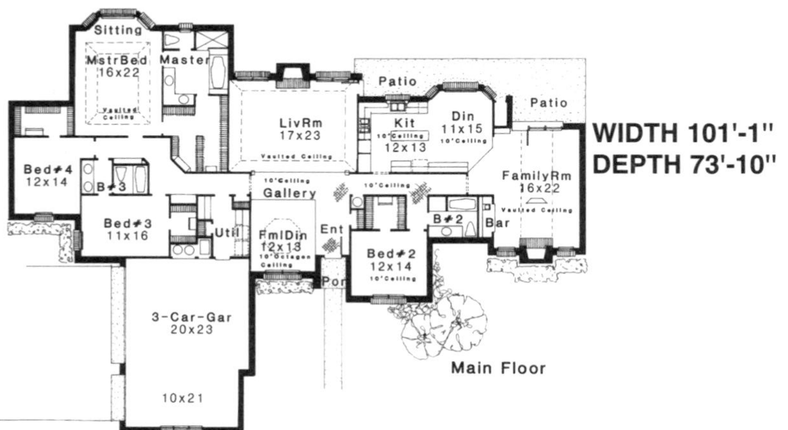

Sitting
MstrBed 16x22
Master
Patio
LivRm 17x23
Kit 12x13
Din 11x15
Patio
Bed#4 12x14
B#3
Gallery
FamilyRm 16x22
Bed#3 11x16
Util
FmlDin 12x13
Ent
Bed#2 12x14
B#2
Bar
Por
3-Car-Gar 20x23
10x21
Main Floor
WIDTH 101'-1"
DEPTH 73'-10"

Refer to **Pricing Schedule F** on the order form for pricing information

Design by **Homeplanners**

PLAN NO. 99278

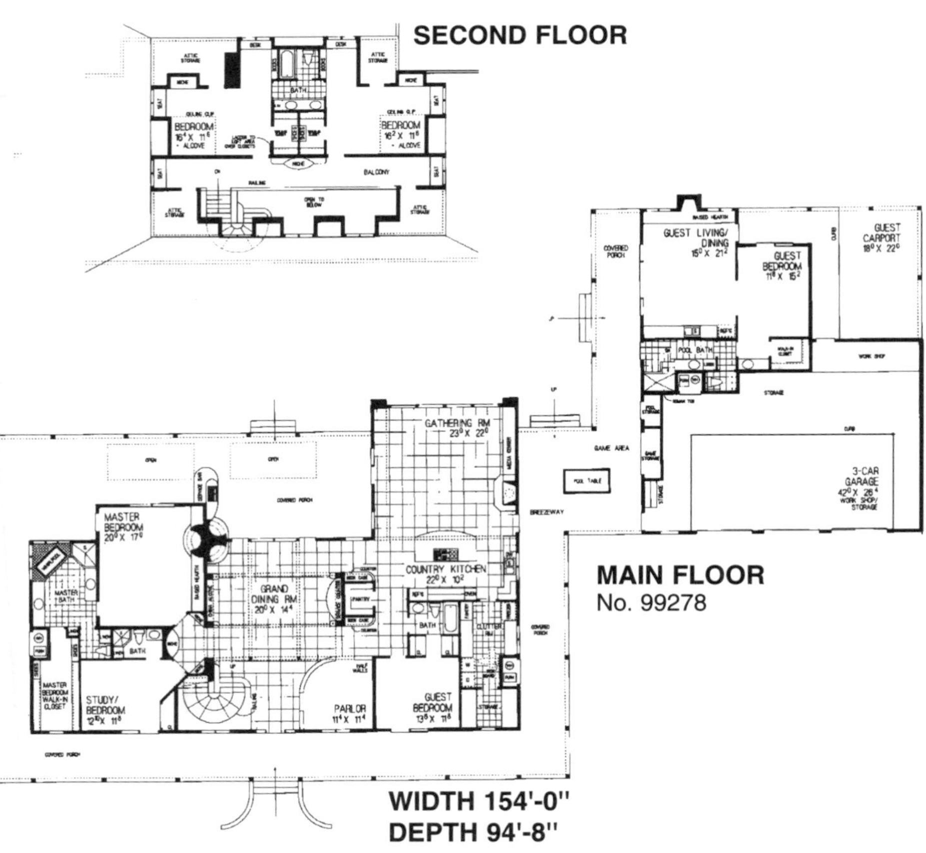
SECOND FLOOR
MAIN FLOOR
No. 99278
WIDTH 154'-0"
DEPTH 94'-8"
GUEST CARPORT
3-CAR GARAGE
GATHERING RM
COUNTRY KITCHEN
GRAND DINING RM
MASTER BEDROOM
PARLOR
GUEST BEDROOM
STUDY/ BEDROOM

Western Farmhouse with Many Comforts

- This plan features:
- — Six bedrooms
- — Five full baths
- A Covered Porch surrounds home
- Central entrance enhanced by circular stairway
- Formal Dining Room offers a built-in china alcove, service counter and fireplace
- Country Kitchen with a large cooktop island overlooks expansive Gathering Room
- Master Bedroom has a raised hearth fireplace and a plush Bath
- Separate Guest accommodations include Living/Dining Area, Bedroom and pool Bath

MAIN FLOOR — 3,166 SQ. FT.
SECOND FLOOR — 950 SQ. FT.
GUEST HOUSE/CARPORT — 680 SQ. FT.

TOTAL LIVING AREA:
4,116 SQ. FT.

PLAN NO. 99443

Design by
Design Basics, Inc.

Refer to **Pricing Schedule F** on the order form for pricing information

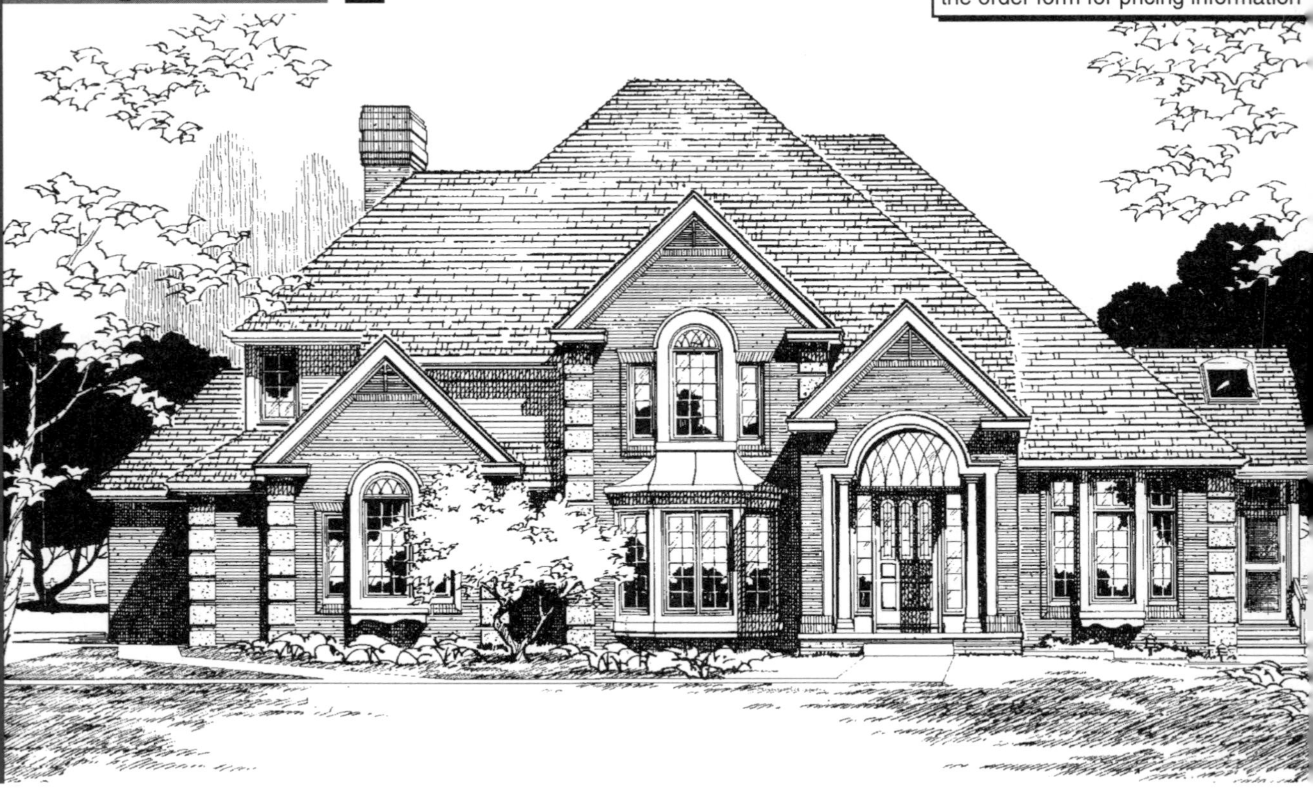

Grandeur Within

- This plan features:
- — Four bedrooms
- — Two full, one three-quarter and one half baths
- Cascading staircase dominates the tiled front entry hall
- Den has a bay window and built-in bookcases
- The Living and Dining Rooms have ten foot ceilings and access a Screened Porch
- The upstairs Master Suite has built-ins, a Sitting Area and a wonderful Bath
- Three secondary Bedrooms all have walk-in closets and share two Baths

FIRST FLOOR — 1,923 SQ. FT.
SECOND FLOOR — 1,852 SQ. FT.
BASEMENT — 1,923 SQ. FT.
GARAGE — 726 SQ. FT.

TOTAL LIVING AREA:
3,775 SQ. FT.

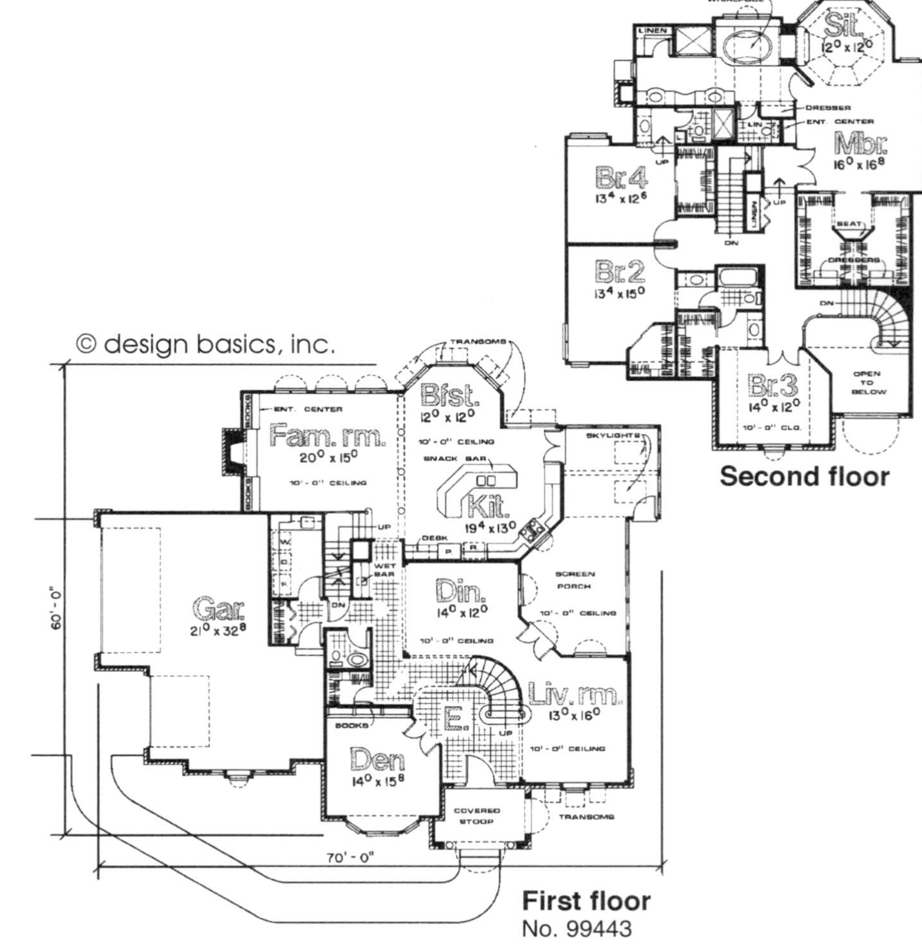

© design basics, inc.
Sit.
12⁰ x 12⁰
Mbr.
16⁰ x 16⁸
Br. 4
13⁴ x 12⁶
Br. 2
13⁴ x 15⁰
Br. 3
14⁰ x 12⁰
Second floor
Bfst.
12⁰ x 12⁰
Fam. rm.
20⁰ x 15⁰
Kit.
19⁴ x 13⁰
Gar.
21⁰ x 32⁸
Din.
14⁰ x 12⁰
Liv. rm.
13⁰ x 16⁰
Den
14⁰ x 15⁸
E.
60'-0"
70'-0"
First floor
No. 99443

To order your Blueprints, call 1-800-235-5700

Refer to **Pricing Schedule E** on the order form for pricing information

Design by
Corley Plan Service

PLAN NO. 90470

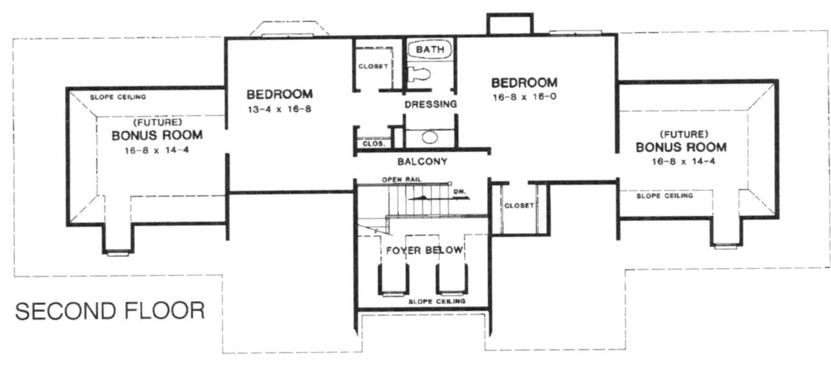
SLOPE CEILING
(FUTURE)
BONUS ROOM
16-8 x 14-4
BEDROOM
13-4 x 16-8
CLOSET
BATH
DRESSING
CLOS.
BEDROOM
16-8 x 18-0
(FUTURE)
BONUS ROOM
16-8 x 14-4
BALCONY
OPEN RAIL
DN.
CLOSET
SLOPE CEILING
FOYER BELOW
SLOPE CEILING
SECOND FLOOR

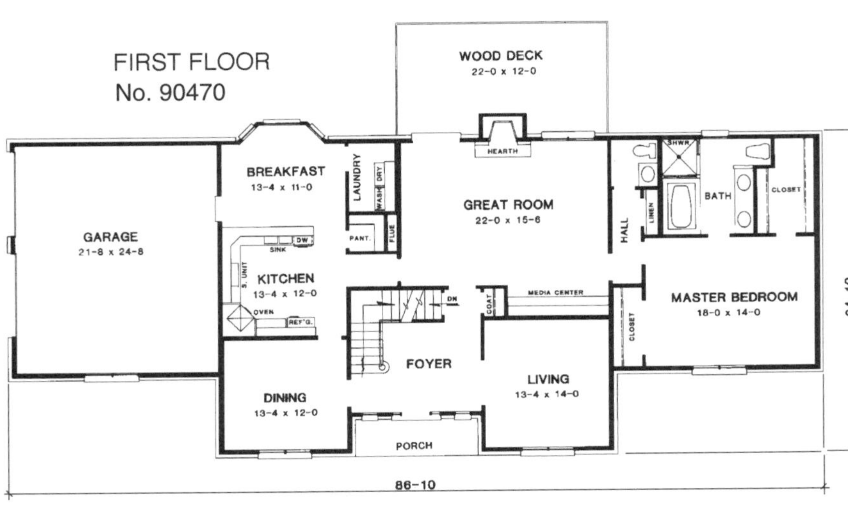
FIRST FLOOR
No. 90470
WOOD DECK
22-0 x 12-0
HEARTH
BREAKFAST
13-4 x 11-0
LAUNDRY
WASH
DRY
PANT.
FLUE
GREAT ROOM
22-0 x 15-6
HALL
LINEN
SHWR
BATH
CLOSET
GARAGE
21-8 x 24-8
DW
SINK
KITCHEN
13-4 x 12-0
OVEN
REF'G.
DN
COAT
MEDIA CENTER
MASTER BEDROOM
18-0 x 14-0
CLOSET
FOYER
LIVING
13-4 x 14-0
DINING
13-4 x 12-0
PORCH
34-10
86-10

Country French Design

- This plan features:
  - — Three bedrooms
  - — Two full and one half baths
- Open Foyer receives light from the dormer above
- Formal Living and Dining Rooms are on either side of the Foyer
- Great Room features rear wall hearth fireplace and a built-in Media Center
- Breakfast Bay is open into the fully equipped U-shaped Kitchen
- First floor Master Bedroom is in it's own wing for privacy
- An optional basement or a crawl space foundation — please specify when ordering

FIRST FLOOR — 1,997 SQ. FT.
SECOND FLOOR — 717 SQ. FT.
BONUS ROOM — 541 SQ. FT.
BASEMENT — 1,997 SQ. FT.
GARAGE — 575 SQ. FT.

TOTAL LIVING AREA:
2,714 SQ. FT.

PLAN NO. 94999

Design by
Design Basics, Inc.

Refer to **Pricing Schedule F** on the order form for pricing information

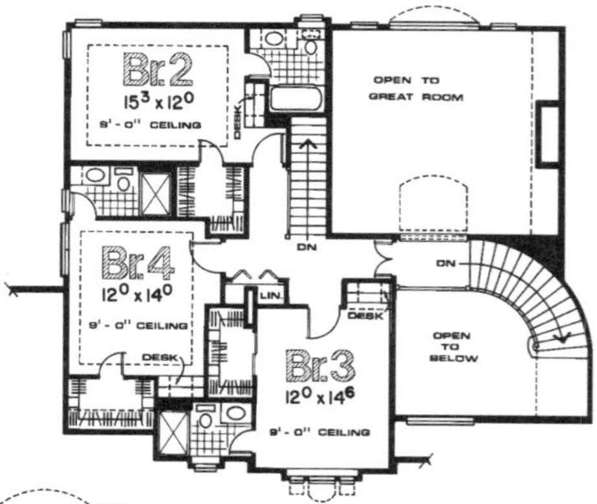

SECOND FLOOR

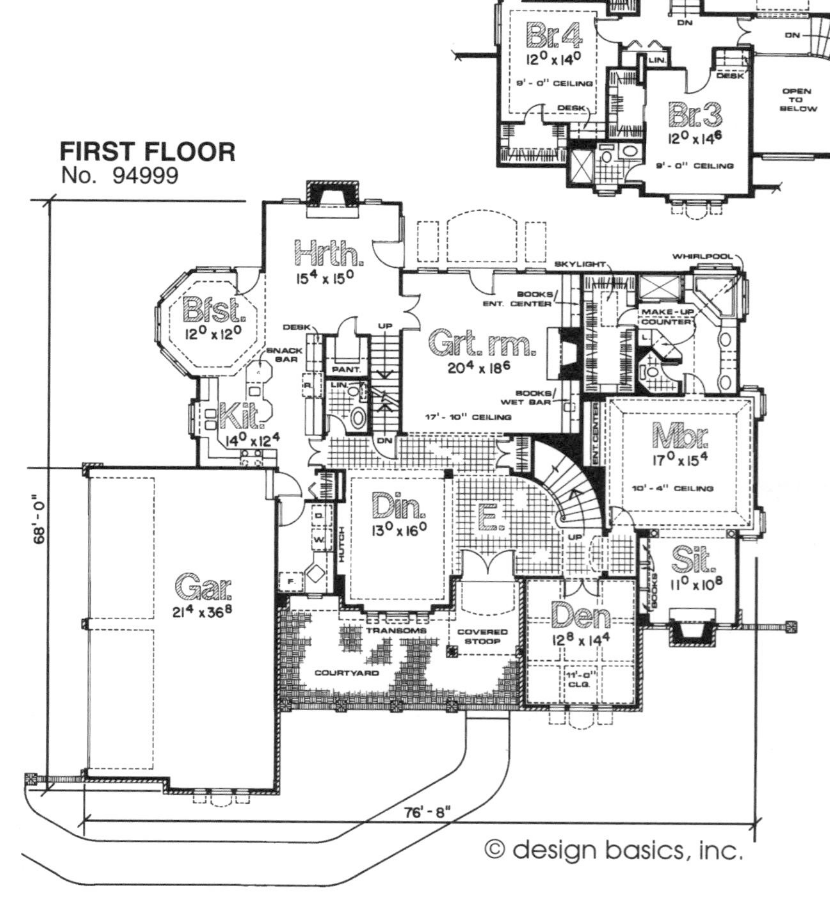

Br.2
15^{3} x 12^{0}
9'-0" CEILING
DESK
OPEN TO GREAT ROOM
Br.4
12^{0} x 14^{0}
9'-0" CEILING
DESK
LIN
DN
DESK
Br.3
12^{0} x 14^{6}
9'-0" CEILING
OPEN TO BELOW
FIRST FLOOR
No. 94999
Hrth.
15^{4} x 15^{0}
Bfst.
12^{0} x 12^{0}
DESK
SNACK BAR
UP
PANT.
LIN
Kit.
14^{0} x 12^{4}
Grt. rm.
20^{4} x 18^{6}
17'-10" CEILING
BOOKS/ ENT. CENTER
BOOKS/ WET BAR
SKYLIGHT
WHIRLPOOL
MAKE-UP COUNTER
ENT. CENTER
Mbr.
17^{0} x 15^{4}
10'-4" CEILING
DN
HUTCH
Din.
13^{0} x 16^{0}
E.
UP
Sit.
11^{0} x 10^{8}
BOOKS
Gar.
21^{4} x 36^{8}
68'-0"
TRANSOMS
COVERED STOOP
COURTYARD
Den
12^{8} x 14^{4}
11'-0" CLG.
76'-8"
© design basics, inc.

Brick and Stucco

- This plan features:
  - Four bedrooms
  - Two full, two three-quarter and one half baths
- The spider beamed Den with French doors includes arched transom windows
- The formal Dining Room opens to a dramatic high ceiling in the entry
- The Great Room features a fire-placed wall with entertainment center, bookcases and wetbar
- Secondary Bedrooms include a built-in desk and a private Bath
- The exquisite first floor Master Suite includes a Sitting Room with a built-in bookcase and a fireplace

FIRST FLOOR — 2,603 SQ. FT.
SECOND FLOOR — 1,020 SQ. FT.
BASEMENT — 2,603 SQ. FT.
GARAGE — 801 SQ. FT.

TOTAL LIVING AREA:
3,623 SQ. FT.

Refer to **Pricing Schedule F** on
e order form for pricing information

Design by
Rick Garner

PLAN NO. 92500

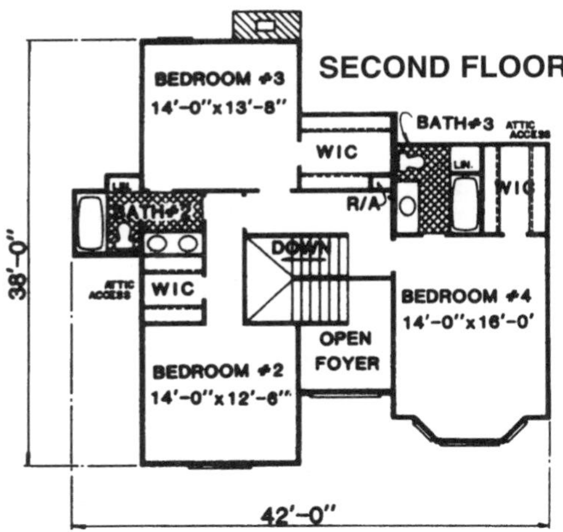
SECOND FLOOR
BEDROOM #3
14'-0"x13'-8"
WIC
BATH#3
ATTIC ACCESS
LIN.
WIC
R/A
BATH#2
DOWN
ATTIC ACCESS
WIC
BEDROOM #4
14'-0"x16'-0'
OPEN FOYER
BEDROOM #2
14'-0"x12'-6"
38'-0"
42'-0"

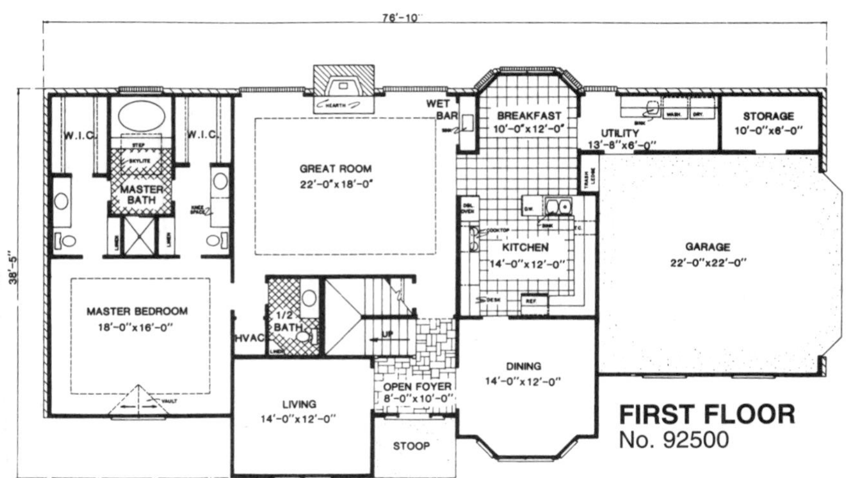
76'-10
W.I.C.
W.I.C.
MASTER BATH
GREAT ROOM
22'-0"x18'-0"
WET BAR
BREAKFAST
10'-0"x12'-0"
UTILITY
13'-8"x6'-0"
STORAGE
10'-0"x6'-0"
KITCHEN
14'-0"x12'-0"
GARAGE
22'-0"x22'-0"
38'-5"
MASTER BEDROOM
18'-0"x16'-0"
HVAC
1/2 BATH
UP
DINING
14'-0"x12'-0"
LIVING
14'-0"x12'-0"
OPEN FOYER
8'-0"x10'-0"
STOOP

FIRST FLOOR
No. 92500

European Styling

- This plan features:
  - — Four bedrooms
  - — Three full and two half baths
- Grand two-story Foyer with graceful, landing staircase, opens to formal Living and Dining Rooms
- Central Great Room with a decorative ceiling, inviting fireplace, wetbar and back yard views
- Country-size Kitchen with peninsula counter serving bright Breakfast Area and nearby Utility/Garage entry
- Master Bedroom wing enhanced by a decorative ceiling, arched window, dual walk-in closets and vanities, and a sky-light whirlpool tub
- Three additional Bedrooms with walk-in closets and access to a full Bath
- An optional slab, or crawl space foundation — please specify when ordering

FIRST FLOOR — 1,981 SQ. FT.
SECOND FLOOR — 1,103 SQ. FT.
GARAGE — 544 SQ. FT.

TOTAL LIVING AREA:
3,084 SQ. FT.

PLAN NO. 94990

Design by
Design Basics, Inc.

Refer to **Pricing Schedule F** on the order form for pricing information

Grandeur Personified

- This plan features:
- — Four bedrooms
- — Two full, one three-quarter and one half baths
- A Master Bedroom topped by a decorative ceiling and a luxurious Bath
- Upstairs, three additional Bedrooms with ample closet space and two full Baths
- French doors and an arched window accenting the Den
- A Dining Room with a built-in hutch and an adjacent butler's Pantry
- A Great Room with an 11-foot ceiling has bowed transom windows and a fireplace

FIRST FLOOR — 2,375 SQ. FT.
SECOND FLOOR — 1,073 SQ. FT.
BASEMENT — 2,375 SQ. FT.
GARAGE — 672 SQ. FT.

TOTAL LIVING AREA:
3,448 SQ. FT.

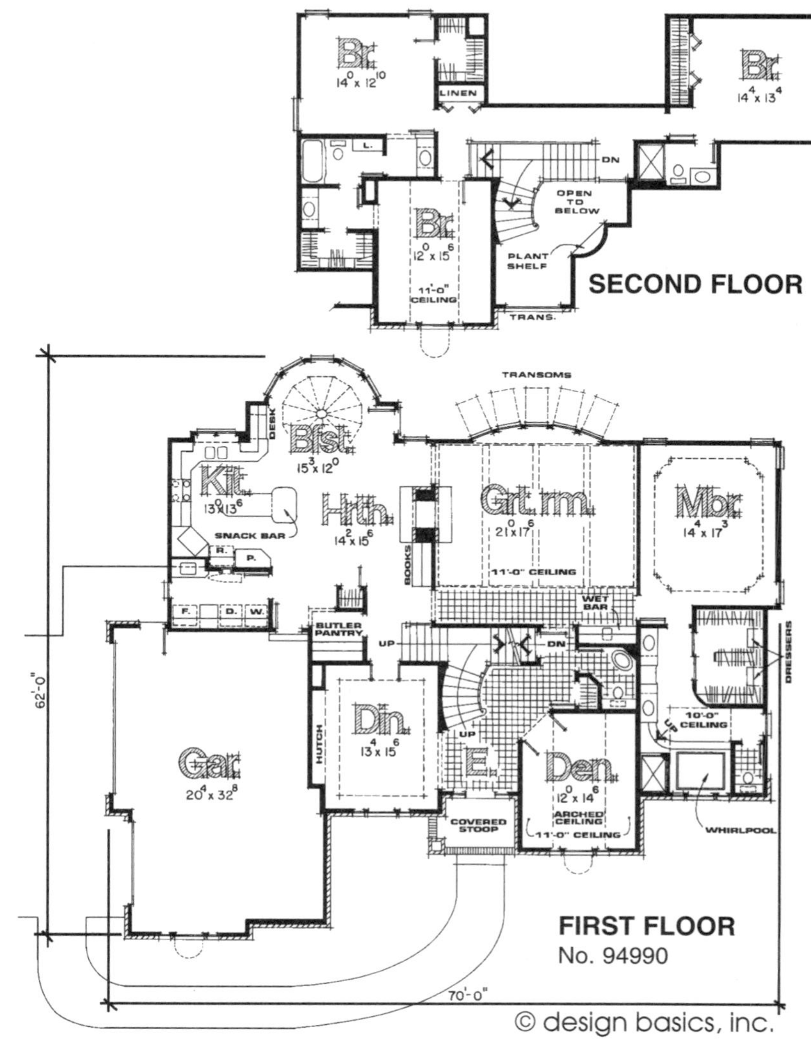

Br. 14⁰ x 12¹⁰
LINEN
Br. 14⁴ x 13⁴
L.
DN
OPEN TO BELOW
Br. 12⁰ x 15⁶
PLANT SHELF
11'-0" CEILING
TRANS.
SECOND FLOOR
TRANSOMS
DESK
Bfst. 15³ x 12⁰
Kit. 13⁰ x 13⁶
SNACK BAR
Hrth. 14² x 15⁶
BOOKS
Grt. rm. 21⁰ x 17⁶
11'-0" CEILING
Mbr. 14⁴ x 17³
WET BAR
F. D. W.
BUTLER PANTRY
UP
DN
DRESSERS
62'-0"
HUTCH
Din. 13⁴ x 15⁶
Gar. 20⁴ x 32⁸
E.
UP
Den. 12⁰ x 14⁶
ARCHED CEILING
11'-0" CEILING
10'-0" CEILING
WHIRLPOOL
COVERED STOOP
FIRST FLOOR
No. 94990
70'-0"

Refer to **Pricing Schedule F** on the order form for pricing information

Design by
Ahmann Design, Inc.

PLAN NO. 93182

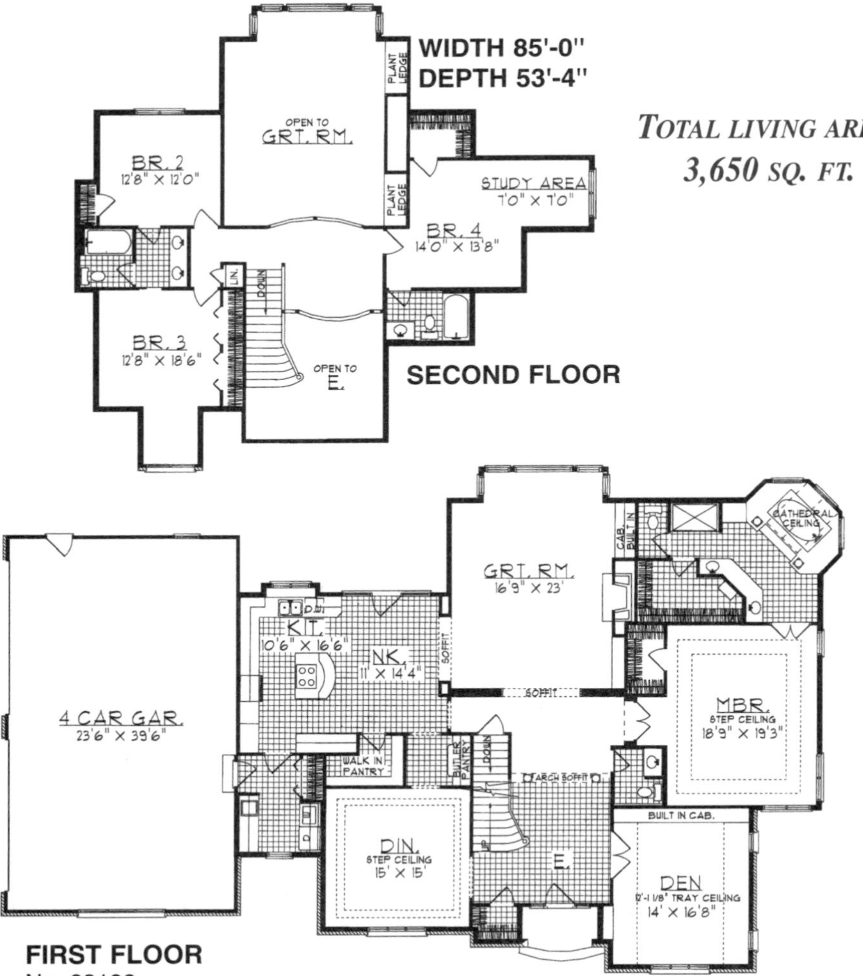

WIDTH 85'-0"
DEPTH 53'-4"
OPEN TO GRT. RM.
PLANT LEDGE
BR. 2
12'8" X 12'0"
STUDY AREA
7'0" X 7'0"
BR. 4
14'0" X 13'8"
LIN.
DOWN
BR. 3
12'8" X 18'6"
OPEN TO E.
SECOND FLOOR
GRT. RM.
16'9" X 23'
CAB. BUILT IN
CATHEDRAL CEILING
KIT.
10'6" X 16'6"
NK.
11' X 14'4"
SOFFIT
4 CAR GAR.
23'6" X 39'6"
MBR.
STEP CEILING
18'9" X 19'3"
WALK IN PANTRY
BUTLER PANTRY
DOWN
ARCH SOFFIT
BUILT IN CAB.
DIN.
STEP CEILING
15' X 15'
E.
DEN
9'-1 1/8" TRAY CEILING
14' X 16'8"
FIRST FLOOR
No. 93182

TOTAL LIVING AREA:
3,650 SQ. FT.

Traditional French Touches

- This plan features:
  - — Four bedrooms
  - — Three full and one half baths
- Traditional French touches adorn the exterior
- Interior details include a tiled Entry with columns
- The Den and Dining Room have decorative ceiling treatments
- The Great Room has a fireplace
- The Nook adjoins the Kitchen
- The Kitchen has a walk-in Pantry and a cooktop island
- The Master Bedroom is located on the first floor for privacy
- No materials list is available for this plan

FIRST FLOOR — 2,575 SQ. FT.
SECOND FLOOR — 1,075 SQ. FT.
BASEMENT — 2,575 SQ. FT.

This plan is not to be built within a 75 mile radius of Cedar Rapids, IA.

PLAN NO. 98439

Design by
Frank Betz Associates, Inc.

Refer to **Pricing Schedule F** on the order form for pricing information

Impressive Entrance

- This plan features:
- — Five bedrooms
- — Four full and one half baths
- An impressive two-story Foyer leads through arched openings
- The Island Kitchen has an abundance of space
- The Breakfast Room opens to the Kitchen
- A fireplace and built-in shelving highlight the Family Room
- A secondary Bedroom has a double door entrance
- The Master Suite has a sitting room
- An optional basement or crawl space foundation — please specify when ordering

FIRST FLOOR — 2,058 SQ. FT.
SECOND FLOOR — 2,067 SQ. FT.
BASEMENT — 2,058 SQ. FT.
GARAGE — 819 SQ. FT.

TOTAL LIVING AREA:
4,125 SQ. FT.

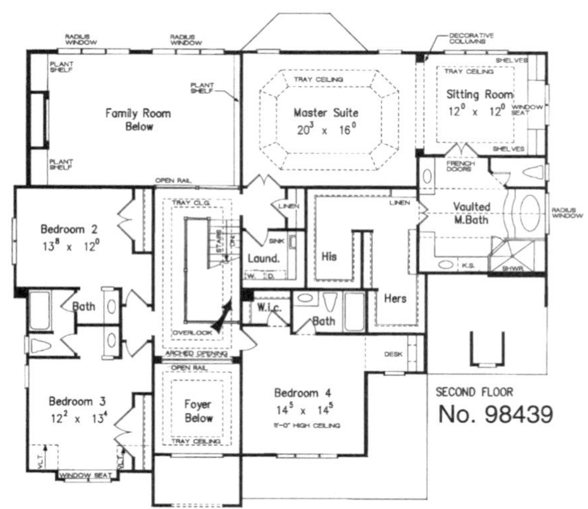

Family Room Below
Master Suite 20³ x 16⁰
Sitting Room 12⁰ x 12⁰
Bedroom 2 13⁸ x 12⁰
Laund.
His
Hers
Vaulted M.Bath
Bath
W.I.c.
Bath
Bedroom 3 12² x 13⁴
Foyer Below
Bedroom 4 14⁵ x 14⁵
SECOND FLOOR
No. 98439

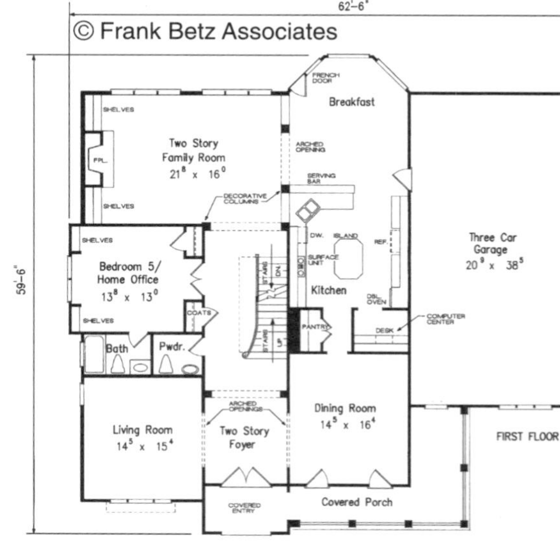

62'-6"
© Frank Betz Associates
59'-6"
Breakfast
Two Story Family Room 21⁸ x 16⁰
Bedroom 5/ Home Office 13⁸ x 13⁰
Kitchen
Three Car Garage 20⁹ x 38⁵
Bath
Pwdr.
Living Room 14⁵ x 15⁴
Two Story Foyer
Dining Room 14⁵ x 16⁴
Covered Porch
FIRST FLOOR

Refer to **Pricing Schedule E** on the order form for pricing information

Design by
Patrick Morabito A.I.A.

PLAN NO. 93333

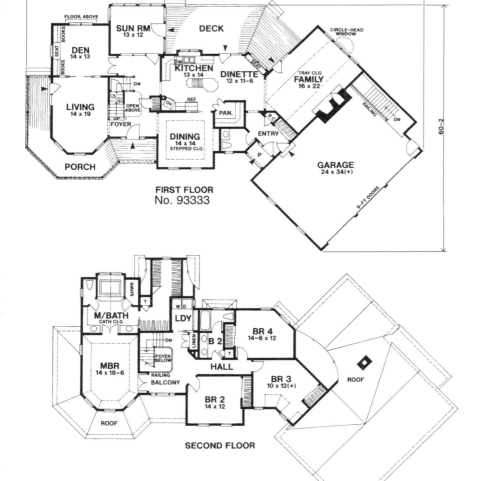

94-6
60-2
FLOOR ABOVE
SUN RM 13 x 12
DECK
CIRCLE-HEAD WINDOW
BOOKS
SEAT
DEN 14 x 13
KITCHEN 13 x 14
DINETTE 12 x 11-6
SEAT
TRAY CLG
FAMILY 16 x 22
DW
DN
REF
OV
LIVING 14 x 19
OPEN ABOVE
UP
FOYER
PAN.
B.C.
RAILING
DN
DINING 14 x 14 STEPPED CLG
ENTRY
P
PORCH
GARAGE 24 x 34(+)
9-FT DOORS

FIRST FLOOR
No. 93333

SHWR
M/BATH CATH CLG
W D
LDY
LINEN
B 2
BR 4 14-6 x 12
T
DN
MBR 14 x 18-6
FOYER BELOW
HALL
RAILING
BALCONY
BR 3 10 x 12(+)
ROOF
BR 2 14 x 12
ROOF

SECOND FLOOR

A Whisper of Victorian Styling

- This plan features:
  - — Four bedrooms
  - — Two full and one half baths
- Formal Living Room features wrap-around windows and direct access to the front Porch
- An elegant, formal Dining Room accented by a stepped ceiling
- A bright, all-purpose Sun Room adjoins an expansive Deck
- Family Room, with a tray ceiling topping a circle head window and a massive, hearth fireplace
- Private Master Suite has a decorative ceiling and a luxurious Bath with a raised, atrium tub
- No materials list is available for this plan

FIRST FLOOR — 1,743 SQ. FT.
SECOND FLOOR — 1,455 SQ. FT.

TOTAL LIVING AREA:
3,198 SQ. FT.

PLAN NO. 91109

Design by
Ryan & Associates

Refer to **Pricing Schedule E** on the order form for pricing informatior

Family Matters

- This plan features:
  - — Five bedrooms
  - — Three full baths
- A beautiful brick exterior is accentuated by double transoms over double windows
- Big bedrooms and an oversized Great Room, desirable for a large family
- Volume ceilings in the Master Suite, Great Room, Dining Room, Kitchen, Breakfast Nook and Bedroom Four
- Three bathrooms, including a plush Master Bath, with a double vanity and knee space
- No materials list available for this plan

FIRST FLOOR — 2,307 SQ. FT.
SECOND FLOOR — 440 SQ. FT.
GARAGE & STORAGE — 517 SQ. FT.

TOTAL LIVING AREA:
2,747 SQ. FT.

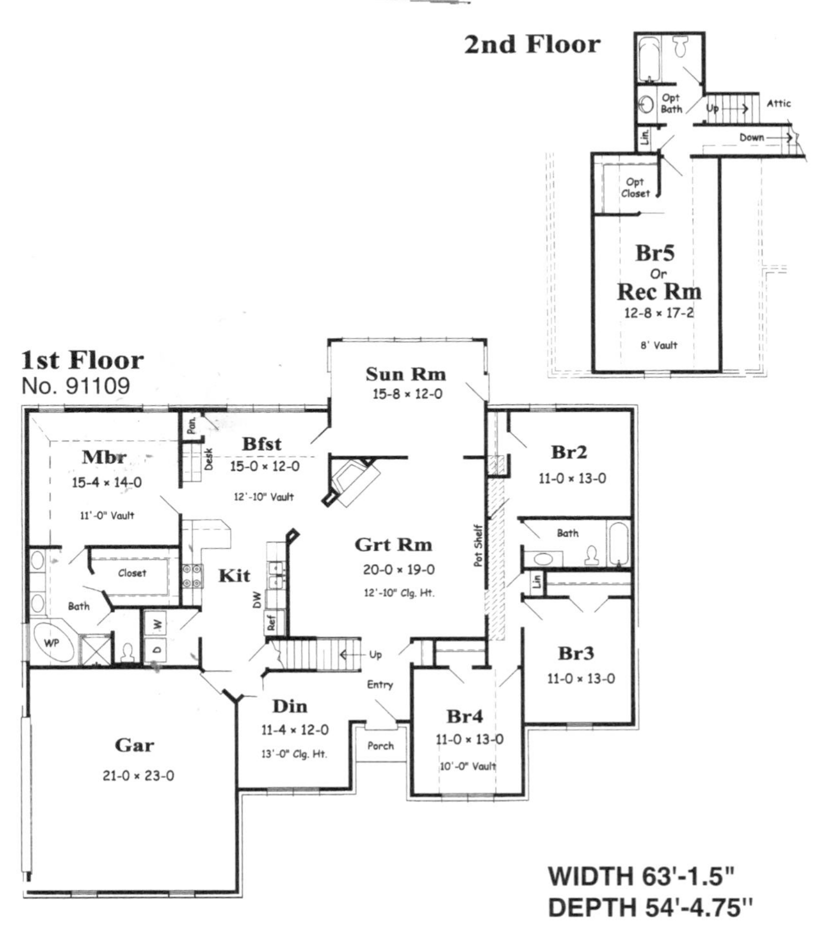

2nd Floor
Opt Bath
Up
Attic
Down
Lin.
Opt Closet
Br5
Or
Rec Rm
12-8 × 17-2
8' Vault
1st Floor
No. 91109
Sun Rm
15-8 × 12-0
Pan.
Desk
Bfst
15-0 × 12-0
12'-10" Vault
Mbr
15-4 × 14-0
11'-0" Vault
Closet
Bath
WP
W
D
Kit
DW
Ref
Grt Rm
20-0 × 19-0
12'-10" Clg. Ht.
Pot Shelf
Up
Entry
Br2
11-0 × 13-0
Bath
Lin
Br3
11-0 × 13-0
Br4
11-0 × 13-0
10'-0" Vault
Din
11-4 × 12-0
13'-0" Clg. Ht.
Porch
Gar
21-0 × 23-0

WIDTH 63'-1.5"
DEPTH 54'-4.75"

Refer to **Pricing Schedule F** on the order form for pricing information

Design by
Frank Betz Associates, Inc

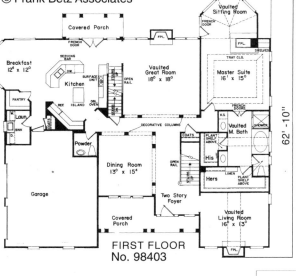

PLAN NO. 98403

64' - 6"

Covered Porch
French Door
FPL.
Vaulted Sitting Room
French Door
Breakfast 12⁶ x 12⁰
Serving Bar
Kitchen
Island
Pantry
Laun.
Vaulted Great Room 18⁰ x 18⁰
Open Rail
Decorative Columns
Master Suite 16¹ x 15⁰
Tray Clg.
Shelves
French Doors
Vaulted M. Bath
Shower
His
Hers
Linen
Plant Shelf Above
Coats
Powder
Dining Room 13⁰ x 15⁴
Open Rail
Two Story Foyer
Garage
Covered Porch
Vaulted Living Room 16⁰ x 13⁰
FPL.
62' - 10"

FIRST FLOOR
No. 98403

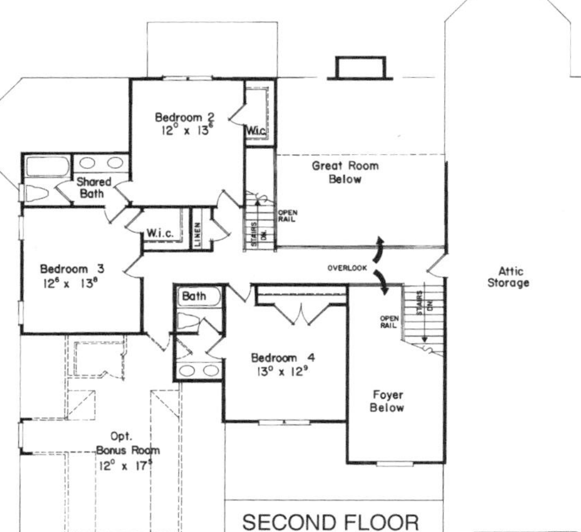
Bedroom 2
12⁰ x 13⁶
W.i.c.
Shared Bath
Great Room Below
W.i.c.
Linen
Open Rail
Bedroom 3
12⁶ x 13⁸
Overlook
Attic Storage
Bath
Bedroom 4
13⁰ x 12⁹
Open Rail
Foyer Below
Opt. Bonus Room
12⁰ x 17⁵

SECOND FLOOR

Luxurious Yet Cozy

- This plan features:
  - — Four bedrooms
  - — Three full and one half baths
- Covered Porch offers a warm welcome
- Decorative columns define Dining Room and Great Room
- Inviting fireplace windows, and a vaulted ceiling in the Great Room
- Kitchen with a work island, serving bar, Breakfast Area and walk-in Pantry
- Corner Master Suite includes a cozy fireplace and a lavish Dressing Area
- An optional basement, crawl space or slab foundation — please specify when ordering

FIRST FLOOR — 2,467 SQ. FT.
SECOND FLOOR — 928 SQ. FT.
BONUS — 296 SQ. FT.
BASEMENT — 2,467 SQ. FT.
GARAGE — 566 SQ. FT.

TOTAL LIVING AREA:
3,395 SQ. FT.

Design by
United Design Associates

Refer to **Pricing Schedule E** on the order form for pricing information

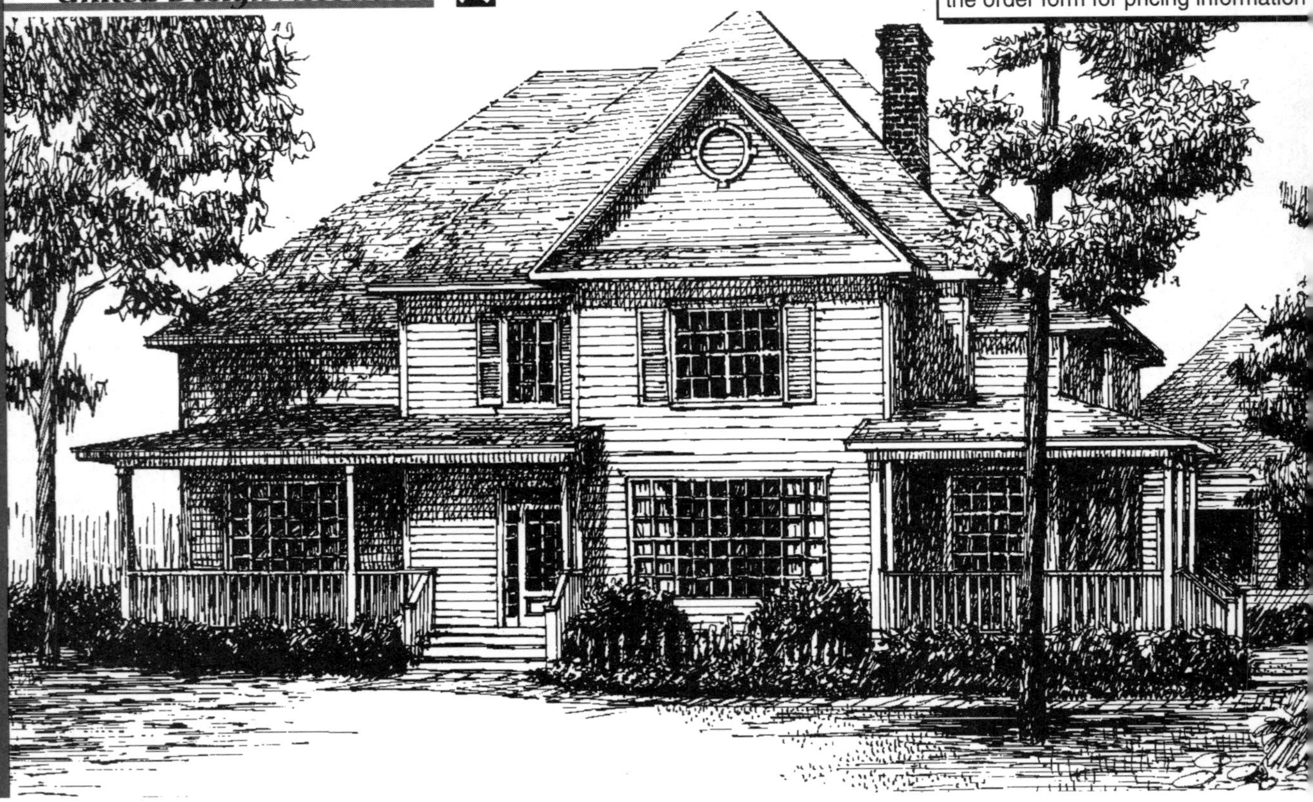

Classic Victorian

- This plan features:
  - — Four bedrooms
  - — Three full and one half baths
- Large open areas that are bright and free flowing
- Great Room accented by a fireplace and large front window
- Sun Room off of the Great Room viewing the Porch
- Dining Room in close proximity to the Kitchen
- Efficient Kitchen flows into informal Breakfast Nook
- Private first floor Master Suite highlighted by a plush Master Bath
- Three Bedrooms on the second floor, two with walk-in closets and one with a private Bath

FIRST FLOOR—1,868 SQ. FT.
SECOND FLOOR—964 SQ. FT.
GARAGE—460 SQ. FT.

TOTAL LIVING AREA:
2,832 SQ. FT.

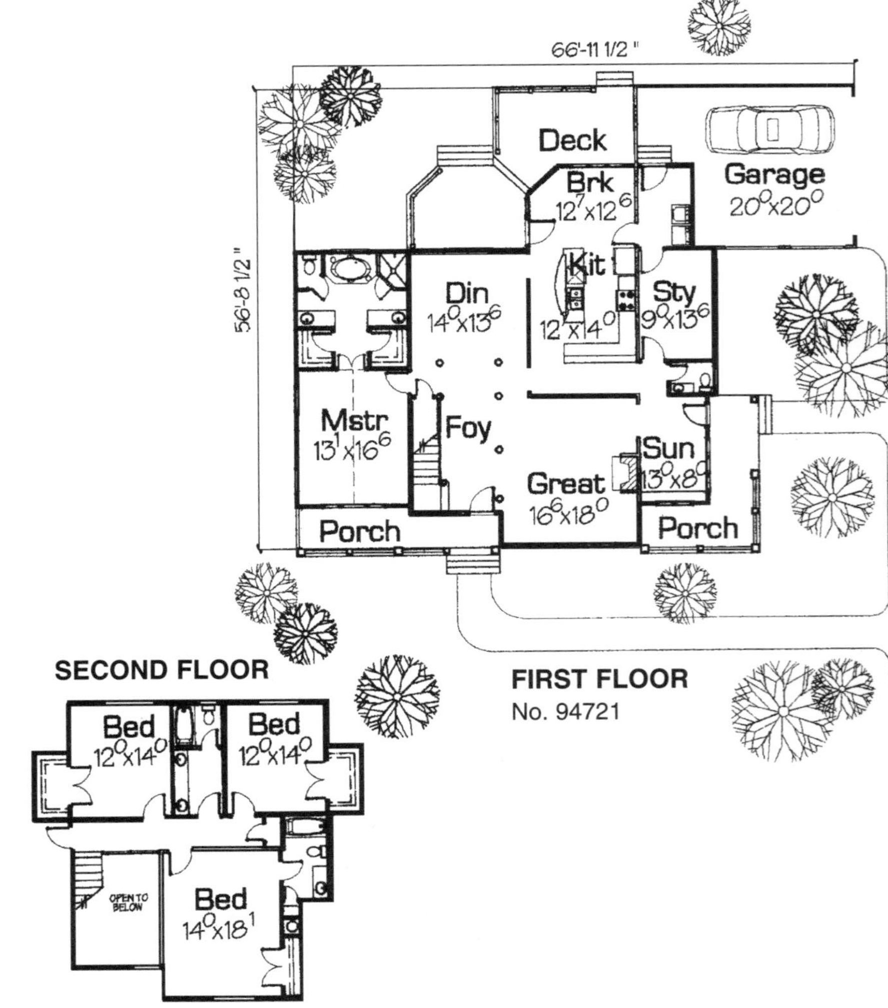
66'-11 1/2"
56'-8 1/2"
Deck
Garage
$20^{0}x20^{0}$
Brk
$12^{7}x12^{6}$
Kit
$12^{7}x14^{0}$
Din
$14^{0}x13^{6}$
Sty
$9^{0}x13^{6}$
Mstr
$13^{1}x16^{6}$
Foy
Sun
$13^{0}x8^{0}$
Great
$16^{6}x18^{0}$
Porch
Porch
SECOND FLOOR
Bed
$12^{0}x14^{0}$
Bed
$12^{0}x14^{0}$
OPEN TO BELOW
Bed
$14^{0}x18^{1}$

FIRST FLOOR
No. 94721

Refer to **Pricing Schedule E** on the order form for pricing information

Design by
Jannis Vann & Associates, Inc.

PLAN NO. 93241

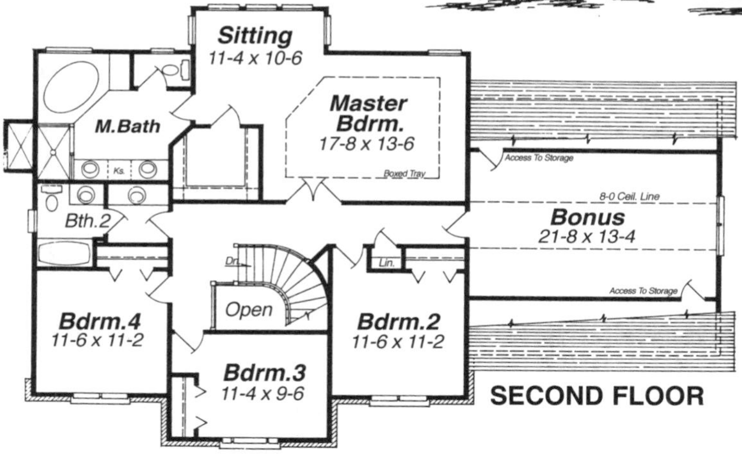

Sitting
11-4 x 10-6
M.Bath
Master Bdrm.
17-8 x 13-6
Boxed Tray
Access To Storage
8-0 Ceil. Line
Bonus
21-8 x 13-4
Access To Storage
Bth.2
Lin.
Open
Bdrm.4
11-6 x 11-2
Bdrm.2
11-6 x 11-2
Bdrm.3
11-4 x 9-6
SECOND FLOOR

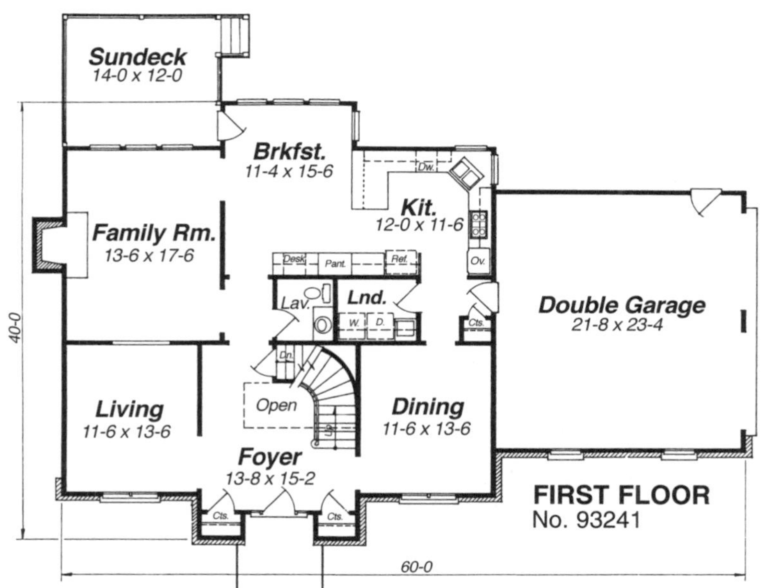
Sundeck
14-0 x 12-0
Brkfst.
11-4 x 15-6
Kit.
12-0 x 11-6
Family Rm.
13-6 x 17-6
Desk
Pant.
Ref.
Ov.
Lav.
Lnd.
Double Garage
21-8 x 23-4
Open
Living
11-6 x 13-6
Dining
11-6 x 13-6
Foyer
13-8 x 15-2
Cts.
Cts.
40-0
60-0
FIRST FLOOR
No. 93241

Elegant Master Suite

- This plan features:
- — Four bedrooms
- — Two full and one half baths
- Comfortable Family Room with a fireplace
- Efficient Kitchen with built-in Pantry and serving counter
- Master Suite with decorative ceiling, Sitting Room and a plush Bath
- An optional basement, slab, or crawl space foundation — please specify when ordering
- No materials list is available for this plan

FIRST FLOOR — 1,307 SQ. FT.
SECOND FLOOR — 1,333 SQ. FT.
BONUS — 308 SQ. FT.
BASEMENT — 1,307 SQ. FT.
GARAGE — 528 SQ. FT.

TOTAL LIVING AREA:
2,640 SQ. FT.

PLAN NO. 99438

Design by
Design Basics, Inc. 

Refer to **Pricing Schedule E** on the order form for pricing information

Eye Catching Tower

- This plan features:
- — Four bedrooms
- — Four full and one half baths
- Dining Room with Bay perfect for special dinner parties
- Study with a high ceiling
- Family Room with fireplace is open to the Breakfast Bay and gourmet Kitchen
- First floor Master Bedrooms spans the width of the home and contains every luxury imaginable
- Located upstairs are three Bedrooms, a Game Room, a Sun Deck and two full Baths
- This plan has a three-car Garage with storage space

FIRST FLOOR — 2,117 SQ. FT.
SECOND FLOOR — 1,206 SQ. FT.
GARAGE — 685 SQ. FT.

TOTAL LIVING AREA:
3,323 SQ. FT.

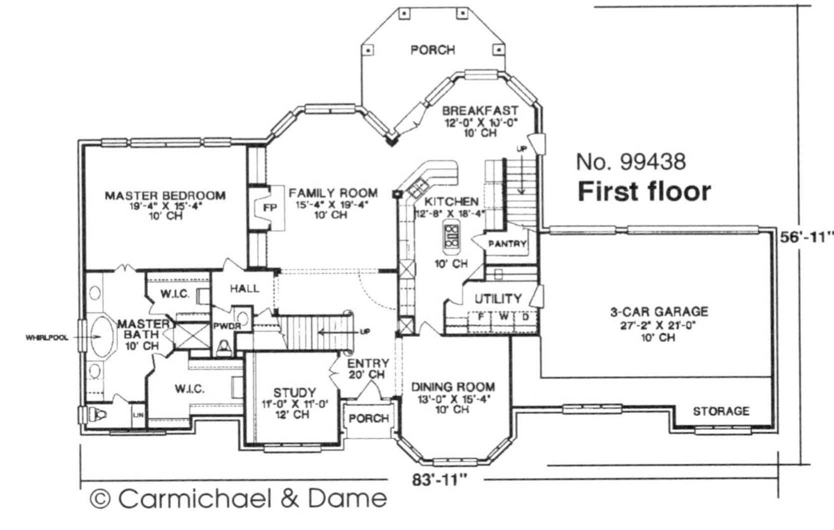
PORCH
BREAKFAST
12'-0" X 10'-0"
10' CH
MASTER BEDROOM
19'-4" X 15'-4"
10' CH
FP
FAMILY ROOM
15'-4" X 19'-4"
10' CH
KITCHEN
12'-8" X 18'-4"
10' CH
PANTRY
UP
No. 99438
First floor
56'-11"
W.I.C.
HALL
UTILITY
F W D
3-CAR GARAGE
27'-2" X 21'-0"
10' CH
WHIRLPOOL
MASTER BATH
10' CH
PWDR
UP
ENTRY
20' CH
W.I.C.
STUDY
11'-0" X 11'-0"
12' CH
PORCH
DINING ROOM
13'-0" X 15'-4"
10' CH
STORAGE
83'-11"
© Carmichael & Dame

Optional Basement Access
KITCHEN
12'-8" X 18'-4"
10' CH
PANTRY
UTILITY
F W D
DOWN TO BASEMENT

SUN DECK
BEDROOM 3
14'-0" X 12'-4"
9' CH
GAME ROOM
15'-0" X 19'-8"
9' CH
W.I.C.
W.I.C.
BATH
LIN
BEDROOM 4
13'-4" X 11'-4"
9' CH
BATH
DN
HALL
DN
W.I.C.
OPEN TO BELOW
BEDROOM 2
13'-0" X 13'-4"
9' CH
Second floor

Refer to **Pricing Schedule F** on the order form for pricing information

Design by
Design Basics, Inc.

PLAN NO. 99402

SECOND FLOOR
No. 99402

© design basics, inc.

FIRST FLOOR

"English Manor" House

- This plan features:
- — Four bedrooms
- — Two full, one three quarter and one half baths
- Stone facade enhances covered Stoop
- Double doors open to private Den with built-in bookshelves
- Formal Dining Room accented by a decorative ceiling
- Bow window and a raised, hearth fireplace highlight Living Room
- Kitchen with walk-in Pantry, angled serving counter/snack bar, bright Breakfast Alcove
- Master Suite includes a Sitting Area and a luxurious Bath

FIRST FLOOR — 2,813 SQ. FT.
SECOND FLOOR — 1,091 SQ. FT.
BASEMENT — 2,813 SQ. FT.
GARAGE — 1,028 SQ. FT.

TOTAL LIVING AREA:
3,904 SQ. FT.

Design by
The Meredith Corporation

Refer to **Pricing Schedule F** on the order form for pricing information

Photography by The Meredith Corporation

Mansion Mystique

- This plan features:
- — Four bedrooms
- — Four full and one half baths
- A beautiful exterior includes multiple rooflines and a covered Porch
- The Entry includes a curved staircase
- Multi purpose rooms include a Guest Room/Study and an upstairs Office
- Both the Family Room and the Great Room have fireplaces
- The L-shaped Kitchen opens to the Breakfast Nook
- Upstairs find multiple Bedrooms, Baths, and a bonus space

MAIN LEVEL — 2,727 SQ. FT.
UPPER LEVEL — 1,168 SQ. FT.
BONUS — 213 SQ. FT.
BASEMENT — 2,250 SQ. FT.
GARAGE — 984 SQ. FT.

TOTAL LIVING AREA:
3,895 SQ. FT.

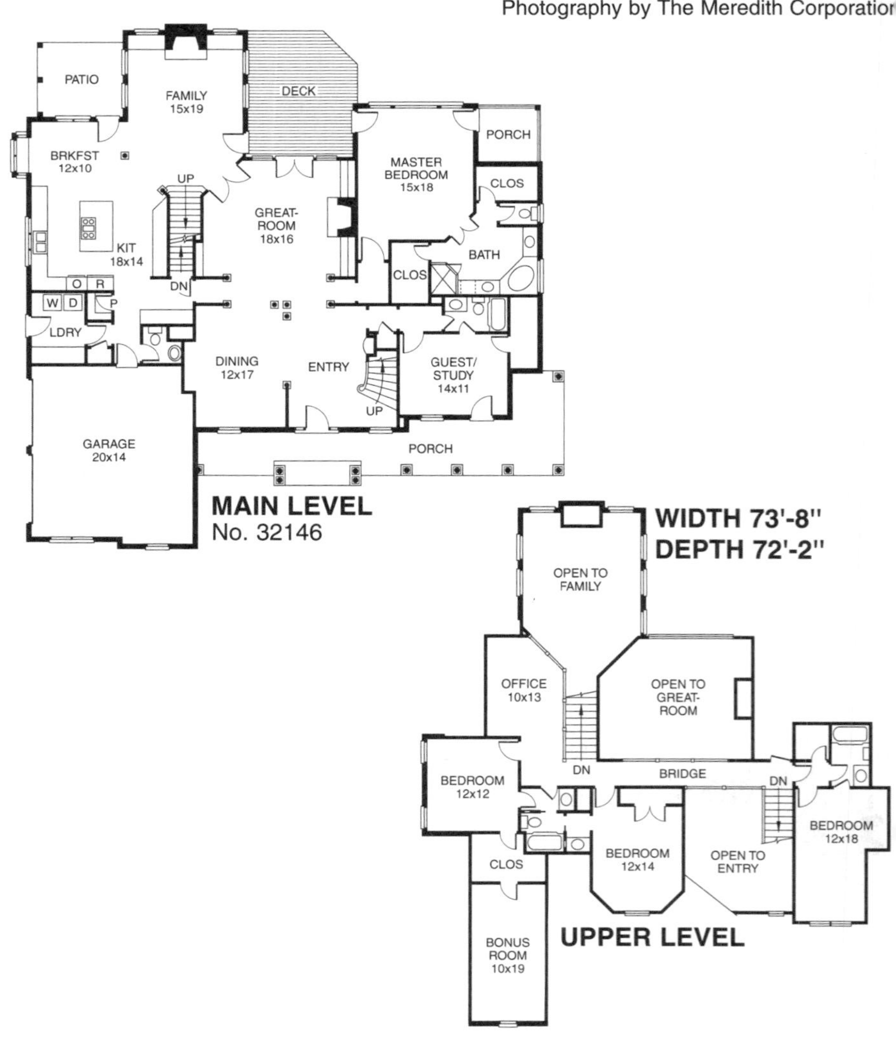
PATIO
FAMILY 15x19
DECK
PORCH
MASTER BEDROOM 15x18
CLOS
BRKFST 12x10
UP
GREAT-ROOM 18x16
KIT 18x14
BATH
CLOS
DN
O R
W D
P
LDRY
DINING 12x17
ENTRY
GUEST/ STUDY 14x11
UP
GARAGE 20x14
PORCH
MAIN LEVEL
No. 32146
WIDTH 73'-8''
DEPTH 72'-2''
OPEN TO FAMILY
OFFICE 10x13
OPEN TO GREAT-ROOM
DN
BRIDGE
DN
BEDROOM 12x12
BEDROOM 12x14
OPEN TO ENTRY
BEDROOM 12x18
CLOS
BONUS ROOM 10x19
UPPER LEVEL

To order your Blueprints, call 1-800-235-5700

Refer to **Pricing Schedule F** on
he order form for pricing information

Design by
Filmore Design Group

PLAN NO. 92237

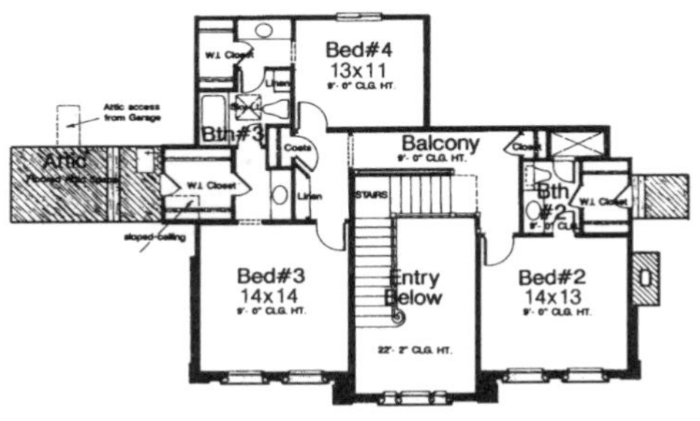

Bed#4
13x11
Bth#3
Balcony
Attic
Bth #2
Bed#3
14x14
Entry Below
Bed#2
14x13

SECOND FLOOR

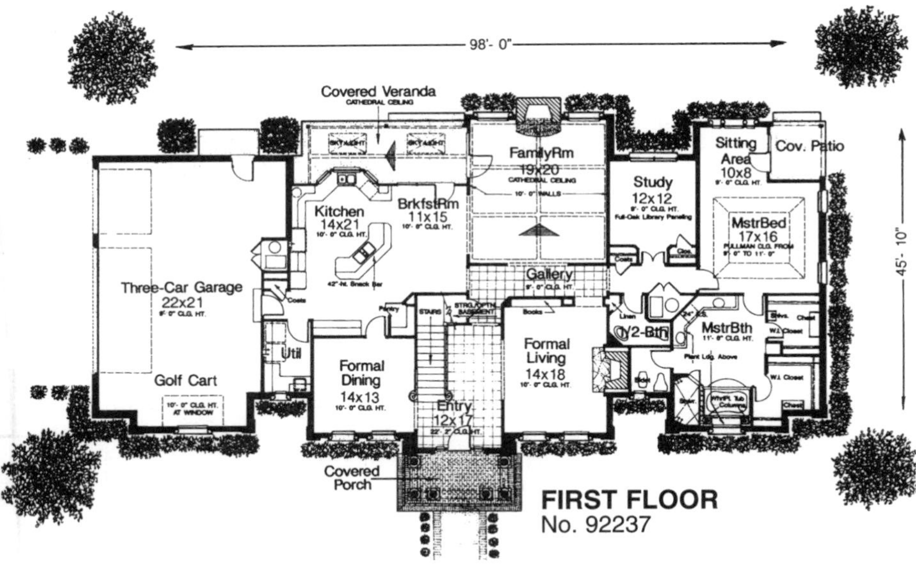

98'- 0"
45'- 10"
Covered Veranda
FamilyRm
19x20
Sitting Area
10x8
Cov. Patio
Study
12x12
Kitchen
14x21
BrkfstRm
11x15
MstrBed
17x16
Three-Car Garage
22x21
Gallery
1/2-Bth
MstrBth
Formal Living
14x18
Util
Formal Dining
14x13
Golf Cart
Entry
12x17
Covered Porch

FIRST FLOOR
No. 92237

Opulent Luxury

- This plan features:
  - Four bedrooms
  - Three full and one half baths
- Magnificent columns frame elegant two-story Entry with a graceful banister staircase
- A stone hearth fireplace and built-in book shelves enhance the Living Room
- Family Room with a huge fireplace and cathedral ceiling
- Spacious Kitchen with cooktop island/snackbar, built-in Pantry and Breakfast Room
- Lavish Master Bedroom wing with a pullman ceiling, Sitting Area, and a private Covered Patio
- No materials list is available for this plan

FIRST FLOOR — 2,804 SQ. FT.
SECOND FLOOR — 979 SQ. FT.
BASEMENT — 2,804 SQ. FT.
GARAGE — 802 SQ. FT.

TOTAL LIVING AREA:
3,783 SQ. FT.

PLAN NO.99087

Design by
National Home Planning Service

Full Length Covered Porch

Price Code: F

- This plan features:
- — Four bedrooms
- — Three full and one half baths
- Natural light floods the entrance Foyer through the dramatic palladium style window
- A grand Family Room with a fireplace and a full length, covered entrance Porch
- The first floor Master Suite features a large walk-in closet and a Bath with a separate Bath tub and stall shower
- Three additional Bedrooms, a Guest Room and two Bathrooms are on the second floor
- No materials list is available for this plan

FIRST FLOOR — 2,538 SQ. FT.
SECOND FLOOR — 1,295 SQ. FT.
BASEMENT — 2,538 SQ. FT.
GARAGE — 900 SQ. FT.

TOTAL LIVING AREA:
3,833 SQ. FT.

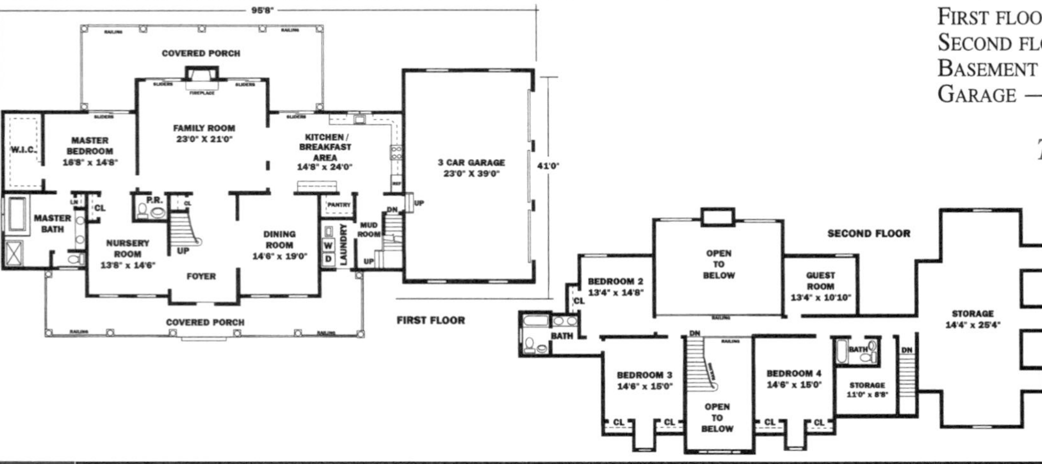
95'8"
COVERED PORCH
W.I.C.
MASTER BEDROOM 16'8" x 14'8"
FAMILY ROOM 23'0" X 21'0"
KITCHEN / BREAKFAST AREA 14'8" x 24'0"
3 CAR GARAGE 23'0" X 39'0"
41'0"
MASTER BATH
CL
P.R.
UP
PANTRY
MUD ROOM
LAUNDRY
NURSERY ROOM 13'8" x 14'6"
DINING ROOM 14'6" x 19'0"
FOYER
COVERED PORCH
FIRST FLOOR
SECOND FLOOR
OPEN TO BELOW
BEDROOM 2 13'4" x 14'8"
GUEST ROOM 13'4" x 10'10"
STORAGE 14'4" x 25'4"
BATH
BEDROOM 3 14'6" x 15'0"
BEDROOM 4 14'6" x 15'0"
STORAGE 11'0" x 8'8"
OPEN TO BELOW
CL
DN

PLAN NO.98511

Design by
Fillmore Design Group

Lap of Luxury

Price Code: D

- This plan features:
- — Four bedrooms
- — Three full and one half baths
- Entertaining in grand style in the formal Living Room, the Dining Room, or under the covered patio in the backyard
- A Master Bedroom with a sitting area, huge walk-in closet, private bath, and access to a covered lanai
- The secondary bedroom wing contains three additional bedrooms
- No materials list is available for this plan

MAIN FLOOR — 2,445 SQ. FT.
GARAGE — 630 SQ. FT.

TOTAL LIVING AREA:
2,445 SQ. FT.

FAMILY ROOM 15X17
COVERED
PATIO AREA
BATH
BDRM. #4 13X10
COVERED
BRKFT. 12X11
MSTR. BATH
COVERED LANAI
LIVING ROOM 13X13
KIT. 12X13
W-I-CLOS.
SITTING AREA
BDRM. #3 10X12
HALL
LINEN
GALLERY
HALL
MSTR. BDRM. 14X18
UTI.
PWD.
BATH
ENT.
FORMAL DINING 11X13
BDRM. #2 10X13
POR.
THREE CAR GARAGE

Refer to **Pricing Schedule D** on the order form for pricing information

Design by
Studer Residential Design, Inc.

PLAN NO. 92651

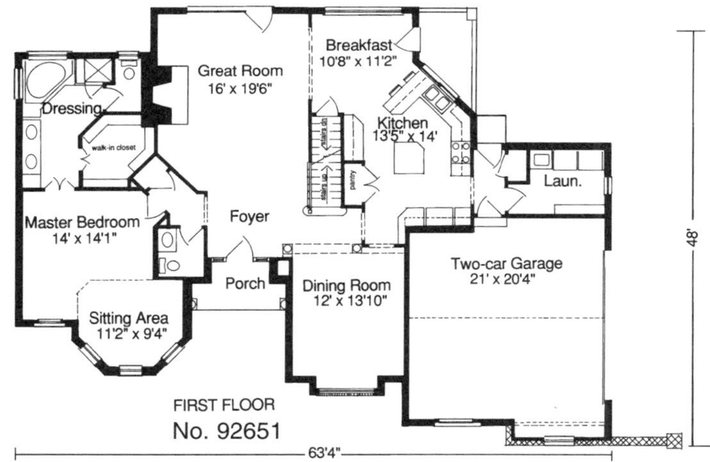

Great Room
16' x 19'6"
Breakfast
10'8" x 11'2"
Dressing
walk-in closet
Kitchen
13'5" x 14'
Laun.
Master Bedroom
14' x 14'1"
Foyer
Porch
Dining Room
12' x 13'10"
Two-car Garage
21' x 20'4"
Sitting Area
11'2" x 9'4"
48'
FIRST FLOOR
No. 92651
63'4"

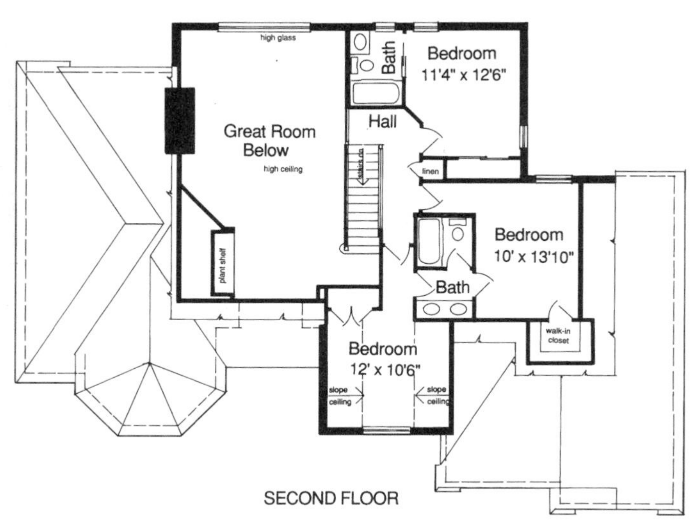

high glass
Bath
Bedroom
11'4" x 12'6"
Hall
Great Room
Below
high ceiling
linen
Bedroom
10' x 13'10"
plant shelf
Bath
walk-in closet
Bedroom
12' x 10'6"
slope ceiling
slope ceiling
SECOND FLOOR

Eye-Catching Turret Adds to Master Suite

- This plan features:
  - — Four bedrooms
  - — Three full and one half baths
- Sheltered entry leads into open Foyer
- Great Room with high ceiling and hearth fireplace
- Columns frame entrance to Dining Room
- Efficient Kitchen with built-in pantry and work island
- Master Bedroom wing with Sitting Area, walk-in closet and private Bath
- No materials list is available for this plan

FIRST FLOOR — 1,710 SQ. FT.
SECOND FLOOR — 693 SQ. FT.
BASEMENT — 1,620 SQ. FT.
GARAGE — 467 SQ. FT.

TOTAL LIVING AREA:
2,403 SQ. FT.

Design by
Ahmann Design, Inc.

Refer to **Pricing Schedule F** on the order form for pricing information

Turn Of The Century Charm

- This plan features:
- — Four bedrooms
- — Three full and one half baths
- Old fashioned turn of the century exterior
- Gourmet Kitchen is open to the Sun Room and the Breakfast Nook
- Large Family Room features a cozy fireplace
- Master Suite has a luxurious Bath and large Sitting Area
- Three additional Bedrooms on the second floor share two full Baths
- No materials list is available for this plan

FIRST FLOOR — 2,470 SQ. FT.
SECOND FLOOR — 1,000 SQ. FT.
BASEMENT — 2,470 SQ. FT.

TOTAL LIVING AREA:
3,470 SQ. FT.

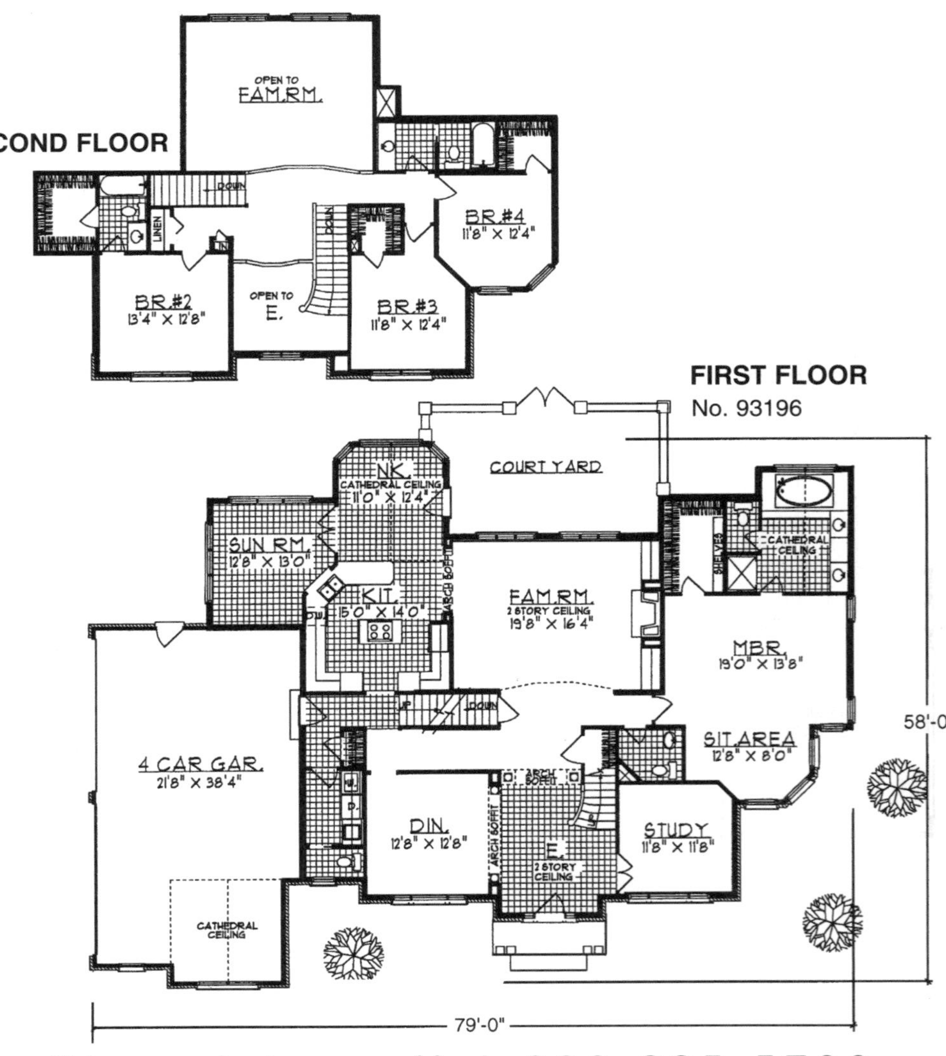
SECOND FLOOR
OPEN TO FAM.RM.
DOWN
LINEN
BR.#2 13'4" X 12'8"
OPEN TO E.
BR.#3 11'8" X 12'4"
BR.#4 11'8" X 12'4"
FIRST FLOOR
No. 93196
COURT YARD
NK. CATHEDRAL CEILING 11'0" X 12'4"
SUN RM. 12'8" X 13'0"
KIT. 15'0" X 14'0"
FAM.RM. 2 STORY CEILING 19'8" X 16'4"
MBR. 13'0" X 13'8"
SIT AREA 12'8" X 8'0"
4 CAR GAR. 21'8" X 38'4"
DIN. 12'8" X 12'8"
E. 2 STORY CEILING
STUDY 11'8" X 11'8"
CATHEDRAL CEILING
58'-0"
79'-0"

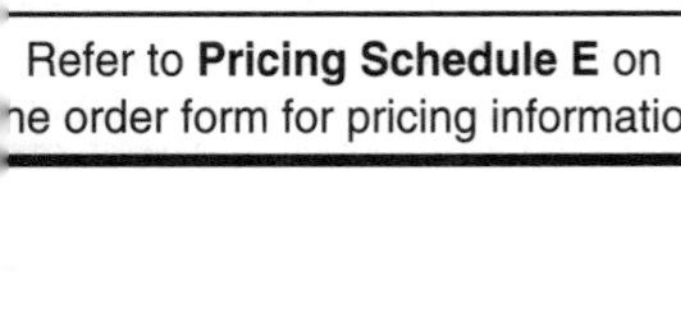
Refer to **Pricing Schedule E** on
the order form for pricing information

Design by
Building Science Associates

PLAN NO. 93709

58'4"

Deck

Morning Room
14'2" x 11'10"

Great Room
20'10" x 16'0"

2-way
f.p.

clos.

M. Bath
13'10" x 11'0"

Kitchen
13'8" x 11'10"

M. Bedroom
17'4" x 13'10"
12' ceil.

storage

Utility
10'2" x 6'4"

Dining Room
15'10" x 12'0"

Foyer
10'6" x 8'4"

Study
13'10" x 12'10"
12' ceil.

Garage
21'10" x 21'10"

58'4"

Main Level Floor Plan

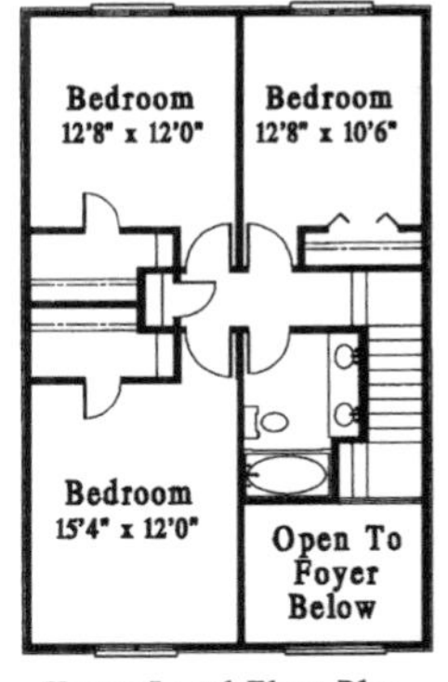
Bedroom
12'8" x 12'0"
Bedroom
12'8" x 10'6"
Bedroom
15'4" x 12'0"
Open To
Foyer
Below

Upper Level Floor Plan

Dramatic Design

- This plan features:
  - — Four bedrooms
  - — Two full and one half baths
- Dramatic two-story foyer flows into the formal Dining Area which is defined by a cluster of columns
- Great Room shares a two-way fireplace with the Morning Room that opens onto the Deck
- The Kitchen features a built-in Pantry, an island and a planning desk
- The Master Bedroom has a private, double vanity Bath and a walk-in closet
- No materials list is available for this plan

MAIN LEVEL — 1,910 SQ. FT.
UPPER LEVEL — 697 SQ. FT.
GARAGE — 536 SQ. FT.

TOTAL LIVING AREA:
2,607 SQ. FT.

PLAN NO. 94231

Design by
Sater Design Group

Refer to **Pricing Schedule E** on the order form for pricing information

Impressive Elevation

- This plan features:
  - — Three bedrooms
  - — Two full and one three-quarter baths
- Glass arch entrance into Foyer and Grand Room accented by fireplace between built-ins and multiple french doors
- Kitchen with walk-in Pantry and peninsula serving counter
- Luxurious Master Suite with step ceiling, Sitting Area, his-n-hers closets and pampering Bath
- Two additional Bedrooms, one with a private Deck, have bay windows and walk-in closets
- No materials list is available for this plan

FIRST FLOOR — 2,181 SQ. FT.
SECOND FLOOR — 710 SQ. FT.
GARAGE —658 SQ. FT.

TOTAL LIVING AREA:
2,891 SQ. FT.

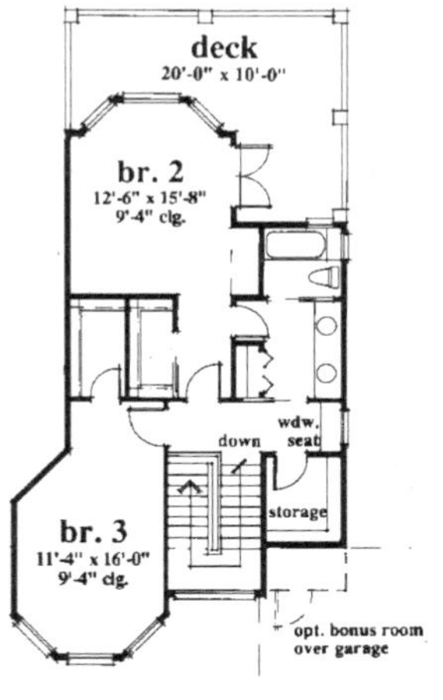

deck
20'-0" x 10'-0"
br. 2
12'-6" x 15'-8"
9'-4" clg.
wdw. seat
down
storage
br. 3
11'-4" x 16'-0"
9'-4" clg.
opt. bonus room over garage

SECOND FLOOR

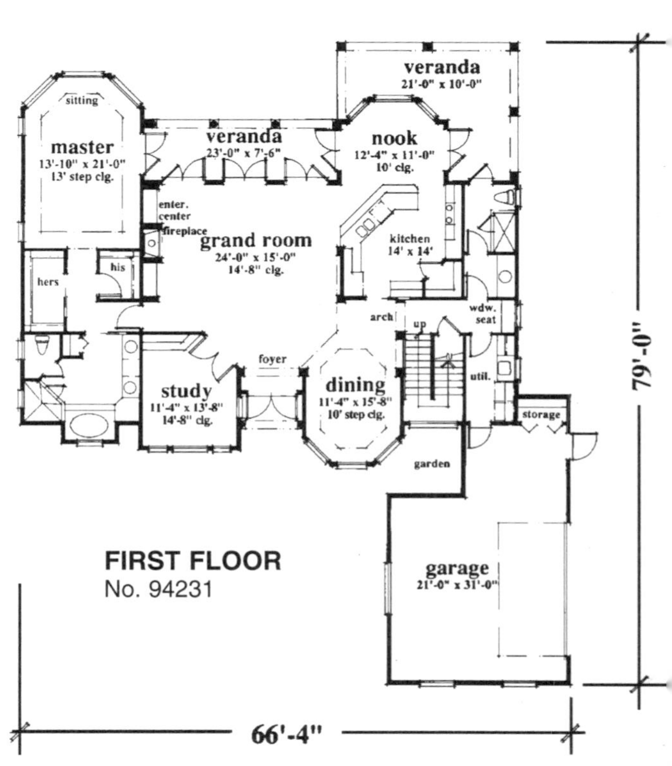

veranda
21'-0" x 10'-0"
sitting
master
13'-10" x 21'-0"
13' step clg.
veranda
23'-0" x 7'-6"
nook
12'-4" x 11'-0"
10' clg.
enter. center
fireplace
grand room
24'-0" x 15'-0"
14'-8" clg.
kitchen
14' x 14'
hers
his
arch
up
wdw. seat
foyer
study
11'-4" x 13'-8"
14'-8" clg.
dining
11'-4" x 15'-8"
10' step clg.
util.
storage
garden
garage
21'-0" x 31'-0"
79'-0"
66'-4"

FIRST FLOOR
No. 94231

Refer to **Pricing Schedule G** on
he order form for pricing information

Design by
Donald A. Gardner Architects, Inc.

PLAN NO. 96443

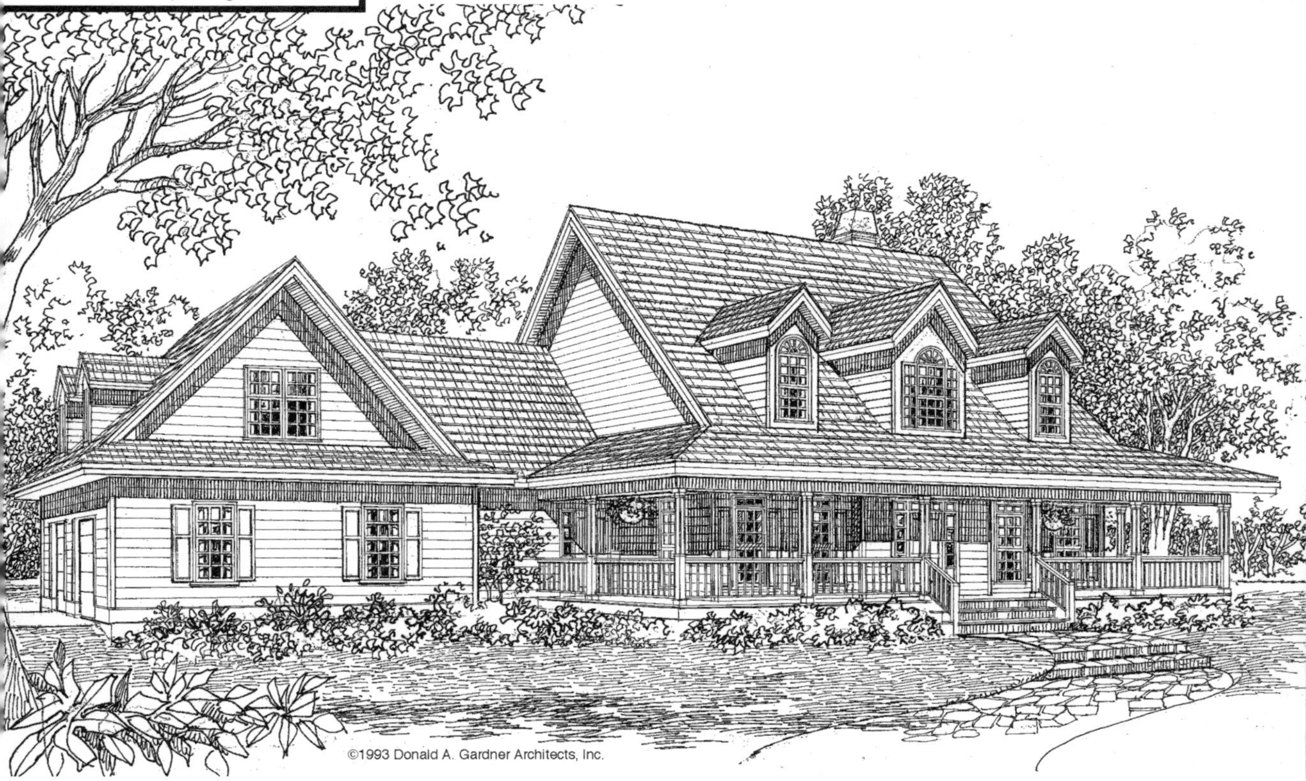

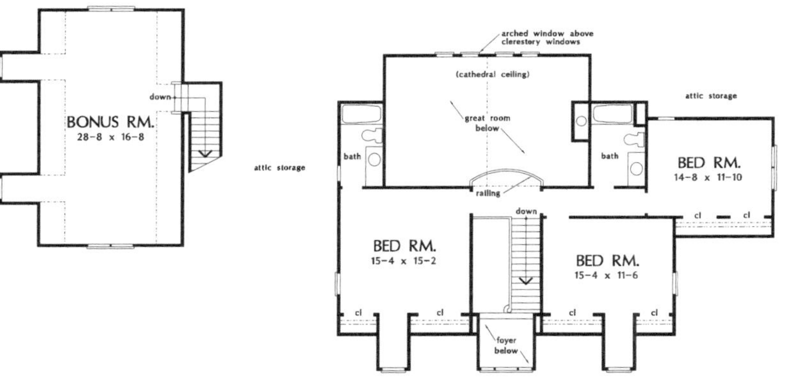

BONUS RM.
28-8 x 16-8
down
attic storage
arched window above clerestory windows
(cathedral ceiling)
great room below
railing
bath
bath
attic storage
BED RM.
14-8 x 11-10
BED RM.
15-4 x 15-2
down
BED RM.
15-4 x 11-6
cl
foyer below

SECOND FLOOR PLAN
No. 96443

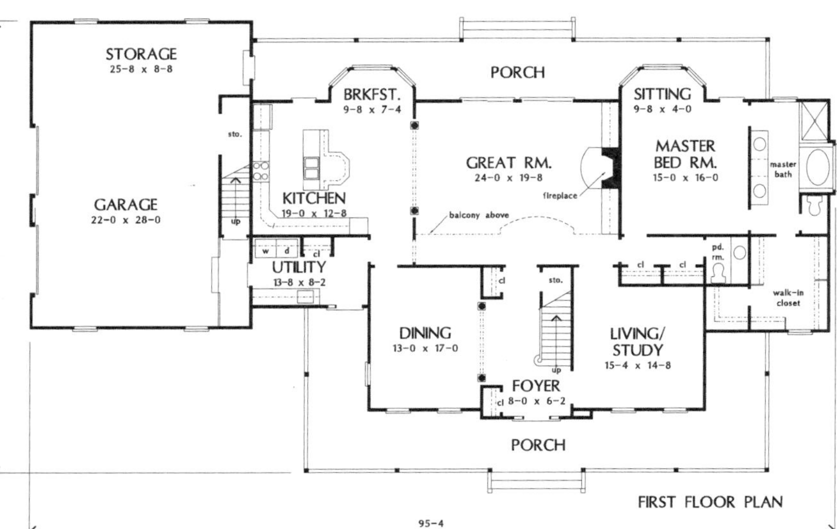

STORAGE
25-8 x 8-8
PORCH
BRKFST.
9-8 x 7-4
SITTING
9-8 x 4-0
GREAT RM.
24-0 x 19-8
MASTER BED RM.
15-0 x 16-0
master bath
fireplace
balcony above
sto.
GARAGE
22-0 x 28-0
KITCHEN
19-0 x 12-8
up
UTILITY
13-8 x 8-2
pd. rm.
walk-in closet
DINING
13-0 x 17-0
LIVING/ STUDY
15-4 x 14-8
FOYER
8-0 x 6-2
PORCH
54-10
95-4
FIRST FLOOR PLAN
© 1993 Donald A Gardner Architects, Inc.

Impressive Spaces Prevail

- This plan features:
- — Four bedrooms
- — Three full and one half baths
- Two-level Foyer with a clerestory window and a curved balcony above the Great Room
- Family Kitchen is convenient to the Breakfast bay, rear Porch, Dining Room and the Utility/Garage
- Master Bedroom retreat offers a Sitting Area, walk-in closet and a double vanity Bath
- The Bonus Room and ample storage space provide additional space for a growing family

FIRST FLOOR — 2,357 SQ. FT.
SECOND FLOOR — 995 SQ. FT.
BONUS ROOM — 545 SQ. FT.
GARAGE & STORAGE — 975 SQ. FT.

TOTAL LIVING AREA:
3,352 SQ. FT.

PLAN NO. 98402

Design by
Frank Betz Associates, Inc.

Refer to **Pricing Schedule F** on the order form for pricing information

Stately Stone and Stucco

- This plan features:
- — Four bedrooms
- — Three full and one half baths
- Two story Foyer with angled staircase
- Expansive two story Great Room enhanced by a fireplace
- Kitchen with a cooktop island with Pantry
- Keeping Room accented by a wall of windows
- Master Suite wing offers a plush Bath and roomy walk-in closet
- An optional basement, crawl space, or slab foundation available — please specify when ordering

FIRST FLOOR — 2,130 SQ. FT.
SECOND FLOOR — 897 SQ. FT.
BASEMENT — 2,130 SQ. FT.
GARAGE — 494 SQ. FT.

TOTAL LIVING AREA:
3,027 SQ. FT.

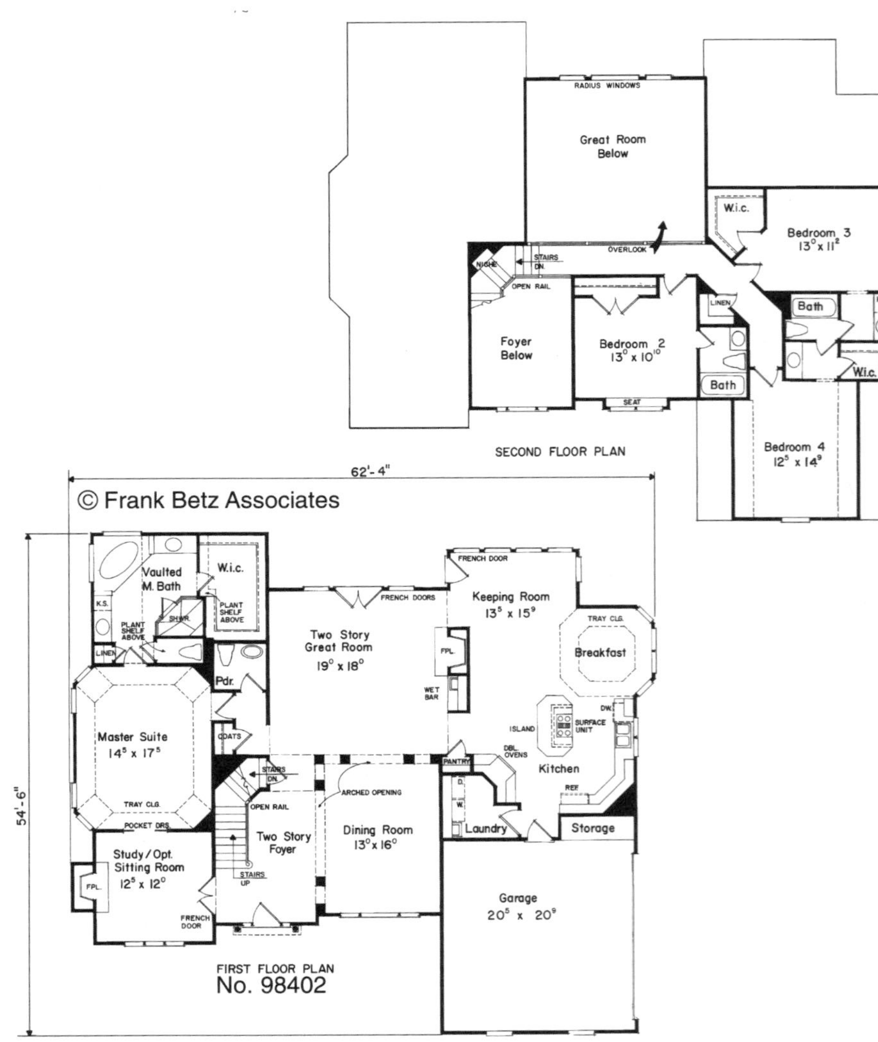
RADIUS WINDOWS
Great Room Below
W.i.c.
Bedroom 3 13° x 11²
STAIRS DN.
OVERLOOK
NICHE
OPEN RAIL
LINEN
Bath
K.S.
Foyer Below
Bedroom 2 13° x 10¹⁰
W.i.c.
Bath
SEAT
Bedroom 4 12⁵ x 14⁹
SECOND FLOOR PLAN
62'- 4"
© Frank Betz Associates
FRENCH DOOR
Vaulted M. Bath
W.i.c.
K.S.
PLANT SHELF ABOVE
LINEN
FRENCH DOORS
Keeping Room 13⁵ x 15⁹
Two Story Great Room 19° x 18°
TRAY CLG.
Breakfast
FPL.
Pdr.
WET BAR
Master Suite 14⁵ x 17⁵
COATS
ISLAND
SURFACE UNIT
DW.
DBL. OVENS
STAIRS DN.
PANTRY
Kitchen
TRAY CLG.
ARCHED OPENING
REF.
OPEN RAIL
POCKET DRS.
Two Story Foyer
Dining Room 13° x 16°
Laundry
Storage
54'-6"
Study / Opt. Sitting Room 12⁵ x 12°
FPL.
STAIRS UP
FRENCH DOOR
Garage 20⁵ x 20⁹
FIRST FLOOR PLAN
No. 98402

Refer to **Pricing Schedule F** on the order form for pricing information

Design by
Donald A. Gardner Architects, Inc.

PLAN NO. 96407

B. NATHAN

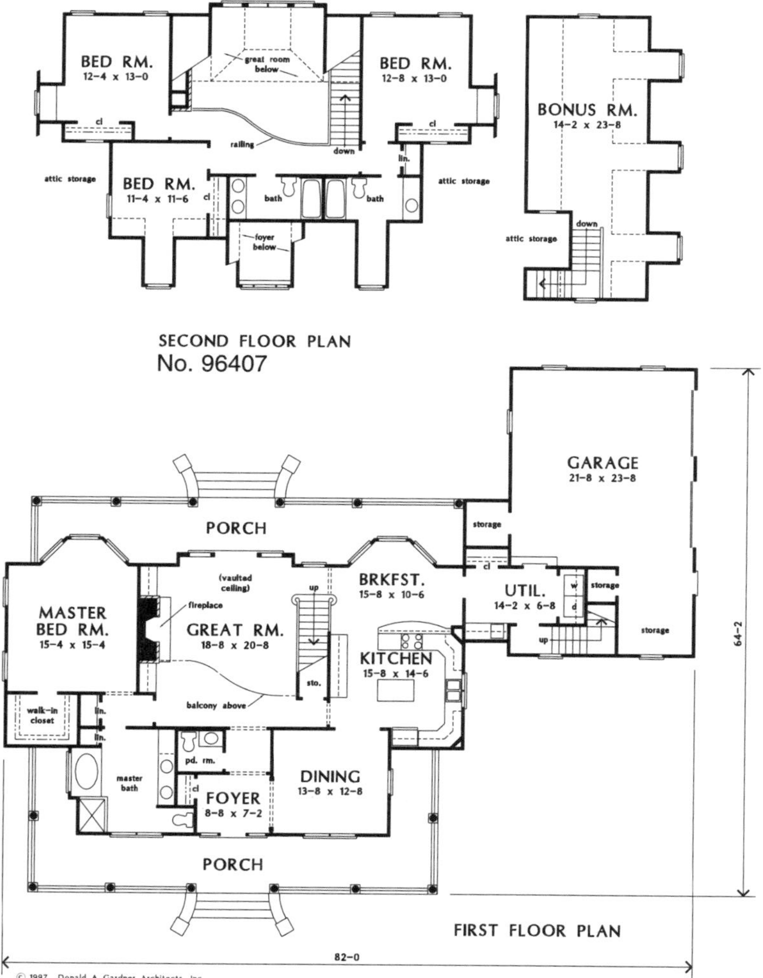
BED RM.
12-4 x 13-0
great room below
BED RM.
12-8 x 13-0
BONUS RM.
14-2 x 23-8
railing
down
attic storage
BED RM.
11-4 x 11-6
bath
bath
attic storage
foyer below
attic storage
down
SECOND FLOOR PLAN
No. 96407
GARAGE
21-8 x 23-8
PORCH
storage
(vaulted ceiling)
BRKFST.
15-8 x 10-6
UTIL.
14-2 x 6-8
storage
MASTER BED RM.
15-4 x 15-4
fireplace
GREAT RM.
18-8 x 20-8
KITCHEN
15-8 x 14-6
storage
walk-in closet
balcony above
pd. rm.
master bath
FOYER
8-8 x 7-2
DINING
13-8 x 12-8
PORCH
64-2
FIRST FLOOR PLAN
82-0
© 1997 Donald A Gardner Architects, Inc.

Perfect for Entertaining

- This plan features:
- — Four bedrooms
- — Three full and one half baths
- With front dormers and wrap-around Porch, the home offers formal entertaining and casual living
- Dramatic Great Room boasts cathedral ceiling and fireplace nestled between built-in shelves
- French doors expand living space to full length rear Porch
- Center island and peninsula counter create an efficient Kitchen/Breakfast Area
- First floor Master Bedroom features a walk-in and spacious Master Bath

FIRST FLOOR — 1,831 SQ. FT.
SECOND FLOOR — 941 SQ. FT.
BONUS ROOM — 539 SQ. FT.
GARAGE & STORAGE — 684 SQ. FT.

TOTAL LIVING AREA:
2,772 SQ. FT.

To order your Blueprints, call 1-800-235-5700

PLAN NO. 99442

Design by
Design Basics, Inc.

Refer to **Pricing Schedule F** on the order form for pricing informatio

Arches Enhance Style

- This plan features:
- — Four bedrooms
- — Three full and one half baths
- Open layout of rooms separated by arched openings
- Living Room is graced by a fireplace and adjoins the Dining Room
- Family Room has a second fireplace and is open to the Breakfast Nook and Kitchen
- A mid level Study is brightened by a large front window
- This plan has four huge Bedrooms and three full Baths upstairs
- No material list is available for this plan

FIRST FLOOR — 1,786 SQ. FT.
SECOND FLOOR — 1,607 SQ. FT
GARAGE — 682 SQ. FT.

TOTAL LIVING AREA:
3,393 SQ. FT.

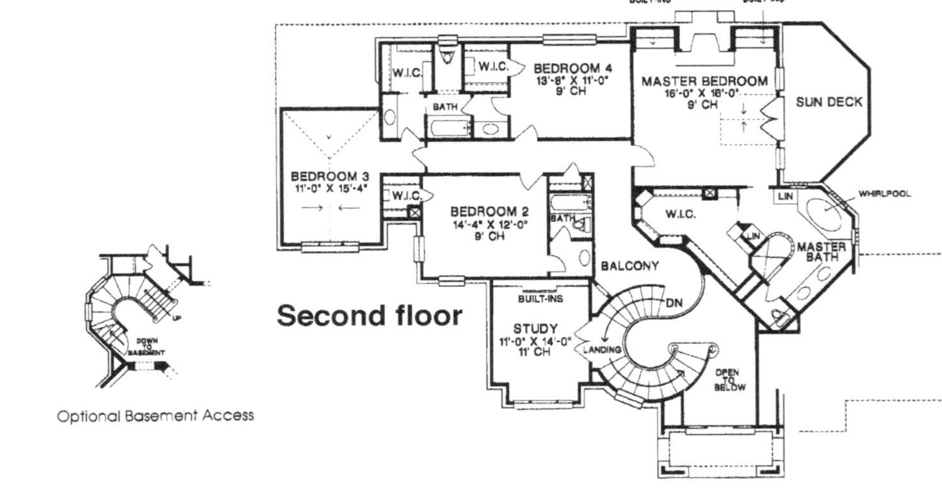
BUILT-INS
BUILT-INS
W.I.C.
W.I.C.
BEDROOM 4
13'-8" X 11'-0"
9' CH
MASTER BEDROOM
16'-0" X 18'-0"
9' CH
SUN DECK
BATH
BEDROOM 3
11'-0" X 15'-4"
W.I.C.
BEDROOM 2
14'-4" X 12'-0"
9' CH
BATH
W.I.C.
LIN
WHIRLPOOL
MASTER BATH
BALCONY
BUILT-INS
STUDY
11'-0" X 14'-0"
11' CH
LANDING
DN
OPEN TO BELOW
Second floor
Optional Basement Access

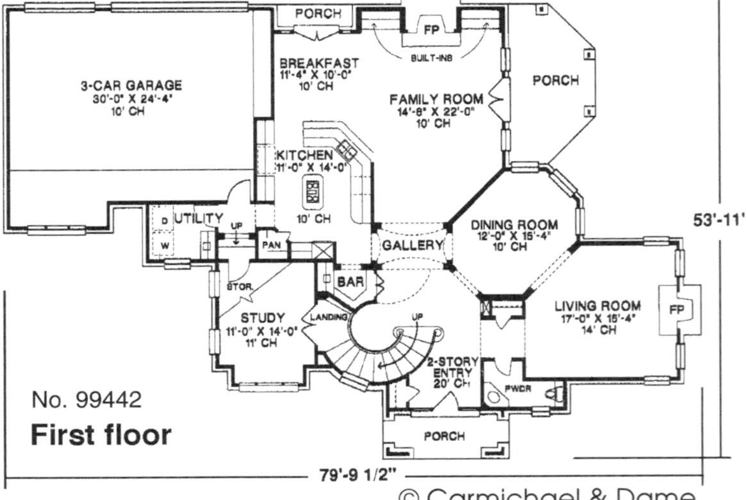
PORCH
FP
BUILT-INS
BREAKFAST
11'-4" X 10'-0"
10' CH
3-CAR GARAGE
30'-0" X 24'-4"
10' CH
FAMILY ROOM
14'-8" X 22'-0"
10' CH
PORCH
KITCHEN
11'-0" X 14'-0"
10' CH
UTILITY
PAN
GALLERY
DINING ROOM
12'-0" X 15'-4"
10' CH
53'-11'
BAR
STUDY
11'-0" X 14'-0"
11' CH
LANDING
UP
LIVING ROOM
17'-0" X 15'-4"
14' CH
FP
2-STORY ENTRY
20' CH
PWDR
No. 99442
First floor
PORCH
79'-9 1/2"

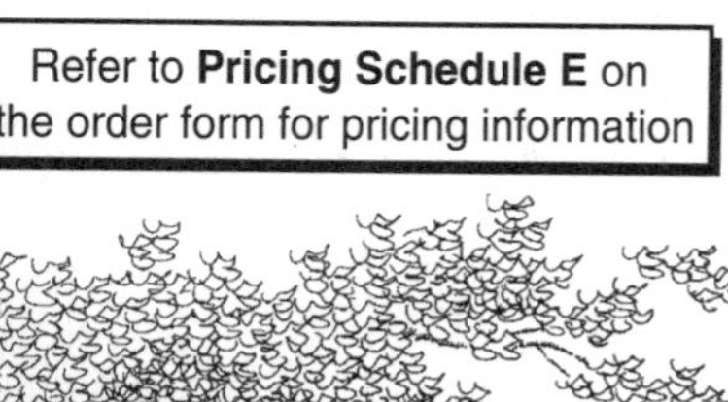
Refer to Pricing Schedule E on
the order form for pricing information

Design by
Frank Betz Associates, Inc.

PLAN NO. 98452

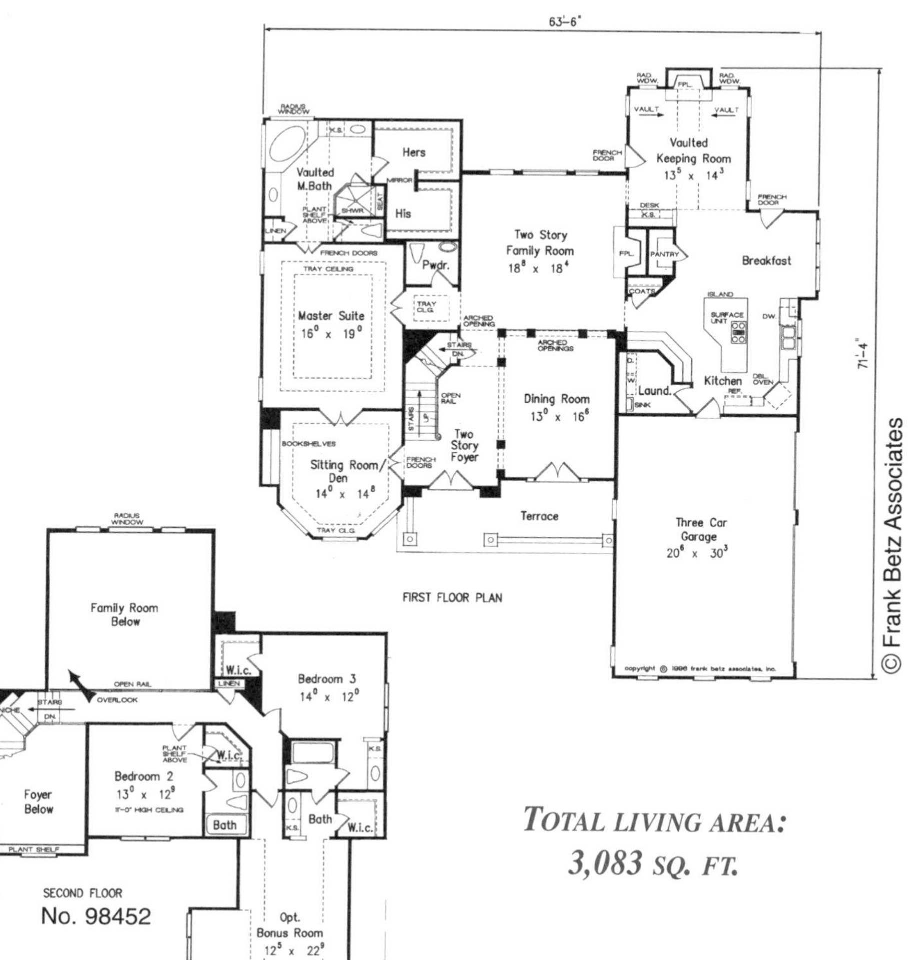
63'-6"
71'-4"
Vaulted Keeping Room 13⁵ x 14³
Vaulted M.Bath
Hers
His
Two Story Family Room 18⁸ x 18⁴
Breakfast
Pwdr.
Master Suite 16⁰ x 19⁰
Kitchen
Laund.
Dining Room 13⁰ x 16⁸
Two Story Foyer
Sitting Room/ Den 14⁰ x 14⁸
Terrace
Three Car Garage 20⁶ x 30³
FIRST FLOOR PLAN
© Frank Betz Associates
Family Room Below
Bedroom 3 14⁰ x 12⁰
Bedroom 2 13⁰ x 12⁹
Foyer Below
Bath
W.i.c.
Opt. Bonus Room 12⁵ x 22⁹
SECOND FLOOR
No. 98452

Splendid Appointments

- This plan features:
- — Three bedrooms
- — Three full and one half baths
- The two-story Foyer is highlighted by a open-railed staircase
- The formal Dining Room opens onto a terrace for expanded dining options
- A private Sitting Room/Den is topped by a tray ceiling
- A two-story Family Room is accented by arched openings from the Dining Room and Foyer
- The spacious Kitchen/Breakfast Room includes a cooktop island
- The Keeping Room has a vaulted ceiling and a cozy fireplace
- An optional basement or crawl space foundation — please specify when ordering

TOTAL LIVING AREA:
3,083 SQ. FT.

FIRST FLOOR — 2,429 SQ. FT.
SECOND FLOOR — 654 SQ. FT.
BONUS ROOM — 420 SQ. FT.
BASEMENT — 2,429 SQ. FT.
GARAGE — 641 SQ. FT.

PLAN NO. 98904

Design by
Jannis Vann & Associates, Inc.

Refer to **Pricing Schedule D** on the order form for pricing information

Quaint Dormers and Columned Porch

- This plan features:
- — Three bedrooms
- — Two full and one half baths
- The Foyer leads into the formal Dining Room that is topped by a decorative ceiling
- A double door entry to the Library overlooks the front Porch
- The cooktop island Kitchen is directly accessed from both Dining Areas
- The Family Room with a fireplace has doors that open to the Deck
- The Master suite has a bay window and a decorative ceiling
- An upstairs bonus space for future consideration

MAIN FLOOR — 2,614 SQ. FT.
BONUS — 1,681 SQ. FT.
BASEMENT — 2,563 SQ. FT.
GARAGE — 596 SQ. FT.

TOTAL LIVING AREA:
2,614 SQ. FT.

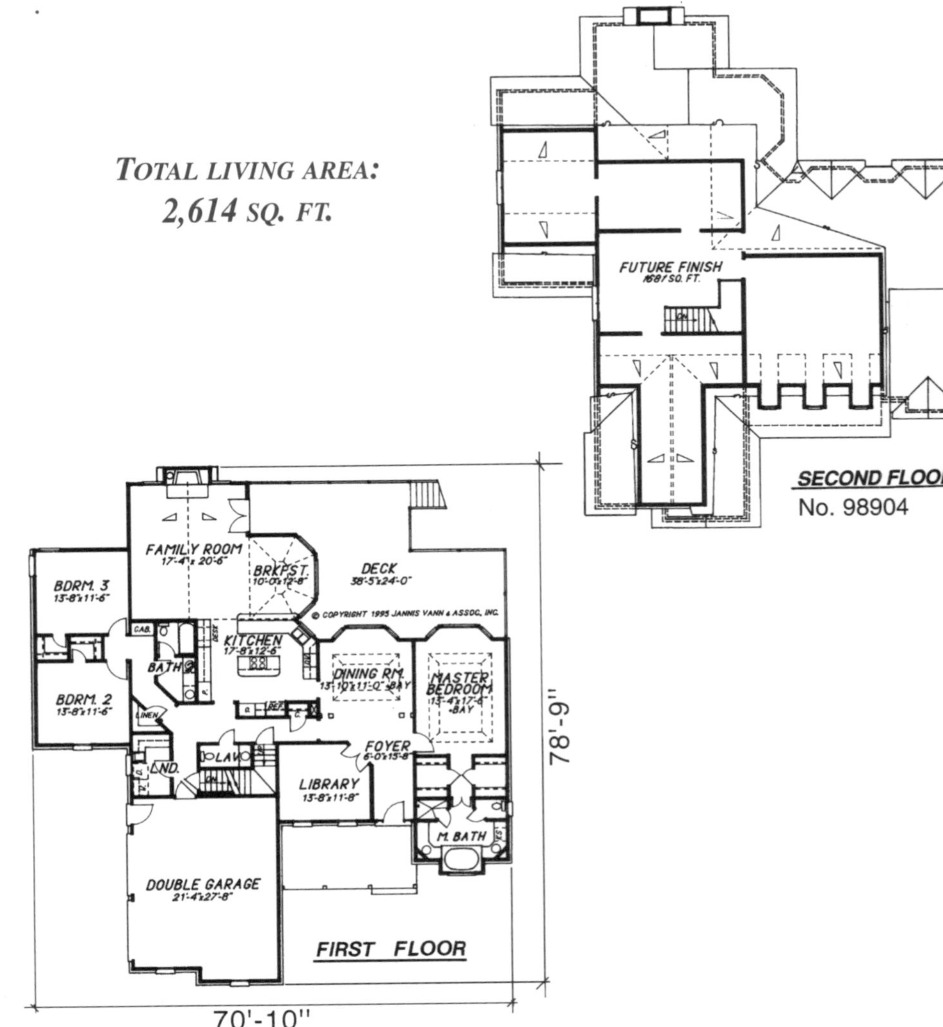

FUTURE FINISH
SECOND FLOOR
No. 98904
FAMILY ROOM
BRKFST.
DECK
BDRM. 3
BDRM. 2
KITCHEN
BATH
DINING RM.
MASTER BEDROOM
FOYER
LIBRARY
M. BATH
DOUBLE GARAGE
FIRST FLOOR
78'-9"
70'-10"

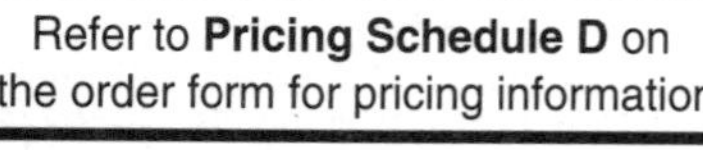
Refer to **Pricing Schedule D** on the order form for pricing information

Design by
Studer Residential Design, Inc.

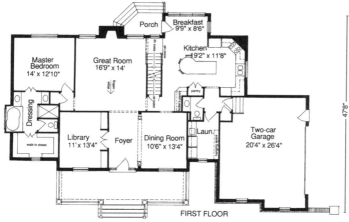

PLAN NO. 92653

Porch
Breakfast 9'9" x 8'6"
Kitchen 19'2" x 11'8"
Master Bedroom 14' x 12'10"
Great Room 16'9" x 14'
Dressing
Library 11' x 13'4"
Foyer
Dining Room 10'6" x 13'4"
Laun.
Two-car Garage 20'4" x 26'4"
47'8"
78'4"

FIRST FLOOR

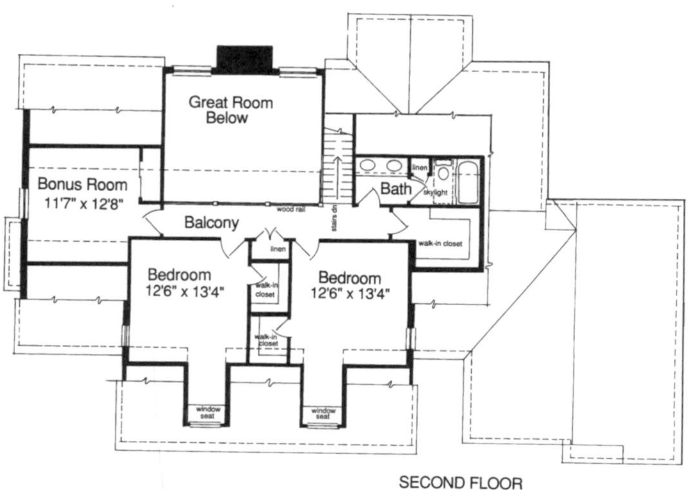
Great Room Below
Bonus Room 11'7" x 12'8"
Bath
Balcony
Bedroom 12'6" x 13'4"
Bedroom 12'6" x 13'4"

SECOND FLOOR
No. 92653

Country Brick

- This plan features:
  - — Three bedrooms
  - — Two full and one half baths
- Library offers a quiet space
- Great Room is enhanced by a fireplace
- Country-size Kitchen with island snackbar
- Private Master Bedroom offers a deluxe Bath
- Two additional Bedrooms with walk-in closets and window seats
- No materials list is available for this plan

First floor — 1,710 sq. ft.
Second floor — 733 sq. ft.
Bonus — 181 sq. ft.
Basement — 1,697 sq. ft.
Garage — 499 sq. ft.

Total living area:
2,443 sq. ft.

PLAN NO. 98400

Design by
Frank Betz Associates, Inc.

Refer to **Pricing Schedule F** on the order form for pricing information

Exquisite Detail

■ This plan features:

— Four bedrooms

— Three full and one half baths

■ Formal Living Room with access to Covered Porch and an arched opening to Family Room

■ Radius windows and arches enhance Family Room

■ Spacious and efficient Kitchen with Pantry, cooktop/serving bar, two-story Breakfast Area and a butler's Pantry

■ Expansive Master Bedroom offers a tray ceiling, a cozy Sitting Room, a luxurious Bath and huge walk-in closet

■ An optional basement or crawl space foundation — please specify when ordering

FIRST FLOOR — 1,418 SQ. FT.
SECOND FLOOR — 1,844 SQ. FT.
BASEMENT — 1,418 SQ. FT.
GARAGE — 840 SQ. FT.

TOTAL LIVING AREA:
3,262 SQ. FT.

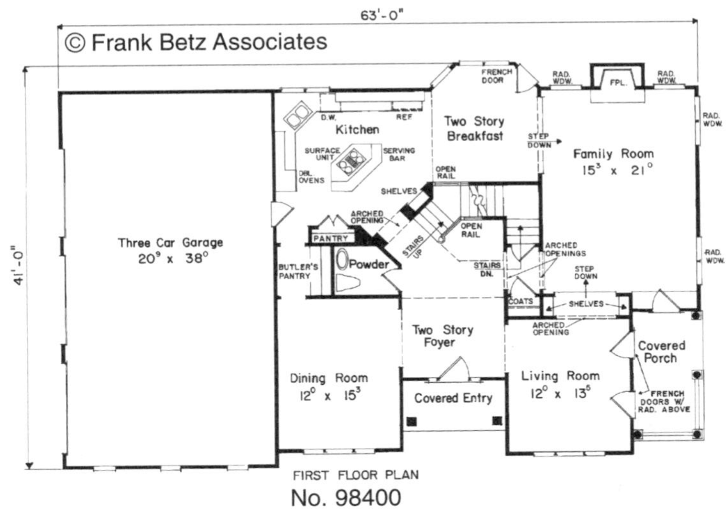
63'-0"
© Frank Betz Associates
41'-0"
Three Car Garage
20⁹ x 38⁰
Kitchen
Two Story Breakfast
Family Room
15³ x 21⁰
Powder
Pantry
Butler's Pantry
Two Story Foyer
Dining Room
12⁰ x 15³
Covered Entry
Living Room
12⁰ x 13⁵
Covered Porch
FIRST FLOOR PLAN

No. 98400

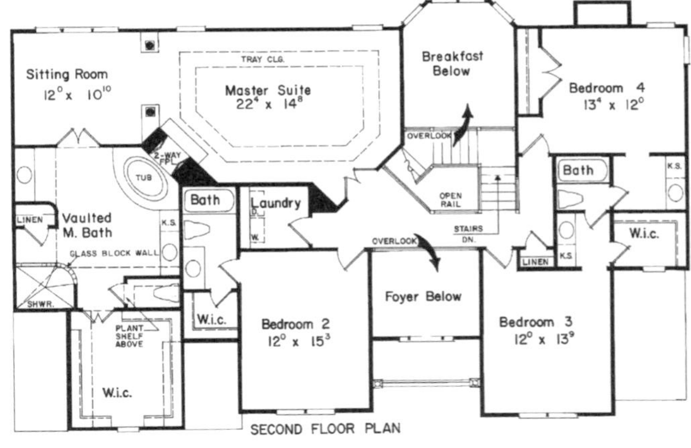
Sitting Room
12⁰ x 10¹⁰
Master Suite
22⁴ x 14⁸
Breakfast Below
Bedroom 4
13⁴ x 12⁰
Vaulted M. Bath
Bath
Laundry
Bath
W.i.c.
W.i.c.
Bedroom 2
12⁰ x 15³
Foyer Below
Bedroom 3
12⁰ x 13⁹
W.i.c.
SECOND FLOOR PLAN

PLAN NO.98426

Design by
Frank Betz Associates, Inc.

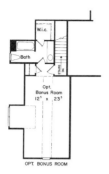

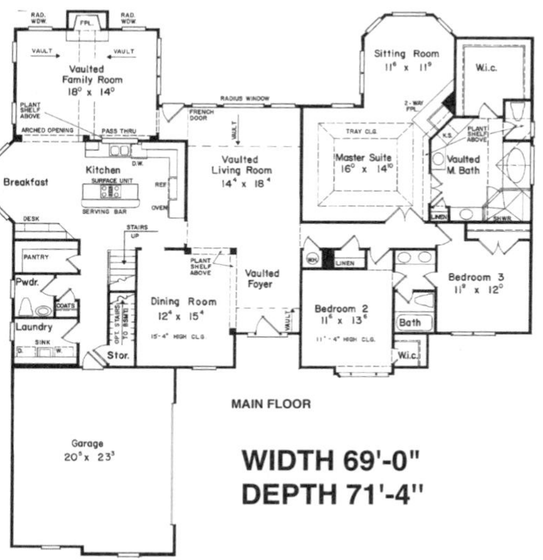

W.i.c.
Bath
Opt. Bonus Room 12⁵ x 23³
OPT. BONUS ROOM
© Frank Betz Associates
Vaulted Family Room 18⁰ x 14⁰
Breakfast
Kitchen
Vaulted Living Room 14⁴ x 18⁴
Sitting Room 11⁶ x 11⁹
Master Suite 16⁰ x 14¹⁰
Vaulted M. Bath
Dining Room 12⁴ x 15⁴
Vaulted Foyer
Bedroom 2 11⁶ x 13⁶
Bedroom 3 11⁶ x 12⁰
Pantry
Pwdr.
Laundry
Stor.
MAIN FLOOR
Garage 20⁵ x 23³

WIDTH 69'-0"
DEPTH 71'-4"

Delightful Detailing

Price Code: E

- This plan features:
- — Three bedrooms
- — Two full and one half baths
- The Dining Room is delineated by columns with a plant shelf above
- Family Room has a vaulted ceiling
- There is an optional bonus room located over the garage
- An optional basement or a crawl space foundation — please specify when ordering

MAIN FLOOR — 2,622 SQ. FT.
BONUS ROOM — 478 SQ. FT.
BASEMENT — 2,622 SQ. FT.
GARAGE — 506 SQ. FT.

TOTAL LIVING AREA:
2,622 SQ. FT.

PLAN NO.98538

Design by
Fillmore Design Group

Exceptional Family Living

Price Code: F

- This plan features:
- — Four bedrooms
- — Three full and one half baths
- A decorative dormer, a bay window and an eyebrow arched window provide for a pleasing Country farmhouse facade
- The cozy Study has its own fireplace and a bay window
- The large formal Living Room has a fireplace and built-in bookcases
- The huge island Kitchen is open to the Breakfast Bay and the Family Room
- The Master Suite includes a large bath with a unique closet
- Three more bedrooms located at the other end of the home each have private access to a full bath
- No materials list is available for this plan

MAIN FLOOR — 4,082 SQ. FT.
GARAGE — 720 SQ. FT.

TOTAL LIVING AREA:
4,082 SQ. FT.

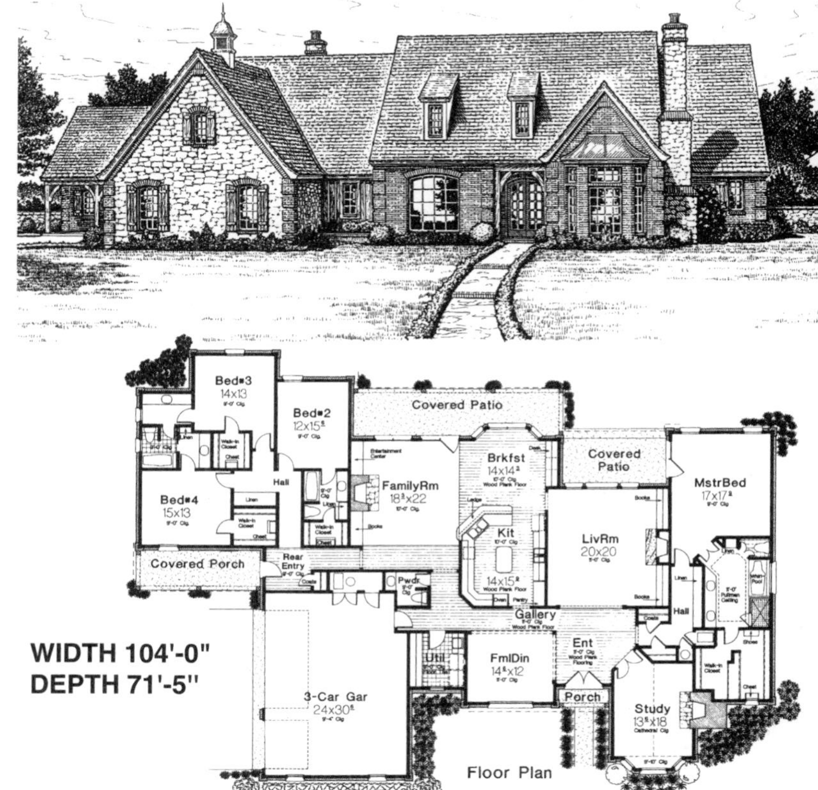

Bed#3 14x13
Bed#2 12x15⁸
Covered Patio
Brkfst 14x14³
FamilyRm 18⁸x22
Covered Patio
MstrBed 17x17³
Bed#4 15x13
Kit
LivRm 20x20
Covered Porch
Rear Entry
Gallery
Ent
FmlDin 14⁸x12
Porch
Study 13⁸x18
3-Car Gar 24x30⁸
Floor Plan

WIDTH 104'-0"
DEPTH 71'-5"

PLAN NO. 92248

Design by
Filmore Design Group

Refer to **Pricing Schedule F** on the order form for pricing information

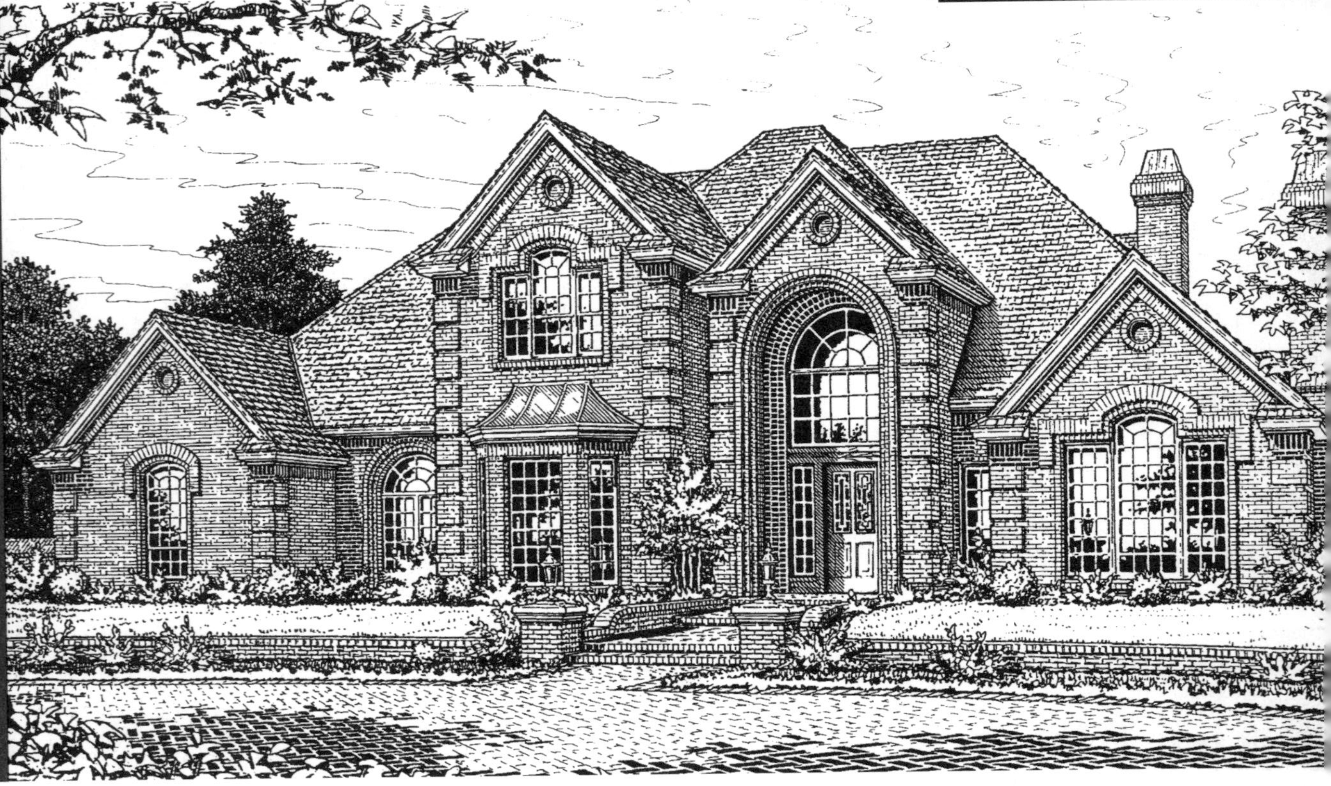

Brick Grandeur

- This plan features:
- — Four bedrooms
- — Three full and one half baths
- Dramatic two-story glass Entry with a curved staircase
- The Living and Family Rooms have high ceilings and fireplaces
- Large Kitchen has a cooktop serving island, walk-in Pantry, a Breakfast Area and Patio access
- Lavish Master Bedroom has a cathedral ceiling, two walk-in closets, and Bath
- Two additional Bedrooms with ample closets, share a double vanity Bath
- No materials list is available for this plan

FIRST FLOOR — 2,506 SQ. FT.
SECOND FLOOR — 1,415 SQ. FT.
BASEMENT — 2,400 SQ. FT.
GARAGE — 660 SQ. FT.

TOTAL LIVING AREA:
3,921 SQ. FT.

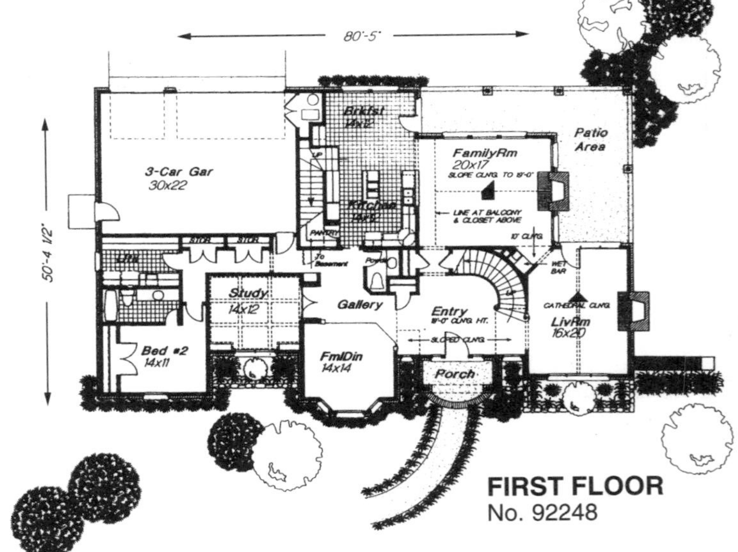
80'-5"
50'-4 1/2"
3-Car Gar
30x22
FamilyRm
20x17
Patio
Area
Study
14x12
Gallery
Entry
LivRm
16x20
Bed #2
14x11
FmlDin
14x14
Porch

FIRST FLOOR
No. 92248

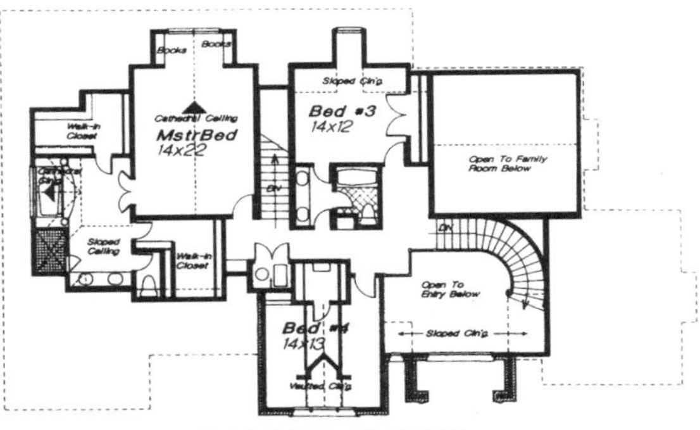
MstrBed
14x22
Bed #3
14x12
Bed #4
14x13
Open To Family Room Below
Open To Entry Below

SECOND FLOOR

Refer to **Pricing Schedule D** on the order form for pricing information

Design by
Larry E. Belk

PLAN NO. 93099

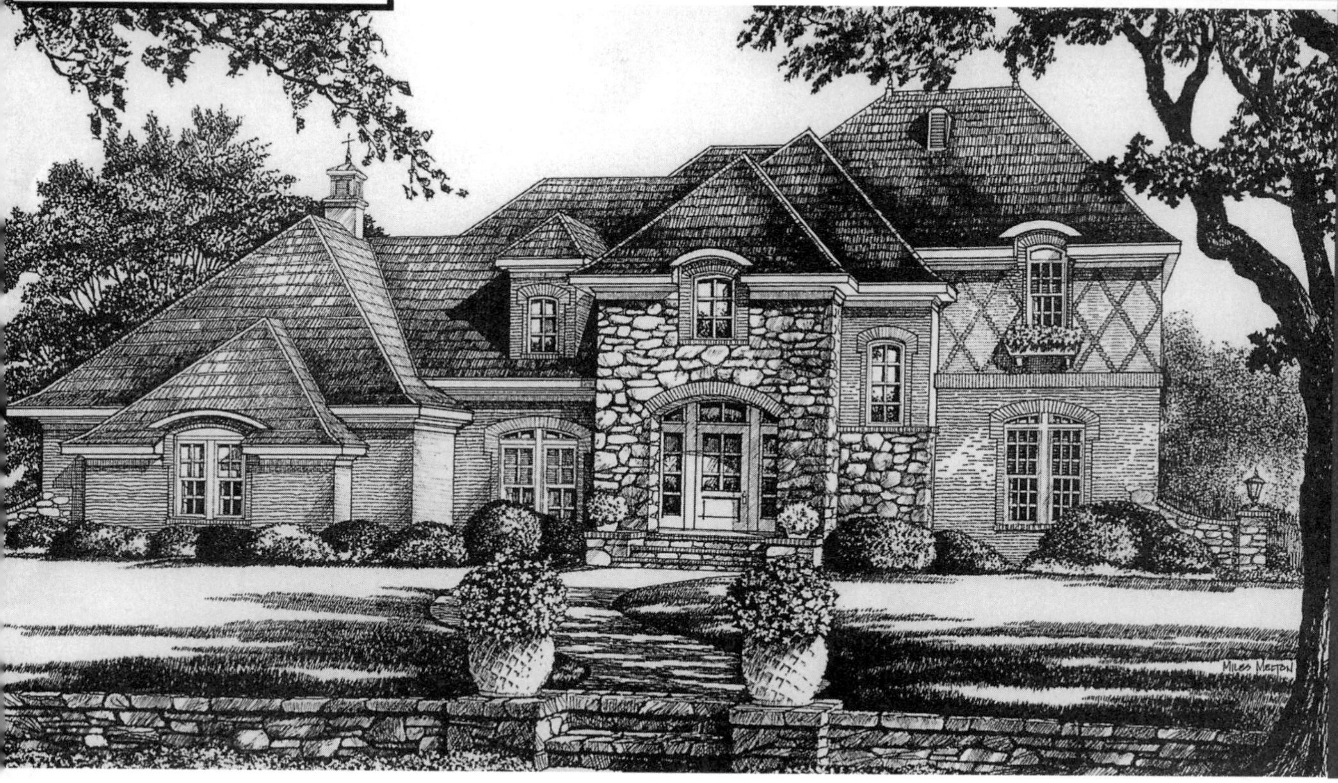

Out of the English Countryside

Total Living Area:
2,611 sq. ft.

- This plan features:
  - — Four bedrooms
  - — Three full baths
- A covered front Porch leads into the two-story Foyer
- From the Foyer find arched entrances into the Dining Room and the Great Room
- The Great Room is at the center of the home and is complimented by a 10-foot tray ceiling
- Located in a secluded part of the first floor is the Master Suite
- The Breakfast Room shares a see-through fireplace with the Great Room
- The Kitchen has a walk-in Pantry
- No materials list is available for this plan

First floor — 2,050 sq. ft.
Second floor — 561 sq. ft.
Bonus — 272 sq. ft.
Garage — 599 sq. ft.

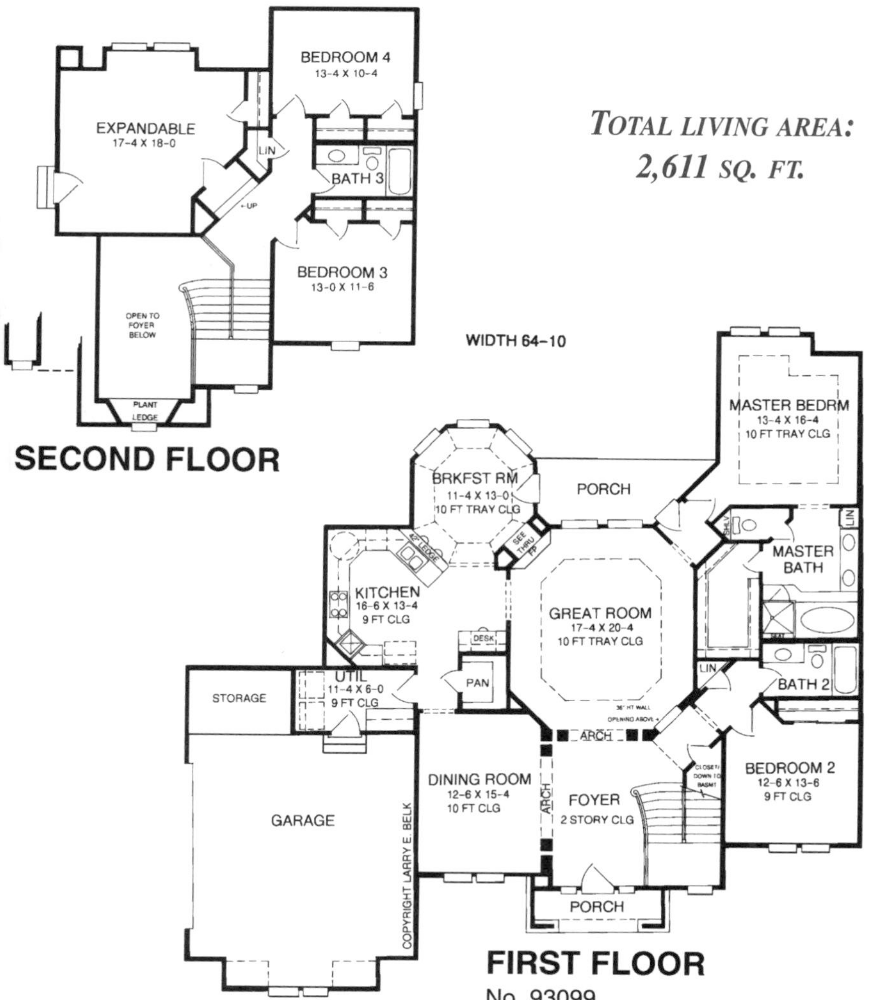
BEDROOM 4
13-4 X 10-4
EXPANDABLE
17-4 X 18-0
LIN
BATH 3
BEDROOM 3
13-0 X 11-6
OPEN TO
FOYER
BELOW
PLANT
LEDGE
SECOND FLOOR
WIDTH 64-10
MASTER BEDRM
13-4 X 16-4
10 FT TRAY CLG
BRKFST RM
11-4 X 13-0
10 FT TRAY CLG
PORCH
MASTER
BATH
KITCHEN
16-6 X 13-4
9 FT CLG
GREAT ROOM
17-4 X 20-4
10 FT TRAY CLG
DEPTH 64-0
DESK
PAN
LIN
BATH 2
STORAGE
UTIL
11-4 X 6-0
9 FT CLG
ARCH
BEDROOM 2
12-6 X 13-6
9 FT CLG
DINING ROOM
12-6 X 15-4
10 FT CLG
FOYER
2 STORY CLG
GARAGE
COPYRIGHT LARRY E. BELK
PORCH
FIRST FLOOR
No. 93099

PLAN NO. 96444

Design by
Donald A. Gardner Architects, Inc.

Refer to **Pricing Schedule G** on the order form for pricing information

Comfortable, Easy Living

■ This plan features:

— Five bedrooms

— Three full and one half baths

■ Great Room is overlooked by a curved balcony and features a fireplace with built-ins on either side

■ Spacious and efficient Kitchen equipped with a cooktop island has direct access to Breakfast Room and Dining Room

■ Swing Room, Bedroom/Study, with private full Bath and closet

■ Master Suite pampered by lavish Bath and large walk-in closet

FIRST FLOOR — 2,176 SQ. FT.
SECOND FLOOR — 861 SQ. FT.
BONUS ROOM — 483 SQ. FT.
GARAGE — 710 SQ. FT.

TOTAL LIVING AREA: 3,037 SQ. FT.

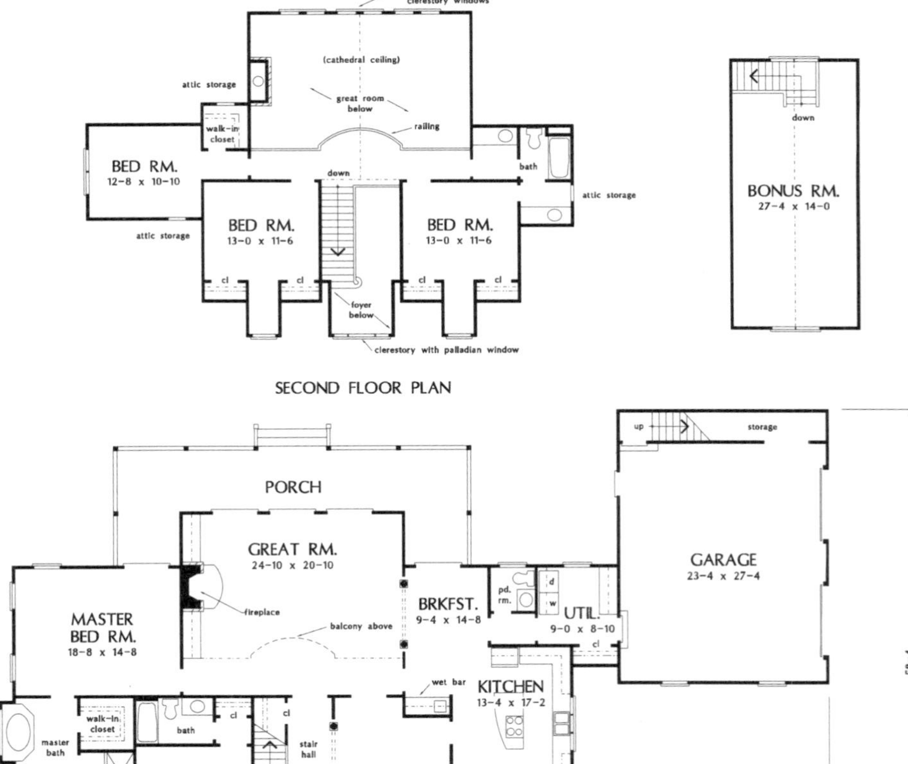
arched windows above clerestory windows
(cathedral ceiling)
attic storage
great room below
walk-in closet
railing
BED RM. 12-8 x 10-10
down
bath
attic storage
BED RM. 13-0 x 11-6
BED RM. 13-0 x 11-6
attic storage
cl
foyer below
clerestory with palladian window
down
BONUS RM. 27-4 x 14-0
up
storage
PORCH
GREAT RM. 24-10 x 20-10
fireplace
balcony above
BRKFST. 9-4 x 14-8
pd. rm.
UTIL. 9-0 x 8-10
GARAGE 23-4 x 27-4
MASTER BED RM. 18-8 x 14-8
wet bar
KITCHEN 13-4 x 17-2
walk-in closet
master bath
bath
stair hall
BED RM./ STUDY 13-0 x 11-8
DINING 13-0 x 15-0
FOYER 8-10 x 6-10
PORCH
58-4
94-0

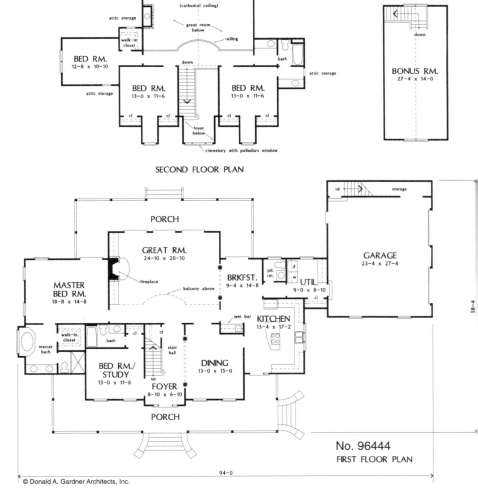

SECOND FLOOR PLAN

No. 96444
FIRST FLOOR PLAN

Refer to **Pricing Schedule D** on the order form for pricing information

Design by
Frank Betz Associates, Inc.

PLAN NO. 98458

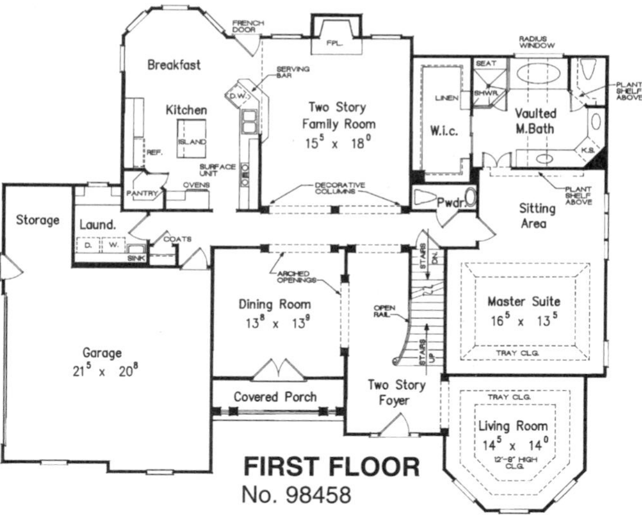

Breakfast
Kitchen
Two Story Family Room 15⁵ x 18⁰
W.i.c.
Vaulted M.Bath
Pwdr.
Sitting Area
Storage
Laund.
Dining Room 13⁸ x 13⁹
Master Suite 16⁵ x 13⁵
Garage 21⁵ x 20⁸
Covered Porch
Two Story Foyer
Living Room 14⁵ x 14⁰

FIRST FLOOR
No. 98458

TOTAL LIVING AREA:
2,940 SQ. FT.

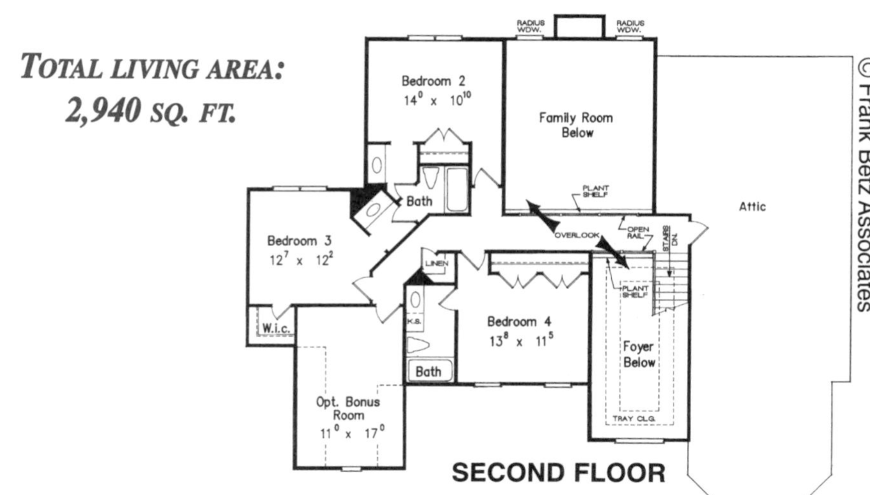

Bedroom 2 14⁰ x 10¹⁰
Family Room Below
Bath
Bedroom 3 12⁷ x 12²
Attic
Bedroom 4 13⁸ x 11⁵
Bath
Foyer Below
Opt. Bonus Room 11⁰ x 17⁰

SECOND FLOOR

Lasting Impression

- This plan features:
  - — Four bedrooms
  - — Three full and one half baths
- The two-story Foyer is enhanced by a cascading staircase with an open rail
- The Living Room is topped by a 12-foot tray ceiling
- Double doors lead from the Dining Room to the covered Porch
- The Master Suite includes a Sitting Area and a five-piece bath
- Three additional Bedrooms have access to a full Bath
- An optional basement, crawl space or slab foundation — please specify when ordering

FIRST FLOOR — 2,044 SQ. FT.
SECOND FLOOR — 896 SQ. FT.
BONUS — 197 SQ. FT.
BASEMENT — 2,044 SQ. FT.
GARAGE — 544 SQ. FT.

PLAN NO. 91588

Design by
Alan Mascord Design Associates

Refer to **Pricing Schedule E** on the order form for pricing information

Let the Sun Shine In

- This plan features:
- — Four bedrooms
- — Two full and one three-quarter baths
- Two-story entrance with a second floor window
- Family Room, Nook and Kitchen are open to each other for a spacious feeling
- Cooktop island/snack bar built-in desk and a pantry highlight the efficient Kitchen
- Family Room has a second fireplace
- Lavish Master Suite with a decorative ceiling in the Bedroom and a private, plush Bath
- No materials list is available for this plan

FIRST FLOOR — 1,575 SQ. FT.
SECOND FLOOR — 1,338 SQ. FT.
GARAGE — 864 SQ. FT.

TOTAL LIVING AREA:
2,913 SQ. FT

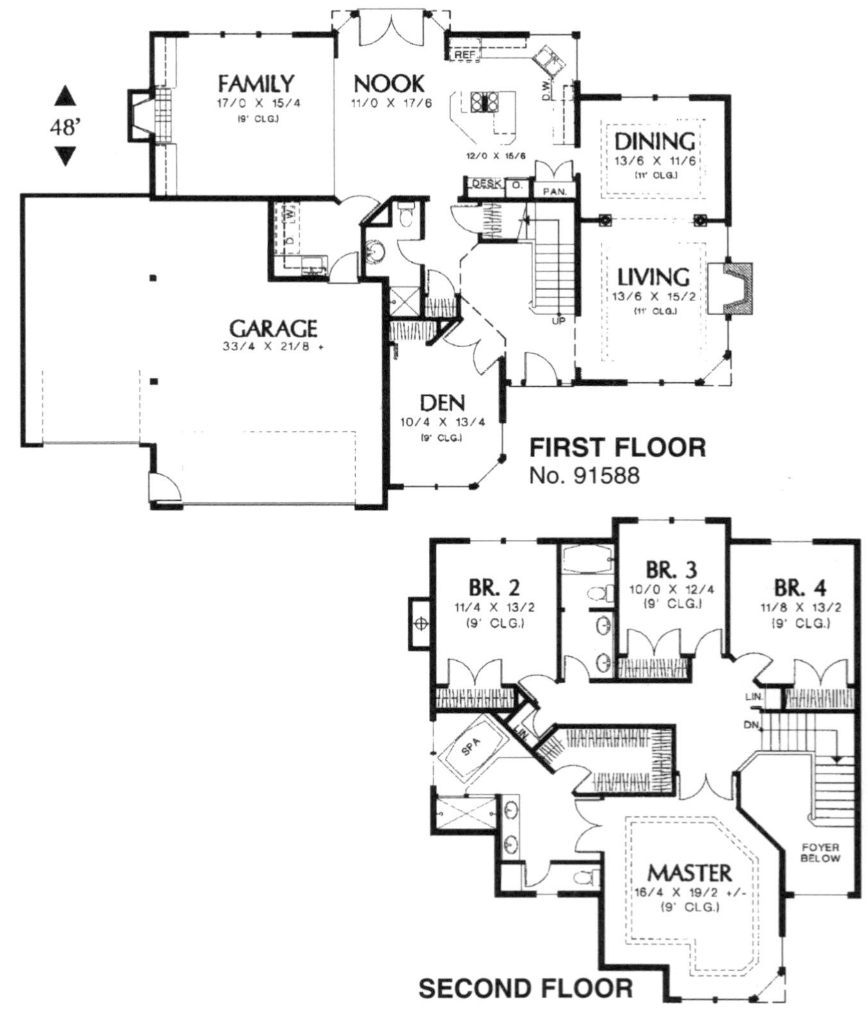

66'
48'
FAMILY
17/0 X 15/4
(9' CLG.)
NOOK
11/0 X 17/6
REF
D.W.
12/0 X 15/6
DESK
PAN.
DINING
13/6 X 11/6
(11' CLG.)
LIVING
13/6 X 15/2
(11' CLG.)
UP
GARAGE
33/4 X 21/8 +
DEN
10/4 X 13/4
(9' CLG.)
FIRST FLOOR
No. 91588
BR. 2
11/4 X 13/2
(9' CLG.)
BR. 3
10/0 X 12/4
(9' CLG.)
BR. 4
11/8 X 13/2
(9' CLG.)
LIN.
DN.
SPA
MASTER
16/4 X 19/2 +/-
(9' CLG.)
FOYER
BELOW
SECOND FLOOR

Refer to **Pricing Schedule E** on the order form for pricing information

Design by
Ahmann Design, Inc.

PLAN NO. 99109

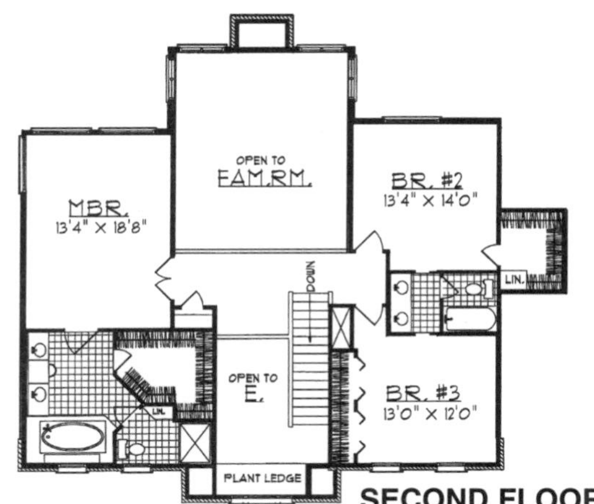
OPEN TO FAM.RM.
MBR.
13'4" X 18'8"
BR. #2
13'4" X 14'0"
LIN.
DOWN
OPEN TO E.
BR. #3
13'0" X 12'0"
PLANT LEDGE

SECOND FLOOR

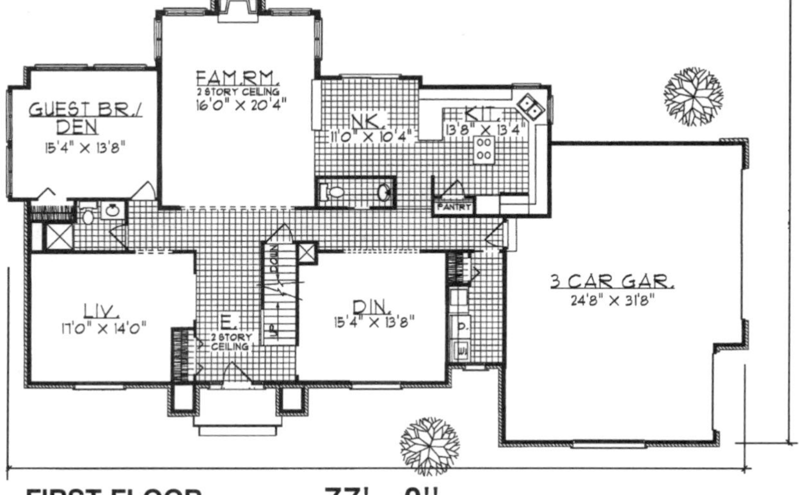
FAM.RM.
2 STORY CEILING
16'0" X 20'4"
GUEST BR./ DEN
15'4" X 13'8"
NK.
11'0" X 10'4"
KIT.
13'8" X 13'4"
PANTRY
3 CAR GAR.
24'8" X 31'8"
48' - 4"
LIV.
17'0" X 14'0"
E.
2 STORY CEILING
DIN.
15'4" X 13'8"
77' - 0"

FIRST FLOOR
No. 99109

Brick Home of Distinction

- This plan features:
- — Four bedrooms
- — Three full and one half baths
- As you enter from the covered front Porch you step into a two-story Entry
- Perfectly sized Living Room and Dining Room allow for entertaining large groups
- Voluminous two-story Family Room has a fireplace centered along the back wall
- Master Bedroom has a private Bath and a large walk-in closet
- Two additional Bedrooms upstairs with ample closet space that share a full Bath
- No materials list is available for this plan

FIRST FLOOR — 1,873 SQ. FT.
SECOND FLOOR — 1,150 SQ. FT.
BASEMENT — 1,810 SQ. FT.

TOTAL LIVING AREA:
3,023 SQ. FT.

PLAN NO.94222

Design by
Sater Design Group

built ins
guest 14'-4" x 14'-6" tray clg.
books
entertainment center
leisure 25'-0" x 19'-10" 13'-4" flat clg.
fireplace
nook 11'-0" x 11'-0" 13'-4" flat clg.
outdoor kitchen
lanai
sitting
am kitchen
corner fireplace
master suite 17'-0" x 32'-0" 13'-4" flat clg.
his
hers
sauna
wetbar
exer. 10' x 14'
guest 12'-8" x 12'-4" 9'-4" flat clg.
kitchen 14'-0" x 18'-0"
living 15'-0" x 14'-0" vaulted clg.
utility
gallery
dining 11'-4" x 15'-0" vaulted clg.
foyer
study 14'-1" x 20'-0" 13'-4" flat clg.
garage 22'-8" x 30'-8"
workbench
entry
95'-0"
88'-0"
MAIN AREA

Luxurious Residence

Price Code: F

- This plan features:
- — Three bedrooms
- — Three full and one half baths
- High ceilings in the formal Living and Dining areas
- Gallery leads to the family gathering and secondary Bedroom areas
- Kitchen with cooking island opens to the round Nook and the Leisure Room
- Round columns grace the rear elevation adding drama to the overall appearance
- No materials list is available for this plan

MAIN FLOOR — 4,656 SQ. FT.
GARAGE — 757 SQ. FT.

TOTAL LIVING AREA:
4,565 SQ. FT.

PLAN NO.94273

Design by
Studer Residential Design, Inc.

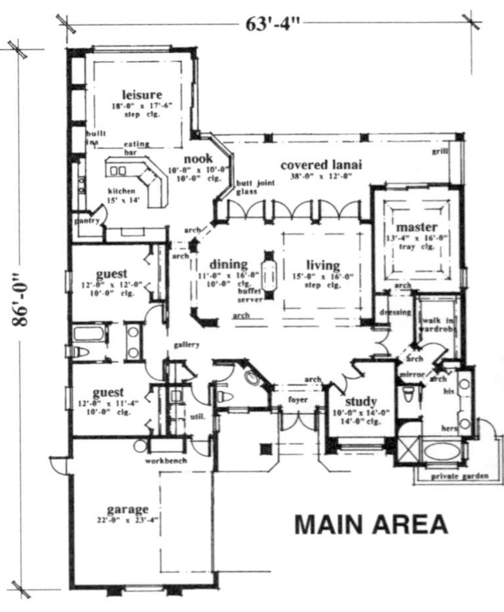
63'-4"
leisure 18'-0" x 17'-6" step clg.
built ins
eating bar
nook 10'-0" x 10'-0" 10'-0" clg.
kitchen 15' x 14'
pantry
covered lanai 38'-0" x 12'-0"
grill
butt joint glass
master 13'-4" x 16'-0" tray clg.
arch
dining 11'-0" x 16'-0" 10'-0" clg.
buffet server
living 15'-0" x 16'-0" step clg.
guest 12'-0" x 12'-0" 10'-0" clg.
dressing
walk in wardrobe
gallery
guest 12'-0" x 11'-4" 10'-0" clg.
util.
foyer
study 10'-0" x 14'-0" 14'-0" clg.
mirror
his
hers
workbench
private garden
garage 22'-0" x 23'-4"
86'-0"
MAIN AREA

Unique Traditional

Price Code: E

- This plan features:
- — Three bedrooms
- — Two full and one half baths
- Slump arched-top windows at the entry and study give a custom look
- Two Guest Suites share a full bath and are separated from the owner's wing
- The Master Suite has glass doors to the Lanai
- Master Bath is highlighted by a dressing area, walk-in wardrobe and his-n-her lavatories
- No materials list is available for this plan

MAIN FLOOR — 2,850 SQ. FT.
GARAGE — 588 SQ. FT.

TOTAL LIVING AREA:
2,850 SQ. FT.

Refer to **Pricing Schedule F** on the order form for pricing information

Design by
Alan Mascord Design Associates

PLAN NO. 91562

WIDTH 63'-0"
DEPTH 48'-0"

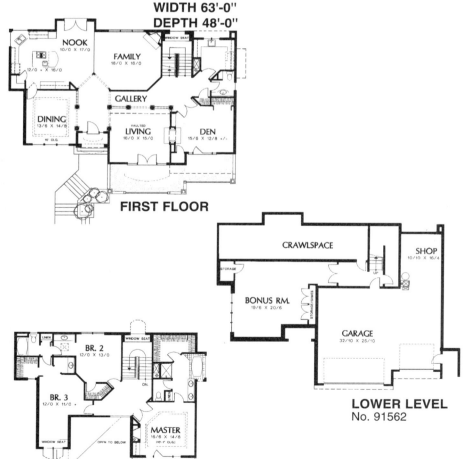

NOOK 10/0 X 17/0
12/0 x 16/0
FAMILY 18/0 X 16/0
WINDOW SEAT
GALLERY
DINING 13/6 X 14/8
10' CLG.
VAULTED LIVING 16/0 X 15/0
DEN 15/6 X 12/8 +/-

FIRST FLOOR

CRAWLSPACE
SHOP 10/10 X 16/4
STORAGE
UP
BONUS RM. 19/6 X 20/6
STORAGE/GAMES
GARAGE 32/10 X 25/10

LOWER LEVEL
No. 91562

LINEN
BR. 2 12/0 X 13/0
WINDOW SEAT
DN.
BR. 3 12/0 X 11/0
WINDOW SEAT
OPEN TO BELOW
MASTER 16/6 X 14/8
(10'-1" CLG.)

SECOND FLOOR

Beautiful Balconies

- This plan features:
- — Three bedrooms
- — Two full and one half baths
- Entrance into formal Dining and Living Rooms defined by columns
- Vaulted Living Room enhanced by French doors
- Elegant ceiling tops decorative window in Dining Room
- Kitchen has a cooktop island/snack bar
- Corner fireplace and a triple window accent the Family Room
- Corner Master Bedroom has decorative ceiling and Dressing Area
- No materials list is available for this plan

FIRST FLOOR — 1,989 SQ. FT.
SECOND FLOOR — 1,349 SQ. FT.
LOWER LEVEL — 105 SQ. FT.
BONUS ROOM — 487 SQ. FT.

TOTAL LIVING AREA:
3,443 SQ. FT.

PLAN NO. 93200

Design by
Jannis Vann & Associates, Inc.

Refer to **Pricing Schedule F** on the order form for pricing information

A Country Estate

- This plan features:
  - — Four bedrooms
  - — Four full and one half baths
- A gorgeous two-story Foyer
- A formal Living Room and Dining Room located at opposite sides of the Foyer
- The Guest Room is equipped with a full bath
- A Library is tucked into a corner for quiet study
- The sunken Family Room is highlighted by a fireplace
- The Breakfast Room is warmed by a see-through fireplace
- A gourmet Kitchen has two built-in pantries
- The second floor Master Suite is enhanced by a decorative ceiling
- No materials list is available for this plan

FIRST FLOOR — 3,199 SQ. FT.
SECOND FLOOR — 2,531 SQ. FT.
BASEMENT — 3,199 SQ. FT.
GARAGE — 748 SQ. FT.

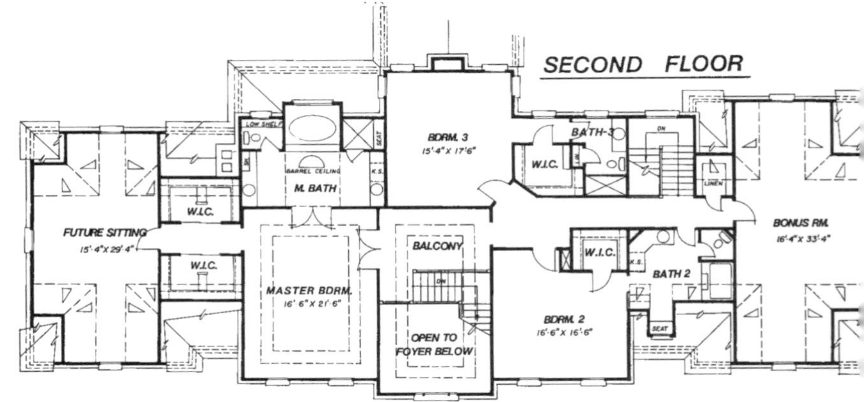
SECOND FLOOR
BDRM. 3
15'4" X 17'6"
BATH-3
W.I.C.
M. BATH
FUTURE SITTING
15'4"X 29'4"
W.I.C.
W.I.C.
BALCONY
MASTER BDRM.
16'6" X 21'6"
OPEN TO FOYER BELOW
BDRM. 2
16'6" X 16'6"
W.I.C.
BATH 2
BONUS RM.
16'4" X 33'4"

TOTAL LIVING AREA:
5,730 SQ. FT.

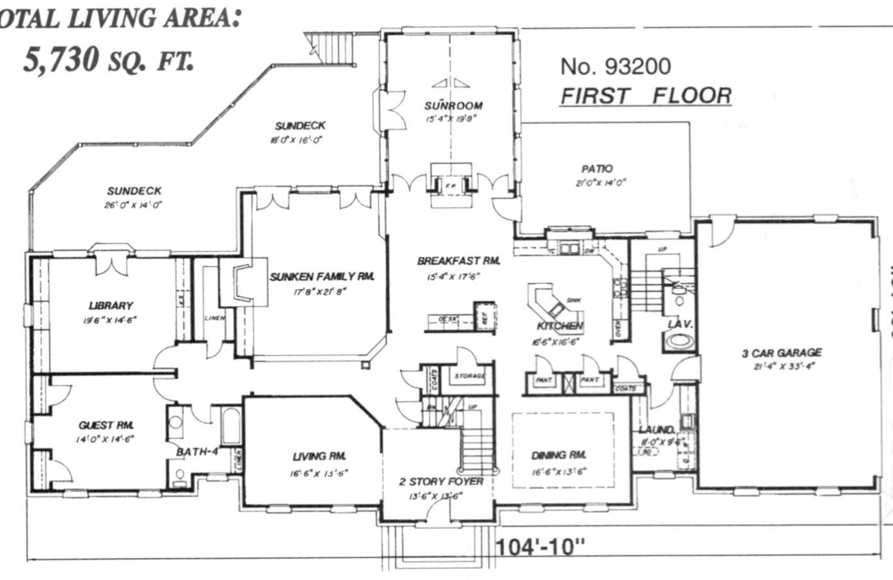
No. 93200
FIRST FLOOR
SUNROOM
15'4" X 19'8"
SUNDECK
18'0" X 16'0"
SUNDECK
26'0" X 14'0"
PATIO
21'0" X 14'0"
LIBRARY
19'6" X 14'6"
SUNKEN FAMILY RM.
17'8" X 21'8"
BREAKFAST RM.
15'4" X 17'6"
KITCHEN
16'6" X 16'6"
LAV.
3 CAR GARAGE
21'4" X 33'4"
GUEST RM.
14'0" X 14'6"
BATH-4
LIVING RM.
16'6" X 13'6"
2 STORY FOYER
13'6" X 13'6"
DINING RM.
16'6" X 13'6"
LAUND.
104'-10"

Refer to **Pricing Schedule D** on the order form for pricing information

Design by
Alan Mascord & Associates

PLAN NO. 91518

◄ 63' ►

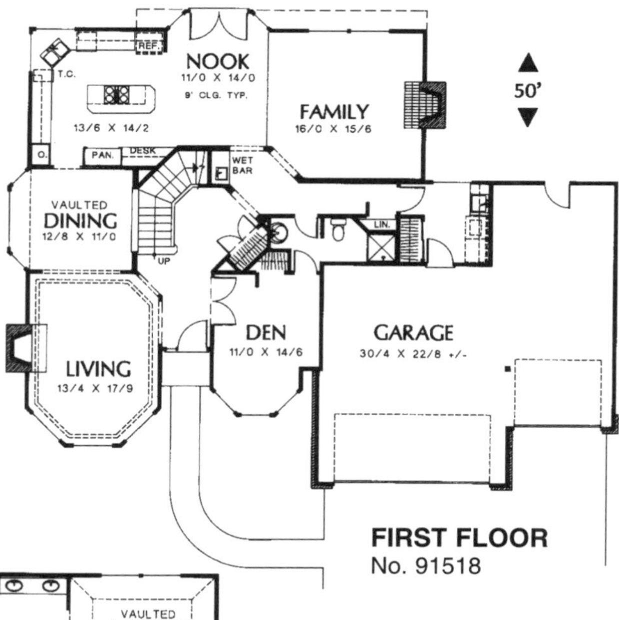
NOOK
11/0 X 14/0
9' CLG. TYP.
13/6 X 14/2
FAMILY
16/0 X 15/6
50'
REF.
T.C.
PAN.
DESK
WET BAR
VAULTED
DINING
12/8 X 11/0
UP
LIN.
DEN
11/0 X 14/6
GARAGE
30/4 X 22/8 +/-
LIVING
13/4 X 17/9

FIRST FLOOR
No. 91518

SPA
VAULTED
MASTER
15/0 X 16/0
DN.
DINING RM. BELOW
FOYER BELOW
BONUS
11/10 X 13/4
BR. 3
11/0 X 14/8
BR. 2
10/0 X 12/2

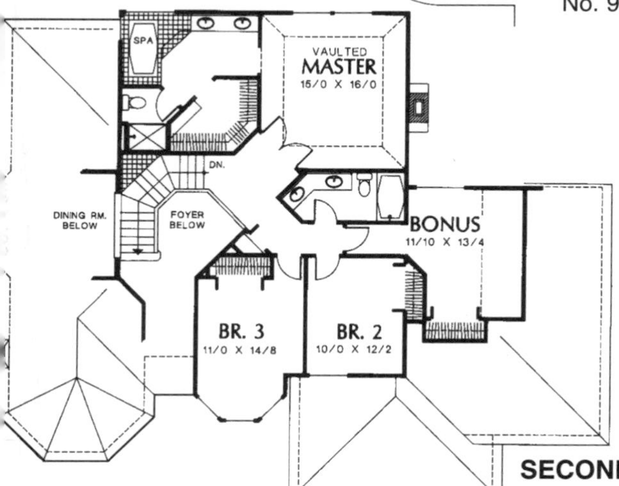

SECOND FLOOR

TOTAL LIVING AREA:
2,550 SQ. FT.

Eye-Catching Glass Turrets

- This plan features:
- — Three bedrooms
- — Three full baths
- Two-story Foyer with a curved staircase, opens to the Living Room with an inviting fireplace
- Alcove of glass and a vaulted ceiling in the open Dining Area
- Kitchen with built-in Pantry and desk, cooktop island/snackbar and a Nook
- Family Room highlighted by another fireplace and wonderful outdoor views
- Vaulted Master Suite offers a Dressing Area with walk-in closet and spa tub
- Bonus Room with a closet

FIRST FLOOR — 1,592 SQ. FT.
SECOND FLOOR — 958 SQ. FT.
BONUS ROOM — 194 SQ. FT.
GARAGE — 956 SQ. FT.

PLAN NO. 93239

Design by
Jannis Vann & Associates, Inc.

Refer to **Pricing Schedule E** on the order form for pricing information

Master Suite on the First Floor

- This plan features:
- — Four bedrooms
- — Two full and one half baths
- The first floor Master Suite is a private retreat
- This home has formal Living and Dining rooms located in the front of the home
- The large Family Room has a rear wall fireplace and accesses the Sun Deck
- Convenient appliance placement highlights the Kitchen
- No materials list is available for this plan
- An optional basement, slab or crawl space foundation — please specify when ordering

FIRST FLOOR — 1,719 SQ. FT.
SECOND FLOOR — 917 SQ. FT.
BONUS — 294 SQ. FT.
BASEMENT — 1,719 SQ. FT.
GARAGE — 614 SQ. FT.

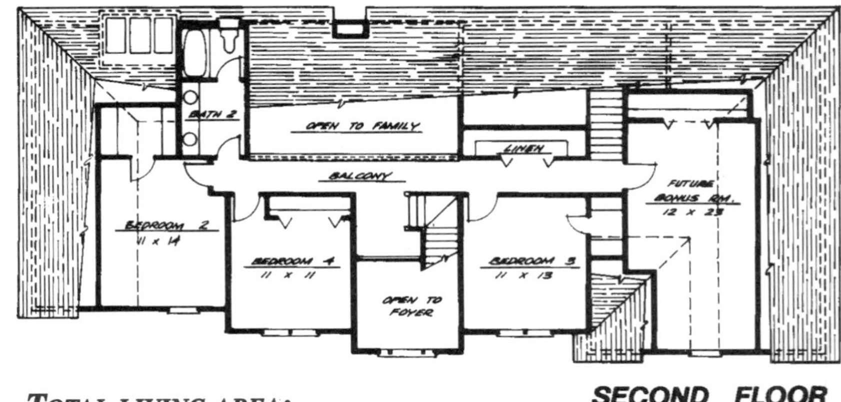
BATH 2
OPEN TO FAMILY
LINEN
BALCONY
FUTURE BONUS RM.
12 x 23
BEDROOM 2
11 x 14
BEDROOM 4
11 x 11
OPEN TO FOYER
BEDROOM 3
11 x 13

SECOND FLOOR

TOTAL LIVING AREA:
2,636 SQ. FT.

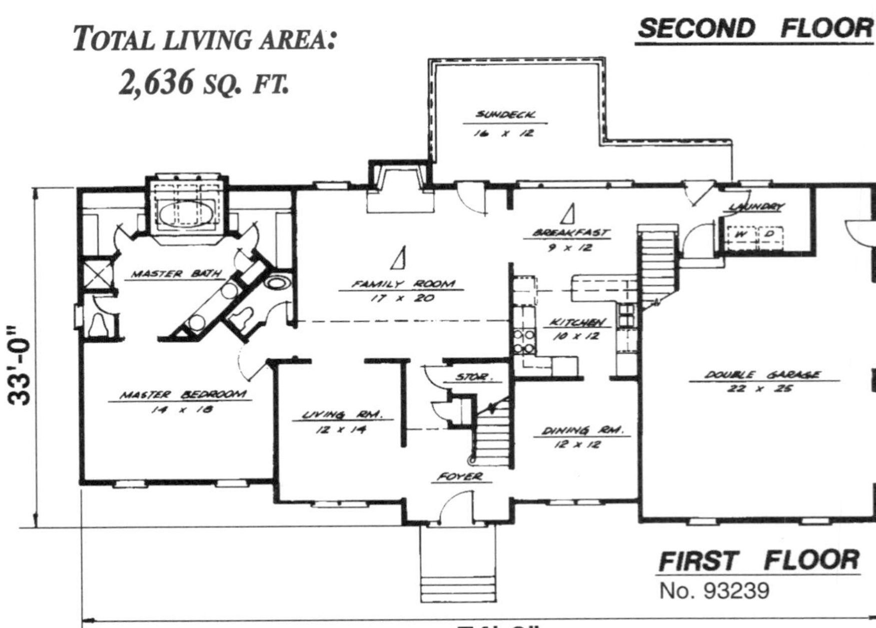
SUNDECK
16 x 12
LAUNDRY
BREAKFAST
9 x 12
MASTER BATH
FAMILY ROOM
17 x 20
KITCHEN
10 x 12
STOR.
DOUBLE GARAGE
22 x 25
MASTER BEDROOM
14 x 18
LIVING RM.
12 x 14
DINING RM.
12 x 12
FOYER
33'-0"
74'-0"

FIRST FLOOR
No. 93239

Refer to **Pricing Schedule F** on the order form for pricing information

Design by
Frank Betz Associates, Inc.

PLAN NO. 98405

55' - 0"

57' - 4"

Two Story Family Room 16^{0} x 19^{2} · FPL.
Breakfast · French Door
Storage
Kitchen · Surface Unit · Serving Bar · D.W. · Ref. · Pantry · Oven
Guest Bedroom/ Study 12^{1} x 12^{0}
Bath · Coats
Stairs Up · Stairs Dn. · Open Rail
3 Car Garage 20^{5} x 31^{6}
Dining Room 12^{0} x 13^{0}
Living Room 12^{1} x 13^{0}
Two Story Foyer

FIRST FLOOR

Radius Window · Radius Window
Family Room Below
Sitting Area
Tray Clg.
Master Suite 19^{6} x 15^{0}
Laundry · Sink · D. · W.
Bedroom 2 12^{1} x 12^{8}
Overlook · Overlook · Open Rail
W.i.c. · W.i.c. · Linen
French Doors
Shwr. · Vaulted M. Bath · VLT. · VLT. · K.S.
Radius Window
Bath · Stairs Dn.
Bedroom 4 12^{0} x 13^{0}
Foyer Below · 20'-6" High Clg.
Bedroom 3 12^{1} x 11^{9}
Plant Shelf
Linen
W.i.c.

SECOND FLOOR
No. 98405

Regal Residence

- This plan features:
  - — Five bedrooms
  - — Four full baths
- Keystone, arched windows accent entrance into two-story Foyer
- Family Room has a fireplace
- Convenient Kitchen with a cook-top island/serving bar walk-in Pantry and Breakfast Area
- First floor Guest Room/Study with roomy closet and adjoining to full Bath
- Luxurious Master Suite offers a tray ceiling, Sitting Area, a walk-in closet and a vaulted Bath
- An optional basement or crawl space foundation — please specify when ordering

FIRST FLOOR — 1,488 SQ. FT.
SECOND FLOOR — 1,551 SQ. FT.
BASEMENT — 1,488 SQ. FT.
GARAGE — 667 SQ. FT.

TOTAL LIVING AREA:
3,039 SQ. FT.

PLAN NO. 92048

Design by
Urban Design Group

Refer to **Pricing Schedule F** on the order form for pricing information

Unusual and Dramatic

- This plan features:
  - Four bedrooms
  - Three full and one half baths
- Elegant Entry with decorative windows, arched openings and a double curved staircase
- Cathedral ceilings crown arched windows in the Den and Living Room
- Spacious Family Room with a vaulted ceiling and a fireplace
- Hub Kitchen with a work island/serving counter
- Secluded Master Suite with a lovely bay window, two walk-in closets and a plush Bath
- Three second floor Bedrooms, one with a private Bath, offer ample closets

FIRST FLOOR — 2,646 SQ. FT.
SECOND FLOOR — 854 SQ. FT.
BASEMENT — 2,656 SQ. FT.

TOTAL LIVING AREA:
3,500 SQ. FT.

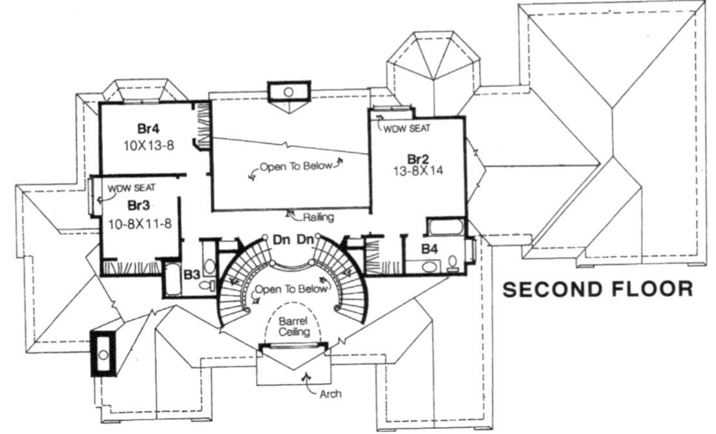
Br4
10X13-8
Open To Below
WDW SEAT
Br2
13-8X14
WDW SEAT
Br3
10-8X11-8
Railing
Dn Dn
B4
B3
Open To Below
Barrel Ceiling
Arch
SECOND FLOOR

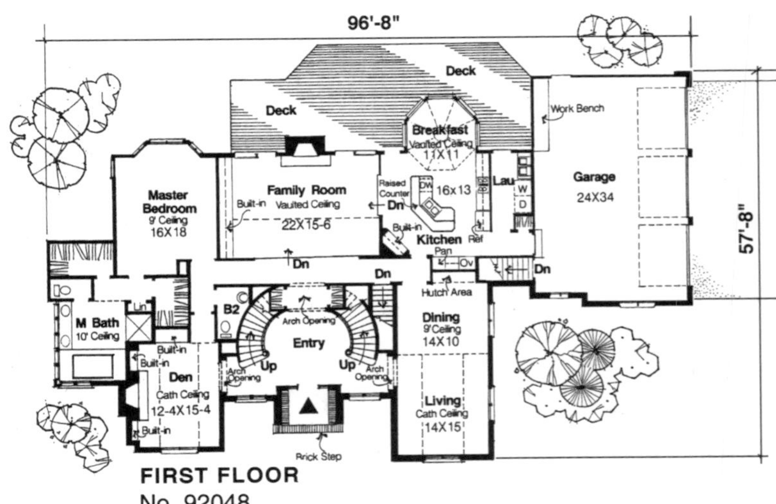
96'-8"
Deck
Deck
Work Bench
Breakfast
Vaulted Ceiling
11X11
Master Bedroom
9' Ceiling
16X18
Family Room
Vaulted Ceiling
22X15-6
Built-in
Raised Counter
16x13
Kitchen
Lau
Garage
24X34
57'-8"
Dn
Dn
Dn
Hutch Area
M Bath
10' Ceiling
B2
Arch Opening
Entry
Dining
9' Ceiling
14X10
Den
Cath Ceiling
12-4X15-4
Up
Up
Living
Cath Ceiling
14X15
Brick Step
FIRST FLOOR
No. 92048

To order your Blueprints, call 1-800-235-5700

Refer to **Pricing Schedule E** on the order form for pricing information

Design by
Ryan & Associates

PLAN NO. 91111

Grand Entrance

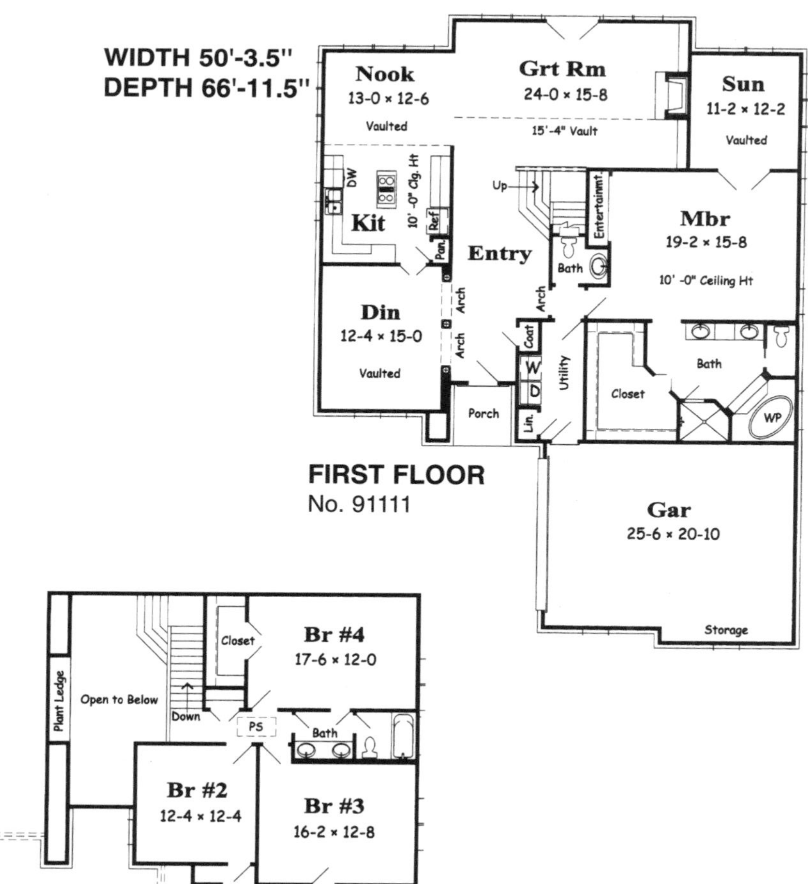

WIDTH 50'-3.5"
DEPTH 66'-11.5"
Nook
13-0 × 12-6
Vaulted
Grt Rm
24-0 × 15-8
15'-4" Vault
Sun
11-2 × 12-2
Vaulted
DW
Kit
10' -0" Clg. Ht
Ref
Pan
Up
Entertainmt
Entry
Bath
Mbr
19-2 × 15-8
10' -0" Ceiling Ht
Din
12-4 × 15-0
Vaulted
Arch
Arch
Arch
Coat
W
D
Utility
Closet
Bath
WP
Porch
Lin.
FIRST FLOOR
No. 91111
Gar
25-6 × 20-10
Storage
Plant Ledge
Open to Below
Closet
Br #4
17-6 × 12-0
Down
PS
Bath
Br #2
12-4 × 12-4
Br #3
16-2 × 12-8
Closet
Closet
SECOND FLOOR

- This plan features:
  - — Four bedrooms
  - — Two full and one half baths
- Dramatic roof lines and a seven-foot tall arched transom above the front door
- Columns, arches, angled stairs and a high ceiling in the Foyer
- Vaulted ceilings and an abundance of windows in the Sun Room, Breakfast Nook and Living Room
- The Master Bedroom has a lavish whirlpool Bath
- Each additional Bedroom features large closets and easy access to a full Bath
- No materials list is available for this plan

FIRST FLOOR — 2,123 SQ. FT.
SECOND FLOOR — 911 SQ. FT.
GARAGE & STORAGE — 565 SQ. FT.

TOTAL LIVING AREA:
3,034 SQ. FT.

PLAN NO. 96500

Design by
Vaughn A. Lauban Designs

Refer to **Pricing Schedule E** on the order form for pricing information

Friendly Front Porch

- This plan features:
- — Three bedrooms
- — Two full and one half baths
- Wrap-around front Porch and double French doors are an inviting sight
- Central Foyer with a lovely landing staircase opens to the Dining and Great rooms
- The fireplace is framed by a built-in credenza in the Great Room
- Kitchen boasts a buffet, Pantry and a peninsula counter/snack bar
- Master Bedroom offers direct access to the Sun Room, a walk-in closet and a luxurious Bath

FIRST FLOOR — 2,361 SQ. FT.
SECOND FLOOR — 650 SQ. FT.
DETACHED CARPORT/WORK SHOP — 864 SQ. FT.

TOTAL LIVING AREA:
3,011 SQ. FT.

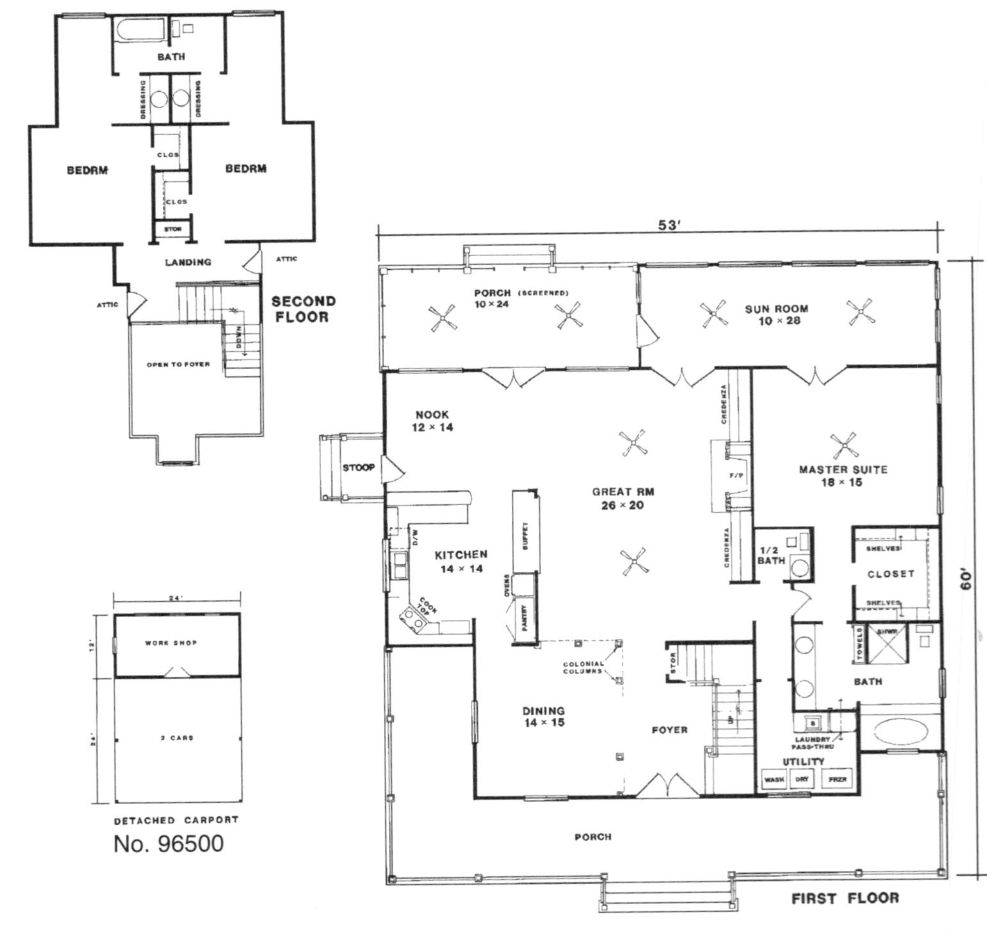

BATH
DRESSING
DRESSING
BEDRM
BEDRM
CLOS
CLOS
STOR
LANDING
ATTIC
ATTIC
DOWN
OPEN TO FOYER
SECOND FLOOR
53'
PORCH (SCREENED) 10 × 24
SUN ROOM 10 × 28
NOOK 12 × 14
STOOP
GREAT RM 26 × 20
CREDENZA
F/P
CREDENZA
MASTER SUITE 18 × 15
KITCHEN 14 × 14
D/W
BUFFET
COOK TOP
OVENS
PANTRY
1/2 BATH
SHELVES
CLOSET
SHELVES
TOWELS
SHWR
BATH
60'
COLONIAL COLUMNS
STOR
DINING 14 × 15
FOYER
LAUNDRY PASS-THRU
UTILITY
WASH
DRY
FRZR
PORCH
FIRST FLOOR
24'
12'
WORK SHOP
24'
2 CARS
DETACHED CARPORT

No. 96500

Refer to **Pricing Schedule E** on the order form for pricing information

Design by
James Fahy, P.E., P.C.

PLAN NO. 94112

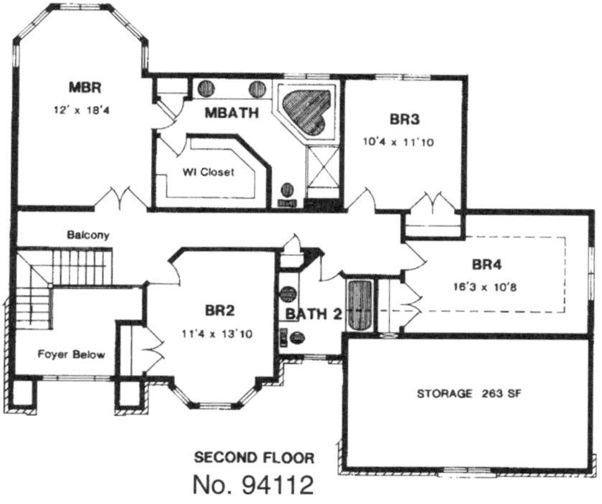

MBR
12' x 18'4
MBATH
WI Closet
BR3
10'4 x 11'10
Balcony
BR4
16'3 x 10'8
BR2
11'4 x 13'10
BATH 2
Foyer Below
STORAGE 263 SF

SECOND FLOOR
No. 94112

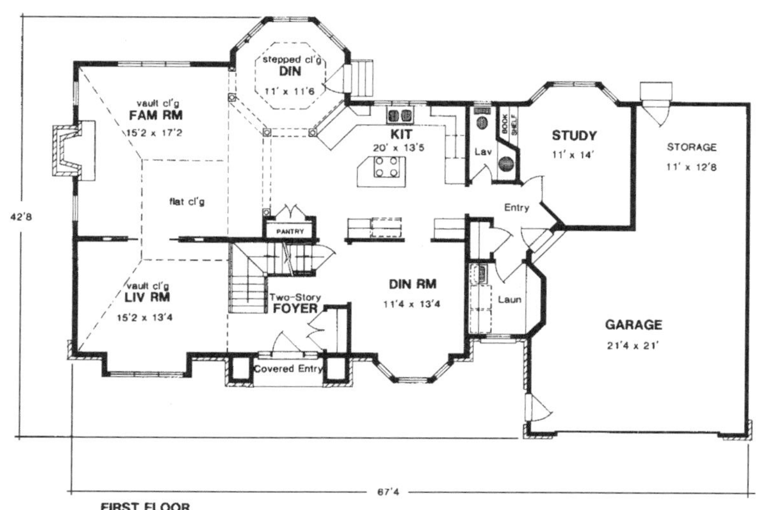

stepped cl'g
DIN
11' x 11'6
vault cl'g
FAM RM
15'2 x 17'2
KIT
20' x 13'5
Lav
STUDY
11' x 14'
STORAGE
11' x 12'8
flat cl'g
42'8
Entry
PANTRY
vault cl'g
LIV RM
15'2 x 13'4
Two-Story
FOYER
DIN RM
11'4 x 13'4
Laun
GARAGE
21'4 x 21'
Covered Entry
67'4

FIRST FLOOR

Distinguished Dwelling

- This plan features:
- — Four bedrooms
- — Two full and one half baths
- Grand two-story Entry into Foyer
- Formal Living Room with a decorative window and a vaulted ceiling
- Beautiful bay window highlights formal Dining Room
- Kitchen with cooktop work island, Pantry, octagon Dining Area, and nearby Study
- Luxurious Master Bedroom offers a Bath with a corner tub
- No materials list is available for this plan

FIRST FLOOR — 1,514 SQ. FT.
SECOND FLOOR — 1,219 SQ. FT.
BASEMENT — 1,465 SQ. FT.
GARAGE — 596 SQ. FT.

TOTAL LIVING AREA:
2,733 SQ. FT.

PLAN NO. 94973

Design by
Design Basics, Inc.

Bricks and Arches Detail this Ranch

Price Code: D

- This plan features:
- — Two bedrooms
- — Two full and one half baths
- A Master Bedroom with a vaulted ceiling and luxurious Bath
- A second bedroom shares a full Bath with the Den/optional Bedroom, which has built-in curio cabinets
- Columns and arched windows define the elegant Dining Room
- The Great Room shares a see-through fireplace with the Hearth Room
- The gazebo-shaped Nook opens into the Kitchen with a center island, snack bar and desk

MAIN FLOOR — 2,512 SQ. FT.
GARAGE — 783 SQ. FT.

TOTAL LIVING AREA:
2,512 SQ. FT.

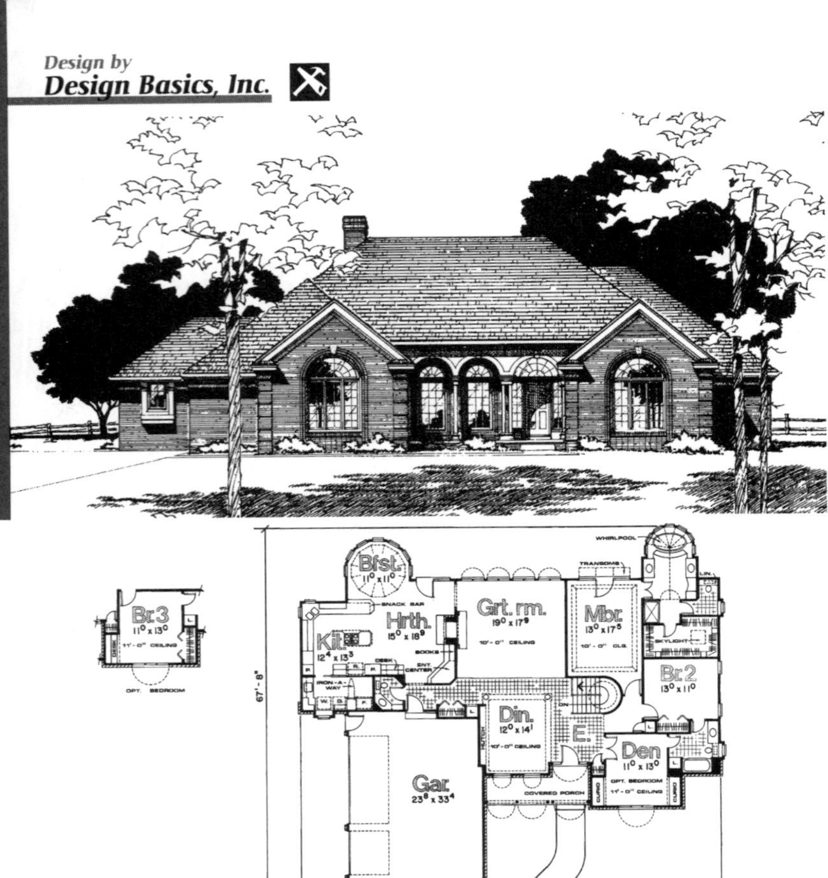
Bfst.
Hrth.
Grt. rm.
Mbr.
Kit.
Br.2
Din.
E.
Den
Gar.
Br.3
74' - 0"
67' - 8"

© design basics, inc.

MAIN AREA

PLAN NO. 10595

Design by
The Garlinghouse Company

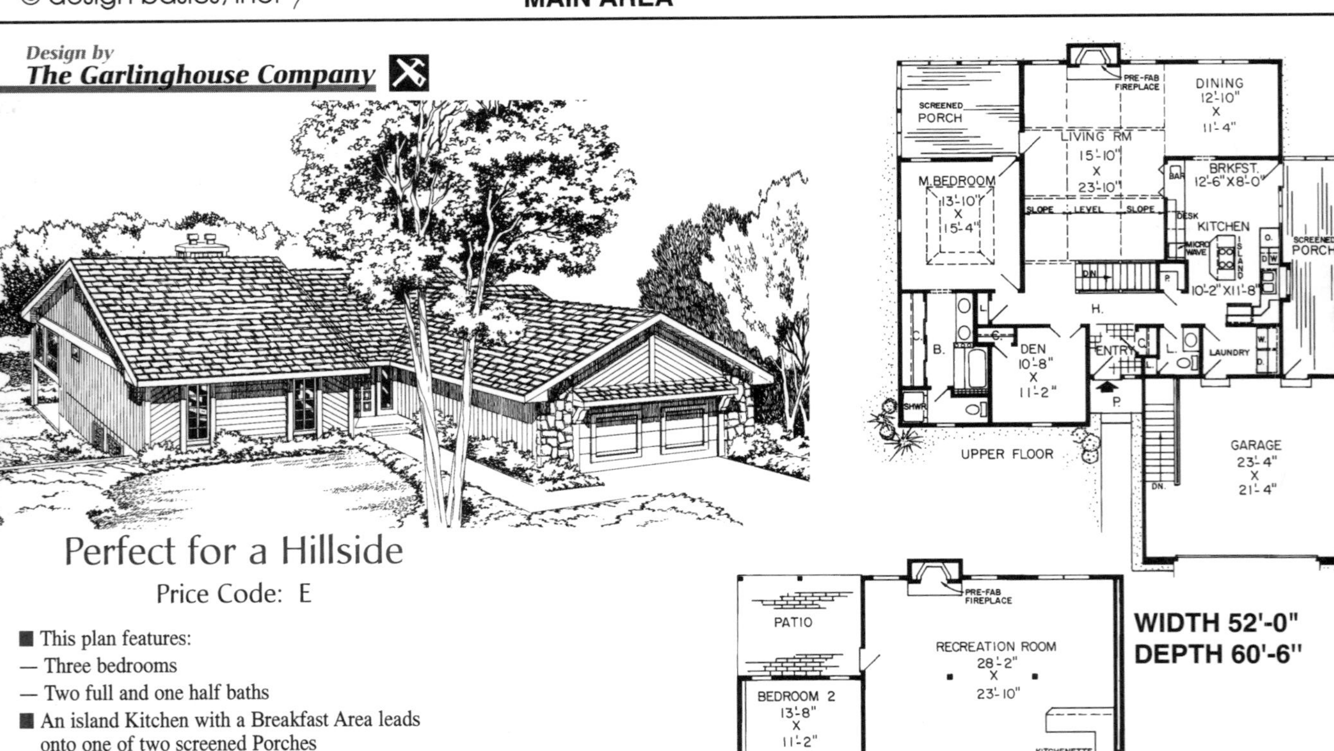
SCREENED PORCH
PRE-FAB FIREPLACE
DINING 12'-10" X 11'-4"
LIVING RM 15'-10" X 23'-10"
M.BEDROOM 13'-10" X 15'-4"
BRKFST. 12'-6"X8'-0"
KITCHEN 10'-2"X11'-8"
DEN 10'-8" X 11'-2"
ENTRY
LAUNDRY
UPPER FLOOR
GARAGE 23'-4" X 21'-4"
PATIO
RECREATION ROOM 28'-2" X 23'-10"
BEDROOM 2 13'-8" X 11'-2"
KITCHENETTE 9'-2" X 12'-0"
STORAGE
MECHANICAL/STOR.
BEDROOM 3 13'-4" X 10'-6"
UP TO GARAGE
LOWER LEVEL

Perfect for a Hillside

Price Code: E

- This plan features:
- — Three bedrooms
- — Two full and one half baths
- An island Kitchen with a Breakfast Area leads onto one of two screened Porches
- A huge Recreation Room with a Kitchenette and a fireplace
- A sloping ceiling and fireplace in the Living Room
- A central staircase directs traffic to all areas of the house

UPPER FLOOR — 1,643 SQ. FT.
LOWER LEVEL — 1,297 SQ. FT.
GARAGE — 528 SQ. FT.

TOTAL LIVING AREA:
2,940 SQ. FT.

WIDTH 52'-0"
DEPTH 60'-6"

Refer to **Pricing Schedule E** on the order form for pricing information

Design by
Northwest Home Designs

PLAN NO. 92156

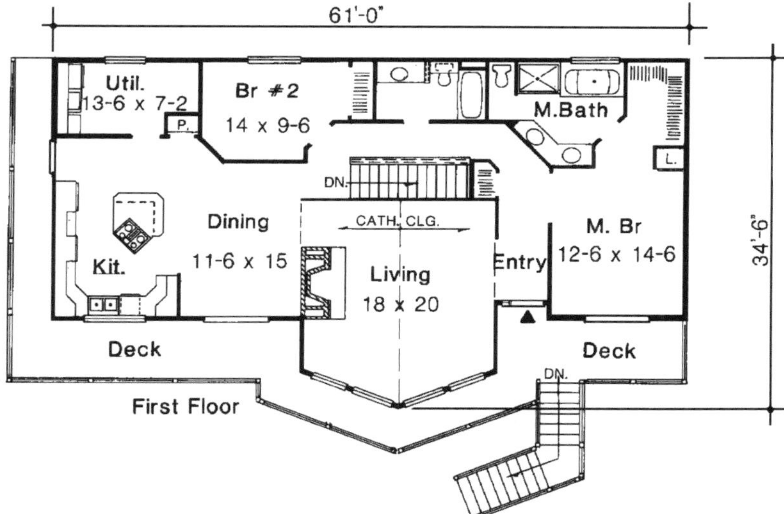

61'-0"
Util.
13-6 x 7-2
P.
Br #2
14 x 9-6
M.Bath
L.
DN.
CATH. CLG.
Dining
11-6 x 15
Kit.
Living
18 x 20
Entry
M. Br
12-6 x 14-6
34'-6"
Deck
Deck
DN.
First Floor

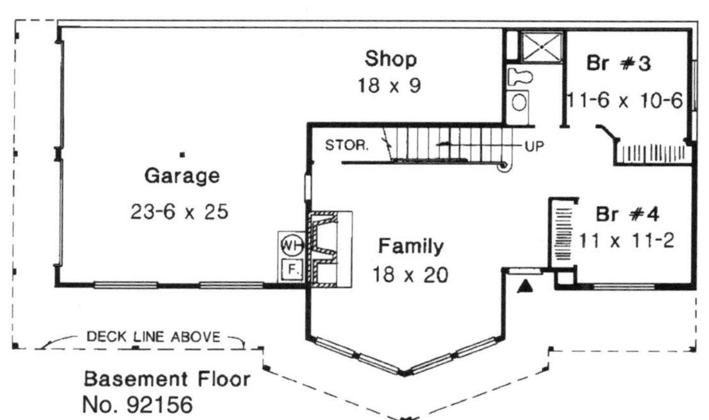

Shop
18 x 9
Br #3
11-6 x 10-6
STOR.
UP
Garage
23-6 x 25
WH
F.
Family
18 x 20
Br #4
11 x 11-2
DECK LINE ABOVE
Basement Floor
No. 92156

Spectacular Views

- This plan features:
- — Four Bedrooms
- — Two full and one three-quarter baths
- Creates an indoor/outdoor relationship with terrific Decks and large glass expanses
- Family Room and Living Room enjoy highly glassed walls taking in the vistas
- Living Room enhanced by a cathedral ceiling and a warm fireplace
- Kitchen has an open layout and highlighted by a center cooktop island/snack bar
- Two additional Bedrooms, a three-quarter Bath and a Family Room complete the basement

FIRST FLOOR — 1,707 SQ. FT.
BASEMENT — 901 SQ. FT.

TOTAL LIVING AREA:
2,608 SQ. FT.

PLAN NO.97206

Design by
Frank Betz Associates, Inc.

Refer to **Pricing Schedule E** on the order form for pricing information

Refinement with Brilliancy

- This plan features:
  - — Four bedrooms
  - — Three full baths
- Two-story foyer dominated by an open rail staircase
- Family Room enhanced by a fireplace
- Walk-in Pantry and ample counter space
- Secluded Study easily becoming an additional Bedroom
- Second floor Master Suite with tray ceiling and bayed Sitting Area
- An optional basement, crawl space or slab foundation — please specify when ordering
- No material list is available for this plan

First floor — 1,548 sq. ft.
Second floor — 1,164 sq. ft.
Bonus — 198 sq. ft.
Basement — 1,548 sq. ft.
Garage — 542 sq. ft.

Total living area:* 2,712 *sq. ft.

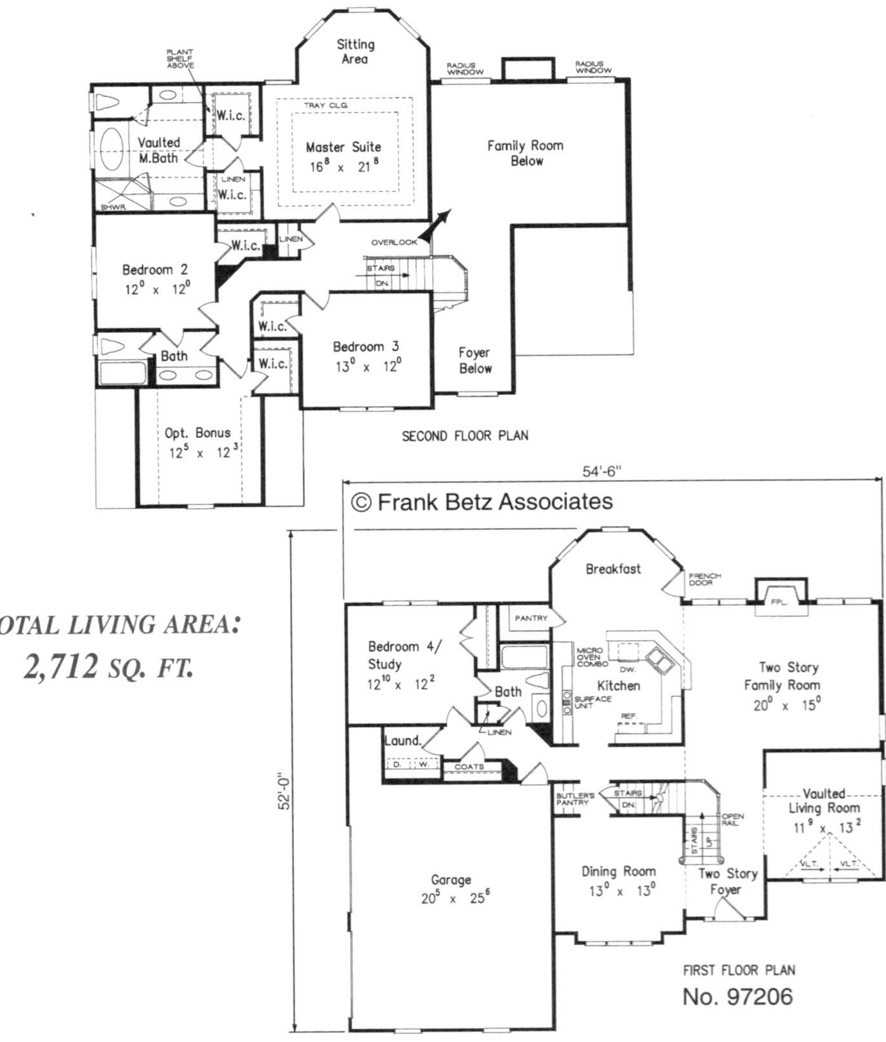

Sitting Area
PLANT SHELF ABOVE
RADIUS WINDOW
RADIUS WINDOW
TRAY CLG.
Master Suite 16^{8} x 21^{8}
W.i.c.
Vaulted M.Bath
LINEN
W.i.c.
SHWR.
Family Room Below
W.i.c.
LINEN
OVERLOOK
STAIRS DN.
Bedroom 2 12^{0} x 12^{0}
W.i.c.
Bath
W.i.c.
Bedroom 3 13^{0} x 12^{0}
Foyer Below
Opt. Bonus 12^{5} x 12^{3}
SECOND FLOOR PLAN
54'-6"
© Frank Betz Associates
Breakfast
FRENCH DOOR
FPL.
PANTRY
Bedroom 4/ Study 12^{10} x 12^{2}
MICRO OVEN COMBO
DW.
Kitchen
SURFACE UNIT
REF.
Two Story Family Room 20^{0} x 15^{0}
Bath
LINEN
Laund.
D. W.
COATS
BUTLER'S PANTRY
STAIRS DN.
OPEN RAIL
STAIRS UP
Vaulted Living Room 11^{9} x 13^{2}
VLT.
VLT.
52'-0"
Garage 20^{5} x 25^{6}
Dining Room 13^{0} x 13^{0}
Two Story Foyer
FIRST FLOOR PLAN
No. 97206

Refer to **Pricing Schedule E** on the order form for pricing information

Design by
Larry E. Belk

PLAN NO. 93034

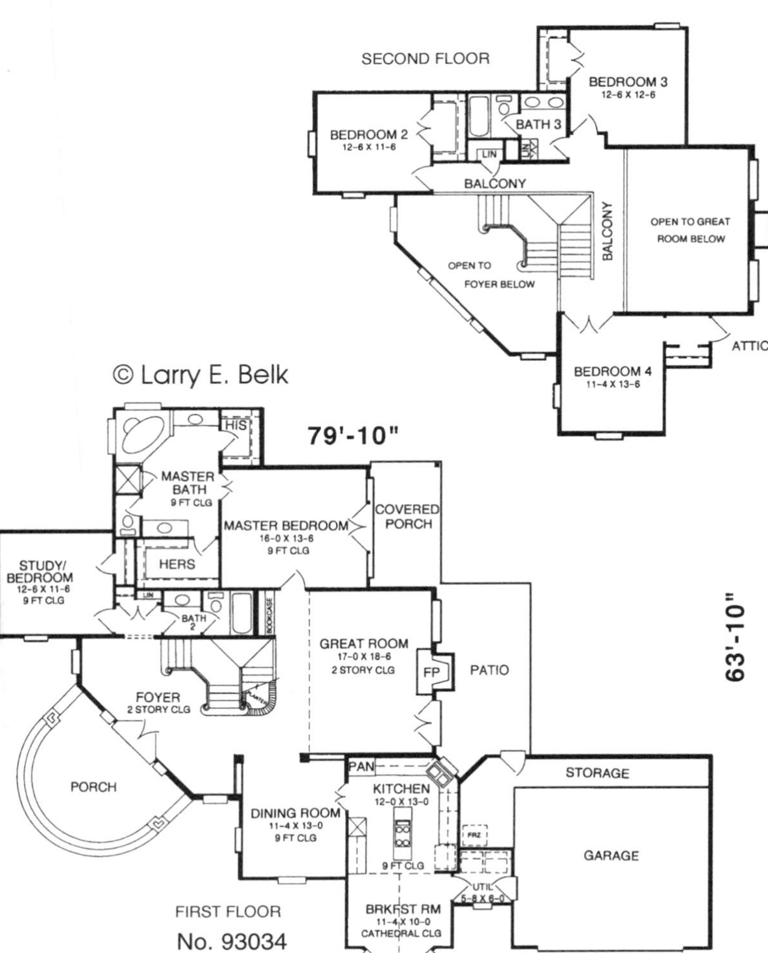

SECOND FLOOR
BEDROOM 3
12-6 X 12-6
BEDROOM 2
12-6 X 11-6
BATH 3
LIN
BALCONY
OPEN TO GREAT ROOM BELOW
OPEN TO FOYER BELOW
ATTIC
BEDROOM 4
11-4 X 13-6
© Larry E. Belk
79'-10"
63'-10"
HIS
MASTER BATH
9 FT CLG
MASTER BEDROOM
16-0 X 13-6
9 FT CLG
COVERED PORCH
STUDY/ BEDROOM
12-6 X 11-6
9 FT CLG
HERS
BATH 2
GREAT ROOM
17-0 X 18-6
2 STORY CLG
FP
PATIO
FOYER
2 STORY CLG
PORCH
PAN
KITCHEN
12-0 X 13-0
STORAGE
DINING ROOM
11-4 X 13-0
9 FT CLG
9 FT CLG
GARAGE
UTIL
5-8 X 6-0
BRKFST RM
11-4 X 10-0
CATHEDRAL CLG
FIRST FLOOR
No. 93034

Towering Windows Enhance Elegance

- This plan features:
  - — Four bedrooms
  - — Three full baths
- Designed for a corner or pie-shaped lot
- Split staircase highlights Foyer
- Expansive Great Room with hearth fireplace
- Study easily another Bedroom or Home Office
- Secluded Master Bedroom has a private Porch, dual vanity, and a corner whirlpool tub
- Three second floor Bedrooms share a balcony and a double vanity Bath
- No materials list is available for this plan

FIRST FLOOR — 1,966 SQ. FT.
SECOND FLOOR — 872 SQ. FT.
GARAGE — 569 SQ. FT.

TOTAL LIVING AREA:
2,838 SQ. FT.

PLAN NO. 98494

Design by
Frank Betz Associates, Inc.

Refer to **Pricing Schedule D** on the order form for pricing information

It's All in the Details

- This plan features:
  — Four bedrooms
  — Three full baths
- The exterior is appointed with keystones, arches and shutters
- The Living Room and Dining Room meet through an arched opening
- The Kitchen, Breakfast and Family Room are open to each other
- Master Suite has a tray ceiling in the bedroom and a vaulted ceiling in the Master Bath
- An optional basement or crawl space foundation — please specify when ordering
- No materials list is available for this plan

FIRST FLOOR — 1,447 SQ. FT.
SECOND FLOOR — 1,325 SQ. FT.
BONUS — 301 SQ. FT.
BASEMENT — 1,447 SQ. FT.
GARAGE — 393 SQ. FT.

TOTAL LIVING AREA:
2,772 SQ. FT.

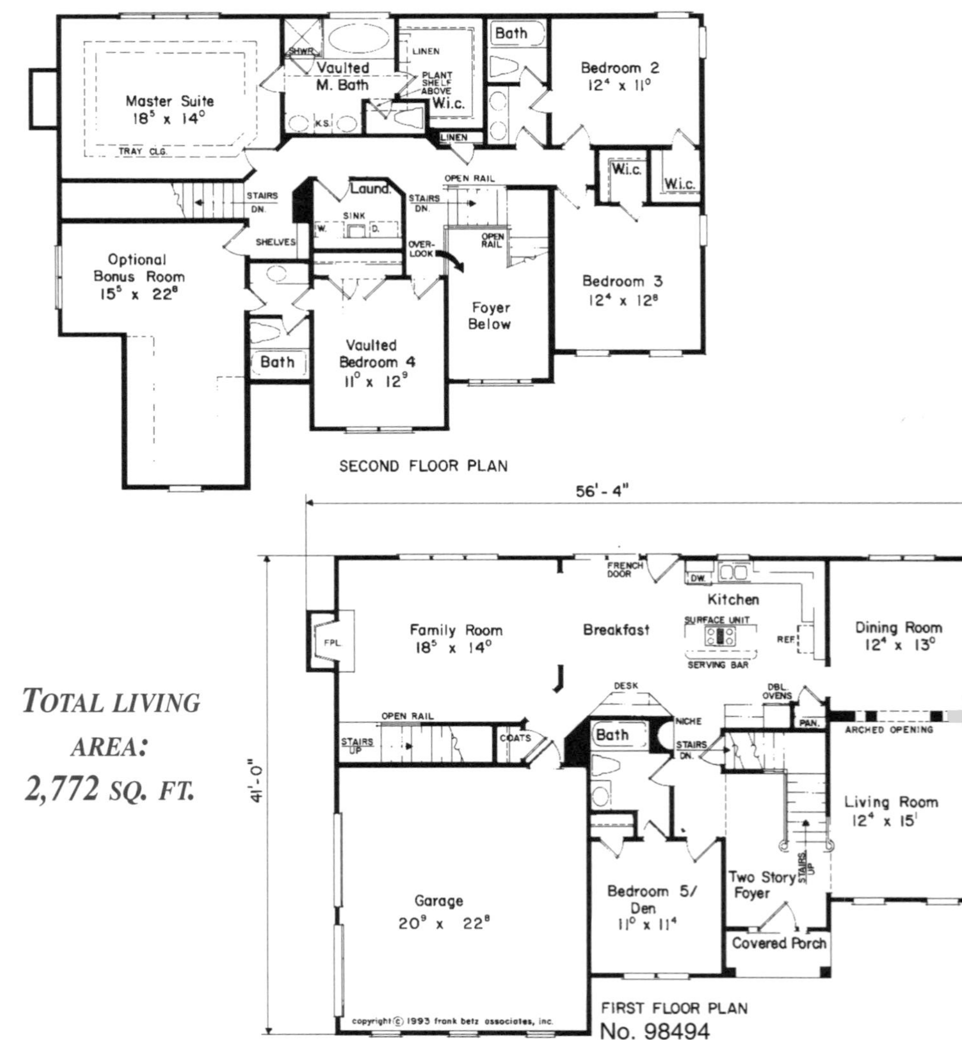

Master Suite
18⁵ x 14⁰
TRAY CLG.
SHWR.
Vaulted
M. Bath
K.S.
LINEN
PLANT SHELF ABOVE
W.i.c.
LINEN
Bath
Bedroom 2
12⁴ x 11⁰
W.i.c.
W.i.c.
STAIRS DN.
Laund.
SINK
W.
D.
SHELVES
STAIRS DN
OPEN RAIL
OVER-LOOK
OPEN RAIL
Optional
Bonus Room
15⁵ x 22⁸
Foyer
Below
Bedroom 3
12⁴ x 12⁸
Bath
Vaulted
Bedroom 4
11⁰ x 12⁹
SECOND FLOOR PLAN
56'- 4"
41'-0"
FRENCH DOOR
DW.
Kitchen
FPL.
Family Room
18⁵ x 14⁰
Breakfast
SURFACE UNIT
SERVING BAR
REF.
Dining Room
12⁴ x 13⁰
DESK
DBL. OVENS
PAN.
OPEN RAIL
STAIRS UP
COATS
Bath
NICHE
STAIRS DN.
ARCHED OPENING
Living Room
12⁴ x 15¹
Garage
20⁹ x 22⁸
Bedroom 5/
Den
11⁰ x 11⁴
Two Story
Foyer
STAIRS UP
Covered Porch
copyright © 1993 frank betz associates, inc.
FIRST FLOOR PLAN
No. 98494

Refer to **Pricing Schedule E** on
he order form for pricing information

Design by
Ahmann Design, Inc.

PLAN NO. 99118

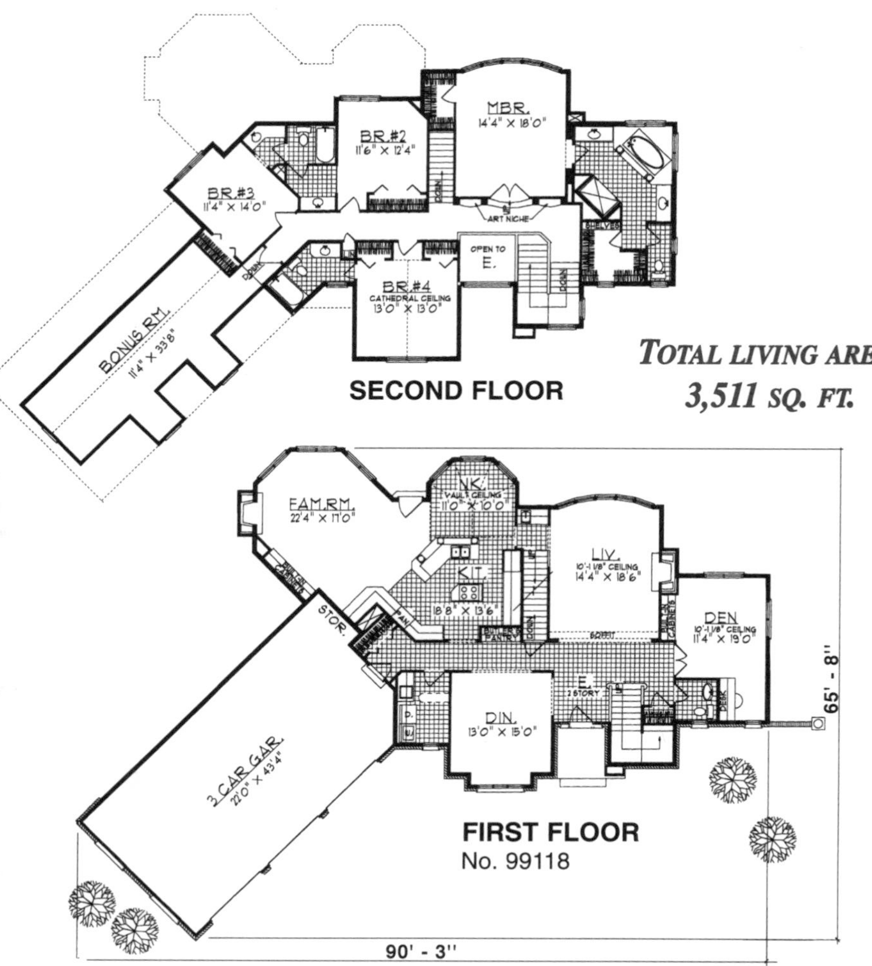

MBR.
14'4" X 18'0"
BR.#2
11'6" X 12'4"
BR.#3
11'4" X 14'0"
BR.#4
CATHEDRAL CEILING
13'0" X 13'0"
OPEN TO
E.
ART NICHE
BONUS RM.
11'4" X 33'8"
SECOND FLOOR
FAM.RM.
22'4" X 17'0"
NK.
VAULT. CEILING
11'0" X 10'0"
KIT.
18'8" X 13'6"
LIV.
10'-1 1/8" CEILING
14'4" X 18'6"
DEN
10'-1 1/8" CEILING
11'4" X 13'0"
DIN.
13'0" X 15'0"
E.
2 STORY
STOR.
3 CAR GAR.
22'0" X 43'4"
FIRST FLOOR
No. 99118
90' - 3"
65' - 8"

Total living area:
3,511 sq. ft.

Lots of Extras

- This plan features:
  - — Four bedrooms
  - — Three full and one half baths
- Enter the Master Bedroom through French doors
- Access the bonus room over the three-car Garage
- The Family Room has a fireplace and built-in cabinets
- The Kitchen has ample counter space, a Pantry and a center island
- The Den has a built-in desk and cabinets
- No materials list is available for this plan

FIRST FLOOR — 1,931 SQ. FT.
SECOND FLOOR — 1,580 SQ. FT.
BONUS — 439 SQ. FT.
BASEMENT — 1,931 SQ. FT.

This plan is not to be built within a 75 mile radius of Cedar Rapids, IA.

PLAN NO. 98419

Design by
Frank Betz Associates, Inc.

Refer to **Pricing Schedule E** on the order form for pricing information

Stucco & Stone

- This plan features:
  - — Three bedrooms
  - — Two full and one half baths
- Decorative columns define the Dining Room
- A built-in Pantry and a radius window in the Kitchen
- A tray ceiling over the Master Bedroom and a vaulted ceiling in the Bath
- An optional basement, crawl space or slab foundation — please specify when ordering
- No material list is available for this plan

FIRST FLOOR — 1,796 SQ. FT.
SECOND FLOOR — 629 SQ. FT.
BONUS ROOM — 208 SQ. FT.
BASEMENT — 1,796 SQ. FT.
GARAGE — 588 SQ. FT.

TOTAL LIVING AREA:
2,425 SQ. FT.

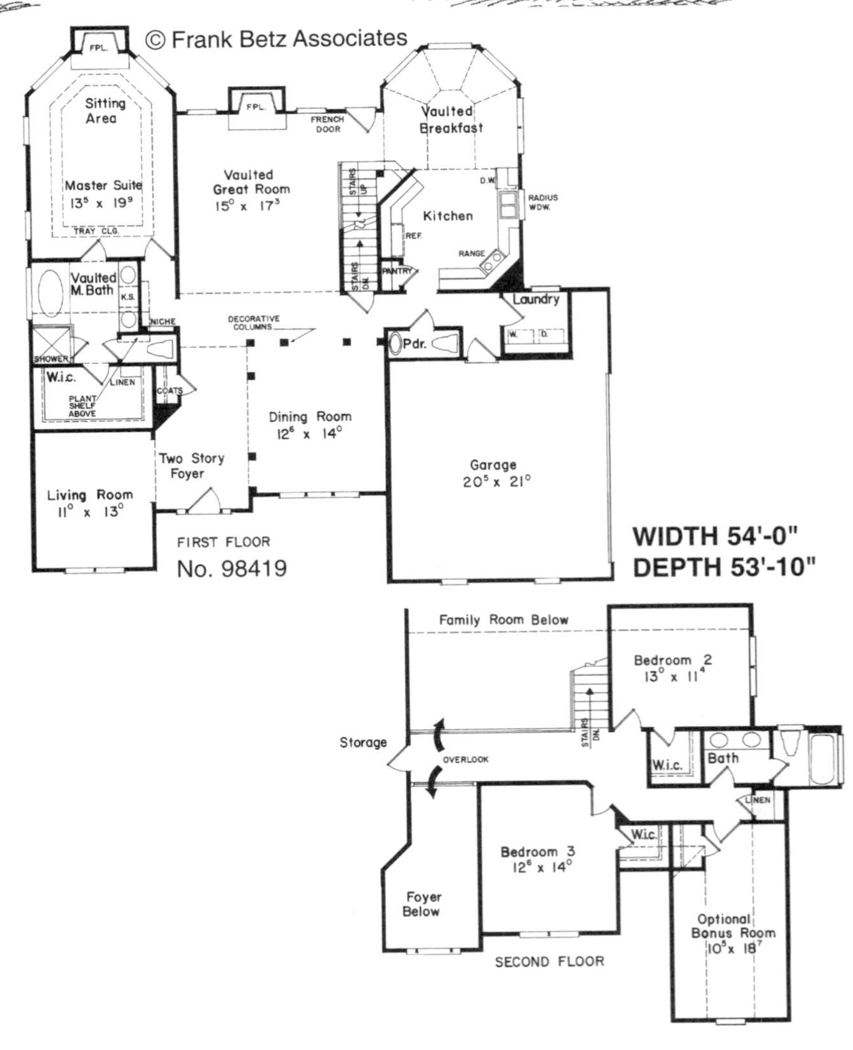
© Frank Betz Associates
FPL.
Sitting Area
Master Suite 13^5 x 19^9
TRAY CLG.
FPL.
FRENCH DOOR
Vaulted Great Room 15^0 x 17^3
Vaulted Breakfast
Kitchen
D.W.
RADIUS WDW.
REF.
RANGE
PANTRY
STAIRS UP
STAIRS DN.
Vaulted M.Bath
K.S.
NICHE
DECORATIVE COLUMNS
Laundry
Pdr.
SHOWER
W.i.c.
LINEN
PLANT SHELF ABOVE
COATS
Dining Room 12^6 x 14^0
Garage 20^5 x 21^0
Two Story Foyer
Living Room 11^0 x 13^0
FIRST FLOOR
No. 98419
WIDTH 54'-0"
DEPTH 53'-10"
Family Room Below
Bedroom 2 13^0 x 11^4
Storage
OVERLOOK
STAIRS DN.
W.i.c.
Bath
LINEN
W.i.c.
Bedroom 3 12^6 x 14^0
Foyer Below
Optional Bonus Room 10^5 x 18^7
SECOND FLOOR

Refer to **Pricing Schedule F** on the order form for pricing information

Design by
Jannis Vann & Associates, Inc.

PLAN NO. 93247

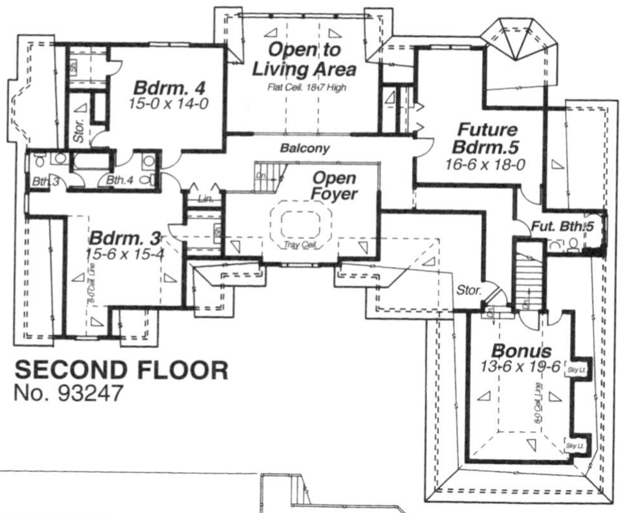

Open to Living Area
Flat Ceil. 18-7 High
Bdrm. 4
15-0 x 14-0
Stor.
Balcony
Future Bdrm.5
16-6 x 18-0
Bth.3
Bth.4
Lin.
Open Foyer
Tray Ceil.
Bdrm. 3
15-6 x 15-4
Fut. Bth.5
Stor.
Bonus
13-6 x 19-6

SECOND FLOOR
No. 93247

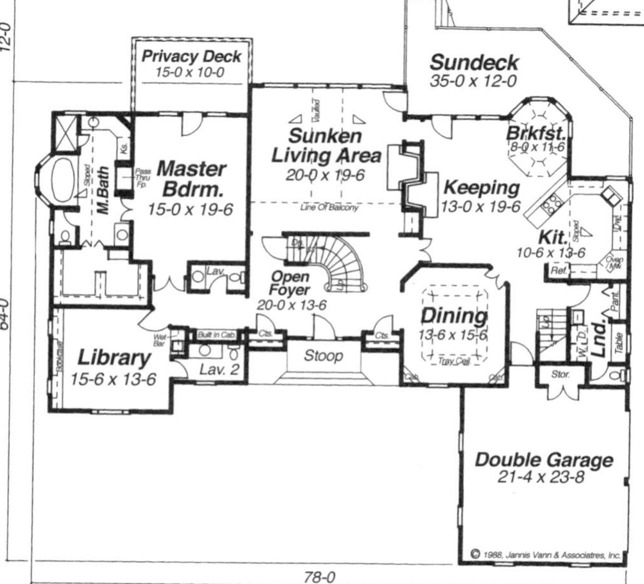

Privacy Deck
15-0 x 10-0
Sundeck
35-0 x 12-0
Sunken Living Area
20-0 x 19-6
Line Of Balcony
Brkfst.
8-0 x 11-6
Master Bdrm.
15-0 x 19-6
M.Bath
Keeping
13-0 x 19-6
Kit.
10-6 x 13-6
Lav.
Open Foyer
20-0 x 13-6
Dining
13-6 x 15-6
Tray Ceil.
Library
15-6 x 13-6
Lav. 2
Stoop
Lnd.
Stor.
Double Garage
21-4 x 23-8
© 1988, Jannis Vann & Associates, Inc.
12-0
64-0
78-0

FIRST FLOOR

Impressive Residence

- This plan features:
  - — Three bedrooms
  - — Two full and four half baths
- Grand entrance with two-story Foyer, curved staircase and Balcony
- Spacious Living Room with a vaulted ceiling above a wall of windows, Sundeck access and an inviting fireplace
- Kitchen with extended cooktop serving counter, octagon glass Breakfast Area and Keeping Room with a fireplace
- Master Bedroom suite with a fireplace, private Deck and spectacular Bath
- No materials list is available for this plan

FIRST FLOOR — 2,656 SQ. FT.
SECOND FLOOR — 1,184 SQ. FT.
BONUS — 508 SQ. FT.
BASEMENT — 2,642 SQ. FT.
GARAGE — 528 SQ. FT.

TOTAL LIVING AREA:
3,840 SQ. FT.

PLAN NO. 24657

Design by
The Garlinghouse Company

Refer to **Pricing Schedule E** on the order form for pricing information

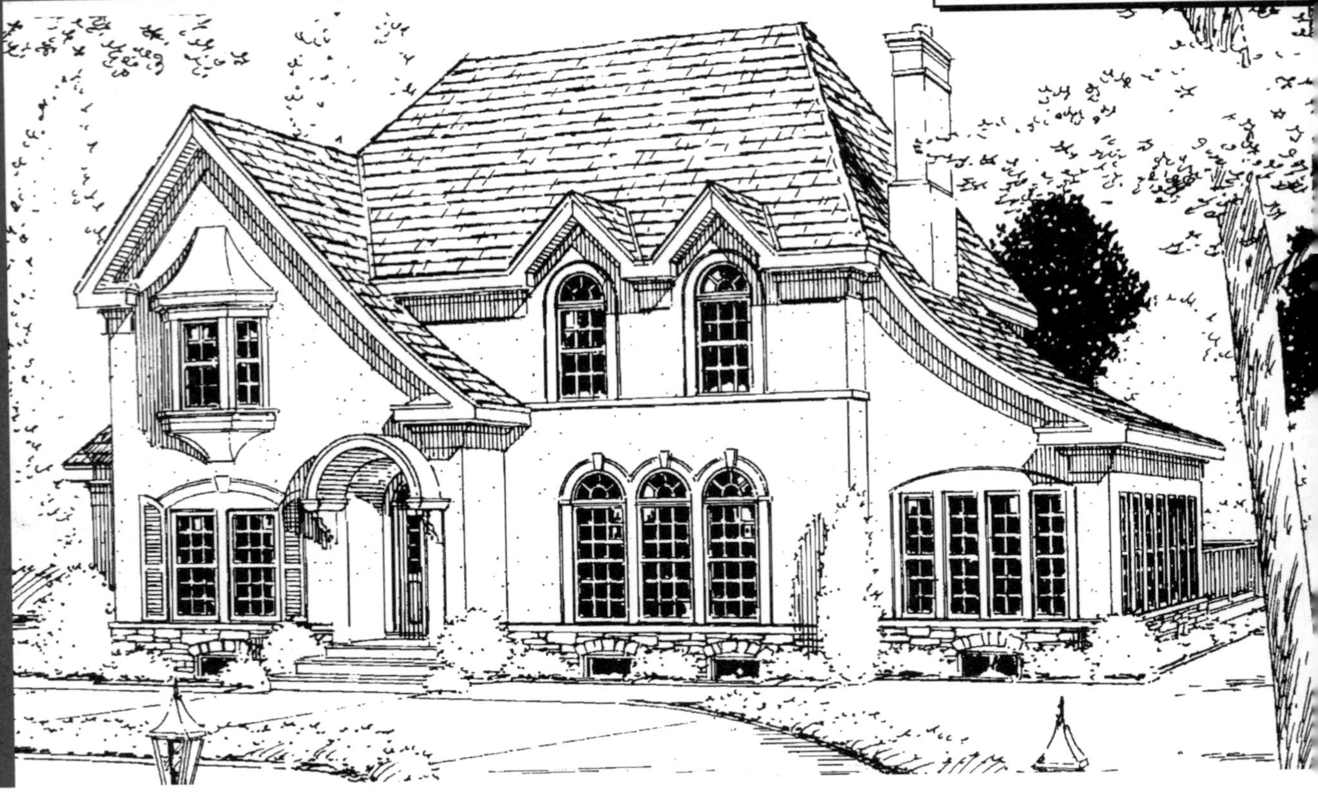

Luxurious Master Suite

- This plan features:
  - — Four bedrooms
  - — Three full and one half baths
- Fireplace in both the Living and Family Rooms
- Optional Sun Room expands living space
- A plush bath with a whirlpool tub highlights the Master Suite
- Two additional Bedrooms, each have private access to a full Bath
- Bonus room available for future expansion

FIRST FLOOR — 1,523 SQ. FT.
SECOND FLOOR — 1,370 SQ. FT.
BONUS — 344 SQ. FT.
BASEMENT — 1,722 SQ. FT.
GARAGE — 484 SQ. FT.

TOTAL LIVING AREA:
2,893 SQ. FT.

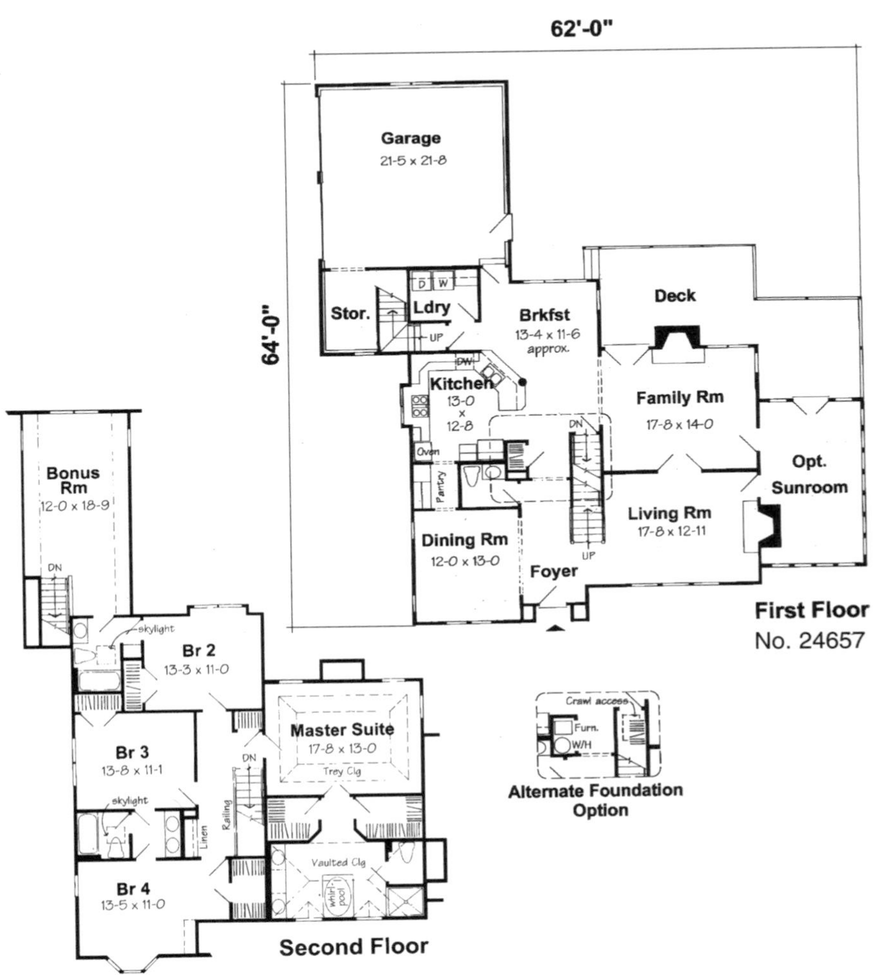

62'-0"
64'-0"
Garage
21-5 x 21-8
Stor.
Ldry
Brkfst
13-4 x 11-6
approx.
Deck
Kitchen
13-0
x
12-8
Family Rm
17-8 x 14-0
Opt.
Sunroom
Pantry
Oven
Dining Rm
12-0 x 13-0
Living Rm
17-8 x 12-11
Foyer
First Floor
No. 24657
Bonus
Rm
12-0 x 18-9
Br 2
13-3 x 11-0
Br 3
13-8 x 11-1
Master Suite
17-8 x 13-0
Trey Clg
Vaulted Clg
Br 4
13-5 x 11-0
skylight
Linen
Railing
Second Floor
Crawl access
Furn.
W/H
Alternate Foundation
Option

Refer to **Pricing Schedule F** on the order form for pricing information

Design by
Donald A. Gardner Architects, Inc.

PLAN NO. 99891

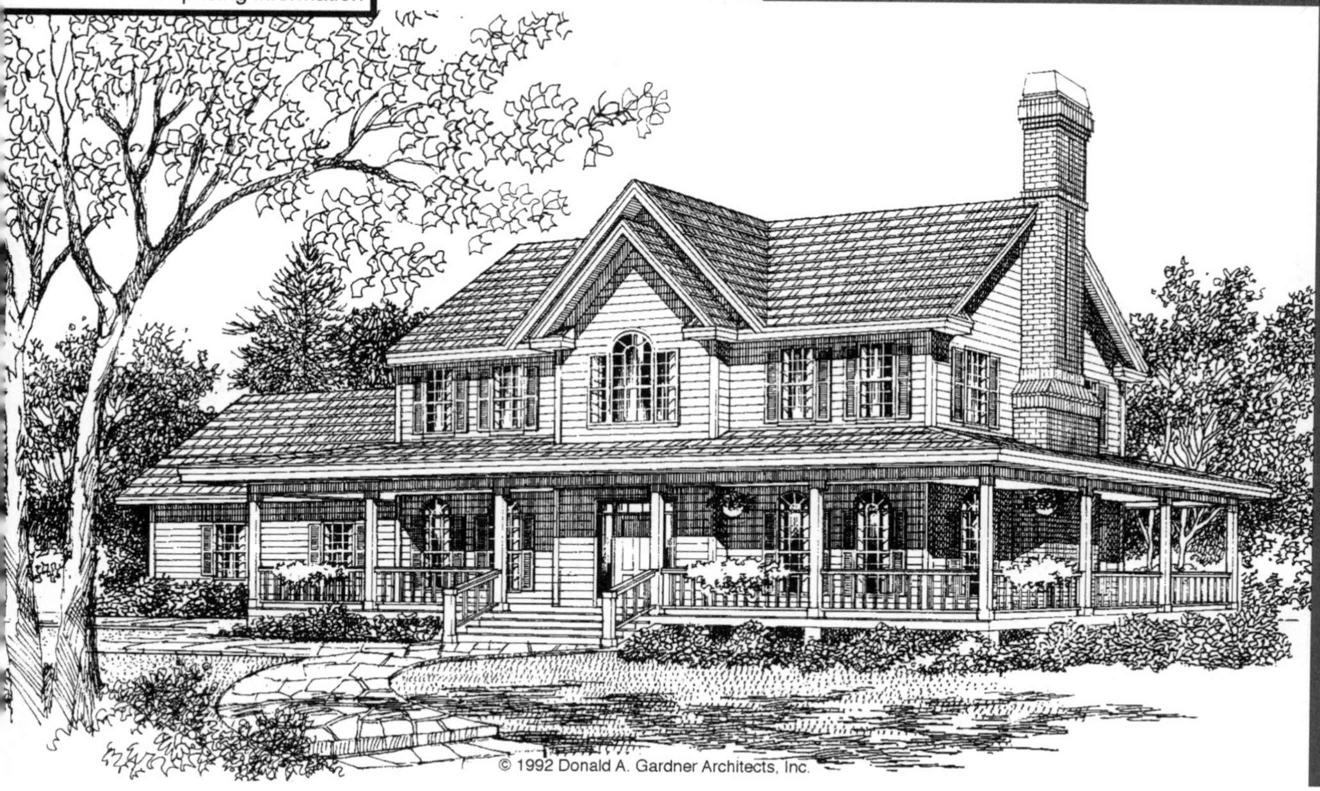

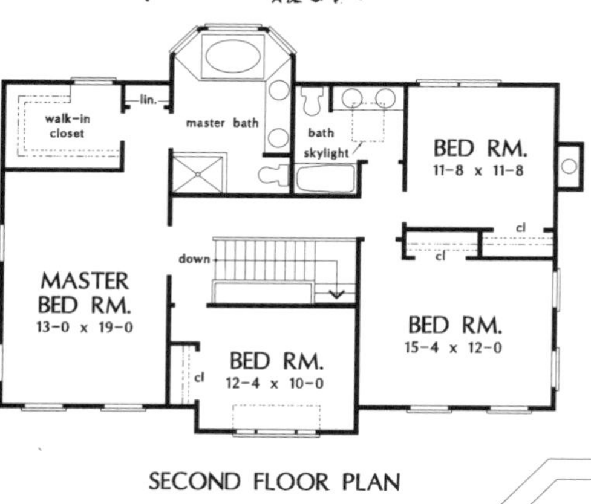

walk-in closet
lin.
master bath
bath
skylight
BED RM.
11-8 x 11-8
cl
down
MASTER BED RM.
13-0 x 19-0
BED RM.
15-4 x 12-0
BED RM.
12-4 x 10-0
cl

SECOND FLOOR PLAN

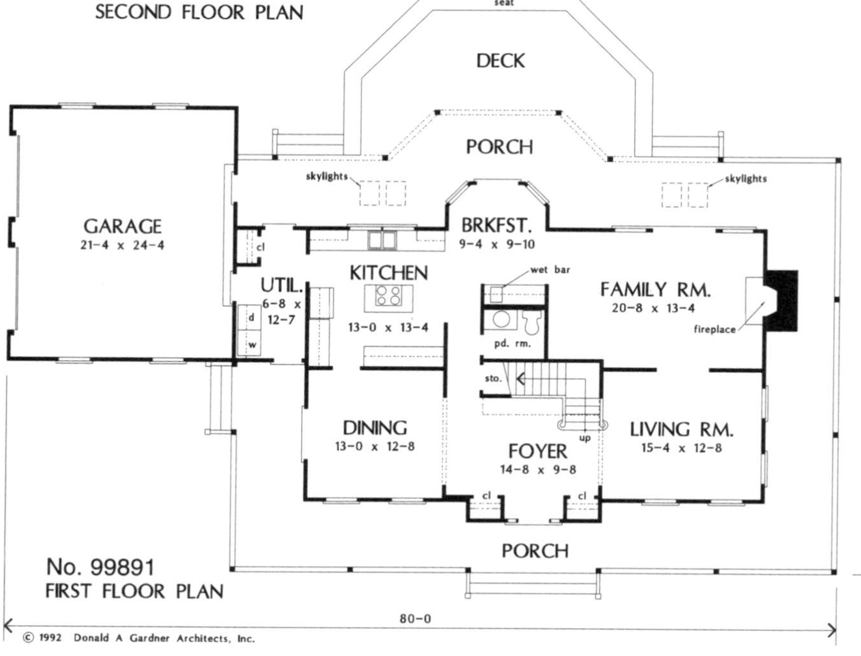

seat
DECK
PORCH
skylights
skylights
GARAGE
21-4 x 24-4
BRKFST.
9-4 x 9-10
cl
UTIL.
6-8 x 12-7
KITCHEN
13-0 x 13-4
wet bar
FAMILY RM.
20-8 x 13-4
fireplace
pd. rm.
sto.
57-0
DINING
13-0 x 12-8
FOYER
14-8 x 9-8
up
LIVING RM.
15-4 x 12-8
cl
cl
PORCH
80-0

No. 99891
FIRST FLOOR PLAN

Grand Four Bedroom Farmhouse

- This plan features:
  - Four bedrooms
  - Two full and one half baths
- Double gables, wrap-around Porch and custom window details add farmhouse appeal
- Formal Living and Dining rooms connected by Foyer in front, while casual living areas are in the rear
- Efficient Kitchen with island cooktop and easy access to all eating areas
- Spacious Master Bedroom features a walk-in closet and pampering bath

FIRST FLOOR — 1,357 SQ. FT.
SECOND FLOOR — 1,204 SQ. FT.
GARAGE & STORAGE — 546 SQ. FT.

TOTAL LIVING AREA:
2,561 SQ. FT.

PLAN NO. 93244

Design by
Jannis Vann & Associates, Inc.

Refer to **Pricing Schedule E** on the order form for pricing information

Exquisite Home

- This plan features:
  - — Four bedrooms
  - — Three full baths
- A two-story Foyer greets you as you enter this home
- The elegant formal Dining Room has a decorative ceiling
- The Kitchen features a cooktop island
- The dramatic sunken Living Room has a rear wall fireplace
- The Master Suite features a private Bath and a walk-in closet
- No materials list is available for this plan
- An optional basement or crawl space foundation — please specify when ordering

FIRST FLOOR — 2,177 SQ. FT.
SECOND FLOOR — 661 SQ. FT.
BONUS — 312 SQ. FT.
BASEMENT — 2,149 SQ. FT.
GARAGE — 534 SQ. FT.

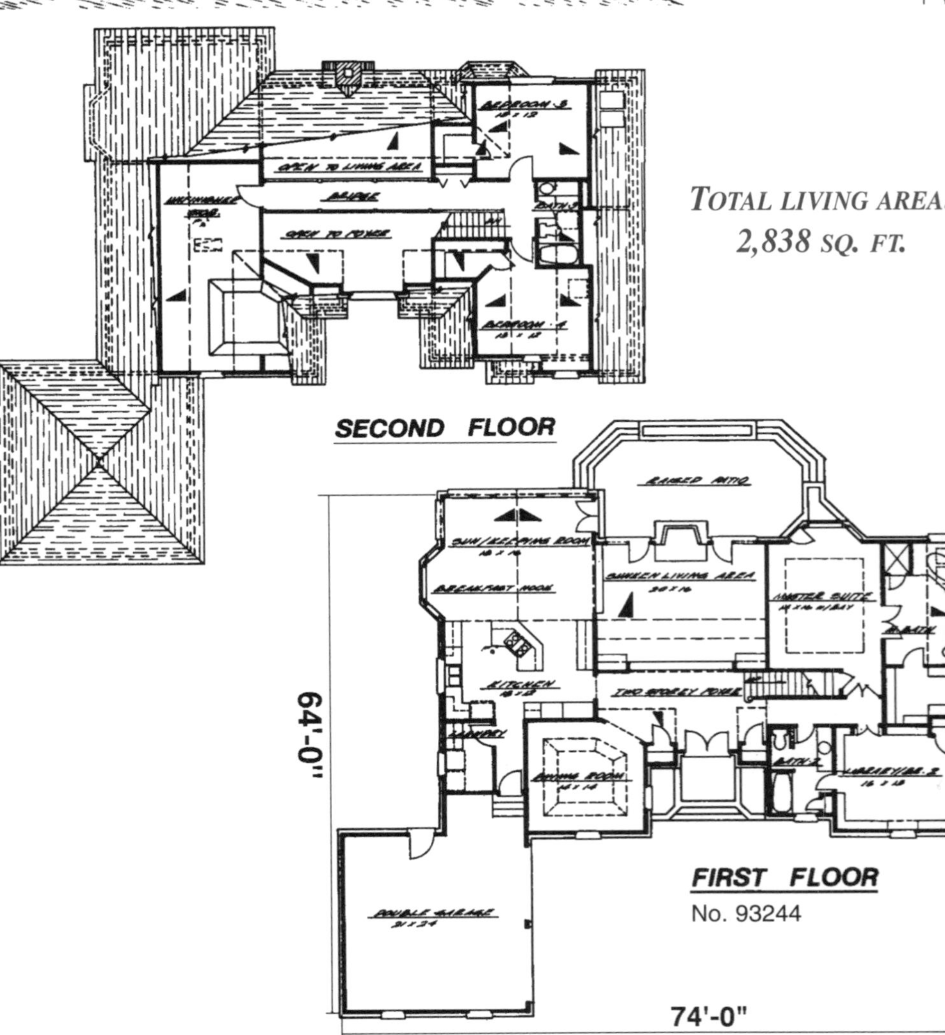
SECOND FLOOR
64'-0"
FIRST FLOOR
No. 93244
74'-0"

TOTAL LIVING AREA:
2,838 SQ. FT.

Refer to **Pricing Schedule E** on the order form for pricing information

Design by
Sater Design Group

PLAN NO. 94242

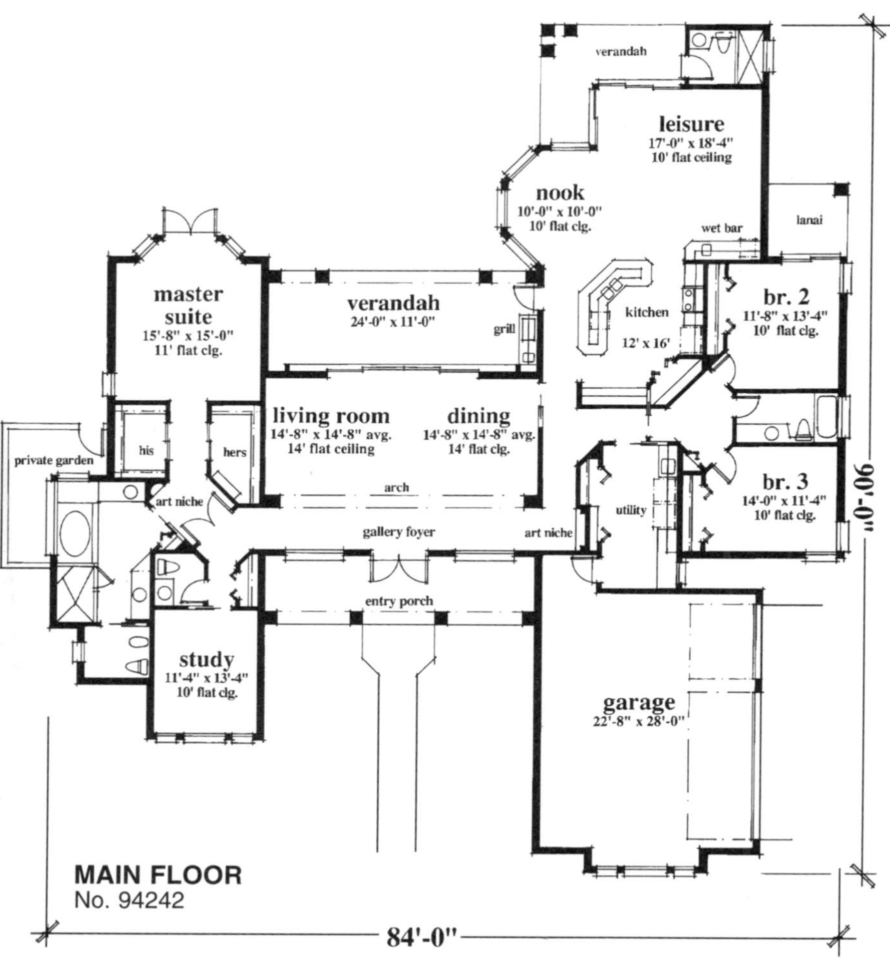

verandah
leisure
17'-0" x 18'-4"
10' flat ceiling
nook
10'-0" x 10'-0"
10' flat clg.
wet bar
lanai
master suite
15'-8" x 15'-0"
11' flat clg.
verandah
24'-0" x 11'-0"
grill
kitchen
12' x 16'
br. 2
11'-8" x 13'-4"
10' flat clg.
private garden
his
hers
living room
14'-8" x 14'-8" avg.
14' flat ceiling
dining
14'-8" x 14'-8" avg.
14' flat clg.
arch
art niche
gallery foyer
art niche
utility
br. 3
14'-0" x 11'-4"
10' flat clg.
90'-0"
entry porch
study
11'-4" x 13'-4"
10' flat clg.
garage
22'-8" x 28'-0"
MAIN FLOOR
No. 94242
84'-0"

A Custom Look

- This plan features:
  - — Three bedrooms
  - — Two full, one half, and one three quarter baths
- Exterior highlighted by triple arched glass in entry Porch
- Triple arches lead into Formal Living and Dining rooms, Verandah and beyond
- Kitchen, Nook, and Leisure Room easily flow together
- Owners' wing has a Master Suite with glass alcove to rear yard, a lavish Bath and a Study
- Two additional Bedrooms with corner windows and over-sized closets access a full Bath
- No materials list is available for this plan

MAIN FLOOR — 2,978 SQ. FT.
GARAGE — 702 SQ. FT.

TOTAL LIVING AREA:
2,978 SQ. FT.

PLAN NO. 97208

Design by
Frank Betz Associates, Inc.

Refer to **Pricing Schedule E** on the order form for pricing information

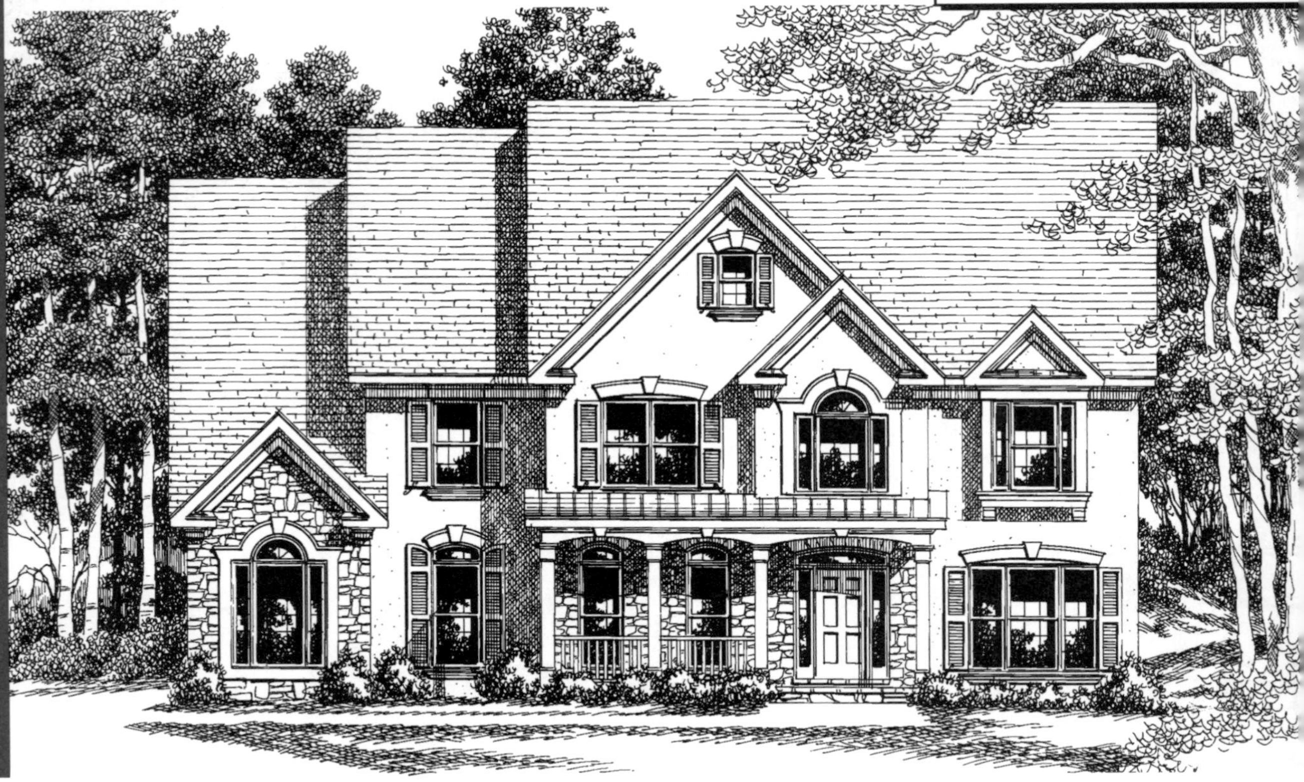

Glorious Arches

- This plan features:
  - — Four bedrooms
  - — Three full and one half baths
- Glorious arched openings distinguish the Family Room
- From the two-story Foyer you may enter either the Living room or the Dining room
- The Kitchen is open to the Breakfast Area and has a center island
- The Master Suite has a tray ceiling and its Baths has a vaulted ceiling
- One secondary Bedroom has a window seat, a walk-in closet and a private Bath
- No materials list is available for this plan
- An optional basement or crawl space foundation — please specify when ordering

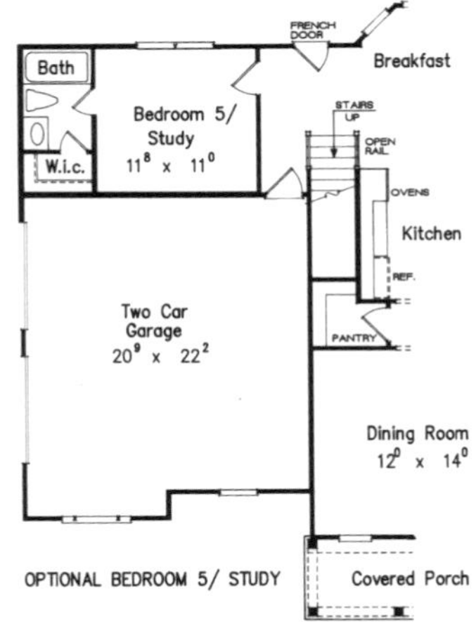

Bath
W.i.c.
Bedroom 5/ Study
11^{8} x 11^{0}
French Door
Breakfast
Stairs Up
Open Rail
Ovens
Kitchen
Ref.
Pantry
Two Car Garage
20^{8} x 22^{2}
Dining Room
12^{0} x 14^{0}
Covered Porch
OPTIONAL BEDROOM 5/ STUDY

WIDTH 58'-4"
DEPTH 46'-6"

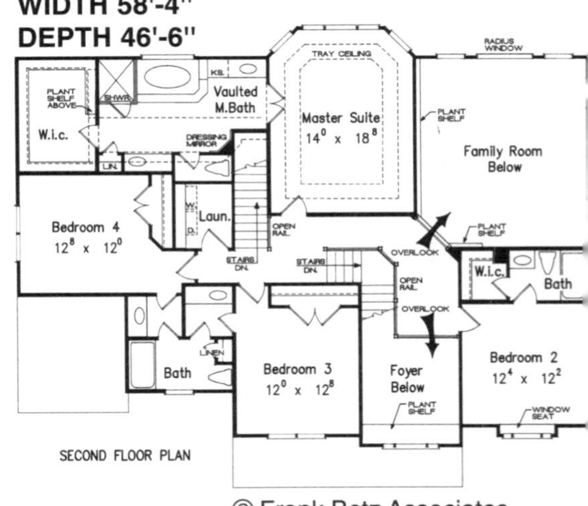

W.i.c.
Vaulted M.Bath
Tray Ceiling
Master Suite
14^{0} x 18^{8}
Radius Window
Family Room Below
Bedroom 4
12^{8} x 12^{0}
Laun.
W.i.c.
Bath
Bath
Bedroom 3
12^{0} x 12^{8}
Foyer Below
Bedroom 2
12^{4} x 12^{2}
Window Seat
SECOND FLOOR PLAN

© Frank Betz Associates

FIRST FLOOR — 1,347 SQ. FT.
SECOND FLOOR — 1,493 SQ. FT.
BONUS — 243 SQ. FT.
BASEMENT — 1,347 SQ. FT.
GARAGE — 778 SQ. FT.

TOTAL LIVING AREA:
2,840 SQ. FT.

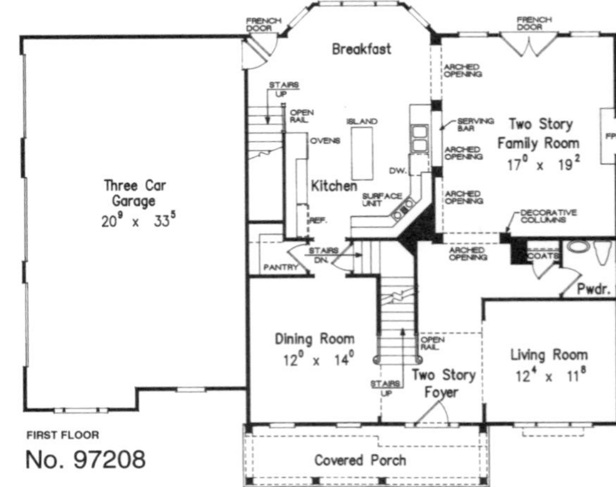

French Door
Breakfast
French Door
Three Car Garage
20^{9} x 33^{5}
Island
Kitchen
Two Story Family Room
17^{0} x 19^{2}
Pantry
Pwdr.
Dining Room
12^{0} x 14^{0}
Two Story Foyer
Living Room
12^{4} x 11^{8}
Covered Porch
FIRST FLOOR

No. 97208

PLAN NO.94269

Design by
Sater Design Group

WIDTH 65'-0"
DEPTH 88'-0"

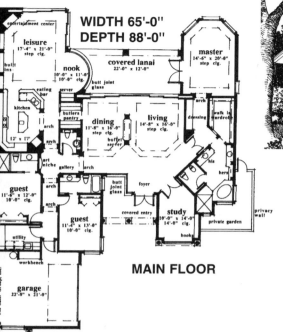

MAIN FLOOR

Stunning Home

Price Code: F

- This plan features:
- — Three bedrooms
- — Three full baths and one half baths
- Twin arched covered entry leads through double doors into a grand Foyer
- Side by side formal Living and Dining rooms
- Arches and niche space highlighting the Gallery hallways
- Nook with curved glass wall
- Master Suite with bayed Sitting Room, French doors to the covered Lanai, and a step ceiling
- No material list is available for this plan

MAIN FLOOR — 3,250 SQ. FT.

TOTAL LIVING AREA:
3,250 SQ. FT.

PLAN NO.97714

Design by
Studer Residential Design, Inc.

Multiple Gables

Price Code: D

- This plan features:
- — Three bedrooms
- — Three full and one half baths
- Impressive Foyer offers dramatic view past the Dining Room and open stairs through the Great Room to the rear yard
- Exquisite columns, 13-foot ceiling heights and detailed ceiling treatments decorate the Dining Room and Great Room
- Gourmet Kitchen with island and snack bar combines with the spacious Breakfast Room and the Hearth Room to create a warm atmosphere
- The Master Suite has a fireplace complemented by a deluxe dressing room with whirlpool tub, shower and dual vanity
- No materials list is available for this plan

MAIN FLOOR — 3,570 SQ. FT.
BONUS — 2,367 SQ. FT.
BASEMENT — 1,203 SQ. FT.

TOTAL LIVING AREA:
3,570 SQ. FT.

LOWER FLOOR

WIDTH 84'-6"
DEPTH 69'-4"

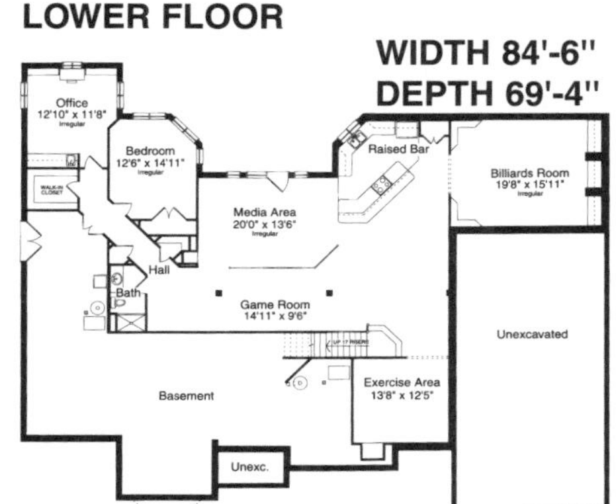
Office
Bedroom
Media Area
Raised Bar
Billiards Room
Hall
Bath
Game Room
Unexcavated
Basement
Exercise Area
Unexc.

MAIN FLOOR

PLAN NO. 98514

Design by
Filmore Design Group

Refer to **Pricing Schedule F** on the order form for pricing information

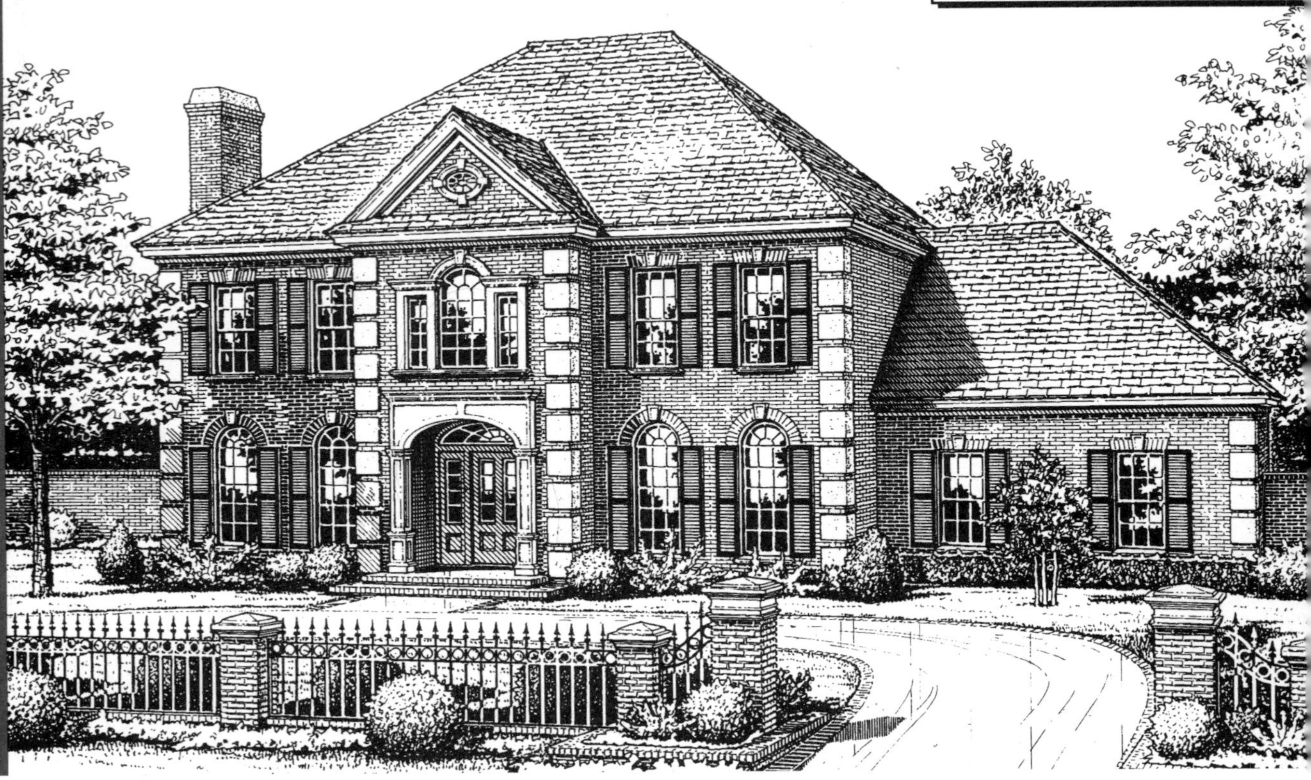

Mind Your Manor

- This plan features:
  - — Five bedrooms
  - — Three full and one half baths
- The Entry/Gallery features a grand spiral staircase
- The Study has built-in bookcases
- The Family Room has a fireplace and a built in stereo cabinet
- The bayed Breakfast Nook leads to the covered Patio
- The Master Bedroom has a built-in chest of drawers and a Bath with a cathedral ceiling
- An optional slab or crawl space foundation — please specify when ordering
- No materials list is available for this plan

MAIN FLOOR — 2,208 SQ. FT.
UPPER FLOOR — 1,173 SQ. FT.
BONUS — 224 SQ. FT.
GARAGE — 520 SQ. FT.

TOTAL LIVING AREA:
3,381 SQ. FT.

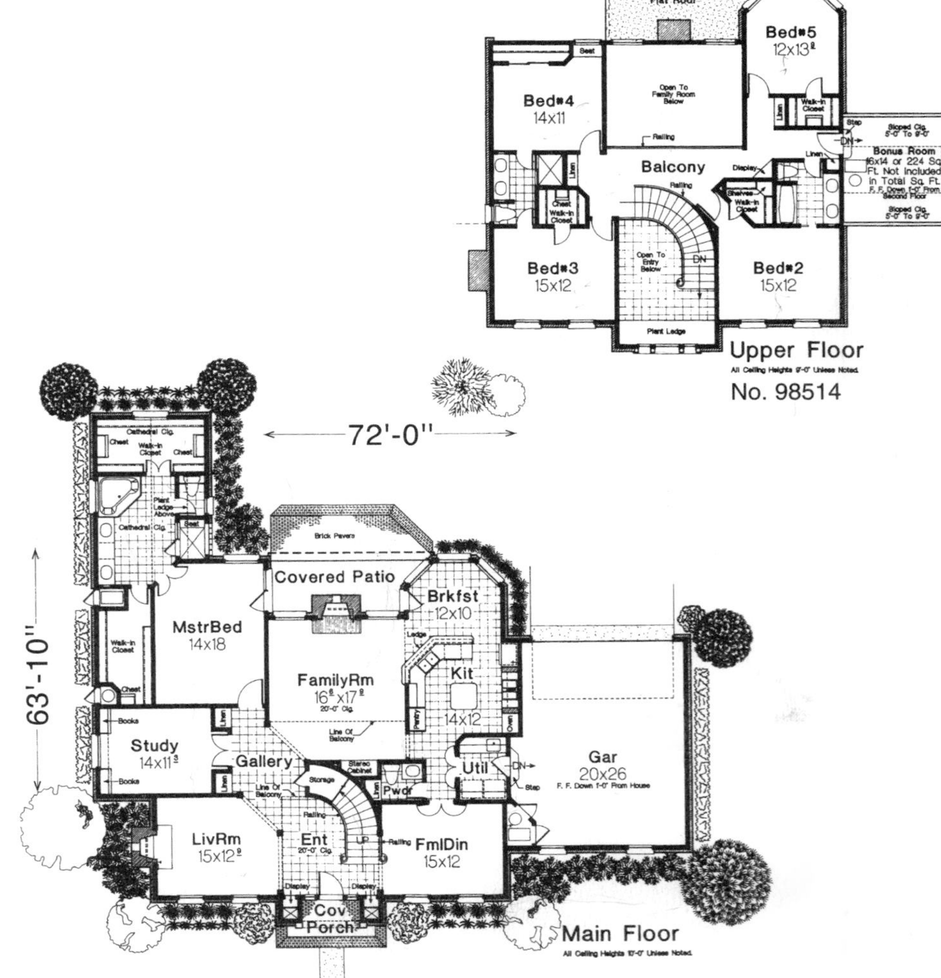

Flat Roof
Bed#5
12x13
Bed#4
14x11
Open To Family Room Below
Balcony
Bonus Room
Bed#3
15x12
Bed#2
15x12
Upper Floor
No. 98514
72'-0"
63'-10"
MstrBed
14x18
Covered Patio
Brkfst
12x10
FamilyRm
Kit
14x12
Study
Gallery
Util
Gar
20x26
Pwdr
LivRm
Ent
FmlDin
15x12
Cov Porch
Main Floor

Refer to **Pricing Schedule E** on the order form for pricing information

Design by L.M. Brunier & Associates, Inc.

PLAN NO. 91319

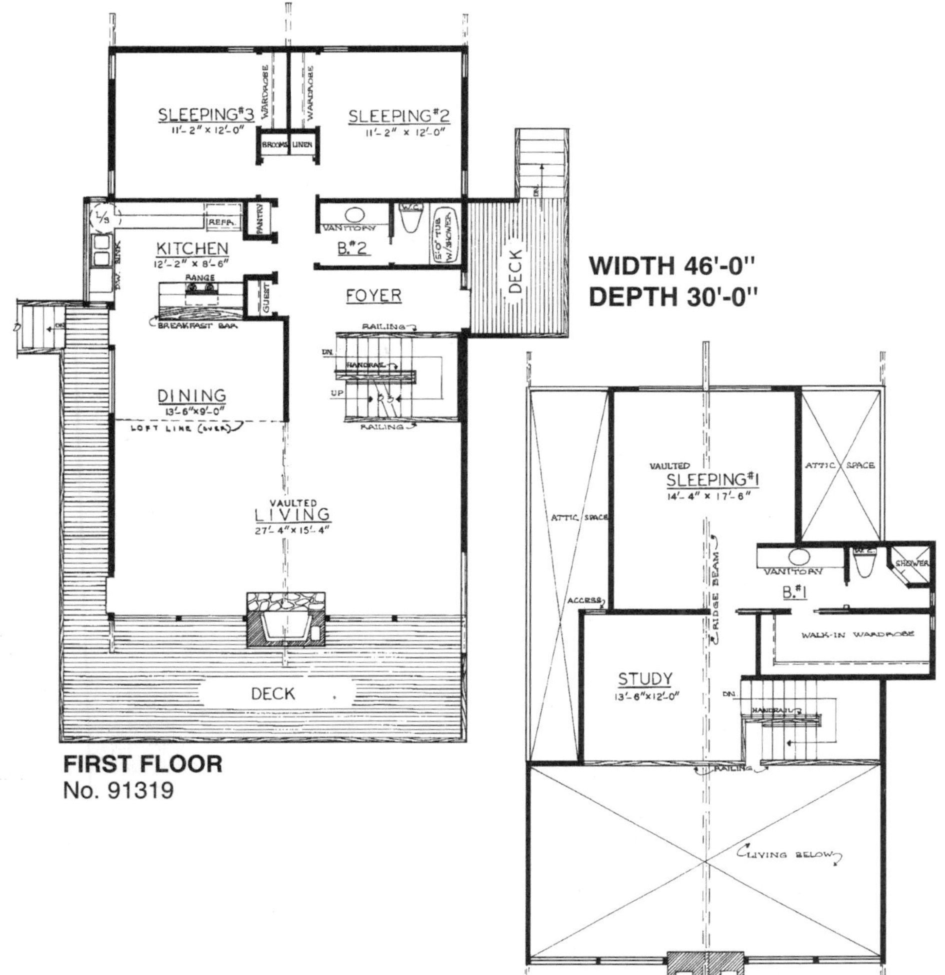
SLEEPING#3
11'-2" x 12'-0"
SLEEPING#2
11'-2" x 12'-0"
KITCHEN
12'-2" x 8'-6"
B.#2
FOYER
DECK
DINING
13'-6"x9'-0"
VAULTED
LIVING
27'-4"x15'-4"
DECK
VAULTED
SLEEPING#1
14'-4" x 17'-6"
ATTIC SPACE
B.#1
WALK-IN WARDROBE
STUDY
13'-6"x12'-0"
LIVING BELOW
SECOND FLOOR

FIRST FLOOR
No. 91319

WIDTH 46'-0"
DEPTH 30'-0"

All Seasons

- This plan features:
- — Three bedrooms
- — One full, one half and one three quarter baths
- A wall of windows takes full advantage of the front view
- An open stairway to the upstairs Study and the Master Bedroom
- The Master Bedroom has a private master Bath and a walk-in wardrobe
- The efficient Kitchen includes a breakfast bar and opens into the Dining Area
- The formal Living Room next a vaulted ceiling and a stone fireplace

FIRST FLOOR — 1,306 SQ. FT.
SECOND FLOOR — 598 SQ. FT.
LOWER FLOOR — 1,288 SQ. FT.

TOTAL LIVING AREA:
3,192 SQ. FT.

PLAN NO. 91339

Design by
L.M. Brunier & Associates

Refer to **Pricing Schedule F** on the order form for pricing information

Traditional Splendor

- This plan features:
  - — Six bedrooms
  - — Four full and one half baths
- Two-story Entry illuminated by palladian window opens to gracious Living Room
- Bright and efficient Kitchen with angled counter/eating bar and walk-in Pantry opens to Family Room and Deck
- Luxurious Master Bedroom Suite shares two-way fireplace with Den
- Four second floor Bedrooms share two full Baths
- No materials list is available for this plan

FIRST FLOOR — 2,498 SQ. FT.
SECOND FLOOR — 1,190 SQ. FT.
BASEMENT — 1,464 SQ. FT.

TOTAL LIVING AREA: 3,688 SQ. FT.

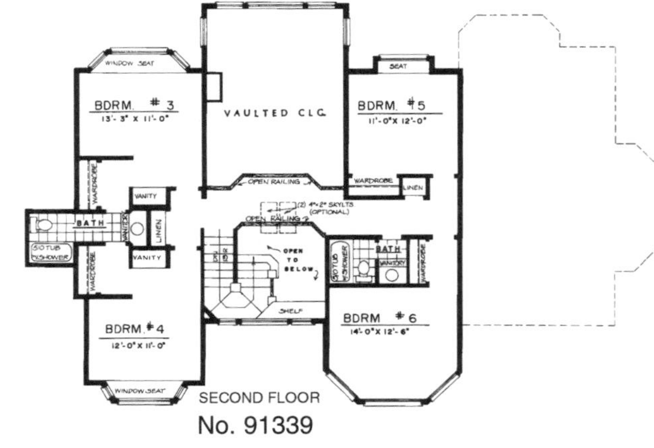
BDRM. #3
13'-3" X 11'-0"
VAULTED CLG.
BDRM. #5
11'-0" X 12'-0"
BATH
BDRM. #4
12'-0" X 11'-0"
BDRM. #6
14'-0" X 12'-6"
SECOND FLOOR
No. 91339

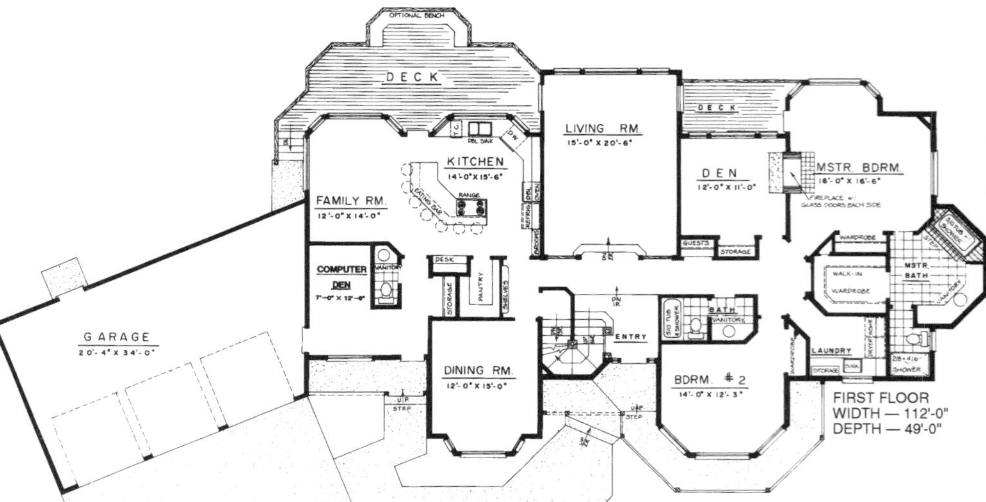
DECK
LIVING RM
15'-0" X 20'-6"
KITCHEN
14'-0" X 15'-6"
FAMILY RM.
12'-0" X 14'-0"
DEN
12'-0" X 11'-0"
MSTR. BDRM.
16'-0" X 16'-6"
COMPUTER DEN
7'-0" X 12'-6"
GARAGE
20'-4" X 34'-0"
DINING RM.
12'-0" X 15'-0"
ENTRY
BDRM. #2
14'-0" X 12'-3"
LAUNDRY
FIRST FLOOR
WIDTH — 112'-0"
DEPTH — 49'-0"

Design by
Filmore Design Group

PLAN NO. 98518

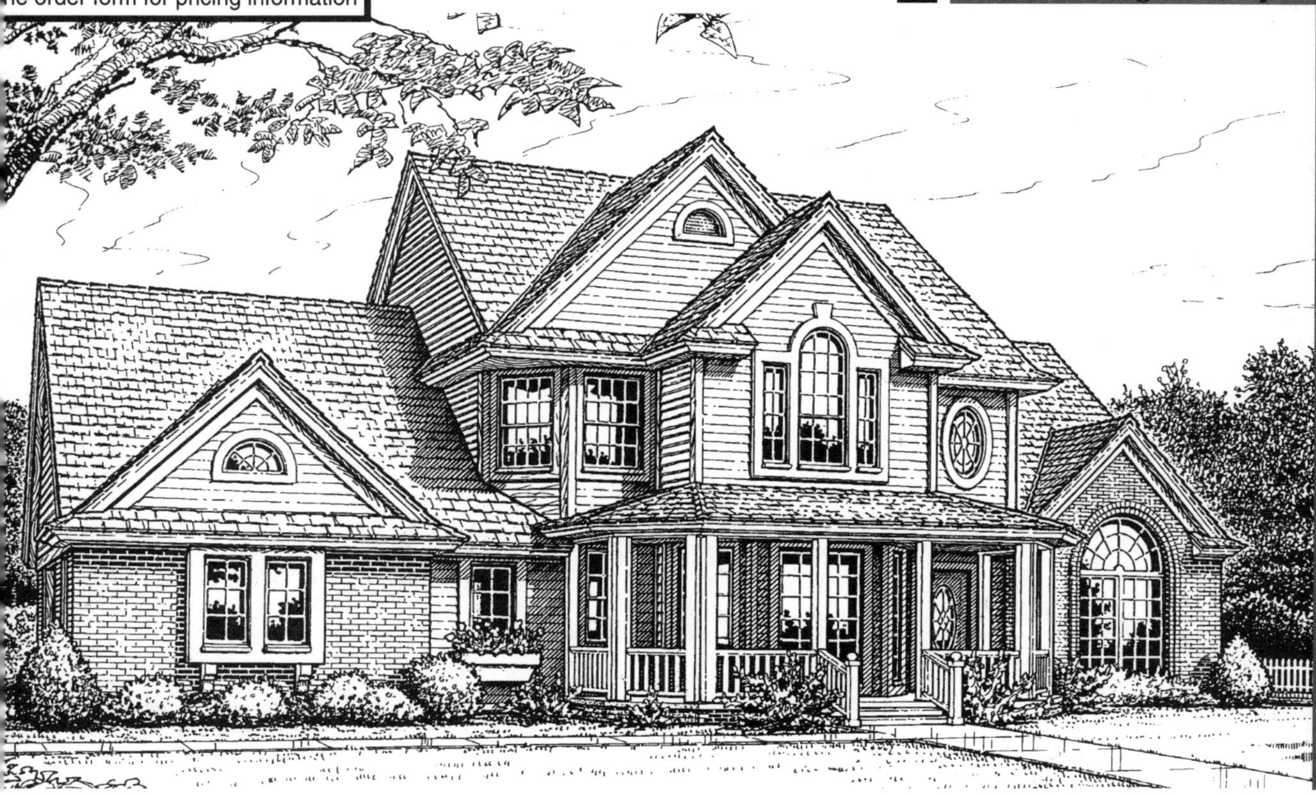

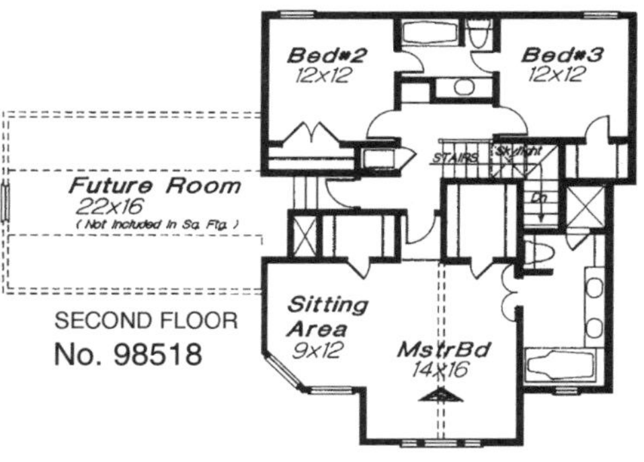
Bed#2
12x12
Bed#3
12x12
Future Room
22x16
(Not Included In Sq. Ftg.)
Sitting Area
9x12
MstrBd
14x16
SECOND FLOOR
No. 98518

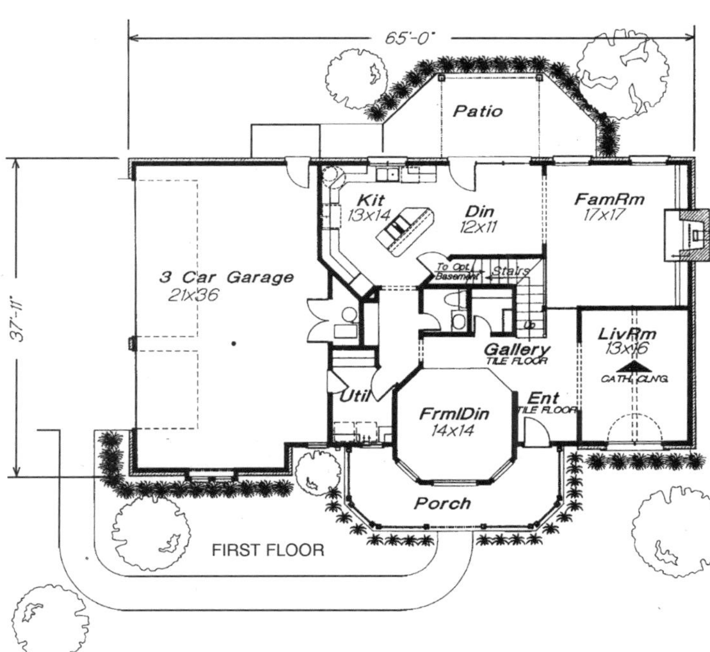
65'-0"
37'-11"
Patio
Kit
13x14
Din
12x11
FamRm
17x17
3 Car Garage
21x36
To Opt. Basement
Stairs
LivRm
13x16
CATH. CLNG.
Gallery
TILE FLOOR
Util
FrmlDin
14x14
Ent
TILE FLOOR
Porch
FIRST FLOOR

Elegant Victorian

- This plan features:
  - — Three bedrooms
  - — Two full and one half baths
- Serve guests dinner in the bayed Dining Room and then gather in the Living Room which features a cathedral ceiling
- There is plenty of space for activities in the Family Room which is accented by a fireplace
- The Master Bedroom has a Sitting Area, walk-in closet, and a private Bath
- An optional basement or slab foundation — please specify when ordering
- No materials list is available for this plan

FIRST FLOOR — 1,447 SQ. FT.
SECOND FLOOR — 1,008 SQ. FT.
GARAGE — 756 SQ. FT.

TOTAL LIVING AREA:
2,455 SQ. FT.

PLAN NO. 99119

Design by
Ahmann Design, Inc.

Refer to **Pricing Schedule E** on the order form for pricing information

Picture Perfect

- This plan features:
  - — Four bedrooms
  - — Two full and one half baths
- The Living Room has a vaulted ceiling and a see-through fireplace
- The large Kitchen is highlighted by an abundant Pantry area and a breakfast bar
- The bright and sunny Nook adjoins the screened Porch
- The Family Room has built-in cabinetry and a see-through fireplace
- The Master Bedroom has a deep walk-in closet and bath with a spa tub
- No materials list is available for this plan

FIRST FLOOR — 2,157 SQ. FT.
SECOND FLOOR — 956 SQ. FT.
BASEMENT — 2,157 SQ. FT.

TOTAL LIVING AREA:
3,113 SQ. FT.

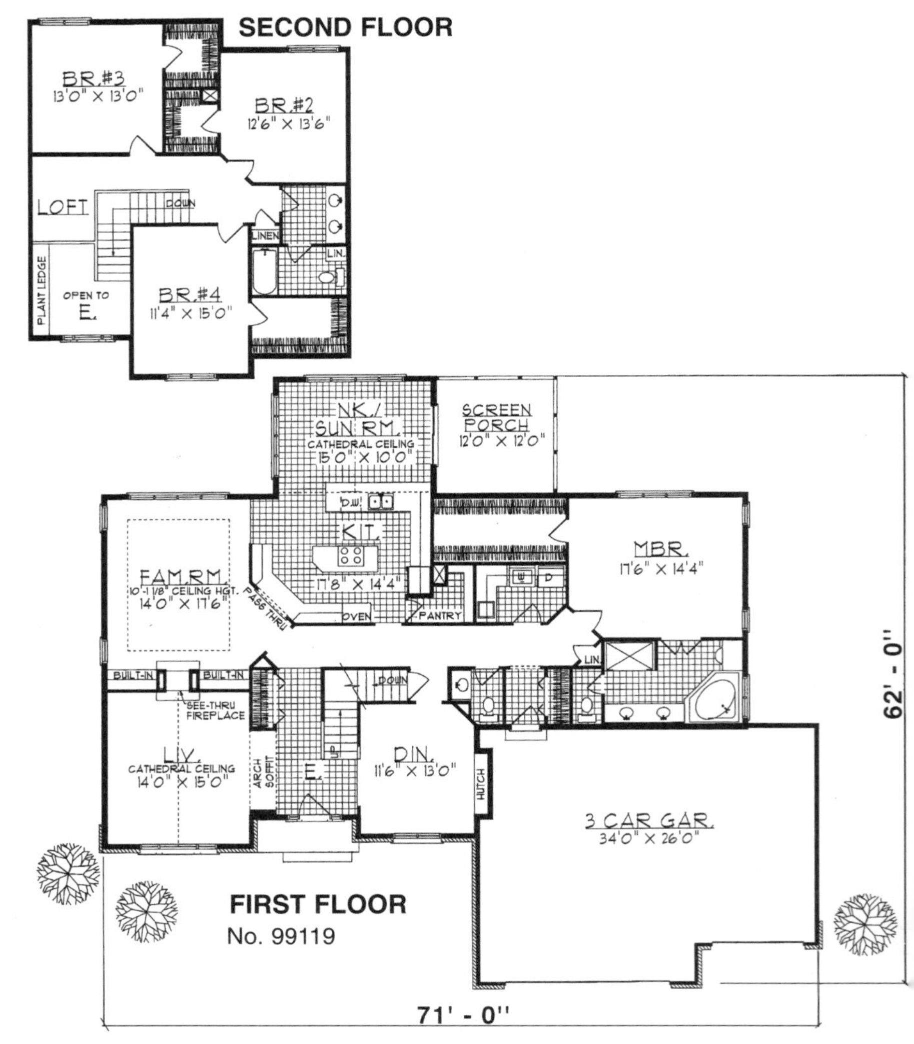
SECOND FLOOR
BR.#3
13'0" X 13'0"
BR.#2
12'6" X 13'6"
LOFT
DOWN
LINEN
LIN.
PLANT LEDGE
OPEN TO
E.
BR.#4
11'4" X 15'0"
NK./
SUN RM.
CATHEDRAL CEILING
15'0" X 10'0"
SCREEN
PORCH
12'0" X 12'0"
KIT.
11'8" X 14'4"
FAM.RM.
10'-1 1/8" CEILING HGT.
14'0" X 17'6"
PASS THRU
OVEN
PANTRY
MBR.
17'6" X 14'4"
LIN.
BUILT-IN
BUILT-IN
SEE-THRU
FIREPLACE
DOWN
UP
LIV.
CATHEDRAL CEILING
14'0" X 15'0"
ARCH
SOFFIT
E.
DIN.
11'6" X 13'0"
HUTCH
3 CAR GAR.
34'0" X 26'0"
62' - 0"
FIRST FLOOR
No. 99119
71' - 0"

To order your Blueprints, call 1-800-235-5700

Refer to **Pricing Schedule E** on the order form for pricing information

Design by
Design Basics, Inc.

PLAN NO. 99446

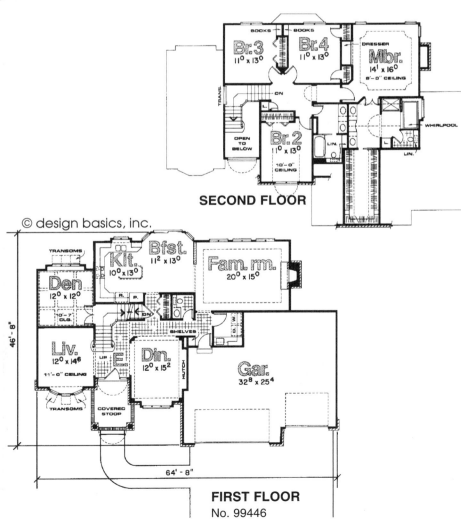

© design basics inc.

BOOKS
BOOKS
Br.3
11⁰ x 13⁰
Br.4
11⁰ x 13⁰
DRESSER
Mbr.
14¹ x 16⁰
9'-0" CEILING
TRANS.
DN
OPEN TO BELOW
Br.2
11⁰ x 13⁰
10'-0" CEILING
LIN.
WHIRLPOOL
LIN.
SECOND FLOOR

© design basics, inc.

TRANSOMS
Kit.
10⁰ x 13⁰
Bfst.
11² x 13⁰
Fam.rm.
20⁰ x 15⁰
Den
12⁰ x 12⁰
10'-7" CLG.
R.
P.
DN
SHELVES
W.
D.
Liv.
12⁰ x 14⁶
11'-0" CEILING
UP
E.
Din.
12⁰ x 15²
HUTCH
Gar.
32⁸ x 25⁴
TRANSOMS
COVERED STOOP
46' - 8"
64' - 8"

FIRST FLOOR
No. 99446

Classical Details

- This plan features:
  - — Four bedrooms
  - — Two full and one half baths
- Decorative windows and dignified brick exterior
- The volume Living Room and formal Dining Room reflect elegance with large bay windows
- The sensible Kitchen provides a large Pantry and a center work island
- The distinctive Master Suite is highlighted by a built-in dresser

FIRST FLOOR — 1,469 SQ. FT.
SECOND FLOOR — 1,306 SQ. FT.
BASEMENT — 1,469 SQ. FT.
GARAGE — 814 SQ. FT.

TOTAL LIVING AREA:
2,775 SQ. FT.

PLAN NO.92285

Design by
Fillmore Design Group

Attractive Roof Line

Price Code: E

- This plan features:
  - — Four bedrooms
  - — Two full and one three-quarter baths
- The Foyer flows easily across the tiled Galley into the formal Living Room
- An island in the center of the U-shaped Kitchen adds to the abundance of work area
- Tiling in the Breakfast Room adds style
- A cathedral ceiling tops the Family Room, which includes a fireplace
- No materials list is available for this plan

MAIN FLOOR — 2,620 SQ. FT.
GARAGE — 567 SQ. FT.

TOTAL LIVING AREA:
2,620 SQ. FT.

73'-0"
MstrBed 14x17 PULLMAN CEILING
Patio
FamilyRm 16x17
Bed #4 12x13
LivRm 14x15
Bed #3 11x13
FmlDin 11x12
3-Car Gar 22x28
Study/ Bed #2 11x12
MAIN FLOOR

PLAN NO.91749

Design by
Landmark Designs, Inc. 

Relax on the Veranda

Price Code: E

- This plan features:
  - — Four bedrooms
  - — Three full and one half baths
- A wrap-around Veranda
- The sky-lit Master Suite has an elevated custom spa, twin basins, a walk-in closet, and an additional vanity outside the bathroom
- A vaulted ceiling in the Den
- A fireplace in both the Family Room and the formal Living Room
- An efficient Kitchen has a peninsula counter and a double sink
- Two additional bedrooms has walk-in closets, served by a compartmentalized bath
- A Guest Suite with a private bath

MAIN FLOOR — 3,051 SQ. FT.
GARAGE — 646 SQ. FT.

TOTAL LIVING AREA:
3,051 SQ. FT.

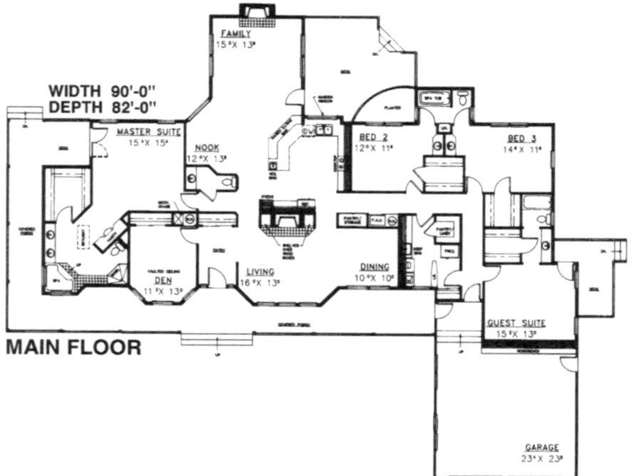
WIDTH 90'-0"
DEPTH 82'-0"
MAIN FLOOR

To order your Blueprints, call 1-800-235-5700

Refer to **Pricing Schedule F** on the order form for pricing information

Design by
Jannis Vann & Associates, Inc.

PLAN NO. 93243

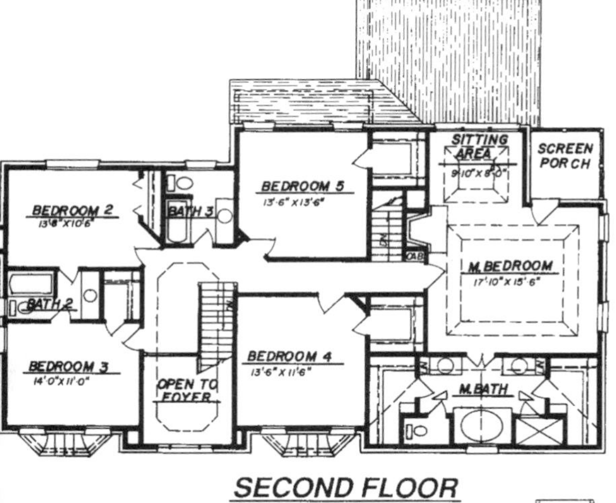

SITTING AREA
9'10"x8'0"
SCREEN PORCH
BEDROOM 5
13'6"x13'6"
BEDROOM 2
13'8"x10'6"
BATH 3
M.BEDROOM
17'10"x15'6"
BATH 2
BEDROOM 3
14'0"x11'0"
OPEN TO FOYER
BEDROOM 4
13'6"x11'6"
M.BATH

SECOND FLOOR

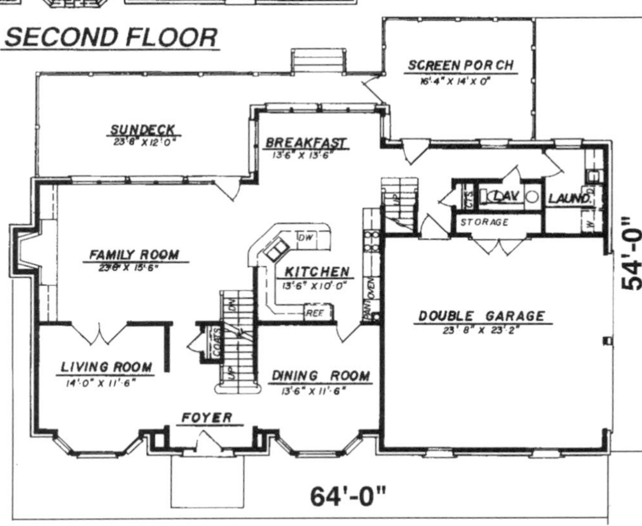

SCREEN PORCH
16'4" x 14' 0"
SUNDECK
23'8" x 12'0"
BREAKFAST
13'6" x 13'6"
LAV
LAUND
STORAGE
FAMILY ROOM
23'8" x 15'6"
KITCHEN
13'6" x 10'0"
DOUBLE GARAGE
23' 8" x 23' 2"
LIVING ROOM
14'0" x 11'-6"
DINING ROOM
13'6" x 11'-6"
FOYER
54'-0"
64'-0"

FIRST FLOOR

No. 93243

Luxurious Bedrooms Abound

- This plan features:
  - — Five bedrooms
  - — Three full and one half baths
- The Family Room has a focal point fireplace and access to the rear Sun Deck
- The Kitchen, Family Room and Breakfast Nook open to each other
- The first floor Screen Porch adds to the living space
- The Master Suite has a decorative ceiling, a fireplace enjoyed also from the Sitting Area, a private Master Bath and a screen Porch
- No materials list is available for this plan

FIRST FLOOR — 1,491 SQ. FT.
SECOND FLOOR — 1,811 SQ. FT.
BASEMENT — 1,164 SQ. FT.
GARAGE — 564 SQ. FT.

TOTAL LIVING AREA:
3,302 SQ. FT.

PLAN NO. 97400

Design by
Design Basics, Inc.

Refer to **Pricing Schedule E** on the order form for pricing informatio

A Sense of Stature

- This plan features:
- — Four bedrooms
- — Three full and one half baths
- A bayed turret and bold double doors add stature to this home
- A bay shaped Study is located in the front of the home
- The Dining Room features a distinctive front window
- The unique Living Room has a fireplace
- The Family Room, Breakfast Nook and Kitchen are arranged in an open manner
- The first floor Master Bedroom has a decorative ceiling
- No materials list is available for this plan
- An optional basement or slab foundation — please specify when ordering

FIRST FLOOR — 2,112 SQ. FT.
SECOND FLOOR — 982 SQ. FT.
GARAGE — 650 SQ. FT.

TOTAL LIVING AREA:
3,094 SQ. FT.

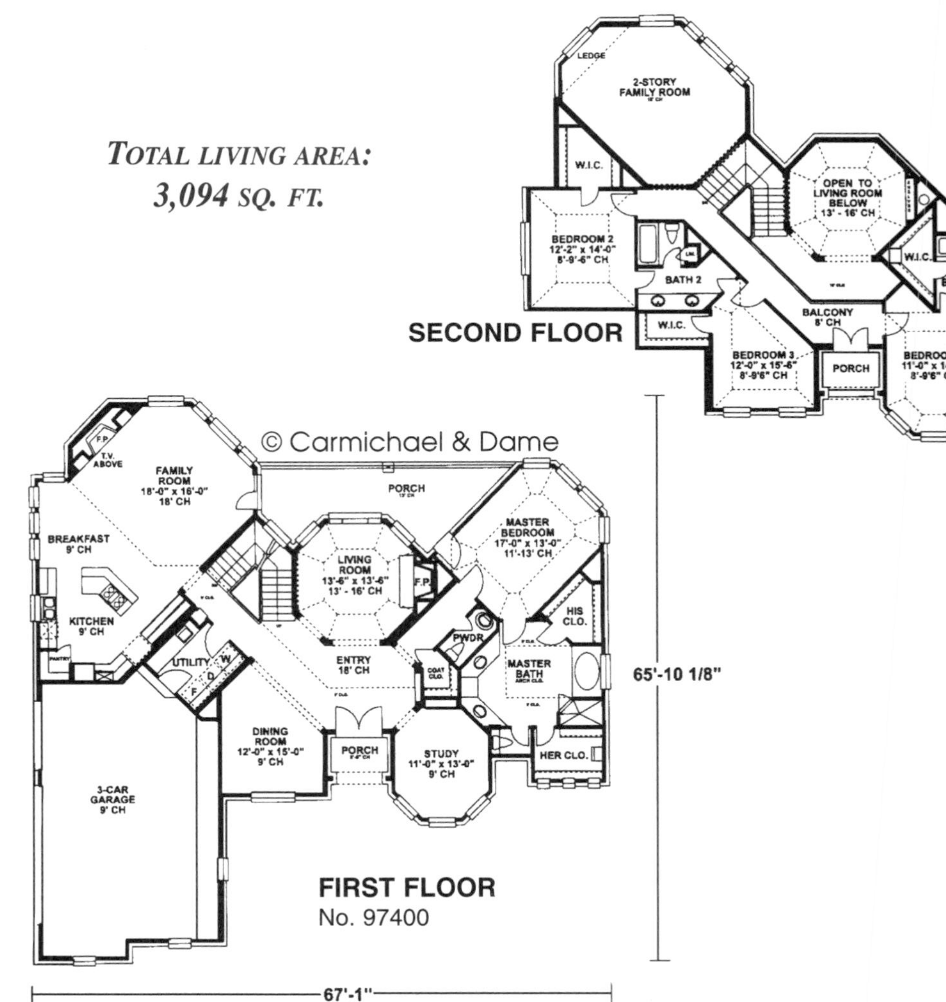

SECOND FLOOR
2-STORY FAMILY ROOM
LEDGE
W.I.C.
BEDROOM 2
12'-2" x 14'-0"
OPEN TO LIVING ROOM BELOW
13' - 16' CH
BATH 2
BALCONY
8' CH
W.I.C.
BEDROOM 3
12'-0" x 15'-6"
PORCH
BEDROOM 4
11'-0" x 14'-4"
© Carmichael & Dame
FAMILY ROOM
18'-0" x 16'-0"
18' CH
T.V. ABOVE
F.P.
PORCH
BREAKFAST
9' CH
KITCHEN
9' CH
LIVING ROOM
13'-6" x 13'-6"
13' - 16' CH
MASTER BEDROOM
17'-0" x 13'-0"
11'-13' CH
HIS CLO.
UTILITY
ENTRY
18' CH
PWDR
COAT CLO.
MASTER BATH
DINING ROOM
12'-0" x 15'-0"
9' CH
PORCH
STUDY
11'-0" x 13'-0"
9' CH
HER CLO.
3-CAR GARAGE
9' CH
65'-10 1/8"
67'-1"
FIRST FLOOR
No. 97400

Refer to **Pricing Schedule D** on
e order form for pricing information

Design by
Alan Mascord Design Associates

PLAN NO. 91535

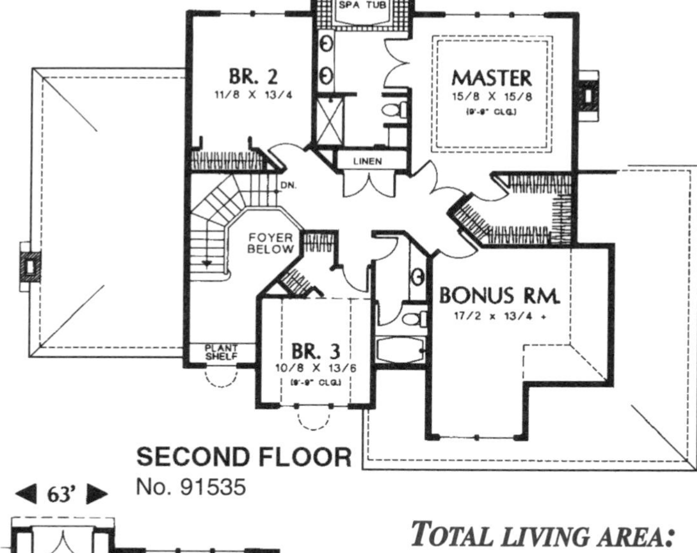

SPA TUB
BR. 2
11/8 X 13/4
MASTER
15/8 X 15/8
(9'-8" CLG.)
LINEN
DN.
FOYER BELOW
BONUS RM.
17/2 x 13/4 +
PLANT SHELF
BR. 3
10/8 X 13/6
(9'-9" CLG.)
SECOND FLOOR
No. 91535

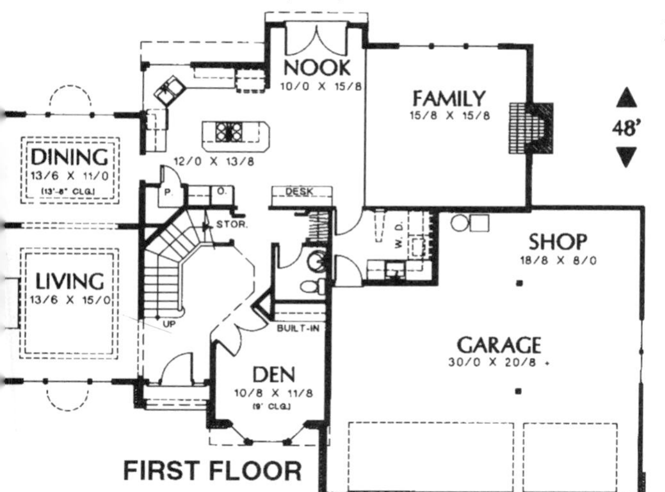

63'
NOOK
10/0 X 15/8
FAMILY
15/8 X 15/8
48'
DINING
13/6 X 11/0
12/0 X 13/8
P.
DESK
STOR.
W.D.
SHOP
18/8 X 8/0
LIVING
13/6 X 15/0
UP
BUILT-IN
GARAGE
30/0 X 20/8 +
DEN
10/8 X 11/8
(9' CLG.)
FIRST FLOOR

Total Living Area:
2,568 Sq. ft.

A Traditional Home with Modern Features

- This plan features:
  - — Three bedrooms
  - — Two full and one half baths
- A bay window and built in shelves in the Den
- A decorative ceiling and a fireplace in the Living Room
- The Dining Room is enhanced by a decorative ceiling treatment
- A cooktop island/eating bar, walk-in Pantry, planning Desk and informal Nook Area in the spacious Kitchen
- A cozy fireplace in the Family Room
- Master Suite equipped with a compartmented bath
- A Bonus Room for future expansion

First floor — 1,465 sq. ft.
Second floor — 1,103 sq. ft.
Bonus room — 303 sq. ft.

PLAN NO. 90456

Design by
Corley Plan Service

Refer to **Pricing Schedule E** on the order form for pricing informatio

Maintenance Free Brick Exterior

- This plan features:
- — Four bedrooms
- — Four full baths
- This Traditionally styled brick home has a wrap-around Porch
- Upon entering the two-story Foyer an open rail staircase comes into view
- On either side of the Foyer are the identically sized Living and Dining rooms
- In the rear find the Great Room which offers a fireplace and built in cabinets
- The U-shaped Kitchen with a center island is located adjacent to the Nook
- The Study is located in a quiet rear corner of the home
- An optional basement or crawl space foundation — please specify when ordering

FIRST FLOOR — 1,609 SQ. FT.
SECOND FLOOR — 1,445 SQ. FT.
BASEMENT — 1,609 SQ. FT.
GARAGE — 527 SQ. FT.

TOTAL LIVING AREA: 3,054 SQ. FT.

COVERED DECK
MASTER BEDROOM 13-0 x 19-2
GREAT ROOM (below)
PLANT SHELF
BEDROOM 11-0 x 12-0
CLOSET
SITTING AREA
OPEN RAIL
BALCONY
BATH
SLOPE CLG.
SPA TUB
BATH 12' CLG.
SHOWER
STOR
LINEN
CLOSET
BEDROOM 11-0 x 13-6 10' CLG
SLOPE CLG.
OPEN RAIL
ENTRY (below)
BEDROOM 11-0 x 12-0 10' CLG.
KNEE SPACE
CLOSET
SECOND FLOOR
8' CEILING UNLESS NOTED OTHERWISE
No. 90456

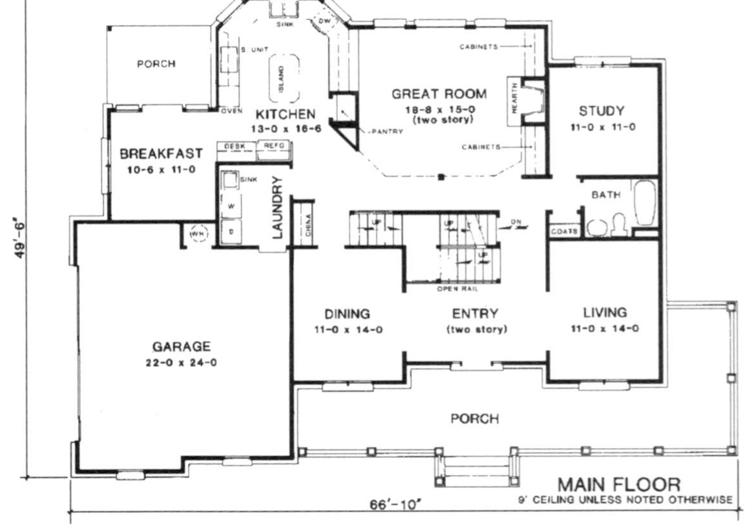
SINK
DW
PORCH
S. UNIT
ISLAND
CABINETS
KITCHEN 13-0 x 16-6
OVEN
PANTRY
GREAT ROOM 18-8 x 15-0 (two story)
HEARTH
STUDY 11-0 x 11-0
BREAKFAST 10-6 x 11-0
DESK
REFG
LAUNDRY
CHINA
BATH
COATS
DN
UP
OPEN RAIL
49'-6"
DINING 11-0 x 14-0
ENTRY (two story)
LIVING 11-0 x 14-0
GARAGE 22-0 x 24-0
PORCH
MAIN FLOOR
9' CEILING UNLESS NOTED OTHERWISE
66'-10"

Refer to **Pricing Schedule D** on the order form for pricing information

Design by
Landmark Design, Inc.

PLAN NO. 91700

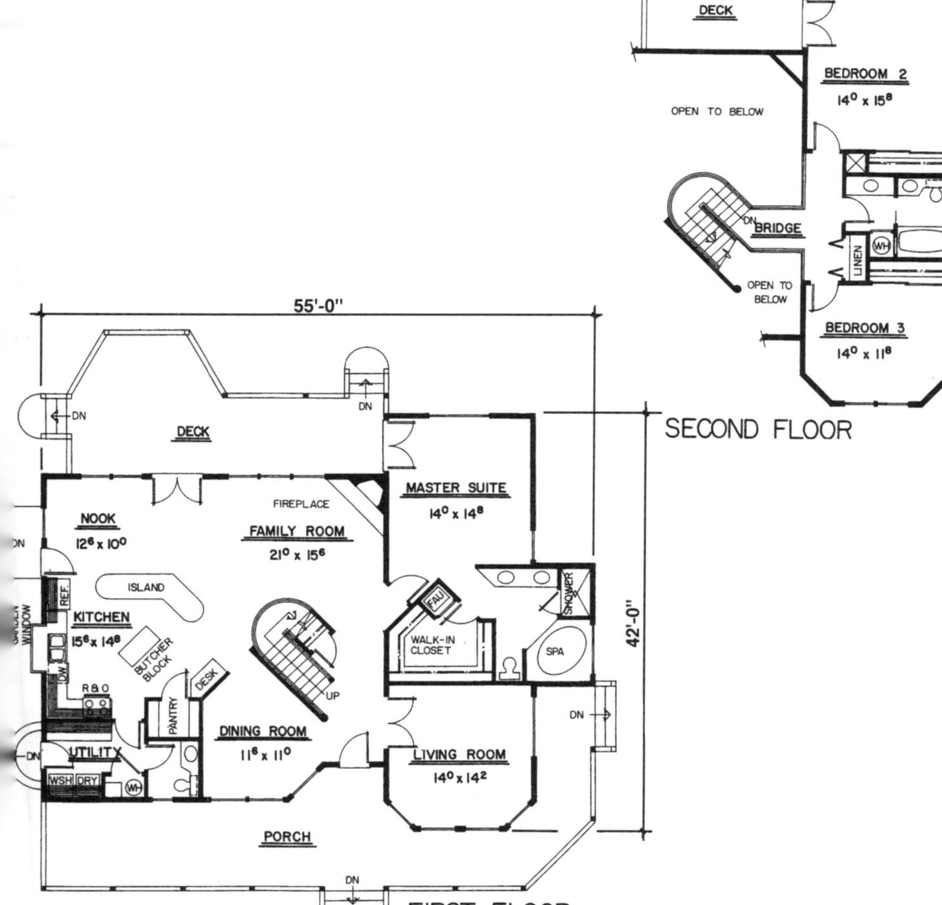

DECK
OPEN TO BELOW
BEDROOM 2
14⁰ x 15⁸
DN
BRIDGE
LINEN
WH
OPEN TO BELOW
BEDROOM 3
14⁰ x 11⁸
SECOND FLOOR
55'-0"
DECK
DN
NOOK
12⁶ x 10⁰
FIREPLACE
FAMILY ROOM
21⁰ x 15⁶
MASTER SUITE
14⁰ x 14⁸
ISLAND
REF.
KITCHEN
15⁶ x 14⁸
BUTCHER BLOCK
DW
R&O
DESK
PANTRY
FAU
WALK-IN CLOSET
SHOWER
SPA
UP
42'-0"
DINING ROOM
11⁶ x 11⁰
UTILITY
WSH
DRY
WH
LIVING ROOM
14⁰ x 14²
PORCH
DN

FIRST FLOOR
No. 91700

Country Style For Today

- This plan features:
  - — Three bedrooms
  - — Two full and one half baths
- A wide wrap-around Porch for a farmhouse style
- A spacious Living Room with double doors and a large front window
- A garden window over the double sink in the huge, country Kitchen with two islands, one a butcher block, and the other an eating bar
- A corner fireplace in the Family Room enjoyed throughout the Nook and Kitchen, thanks to an open layout
- A Master Suite with a spa tub, and a huge walk-in closet as well as a shower and double vanity

FIRST FLOOR — 1,785 SQ. FT.
SECOND FLOOR — 621 SQ. FT.

TOTAL LIVING AREA:
2,406 SQ. FT.

PLAN NO. 93254

Design by
Jannis Vann & Associates, Inc.

Refer to **Pricing Schedule D** on the order form for pricing information

Rewards of Success

TOTAL LIVING AREA:
2,509 SQ. FT.

- This plan features:
- — Three bedrooms
- — Three full and one half baths
- The Living Room and Dining Room are each enhanced by a bay window
- An expansive Family Room includes a fireplace
- An open layout between the Family Room, Breakfast Bay and the Kitchen
- The lavish Master Suite is crowned by a decorative ceiling
- An optional basement, crawl space or slab foundation — please specify when ordering
- No materials list is available for this plan

FIRST FLOOR — 1,282 SQ. FT.
SECOND FLOOR — 1,227 SQ. FT.
BONUS ROOM — 314 SQ. FT.
GARAGE — 528 SQ. FT.
BASEMENT — 1,154 SQ. FT.

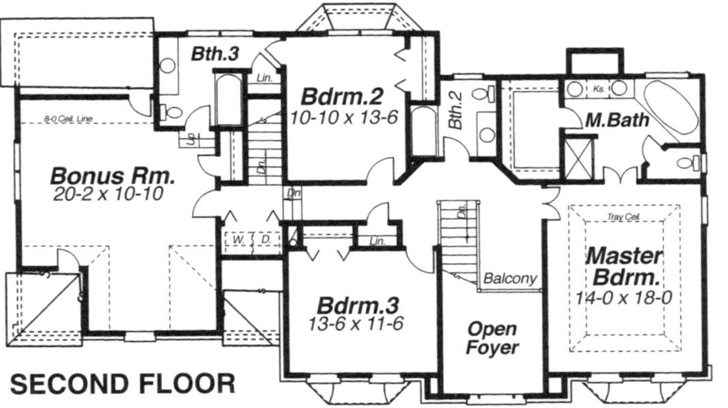
Bth.3
Lin.
Bdrm.2
10-10 x 13-6
Bth.2
M.Bath
Bonus Rm.
20-2 x 10-10
W. D.
Lin.
Bdrm.3
13-6 x 11-6
Balcony
Master
Bdrm.
14-0 x 18-0
Open
Foyer
SECOND FLOOR

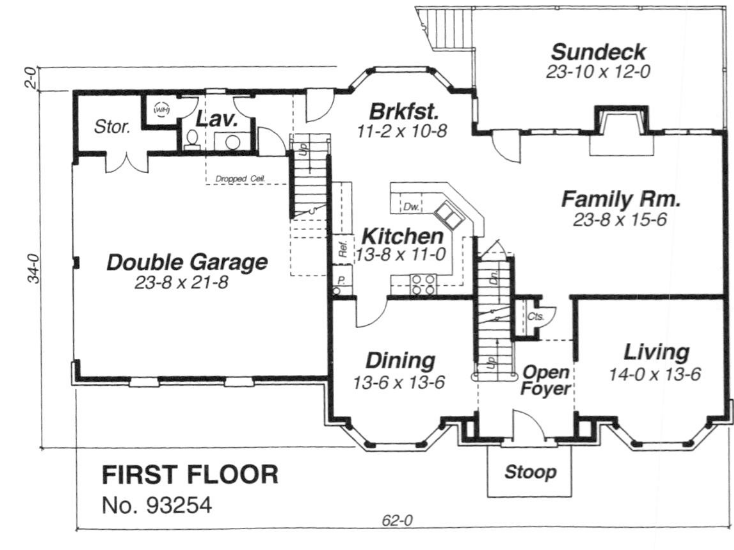
Sundeck
23-10 x 12-0
2-0
Stor.
Lav.
Brkfst.
11-2 x 10-8
Family Rm.
23-8 x 15-6
Kitchen
13-8 x 11-0
Double Garage
23-8 x 21-8
34-0
Dining
13-6 x 13-6
Open
Foyer
Living
14-0 x 13-6
Stoop
FIRST FLOOR
No. 93254
62-0

Refer to **Pricing Schedule F** on
ne order form for pricing information

Design by
The Meredith Corporation

PLAN NO. 32063

otography by The Meredith Corporation

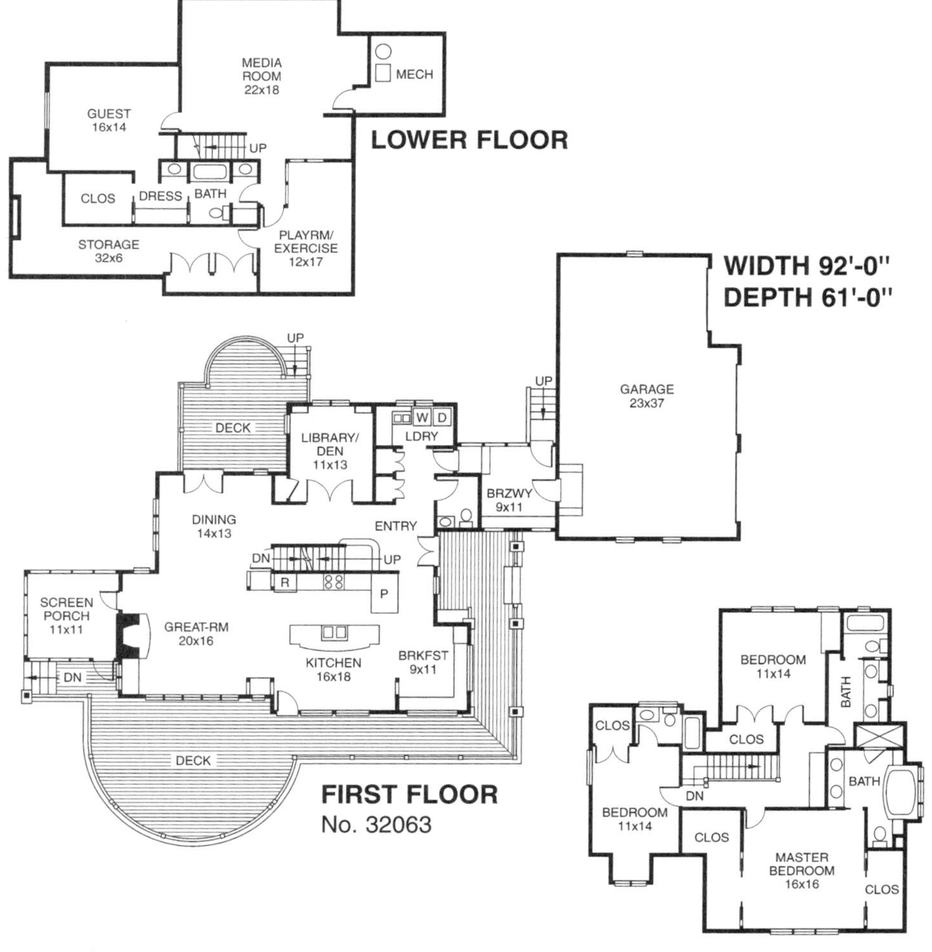

MEDIA ROOM 22x18
MECH
GUEST 16x14
UP
CLOS
DRESS
BATH
STORAGE 32x6
PLAYRM/ EXERCISE 12x17
LOWER FLOOR
WIDTH 92'-0"
DEPTH 61'-0"
GARAGE 23x37
DECK
LIBRARY/ DEN 11x13
LDRY
W D
BRZWY 9x11
DINING 14x13
ENTRY
DN
R
P
SCREEN PORCH 11x11
GREAT-RM 20x16
KITCHEN 16x18
BRKFST 9x11
DECK
FIRST FLOOR
No. 32063
BEDROOM 11x14
BATH
CLOS
BEDROOM 11x14
MASTER BEDROOM 16x16
SECOND FLOOR

Forest Cottage

- This plan features:
- — Four Bedrooms
- — Four full and one half baths
- The bow shaped front Deck mirrors the home's eyebrow dormer and large arched window
- The Kitchen has an island and a built-in Pantry
- The Great Room is highlighted by a fireplace
- The Master Suite is pampered by a five-piece Bath
- The lower floor contains a Media Room, a Play Room and a Guest Suite

FIRST FLOOR — 1,642 SQ. FT.
SECOND FLOOR — 1411 SQ. FT.
LOWER FLOOR — 1,230 SQ. FT.
BASEMENT — 412 SQ. FT.

TOTAL LIVING AREA:
4,283 SQ. FT.

PLAN NO.91139

Design by
Ryan & Associates

Nothing Short Of Luxury

Price Code: D

- This plan features:
- — Four bedrooms
- — Two full and one half baths
- There are arched entrances to the Dining and Great rooms, adding sophistication
- The Study has French doors, built-in book-shelves and a vaulted ceiling
- Connected to the Breakfast Area and the snack bar off the Kitchen, the Great Room has an open, warm feel
- The Master Suite is set off from the rest of the house, and has a tray ceiling
- On the second floor, there are four additional Bedrooms and a Game Room that overlooks the entry
- No materials list is available for this plan

FIRST FLOOR — 1,822 SQ. FT.
SECOND FLOOR — 716 SQ. FT.
BONUS — 540 SQ. FT.
GARAGE & STORAGE — 479 SQ. FT.

TOTAL LIVING AREA:
2,538 SQ. FT.

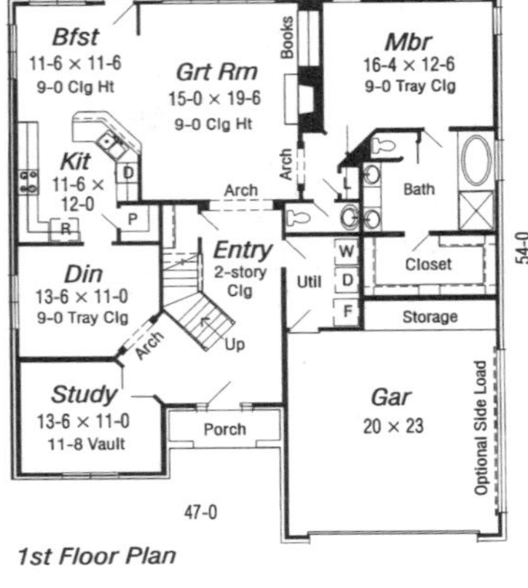

Bfst
11-6 × 11-6
9-0 Clg Ht
Grt Rm
15-0 × 19-6
9-0 Clg Ht
Books
Mbr
16-4 × 12-6
9-0 Tray Clg
Kit
11-6 ×
12-0
Arch
Bath
Entry
2-story
Clg
Closet
Din
13-6 × 11-0
9-0 Tray Clg
Util
Storage
54-0
Study
13-6 × 11-0
11-8 Vault
Porch
Gar
20 × 23
Optional Side Load
47-0
1st Floor Plan

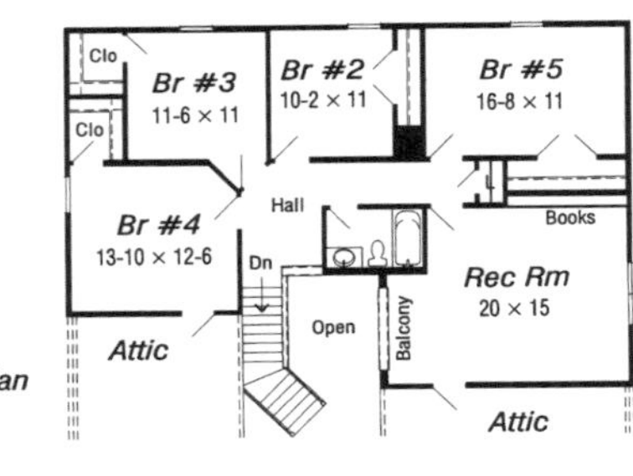

Clo
Br #3
11-6 × 11
Br #2
10-2 × 11
Br #5
16-8 × 11
Br #4
13-10 × 12-6
Hall
Books
Rec Rm
20 × 15
Dn
Open
Balcony
Attic
Attic

2nd Floor Plan

PLAN NO.92501

Design by
Rick Garner

European Style

Price Code: F

- This plan features:
- — Four bedrooms
- — Three full and one half baths
- Central Foyer between spacious Living and Dining rooms with arched windows
- Hub Kitchen with extended counter and nearby Utility/Garage entry, easily serves Breakfast area and Dining Room
- Spacious Den with a hearth fireplace between built-ins and sliding glass doors to Porch
- Master Bedroom wing with decorative ceiling, plush bath and two walk-in closets
- Three additional bedrooms with ample closets and private access to a full bath
- An optional crawl space or slab foundation — please specify when ordering

MAIN AREA — 2,727 SQ. FT.
GARAGE — 569 SQ. FT.

TOTAL LIVING AREA:
2,727 SQ. FT.

MAIN AREA

WIDTH 70'-10"
DEPTH 64'-5"

br 4 12 x 12 · porch 32 x 6 · eating 12 x 12 · mbr 22 x 16 · den 20 x 18 · util · sto · br 3 12 x 12 · kit 12x12 · garage 22 x 22 · living 12 x 14 · dining 12 x 14 · foy · br 2 12 x 12

To order your Blueprints, call 1-800-235-5700

Refer to **Pricing Schedule F** on the order form for pricing information

Design by
Sater Design Group

PLAN NO. 94239

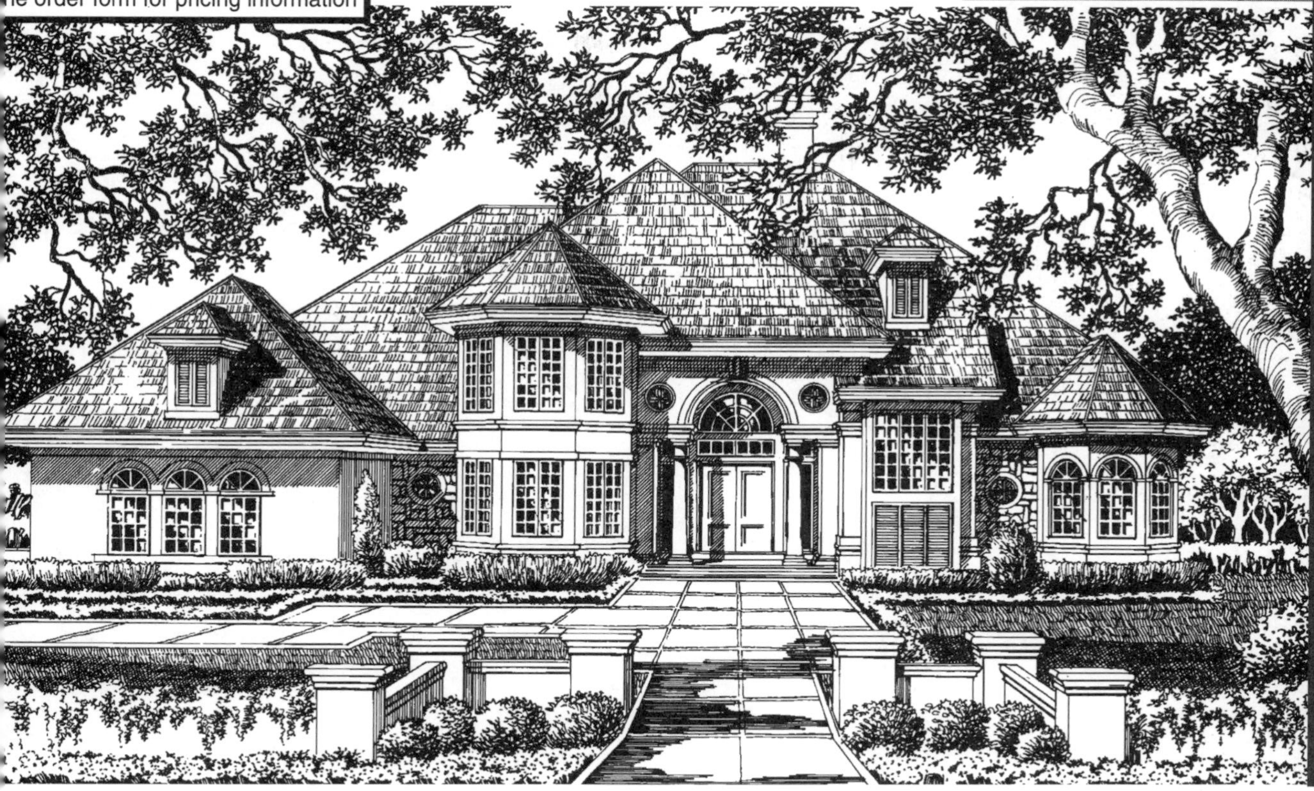

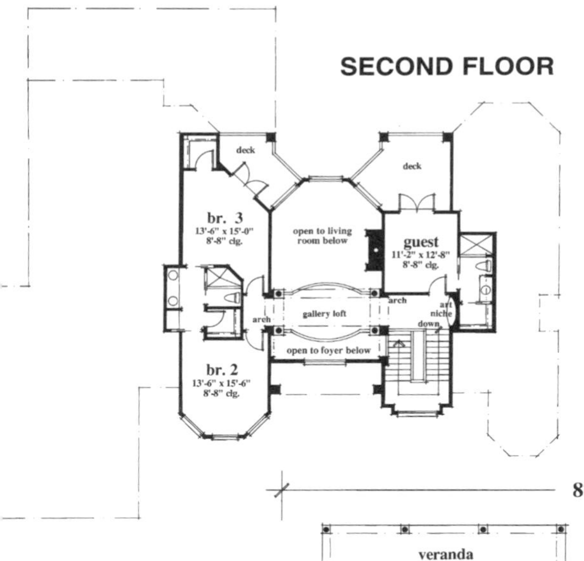
SECOND FLOOR
deck
deck
br. 3
13'-6" x 15'-0"
8'-8" clg.
open to living room below
guest
11'-2" x 12'-8"
8'-8" clg.
gallery loft
arch
art niche
down
open to foyer below
br. 2
13'-6" x 15'-6"
8'-8" clg.

FIRST FLOOR — 3,027 SQ. FT.
SECOND FLOOR — 1,079 SQ. FT.
BASEMENT — 3,027 SQ. FT.
GARAGE — 802 SQ. FT.

TOTAL LIVING AREA:
4,106 SQ. FT.

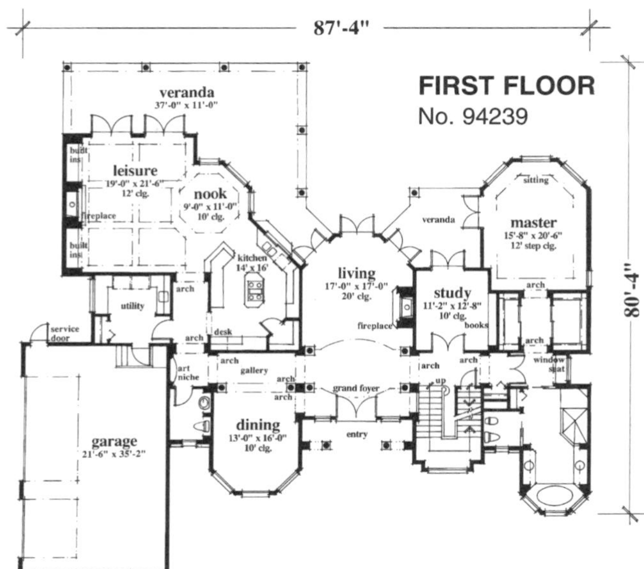
87'-4"
FIRST FLOOR
No. 94239
veranda
37'-0" x 11'-0"
leisure
19'-0" x 21'-6"
12' clg.
built ins
fireplace
nook
9'-0" x 11'-0"
10' clg.
kitchen
14' x 16'
living
17'-0" x 17'-0"
20' clg.
fireplace
veranda
master
15'-8" x 20'-6"
12' step clg.
sitting
study
11'-2" x 12'-8"
10' clg.
books
utility
service door
desk
gallery
grand foyer
entry
window seat
art niche
dining
13'-0" x 16'-0"
10' clg.
garage
21'-6" x 35'-2"
80'-4"

Spectacular Stucco and Stone

- This plan features:
  - — Four bedrooms
  - — One full, two three-quarter and one half baths
- Arches and columns accent formal spaces
- Open Living Room with fireplace and multiple doors to rear grounds
- Formal Dining Room has a bay window conveniently located
- Angled Kitchen with walk-in Pantry and peninsula counter
- Master wing offers a step ceiling, two walk-in closets and a lavish Bath
- Two additional Bedrooms and a Guest Suite share second floor and Decks
- No materials list is available with this plan

PLAN NO. 92504

Design by
Rick Garner

Refer to **Pricing Schedule F** on the order form for pricing information

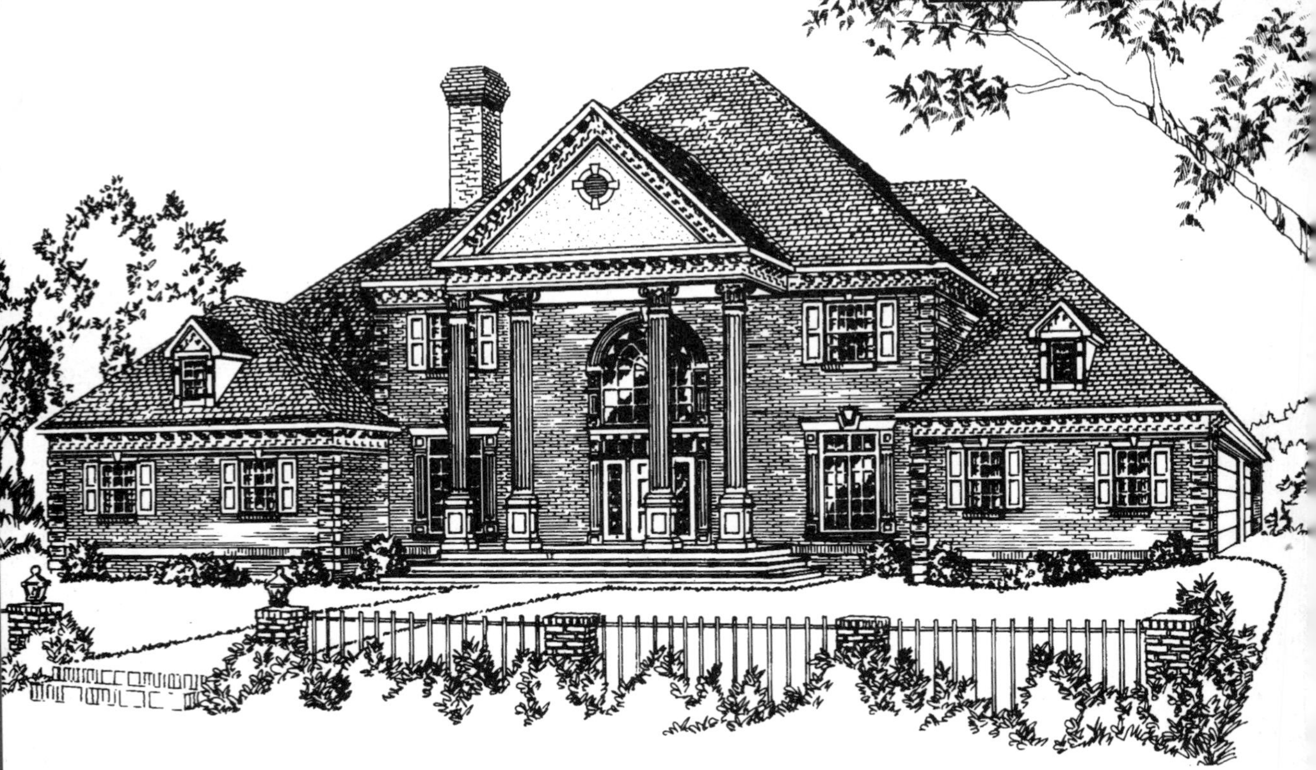

Traditional Elegance

- This plan features:
- — Four bedrooms
- — Three full and one half baths
- An elegant entrance leads to an impressive two-story Foyer
- Floor to ceiling windows in the formal Living and Dining Rooms
- The spacious Den has a hearth fireplace, built-in book shelves and a wetbar
- The Kitchen is equipped with lots of counter and storage space
- The grand Master Suite has decorative ceilings, a private Porch and an elaborate Bath
- An optional slab or crawl space foundation — please specify when ordering

FIRST FLOOR — 2,553 SQ. FT.
SECOND FLOOR — 1,260 SQ. FT.
GARAGE — 714 SQ. FT.

TOTAL LIVING AREA:
3,813 SQ. FT.

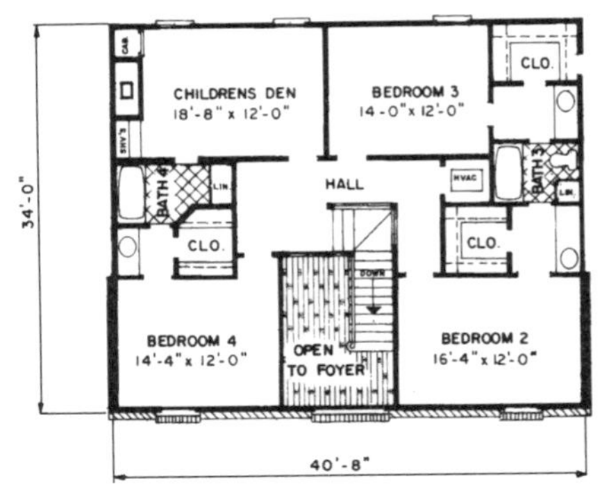

CHILDRENS DEN
18'-8" x 12'-0"
BEDROOM 3
14'-0" x 12'-0"
CLO.
HALL
BATH 4
BATH 3
CLO.
CLO.
BEDROOM 4
14'-4" x 12'-0"
OPEN TO FOYER
BEDROOM 2
16'-4" x 12'-0"
34'-0"
40'-8"

SECOND FLOOR PLAN

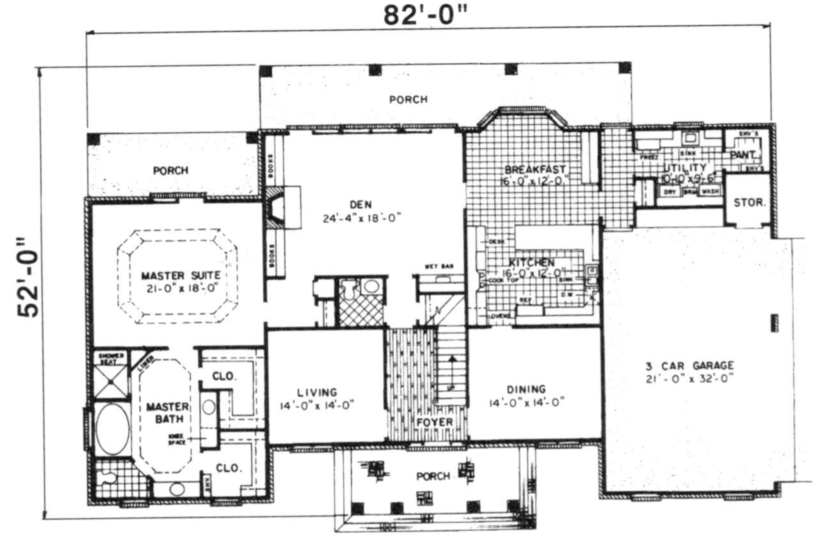

82'-0"
52'-0"
PORCH
PORCH
DEN
24'-4" x 18'-0"
BREAKFAST
16'-0" x 12'-0"
UTILITY
10'-0" x 9'-6"
STOR.
MASTER SUITE
21'-0" x 18'-0"
KITCHEN
16'-0" x 12'-0"
3 CAR GARAGE
21'-0" x 32'-0"
MASTER BATH
CLO.
CLO.
LIVING
14'-0" x 14'-0"
FOYER
DINING
14'-0" x 14'-0"
PORCH

FIRST FLOOR PLAN
No. 92504

Refer to **Pricing Schedule E** on the order form for pricing information

Design by
Garrell Associates Inc.

PLAN NO. 93603

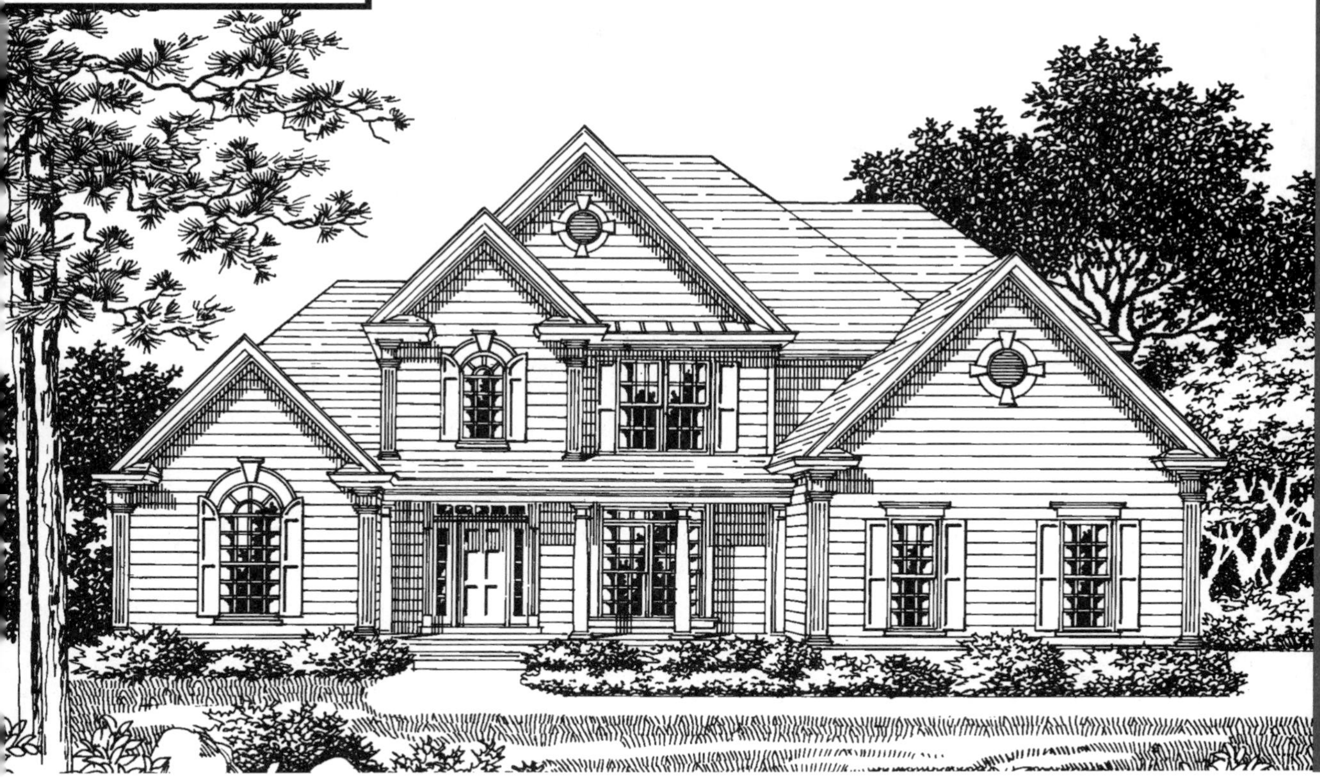

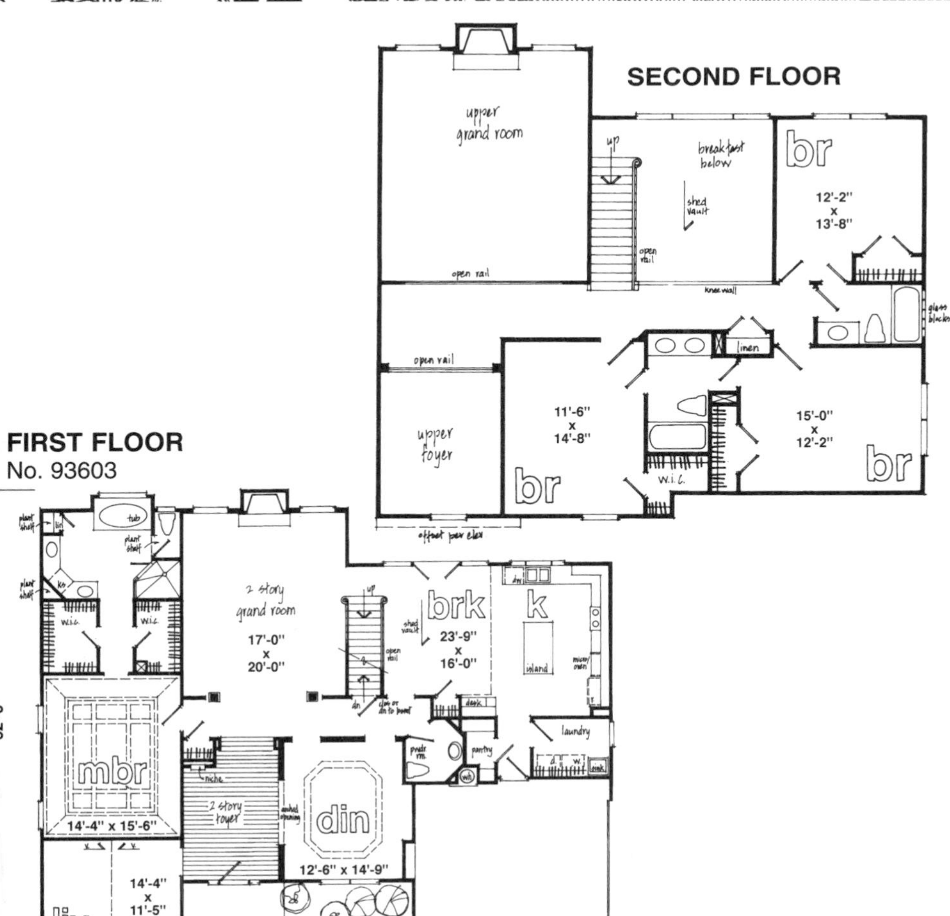

SECOND FLOOR
upper grand room
open rail
up
breakfast below
shed vault
open rail
knee wall
br
12'-2"
x
13'-8"
glass blocks
linen
open rail
upper foyer
11'-6"
x
14'-8"
br
w.i.c.
15'-0"
x
12'-2"
br
FIRST FLOOR
No. 93603
tub
w.i.c.
w.i.c.
2 story grand room
17'-0"
x
20'-0"
up
brk
23'-9"
x
16'-0"
k
island
laundry
pantry
mbr
14'-4" x 15'-6"
2 story foyer
din
12'-6" x 14'-9"
liv
14'-4"
x
11'-5"
gar
60'-0"

Stately Columns and Keystones

- This plan features:
- — Four bedrooms
- — Three full and one half baths
- Gracious two-story Foyer opens to vaulted Living Room and arched Dining Room
- Expansive, two-story Grand Room with impressive fireplace
- Spacious and efficient Kitchen with a work island
- Private Master Bedroom offers a decorative ceiling, two walk-in closets and vanities, and a garden window tub
- No materials list is available for this plan

FIRST FLOOR — 2,115 SQ. FT.
SECOND FLOOR — 914 SQ. FT.
BASEMENT — 2,115 SQ. FT.
GARAGE — 448 SQ. FT.

TOTAL LIVING AREA:
3,029 SQ. FT.

PLAN NO. 99452

Design by
Design Basics, Inc.

Refer to **Pricing Schedule E** on the order form for pricing information

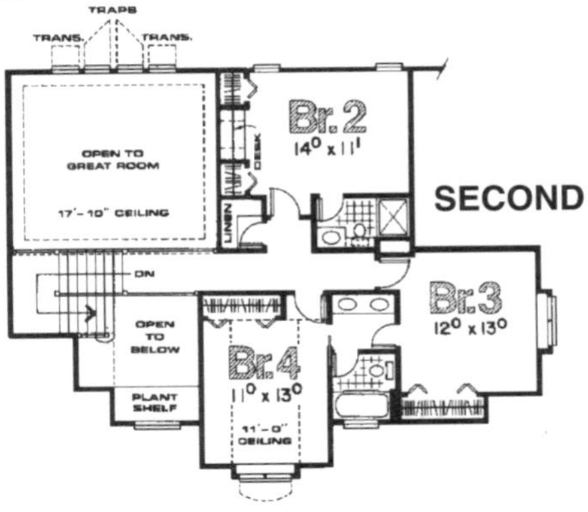

TRAPS
TRANS.
TRANS.
OPEN TO GREAT ROOM
17'-10" CEILING
Br. 2
$14^0 \times 11^1$
DESK
LINEN
DN
OPEN TO BELOW
PLANT SHELF
Br. 4
$11^0 \times 13^0$
11'-0" CEILING
Br. 3
$12^0 \times 13^0$

SECOND FLOOR

Traditional Home

- This plan features:
- — Four bedrooms
- — Two full, one three quarter and one half baths
- Dining Room has a built-in hutch and a bay window
- Cozy Den and Great Room have high ceilings and transom windows
- Conveniently arranged Kitchen adjoins the Breakfast Nook
- The Gathering Room features a fireplace and a cathedral ceiling
- The secluded Master Bedroom is a world away from the busy areas
- Upstairs are three Bedrooms and two full Baths

FIRST FLOOR — 2,158 SQ. FT.
SECOND FLOOR — 821 SQ. FT.
BASEMENT — 2,158 SQ. FT.
GARAGE — 692 SQ. FT.

TOTAL LIVING AREA:
2,979 SQ. FT.

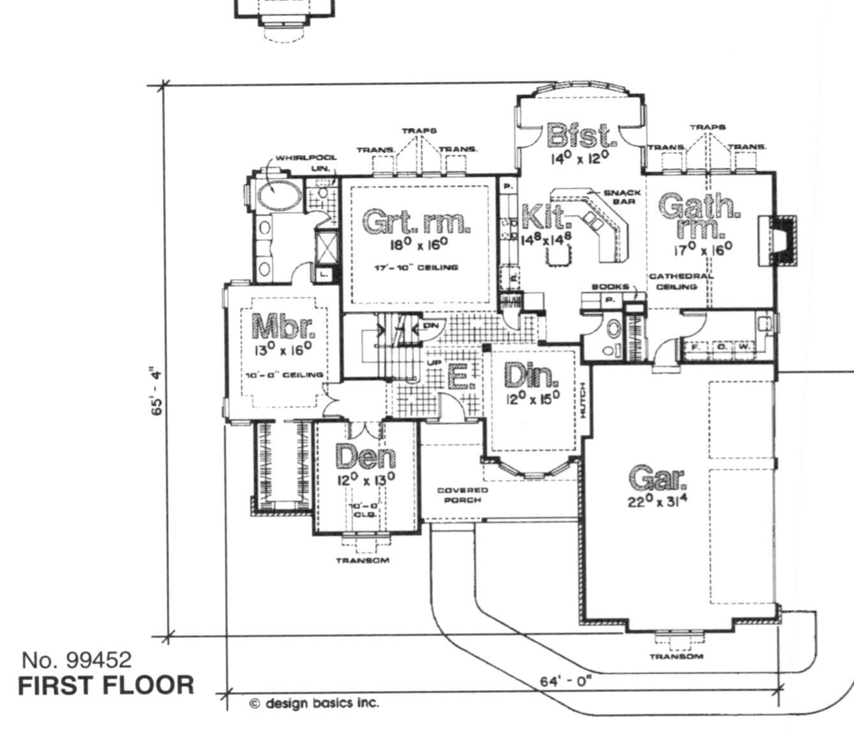
TRAPS
TRANS.
TRANS.
WHIRLPOOL
LIN.
Bfst.
$14^0 \times 12^0$
Grt. rm.
$18^0 \times 16^0$
17'-10" CEILING
SNACK BAR
Kit.
$14^8 \times 14^8$
Gath. rm.
$17^0 \times 16^0$
CATHEDRAL CEILING
BOOKS
Mbr.
$13^0 \times 16^0$
10'-0" CEILING
DN
UP
E.
Din.
$12^0 \times 15^0$
HUTCH
Den
$12^0 \times 13^0$
10'-0" CLG.
COVERED PORCH
TRANSOM
Gar.
$22^0 \times 31^4$
TRANSOM
65'-4"
64'-0"
No. 99452
FIRST FLOOR
© design basics inc.

To order your Blueprints, call 1-800-235-5700

Refer to **Pricing Schedule F** on the order form for pricing information

Design by
Patrick Morabito A.I.A.

PLAN NO. 93321

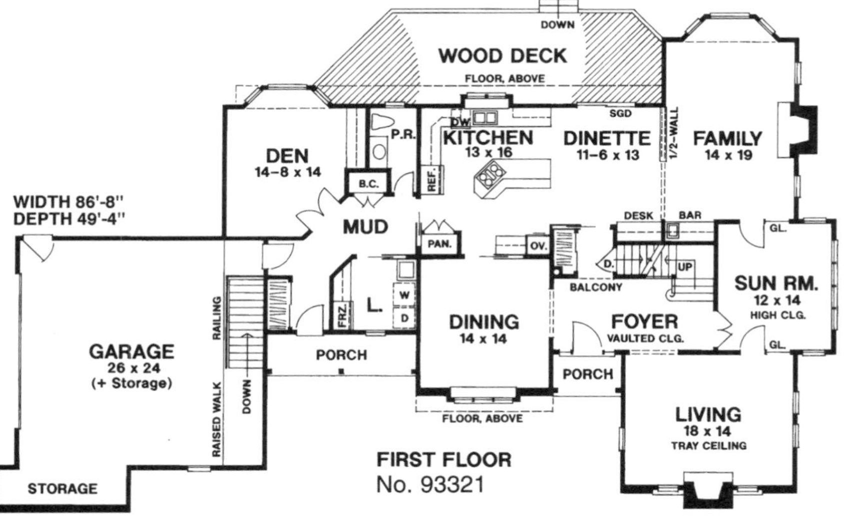

DOWN
WOOD DECK
FLOOR ABOVE
DEN
14-8 x 14
P.R.
KITCHEN
13 x 16
DINETTE
11-6 x 13
SGD
1/2-WALL
FAMILY
14 x 19
WIDTH 86'-8"
DEPTH 49'-4"
B.C.
REF.
MUD
DESK
BAR
PAN.
OV.
GL.
GARAGE
26 x 24
(+ Storage)
RAILING
L.
FRZ.
DINING
14 x 14
BALCONY
FOYER
VAULTED CLG.
SUN RM.
12 x 14
HIGH CLG.
PORCH
PORCH
RAISED WALK
DOWN
FLOOR ABOVE
LIVING
18 x 14
TRAY CEILING
STORAGE
FIRST FLOOR
No. 93321

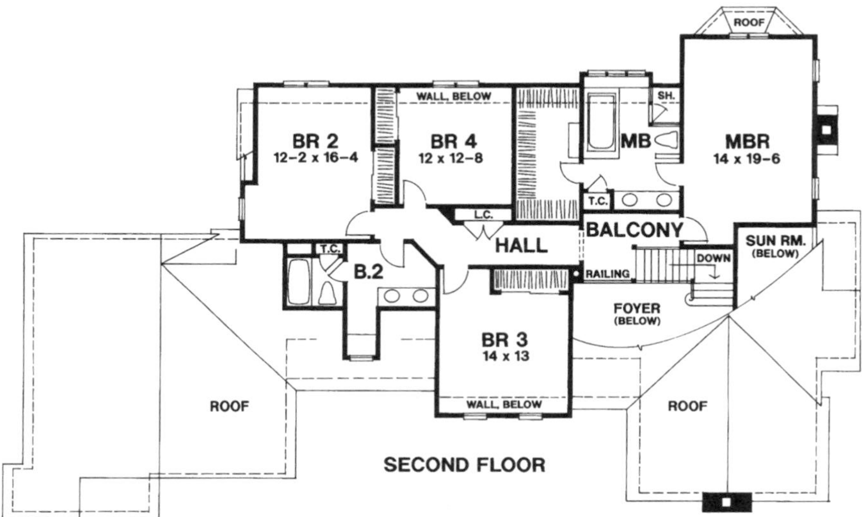

ROOF
WALL BELOW
BR 2
12-2 x 16-4
BR 4
12 x 12-8
SH.
MB
MBR
14 x 19-6
T.C.
L.C.
HALL
BALCONY
SUN RM.
(BELOW)
T.C.
B.2
RAILING
DOWN
FOYER
(BELOW)
BR 3
14 x 13
ROOF
WALL BELOW
ROOF
SECOND FLOOR

A Tasteful Elegance

- This plan features:
- — Four bedrooms
- — Two full and one half baths
- A Foyer with a vaulted ceiling
- A Kitchen with a cooktop island
- The Dinette has sliding glass doors to a wooden Deck
- A Family Room with a beamed ceiling and a cozy fireplace
- A tray ceiling in the formal Living Room and a fireplace
- A Master Bedroom with a stepped ceiling, double vanity private Bath and a huge walk-in closet
- No materials list is available for this plan

FIRST FLOOR — 1,947 SQ. FT.
SECOND FLOOR — 1,390 SQ. FT.
BASEMENT — 1,947 SQ. FT.
GARAGE — 680 SQ. FT.
DECK — 322 SQ. FT.

TOTAL LIVING AREA:
3,337 SQ. FT.

PLAN NO. 94233

Design by
Sater Design Group

Refer to **Pricing Schedule D** on the order form for pricing information

Soft Arches Accent Country Design

- This plan features:
  - — Four or five bedrooms
  - — Two full and one half baths
- Entry Porch with double doors
- Pillared arches frame Foyer, Dining Room and Great Room
- Open Great Room with optional built-ins and sliding glass doors
- Compact Kitchen has walk-in Pantry and a counter/snackbar
- Second floor Bedrooms share a computer loft and full Bath
- No materials list is available for this plan
- An optional basement or slab foundation — please specify when ordering

FIRST FLOOR — 1,676 SQ. FT.
SECOND FLOOR — 851 SQ. FT.
GARAGE — 304 SQ. FT.

TOTAL LIVING AREA:
2,527 SQ. FT.

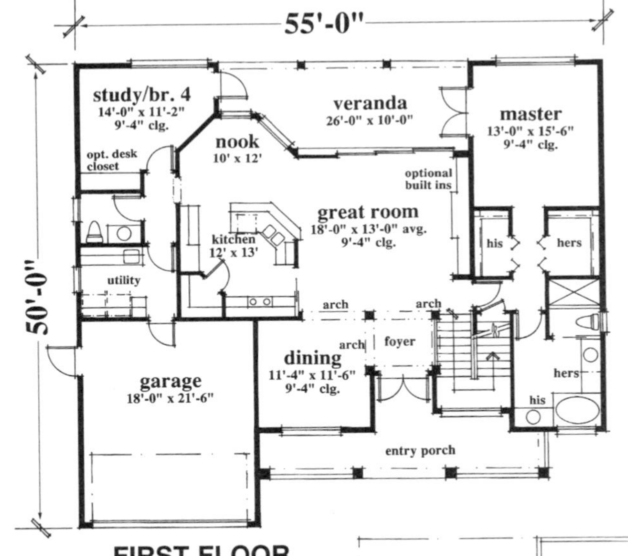

55'-0"
50'-0"
study/br. 4
14'-0" x 11'-2"
9'-4" clg.
veranda
26'-0" x 10'-0"
master
13'-0" x 15'-6"
9'-4" clg.
nook
10' x 12'
opt. desk closet
optional built ins
great room
18'-0" x 13'-0" avg.
9'-4" clg.
kitchen
12' x 13'
his
hers
utility
arch
arch
arch
foyer
dining
11'-4" x 11'-6"
9'-4" clg.
garage
18'-0" x 21'-6"
hers
his
entry porch

FIRST FLOOR
No. 94233

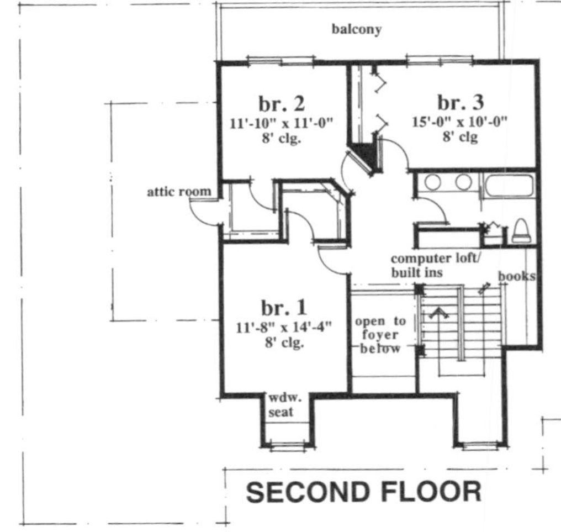

balcony
br. 2
11'-10" x 11'-0"
8' clg.
br. 3
15'-0" x 10'-0"
8' clg
attic room
computer loft/
built ins
books
br. 1
11'-8" x 14'-4"
8' clg.
open to foyer below
wdw. seat

SECOND FLOOR

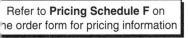

Refer to Pricing Schedule F on
the order form for pricing information

Design by
Landmark Designs, Inc.

PLAN NO.91724

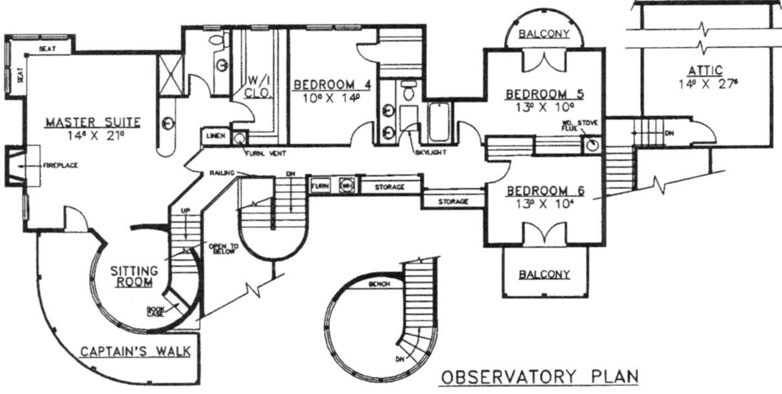

BALCONY
ATTIC
14⁰ X 27⁶
SEAT
W/I CLO.
BEDROOM 4
10⁶ X 14⁰
BEDROOM 5
13⁰ X 10⁰
MASTER SUITE
14⁶ X 21⁰
FIREPLACE
BEDROOM 6
13⁰ X 10⁴
STORAGE
SITTING ROOM
BALCONY
CAPTAIN'S WALK
OBSERVATORY PLAN

SECOND FLOOR PLAN
No. 91724

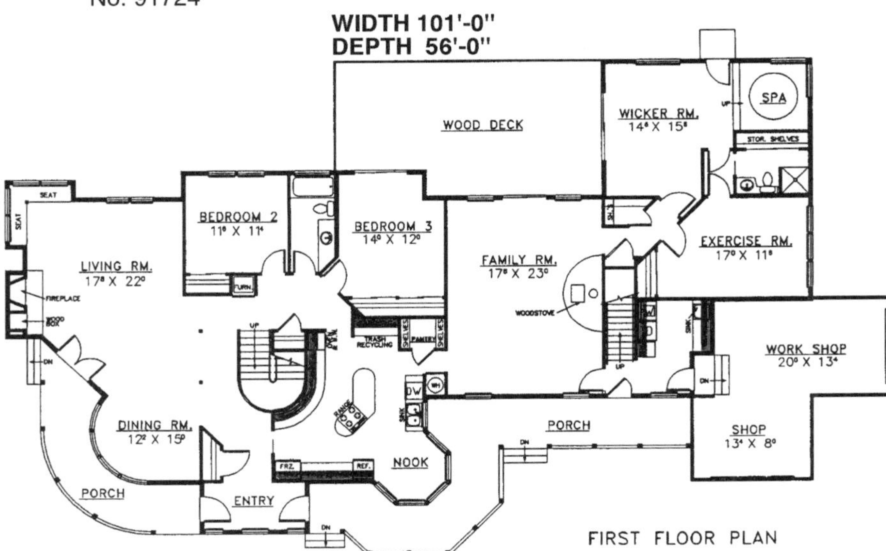

WIDTH 101'-0"
DEPTH 56'-0"
SPA
WOOD DECK
WICKER RM.
14⁶ X 15⁸
BEDROOM 2
11⁰ X 11⁴
BEDROOM 3
14⁰ X 12⁰
FAMILY RM.
17⁸ X 23⁰
EXERCISE RM.
17⁰ X 11⁸
LIVING RM.
17⁸ X 22⁰
FIREPLACE
WOODSTOVE
WORK SHOP
20⁰ X 13⁴
DINING RM.
12⁰ X 15⁰
PORCH
NOOK
SHOP
13⁴ X 8⁰
PORCH
ENTRY

FIRST FLOOR PLAN

Spectacular Victorian

- This plan features:
  - — Six bedrooms
  - — Four full baths
- A multitude of Porches, Decks, balconies, and a Captain's Walk
- L-shaped Kitchen with an angled range/counter
- A large, windowed Exercise Room and Wicker Room with a luxurious step-up Spa
- Living Room with corner window seats and a fireplace
- A Family Room with a woodstove
- A fireplaced Master Suite with corner window seats, a circular Sitting Room, and access to the Captain's Walk

FIRST FLOOR — 3,031 SQ. FT.
SECOND FLOOR — 1,578 SQ. FT.
GARAGE — 514 SQ. FT.

TOTAL LIVING AREA:
4,609 SQ. FT.

PLAN NO. 24403

Design by
The Garlinghouse Company

Refer to **Pricing Schedule E** on the order form for pricing information

Large Wrap-Around Porch

- This plan features:
- — Three or four bedrooms
- — Two full and one three quarter baths
- A large wrap-around Porch adds an old-fashioned feel
- A large entrance Foyer has an attractive staircase
- An elegant Dining Room is topped by a decorative ceiling treatment
- The Family Room is equipped with a fireplace
- The informal Breakfast Room is enhanced by a planning Desk
- Find a peninsula counter/eating bar and ample counter space in the Kitchen
- A cathedral ceiling crowns the Master Suite

FIRST FLOOR — 1,378 SQ. FT.
SECOND FLOOR — 1,269 SQ. FT.
BASEMENT — 1,378 SQ. FT.
GARAGE — 717 SQ. FT.

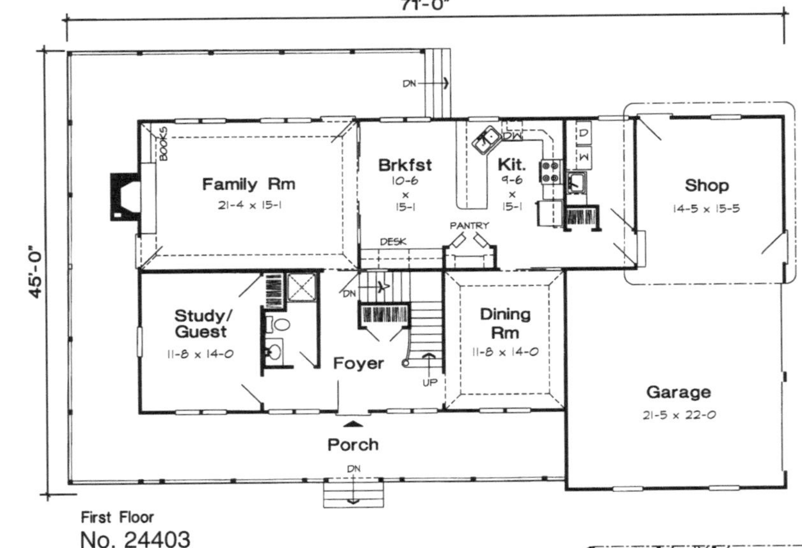

71'-0"
45'-0"
DN
BOOKS
Family Rm
21-4 x 15-1
Brkfst
10-6 x 15-1
Kit.
9-6 x 15-1
DW
PANTRY
DESK
Shop
14-5 x 15-5
Study/
Guest
11-8 x 14-0
Foyer
UP
Dining
Rm
11-8 x 14-0
Garage
21-5 x 22-0
Porch
DN

First Floor
No. 24403

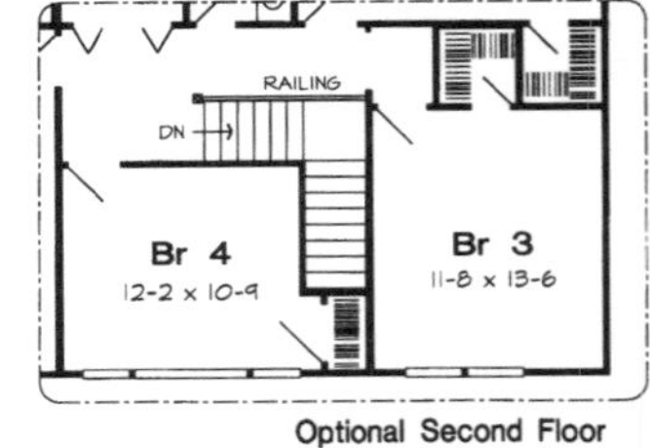

RAILING
DN
Br 4
12-2 x 10-9
Br 3
11-8 x 13-6

Optional Second Floor

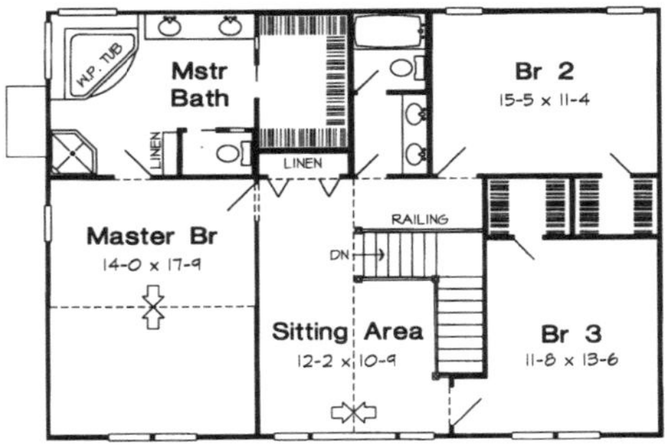

TOTAL LIVING AREA:
2,647 SQ. FT.

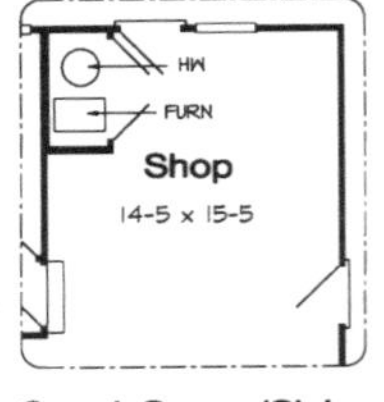

HW
FURN
Shop
14-5 x 15-5

Crawl Space/Slab Option

To order your Blueprints, call 1-800-235-5700

Refer to **Pricing Schedule F** on
e order form for pricing information

Design by
Filmore Design Group

PLAN NO. 98508

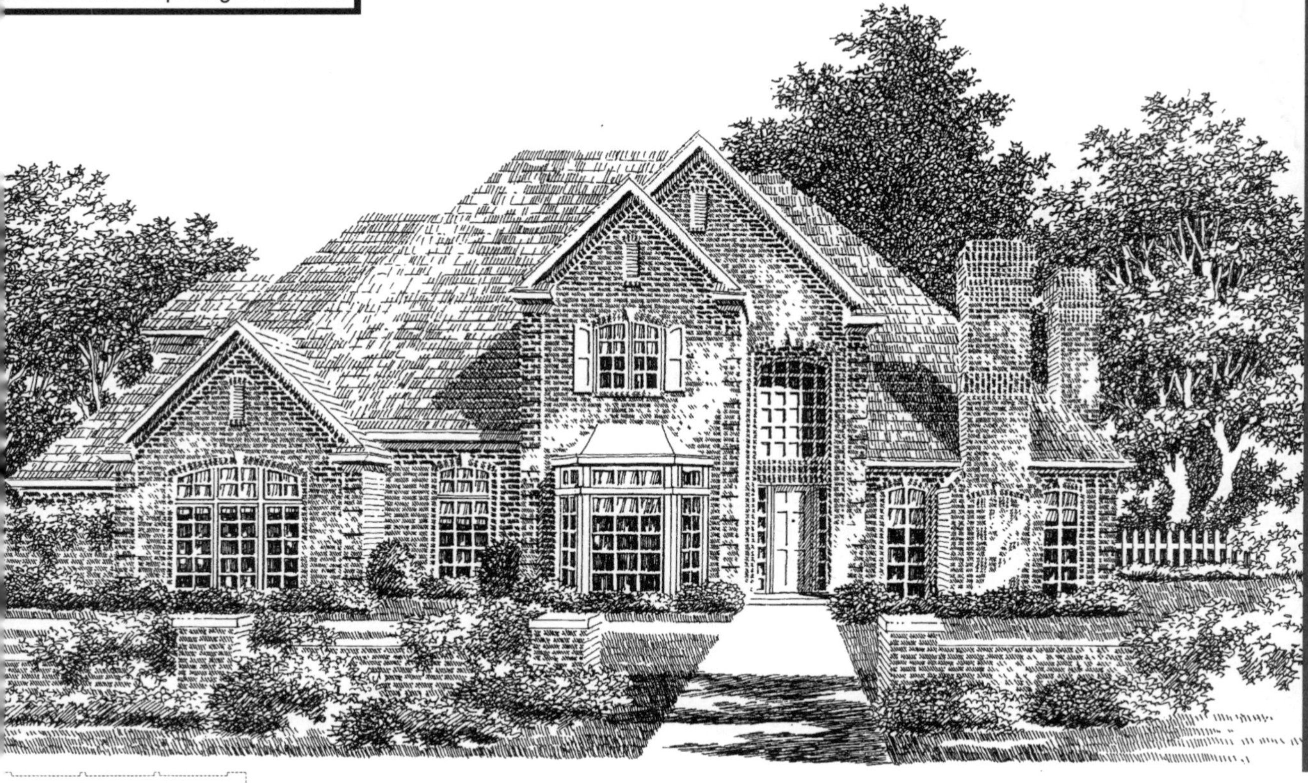

Attic Storage
Bed#4 13x14[6]
Future Playroom 271 Sq. Ft. Not Included In Total Square Footage
Bed#3 13x13
Balcony
Bed#2 13x12[6]
No. 98508
Upper Floor

TOTAL LIVING AREA:
3,480 SQ. FT.

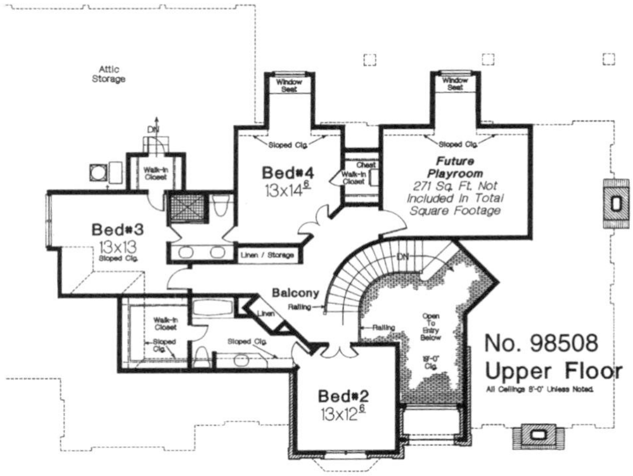

Country Estate Home

- This plan features:
  - — Four bedrooms
  - — Three full and one half baths
- Impressive two-story Entry with a lovely curved staircase
- Formal Living and Dining rooms have columns and decorative windows
- A large fireplace and Veranda access accent Great Room
- Hub Kitchen with brick pavers, extended serving counter, bright Breakfast Area, and nearby Utility/Garage entry
- Private Master Suite offers a Private Lanai and Dressing Area
- Future Playroom offers many options
- No materials list is available for this plan

MAIN FLOOR — 2,441 SQ. FT.
UPPER FLOOR — 1,039 SQ. FT.
GARAGE — 660 SQ. FT.
BONUS — 271 SQ. FT.

73'-0"
56'-6 1/2"
3-Car Gar
30x22
Covered Veranda
Kit
Din
10x14
15x16
GreatRm
19x19
Util
MstrBed
15x18
Study
12x11
FmlDin
13x13
Ent
FmlLiv
17x14
Private Lanai
Por.
Main Floor

PLAN NO. 94246

Design by
Sater Design Group

Refer to **Pricing Schedule F** on the order form for pricing information

Separate Guest Quarters

- This plan features:
  - — Four bedrooms
  - — Three full and one half baths
- Portico Entry way opens to a unique courtyard
- Octagon-shaped Grand Salon overlooks Lanai
- Kitchen with a walk-in Pantry
- Master wing has a large Bedroom with a stepped ceiling, a bayed Sitting Area, glass doors to a Lanai, built-ins and a lavish Bath Area
- Private Guest House offers luxurious accommodations
- No materials list is available for this plan

FIRST FLOOR — 2,853 SQ. FT.
SECOND FLOOR — 627 SQ. FT.
GUEST HOUSE — 312 SQ. FT.
GARAGE — 777 SQ. FT.

TOTAL LIVING AREA:
3,792 SQ. FT.

observation deck
bedroom
11'-2" x 13'-6"
9'-4" clg.
overlook
down
bedroom
15'-2" x 11'-8"
9'-4" clg.
80'-0"
96'-0"
lanai
master
20'-4" x 22'-0"
14' step clg.
grand salon
18'-8" x 19'-8"
17'-8" coffered clg.
dining
11'-8" x 13'-6"
10' clg.
foyer
study
14'-0" x 14'-0"
13' step clg.
kitchen
nook
10'-0" x 12'-0"
10' clg.
garage
11'-6" x 16'-6"
optional pool
leisure
18'-4" x 21'-4"
14'-6" step clg.
entertainment center
portico entry
garage
22'-0" x 23'-6"
motorcourt
guest house
14'-0" x 13'-2"
10' clg.

SECOND FLOOR

FIRST FLOOR
No. 94246

Refer to **Pricing Schedule F** on the order form for pricing information

Design by
Frank Betz Associates, Inc.

PLAN NO. 98404

© Frank Betz Associates

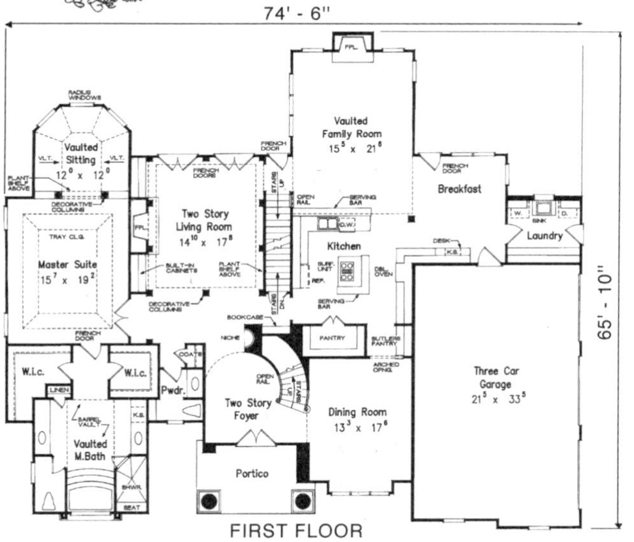

74' - 6"

65' - 10"

FIRST FLOOR
No. 98404

Sensational Entry

- This plan features:
- — Four bedrooms
- — Three full and one half baths
- Two-story Living Room accented by columns, a massive fireplace and French doors to the rear yard
- Vaulted Family Room highlighted by outdoor views and a cozy fireplace
- Kitchen with a cooktop island/serving bar, walk-in Pantry, Breakfast Area and nearby Laundry and Garage entry
- Secluded Master Suite offers a vaulted Sitting area with radius windows and decorative columns, two walk-in closets, and a lavish Bath
- An optional basement or crawlspace foundation — please specify when ordering

FIRST FLOOR — 2,764 SQ. FT.
SECOND FLOOR — 1,598 SQ. FT.
BASEMENT — 2,764 SQ. FT.
GARAGE — 743 SQ. FT.

TOTAL LIVING AREA:
4,362 SQ. FT.

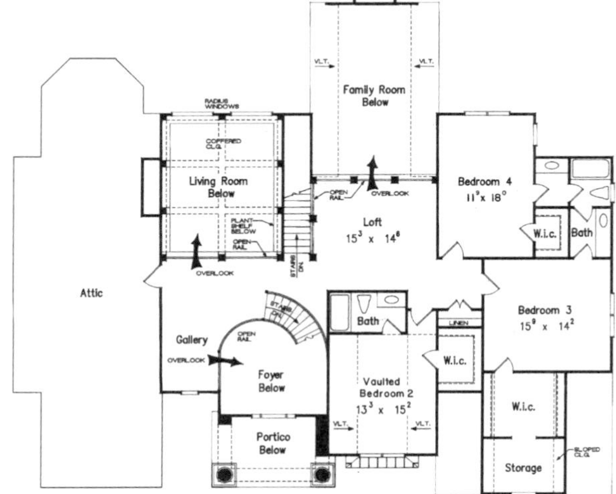
Family Room Below
Living Room Below
Bedroom 4
11° x 18°
Loft
15³ x 14⁸
Bath
Attic
Gallery
Foyer Below
Vaulted Bedroom 2
13³ x 15²
Bedroom 3
15⁹ x 14²
W.I.c.
Storage
Portico Below

SECOND FLOOR

Design by
The Meredith Corporation

Refer to **Pricing Schedule F** on the order form for pricing informatio

Photography by The Meredith Corporat

Luxurious Country

- This plan features:
- — Five bedrooms
- — Four full and one half baths
- A welcoming front Porch adds style to this luxurious country home
- The Living room and the Dining room are located in the front of the home
- The Family room in the rear has a fireplace and doors to the rear porch
- A Playroom is located behind the Garage for the kids
- The Kitchen is designed in a convenient U-shape
- Upstairs find the Master Bedroom which comprises half of the space
- Also upstairs are four secondary bedrooms

FIRST FLOOR — 1,928 SQ. FT.
SECOND FLOOR — 2,364 SQ. FT.
GARAGE — 578 SQ. FT.

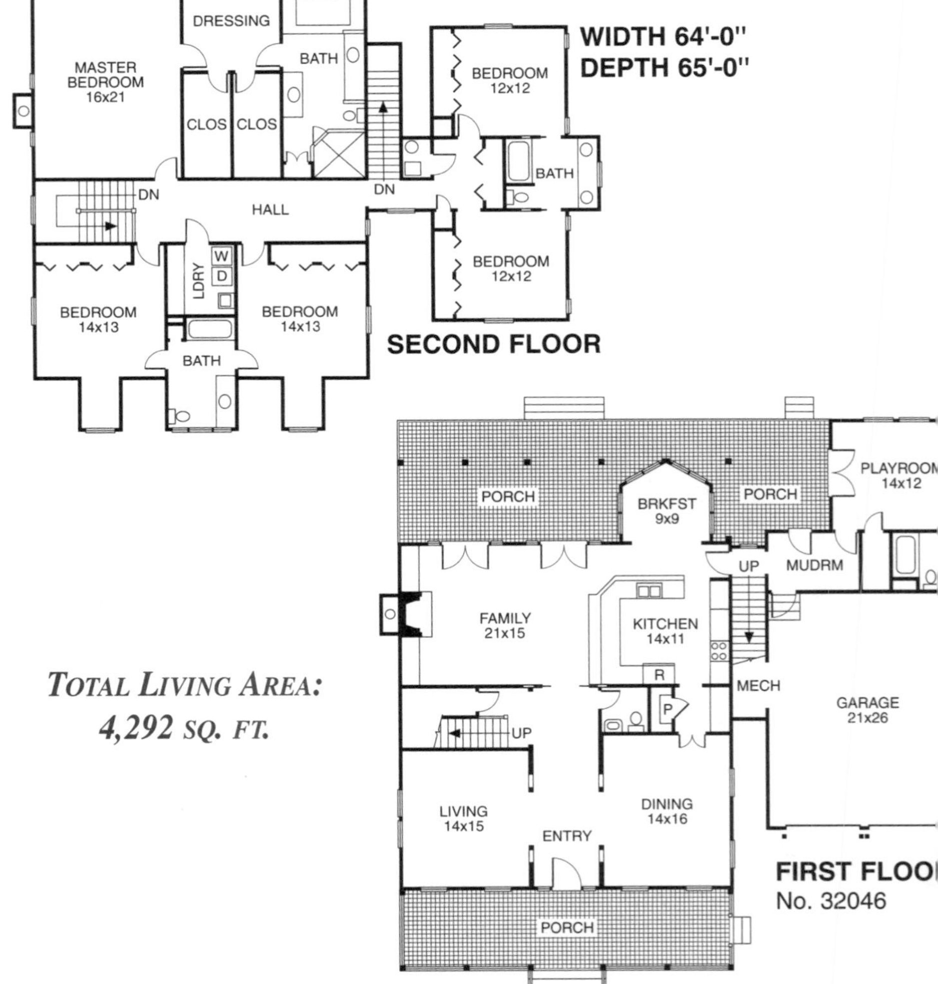
MASTER BEDROOM 16x21
DRESSING
BATH
CLOS
CLOS
DN
HALL
DN
BEDROOM 12x12
BATH
BEDROOM 12x12
LDRY
W
D
BEDROOM 14x13
BEDROOM 14x13
BATH
WIDTH 64'-0"
DEPTH 65'-0"
SECOND FLOOR
PORCH
BRKFST 9x9
PORCH
PLAYROOM 14x12
UP
MUDRM
FAMILY 21x15
KITCHEN 14x11
R
P
MECH
GARAGE 21x26
UP
LIVING 14x15
ENTRY
DINING 14x16
PORCH
FIRST FLOO
No. 32046

TOTAL LIVING AREA:
4,292 SQ. FT.

Refer to **Pricing Schedule E** on the order form for pricing information

Design by
Filmore Design Group

PLAN NO. 92277

Attic Storage
Attic Access
Bed#4 13x14
Bed#3 14x13
Sloping Clg.
Linen/Storage
Attic Access
Balcony
Open To Entry Below
Bed#2 13x12
Plant Ledge

Upper Floor
All Ceilings 8' Unless Noted.

← 69' - 0" →
← 53' - 10" →

Covered Patio
3-Car Gar 30x22 8' Clg.
Covered Area
Din 10x13
GreatRm 16x18 Cathedral Clg.
Books
Kit 15x15
Desk Below Stairs
Walk-in Closet
Util
Linen
Pantry
Sloping Clg.
Entertainment Center
Pwdr
Books
Ent 19' Clg.
MstrBed 14x18 12' Vaulted Clg.
Study 12x11
FmlDin 13x14
LivRm 13x15
Private Lanai
Porch

Main Floor
No. 92277

Impressive Fieldstone Facade

- This plan features:
  - — Four bedrooms
  - — Three full and one half baths
- Double door leads into two-story entry with a curved staircase
- Formal Living Room features a marble hearth fireplace, triple window and built-in book shelves
- Dining Room has columns and a lovely bay window
- Efficient Kitchen has a cooktop/work island
- Great Room with entertainment center and a fieldstone fireplace
- Vaulted ceiling crowns the Master Bedroom
- No materials list is available for this plan

MAIN FLOOR — 2,190 SQ. FT.
UPPER FLOOR — 920 SQ. FT.
GARAGE — 624 SQ. FT.

TOTAL LIVING AREA:
3,110 SQ. FT.

PLAN NO. 97409

Design by
Design Basics, Inc.

Refer to **Pricing Schedule E** on the order form for pricing information

A Home of Distinction

- This plan features:
- — Four bedrooms
- — Three full and one half baths
- The Dining room and the Study are to either side of the Entry
- The Study's entrance is at an angle with a double door entry
- Columns define the Dining room
- The two-story Family room includes a fireplace and a highly windowed rear wall
- The Breakfast Room is open to the Kitchen
- The first floor Master Suite includes a whirlpool tub, separate shower and two vanities
- The three additional Bedrooms have easy access to a full Bath and ample storage space
- An optional basement or slab foundation — please specify when ordering

FIRST FLOOR — 1,844 SQ. FT.
SECOND FLOOR — 794 SQ. FT.

TOTAL LIVING AREA:
2,638 SQ. FT.

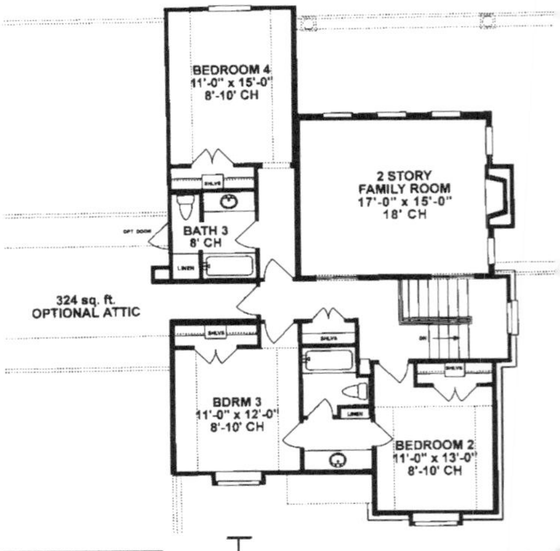

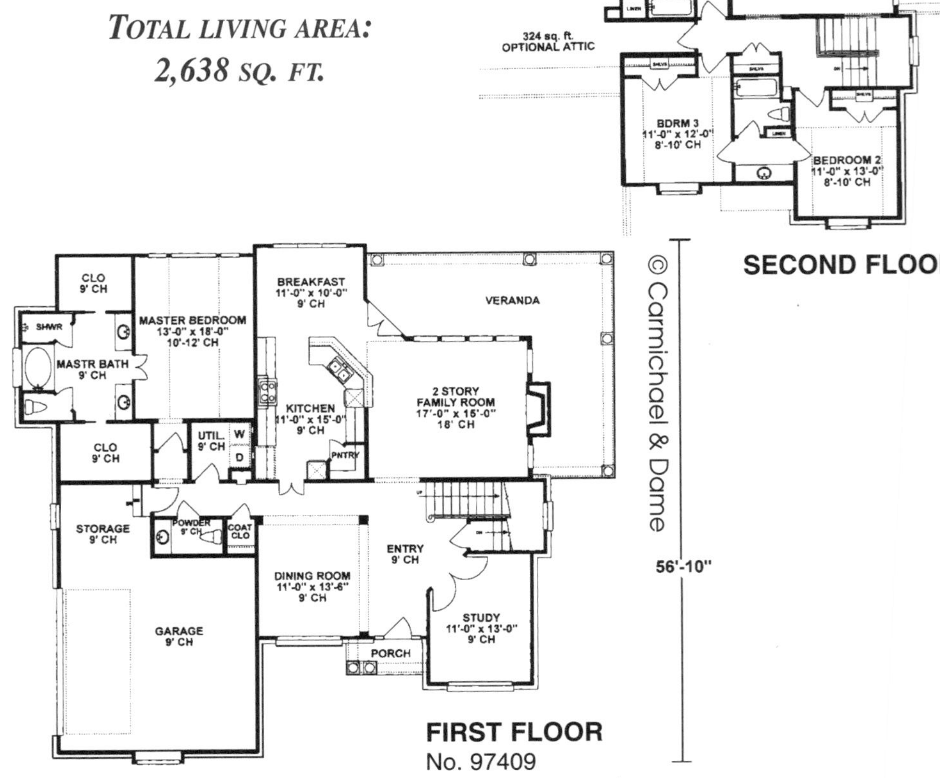
BEDROOM 4
11'-0" x 15'-0"
8'-10' CH
2 STORY FAMILY ROOM
17'-0" x 15'-0"
18' CH
BATH 3
8' CH
324 sq. ft.
OPTIONAL ATTIC
BDRM 3
11'-0" x 12'-0"
8'-10' CH
BEDROOM 2
11'-0" x 13'-0"
8'-10' CH
SECOND FLOOR
CLO
9' CH
MASTER BEDROOM
13'-0" x 18'-0"
10'-12' CH
SHWR
MASTR BATH
9' CH
BREAKFAST
11'-0" x 10'-0"
9' CH
VERANDA
KITCHEN
11'-0" x 15'-0"
9' CH
2 STORY FAMILY ROOM
17'-0" x 15'-0"
18' CH
CLO
9' CH
UTIL.
9' CH
PNTRY
STORAGE
9' CH
POWDER
9' CH
COAT CLO
ENTRY
9' CH
DINING ROOM
11'-0" x 13'-6"
9' CH
STUDY
11'-0" x 13'-0"
9' CH
GARAGE
9' CH
PORCH
© Carmichael & Dame
56'-10"
65'-6"
FIRST FLOOR
No. 97409

Refer to **Pricing Schedule D** on
he order form for pricing information

Design by
Jannis Vann & Associates, Inc.

PLAN NO. 93209

Sundeck
13-6 x 12-0
Screen Porch
8-10 x 11-8
Brkfst.
12-0 x 11-8
Great Rm.
13-6 x 19-6
Kit.
12-0 x 13-8
Lav.
Living
13-6 x 11-6
Open Foyer
7-8 x 13-6
Dining
13-6 x 11-6
Porch
42-0

FIRST FLOOR
No. 93209

Deck
8-10 x 11-8
Master Bdrm.
12-4 x 17-6
Bdrm.4
13-6 x 11-6
M.Bath
Bth.2
Lin.
Balcony
Bdrm.3
13-6 x 11-6
Open To Foyer
Bdrm.2
13-6 x 11-6

SECOND FLOOR

Classic Styling

- This plan features:
  - — Four bedrooms
  - — Two full and one half baths
- A wrap-around Porch adding a cozy touch to this classic style
- A two-story Foyer
- A large Family Room accentuated by columns and a fireplace
- A sunny Breakfast Area with direct access to the Sun Deck
- The Kitchen has an informal Breakfast Area, a Laundry Center and a Pantry
- A private Deck highlights the Master Suite

FIRST FLOOR — 1,250 SQ. FT.
SECOND FLOOR — 1,166 SQ. FT.
FINISHED STAIRCASE — 48 SQ. FT.
BASEMENT — 448 SQ. FT.
GARAGE — 706 SQ. FT.

TOTAL LIVING AREA:
2,464 SQ. FT.

PLAN NO. 93340

Design by
Patrick J. Morabito A.I.A.

Refer to **Pricing Schedule D** on the order form for pricing information

Expansive Family Living Area

- This plan features:
- — Four bedrooms
- — Two full baths and one half baths
- A vaulted ceiling tops the Foyer, achieving a feeling of volume
- The Living Room showcases a tray ceiling, and is enhanced by a boxed bay window
- The Kitchen features a cooktop island and flows into the Dinette
- The Family Room includes a fireplace framed by windows
- Double doors add privacy to the Den
- A tray ceiling tops the Master Bedroom
- No materials list is available for this plan

FIRST FLOOR — 1,378 SQ. FT.
SECOND FLOOR — 1,084 SQ. FT.
BASEMENT — 1,378 SQ. FT.
GARAGE — 448 SQ. FT.

B.R. 2
10-6 X 14-6
B.R. 3
11-6 X 13-0
WHIRLPOOL TUB
M. BATH
M.B.R.
TRAY CLG.
13-8 X 16-8
BALCONY
RAILING
BATH 2
FOYER
BELOW
SLOPED CLG.
B.R. 4
11-0 X 13-0
WALL BELOW
ROOF
ROOF
SECOND FLOOR
No. 93340

TOTAL LIVING AREA:
2,462 SQ. FT.

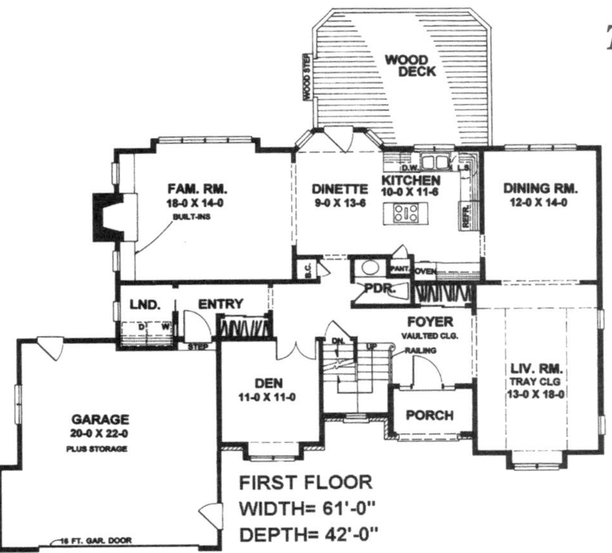
WOOD DECK
FAM. RM.
18-0 X 14-0
BUILT-INS
DINETTE
9-0 X 13-6
KITCHEN
10-0 X 11-6
DINING RM.
12-0 X 14-0
PDR.
LND.
ENTRY
FOYER
VAULTED CLG.
RAILING
DEN
11-0 X 11-0
PORCH
LIV. RM.
TRAY CLG
13-0 X 18-0
GARAGE
20-0 X 22-0
PLUS STORAGE
16 FT. GAR. DOOR
FIRST FLOOR
WIDTH= 61'-0"
DEPTH= 42'-0"

Refer to **Pricing Schedule D** on the order form for pricing information

Design by
Design Basics, Inc.

PLAN NO. 99454

Captivating Colonial

- This plan features:
  - — Four bedrooms
  - — Two full and one half baths
- Decorative windows and brick detailing
- Dining Room highlighted by decorative ceiling, French doors and hutch space
- The Family Room has a fireplace and a bow window
- The Breakfast Nook and Kitchen are perfectly set up for meals on the run
- Upstairs find the Master Bedroom and Bath fully complemented
- An optional basement or slab foundation — please specify when ordering

FIRST FLOOR — 1,362 SQ. FT.
SECOND FLOOR — 1,223 SQ. FT.
BASEMENT — 1,362 SQ. FT.
GARAGE — 734 SQ. FT.

TOTAL LIVING AREA:
2,585 SQ. FT.

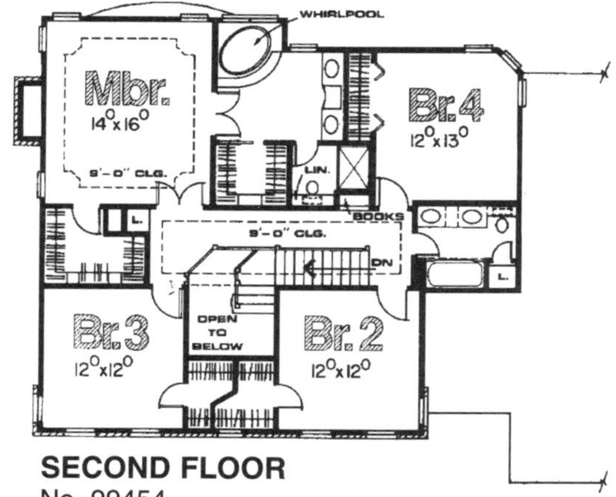
WHIRLPOOL
Mbr.
14^{0}x16^{0}
9'-0" CLG.
Br. 4
12^{0}x13^{0}
LIN.
BOOKS
9'-0" CLG.
DN
OPEN TO BELOW
Br. 3
12^{0}x12^{0}
Br. 2
12^{0}x12^{0}

SECOND FLOOR
No. 99454

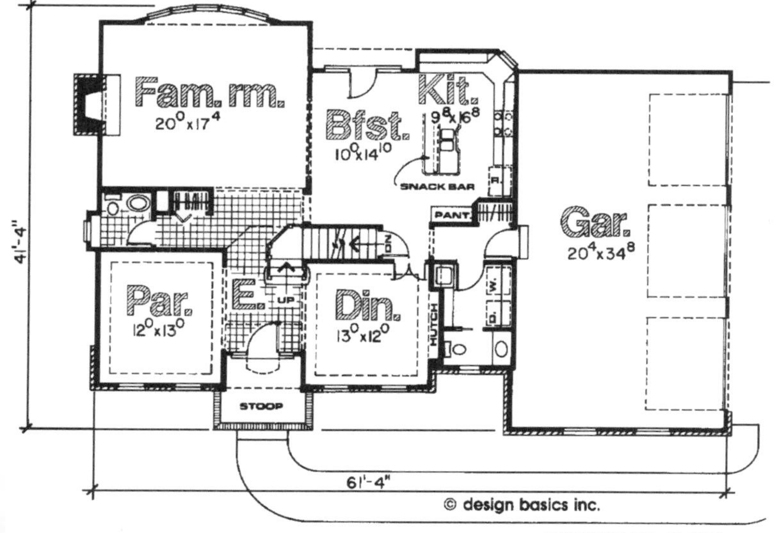
Fam. rm.
20^{0}x17^{4}
Bfst.
10^{0}x14^{10}
Kit.
9^{8}x16^{8}
SNACK BAR
PANT.
Gar.
20^{4}x34^{8}
DN
Par.
12^{0}x13^{0}
E.
UP
Din.
13^{0}x12^{0}
HUTCH
STOOP
41'-4"
61'-4"
© design basics inc.

FIRST FLOOR

PLAN NO. 98525

Design by
Filmore Design Group

Refer to **Pricing Schedule E** on the order form for pricing information

Brick Beauty

- This plan features:
- — Four bedrooms
- — Three full and one half baths
- Living Room and the Dining Room are each distinguished by their impressive front windows
- Kitchen with center island opens into the Breakfast Nook, which has sliding doors to the backyard Patio
- Enormous Family Room with fireplace, will be the central location of family activities
- First floor Master Bedroom is removed from high traffic areas, and is complimented by a spacious Bath and walk-in closet
- No materials list is available for this plan

FIRST FLOOR — 1,842 SQ. FT.
SECOND FLOOR — 843 SQ. FT.
GARAGE — 455 SQ. FT.

TOTAL LIVING AREA:
2,685 SQ. FT.

WIDTH 60'-0"
DEPTH 48'-9"

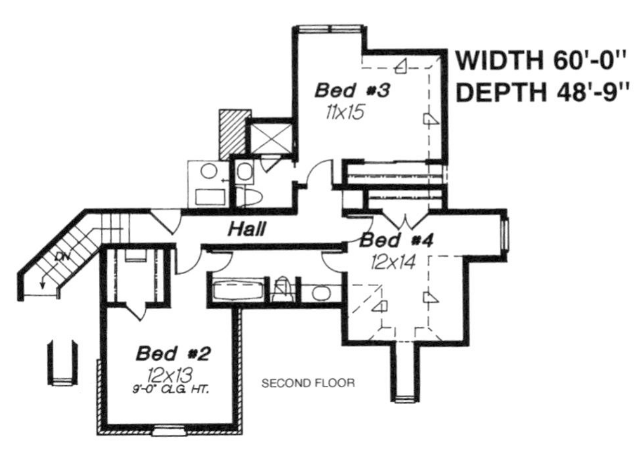

Bed #3
11x15
Hall
Bed #4
12x14
Bed #2
12x13
9'-0" CLG. HT.
SECOND FLOOR

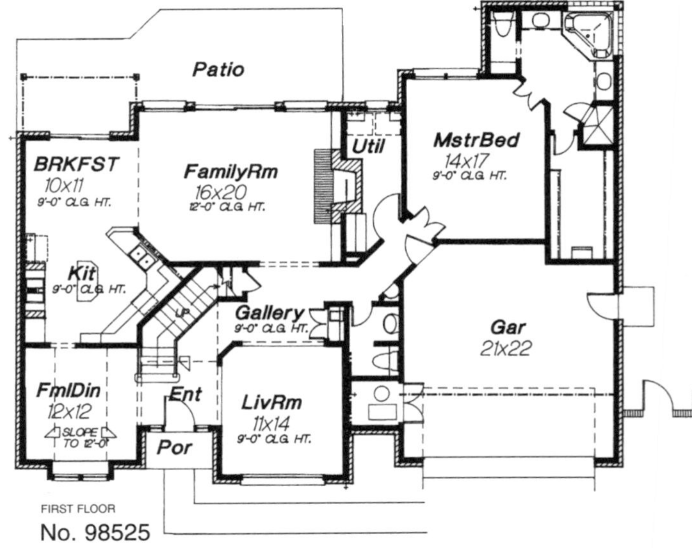

Patio
BRKFST
10x11
9'-0" CLG. HT.
FamilyRm
16x20
12'-0" CLG. HT.
Util
MstrBed
14x17
9'-0" CLG. HT.
Kit
9'-0" CLG. HT.
Gallery
9'-0" CLG. HT.
Gar
21x22
FmlDin
12x12
SLOPE TO 12'-0"
Ent
LivRm
11x14
9'-0" CLG. HT.
Por
FIRST FLOOR

No. 98525

Refer to **Pricing Schedule E** on the order form for pricing information

Design by
Design Basics, Inc.

PLAN NO. 97420

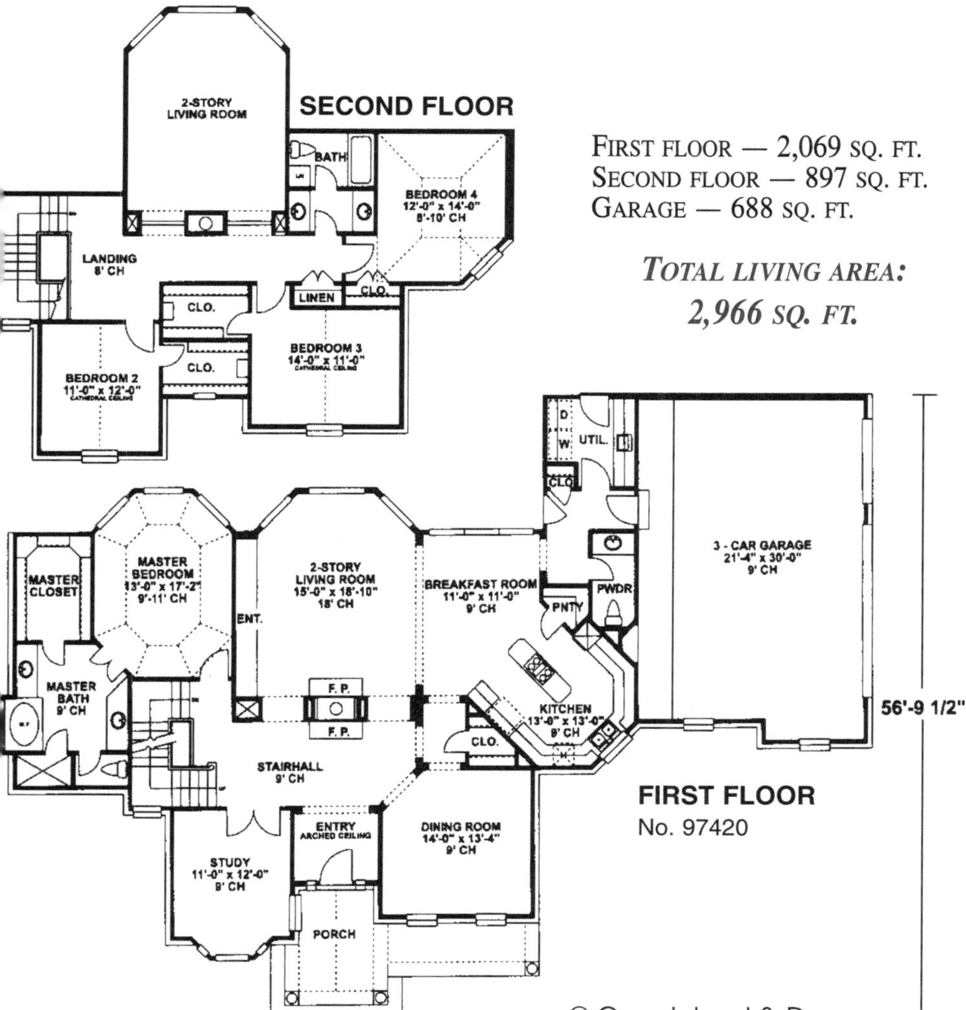

SECOND FLOOR
2-STORY LIVING ROOM
BATH
BEDROOM 4
12'-0" x 14'-0"
8'-10' CH
LANDING
8' CH
CLO.
LINEN
CLO.
BEDROOM 3
14'-0" x 11'-0"
CLO.
BEDROOM 2
11'-0" x 12'-0"
MASTER CLOSET
MASTER BEDROOM
13'-0" x 17'-2"
9'-11' CH
2-STORY LIVING ROOM
15'-0" x 18'-10"
18' CH
ENT.
BREAKFAST ROOM
11'-0" x 11'-0"
9' CH
UTIL.
D
W
CLO
PWDR
PNTY
3 - CAR GARAGE
21'-4" x 30'-0"
9' CH
MASTER BATH
9' CH
F.P.
F.P.
KITCHEN
9' CH
CLO.
STAIRHALL
9' CH
STUDY
11'-0" x 12'-0"
9' CH
ENTRY
ARCHED CEILING
DINING ROOM
14'-0" x 13'-4"
9' CH
PORCH
56'-9 1/2"
82'-7 1/2"
FIRST FLOOR
No. 97420

FIRST FLOOR — 2,069 SQ. FT.
SECOND FLOOR — 897 SQ. FT.
GARAGE — 688 SQ. FT.

TOTAL LIVING AREA:
2,966 SQ. FT.

Manor Styled

- This plan features:
  - — Four bedrooms
  - — Two full and one half baths
- Shutters and round pilasters perfectly contrast the all-brick facade
- The two-story Living room and stair hall share a see-through fireplace
- Bay windows and double doors frame the Study
- An angled Kitchen is positioned to serve the Breakfast Room
- Angled lines in the Master Suite help direct a view to the back towards the Bath
- A wide second-floor landing dramatically overlooks the formal Living Room
- No materials list is available for this plan
- An optional basement or slab foundation — please specify when ordering

PLAN NO. 94145

Design by
James Fahy, P.E., P.C.

Refer to **Pricing Schedule F** on the order form for pricing information

Great Room With Vaulted Ceiling

- This plan features:
- — Four Bedrooms
- — Three full and two half baths
- Cozy covered porch leading into an impressive two-story foyer
- Formal Dining Room accented by a bay window
- A gas fireplace in the Great Room
- Kitchen and Dinette topped by a vaulted ceiling, adjoining with a peninsula counter
- Island Kitchen has an abundance of work and storage space
- First floor Master Suite affords privacy and luxury
- No material list is available for this plan

FIRST FLOOR — 1,845 SQ. FT.
SECOND FLOOR — 876 SQ. FT.
BASEMENT — 1,832 SQ. FT.
GARAGE — 512 SQ. FT.

TOTAL LIVING AREA:
2,721 SQ. FT.

WIDTH 75'-6"
DEPTH 45'-4"

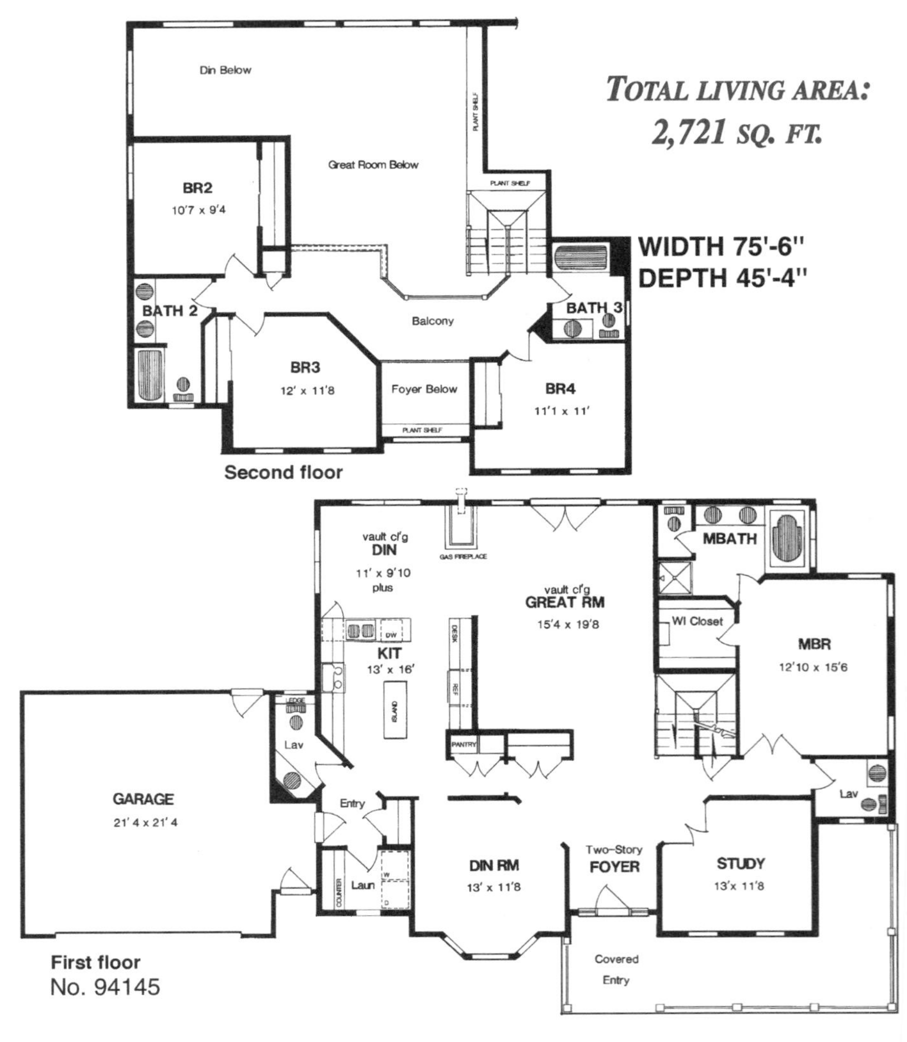

Din Below
Great Room Below
PLANT SHELF
BR2
10'7 x 9'4
BATH 2
Balcony
BATH 3
BR3
12' x 11'8
Foyer Below
BR4
11'1 x 11'
Second floor
vault cl'g
DIN
11' x 9'10
plus
GAS FIREPLACE
vault cl'g
GREAT RM
15'4 x 19'8
MBATH
WI Closet
MBR
12'10 x 15'6
KIT
13' x 16'
ISLAND
DESK
PANTRY
Lav
Entry
GARAGE
21'4 x 21'4
Laun
COUNTER
DIN RM
13' x 11'8
Two-Story
FOYER
STUDY
13'x 11'8
Lav
Covered
Entry
First floor
No. 94145

Refer to **Pricing Schedule E** on the order form for pricing information

Design by
Design Basics, Inc.

PLAN NO. 99489

TOTAL LIVING AREA:
2,613 SQ. FT.

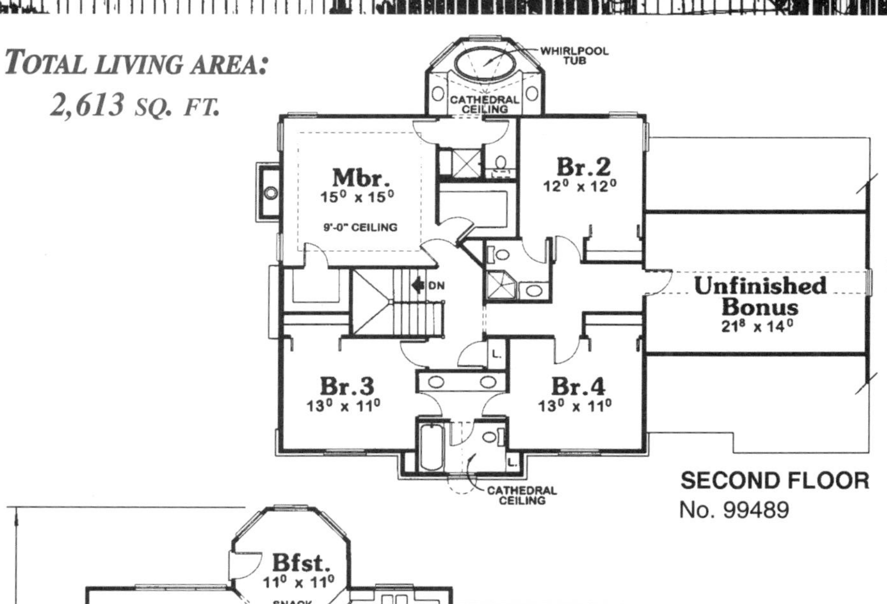

WHIRLPOOL TUB
CATHEDRAL CEILING
Mbr.
15⁰ x 15⁰
9'-0" CEILING
Br.2
12⁰ x 12⁰
DN
Unfinished Bonus
21⁸ x 14⁰
44'-4"
Br.3
13⁰ x 11⁰
Br.4
13⁰ x 11⁰
CATHEDRAL CEILING
SECOND FLOOR
No. 99489
Bfst.
11⁰ x 11⁰
SNACK BAR
Fam. Rm.
18⁰ x 15⁰
Kit.
11⁸ x 12⁰
DESK
WET BAR
SEAT
DN
UP
W. D.
Gar.
21⁸ x 29⁴
OPTIONAL COMPUTER AREA
Liv.
14⁰ x 11⁰
E.
Din.
14⁰ x 11⁰
STOOP
FIRST FLOOR
58'-0"
© design basics inc.

Statuesque in Appearance

- This plan features:
- — Four bedrooms
- — Two full, one three-quarter, one half baths
- The formal rooms flank the Entry and provide views to the front
- An angled snack bar in the Kitchen serves the Breakfast Area
- Bedroom two is the perfect Guest Suite with its own three-quarter Bath
- His-n-her walk-in closets and an extravagant bayed whirlpool tub under a cathedral ceiling set the tone in the Master Suite
- A large bonus room has much potential
- An optional basement or crawl space foundation — please specify when ordering

FIRST FLOOR — 1,333 SQ. FT.
SECOND FLOOR — 1,280 SQ. FT.
BASEMENT — 1,333 SQ. FT.
GARAGE — 687 SQ. FT.

PLAN NO.92273

Design by
Fillmore Design Group

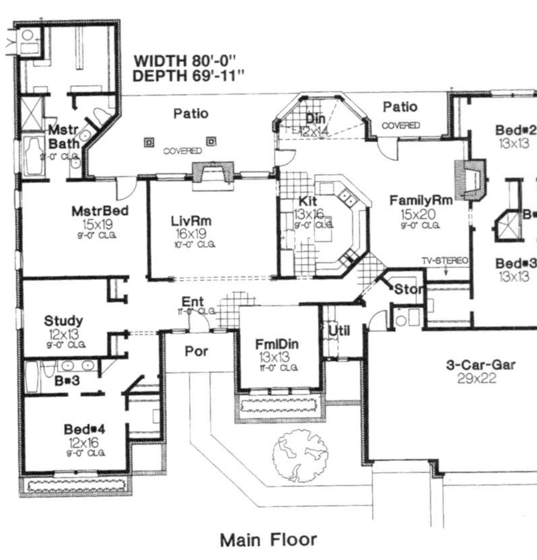
WIDTH 80'-0"
DEPTH 69'-11"
Patio
COVERED
Mstr Bath
Din 12x14
Patio
COVERED
Bed#2 13x13
MstrBed 15x19
LivRm 16x19
Kit 13x16
FamilyRm 15x20
Bed#3 13x13
Study 12x13
Ent
Stor
Util
Por
FmlDin 13x13
B#3
3-Car-Gar 29x22
Bed#4 12x16
Main Floor

Luxurious One Floor Living

Price Code: F

- This plan features:
- — Four bedrooms
- — Three full baths
- Decorative windows enhance the front entrance of this elegant home
- Formal Dining Room is highlighted by a decorative window
- Bright alcove for informal dining, and a Family Room with access to the covered Patio
- No materials list is available for this plan

MAIN FLOOR — 3,254 SQ. FT.
GARAGE — 588 SQ. FT.

TOTAL LIVING AREA:
3,254 SQ. FT.

PLAN NO.10601

Design by
The Garlinghouse Company

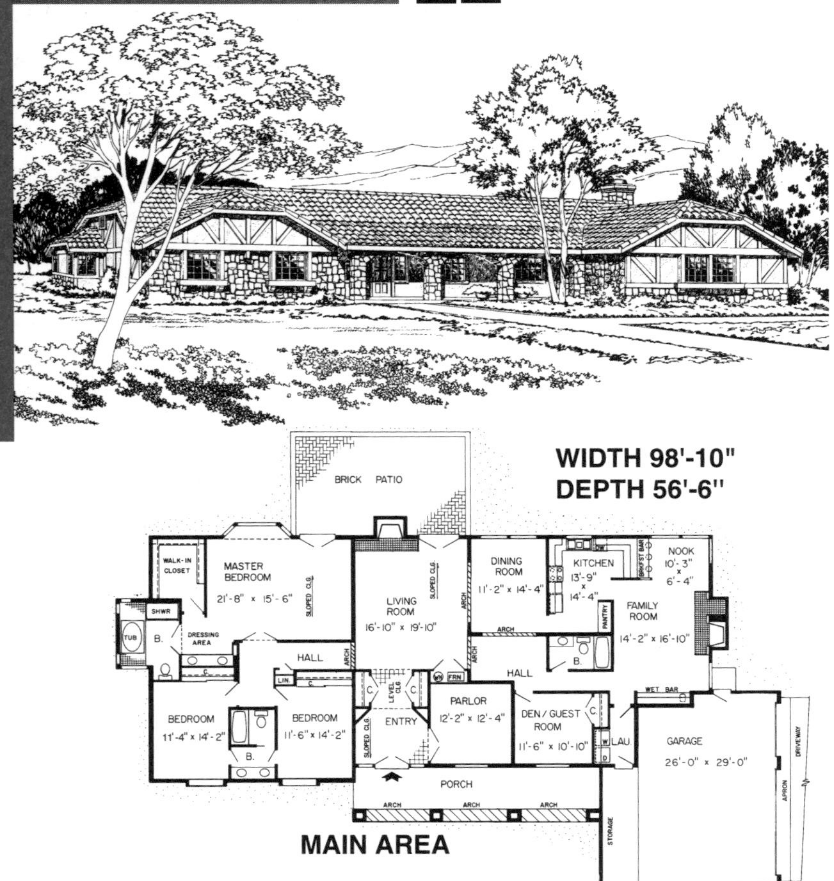
WIDTH 98'-10"
DEPTH 56'-6"
BRICK PATIO
WALK-IN CLOSET
MASTER BEDROOM
21'-8" x 15'-6"
LIVING ROOM
16'-10" x 19'-10"
DINING ROOM
11'-2" x 14'-4"
KITCHEN
NOOK
FAMILY ROOM
14'-2" x 16'-10"
DRESSING AREA
HALL
BEDROOM
11'-4" x 14'-2"
BEDROOM
11'-6" x 14'-2"
ENTRY
PARLOR
12'-2" x 12'-4"
DEN / GUEST ROOM
11'-6" x 10'-10"
GARAGE
26'-0" x 29'-0"
PORCH
MAIN AREA

Unusual Tile Roof

Price Code: E

- This plan features:
- — Three or four bedrooms
- — Three full baths
- Stone arched Porch accesses tiled Entry with sloped ceiling and Parlor through French doors
- Spacious Living Room with sloped ceiling, tiled hearth fireplace, and access to brick Patio
- Convenient Dining Room is enhanced by arches and a double window
- Hub Kitchen has a large Pantry, a breakfast bar and a glass Eating Nook
- Comfortable Family Room offers another fireplace, a wetbar and access to Laundry/Garage
- Den/Guest Room provides many options
- Expansive Master Bedroom has a bay window, Patio access, walk-in closet, dressing area and private bath
- Two additional bedrooms have private access to a full bath

MAIN AREA — 3,025 SQ. FT.
GARAGE — 722 SQ. FT.

TOTAL LIVING AREA:
3,025 SQ. FT.

Refer to **Pricing Schedule E** on the order form for pricing information

Design by
Urban Design Group

PLAN NO. 92053

Total living area:
2,900 sq. ft.

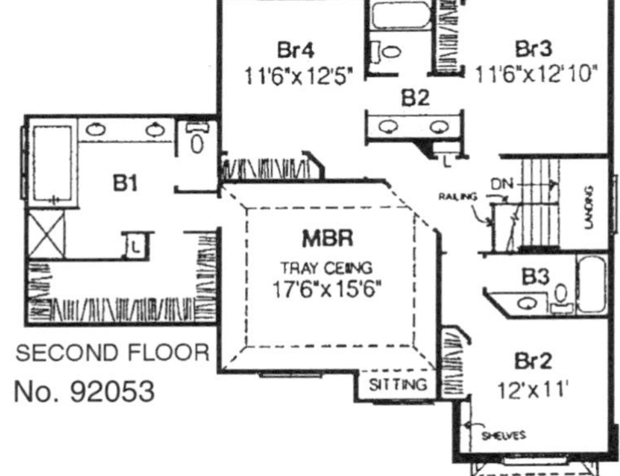

Br4
11'6"x12'5"
Br3
11'6"x12'10"
B2
B1
DN
RAILING
LANDING
MBR
TRAY CEILING
17'6"x15'6"
B3
Br2
12'x11'
SITTING
SHELVES
SECOND FLOOR
No. 92053

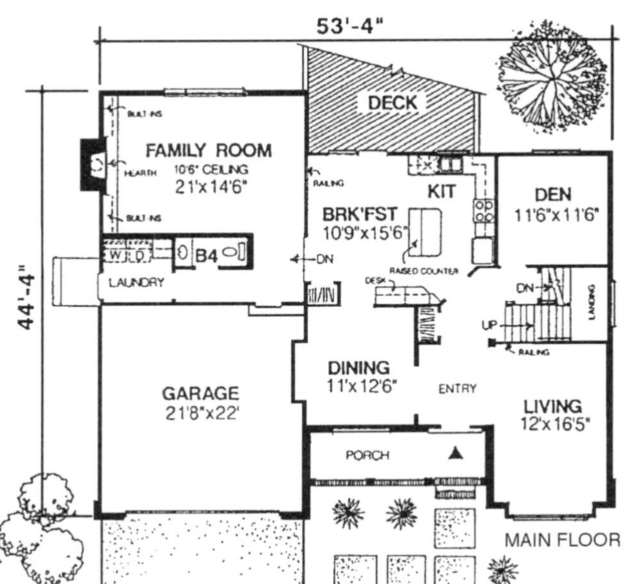

53'-4"
44'-4"
DECK
FAMILY ROOM
10'6" CEILING
21'x14'6"
HEARTH
BUILT-INS
RAILING
KIT
BRK'FST
10'9"x15'6"
RAISED COUNTER
DESK
DEN
11'6"x11'6"
W D
B4
LAUNDRY
DN
UP
GARAGE
21'8"x22'
DINING
11'x12'6"
ENTRY
LIVING
12'x16'5"
PORCH
MAIN FLOOR

Stately Two-Story

- This plan features:
- — Four bedrooms
- — Three full and one half baths
- Refined Colonial styling and the use of brick add a stately presence to this home
- The Living room has a lovely boxed bay window in the front
- In the Dining room find a space specifically for a china hutch
- A railing separates the Nook from the Family room
- The Kitchen has an island with a raised counter on one side
- A private Den is located in a rear corner of the home
- The Family Room features a raised hearth fireplace with built in cabinets on either side
- Upstairs find the Bedrooms all with access to a Bath

First floor — 1,514 sq. ft.
Second floor — 1,386 sq. ft.
Basement — 1,514 sq. ft.

PLAN NO. 90941

Design by
Wesplan Building Design, Inc.

Refer to **Pricing Schedule E** on the order form for pricing information

Exciting Vaulted Sunken Living Room

- This plan features:
- — Four bedrooms
- — Two full and one half baths
- A dramatic, sunken Living Room with a vaulted ceiling, fireplace, and glass walls to enjoy the view
- The well-appointed, Kitchen has a peninsula counter and direct access to the Family Room, Dining Room or the Sun Deck
- The Master Suite has a walk-in closet and a private full Bath
- The Family Room has direct access to the rear Sun Deck

MAIN FLOOR — 1,464 SQ. FT.
BASEMENT — 1,187 SQ. FT.
GARAGE — 418 SQ. FT.

TOTAL LIVING AREA:
2,651 SQ. FT.

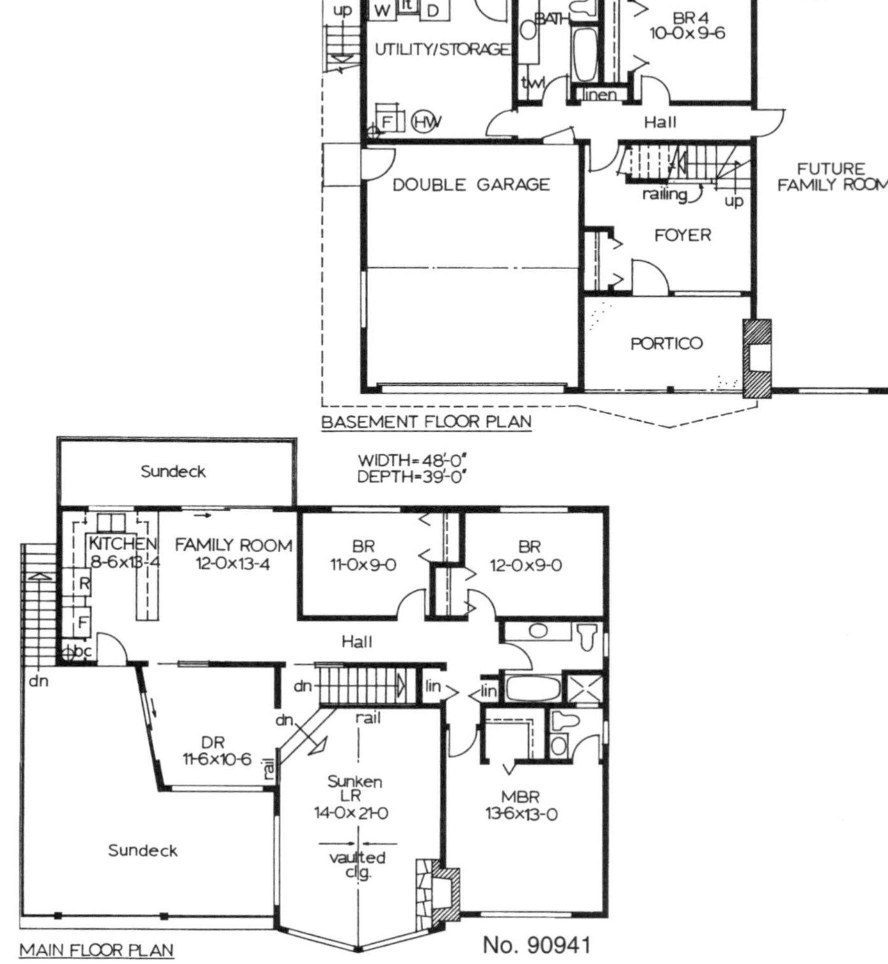

up
W
lt
D
UTILITY/STORAGE
BATH
BR 4
10-0x9-6
twl
linen
F
HW
Hall
DOUBLE GARAGE
railing
up
FUTURE FAMILY ROOM
FOYER
PORTICO
BASEMENT FLOOR PLAN
WIDTH=48'-0"
DEPTH=39'-0"
Sundeck
KITCHEN
8-6x13-4
FAMILY ROOM
12-0x13-4
BR
11-0x9-0
BR
12-0x9-0
R
F
dbc
Hall
dn
dn
lin
lin
dn.
rail
DR
11-6x10-6
rail
Sunken
LR
14-0x21-0
MBR
13-6x13-0
Sundeck
vaulted
clg.
MAIN FLOOR PLAN
No. 90941

Refer to **Pricing Schedule F** on
the order form for pricing information

Design by
The Meredith Corporation

PLAN NO. 32006

otography by The Meredith Corporation

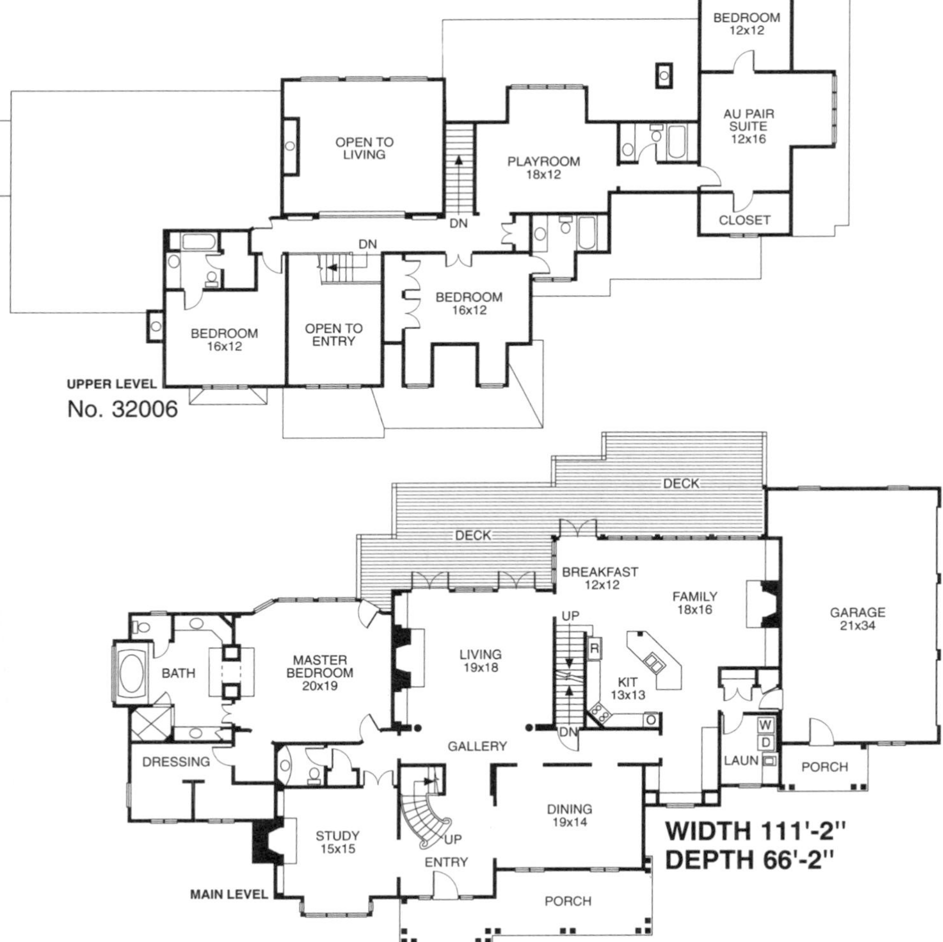

BEDROOM 12x12
AU PAIR SUITE 12x16
OPEN TO LIVING
PLAYROOM 18x12
DN
CLOSET
BEDROOM 16x12
OPEN TO ENTRY
BEDROOM 16x12
UPPER LEVEL
No. 32006
DECK
DECK
BREAKFAST 12x12
FAMILY 18x16
GARAGE 21x34
BATH
MASTER BEDROOM 20x19
LIVING 19x18
UP
KIT 13x13
GALLERY
DRESSING
LAUN
PORCH
STUDY 15x15
DINING 19x14
ENTRY
PORCH
MAIN LEVEL
WIDTH 111'-2"
DEPTH 66'-2"

Country Manor

- This plan features:
  - — Four Bedrooms
  - — Four full and one half baths
- Combined with the Study, the Master Suite occupies an entire wing of the first floor
- Living Room and Dining Room with adjacent locations for ease in entertaining
- Kitchen, Breakfast Nook and Family Room create large informal area
- Three Bedrooms, Au Pair Suite, three Baths and Playroom complete the second floor
- Second floor balcony connects the bedroom wings and overlooks Living Room above Foyer

MAIN LEVEL —3,322 SQ. FT.
UPPER LEVEL — 1,966 SQ. FT.
BASEMENT — 3,275 SQ. FT.
GARAGE — 774 SQ. FT.

TOTAL LIVING AREA:
5,288 SQ. FT.

PLAN NO. 96403

Design by
Donald A. Gardner Architects, Inc.

Refer to **Pricing Schedule F** on the order form for pricing information

B. NATHAN.

Welcoming Exterior

- This plan features:
  - — Four bedrooms
  - — Two full and one half baths
- Columns between the Foyer and Living Room/Study
- Transom windows over French doors open up the Living Room/Study to the Front Porch
- Deluxe Master Suite is topped by a tray ceiling and includes a Bath with a sunny garden tub
- Bonus room is accessed from the second floor and ready to expand for future needs

FIRST FLOOR — 1,483 SQ. FT.
SECOND FLOOR — 1,349 SQ. FT.
BONUS — 486 SQ. FT.
GARAGE — 738 SQ. FT.

TOTAL LIVING AREA:
2,832 SQ. FT.

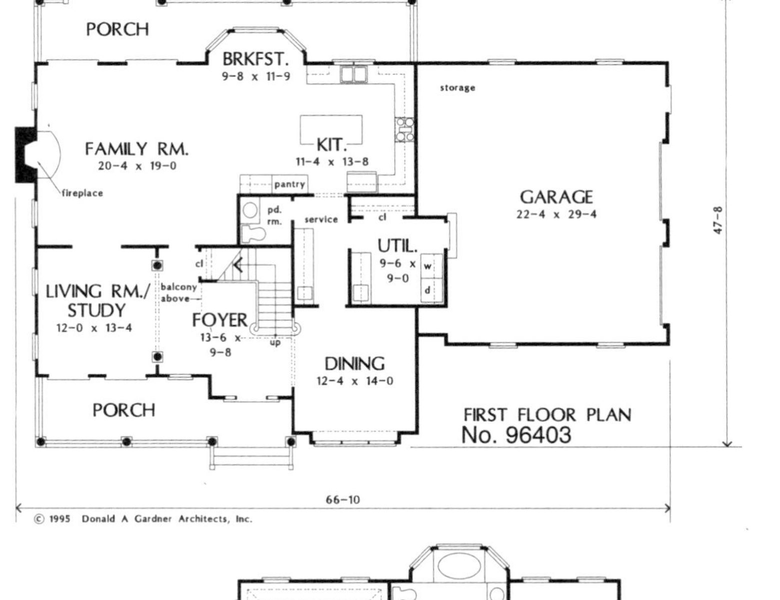
PORCH
BRKFST.
9-8 x 11-9
storage
FAMILY RM.
20-4 x 19-0
fireplace
KIT.
11-4 x 13-8
pantry
GARAGE
22-4 x 29-4
47-8
pd. rm.
service
cl
UTIL.
9-6 x 9-0
w
d
LIVING RM./
STUDY
12-0 x 13-4
balcony above
FOYER
13-6 x 9-8
up
DINING
12-4 x 14-0
PORCH
FIRST FLOOR PLAN
No. 96403
66-10
© 1995 Donald A Gardner Architects, Inc.

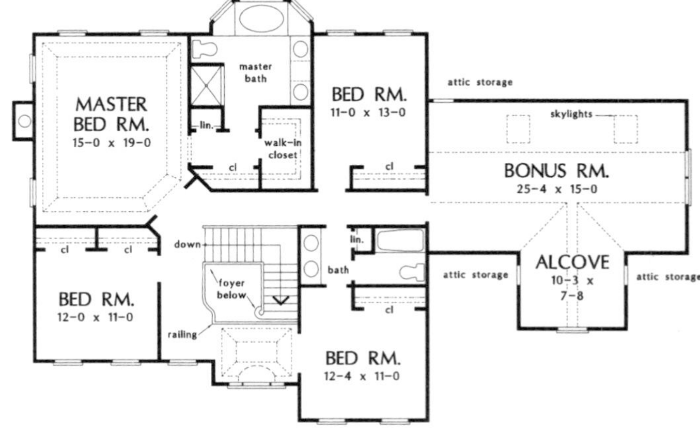
MASTER
BED RM.
15-0 x 19-0
master bath
lin.
walk-in closet
cl
BED RM.
11-0 x 13-0
cl
attic storage
skylights
BONUS RM.
25-4 x 15-0
ALCOVE
10-3 x 7-8
attic storage
attic storage
cl
cl
down
foyer below
railing
BED RM.
12-0 x 11-0
lin.
bath
cl
BED RM.
12-4 x 11-0
SECOND FLOOR PLAN

To order your Blueprints, call 1-800-235-5700

Refer to **Pricing Schedule E** on
the order form for pricing information

Design by
Jannis Vann & Associates, Inc.

PLAN NO. 93206

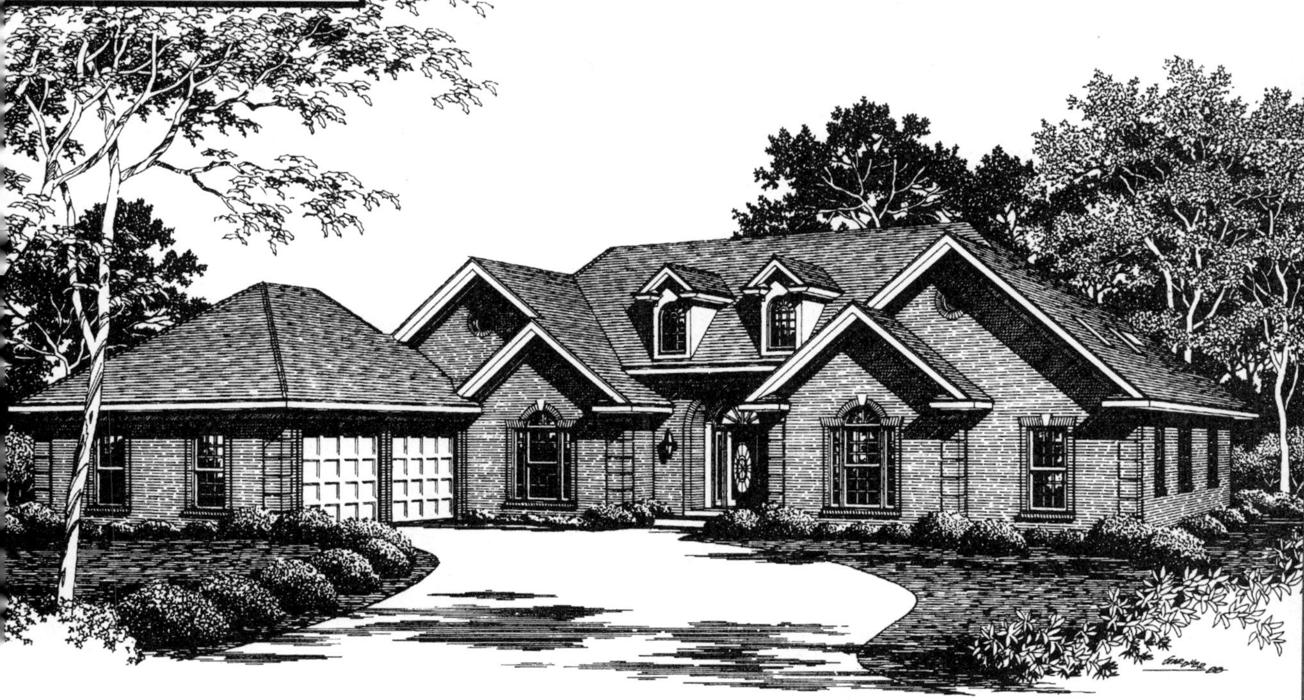

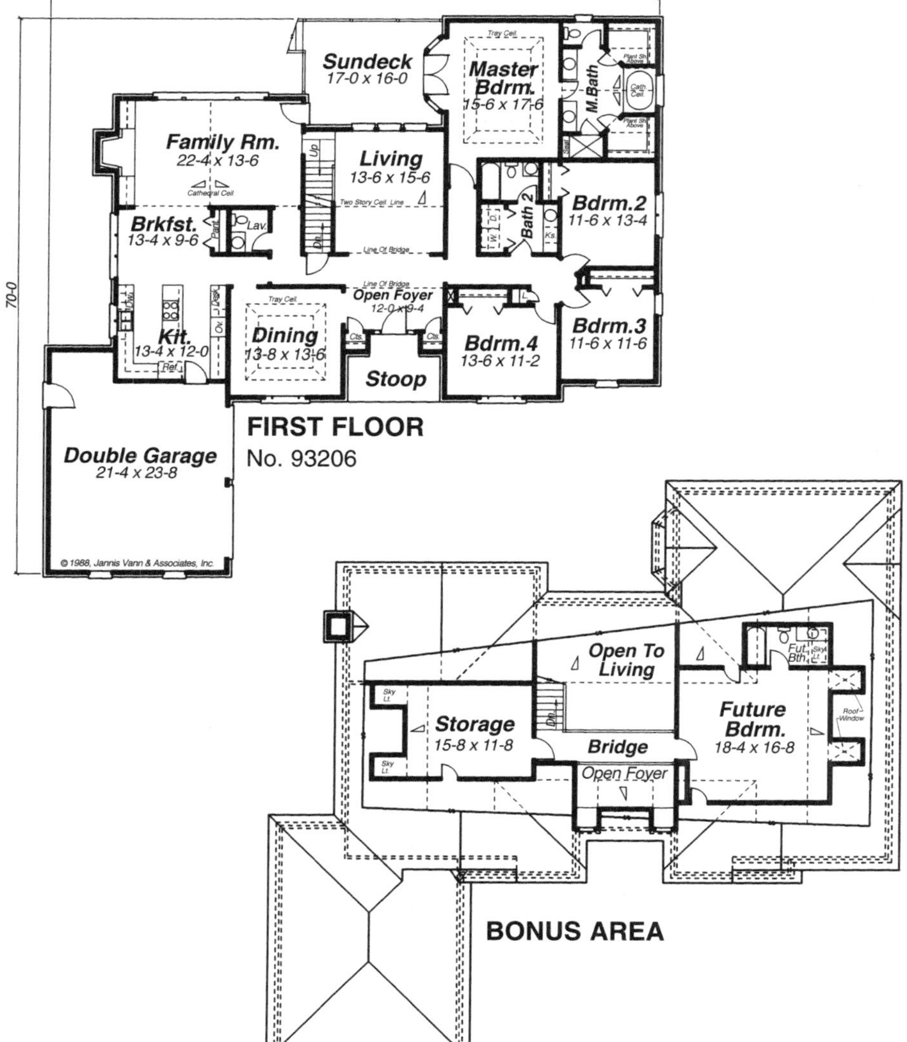

74-0
70-0
Sundeck
17-0 x 16-0
Master Bdrm.
15-6 x 17-6
M.Bath
Family Rm.
22-4 x 13-6
Cathedral Ceil
Living
13-6 x 15-6
Brkfst.
13-4 x 9-6
Lav.
Bath 2
Bdrm.2
11-6 x 13-4
Open Foyer
12-0 x 9-4
Kit.
13-4 x 12-0
Dining
13-8 x 13-6
Bdrm.4
13-6 x 11-2
Bdrm.3
11-6 x 11-6
Stoop
Double Garage
21-4 x 23-8
© 1988, Jannis Vann & Associates, Inc.
FIRST FLOOR
No. 93206
Open To Living
Storage
15-8 x 11-8
Bridge
Open Foyer
Future Bdrm.
18-4 x 16-8
Fut. Bth.
Roof Window
BONUS AREA

Distinctive Brick

- This plan features:
  - — Four bedrooms
  - — Two full and one half baths
- Arched entrance with decorative glass leads into two-story Foyer
- Formal Dining Room with tray ceiling above decorative window
- Kitchen with island cooktop and built-in Desk and Pantry
- Master Bedroom wing topped by tray ceiling with French door to Patio and a huge private Bath
- Second Floor optional space for Future Bedroom with full Bath
- An optional basement, slab or crawl space foundation — please specify when ordering

FIRST FLOOR — 2,577 SQ. FT.
BONUS AREA — 619 SQ. FT.
BASEMENT — 2,561 SQ. FT.
BRIDGE — 68 SQ. FT.
GARAGE — 560 SQ. FT.

TOTAL LIVING AREA:
2,645 SQ. FT.

PLAN NO. 94230

Design by
Sater Design Group

Refer to **Pricing Schedule F** on the order form for pricing information

Grand Design Highlighted by Turrets

- This plan features:
- — Four bedrooms
- — Two full, one three quarter and one half baths
- Triple arches at Entry lead into Grand Foyer and Gallery with arched entries to all areas
- Triple french doors access to rear grounds in Living and Leisure rooms
- Kitchen with large walk-in Pantry, cooktop/work island and angled serving counter/snackbar
- Master Suite wing offers Veranda access, two closets and vanities, and a garden window tub
- No materials list is available for this plan

FIRST FLOOR — 3,546 SQ. FT.
SECOND FLOOR — 1,213 SQ. FT.
GARAGE — 822 SQ. FT.

TOTAL LIVING AREA:
4,759 SQ. FT.

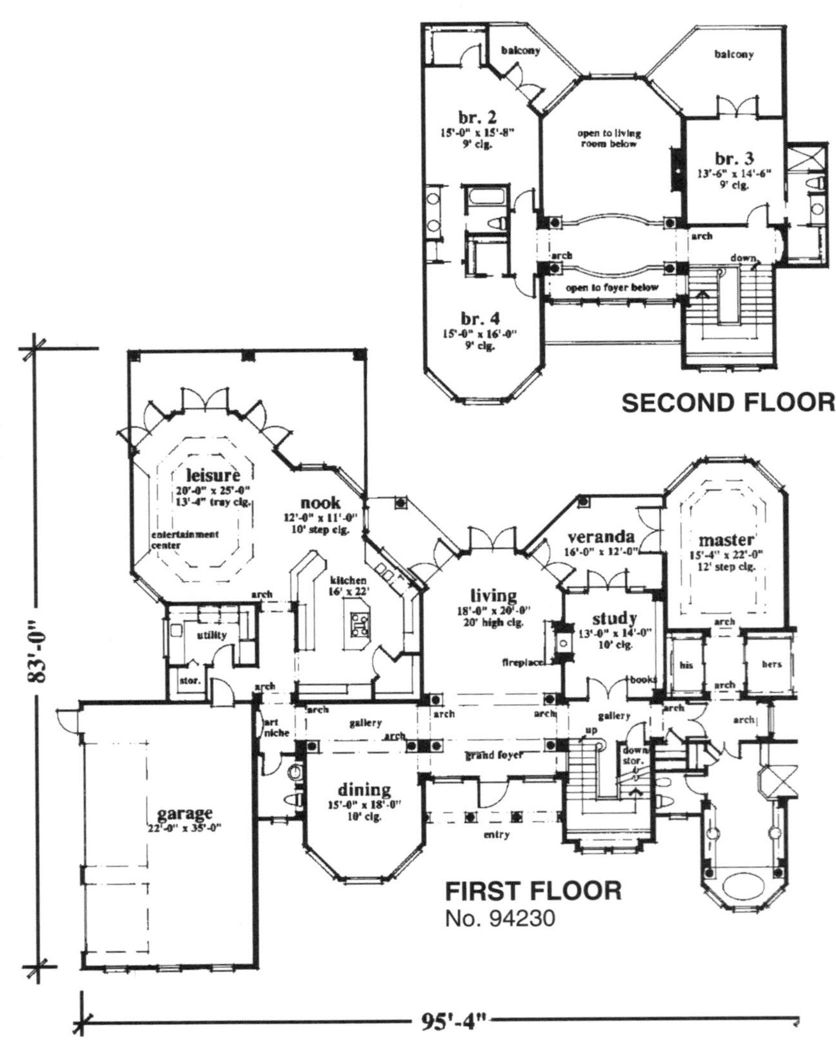
balcony
balcony
br. 2
15'-0" x 15'-8"
9' clg.
open to living room below
br. 3
13'-6" x 14'-6"
9' clg.
arch
down
open to foyer below
br. 4
15'-0" x 16'-0"
9' clg.
SECOND FLOOR
leisure
20'-0" x 25'-0"
13'-4" tray clg.
entertainment center
nook
12'-0" x 11'-0"
10' step clg.
kitchen
16' x 22'
veranda
16'-0" x 12'-0"
master
15'-4" x 22'-0"
12' step clg.
living
18'-0" x 20'-0"
20' high clg.
fireplace
study
13'-0" x 14'-0"
10' clg.
books
his
hers
utility
stor.
art niche
gallery
grand foyer
dining
15'-0" x 18'-0"
10' clg.
entry
garage
22'-0" x 35'-0"
83'-0"
95'-4"
FIRST FLOOR
No. 94230

Refer to **Pricing Schedule C** on the order form for pricing information

Design by
Garrell Associates Inc.

PLAN NO. 93609

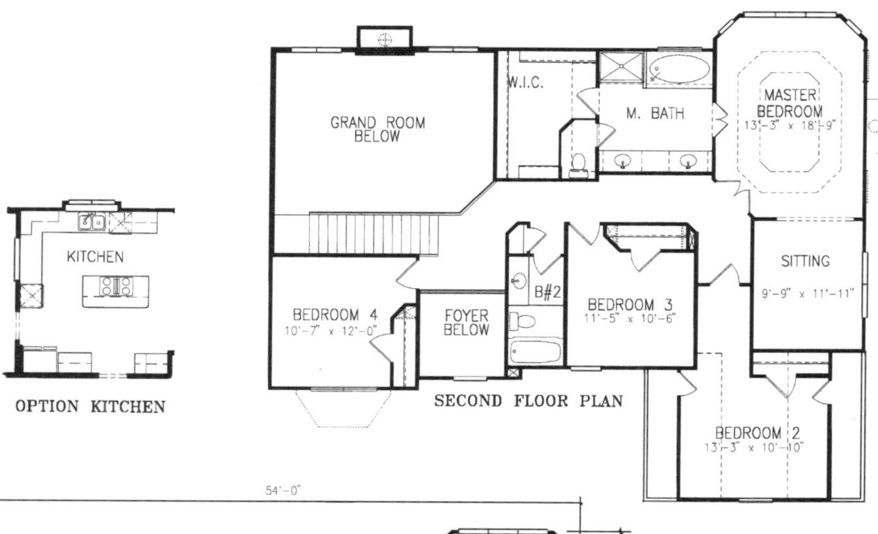

KITCHEN
OPTION KITCHEN
W.I.C.
M. BATH
MASTER BEDROOM
13'-3" x 18'-9"
GRAND ROOM BELOW
SITTING
9'-9" x 11'-11"
BEDROOM 4
10'-7" x 12'-0"
FOYER BELOW
B#2
BEDROOM 3
11'-5" x 10'-6"
BEDROOM 2
13'-3" x 10'-10"
SECOND FLOOR PLAN

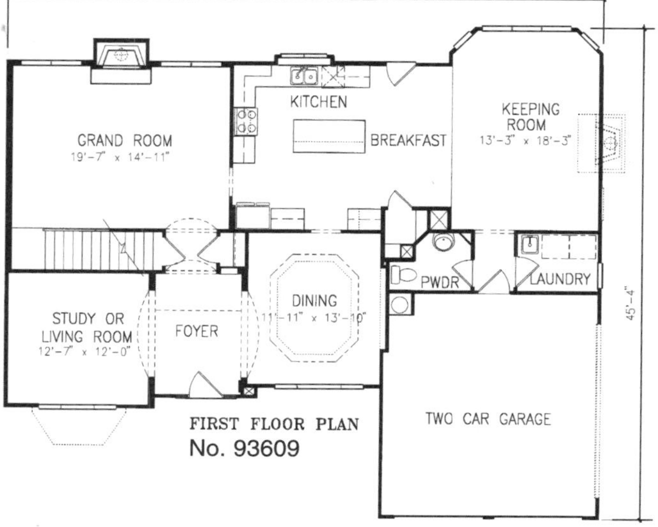

54'-0"

GRAND ROOM
19'-7" x 14'-11"

KITCHEN

BREAKFAST

KEEPING ROOM
13'-3" x 18'-3"

PWDR

LAUNDRY

STUDY OR LIVING ROOM
12'-7" x 12'-0"

FOYER

DINING
11'-11" x 13'-10"

TWO CAR GARAGE

45'-4"

FIRST FLOOR PLAN
No. 93609

Ideal Family Home

- This plan features:
- — Four bedrooms
- — Two full and one half baths
- Inside, from the two-story foyer enter either the Living Room or the Dining Room
- In the rear of the home there is the Grand Room and the Keeping room both with fireplaces
- The L-shaped Kitchen has a center island and is open to the Breakfast Nook
- Upstairs the Master Bedroom has a decorative ceiling and a huge walk-in closet
- No materials list is available for this plan
- An optional basement or slab foundation — please specify when ordering

FIRST FLOOR — 1,534 SQ. FT.
SECOND FLOOR — 1,236 SQ. FT.
GARAGE — 418 SQ. FT.

TOTAL LIVING AREA:
2,771 SQ. FT.

To order your Blueprints, call 1-800-235-5700

PLAN NO. 98524

Design by
Filmore Design Group

Refer to **Pricing Schedule E** on the order form for pricing information

Essence of Style & Grace

- This plan features:
  - — Four bedrooms
  - — Three full and one half baths
- French doors introduce Study and columns define the Gallery and formal areas
- The Family Room has a fireplace and a cathedral ceiling
- The Kitchen features a cooktop island, butler's Pantry, Breakfast Area and Patio access
- The Master Bedroom has a vaulted ceiling and a dual vanity
- No materials list is available for this plan
- An optional basement or slab foundation — please specify when ordering

FIRST FLOOR — 2,036 SQ. FT.
SECOND FLOOR — 866 SQ. FT.
GARAGE — 720 SQ. FT.

TOTAL LIVING AREA:
2,902 SQ. FT.

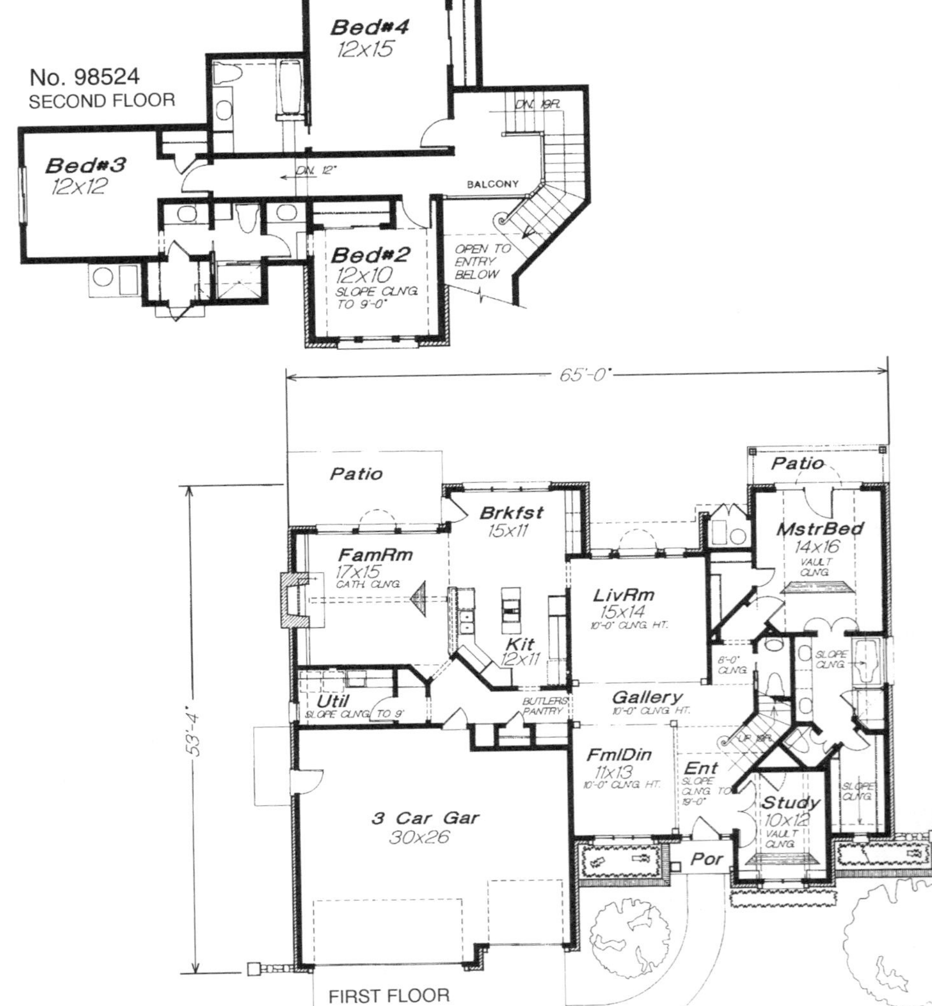
No. 98524
SECOND FLOOR
Bed#4
12x15
Bed#3
12x12
Bed#2
12x10
SLOPE CLNG. TO 9'-0"
BALCONY
OPEN TO ENTRY BELOW
65'-0"
53'-4"
Patio
Patio
Brkfst
15x11
FamRm
17x15
CATH. CLNG.
MstrBed
14x16
VAULT CLNG.
LivRm
15x14
10'-0" CLNG. HT.
Kit
12x11
Util
SLOPE CLNG. TO 9'
BUTLERS PANTRY
Gallery
10'-0" CLNG. HT.
FmlDin
11x13
10'-0" CLNG. HT.
Ent
Study
10x12
VAULT CLNG.
3 Car Gar
30x26
Por
FIRST FLOOR

To order your Blueprints, call 1-800-235-5700

Refer to **Pricing Schedule E** on the order form for pricing information

Design by
Filmore Design Group

PLAN NO. 92207

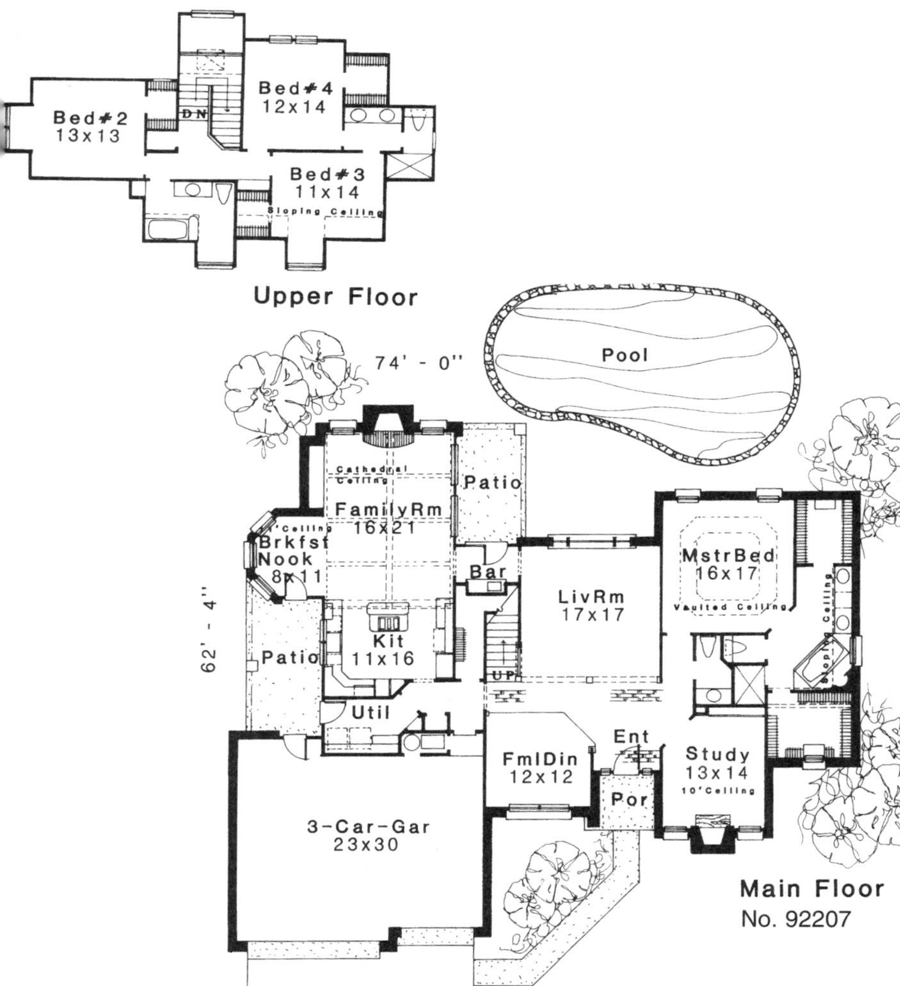

Bed#4
12x14
Bed#2
13x13
DN
Bed#3
11x14
Sloping Ceiling
Upper Floor
Pool
74' - 0"
Cathedral Ceiling
Patio
FamilyRm
16x21
Brkfst
Nook
8x11
Bar
LivRm
17x17
MstrBed
16x17
Vaulted Ceiling
62' - 4"
Patio
Kit
11x16
UP
Sloping Ceiling
Util
Ent
FmlDin
12x12
Study
13x14
10' Ceiling
Por
3-Car-Gar
23x30
Main Floor
No. 92207

Uncommon Brickwork Enhances Facade

- This plan features:
  - — Four bedrooms
  - — Three full and one half baths
- Sheltered Porch leads into Entry and spacious Living Room
- Quiet Study with focal point fireplace and open formal Dining Room
- Expansive Kitchen with cooktop work island, efficiently serves Breakfast Nook, Patio and Dining Room
- Master Bedroom wing offers a vaulted ceiling, two walk-in closets and a corner window tub
- No materials list is available for this plan

MAIN FLOOR — 2,304 SQ. FT.
UPPER FLOOR — 852 SQ. FT.
GARAGE — 690 SQ. FT.

TOTAL LIVING AREA:
3,156 SQ. FT.

PLAN NO. 24594

Design by
The Garlinghouse Company

Refer to **Pricing Schedule E** on the order form for pricing information

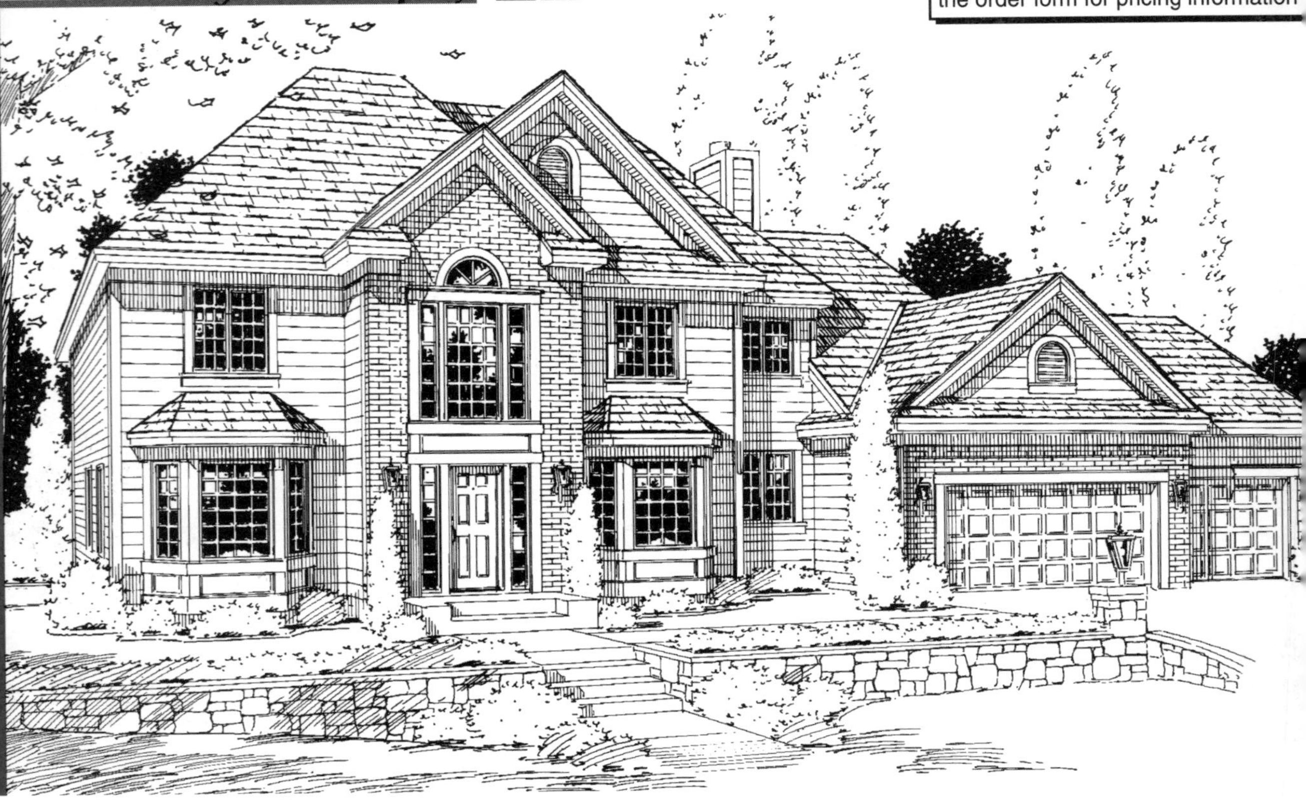

Impressive Two-Story Entrance

■ This plan features:

— Four bedrooms

— Two full and one half baths

■ Two-story Foyer highlighted by lovely, angled staircase and decorative window

■ Bay windows enhance Dining and Living Rooms

■ Efficient Kitchen with work island and an open Breakfast Area with backyard access

■ Spacious, yet cozy Family Room with a fireplace and Future Sun Room access

■ Private Master Suite has a walk-in closet and pampering Bath

First floor — 1,497 sq. ft.
Second floor — 1,460 sq. ft.
Future Sun room — 210 sq. ft.
Garage — 680 sq. ft.
Basement — 1,456 sq. ft.

Total living area:
2,957 sq. ft.

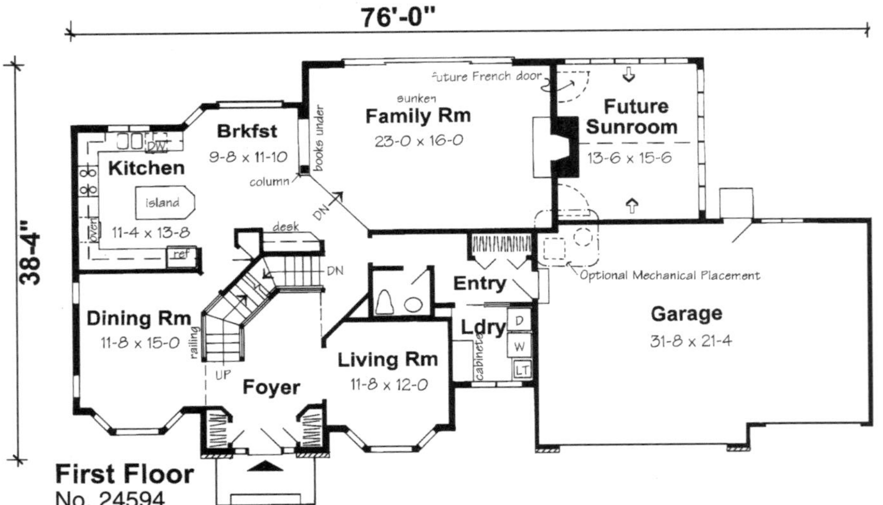

76'-0"
38'-4"
future French door
sunken
Family Rm
23-0 x 16-0
Future Sunroom
13-6 x 15-6
Brkfst
9-8 x 11-10
books under
column
Kitchen
Island
11-4 x 13-8
DW
oven
ref
desk
DN
Optional Mechanical Placement
Entry
Garage
31-8 x 21-4
Ldry
D
W
LT
cabinets
Dining Rm
11-8 x 15-0
railing
UP
Foyer
Living Rm
11-8 x 12-0

First Floor
No. 24594

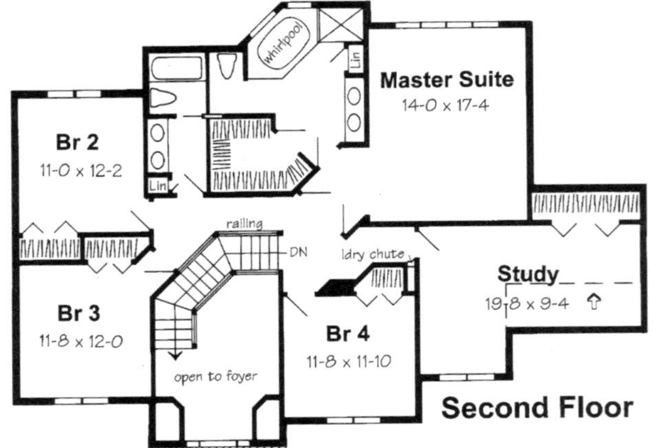

whirlpool
Lin
Master Suite
14-0 x 17-4
Br 2
11-0 x 12-2
Lin
railing
DN
ldry chute
Study
19-8 x 9-4
Br 3
11-8 x 12-0
Br 4
11-8 x 11-10
open to foyer

Second Floor

Refer to **Pricing Schedule F** on the order form for pricing information

Design by
Rick Garner

PLAN NO. 92535

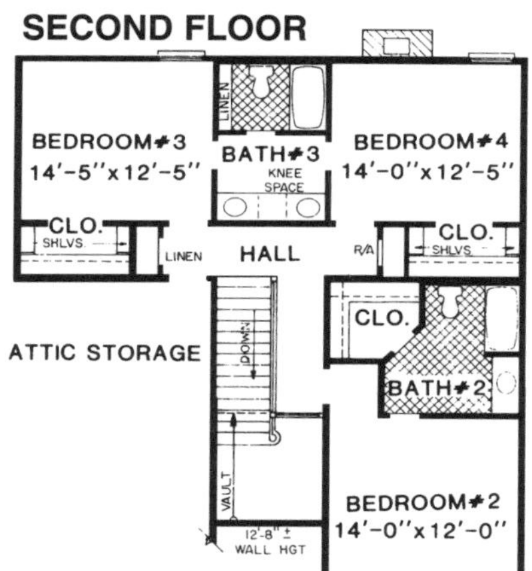

SECOND FLOOR
BEDROOM#3
14'-5"x12'-5"
BATH#3
KNEE SPACE
LINEN
BEDROOM#4
14'-0"x12'-5"
CLO.
SHLVS
LINEN
HALL
R/A
CLO.
SHLVS
ATTIC STORAGE
DOWN
CLO.
BATH#2
VAULT
12'-8" ± WALL HGT
BEDROOM#2
14'-0"x12'-0"

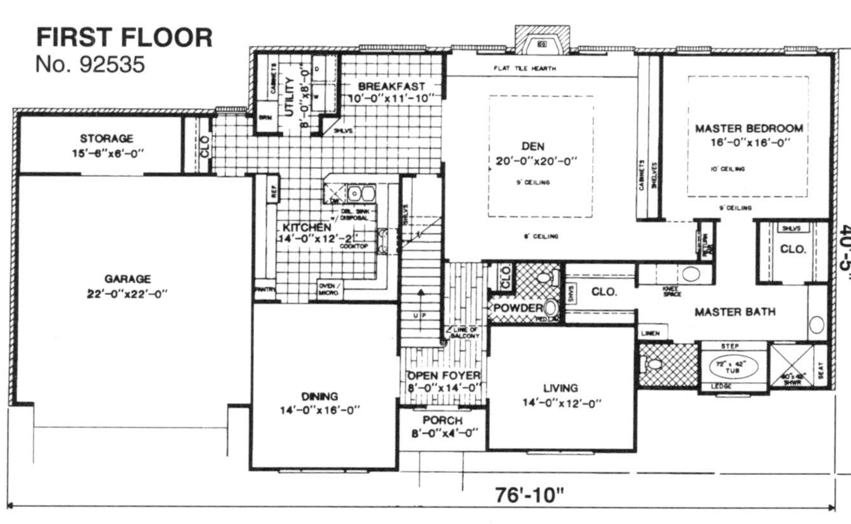

FIRST FLOOR
No. 92535
UTILITY
8'-0"x8'-0"
BREAKFAST
10'-0"x11'-10"
FLAT TILE HEARTH
STORAGE
15'-6"x6'-0"
CLO
DEN
20'-0"x20'-0"
9' CEILING
MASTER BEDROOM
16'-0"x16'-0"
10' CEILING
9' CEILING
KITCHEN
14'-0"x12'-2"
8' CEILING
CLO.
GARAGE
22'-0"x22'-0"
CLO
POWDER
CLO.
MASTER BATH
UP
DINING
14'-0"x16'-0"
OPEN FOYER
8'-0"x14'-0"
LIVING
14'-0"x12'-0"
PORCH
8'-0"x4'-0"
76'-10"
40'-5"

Rewards of Success

- This plan features:
  - — Four bedrooms
  - — Three full and one half baths
- An open Foyer flanked by formal areas, left to the Dining Room, right to the Living Room
- The Den has a large fireplace with a flat tiled hearth
- Built-in cabinets and shelves in the Den
- A well-appointed Kitchen serves the formal Dining Room and provides a snack bar for meals on the run
- The Master Bedroom has a lavish Bath and a walk-in closet
- An optional crawl space or slab foundation — please specify when ordering

FIRST FLOOR — 2,019 SQ. FT.
SECOND FLOOR — 946 SQ. FT.
GARAGE — 577 SQ. FT.

TOTAL LIVING AREA:
2,965 SQ. FT.

PLAN NO. 99895

Design by
Donald A. Gardner Architects, Inc.

Refer to **Pricing Schedule E** on the order form for pricing information

Elegance And A Relaxed Lifestyle

- This plan features:
  - — Four bedrooms
  - — Three full baths
- Open two-level Foyer has a palladian window which visually ties the formal Dining Area to the expansive Great Room
- Bay windows in Master Bedroom Suite and Breakfast Area provide natural light, while 9-foot ceilings create volume
- Master Bedroom features a whirlpool tub, separate shower and his-n-her vanities

FIRST FLOOR — 1,841 SQ. FT.
SECOND FLOOR — 594 SQ. FT.
BONUS ROOM — 411 SQ. FT.
GARAGE & STORAGE — 596 SQ. FT.

TOTAL LIVING AREA:
2,435 SQ. FT.

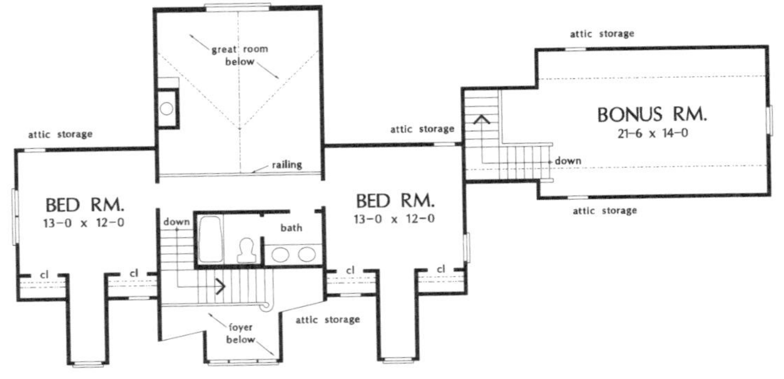
great room below
attic storage
BONUS RM.
21-6 x 14-0
down
BED RM.
13-0 x 12-0
railing
bath
cl
foyer below

SECOND FLOOR PLAN

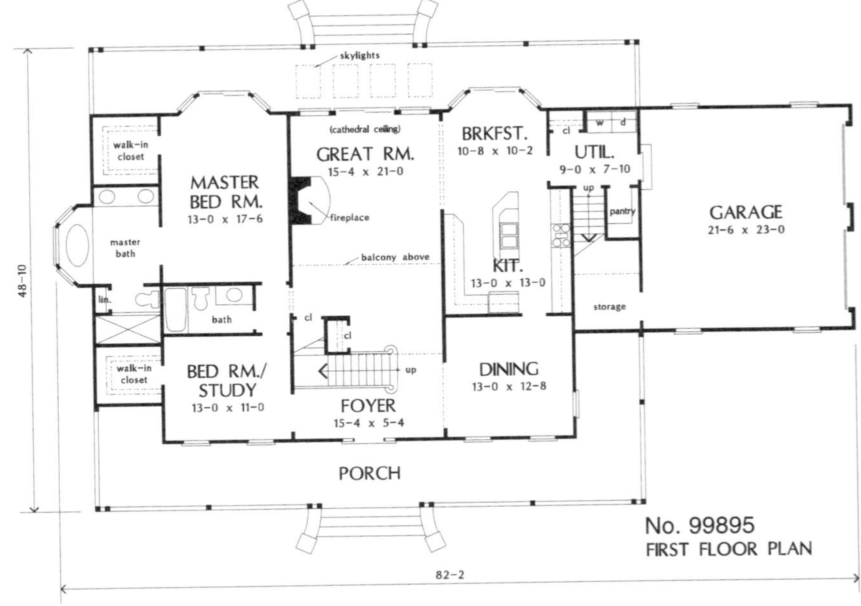
skylights
(cathedral ceiling)
GREAT RM.
15-4 x 21-0
fireplace
balcony above
walk-in closet
MASTER BED RM.
13-0 x 17-6
master bath
lin.
bath
BRKFST.
10-8 x 10-2
UTIL.
9-0 x 7-10
w d
pantry
GARAGE
21-6 x 23-0
KIT.
13-0 x 13-0
storage
BED RM./ STUDY
13-0 x 11-0
FOYER
15-4 x 5-4
up
DINING
13-0 x 12-8
PORCH
48-10
82-2

No. 99895
FIRST FLOOR PLAN

To order your Blueprints, call 1-800-235-5700

Refer to **Pricing Schedule E** on the order form for pricing information

Design by
Design Basics, Inc.

PLAN NO. 99461

Magnificent Grandeur

- This plan features:
- — Four bedrooms
- — Two full, one three-quarter and one half baths
- Decorative ceilings and built-ins enhance the Living Room and the Dining Room
- The island Kitchen serves the Dining Room and the Breakfast Area with equal ease
- Great Room is topped by a valley cathedral ceiling and highlighted by a fireplace
- The Master Suite includes a decorative ceiling, a whirlpool tub and separate shower and a walk-in closet

FIRST FLOOR — 1,972 SQ. FT.
SECOND FLOOR — 893 SQ. FT.
GARAGE — 658 SQ. FT.

TOTAL LIVING AREA:
2,865 SQ. FT.

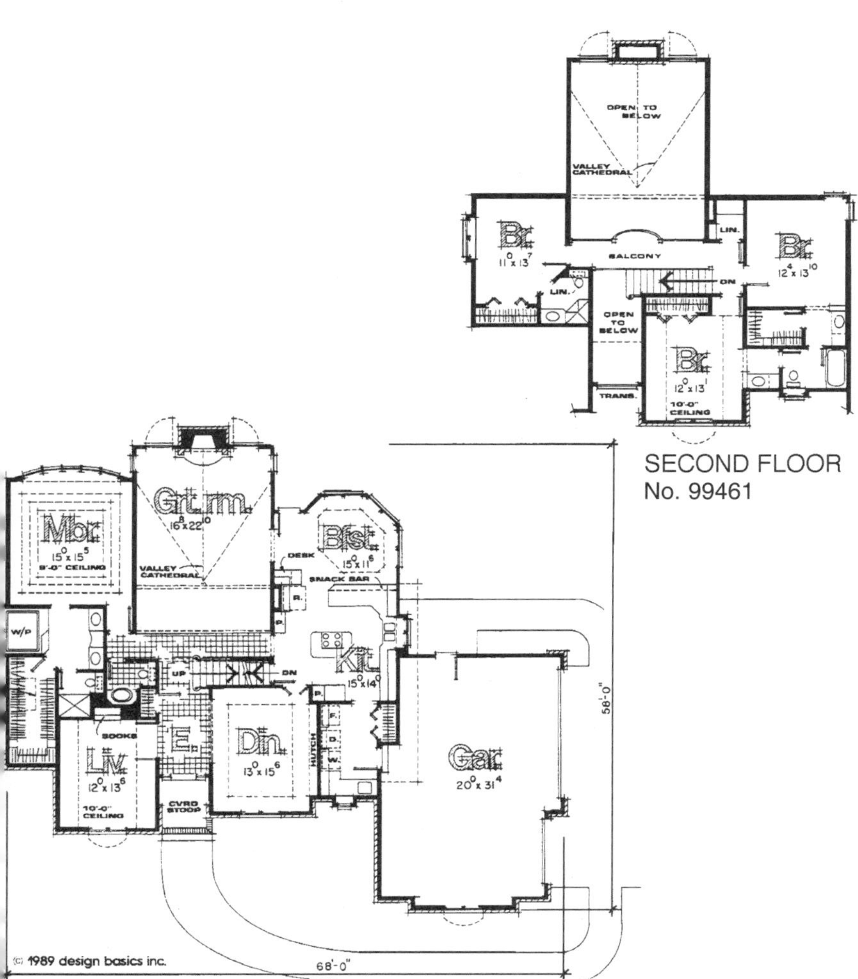

OPEN TO BELOW
VALLEY CATHEDRAL
Br.
BALCONY
LIN.
DN
OPEN TO BELOW
TRANS.
10'-0" CEILING
Grt.rm.
Mbr.
8'-0" CEILING
VALLEY CATHEDRAL
Bfst.
DESK
SNACK BAR
Kit.
UP
DN
W/P
BOOKS
Liv.
10'-0" CEILING
CVRD STOOP
Din.
HUTCH
Gar.
58'-0"
68'-0"
(c) 1989 design basics inc.

SECOND FLOOR
No. 99461

FIRST FLOOR

PLAN NO. 92550

Design by
Rick Garner

Refer to **Pricing Schedule F** on the order form for pricing information

Curb Appeal

- This plan features:
  - — Four bedrooms
  - — Three full baths
- A private Master Bedroom with a raised ceiling and attached Bath with a spa tub
- A wing of three Bedrooms that share two full Baths on the right side of the home
- An efficient Kitchen is straddled by an Eating Nook and a Dining Room
- A cozy Den with a raised ceiling and a fireplace that is the focal point of the home
- A two-car Garage has a storage area
- An optional crawl space or slab foundation — please specify when ordering

MAIN FLOOR — 2,735 SQ. FT.
GARAGE — 561 SQ. FT.

TOTAL LIVING AREA:
2,735 SQ. FT.

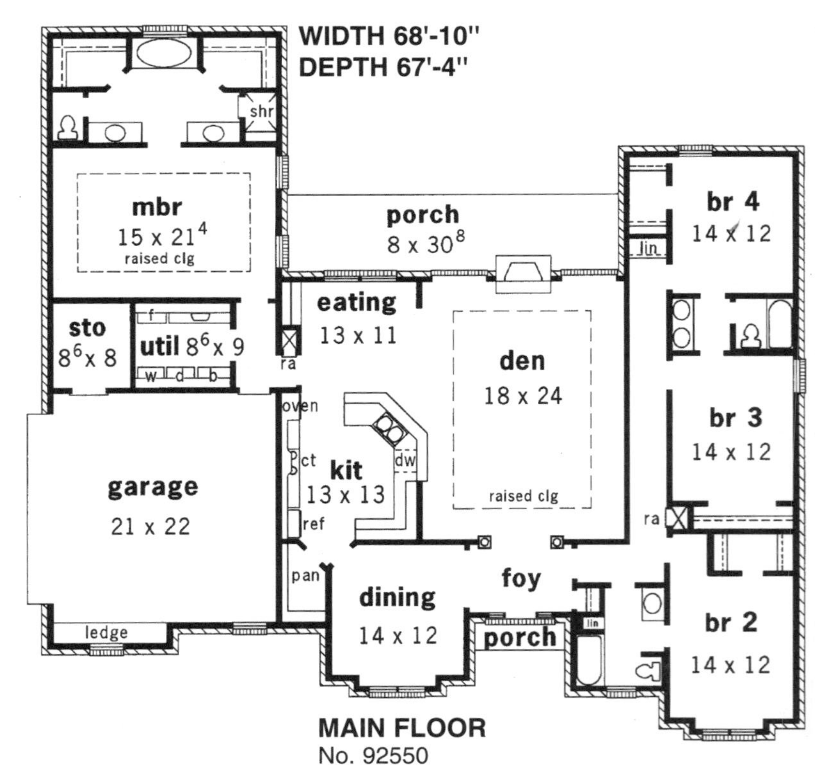
WIDTH 68'-10"
DEPTH 67'-4"
shr
mbr
15 x 21⁴
raised clg
porch
8 x 30⁸
br 4
14 x 12
lin
eating
13 x 11
sto
8⁶x 8
util 8⁶x 9
ra
den
18 x 24
raised clg
oven
kit
13 x 13
dw
ref
br 3
14 x 12
ra
garage
21 x 22
pan
dining
14 x 12
foy
br 2
14 x 12
lin
porch
ledge
MAIN FLOOR
No. 92550

Refer to **Pricing Schedule E** on the order form for pricing information

Design by
Frank Betz Associates, Inc.

PLAN NO. 98457

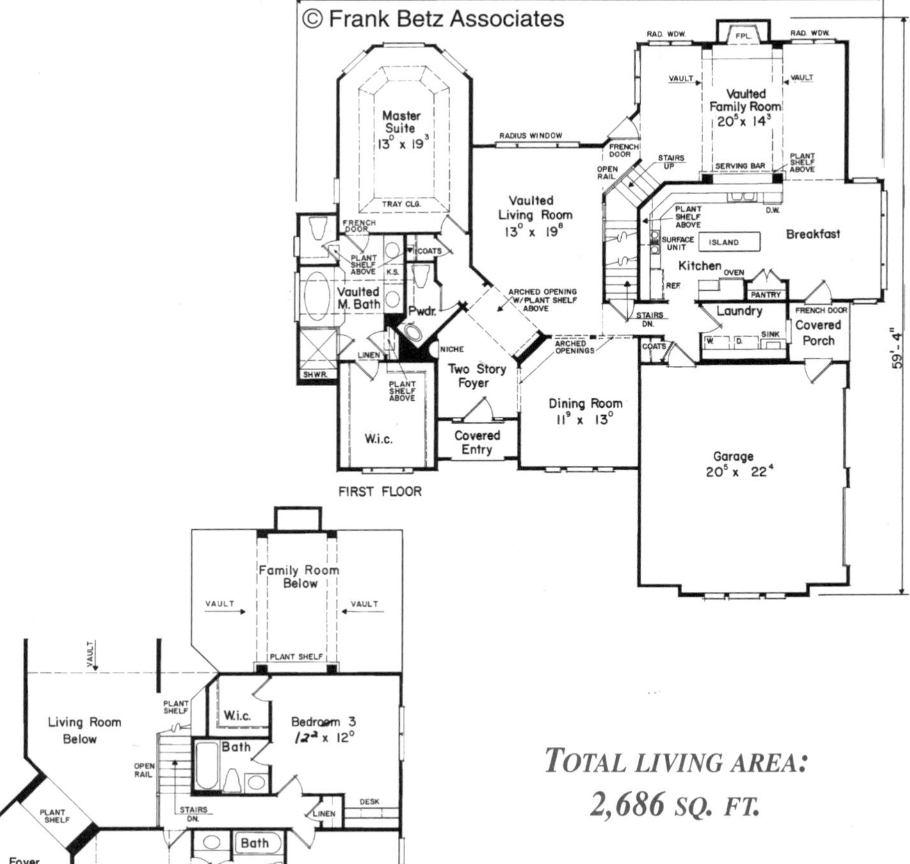

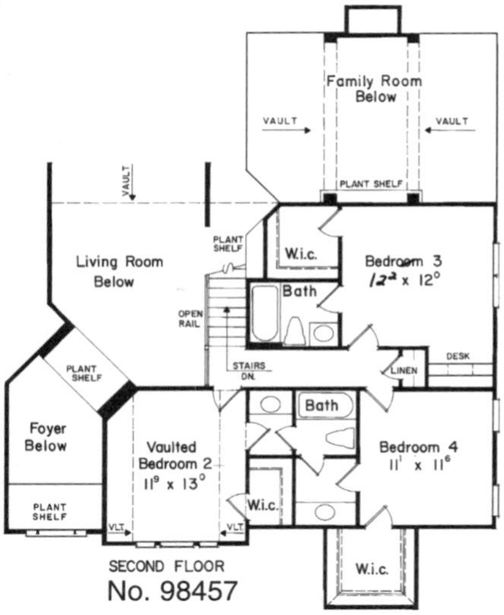

58'-6"
© Frank Betz Associates
Master Suite 13⁰ x 19³
Vaulted Living Room 13⁰ x 19⁸
Vaulted Family Room 20⁵ x 14³
Breakfast
Kitchen
Laundry
Covered Porch
Vaulted M. Bath
Pwdr.
Two Story Foyer
Dining Room 11⁹ x 13⁰
W.i.c.
Covered Entry
Garage 20⁵ x 22⁴
59'-4"
FIRST FLOOR
Family Room Below
Living Room Below
Bedroom 3 12³ x 12⁰
Bath
Foyer Below
Vaulted Bedroom 2 11⁹ x 13⁰
Bedroom 4 11¹ x 11⁶
W.i.c.
SECOND FLOOR
No. 98457

Modern Luxury

- This plan features:
  - Four bedrooms
  - Three full and one half baths
- A feeling of spaciousness is created by the two-story Foyer and volume ceilings in many of the other rooms in this home
- Arched openings and decorative windows enhance the Dining and Living rooms
- The efficient Kitchen has a work island, Pantry and a Breakfast area open to the Family Room
- The plush Master Suite features a tray ceiling above, an alcove of windows and a whirlpool Bath
- An optional basement or crawl space foundaion — please specify when ordering

FIRST FLOOR — 1,883 SQ. FT.
SECOND FLOOR — 803 SQ. FT.
BASEMENT — 1,883 SQ. FT.
GARAGE — 495 SQ. FT.

TOTAL LIVING AREA:
2,686 SQ. FT.

PLAN NO. 94247

Design by
Sater Design Group

Refer to **Pricing Schedule E** on the order form for pricing information

Designed for Entertaining

- This plan features:
  - — Three bedrooms
  - — Three full and one half baths
- Large, open floor plan with an array of amenities
- Grand Room and Dining Area separated by 3-sided fireplace
- Spacious Kitchen with a cooktop island and Eating Nook
- Secluded Master Suite enhanced by a private Spa Deck
- Study and two additional Bedrooms have private access to full Baths
- No materials list is available for this plan

MAIN FLOOR — 2,066 SQ. FT.
SECOND FLOOR — 809 SQ. FT.
BONUS — 1,260 SQ. FT.
GARAGE — 798 SQ. FT.

TOTAL LIVING AREA:
2,875 SQ. FT.

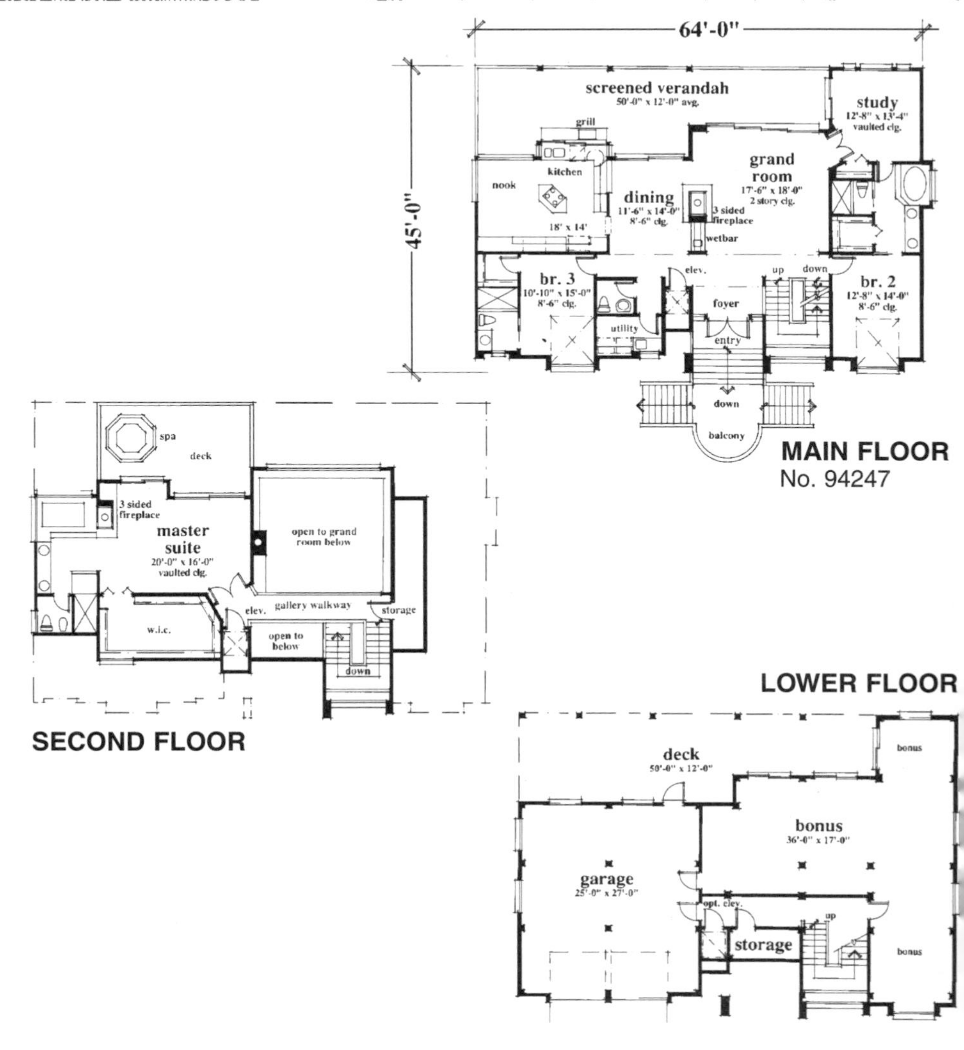

64'-0"
45'-0"
screened verandah
50'-0" x 12'-0" avg.
study
12'-8" x 13'-4"
vaulted clg.
grill
kitchen
nook
18' x 14'
dining
11'-6" x 14'-0"
8'-6" clg.
grand
room
17'-6" x 18'-0"
2 story clg.
3 sided
fireplace
wetbar
br. 3
10'-10" x 15'-0"
8'-6" clg.
utility
elev.
foyer
entry
up
down
br. 2
12'-8" x 14'-0"
8'-6" clg.
down
balcony
MAIN FLOOR
No. 94247
spa
deck
3 sided
fireplace
master
suite
20'-0" x 16'-0"
vaulted clg.
open to grand
room below
w.i.c.
elev.
gallery walkway
storage
open to
below
down
SECOND FLOOR
LOWER FLOOR
deck
59'-0" x 12'-0"
bonus
bonus
36'-0" x 17'-0"
garage
25'-0" x 27'-0"
opt. elev.
up
storage
bonus

Brick Magnificence

Price Code: E

Design by
Fillmore Design Group

PLAN NO.92243

- This plan features:
- — Four bedrooms
- — Three full baths
- Large windows and attractive brick detailing using segmented arches give fantastic curb appeal
- Convenient Ranch layout allows for step-saving one floor ease
- A fireplace in the Living Room adds a warm ambience
- The Family Room sports a second fireplace and built-in shelving
- Two additional Bedrooms include private access to a full double vanity Bath
- No materials list is available for this plan

MAIN FLOOR — 2,858 SQ. FT.
GARAGE — 768 SQ. FT.

TOTAL LIVING AREA:
2,858 SQ. FT.

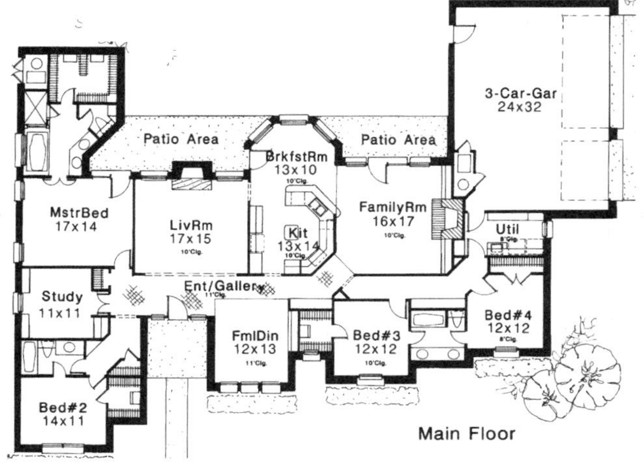

3-Car-Gar
24x32
Patio Area
BrkfstRm
13x10
Patio Area
MstrBed
17x14
LivRm
17x15
Kit
13x14
FamilyRm
16x17
Util
Ent/Gallery
Study
11x11
FmlDin
12x13
Bed#3
12x12
Bed#4
12x12
Bed#2
14x11
Main Floor

WIDTH 89'-7"
DEPTH 68'-4"

Design by
Kent & Kent, Inc.

PLAN NO.92902

SCREENED PORCH
13'-0"x17'-0"
MASTER SUITE
15'-0" x 17'-8"
COV PATIO
BREAKFAST
15'-8" x 10'-4"
MST BATH
STUDY / BEDROOM 2
11'-8"x10'-8"
FAMILY RM
19'-0" x 19'-6"
KITCHEN
BAR
UTILITY
BATH 2
FOYER
BATH
DRSG
SHOP
DINING
13'-0"x15'-0"
PORCH
BEDROOM 3
11'-8" x 12'-4"
BEDROOM 4
12'-0" x 12'-6"
OLF CART
TWO CAR GARAGE
21'-6" x 24'-0"
MAIN AREA

WIDTH 78'-0"
DEPTH 78'-6"

A Home for Today's Lifestyle

Price Code: E

- This plan features:
- — Four bedrooms
- — Three full baths
- Family living area comprised of a Family Room, Breakfast Area, and island kitchen
- Pampering Master Suite with private Master Bath and an abundance of storage space
- Three additional Bedrooms have ample closet space
- No materials list is available for this plan

MAIN FLOOR — 2,787 SQ. FT.
GARAGE — 685 SQ. FT.

TOTAL LIVING AREA:
2,787 SQ. FT.

PLAN NO. 96600

Design by
Larry E. Belk

Refer to **Pricing Schedule E** on the order form for pricing information

A Classic Design

- This plan features:
  - — Four bedrooms
  - -- Two full and one half baths
- An elegant arched opening graces the entrance of this classic design
- The dramatic arch detail is repeated at the Dining Room entrance
- The Kitchen, Breakfast Room and Family Room are open to one another
- The Kitchen has amenities including a walk-in Pantry, double ovens and an eating bar
- The Master Suite is designed apart from the other Bedrooms for privacy
- No materials list is available for this plan

MAIN FLOOR — 2,678 SQ. FT
GARAGE — 474 SQ. FT.

TOTAL LIVING AREA:
2,678 SQ. FT.

HERS
HIS
K.S.
STEP
MASTER BATH
11 FT TRAY CLG
SEAT
FP
PORCH
9 FT CLG
COVERED PORCH
9 FT CLG
FAMILY ROOM
13-6 X 16-6
9 FT CLG
BRKFST RM
10-8 X 11-6
9 FT CLG
MASTER BEDRM
15-0 X 17-4
11 FT TRAY CLG
BEDRM 4
14-8 X 12-8
9 FT CLG
ARCH
42" LEDGE
KITCHEN
13-6 X 11-4
9 FT CLG
PWDR
UTIL
12-6 X 5-8
9 FT CLG
DEPTH 67-9
LIVING ROOM
18-4 X 18-6
11 FT CLG
BATH 2
PAN
GARAGE
BEDRM 3
11-0 X 13-4
9 FT CLG
BEDRM 2/ STUDY
11-6 X 13-0
11 FT TRAY CLG
FOYER
11 FT CLG
DINING ROOM
14-0 X 13-6
11 FT CLG
COPYRIGHT LARRY E. BELK
PORCH
9 FT CLG
WIDTH 70-2

MAIN FLOOR
No. 96600

Refer to **Pricing Schedule F** on the order form for pricing information

Design by
Rick Garner

PLAN NO. 92508

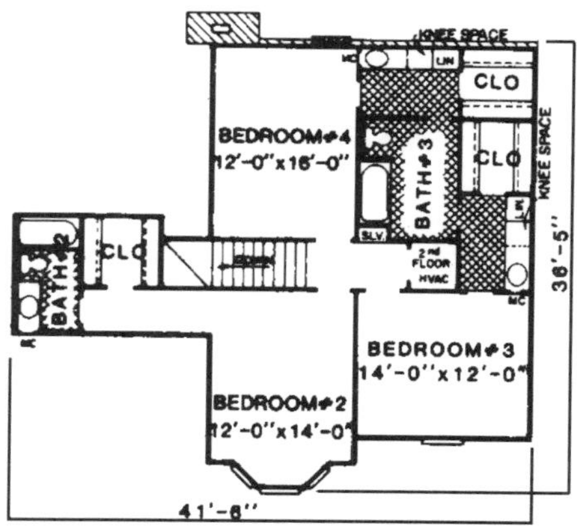

KNEE SPACE
CLO
BEDROOM#4
12'-0"x16'-0"
BATH#3
CLO
KNEE SPACE
CLO
BATH#2
2nd FLOOR HVAC
36'-5"
BEDROOM#3
14'-0"x12'-0"
BEDROOM#2
12'-0"x14'-0"
41'-8"

SECOND FLOOR

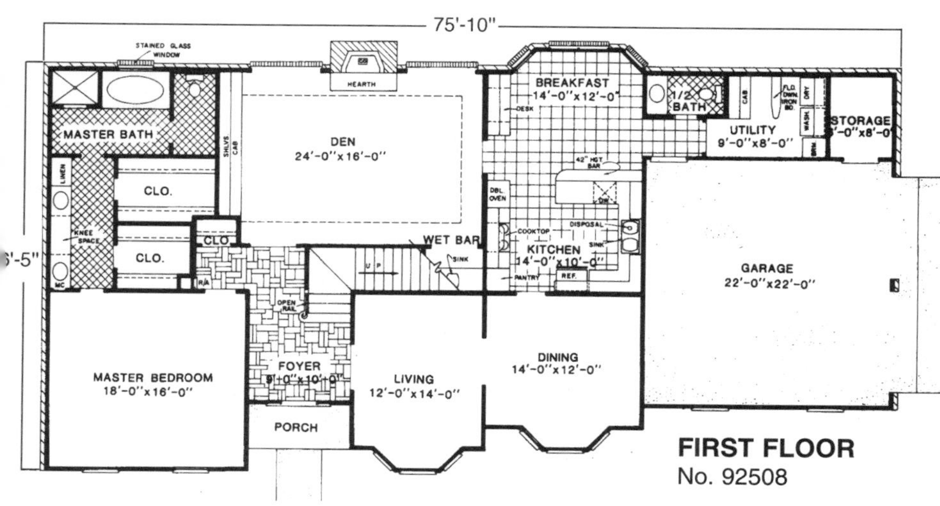

75'-10"
STAINED GLASS WINDOW
HEARTH
BREAKFAST
14'-0"x12'-0"
1/2 BATH
UTILITY
9'-0"x8'-0"
STORAGE
MASTER BATH
DEN
24'-0"x16'-0"
CLO.
CLO.
CLO
WET BAR
KITCHEN
14'-0"x10'-0"
GARAGE
22'-0"x22'-0"
FOYER
MASTER BEDROOM
18'-0"x16'-0"
LIVING
12'-0"x14'-0"
DINING
14'-0"x12'-0"
PORCH

FIRST FLOOR
No. 92508

Lasting Elegance

- This plan features:
  - — Four bedrooms
  - — Three full and one half baths
- Rich lines, bays and detailed window treatments add lasting elegance to this home
- Large Foyer leads directly into huge Den with hearth fireplace and built-ins
- Both the Living and Dining Rooms have bays which add style and character
- The U-shaped Kitchen is fully equipped and opens into a Nook
- The Master Suite is second to none and features a private Bath
- An optional crawl space or a slab foundation — please specify when ordering

FIRST FLOOR — 2,008 SQ. FT.
SECOND FLOOR — 943 SQ. FT.
GARAGE — 556 SQ. FT.

TOTAL LIVING AREA:
2,951 SQ. FT.

PLAN NO. 24550

Design by
The Garlinghouse Company

Refer to **Pricing Schedule E** on the order form for pricing information

Impressive Brick

■ This plan features:

— Four bedrooms

— Two full and one half baths

■ A two-story, raised Foyer with a splendid, curved staircase

■ A dramatic cathedral ceiling and a two-way fireplace in the Living Room

■ A formal Dining Room accented by a lovely bay window

■ A Family Room with the unique fireplace and built-in entertainment center

■ Kitchen with an atrium sink, walk-in Pantry and built-in Desk

■ A Master Suite with a vaulted ceiling and a plush Bath with a corner window tub

FIRST FLOOR — 1,433 SQ. FT.
SECOND FLOOR — 1,283 SQ. FT.
BASEMENT — 1,433 SQ. FT.
GARAGE — 923 SQ. FT.

TOTAL LIVING AREA:
2,716 SQ. FT.

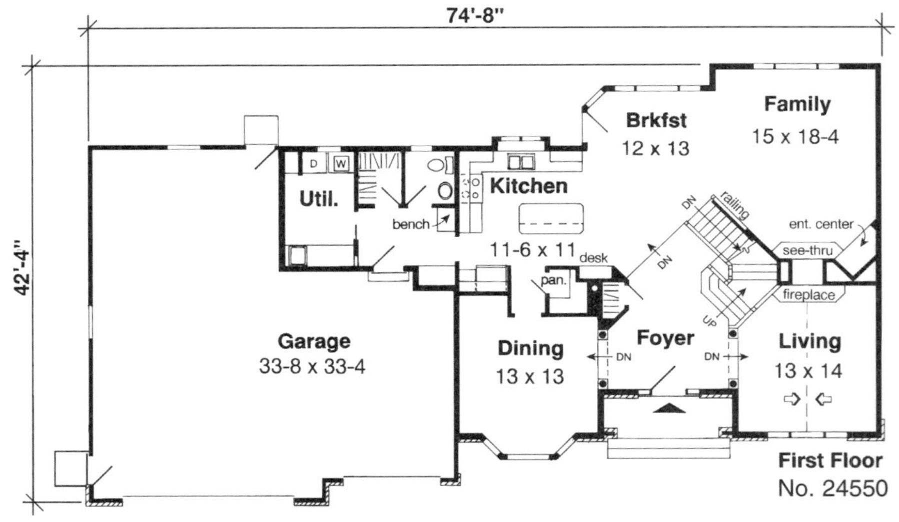
74'-8"
42'-4"
Family
15 x 18-4
Brkfst
12 x 13
Kitchen
11-6 x 11
Util.
bench
desk
pan.
railing
ent. center
see-thru
fireplace
DN
UP
Garage
33-8 x 33-4
Dining
13 x 13
Foyer
Living
13 x 14

First Floor
No. 24550

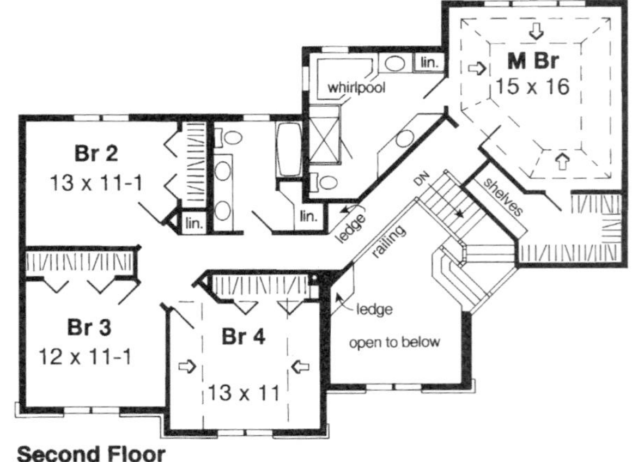
M Br
15 x 16
whirlpool
lin.
Br 2
13 x 11-1
shelves
ledge
railing
DN
Br 3
12 x 11-1
Br 4
13 x 11
ledge
open to below

Second Floor

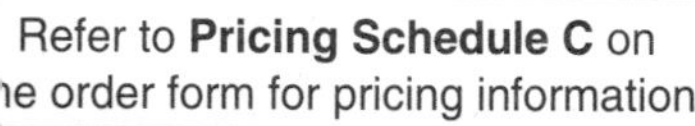
Refer to **Pricing Schedule C** on
the order form for pricing information

Design by
Sater Design Group

PLAN NO. 94259

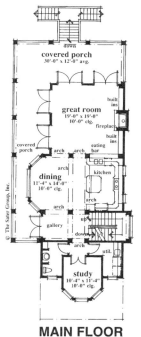

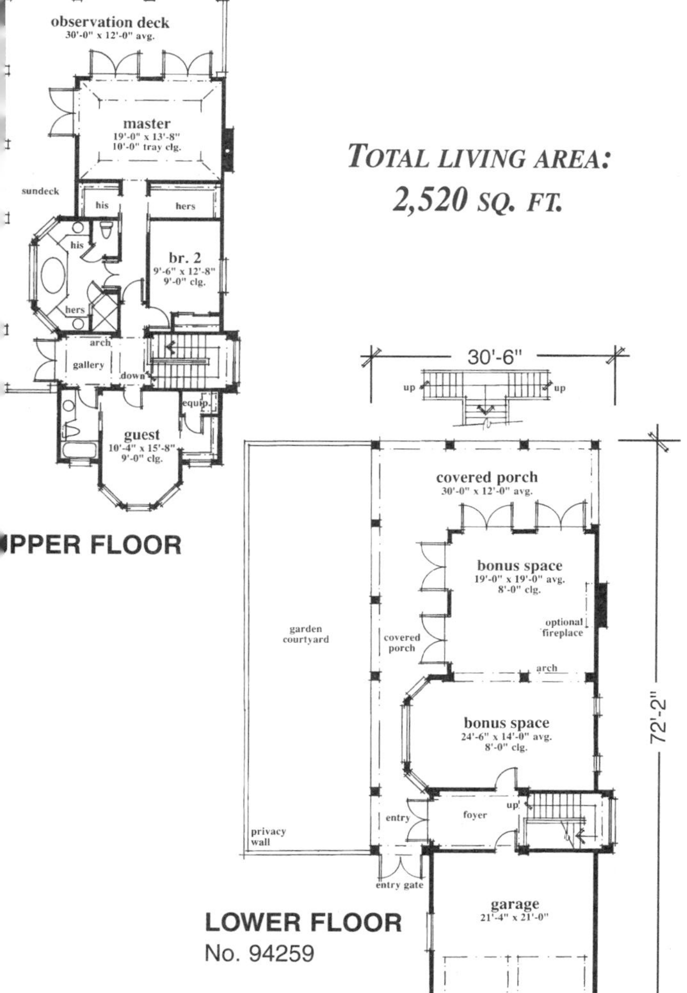
observation deck
30'-0" x 12'-0" avg.
master
19'-0" x 13'-8"
10'-0" tray clg.
sundeck
his
hers
br. 2
9'-6" x 12'-8"
9'-0" clg.
arch
gallery
down
equip.
guest
10'-4" x 15'-8"
9'-0" clg.
UPPER FLOOR
30'-6"
up
covered porch
30'-0" x 12'-0" avg.
bonus space
19'-0" x 19'-0" avg.
8'-0" clg.
optional fireplace
covered porch
garden courtyard
arch
bonus space
24'-6" x 14'-0" avg.
8'-0" clg.
72'-2"
entry
foyer
privacy wall
entry gate
garage
21'-4" x 21'-0"
LOWER FLOOR
No. 94259
down
covered porch
30'-0" x 12'-0" avg.
great room
19'-0" x 19'-0"
10'-0" clg.
built ins
fireplace
eating bar
arch
dining
11'-4" x 14'-0"
10'-0" clg.
kitchen
gallery
util.
study
10'-4" x 11'-4"
10'-0" clg.
© The Sater Group, Inc.
MAIN FLOOR

TOTAL LIVING AREA:
2,520 SQ. FT.

Elegant Row House

- This plan features:
  - — Three bedrooms
  - — Two full and one half baths
- Arched columns define the formal and casual spaces
- Wrap-around Porticos on two levels provide views to the living areas
- Four sets of French doors let the outside in to the Great Room
- The Master Suite features a private bath designed for two people
- Generous bonus space awaits your ideas for completion
- The Guest Bedroom leads to a gallery hallway with Deck access
- An optional slab or post foundation — please specify when ordering
- No materials list is available for this plan

MAIN FLOOR — 1,305 SQ. FT.
UPPER FLOOR — 1,215 SQ. FT.
BONUS — 935 SQ. FT.
GARAGE — 480 SQ. FT.

PLAN NO.96435

Design by
Donald A. Gardner Architects, Inc.

Stately Home

Price Code: F

© 1992 Donald A. Gardner Architects, Inc.

- This plan features:
- — Four bedrooms
- — Two full and one half baths
- An elegant brick exterior and careful detailing
- Light floods through the arched window in the clereste dormer above the Foyer
- Great Room topped by a cathedral ceiling boasts built-cabinets and bookshelves
- Through glass doors capped by an arched window the Sun Room is accessed from the Great Room
- Both the Dining Room and the Bedroom/Study have t ceilings
- Master Suite includes a fireplace, access to the Deck, his-n-her vanities and a whirlpool tub
- An optional basement or crawl space foundation — please specify when ordering

MAIN FLOOR — 2,526 SQ. FT.
GARAGE — 611 SQ. FT.

TOTAL LIVING AREA:
2,526 SQ. FT.

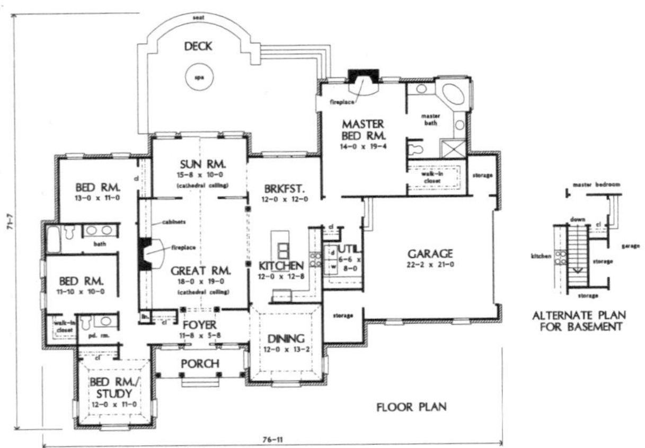
DECK
MASTER BED RM. 14-0 x 19-4
SUN RM. 15-8 x 10-0 (cathedral ceiling)
BRKFST. 12-0 x 12-0
BED RM. 13-0 x 11-0
GREAT RM. 18-0 x 19-0 (cathedral ceiling)
KITCHEN 12-0 x 12-8
GARAGE 22-2 x 21-0
BED RM. 11-10 x 10-0
FOYER 11-8 x 5-8
DINING 12-0 x 13-2
PORCH
BED RM./ STUDY 12-0 x 11-0
FLOOR PLAN
ALTERNATE PLAN FOR BASEMENT
71-7
76-11
© Donald A. Gardner Architects, Inc.

PLAN NO.98513

Design by
Filmore Design Group

French Country Styling

Price Code: F

- This plan features:
- — Four bedrooms
- — Three full and one half baths
- Brick and stone blend masterfully for an impressive French Country exterior
- Separate Master Suite has an expansive Bath and clos
- Study contains a built-in desk and a bookcase
- Angled island Kitchen is highlighted by a walk-in Pa
- Fantastic Family Room includes a brick fireplace and built-in entertainment center
- Three additional Bedrooms have private access to a f Bath
- No material list is available for this plan

MAIN FLOOR — 3,352 SQ. FT.
GARAGE — 672 SQ. FT.

TOTAL LIVING AREA:
3,352 SQ. FT.

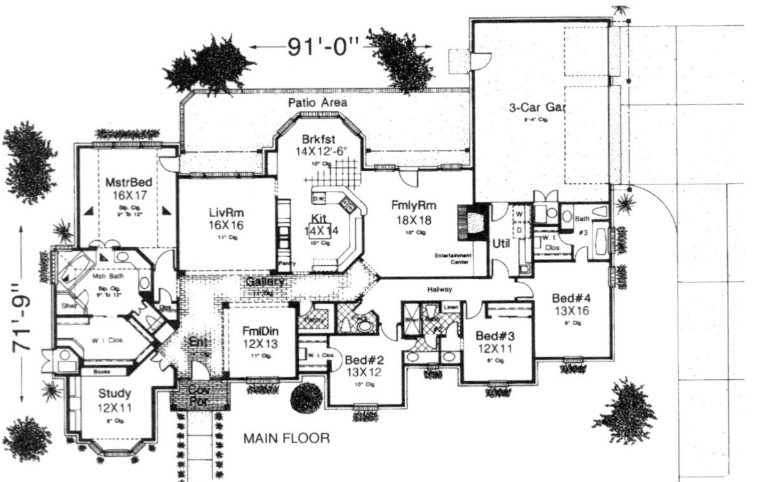
91'-0"
71'-9"
Patio Area
3-Car Gar
Brkfst 14X12'-6"
MstrBed 16X17
LivRm 16X16
Kit 14X14
FmlyRm 18X18
Util
Bed#4 13X16
Gallery
FmlDin 12X13
Bed#3 12X11
Bed#2 13X12
Study 12X11
MAIN FLOOR

Refer to **Pricing Schedule E** on the order form for pricing information

Design by
Design Basics, Inc.

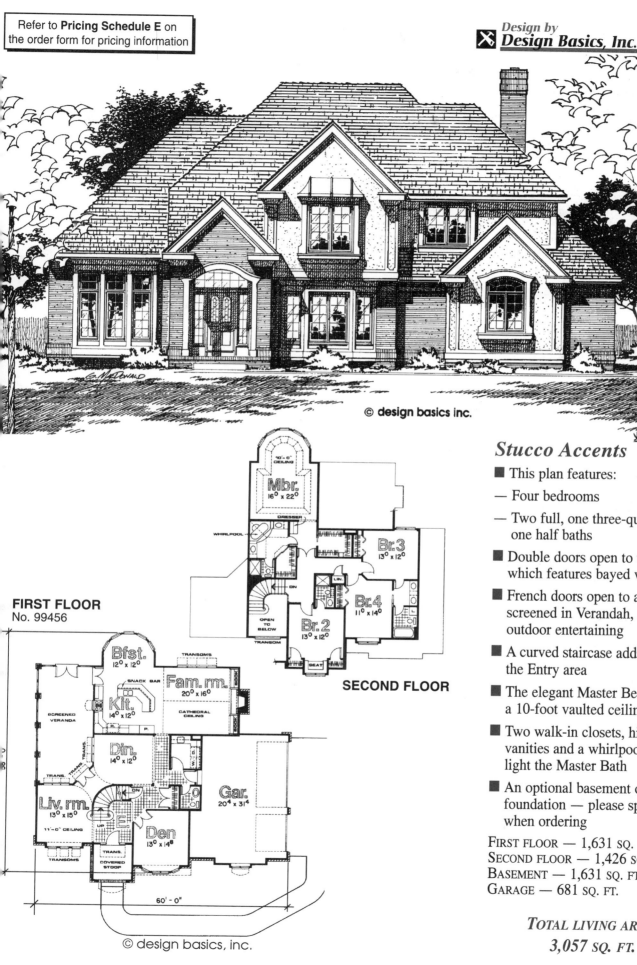

PLAN NO. 99456

© design basics inc.

Stucco Accents

- This plan features:
- — Four bedrooms
- — Two full, one three-quarter and one half baths
- Double doors open to the Den which features bayed windows
- French doors open to a large screened in Verandah, ideal for outdoor entertaining
- A curved staircase adds drama to the Entry area
- The elegant Master Bedroom has a 10-foot vaulted ceiling
- Two walk-in closets, his-n-her vanities and a whirlpool tub highlight the Master Bath
- An optional basement or slab foundation — please specify when ordering

FIRST FLOOR — 1,631 SQ. FT.
SECOND FLOOR — 1,426 SQ. FT.
BASEMENT — 1,631 SQ. FT.
GARAGE — 681 SQ. FT.

TOTAL LIVING AREA:
***3,057** SQ. FT.*

FIRST FLOOR
No. 99456

SECOND FLOOR

PLAN NO. 94261

Design by
Sater Design Group

Refer to **Pricing Schedule E** on the order form for pricing information

Poetic Symmetry

- This plan features:
- — Three bedrooms
- — Three full and one half baths
- The open Living and Dining areas are defined by French doors
- The Kitchen has a center island and loads of cabinets
- The Master Suite is located for maximum in privacy
- Upstairs find two Guest Rooms each with a private Bath and Sun Deck
- Also upstairs is a Gallery Loft and a Computer Loft, which overlooks the Grand Room
- The ground level features a two-car Garage and plenty of storage space
- No materials list is available for this plan

MAIN FLOOR — 1,642 SQ. FT.
UPPER FLOOR — 1,165 SQ. FT.
LOWER — 150 SQ. FT.

TOTAL LIVING AREA:
2,957 SQ. FT.

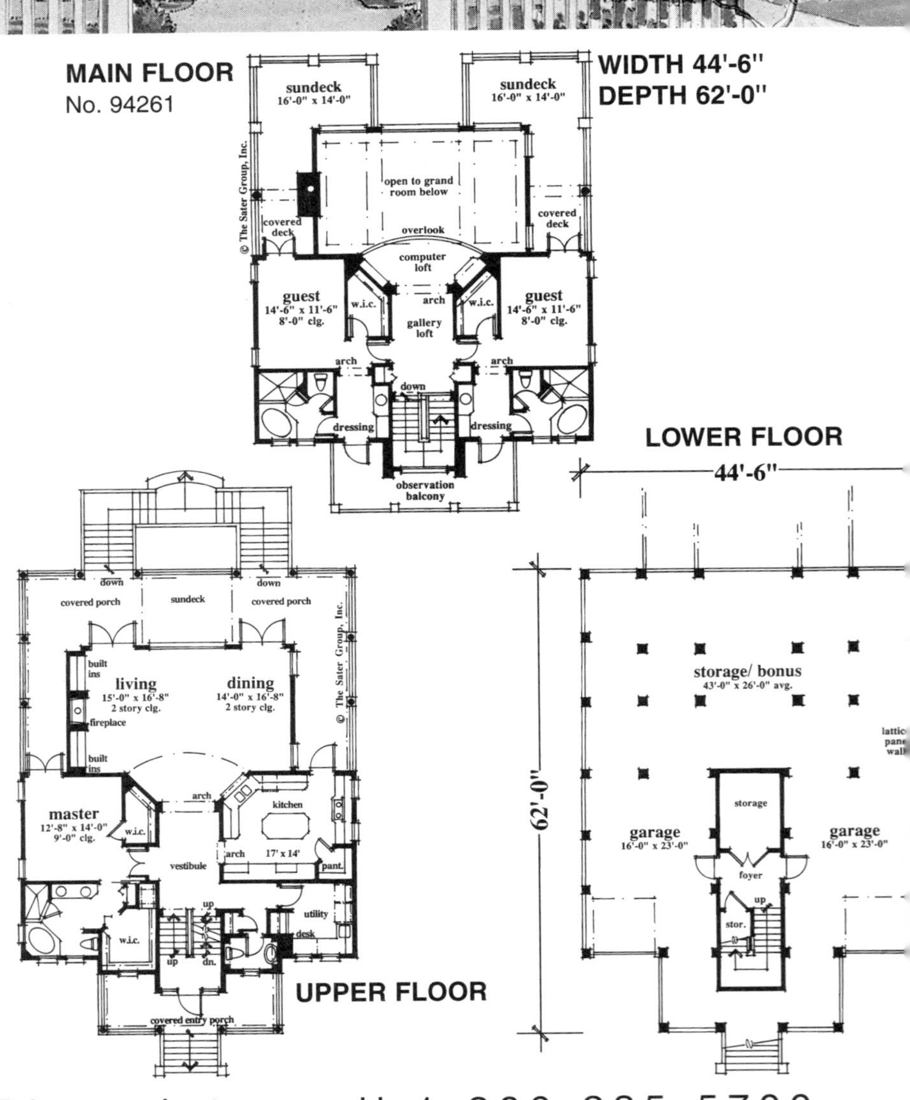
MAIN FLOOR
No. 94261
WIDTH 44'-6"
DEPTH 62'-0"
sundeck
16'-0" x 14'-0"
sundeck
16'-0" x 14'-0"
open to grand room below
covered deck
covered deck
overlook
computer loft
guest
14'-6" x 11'-6"
8'-0" clg.
guest
14'-6" x 11'-6"
8'-0" clg.
w.i.c.
arch
gallery loft
arch
down
dressing
dressing
observation balcony
© The Sater Group, Inc.
LOWER FLOOR
44'-6"
62'-0"
storage/ bonus
43'-0" x 26'-0" avg.
storage
garage
16'-0" x 23'-0"
garage
16'-0" x 23'-0"
foyer
up
stor.
down
covered porch
sundeck
covered porch
built ins
living
15'-0" x 16'-8"
2 story clg.
dining
14'-0" x 16'-8"
2 story clg.
fireplace
master
12'-8" x 14'-0"
9'-0" clg.
arch
kitchen
17' x 14'
pant.
vestibule
utility
desk
up
dn.
covered entry porch
UPPER FLOOR

Refer to **Pricing Schedule E** on the order form for pricing information

Design by
Studer Residential Design, Inc.

PLAN NO. 97717

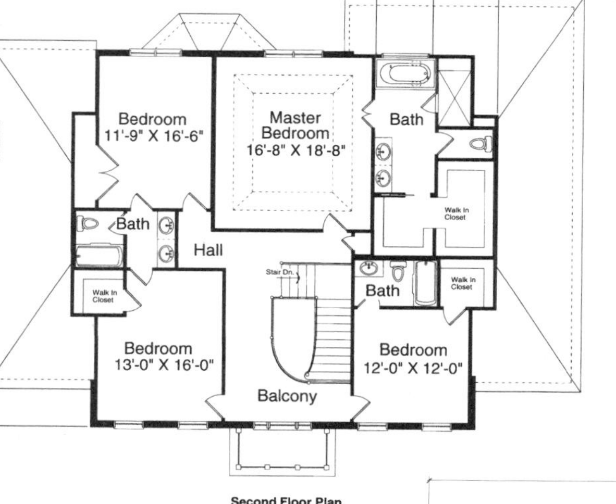
Bedroom
11'-9" X 16'-6"
Master Bedroom
16'-8" X 18'-8"
Bath
Walk In Closet
Bath
Hall
Stair Dn.
Bath
Walk In Closet
Walk In Closet
Bedroom
13'-0" X 16'-0"
Bedroom
12'-0" X 12'-0"
Balcony

Second Floor Plan
No. 97717

FIRST FLOOR — 1,670 SQ. FT.
SECOND FLOOR — 1,641 SQ. FT.
BASEMENT — 1,670 SQ. FT.
GARAGE — 750 SQ. FT.

TOTAL LIVING AREA:
3,311 SQ. FT.

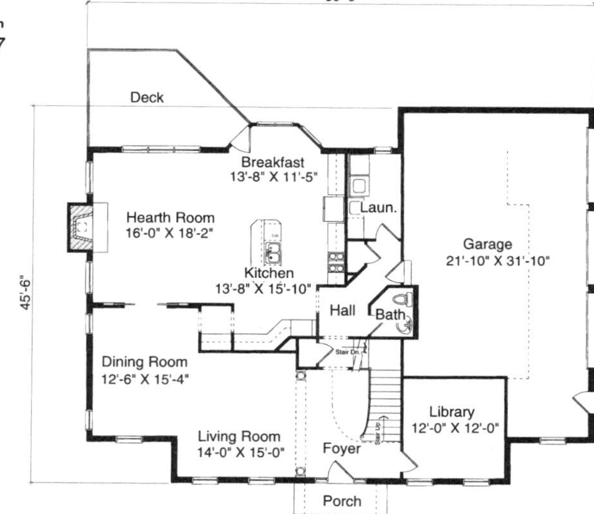
60'-0"
Deck
Breakfast
13'-8" X 11'-5"
Hearth Room
16'-0" X 18'-2"
Laun.
Garage
21'-10" X 31'-10"
Kitchen
13'-8" X 15'-10"
45'-6"
Hall
Bath
Stair Dn.
Dining Room
12'-6" X 15'-4"
Library
12'-0" X 12'-0"
Living Room
14'-0" X 15'-0"
Foyer
Porch

First Floor Plan

The Perfect Balance

- This plan features:
  - — Four bedrooms
  - — Three full and one half baths
- This delightful two-story home offers formal and informal spaces
- The Entry includes a graceful curved staircase
- Colonial columns at the Living Room entry
- Pocket doors introduce you to the spacious Hearth Room
- An island with seating defines the functional Kitchen
- A Library located for privacy completes the first floor
- Highlighting the second floor is the balcony
- The spacious Master Bedroom has a tray ceiling and deluxe Dressing Room
- No materials list is available for this plan

PLAN NO. 98016

Design by
Donald A. Gardner Architects, Inc.

Refer to **Pricing Schedule F** on the order form for pricing information

B.NATHAN

Family Farmhouse

- This plan features:
  - Four bedrooms
  - Two full and one half baths
- An arched entry and a wrapping front Porch provide charm to this family farmhouse
- The Foyer and the Great Room are each brightened by clerestory windows
- Bay windows grace the Dining Room, Breakfast Area and Master Suite
- Generous front and back Porches afford options for outdoor relaxation
- A fabulous, first floor Master Suite features a bayed Sitting Area and a private Bath
- Upstairs find three Bedrooms and a bonus room

FIRST FLOOR — 1,614 SQ. FT.
SECOND FLOOR — 892 SQ. FT.
BONUS ROOM — 341 SQ. FT.
GARAGE & STORAGE — 510 SQ. FT.

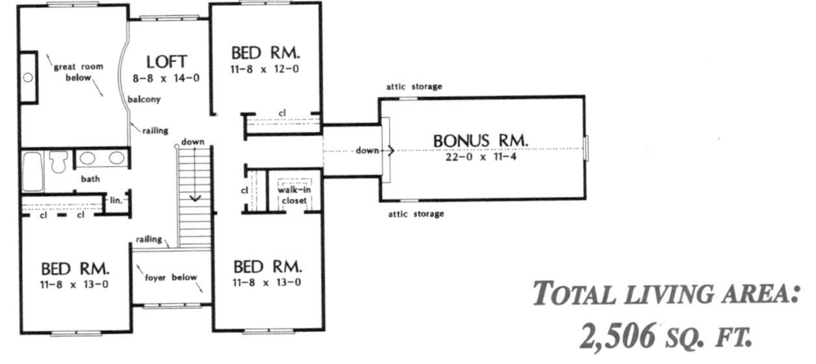

great room below
LOFT
8-8 x 14-0
balcony
railing
BED RM.
11-8 x 12-0
cl
attic storage
BONUS RM.
22-0 x 11-4
down
bath
lin.
cl
cl
walk-in closet
attic storage
railing
BED RM.
11-8 x 13-0
foyer below
BED RM.
11-8 x 13-0

No. 98016
SECOND FLOOR PLAN

TOTAL LIVING AREA:
2,506 SQ. FT.

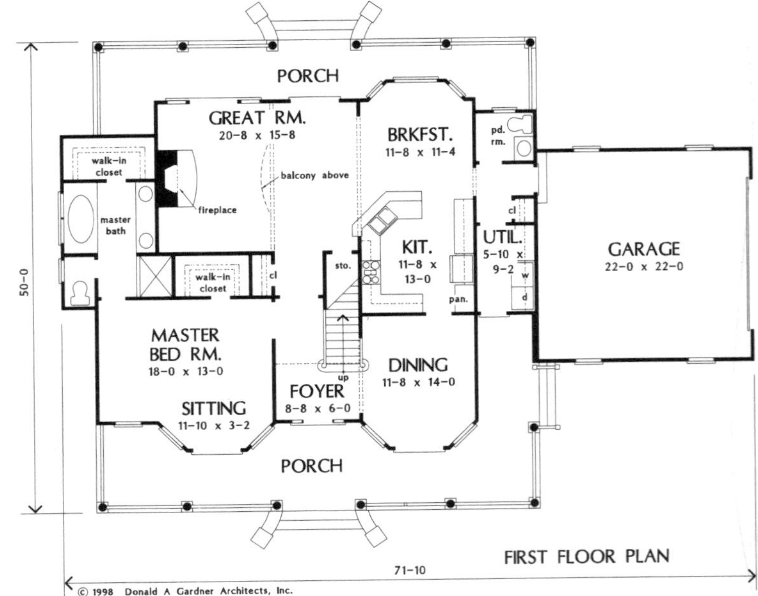

PORCH
GREAT RM.
20-8 x 15-8
BRKFST.
11-8 x 11-4
pd. rm.
walk-in closet
balcony above
fireplace
master bath
KIT.
11-8 x 13-0
sto.
UTIL.
5-10 x 9-2
GARAGE
22-0 x 22-0
walk-in closet
cl
pan.
50-0
MASTER
BED RM.
18-0 x 13-0
up
DINING
11-8 x 14-0
FOYER
8-8 x 6-0
SITTING
11-10 x 3-2
PORCH
71-10

FIRST FLOOR PLAN

To order your Blueprints, call 1-800-235-5700

Refer to **Pricing Schedule F** on
the order form for pricing information

Design by
Filmore Design Group

PLAN NO. 98527

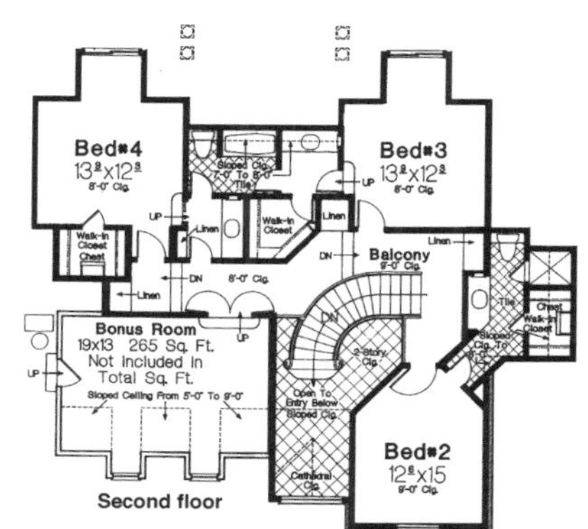
Bed#4
13⁸x12⁸
Bed#3
13⁸x12⁸
Balcony
Bonus Room
19x13 265 Sq. Ft.
Not Included In
Total Sq. Ft.
Bed#2
12⁸x15
Second floor

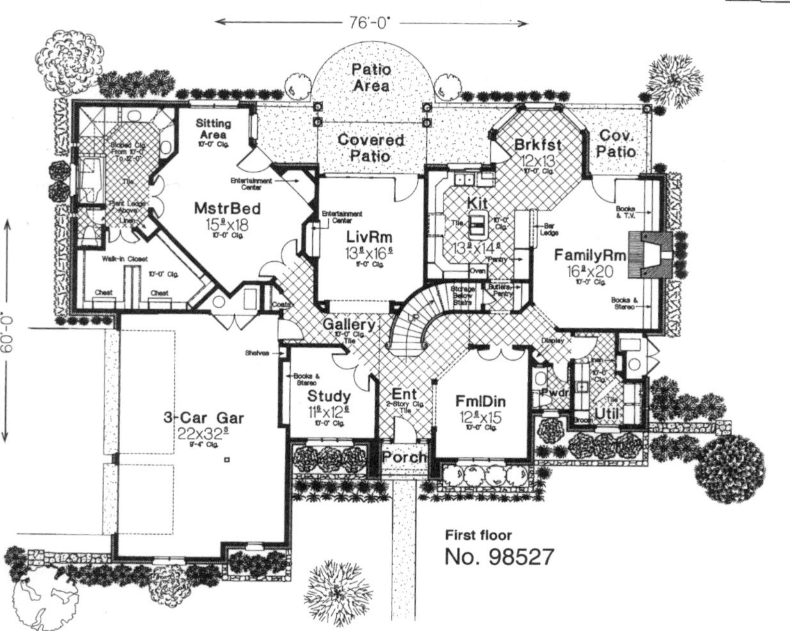
76'-0"
60'-0"
Patio
Area
Covered
Patio
Sitting
Area
MstrBed
15⁸x18
LivRm
13⁸x16⁸
Brkfst
12x13
Cov.
Patio
Kit
13⁸x14⁸
FamilyRm
16⁸x20
Gallery
3-Car Gar
22x32⁸
Study
11⁸x12⁸
Ent
FmlDin
12⁸x15
Pwdr
Util
Porch
First floor
No. 98527

Executive Estate

- This plan features:
  - — Four bedrooms
  - — Three full and one half baths
- A two-story Foyer highlighted by a curved staircase
- The formal Dining Room has a large front window and decorative columns
- The Study offers built-in shelves for books and electronic equipment
- The sumptuous Master Suite features a large closet, Sitting Area, and entertainment center
- No materials list is available for this plan

FIRST FLOOR — 2,655 SQ. FT.
SECOND FLOOR — 1,090 SQ. FT.
BONUS — 265 SQ. FT.
GARAGE — 704 SQ. FT.

TOTAL LIVING AREA:
3,745 SQ. FT.

PLAN NO. 94933

Design by
Design Basics, Inc.

Refer to **Pricing Schedule F** on the order form for pricing information

SECOND FLOOR

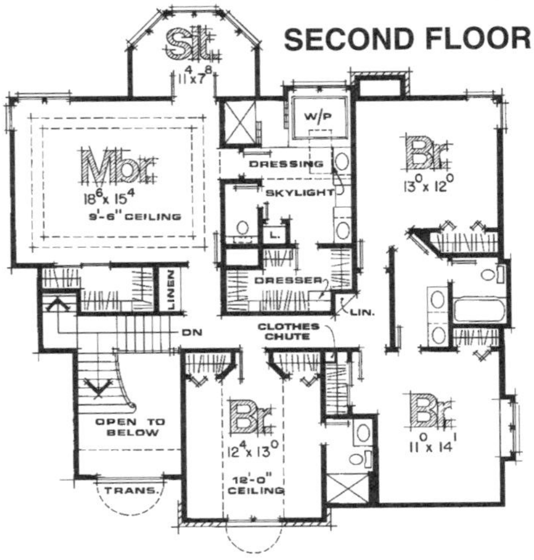

Sit. 11^4x7^8

Mbr. 18^6x 15^4 9'-6" CEILING

W/P DRESSING SKYLIGHT DRESSER LIN. CLOTHES CHUTE LINEN DN

Br. 13^0x 12^0

Br. 12^4x 13^0 12'-0" CEILING

Br. 11^0x 14^1

OPEN TO BELOW TRANS.

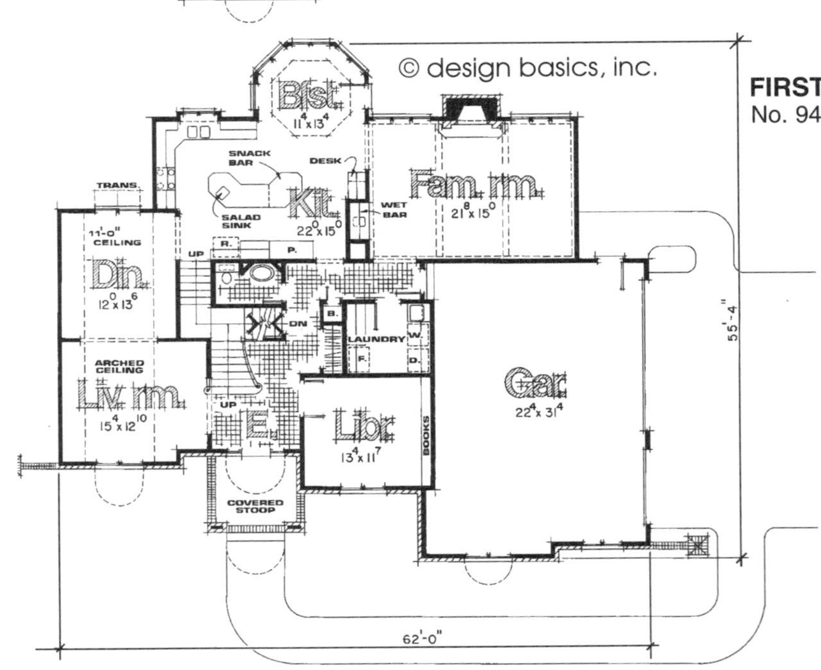

© design basics, inc.
Brkfst. 11^4x13^4
SNACK BAR
DESK
Kit. 22^0x15^0
SALAD SINK
WET BAR
Fam. rm. 21^8x15^0
TRANS.
11'-0" CEILING
Din. 12^0x13^6
UP
R.
P.
DN
B.
LAUNDRY
W.
F.
D.
ARCHED CEILING
Liv. rm. 15^4x12^{10}
UP
E.
Libr. 13^4x11^7
BOOKS
Gar. 22^4x31^4
COVERED STOOP
55'-4"
62'-0"

FIRST FLOOR
No. 94933

Glorious Gables

- This plan features:
- — Four bedrooms
- — Two full, one three-quarter and one half baths
- Arched windows and entry lead to tiled Entry with cascading staircase
- Arched ceiling topping Living and Dining room
- Double door leads into quiet Library with book shelves
- Hub Kitchen with angled, work island/snackbar, built-in Pantry and desk
- Comfortable Family Room with hearth fireplace
- Private Master Bedroom suite offers a Sitting Area

FIRST FLOOR — 1,709 SQ. FT.
SECOND FLOOR — 1,597 SQ. FT.
GARAGE — 721 SQ. FT.
BASEMENT — 1,709 SQ. FT.

TOTAL LIVING AREA:
3,306 SQ. FT.

Refer to **Pricing Schedule F** on the order form for pricing information

Design by
Donald A. Gardner Architects, Inc.

PLAN NO. 96411

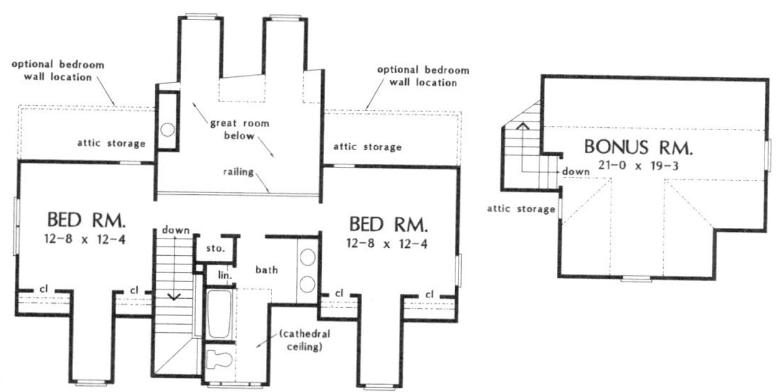

optional bedroom wall location
great room below
optional bedroom wall location
attic storage
railing
attic storage
BED RM.
12-8 x 12-4
down
sto.
lin.
bath
BED RM.
12-8 x 12-4
cl
(cathedral ceiling)
BONUS RM.
21-0 x 19-3
down
attic storage

SECOND FLOOR PLAN

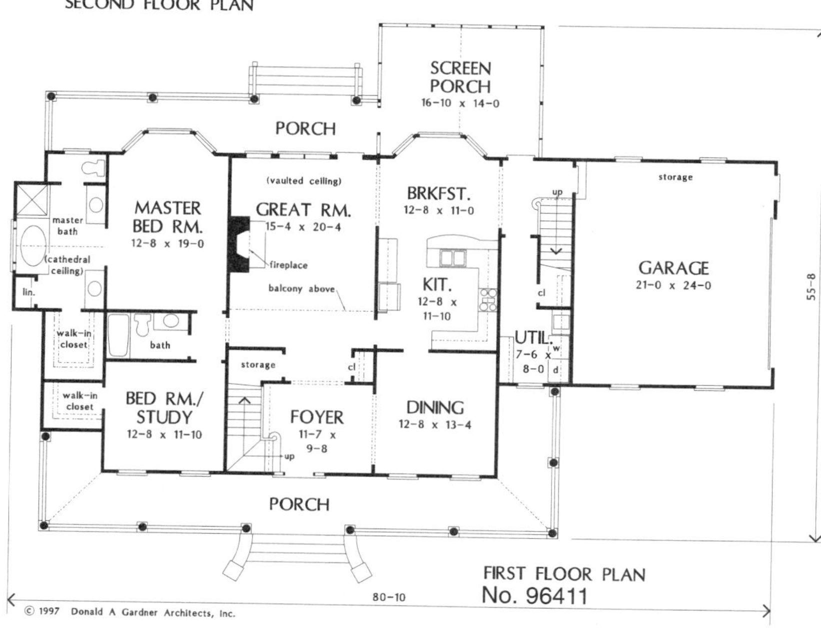

SCREEN PORCH
16-10 x 14-0
PORCH
(vaulted ceiling)
MASTER BED RM.
12-8 x 19-0
master bath
(cathedral ceiling)
lin.
GREAT RM.
15-4 x 20-4
fireplace
balcony above
BRKFST.
12-8 x 11-0
KIT.
12-8 x 11-10
storage
GARAGE
21-0 x 24-0
UTIL.
7-6 x 8-0
walk-in closet
bath
walk-in closet
BED RM./ STUDY
12-8 x 11-10
storage
FOYER
11-7 x 9-8
up
DINING
12-8 x 13-4
PORCH
55-8
80-10
© 1997 Donald A Gardner Architects, Inc.

FIRST FLOOR PLAN
No. 96411

Wrapping Front Porch and Gabled Dormers

- This plan features:
  - — Four bedrooms
  - — Three full baths
- Generous Great Room with a fireplace, cathedral ceiling, and a balcony above
- Flexible Bedroom/Study with a walk-in closet and an adjacent full Bath
- First floor Master Suite with a sunny bay window and a private Bath with cathedral ceiling, his-n-her vanity, and a separate tub and shower
- Bonus room over the Garage for future expansion

FIRST FLOOR — 1,939 SQ. FT.
SECOND FLOOR — 657 SQ. FT.
GARAGE & STORAGE — 526 SQ. FT.
BONUS ROOM — 386 SQ. FT.

TOTAL LIVING AREA:
2,596 SQ. FT.

PLAN NO. 99149

Design by
Ahmann Design, Inc.

Refer to **Pricing Schedule E** on the order form for pricing information

Elegant Stone Two-Story

- This plan features:
- — Four bedrooms
- — Two full and one half baths
- The two-story entry leads directly into the Great Room
- The Kitchen has a center island and is open to the large Nook
- The Master Bedrooms has an access door to the rear Deck
- Upstairs are two Bedrooms that are serviced by a full Bath
- Also upstairs is a large Game Room for all the kid's toys
- A Three-Season Porch with a cathedral ceiling rounds out this plan
- No materials list is available for this plan

MAIN FLOOR — 2,039 SQ. FT.
SECOND FLOOR — 613 SQ. FT.

TOTAL LIVING AREA:
2,652 SQ. FT.

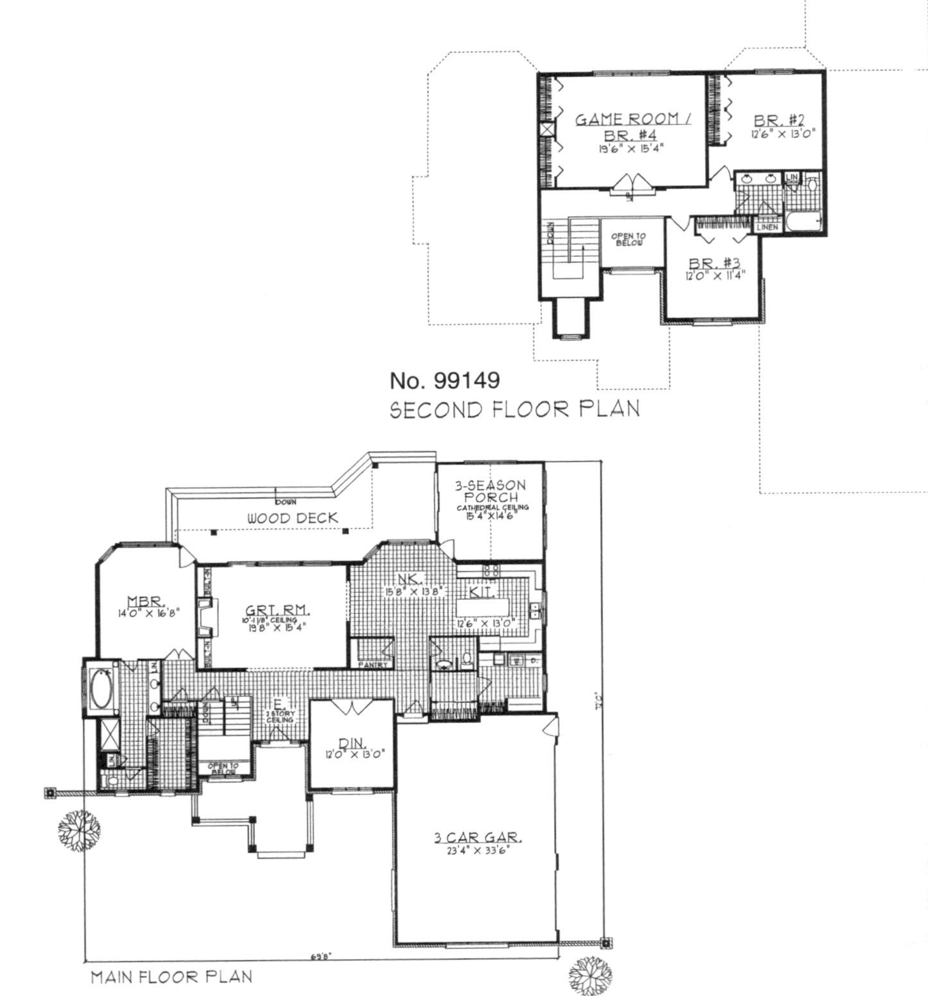
GAME ROOM / BR. #4
19'6" X 15'4"
BR. #2
12'6" X 13'0"
LIN
LINEN
OPEN TO BELOW
BR. #3
12'0" X 11'4"
No. 99149
SECOND FLOOR PLAN
3-SEASON PORCH
15'4" X 14'6"
DOWN
WOOD DECK
MBR.
14'0" X 16'8"
GRT. RM.
19'8" X 15'4"
NK.
15'8" X 13'8"
KIT.
12'6" X 13'0"
PANTRY
DIN.
12'0" X 13'0"
3 CAR GAR.
23'4" X 33'6"
MAIN FLOOR PLAN

To order your Blueprints, call 1-800-235-5700

Design by
Fillmore Design Group

PLAN NO. 92265

Luxurious Masterpiece

Price Code: F

- This plan features:
- — Four bedrooms
- — Three full and one half baths
- An elegant and distinguished exterior
- An expansive formal Living Room with a fourteen foot ceiling and a raised hearth fireplace
- Informal Family Room offers another fireplace, wet bar, cathedral ceiling and access to the Covered Patio
- A hub Kitchen with a cooktop island, peninsula counter/snackbar, and a bright breakfast area
- French doors lead into a quiet Study offering many uses
- Private Master Bedroom enhanced by a pullman ceiling, lavish his-n-her baths, and a garden window tub
- Three additional bedrooms with walk-in closets have private access to a full bath
- No materials list is available for this plan

MAIN FLOOR — 3,818 SQ. FT.
GARAGE — 816 SQ. FT.

TOTAL LIVING AREA:
3,818 SQ. FT.

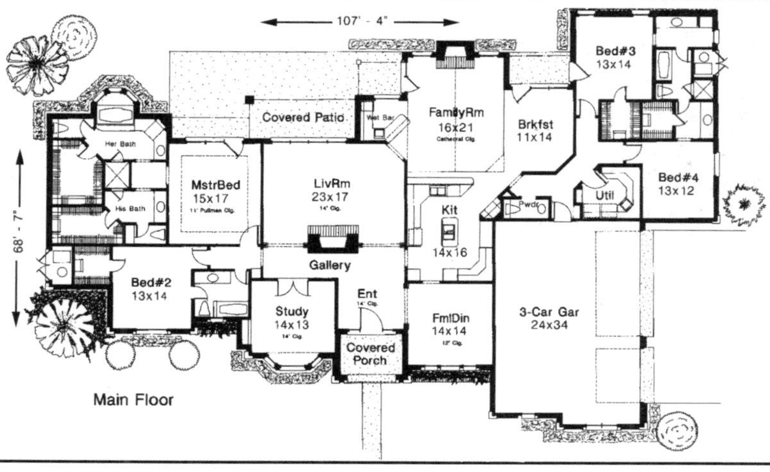

107' - 4"
68' - 7"
Covered Patio
FamilyRm
16x21
Brkfst
11x14
Bed#3
13x14
Bed#4
13x12
Util
Pwdr
Kit
14x16
LivRm
23x17
MstrBed
15x17
Her Bath
His Bath
Bed#2
13x14
Gallery
Ent
Study
14x13
Covered Porch
FmlDin
14x14
3-Car Gar
24x34
Main Floor

Design by
Sater Design Group

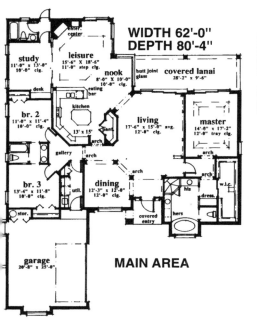

PLAN NO. 94271

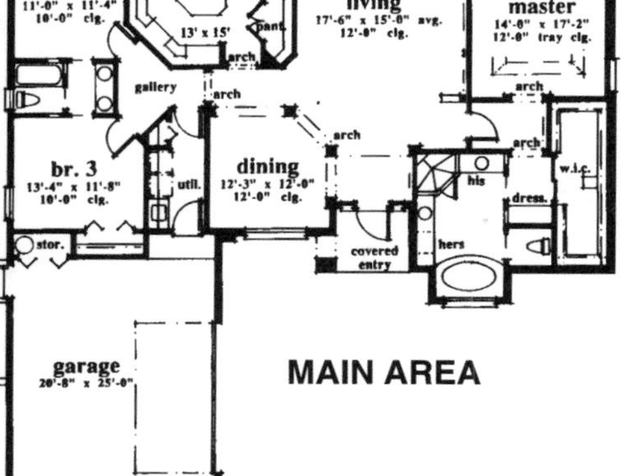

WIDTH 62'-0"
DEPTH 80'-4"
enter. center
leisure
15'-6" X 18'-6"
11'-0" step clg.
study
11'-0" x 13'-0"
10'-0" clg.
nook
8'-0" X 10'-0"
10'-0" clg.
butt joint glass
covered lanai
28'-2" x 9'-6"
desk
eating bar
kitchen
13' x 15'
br. 2
11'-0" x 11'-4"
10'-0" clg.
living
17'-6" x 15'-0" avg.
12'-0" clg.
master
14'-0" x 17'-2"
12'-0" tray clg.
pant
arch
gallery
br. 3
13'-4" x 11'-8"
10'-0" clg.
util.
dining
12'-3" x 12'-0"
12'-0" clg.
his
dress.
w.i.c.
hers
covered entry
stor.
garage
20'-8" x 25'-0"
MAIN AREA

High Pitched Roof Lines

Price Code: E

- This plan features:
- — Three bedrooms
- — Three full baths
- The facade is elegant with a mix of brick and stucco and high pitched roof lines
- Interior detailing and arches highlight the formal spaces
- The Living Room opens to a covered Lanai facing the rear yard
- An open Kitchen, Nook and Leisure Room
- No materials list is available for this plan

MAIN FLOORS — 2,802 SQ. FT.
GARAGE — 619 SQ. FT.

TOTAL LIVING AREA:
2,802 SQ. FT.

PLAN NO. 99290

Design by **Homeplanners**

Refer to **Pricing Schedule E** on the order form for pricing information

Unique Angles and Lots of Light

- This plan features:
  - — Three bedrooms
  - — Two full and one half baths
- Unusual angles and windows highlight the formal Living and Dining rooms
- Expansive Family Room has an angled fireplace
- Dream Kitchen offers a breakfast bar/work island, walk-in Pantry, recipe corner, Laundry Room, Garage entry and Breakfast Lanai
- Master Suite opens to private Lanai with a spa and a plush Master Bath with a whirlpool window tub
- Large Den/Study offers many uses, even double as another Bedroom

FIRST FLOOR — 2,137 SQ. FT.
SECOND FLOOR — 671 SQ. FT.

TOTAL LIVING AREA:
2,808 SQ. FT.

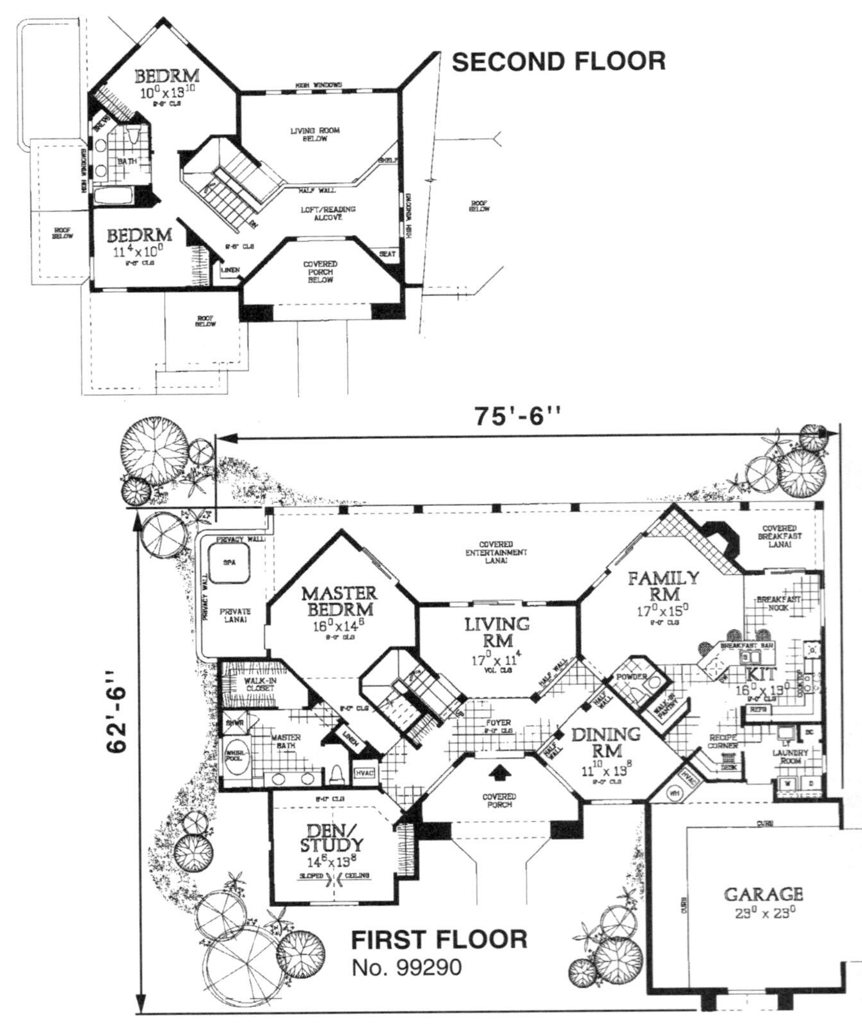

SECOND FLOOR
BEDRM
10^0x13^{10}
LIVING ROOM BELOW
LOFT/READING ALCOVE
BATH
BEDRM
11^4x10^0
LINEN
COVERED PORCH BELOW
SEAT
ROOF BELOW
75'-6''
62'-6''
COVERED ENTERTAINMENT LANAI
COVERED BREAKFAST LANAI
SPA
PRIVATE LANAI
MASTER BEDRM
16^0x14^6
LIVING RM
17^0x11^4
FAMILY RM
17^0x15^0
BREAKFAST NOOK
BREAKFAST BAR
KIT
16^0x13^0
WALK-IN CLOSET
MASTER BATH
FOYER
DINING RM
11^{10}x13^8
POWDER
RECIPE CORNER
LAUNDRY ROOM
COVERED PORCH
DEN/ STUDY
14^6x13^8
GARAGE
23^0 x 23^0
FIRST FLOOR
No. 99290

To order your Blueprints, call 1-800-235-5700

Refer to **Pricing Schedule E** on the order form for pricing information

Design by
Patrick Morabito A.I.A.

PLAN NO. 93332

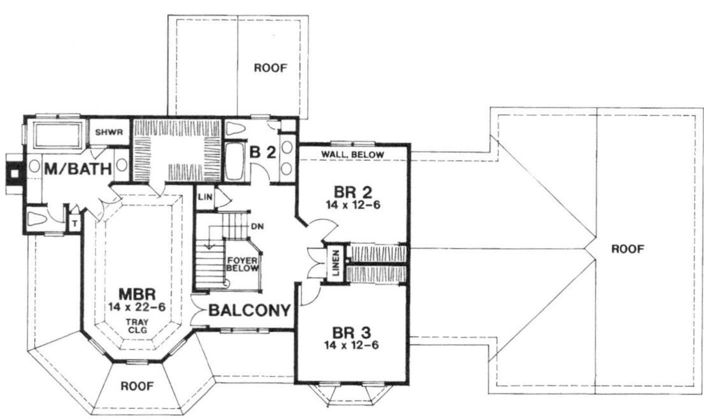

ROOF
SHWR
M/BATH
B 2
WALL BELOW
BR 2
14 x 12-6
LIN
DN
FOYER BELOW
LINEN
ROOF
MBR
14 x 22-6
TRAY CLG
BALCONY
BR 3
14 x 12-6
ROOF

SECOND FLOOR

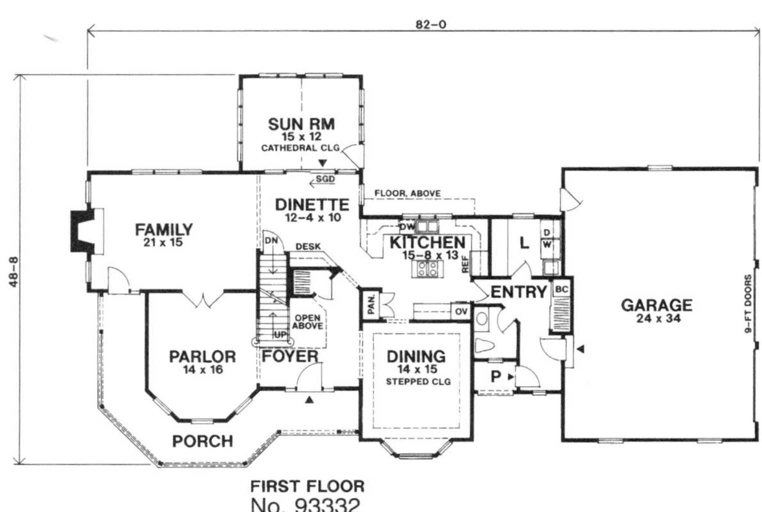

82-0
48-8
SUN RM
15 x 12
CATHEDRAL CLG
SGD
FLOOR ABOVE
DINETTE
12-4 x 10
FAMILY
21 x 15
DN
DESK
DW
KITCHEN
15-8 x 13
REF
L
D
W
ENTRY
BC
GARAGE
24 x 34
9-FT DOORS
OPEN ABOVE
PAN
OV
UP
PARLOR
14 x 16
FOYER
DINING
14 x 15
STEPPED CLG
P
PORCH

FIRST FLOOR
No. 93332

That Old-Fashioned Feeling

- This plan features:
  - — Three bedrooms
  - — Two full and one half baths
- A formal Parlor opens into the Family Room, with a hearth fireplace
- A stepped ceiling and a bay window accent the formal Dining Room
- A large Kitchen with a double sink, built-in Pantry, island and peninsula counter is a delight
- Elegant Master Suite includes a tray ceiling and a plush Bath featuring a raised, corner window tub and two vanities
- No materials list is available for this plan

FIRST FLOOR — 1,484 SQ. FT.
SECOND FLOOR — 1,223 SQ. FT.
BASEMENT — 1,484 SQ. FT.

TOTAL LIVING AREA:
2,707 SQ. FT.

PLAN NO. 24265

Design by
The Garlinghouse Company

Refer to **Pricing Schedule E** on the order form for pricing information

Comfortable Living

- This plan features:
  - — Three or Four Bedrooms
  - — Three full baths
- Easy access between Living Room and Dining Room for ease in entertaining
- Modern Kitchen with double sink, built-in Pantry and peninsula counter
- Vaulted ceiling in the Family Room which also features a fireplace
- A Master Suite with vaulted ceiling, optional fireplace, his-and-her walk-in closets and lavish Master Bath

FIRST FLOOR — 1,574 SQ. FT.
SECOND FLOOR — 1,098 SQ. FT.

TOTAL LIVING AREA:
2,672 SQ. FT.

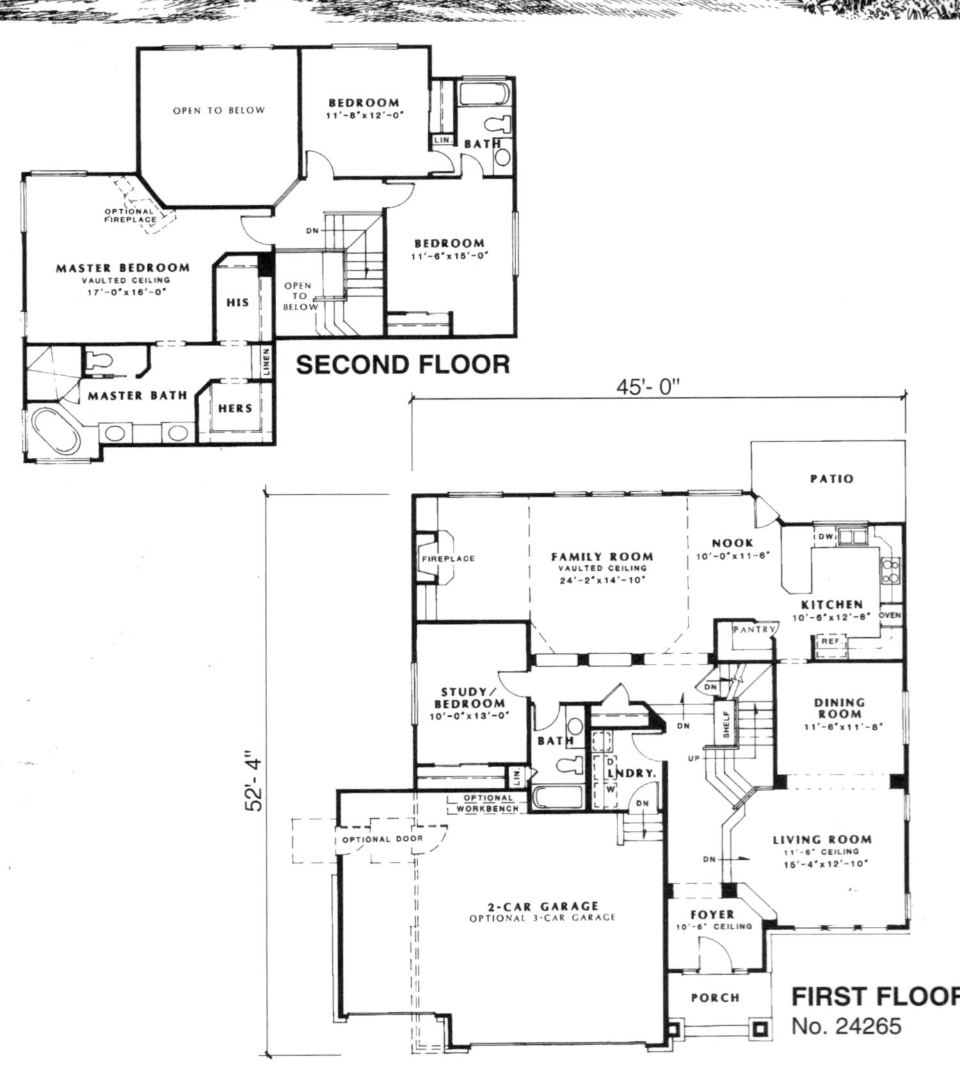

OPEN TO BELOW
BEDROOM 11'-8"x12'-0"
LIN
BATH
OPTIONAL FIREPLACE
DN
BEDROOM 11'-6"x15'-0"
MASTER BEDROOM VAULTED CEILING 17'-0"x16'-0"
HIS
OPEN TO BELOW
LINEN
MASTER BATH
HERS
SECOND FLOOR
45'- 0"
PATIO
FIREPLACE
FAMILY ROOM VAULTED CEILING 24'-2"x14'-10"
NOOK 10'-0"x11-6"
DW
KITCHEN 10'-6"x12'-6"
OVEN
PANTRY
REF.
STUDY/ BEDROOM 10'-0"x13'-0"
DN
SHELF
DINING ROOM 11'-6"x11'-8"
BATH
LNDRY.
UP
LIN
OPTIONAL WORKBENCH
52'- 4"
OPTIONAL DOOR
LIVING ROOM 11'-6" CEILING 15'-4"x12'-10"
2-CAR GARAGE OPTIONAL 3-CAR GARAGE
FOYER 10'-6" CEILING
PORCH
FIRST FLOOR
No. 24265

Refer to **Pricing Schedule H** on the order form for pricing information

Design by
Donald A. Gardner Architects, Inc.

PLAN NO. 98022

LOWER LEVEL

COVERED PATIO
BED RM. 13-0 x 14-0
FAMILY RM. 16-4 x 20-0
BED RM. 12-4 x 14-8
STORAGE (unfinished)

DECK
BRKFST. 10-0 x 14-0
KIT. 11-10 x 14-0
LIVING RM. 16-4 x 20-0 (cathedral ceiling)
MASTER BED RM. 14-0 x 17-0
DINING 13-0 x 14-4
FOYER 6-8 x 13-2
BED RM./STUDY 13-0 x 13-0
BED RM. 12-0 x 13-0
UTIL. 7-4 x 9-0
PORCH
GARAGE 22-0 x 22-8

FIRST FLOOR
No. 98022

European Style for a Sloping Lot

■ This plan features:
— Five bedrooms
— Five full and one half baths
■ Cedar shake, stone, and siding embellish the sophisticated exterior
■ The expansive Deck allows spectacular rear views
■ Special ceiling treatments enhance the open Living and Dining rooms
■ The Kitchen features a smart layout with a center cooktop island
■ Located on the lower level are the Family Room and two Bedrooms
■ Three Bedrooms and three Baths are located on the first floor including the Master Suite

FIRST FLOOR — 2,297 SQ. FT.
LOWER LEVEL — 1,212 SQ. FT.
GARAGE — 626 SQ. FT.

TOTAL LIVING AREA:
3,509 SQ. FT.

PLAN NO. 96602

Design by
Larry E. Belk

Refer to **Pricing Schedule E** on the order form for pricing information

With A European Influence

- This plan features:
- — Four bedrooms
- — Two full and one half baths
- The Old World country French influence in this home is evident
- The Foyer opens to the well-proportioned Dining Room
- Double French doors with transoms lead off the Living Room to the rear Porch
- The spacious Kitchen is adjacent to the Breakfast and Family Room
- The Master Bedroom features a tray ceiling and a luxurious Master Bath
- An optional basement, crawl space or slab foundation — please specify when ordering
- No materials list is available for this plan

MAIN FLOOR — 2,745 SQ. FT.
GARAGE — 525 SQ. FT.

TOTAL LIVING AREA:
2,745 SQ. FT.

WIDTH 69–6
DEPTH 76–6
COVERED PORCH
MASTER BATH
K.S.
FAMILY ROOM
15–4 X 16–0
12 FT VAULTED CLG
LIVING ROOM
17–0 X 16–0
12 FT CLG
BEDRM 4/STUDY
13–4 X 14–8
10 FT CLG
MASTER BEDROOM
15–4 X 15–4
12 FT TRAY CLG
BRKFST RM
15–4 X 7–6
12 FT VAULTED CLG
42" LEDGE
UP
DOWN
BATH 2
PWDR
KITCHEN
15–4 X 16–4
10 FT CLG
DINING ROOM
12–8 X 14–4
12 FT CLG
FOYER
12 FT CLG
BEDROOM 2
12–8 X 12–6
10 FT CLG
BEDROOM 3
12–4 X 13–6
10 FT CLG
PORCH
UTIL
PAN
COPYRIGHT LARRY E. BELK
GARAGE

MAIN FLOOR
No. 96602

Refer to **Pricing Schedule D** on
the order form for pricing information

Design by
Filmore Design Group

PLAN NO. 98533

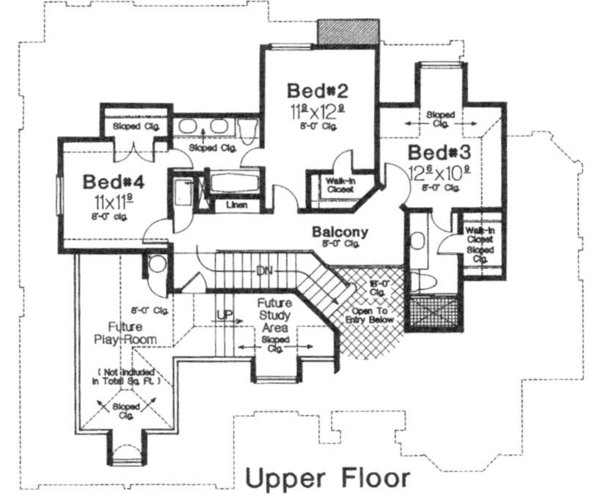
Bed#2
Bed#3
Bed#4
Sloped Clg.
Walk-In Closet
Linen
Balcony
DN
UP
Future Study Area
Future Play Room
(Not Included In Total Sq. Ft.)
Open To Entry Below
Upper Floor

TOTAL LIVING AREA:
2,567 SQ. FT.

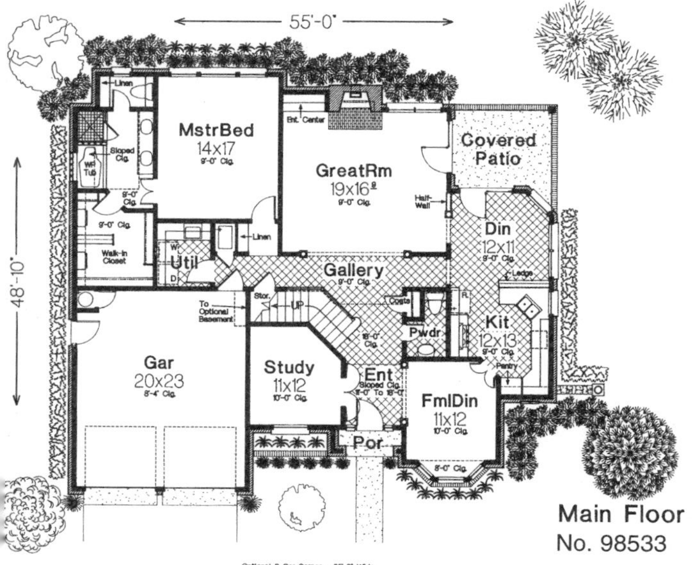
55'-0"
48'-10"
MstrBed
14x17
GreatRm
Covered Patio
Din
12x11
Gallery
Util
Walk-In Closet
Linen
Kit
12x13
Pwdr
Gar
20x23
Study
11x12
Ent
FmlDin
11x12
Por
Main Floor
No. 98533
Optional 3-Car Garage = 65'-0" Wide

French Country Styling

- This plan features:
  - — Four bedrooms
  - — Two full, one half, and one three quarter baths
- A bay window with a copper roof and an arched covered entry add Country flavor
- The Great Room includes a brick fireplace
- An elegant Dining Room and angled Study are located off the entry
- The convenient Kitchen has a Dining Area
- The Master Suite has a large Bath
- An optional basement or slab foundation — please specify when ordering
- No materials list is available for this plan

MAIN FLOOR — 1,765 SQ. FT.
UPPER FLOOR — 802 SQ. FT.
BONUS ROOM — 275 SQ. FT.
GARAGE — 462 SQ. FT.

PLAN NO. 94270

Design by
Sater Design Group

Refer to **Pricing Schedule F** on the order form for pricing information

In the Grandest of Style

- This plan features:
- — Four bedrooms
- — Three full and one half baths
- The Living Room has corner glass doors out to the rear Lanai
- The Dining Room features a step ceiling and a built-in server
- In the rear of the home find the Leisure Room with a built-in entertainment center
- The unique Kitchen has an island and a walk-in Pantry
- The Master Suite is impeccable and has a private outdoor garden
- There are three guest Bedrooms, two of which are on the second floor
- Also upstairs, find a loft which accesses a covered Observation Deck
- No materials list is available for this plan

FIRST FLOOR — 3,010 SQ. FT.
SECOND FLOOR — 948 SQ. FT.
GARAGE — 604 SQ. FT.

TOTAL LIVING AREA:
3,958 SQ. FT.

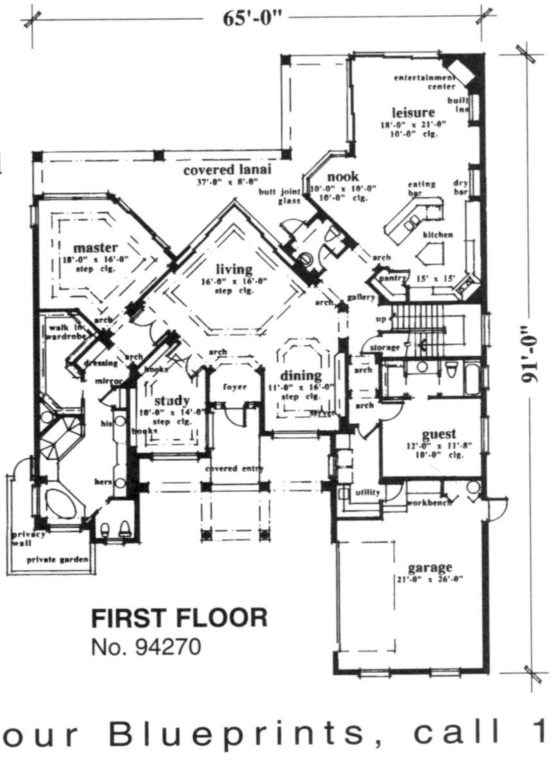

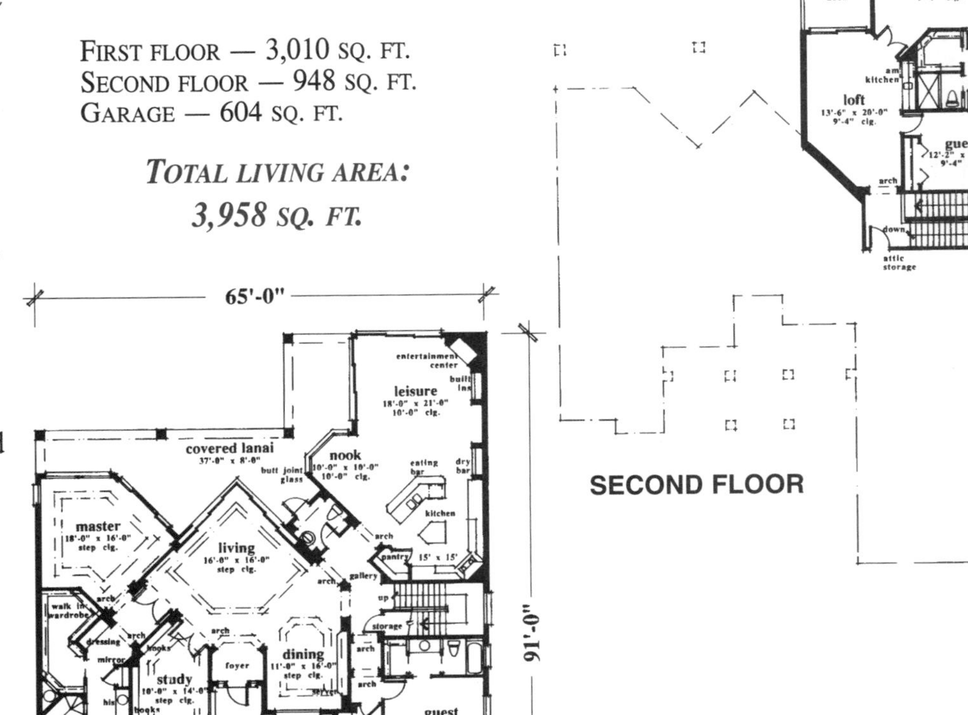

65'-0"
91'-0"
covered lanai
master
living
leisure
nook
kitchen
study
foyer
dining
guest
garage
covered entry
private garden
loft
covered observation deck
SECOND FLOOR
FIRST FLOOR
No. 94270

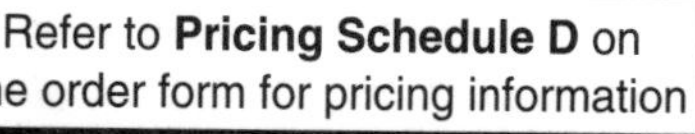
Refer to **Pricing Schedule D** on
he order form for pricing information

Design by
The Garlinghouse Company

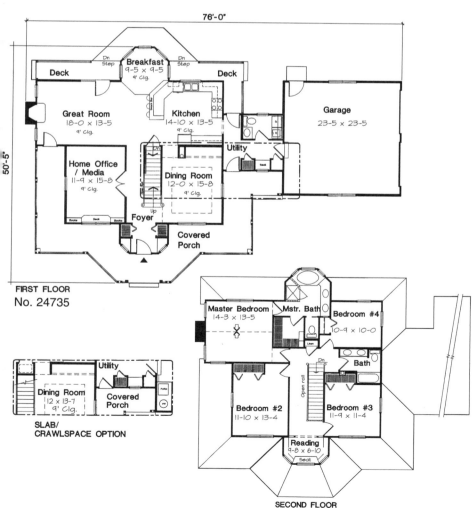

PLAN NO. 24735

76'-0"
50'-5"
Deck
Dn Step
Breakfast 9-5 x 9-5 9' Clg.
Dn Step
Deck
Great Room 18-0 x 13-5 9' Clg.
Kitchen 14-10 x 13-5 9' Clg.
Garage 23-5 x 23-5
Utility
Home Office / Media 11-9 x 15-8 9' Clg.
Dining Room 12-0 x 15-8 9' Clg.
Foyer
Covered Porch

FIRST FLOOR
No. 24735

Utility
Dining Room 12 x 13-7 9' Clg.
Covered Porch

SLAB/
CRAWLSPACE OPTION

Master Bedroom 14-3 x 13-5
Mstr. Bath
Bedroom #4 10-9 x 10-0
Bath
Bedroom #2 11-10 x 13-4
Bedroom #3 11-9 x 11-4
Reading 9-8 x 6-10
Seat

SECOND FLOOR

A Splendid Porch

- This plan features:
  - — Four bedrooms
  - — Two full and one half baths
- A stylish front Porch enhances this attractive home
- Dual closets and an attractive staircase greet you upon entering
- There is a room devoted to a Home Office or a Media Center
- The Great Room is open to the Kitchen and they share a serving bar
- The Breakfast Nook overlooks the rear Deck
- Upstairs find the Bedrooms and a Reading Nook
- No materials list is available for this plan

FIRST FLOOR — 1,305 SQ. FT.
SECOND FLOOR — 1,121 SQ. FT.
BASEMENT — 1,194 SQ. FT.
GARAGE — 576 SQ. FT.

TOTAL LIVING AREA:
2,426 SQ. FT.

PLAN NO. 20507

Design by
The Garlinghouse Company

Refer to **Pricing Schedule E** on the order form for pricing information

Luxury and Style

- This plan features:
  - — Three bedrooms
  - — Two full and one half baths
- A two story ceiling and two-way fireplace in the formal Living Room and the Family Room
- A cooktop island, built-in Pantry, peninsula counter/eating bar in the Kitchen
- A first floor Master Suite crowned by a tray ceiling and enhanced by a lavish Bath and walk-in closet
- A tray ceiling adds elegance to the formal Dining Room
- Two additional Bedrooms, one with a sloped ceiling and built-in Desk, on the second floor
- A second floor Game Room
- No materials list is available for this plan

FIRST FLOOR — 1,979 SQ. FT.
SECOND FLOOR — 948 SQ. FT.

TOTAL LIVING AREA:
2,927 SQ. FT.

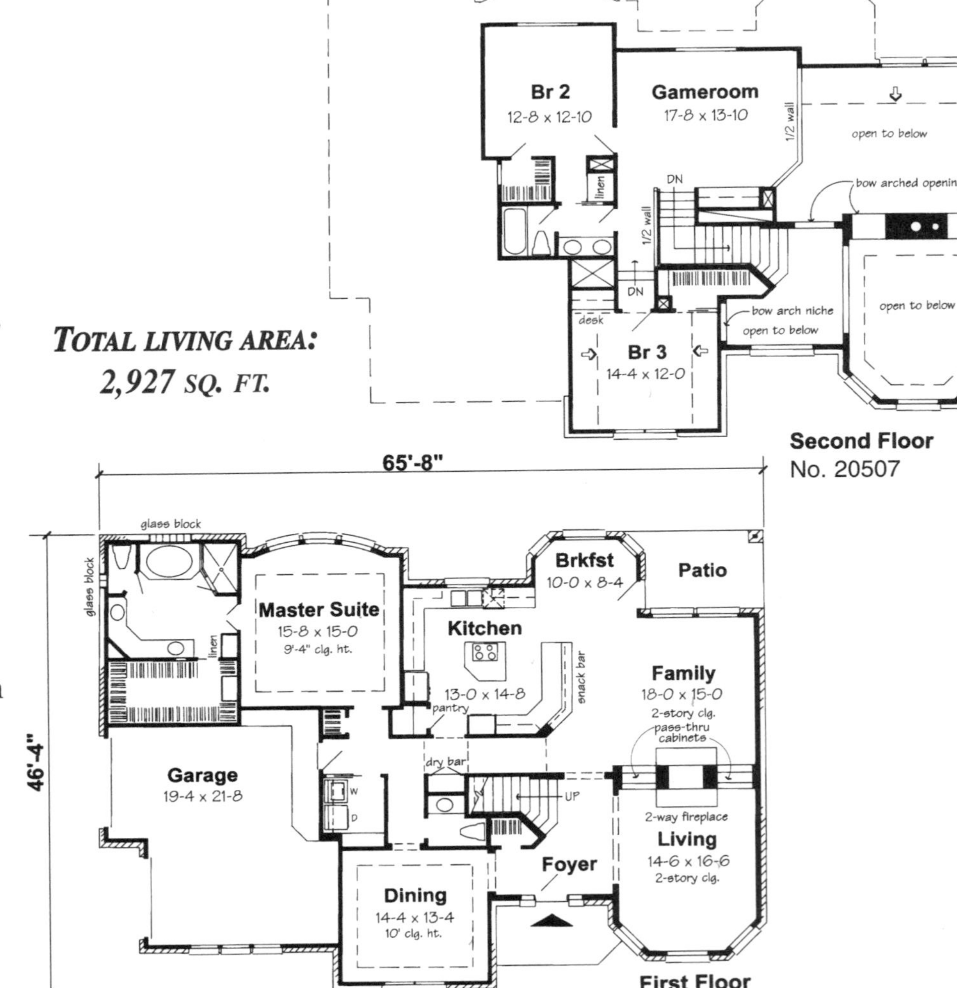

Br 2
12-8 x 12-10
Gameroom
17-8 x 13-10
1/2 wall
open to below
bow arched openings
DN
linen
1/2 wall
DN
desk
bow arch niche
open to below
open to below
Br 3
14-4 x 12-0
Second Floor
No. 20507
65'-8"
46'-4"
glass block
glass block
linen
Master Suite
15-8 x 15-0
9'-4" clg. ht.
Brkfst
10-0 x 8-4
Patio
Kitchen
13-0 x 14-8
pantry
snack bar
Family
18-0 x 15-0
2-story clg.
pass-thru cabinets
Garage
19-4 x 21-8
dry bar
UP
W
D
2-way fireplace
Living
14-6 x 16-6
2-story clg.
Foyer
Dining
14-4 x 13-4
10' clg. ht.
First Floor

To order your Blueprints, call 1-800-235-5700

Refer to **Pricing Schedule F** on the order form for pricing information

Design by
Rick Garner

PLAN NO. 92582

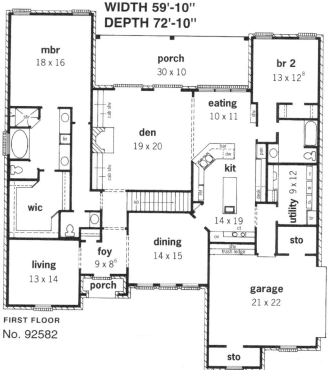

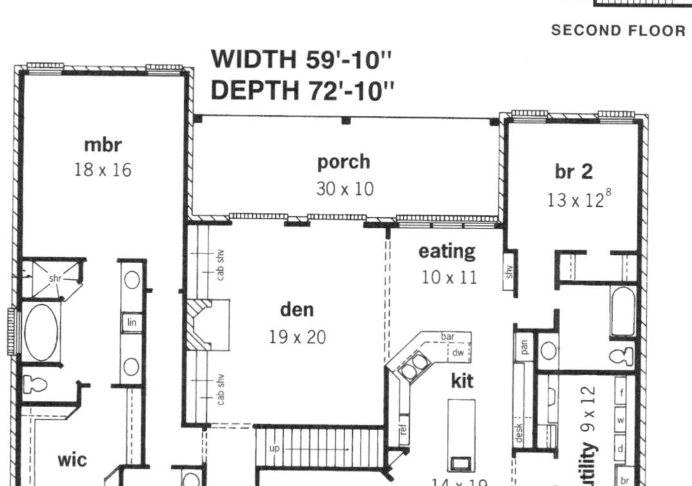

br 3
16 x 12
lin
hvac
attic access
br 4
16 x 12
desk
SECOND FLOOR
WIDTH 59'-10"
DEPTH 72'-10"
mbr
18 x 16
porch
30 x 10
br 2
13 x 12[8]
eating
10 x 11
den
19 x 20
cab shv
shr
lin
bar
dw
pan
kit
wic
ref
desk
utility 9 x 12
up
14 x 19
ct
ov
shv
trash ledge
sto
dining
14 x 15
foy
9 x 8[6]
living
13 x 14
porch
garage
21 x 22
sto
FIRST FLOOR
No. 92582

Plenty of Attention to Detail

- This plan features:
  - — Four bedrooms
  - — Three full and one half baths
- The Dining Room has three windows with segmented keystone arches above them
- The long Kitchen is a chef's delight with a center island
- The centrally located Den has a fireplace with built-in cabinets and shelves to either side
- The Master Bedroom is located in its own wing and has a huge walk-in closet
- No materials list is available for this plan
- An optional slab or crawl space foundation — please specify when ordering

FIRST FLOOR — 2,545 SQ. FT.
SECOND FLOOR — 711 SQ. FT.
GARAGE — 484 SQ. FT.

TOTAL LIVING AREA:
3,256 SQ. FT.

Design by
Sater Design Group

Refer to **Pricing Schedule E** on the order form for pricing information

Wonderful Presence

- This plan features:
  - — Four bedrooms
  - — Four full baths
- Double front doors welcome you into this spacious home
- The Dining Room has a bay of windows at its front and also sports a step ceiling
- Across the Foyer is the Study with a barrel vaulted ceiling and an immense front window
- The Great Room is truly that with its fireplace, entertainment center and high ceiling
- The Master Suite comprises the width of one side of the home
- There are two separate covered Lanais in the rear
- Upstairs find two Bedrooms and an optional bonus room
- No materials list is available for this plan

FIRST FLOOR — 2,341 SQ. FT.
SECOND FLOOR — 797 SQ. FT.
GARAGE — 635 SQ. FT.

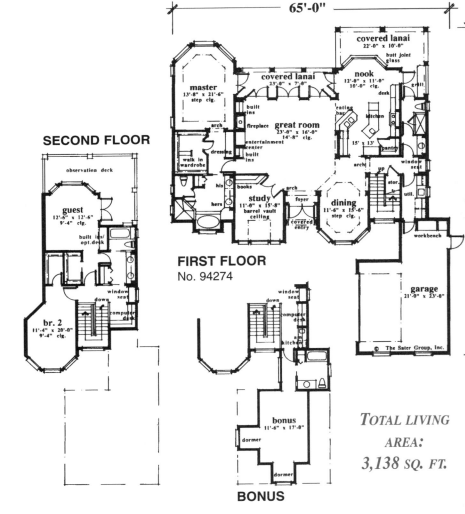

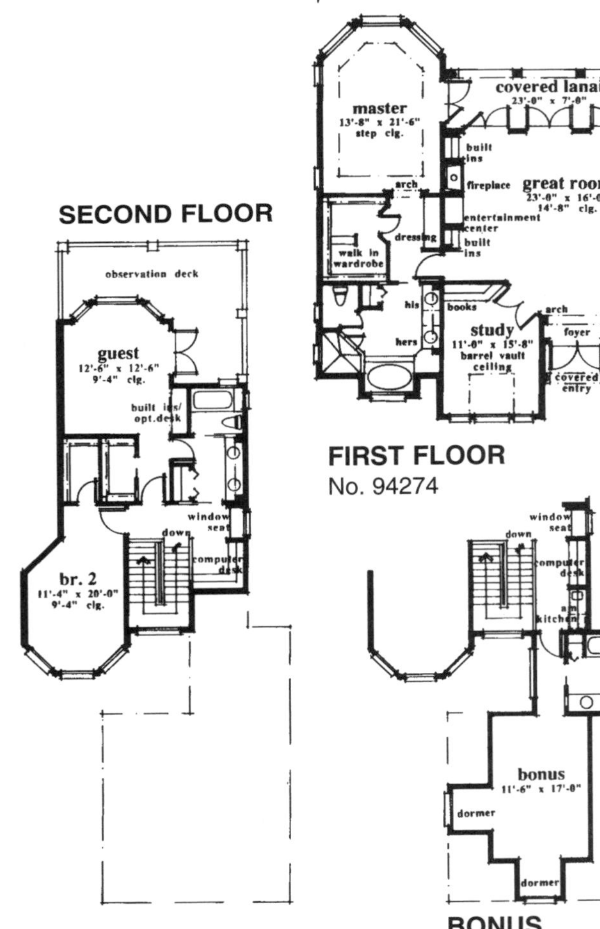
65'-0"
SECOND FLOOR
observation deck
guest
12'-6" x 12'-6"
9'-4" clg.
br. 2
11'-4" x 20'-0"
9'-4" clg.
covered lanai
22'-0" x 10'-0"
covered lanai
23'-0" x 7'-0"
master
13'-8" x 21'-6"
step clg.
nook
12'-0" x 11'-0"
10'-0" clg.
great room
23'-0" x 16'-0"
14'-8" clg.
kitchen
15' x 13'
study
11'-0" x 15'-8"
barrel vault ceiling
foyer
covered entry
dining
11'-6" x 15'-6"
step clg.
garage
21'-0" x 23'-0"
workbench
© The Sater Group, Inc.
FIRST FLOOR
No. 94274
bonus
11'-6" x 17'-0"
dormer
BONUS

TOTAL LIVING AREA: 3,138 SQ. FT.

Refer to **Pricing Schedule E** on the order form for pricing information

Design by
Design Basics, Inc.

PLAN NO. 94965

A Livable Home

- This plan features:
- — Four bedrooms
- — Two full, one three quarter and one half baths
- The Dining and Living Rooms both have decorative windows that let in plenty of light
- The Family Room has a beamed ceiling and a fireplace
- The Master Bedroom is complete with a tray ceiling, two walk-in closets and a large Bath
- Three additional Bedrooms upstairs share two full Baths
- A three car Garage with plenty of storage space
- No materials list is available for this plan

FIRST FLOOR — 1,400 SQ. FT.
SECOND FLOOR — 1,315 SQ. FT.
BASEMENT — 1,400 SQ. FT.
GARAGE — 631 SQ. FT.

TOTAL LIVING AREA:
2,715 SQ. FT.

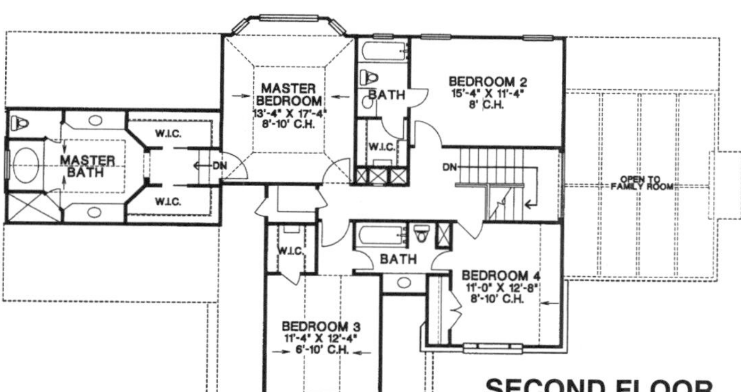
MASTER BEDROOM
13'-4" X 17'-4"
8'-10' C.H.
BATH
BEDROOM 2
15'-4" X 11'-4"
8' C.H.
W.I.C.
MASTER BATH
W.I.C.
W.I.C.
DN
DN
OPEN TO FAMILY ROOM
W.I.C.
BATH
BEDROOM 4
11'-0" X 12'-8"
8'-10' C.H.
BEDROOM 3
11'-4" X 12'-4"
6'-10' C.H.

SECOND FLOOR

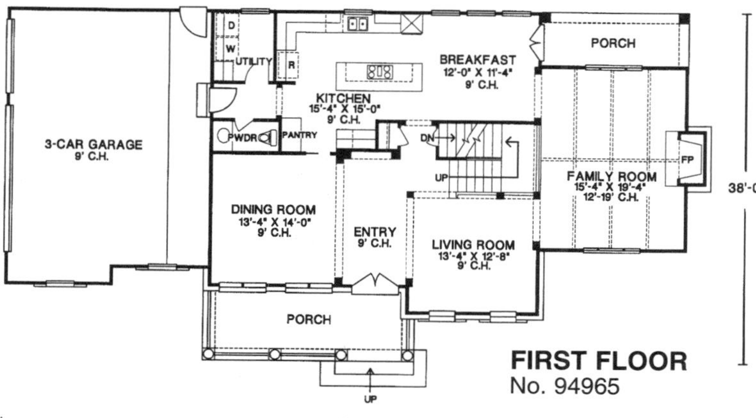
3-CAR GARAGE
9' C.H.
D
W
UTILITY
R
KITCHEN
15'-4" X 15'-0"
9' C.H.
BREAKFAST
12'-0" X 11'-4"
9' C.H.
PORCH
PWDR
PANTRY
DN
UP
FAMILY ROOM
15'-4" X 19'-4"
12'-19' C.H.
FP
38'-0"
DINING ROOM
13'-4" X 14'-0"
9' C.H.
ENTRY
9' C.H.
LIVING ROOM
13'-4" X 12'-8"
9' C.H.
PORCH
UP
75'-1 1/2"

FIRST FLOOR
No. 94965

PLAN NO. 98038

Design by
Donald A. Gardner Architects, Inc.

Refer to **Pricing Schedule G** on the order form for pricing information

Southern Plantation

- This plan features:
  - — Four bedrooms
  - — Three full and one half baths
- A wide front Porch creates a southern plantation feel
- Columns add elegance to the formal Dining Room
- The generous Great Room features a cathedral ceiling
- The spacious Kitchen is open to a sunny breakfast bay
- The Master Suite is on the first floor and has back Porch access
- The Bedroom/Study has its own full Bath and walk-in closet
- Upstairs, two more Bedrooms share another full Bath

FIRST FLOOR — 2,516 SQ. FT.
SECOND FLOOR — 722 SQ. FT.
BONUS ROOM — 513 SQ. FT.

TOTAL LIVING AREA:
3,238 SQ. FT.

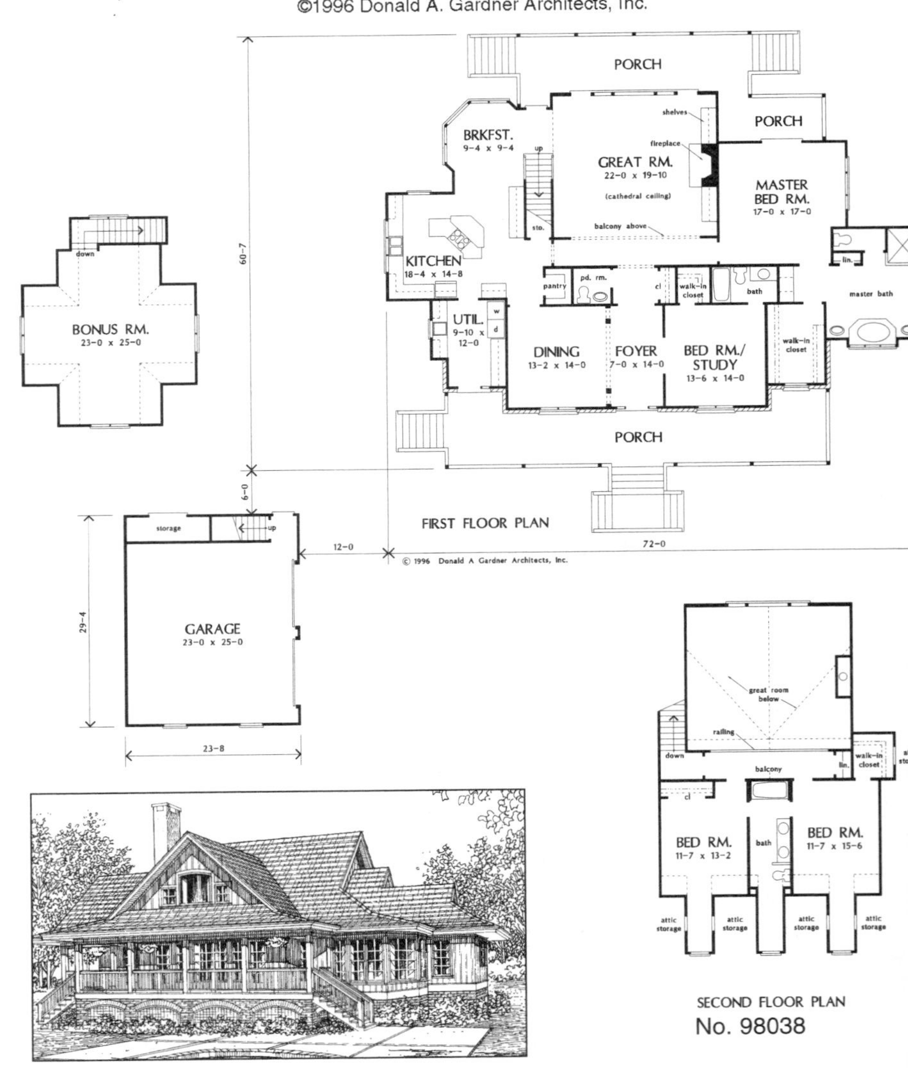
PORCH
PORCH
BRKFST.
9-4 x 9-4
GREAT RM.
22-0 x 19-10
(cathedral ceiling)
fireplace
shelves
balcony above
MASTER
BED RM.
17-0 x 17-0
KITCHEN
18-4 x 14-8
pantry
pd. rm.
walk-in closet
bath
master bath
UTIL.
9-10 x 12-0
DINING
13-2 x 14-0
FOYER
7-0 x 14-0
BED RM./
STUDY
13-6 x 14-0
walk-in closet
PORCH
BONUS RM.
23-0 x 25-0
60-7
6-0
12-0
72-0
FIRST FLOOR PLAN
© 1996 Donald A Gardner Architects, Inc.
storage
GARAGE
23-0 x 25-0
29-4
23-8
great room below
railing
down
balcony
walk-in closet
BED RM.
11-7 x 13-2
bath
BED RM.
11-7 x 15-6
attic storage
attic storage
attic storage
attic storage

SECOND FLOOR PLAN
No. 98038

To order your Blueprints, call 1-800-235-5700

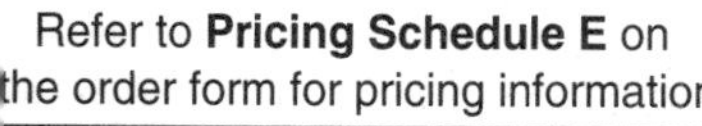
Refer to **Pricing Schedule E** on
the order form for pricing information

Design by
Filmore Design Group

PLAN NO. 98534

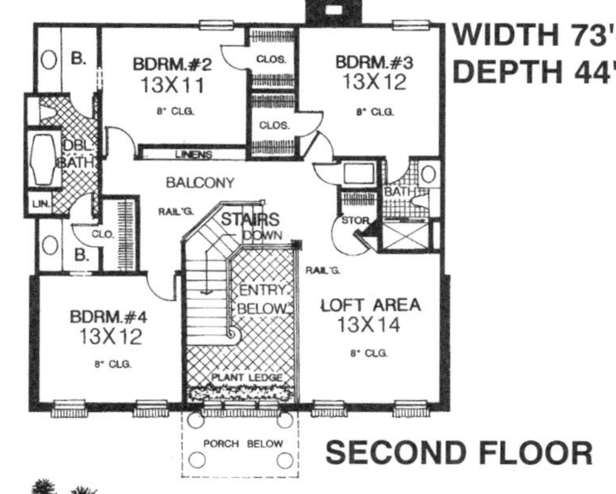
B.
BDRM.#2
13X11
8" CLG.
CLOS.
BDRM.#3
13X12
8" CLG.
CLOS.
DBL. BATH
LINENS
BALCONY
BATH
LIN.
RAIL'G.
STAIRS DOWN
STOR.
CLO.
B.
RAIL'G.
ENTRY BELOW
BDRM.#4
13X12
8" CLG.
LOFT AREA
13X14
8" CLG.
PLANT LEDGE
PORCH BELOW

WIDTH 73'-4"
DEPTH 44'-0"

SECOND FLOOR

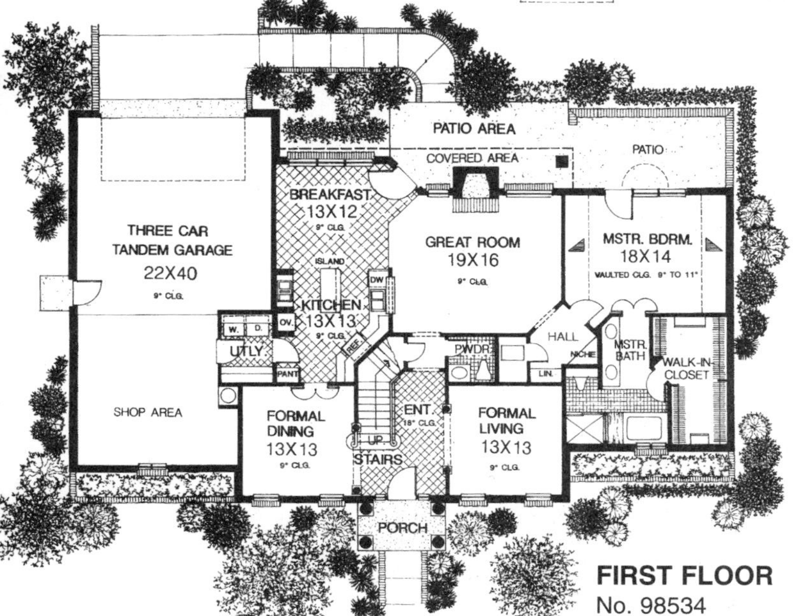
PATIO AREA
COVERED AREA
PATIO
BREAKFAST
13X12
9" CLG.
THREE CAR
TANDEM GARAGE
22X40
9" CLG.
ISLAND
GREAT ROOM
19X16
9" CLG.
MSTR. BDRM.
18X14
VAULTED CLG. 9" TO 11"
DW
KITCHEN
13X13
9" CLG.
W.
D.
OV.
UTLY
PANT
PWDR
HALL
NICHE
MSTR. BATH
WALK-IN-CLOSET
LIN.
SHOP AREA
FORMAL DINING
13X13
9" CLG.
ENT.
18" CLG.
FORMAL LIVING
13X13
9" CLG.
UP
STAIRS
PORCH

FIRST FLOOR
No. 98534

Stately Colonial Home

- This plan features:
  - — Four bedrooms
  - — Three full and one half baths
- Stately columns and arched windows project luxury and quality that is evident throughout this home
- The entry is highlighted by a palladian window, a plant shelf and an angled staircase
- The comfortable Great Room has an inviting fireplace and opens to Kitchen/Breakfast Area and the Patio
- The Master Bedroom wing offers Patio access, a luxurious Bath and a walk-in closet
- No materials list is available for this plan

FIRST FLOOR — 1,848 SQ. FT.
SECOND FLOOR — 1,111 SQ. FT.
GARAGE & SHOP — 722 SQ. FT.

TOTAL LIVING AREA:
2,959 SQ. FT.

PLAN NO. 99411

Design by
Design Basics, Inc.

Refer to **Pricing Schedule F** on the order form for pricing information

A Picturesque Setting

- This plan features:
- — Three bedrooms
- — Three full and one half baths
- The two-story Entry expands into the Living and Dining rooms
- The informal space includes the open Family Room and Breakfast Nook
- The gourmet Kitchen includes a center island
- The Master Suite is located on the main floor
- The rooms upstairs include a Game Room, a Study and the secondary Bedrooms
- No materials list is available for this plan

FIRST FLOOR — 2,144 SQ. FT.
SECOND FLOOR — 1,253 SQ. FT.
BASEMENT — 2,144 SQ. FT.
GARAGE — 697 SQ. FT.

TOTAL LIVING AREA:
3,397 SQ. FT.

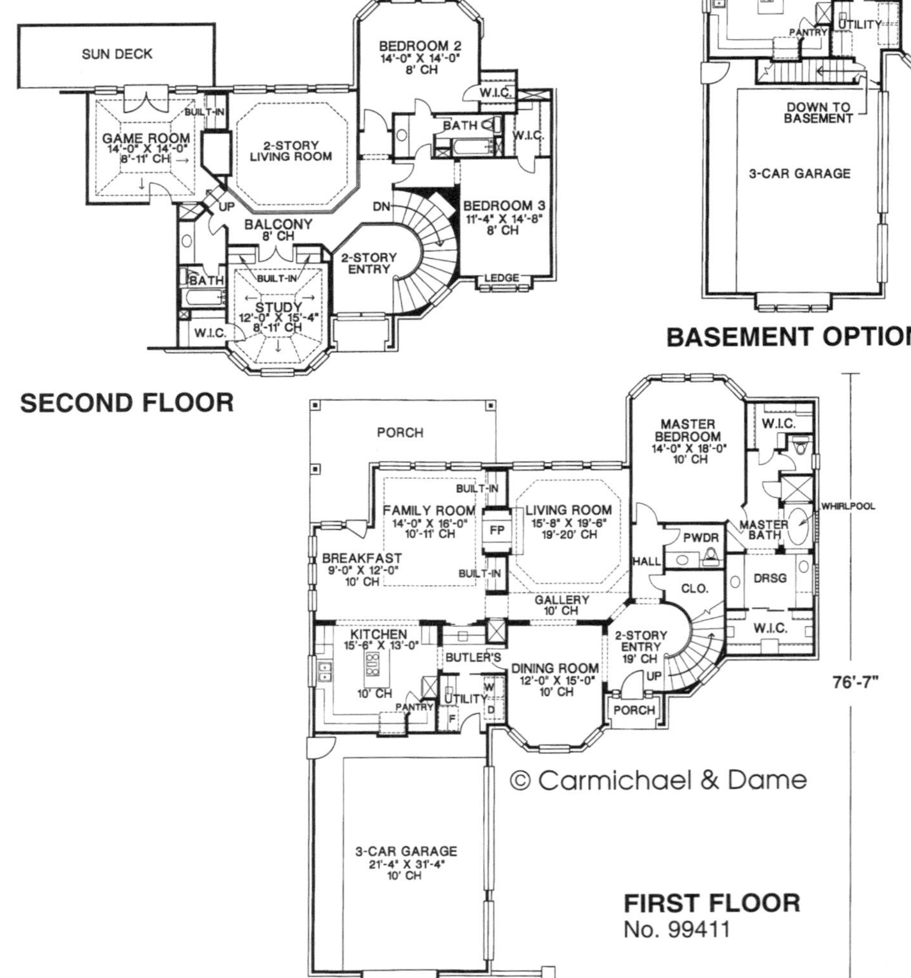
SUN DECK
GAME ROOM 14'-0" X 14'-0" 8'-11' CH
BUILT-IN
2-STORY LIVING ROOM
BEDROOM 2 14'-0" X 14'-0" 8' CH
W.I.C.
BATH
W.I.C.
BEDROOM 3 11'-4" X 14'-8" 8' CH
UP
DN
BALCONY 8' CH
2-STORY ENTRY
LEDGE
BATH
BUILT-IN
STUDY 12'-0" X 15'-4" 8'-11' CH
W.I.C.
SECOND FLOOR
PANTRY
UTILITY
DOWN TO BASEMENT
3-CAR GARAGE
BASEMENT OPTION
PORCH
MASTER BEDROOM 14'-0" X 18'-0" 10' CH
W.I.C.
BUILT-IN
FAMILY ROOM 14'-0" X 16'-0" 10'-11' CH
FP
LIVING ROOM 15'-8" X 19'-6" 19'-20' CH
WHIRLPOOL
MASTER BATH
PWDR
BREAKFAST 9'-0" X 12'-0" 10' CH
BUILT-IN
HALL
CLO.
DRSG
GALLERY 10' CH
KITCHEN 15'-6" X 13'-0"
10' CH
BUTLER'S
DINING ROOM 12'-0" X 15'-0" 10' CH
2-STORY ENTRY 19' CH
UP
W.I.C.
PANTRY
UTILITY
W
D
F
PORCH
76'-7"
© Carmichael & Dame
3-CAR GARAGE 21'-4" X 31'-4" 10' CH
FIRST FLOOR
No. 99411
64'-11"

Refer to **Pricing Schedule E** on
the order form for pricing information

Design by
Studer Residential Design, Inc.

PLAN NO. 92661

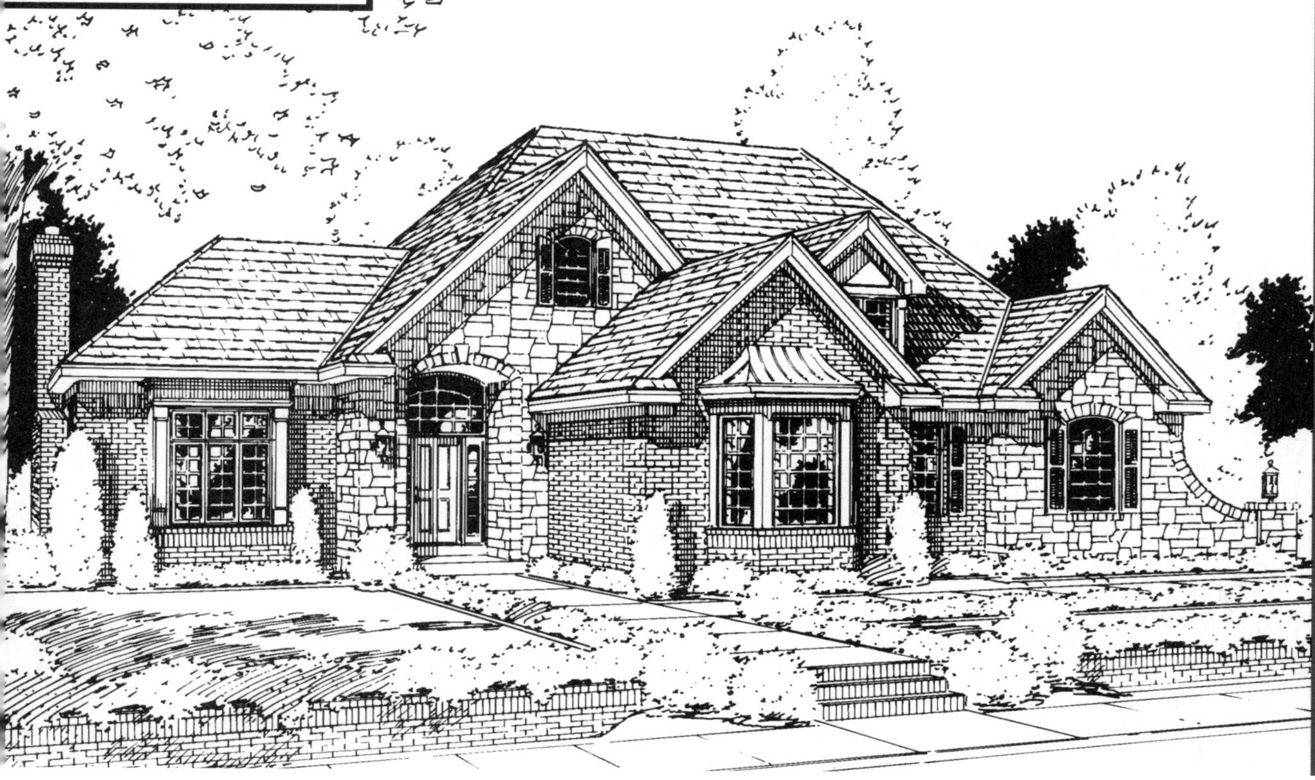

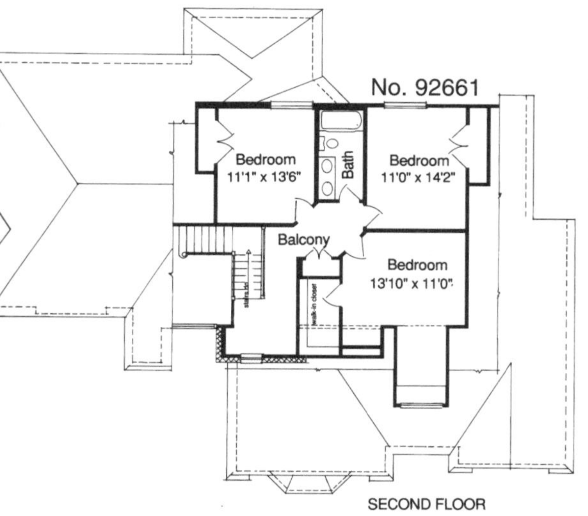
No. 92661
Bedroom
11'1" x 13'6"
Bath
Bedroom
11'0" x 14'2"
Balcony
Bedroom
13'10" x 11'0"
walk-in closet
SECOND FLOOR

First floor — 1,767 sq. ft.
Second floor — 873 sq. ft.
Basement — 1,749 sq. ft.
Garage — 440 sq. ft.

Total living area:
2,640 sq. ft.

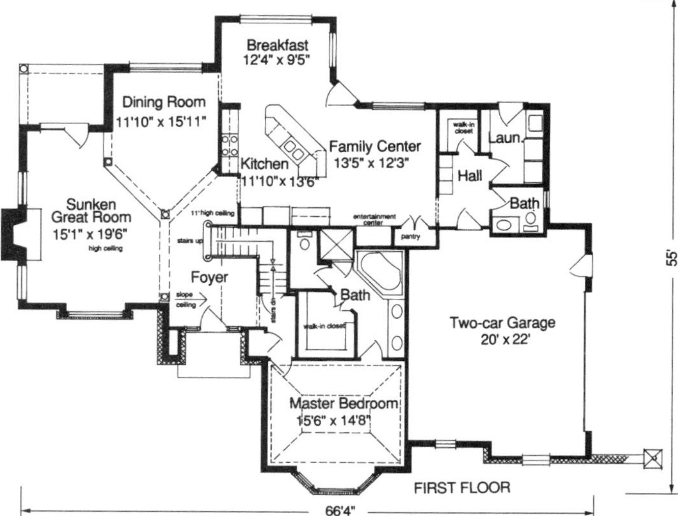
Breakfast
12'4" x 9'5"
Dining Room
11'10" x 15'11"
Family Center
13'5" x 12'3"
Kitchen
11'10" x 13'6"
walk-in closet
Laun.
Hall
Bath
pantry
Sunken
Great Room
15'1" x 19'6"
high ceiling
stairs up
Foyer
slope ceiling
Bath
walk-in closet
Two-car Garage
20' x 22'
Master Bedroom
15'6" x 14'8"
FIRST FLOOR
55'
66'4"

Brick and Stone in Perfect Harmony

- This plan features:
  - — Four bedrooms
  - — Two full and one half baths
- A sheltered front entry has side-light windows beside and a transom window above the door
- Inside the Foyer there is a sloped ceiling and an open rail staircase
- Columns delineate the sunken Living Room and the Dining Room
- Informal space is commingled and includes a Family Center, Kitchen and Nook
- The Master Bedroom is located on the first floor and has a bay window and a tray ceiling
- A service hall behind the Garage contains a walk-in closet, a half bath and a Laundry Room
- No materials list is available for this plan

PLAN NO.10686

Design by
The Garlinghouse Company

Refer to **Pricing Schedule F** on the order form for pricing information

Every Luxurious Feature One Could Want

- This plan features:
- — Four bedrooms
- — Two full and one half baths
- An open staircase leads to the Bedrooms and divides the space between the vaulted Living and Dining rooms
- A wide Family Area includes the Kitchen, Dinette and Family Room complete with built-in bar, bookcases and a fireplace
- The Master Bedroom has a vaulted ceiling, spacious closets and a Jacuzzi

FIRST FLOOR — 1,786 SQ. FT.
SECOND FLOOR — 1,490 SQ. FT.
BASEMENT — 1,773 SQ. FT.
GARAGE — 579 SQ. FT.

TOTAL LIVING AREA:
3,276 SQ. FT.

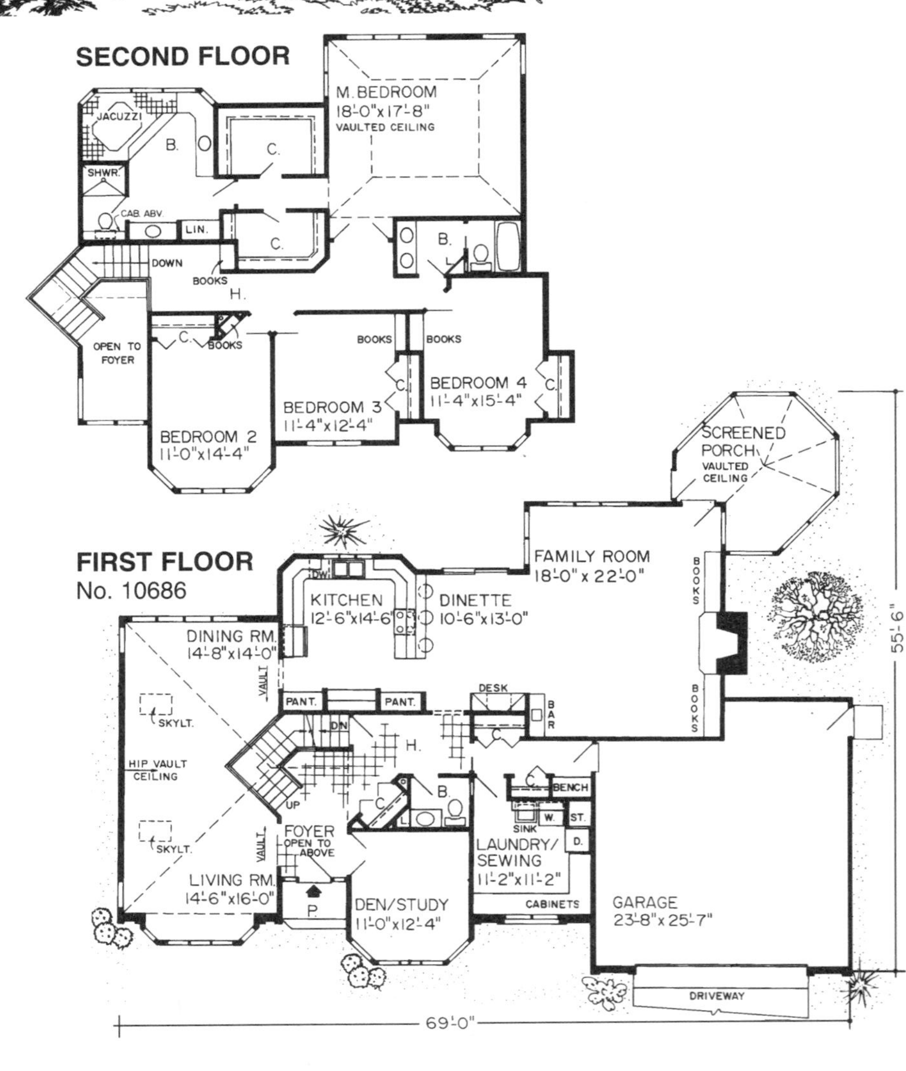
SECOND FLOOR
M. BEDROOM
18'-0"x17'-8"
VAULTED CEILING
JACUZZI
B.
C.
SHWR.
CAB. ABV.
LIN.
C.
DOWN
BOOKS
H.
B.
OPEN TO FOYER
C.
BOOKS
BOOKS
BOOKS
C
BEDROOM 4
11'-4"x15'-4"
C
BEDROOM 3
11'-4"x12'-4"
BEDROOM 2
11'-0"x14'-4"
SCREENED PORCH
VAULTED CEILING
FIRST FLOOR
No. 10686
FAMILY ROOM
18'-0" x 22'-0"
KITCHEN
12'-6"x14'-6"
DINETTE
10'-6"x13'-0"
DINING RM.
14'-8"x14'-0"
BOOKS
BOOKS
55'-6"
VAULT
PANT.
PANT.
DESK
BAR
SKYLT.
DN
H.
HIP VAULT CEILING
C
B.
BENCH
W.
ST.
UP
SINK
D.
SKYLT.
VAULT
FOYER
OPEN TO ABOVE
LAUNDRY/ SEWING
11'-2"x11'-2"
LIVING RM.
14'-6"x16'-0"
P
DEN/STUDY
11'-0"x12'-4"
CABINETS
GARAGE
23'-8"x25'-7"
DRIVEWAY
69'-0"

Refer to **Pricing Schedule E** on the order form for pricing information

Design by
Frank Betz Associates, Inc.

© Frank Betz Associates

PLAN NO. 97210

FIRST FLOOR
No. 97210

SECOND FLOOR

TOTAL LIVING AREA:
2,601 SQ. FT.

Notable Exterior

- This plan features:
- — Four bedrooms
- — Three full baths
- Two-story foyer adds a feeling of volume
- Family Room topped by vaulted ceiling and accented by a fireplace
- Formal Living Room with an eleven-foot ceiling
- Private Master Suite with a five-piece Bath and a large walk-in closet
- Rear Bedroom/Study located close a full bath
- No materials list is available for this plan
- An optional basement, slab or crawl space foundation — please specify when ordering

FIRST FLOOR — 2,003 SQ. FT.
SECOND FLOOR — 598 SQ. FT.
BONUS — 321 SQ. FT.
BASEMENT — 2,003 SQ. FT.
GARAGE — 546 SQ. FT.

PLAN NO.97419

Design by
Design Basics, Inc.

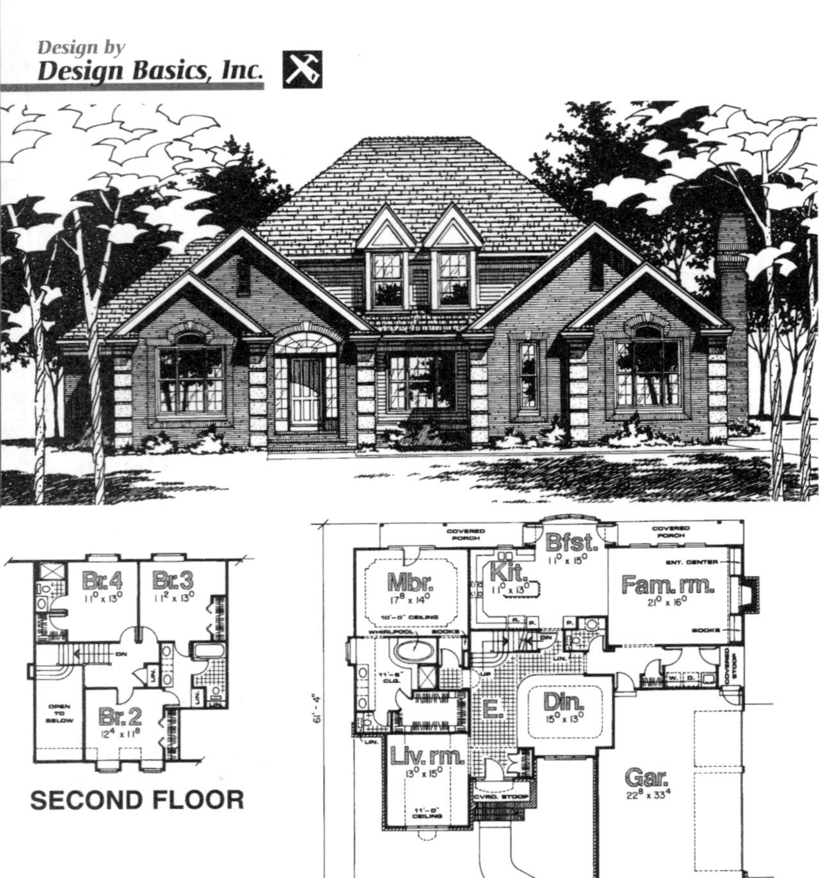
Br.4
Br.3
Br.2
SECOND FLOOR
Mbr.
Kit.
Bfst.
Fam.rm.
Din.
Liv.rm.
Gar.
FIRST FLOOR
© design basics inc.

Spaciousness is Dominating Feature

Price Code: E

- This plan features:
- — Four bedrooms
- — Two full, one three-quarter and one half baths
- Pair of narrow dormers, double gables and extensive detailing highlight the exterior
- An island counter and two Pantries add to the Kitchen's efficiency
- Built-in shelves offer places for electronic equipment or reading material in the Family Room
- Rear covered Porch can be accessed from either the Breakfast Area or Master Suite
- Three additional Bedrooms, each with private access to a Bath, are located on the second floor

FIRST FLOOR — 2,098 SQ. FT.
SECOND FLOOR — 790 SQ. FT.
GARAGE — 739 SQ. FT.

TOTAL LIVING AREA:
2,888 SQ. FT.

PLAN NO.98010

Design by
Donald A. Gardner Architects, Inc.

©1997 Donald A. Gardner Architects, Inc.

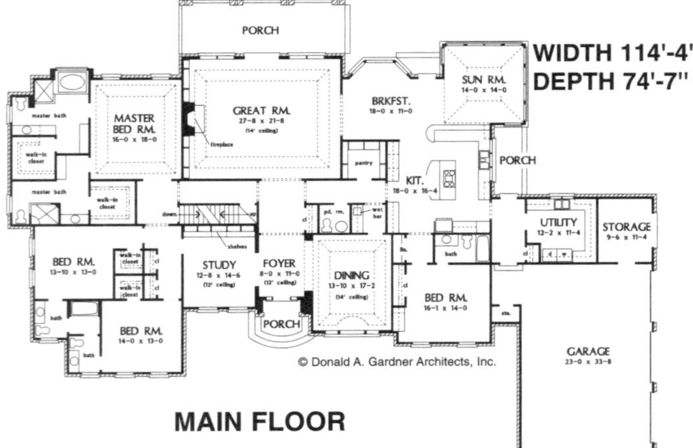
PORCH
GREAT RM.
MASTER BED RM.
BRKFST.
SUN RM.
KIT.
UTILITY
STORAGE
BED RM.
STUDY
FOYER
DINING
BED RM.
BED RM.
GARAGE
© Donald A. Gardner Architects, Inc.

WIDTH 114'-4"
DEPTH 74'-7"

MAIN FLOOR

Always in Style

Price Code: H

- This plan features:
- — Four bedrooms
- — Four full and two half baths
- Brick, gables and a traditional hip roof always seem to be in style
- Dramatic spaces include the Dining Room and the Great Room, both with 14-foot ceilings
- The Study features a wall of built-in book-shelves
- The Kitchen has a center island with a cooktop
- The Sun Room and the Breakfast Nook share a counter with the Kitchen
- The Master Bedroom is opulent with dual baths and closets
- Storage space abounds with a walk-in Pantry, numerous closets, and storage space in the Garage

MAIN FLOOR — 4,523 SQ. FT.
GARAGE — 1,029 SQ. FT.

TOTAL LIVING AREA:
4,523 SQ. FT.

This plan is not to be built in Greenville County, SC

Refer to **Pricing Schedule F** on the order form for pricing information

Design by
Design Basics, Inc.

PLAN NO. 99444

© design basics inc.

SECOND FLOOR

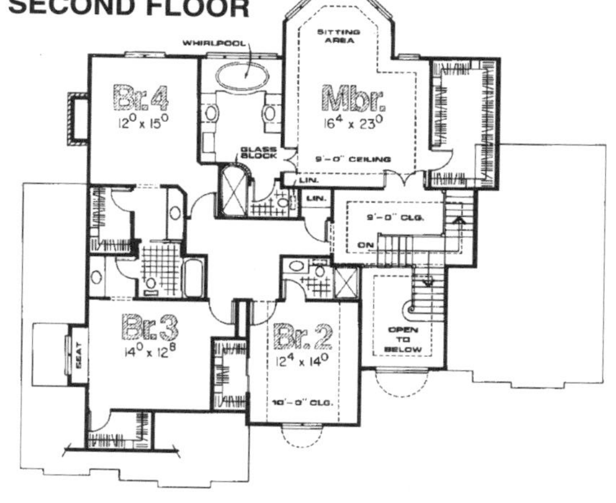

Br.4
Mbr.
Br.3
Br.2
SITTING AREA
WHIRLPOOL
GLASS BLOCK
9'-0" CEILING
LIN.
OPEN TO BELOW
10'-0" CLG.
SEAT

TOTAL LIVING AREA:
3,611 SQ. FT.

FIRST FLOOR
No. 99444

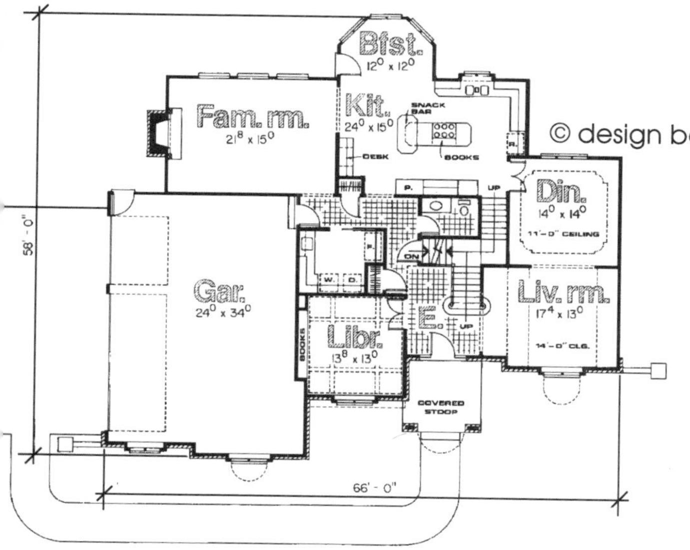

© design basics, inc.

Stone, Stucco & Band Boards

- This plan features:
  - — Four bedrooms
  - — Two full, one three-quarter and one half baths
- The two-story entry reveals French doors to the library and the formal Living Room
- A 14-foot ceiling and an arched transom window highlight the Living Room
- An intriguing ceiling pattern complements the Dining Room
- The gourmet Kitchen presents an expansive island with a triple cooktop
- The spider-beamed library has a built-in bookcase
- Exquisite Master Suite offers a large walk-in closet and a spacious shower with glass block

FIRST FLOOR — 1,857 SQ. FT.
SECOND FLOOR — 1,754 SQ. FT.
BASEMENT — 1,857 SQ. FT.
GARAGE — 633 SQ. FT.

PLAN NO. 99464

Design by
Design Basics, Inc.

Refer to **Pricing Schedule E** on the order form for pricing information

Spectacular Voluminous Entry

- This plan features:
  - — Four bedrooms
  - — Two full, two three-quarter and one half baths
- The spectacular entry has a curving staircase, while defining columns lead into the Living Room
- The dramatic Kitchen is equipped with a large snack bar
- Double doors introduce the Master Suite with a whirlpool and large walk-in closet
- A beautiful arched window in each secondary Bedroom adds natural light

FIRST FLOOR — 2,617 SQ. FT.
SECOND FLOOR — 1,072 SQ. FT.
BASEMENT — 2,617 SQ. FT.
GARAGE — 1,035 SQ. FT.

TOTAL LIVING AREA:
3,689 SQ. FT.

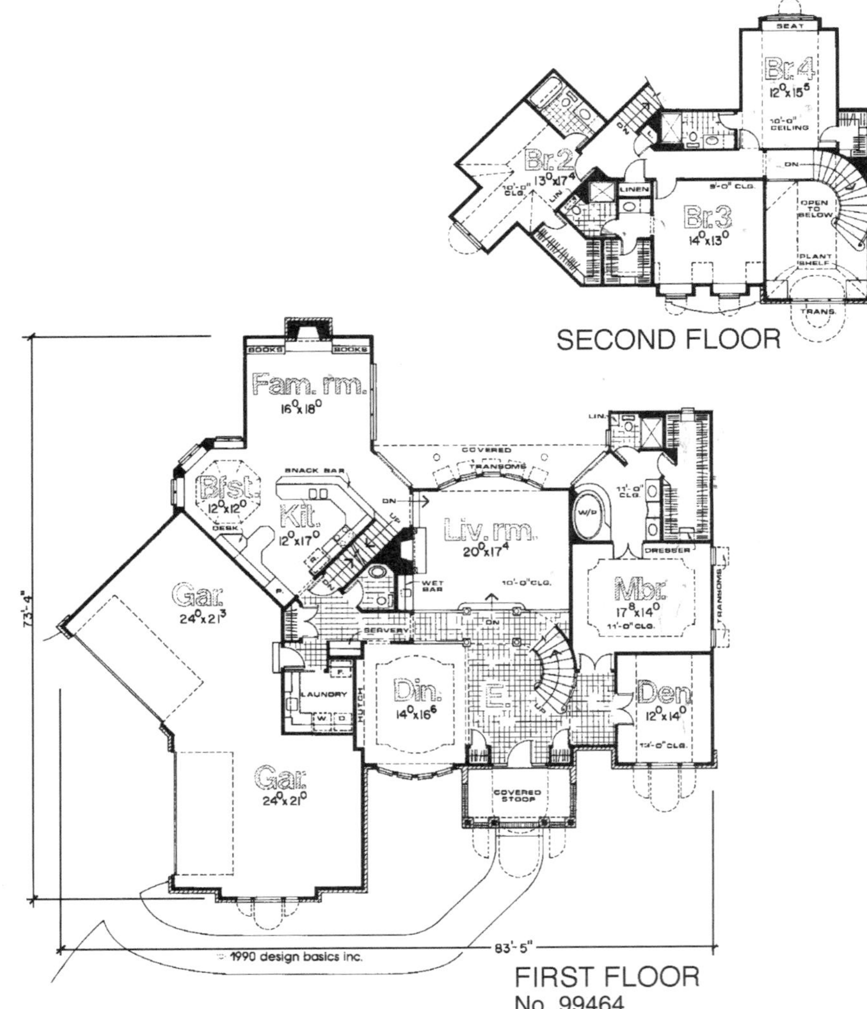

Br.4
SEAT
Br.2
Br.3
LINEN
OPEN TO BELOW
PLANT SHELF
TRANS.
SECOND FLOOR
BOOKS
BOOKS
Fam. rm.
SNACK BAR
Bfst.
Kit.
COVERED
TRANSOMS
Liv. rm.
WET BAR
Mbr.
DRESSER
Gar.
SERVERY
LAUNDRY
Din.
E.
Den
Gar.
COVERED STOOP
73'-4"
83'-5"
© 1990 design basics inc.

FIRST FLOOR
No. 99464

Refer to **Pricing Schedule E** on the order form for pricing information

Design by
Design Basics, Inc.

PLAN NO. 99453

McDONALD
© design basics inc.

SECOND FLOOR

Br. 2 11⁰ x 13⁰
Br. 3 11⁴ x 12⁷
OPEN TO BELOW
DN
LINEN
DN
UNFINISHED BONUS ROOM 22⁴ x 23⁸
Br. 4 11⁰ x 12⁷

FIRST FLOOR
No. 99453

TRANSOMS
WHIRLPOOL
Bfst. 12⁰ x 12⁰
Liv. rm. 15⁰ x 20⁴
14'-5" CEILING
Kit. 12⁸ x 13⁰
P.
DESK
ENT. CENTER
Fam. rm. 21⁰ x 15⁰
BOOKS
UP
WARDROBE
Mbr. 13⁰ x 16⁰
10'-8" CLG.
WARDROBE
DN
UP
Din. 12⁰ x 15⁰
HUTCH
Gar. 33⁴ x 22⁸
E.
Den 12⁰ x 13⁰
TRANS.
TRANSOMS
COVERED STOOP
© design basics inc.
69' - 4"

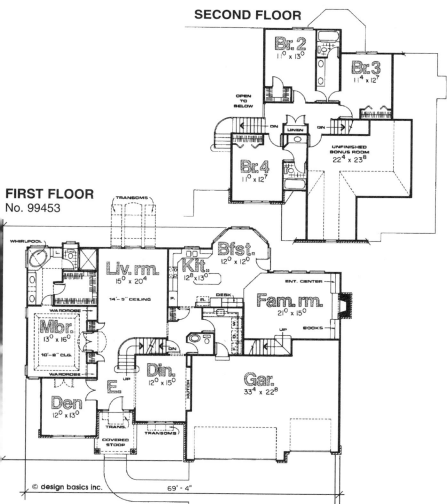

Spacious Living Room

- This plan features:
- — Four bedrooms
- — Three full and one half baths
- The formal Dining Room is highlighted by built-in hutch space
- The spacious Living Room has a high ceiling and is accented by large windows
- The Kitchen/Dinette area boasts an island, a Pantry and a planning desk
- The Family Room features an entertainment center, a built-in bookcase and a cozy fireplace
- The Master Suite includes his-n-her wardrobes and is topped by a decorative ceiling

FIRST FLOOR — 2,179 SQ. FT.
SECOND FLOOR — 838 SQ. FT.
BASEMENT — 2,179 SQ. FT.
GARAGE — 813 SQ. FT.

TOTAL LIVING AREA:
3,017 SQ. FT.

To order your Blueprints, call 1-800-235-5700

PLAN NO. 92663

Design by
Studer Residential Design, Inc.

Refer to **Pricing Schedule E** on the order form for pricing information

Covered Front Porch

- This plan features:
- — Four bedrooms
- — Two full and one half baths
- A covered front Porch coupled with the fieldstone and brick exterior
- A butler's Pantry is located between the Kitchen and Dining Room for ease in serving
- The Kitchen offers an abundance of storage and work area
- A corner fireplace warms the Great Room
- A sloped ceiling in the Master Bedroom along with the luxurious Dressing/Bath Area
- No materials list is available for this plan

FIRST FLOOR — 1,573 SQ. FT.
SECOND FLOOR — 1,152 SQ. FT.
BASEMENT — 1,534 SQ. FT.
GARAGE — 680 SQ. FT.

TOTAL LIVING AREA:
2,725 SQ. FT.

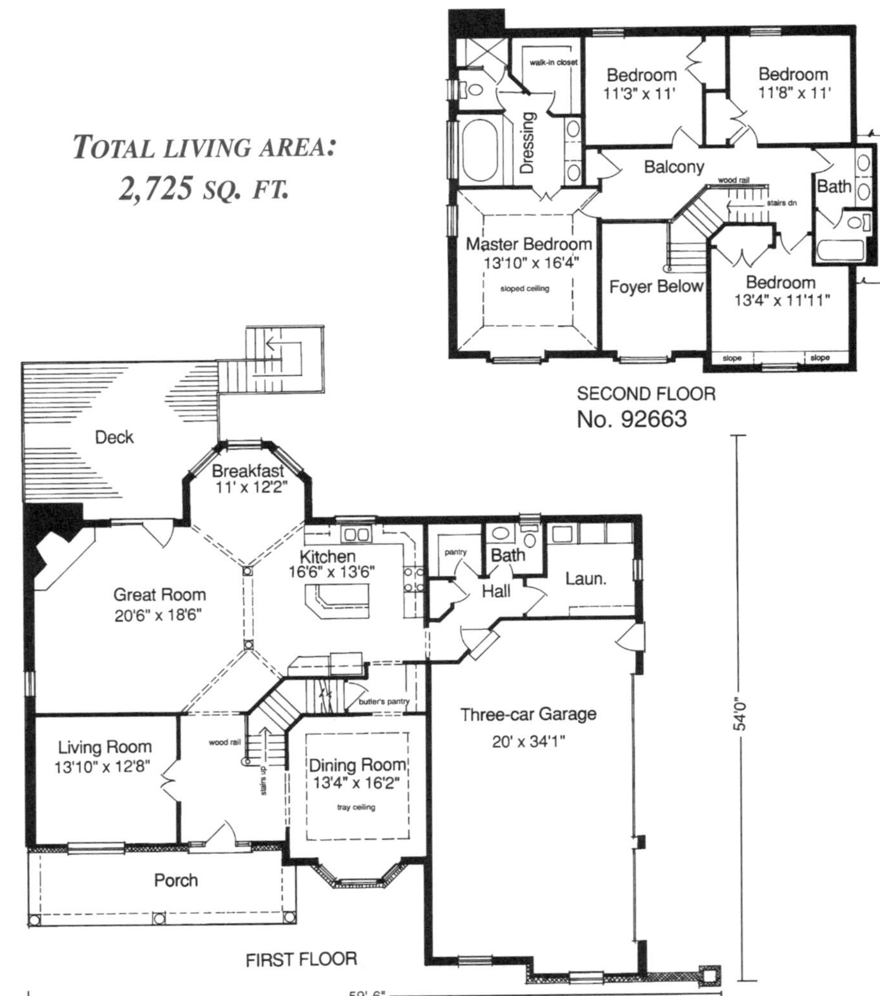

walk-in closet
Bedroom
11'3" x 11'
Bedroom
11'8" x 11'
Dressing
Balcony
wood rail
stairs dn
Bath
Master Bedroom
13'10" x 16'4"
sloped ceiling
Foyer Below
Bedroom
13'4" x 11'11"
slope
slope
SECOND FLOOR
No. 92663
Deck
Breakfast
11' x 12'2"
Kitchen
16'6" x 13'6"
pantry
Bath
Hall
Laun.
Great Room
20'6" x 18'6"
butler's pantry
Three-car Garage
20' x 34'1"
Living Room
13'10" x 12'8"
wood rail
stairs up
Dining Room
13'4" x 16'2"
tray ceiling
Porch
FIRST FLOOR
54'0"
59'-6"

To order your Blueprints, call 1-800-235-5700

Refer to **Pricing Schedule E** on the order form for pricing information

Design by
Design Basics, Inc.

PLAN NO. 99425

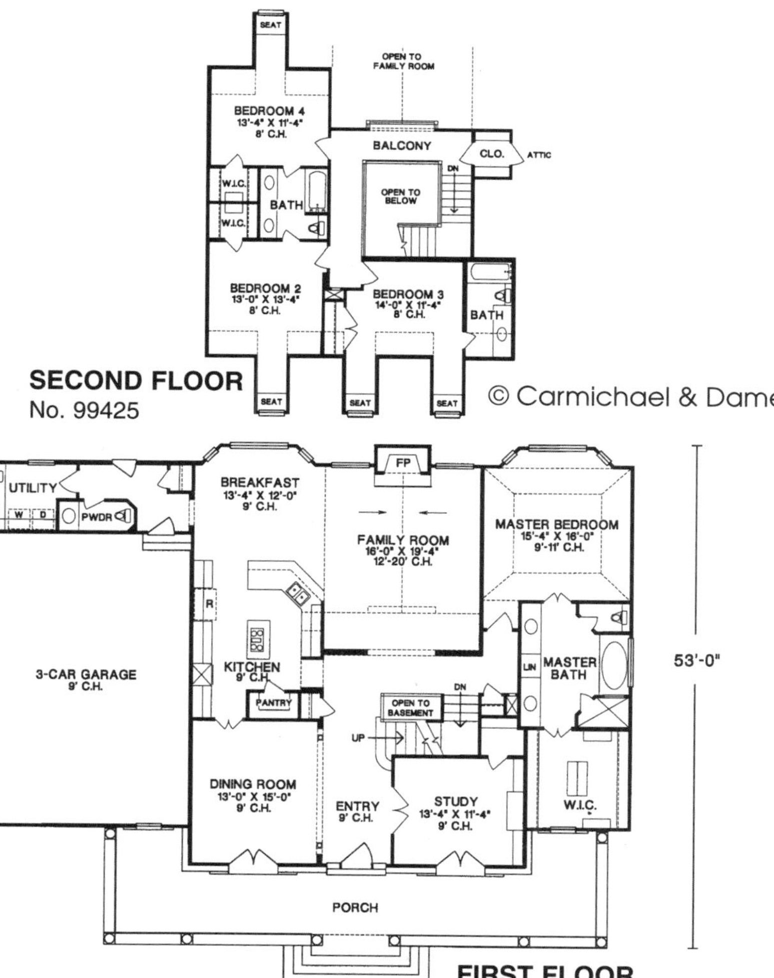

SEAT
OPEN TO FAMILY ROOM
BEDROOM 4
13'-4" X 11'-4"
8' C.H.
BALCONY
CLO.
ATTIC
DN
OPEN TO BELOW
W.I.C.
W.I.C.
BATH
BEDROOM 2
13'-0" X 13'-4"
8' C.H.
BEDROOM 3
14'-0" X 11'-4"
8' C.H.
BATH
SECOND FLOOR
No. 99425
SEAT
SEAT
SEAT
© Carmichael & Dame
UTILITY
W
D
PWDR
BREAKFAST
13'-4" X 12'-0"
9' C.H.
FP
FAMILY ROOM
16'-0" X 19'-4"
12'-20' C.H.
MASTER BEDROOM
15'-4" X 16'-0"
9'-11' C.H.
R
3-CAR GARAGE
9' C.H.
KITCHEN
9' C.H.
PANTRY
LIN
MASTER BATH
53'-0"
OPEN TO BASEMENT
DN
UP
DINING ROOM
13'-0" X 15'-0"
9' C.H.
ENTRY
9' C.H.
STUDY
13'-4" X 11'-4"
9' C.H.
W.I.C.
PORCH
FIRST FLOOR
67'-8"

Dormers and Porch Create Country Atmosphere

- This plan features:
  - — Four bedrooms
  - — Three full and one half baths
- French doors lead from both the Dining Room and the Study onto the front Porch
- The center island Kitchen also has a walk-in Pantry
- The bayed Breakfast Nook opens into the Family Room which features a fireplace
- The Master Bedroom has a bay window, private Bath, and walk in closet
- No materials list is available for this plan

FIRST FLOOR — 2,116 SQ. FT.
SECOND FLOOR — 956 SQ. FT.
BASEMENT — 2,116 SQ. FT.
GARAGE — 675 SQ. FT.

TOTAL LIVING AREA:
3,072 SQ. FT.

PLAN NO. 97216

Design by
Frank Betz Associates, Inc.

Refer to **Pricing Schedule E** on the order form for pricing information

Two-Story Family Room

- This plan features:
  - — Four bedrooms
  - — Two full and one half baths
- The Family Room has a fireplace and a French door to the Porch
- The Kitchen features a convenient serving bar for quick meals and snacks
- The hall from the Kitchen to the Dining Room has a butler's Pantry
- The second floor Master Suite has a tray ceiling and an optional plan for a Sitting Area
- No materials list is available for this plan

FIRST FLOOR — 1,351 SQ. FT.
SECOND FLOOR — 1,257 SQ. FT.
BONUS — 115 SQ. FT.
GARAGE — 511 SQ. FT.
BASEMENT — 1,351 SQ. FT.

TOTAL LIVING AREA:
2,608 SQ. FT.

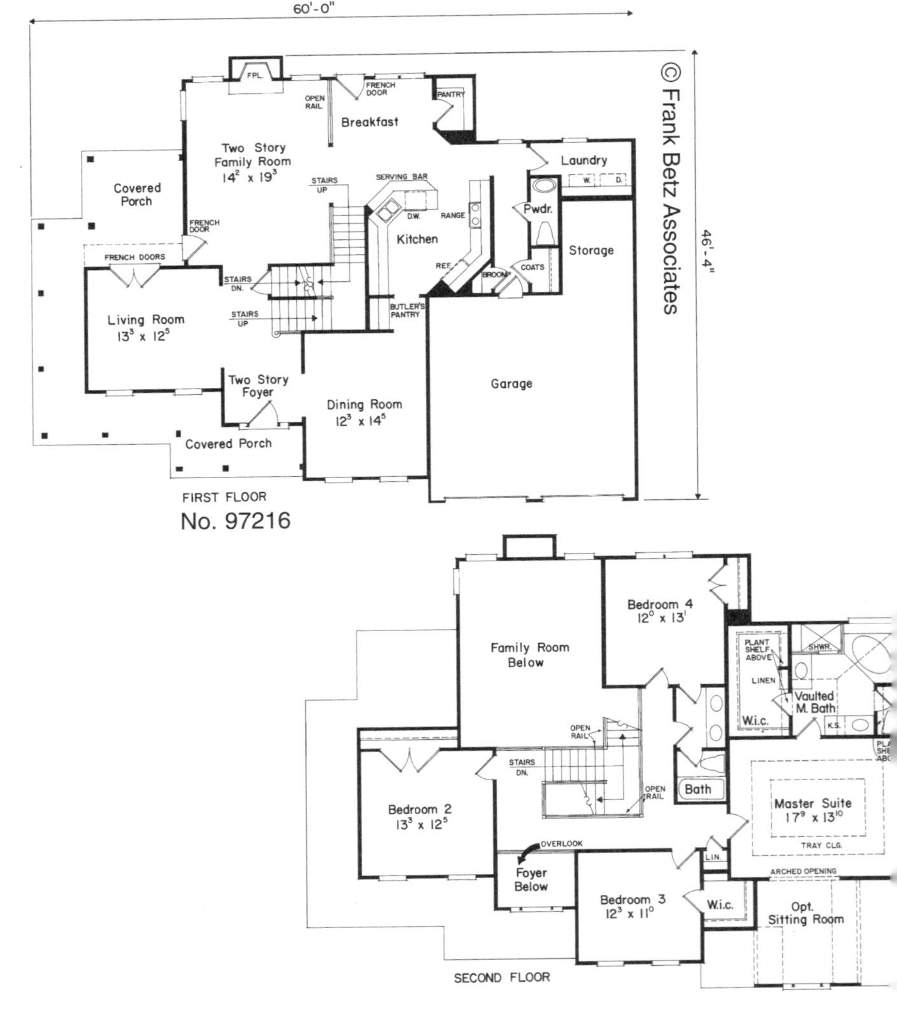
60'-0"
46'-4"
© Frank Betz Associates
FPL.
OPEN RAIL
FRENCH DOOR
PANTRY
Breakfast
Two Story Family Room 14² x 19³
Laundry
Covered Porch
STAIRS UP
SERVING BAR
Kitchen
RANGE
Pwdr.
Storage
FRENCH DOOR
FRENCH DOORS
STAIRS DN.
REF.
BROOM
COATS
Living Room 13³ x 12⁵
STAIRS UP
BUTLER'S PANTRY
Garage
Two Story Foyer
Dining Room 12³ x 14⁵
Covered Porch
FIRST FLOOR
No. 97216
Bedroom 4 12⁰ x 13¹
Family Room Below
PLANT SHELF ABOVE
SHWR.
LINEN
Vaulted M. Bath
W.i.c.
OPEN RAIL
Bedroom 2 13³ x 12⁵
STAIRS DN.
OPEN RAIL
Bath
Master Suite 17⁹ x 13¹⁰
TRAY CLG.
OVERLOOK
LIN.
ARCHED OPENING
Foyer Below
Bedroom 3 12³ x 11⁰
W.i.c.
Opt. Sitting Room
SECOND FLOOR

Luxurious Appointments

Price Code: F

- This plan features:
- — Five bedrooms
- — Four full and one half baths
- Formal areas located conveniently to promote elegant entertaining and family interaction
- Arched openings from the Foyer into the formal Dining Room and the Living Room
- Decorative columns highlight the entrance to the Breakfast Room
- Two-Story ceiling tops the Family Room, highlighted by a fireplace
- Efficiency is emphasized in the island Kitchen with a walk-in Pantry and abundant counter space
- Master Suite with lavish Bath is topped by a vaulted ceiling
- An optional basement or crawl space foundation — please specify when ordering
- No material list is available for this plan

FIRST FLOOR — 1,527 SQ. FT.
SECOND FLOOR — 1,495 SQ. FT.
BASEMENT — 1,527 SQ. FT.
GARAGE — 440 SQ. FT.

TOTAL LIVING AREA:
3,022 SQ. FT.

Design by
Frank Betz Associates, Inc.

PLAN NO.97213

© Frank Betz Associates

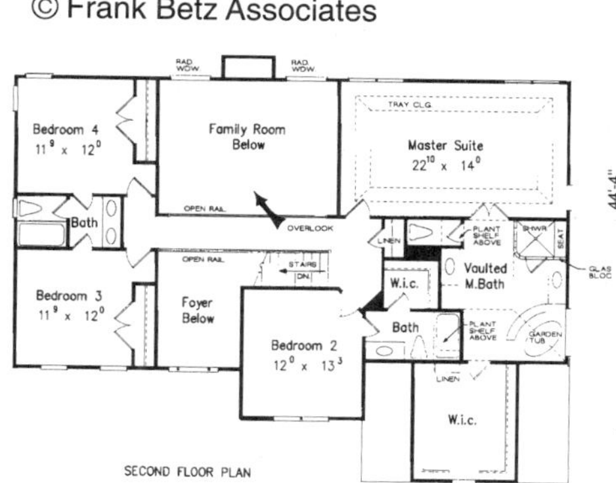
Bedroom 4
11⁹ x 12⁰
Family Room Below
Master Suite
22¹⁰ x 14⁰
Bath
Bedroom 3
11⁹ x 12⁰
Foyer Below
Bedroom 2
12⁰ x 13³
Vaulted M.Bath
W.i.c.
Bath
W.i.c.
SECOND FLOOR PLAN

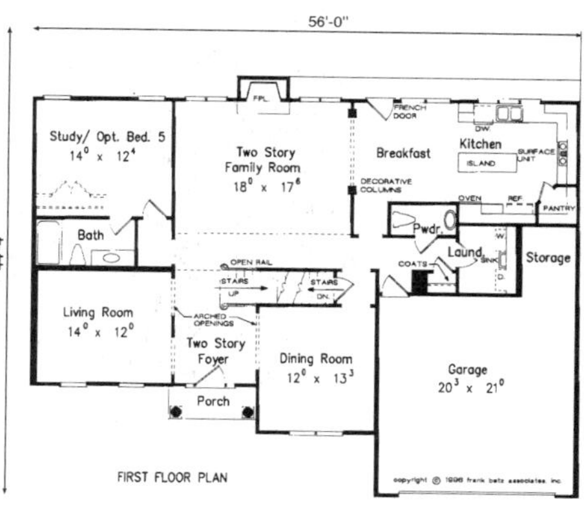
56'-0"
44'-4"
Study/ Opt. Bed. 5
14⁰ x 12⁴
Two Story Family Room
18⁰ x 17⁶
Breakfast
Kitchen
Bath
Pwdr.
Laund.
Storage
Living Room
14⁰ x 12⁰
Two Story Foyer
Dining Room
12⁶ x 13³
Garage
20³ x 21⁰
Porch
FIRST FLOOR PLAN

With Room for All

Price Code: E

- This plan features:
- - Four bedrooms
- - Three full baths
- Corner quoins, segmented arches and shutters create an appealing elevation
- A formal Living Room is directly across from the Entryway
- A Kitchen/Breakfast Bay area with ample cabinet and counter space accesses the Family Room
- A fireplace adds a cozy effect in the Family Room
- A formal Dining Room is located across the Gallery from the Kitchen, which includes a butler's Pantry
- Two secondary Bedrooms are situated to either side of a full Bath
- A Master Suite at the opposite end of the house includes a large compartmented Bath and a walk-in closet
- A third secondary Bedroom has direct access to a full Bath, making a perfect Guest Room
- No materials list is available for this plan

MAIN FLOOR — 2,615 SQ. FT.
GARAGE — 713 SQ. FT.

TOTAL LIVING AREA:
2,615 SQ. FT.

Design by
Filmore Design Group

PLAN NO.92271

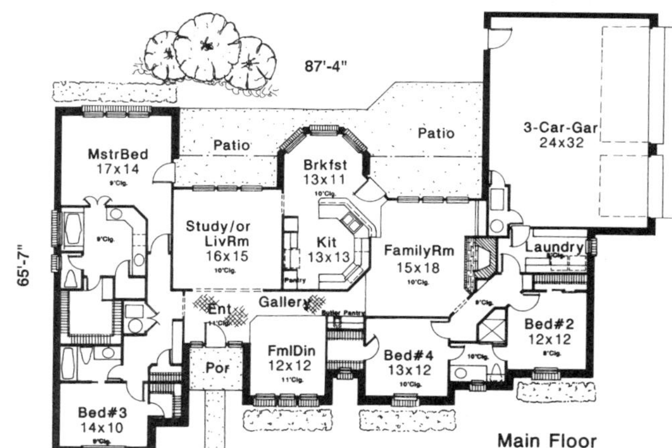
87'-4"
65'-7"
MstrBed
17x14
Patio
Brkfst
13x11
Patio
3-Car-Gar
24x32
Study/or LivRm
16x15
Kit
13x13
FamilyRm
15x18
Laundry
Ent
Gallery
FmlDin
12x12
Bed#4
13x12
Bed#2
12x12
Por
Bed#3
14x10
Main Floor

PLAN NO. 99449

Design by
Design Basics, Inc.

Refer to **Pricing Schedule D** on the order form for pricing information

© design basics inc.

Beautiful See-Through Fireplace

- This plan features:
  - — Four bedrooms
  - — Two full and one half baths
- Large repeating windows to the rear of the Great Room
- The Great Room and the cozy Hearth Room share a beautiful see-through fireplace
- The bayed Breakfast Area is a bright and cheery place
- The gourmet Kitchen includes a Pantry, work Island and a corner sink
- Secluded Master Suite has a skylight in the dressing area and a large walk-in closet

FIRST FLOOR — 1,733 SQ. FT.
SECOND FLOOR — 672 SQ. FT.
BASEMENT — 1,733 SQ. FT.
GARAGE — 613 SQ. FT.

TOTAL LIVING AREA:
2,405 SQ. FT.

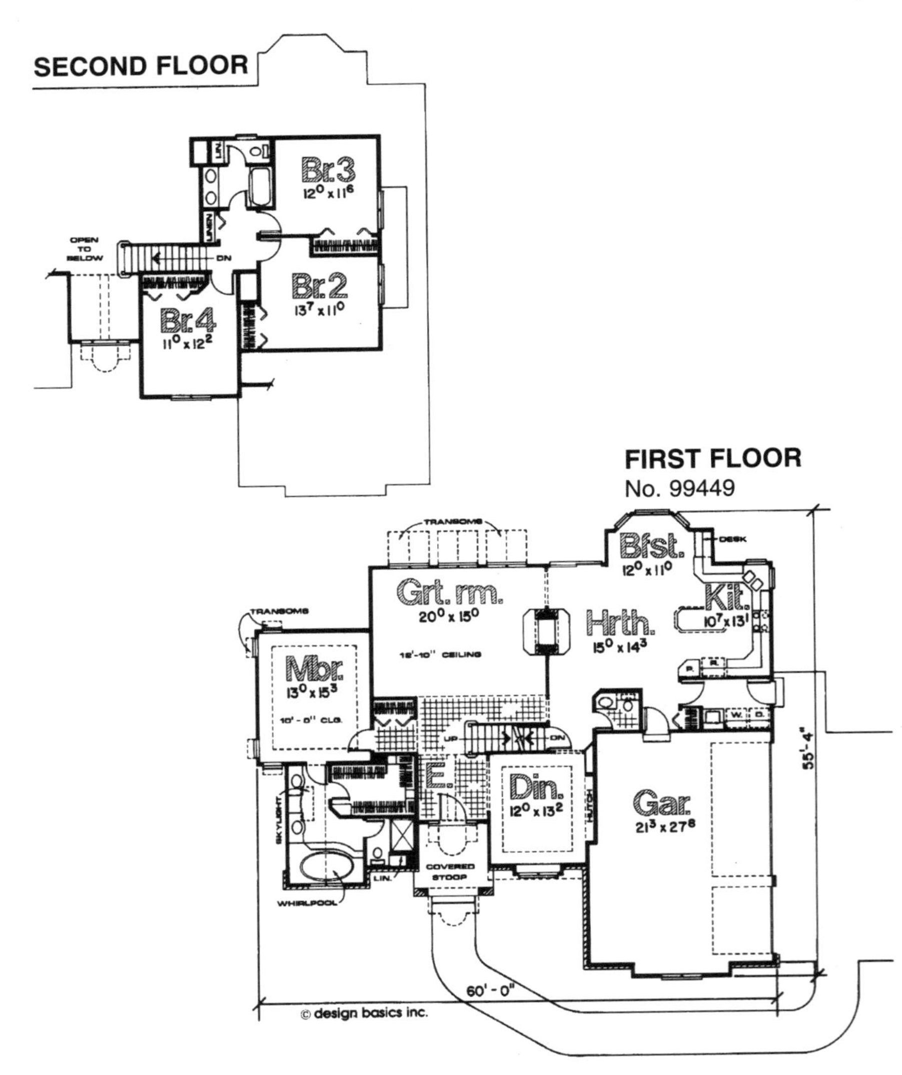

SECOND FLOOR
Br.3
Br.2
Br.4
OPEN TO BELOW
DN
FIRST FLOOR
No. 99449
TRANSOMS
Bfst.
Kit.
Hrth.
Grt. rm.
Mbr.
Din.
Gar.
E.
COVERED STOOP
WHIRLPOOL
SKYLIGHT
LIN.
UP
DN
55'-4"
60'-0"
© design basics inc.

Refer to **Pricing Schedule E** on the order form for pricing information

Design by Design Basics, Inc.

PLAN NO. 99430

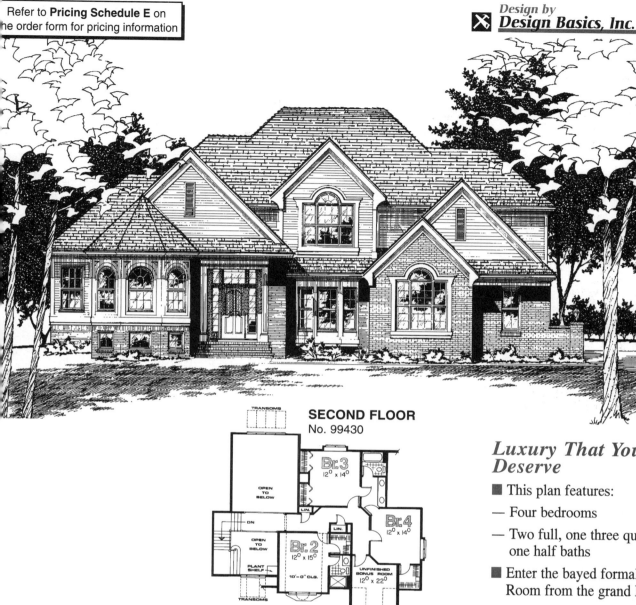

SECOND FLOOR
No. 99430
TRANSOMS
OPEN TO BELOW
Br. 3
12⁰ x 14⁰
Br. 4
12⁰ x 14⁰
Br. 2
12⁰ x 15⁰
10'-0" CLG.
LIN.
DN
PLANT SHELF
UNFINISHED BONUS ROOM
12⁰ x 22⁰
© design basics, inc.
Bfst.
11⁰ x 13⁰
Liv. rm.
16⁰ x 20⁰
18'-0" CEILING
Hrth.
16⁰ x 18⁰
Kit.
13⁴ x 14⁰
SNACK BAR
BOOKS
GLASS BLOCK
WHIRLPOOL
Mbr.
13⁰ x 16⁰
10'-0" CLG.
CURIO
E.
UP
Din.
12⁰ x 16⁸
Gar.
22⁰ x 33⁸
Den
12⁰ x 15⁰
COVERED STOOP
63' - 4"
64' - 0"
FIRST FLOOR

Luxury That You Deserve

- This plan features:
  - — Four bedrooms
  - — Two full, one three quarter and one half baths
- Enter the bayed formal Dining Room from the grand Entry Hall
- The warm hearth room and bright bayed Nook compliment the fully appointed Kitchen
- The Living Room has a see through fireplace and a wall of windows overlooking the backyard
- French doors leading into the Master Suite feature a private Den, Bath with whirlpool tub, and a glass block shower

FIRST FLOOR — 2,235 SQ. FT.
SECOND FLOOR — 1,003 SQ. FT.
GARAGE — 740 SQ. FT.
BASEMENT — 2,235 SQ. FT.

TOTAL LIVING AREA:
3,238 SQ. FT.

To order your Blueprints, call 1-800-235-5700

P L A N   N O .   9 8 5 3 5

Design by
Filmore Design Group

Refer to **Pricing Schedule F** on the order form for pricing information

A Home with Tremendous Appeal

- This plan features:
- — Four bedrooms
- — Three full and one half baths
- The circular stairway highlights the entry
- The formal Dining Room has a bay window
- A Study with a double door entry
- Formal Living Room has a fireplace and elegant columns
- The large Family Room boasts a brick fireplace and a built-in TV cabinet
- The angled Kitchen contains a built-in Pantry
- The Master Suite occupies one wing of the house
- No materials list is available for this plan

MAIN FLOOR — 2,658 SQ. FT.
UPPER FLOOR — 854 SQ. FT.
GARAGE — 660 SQ. FT.

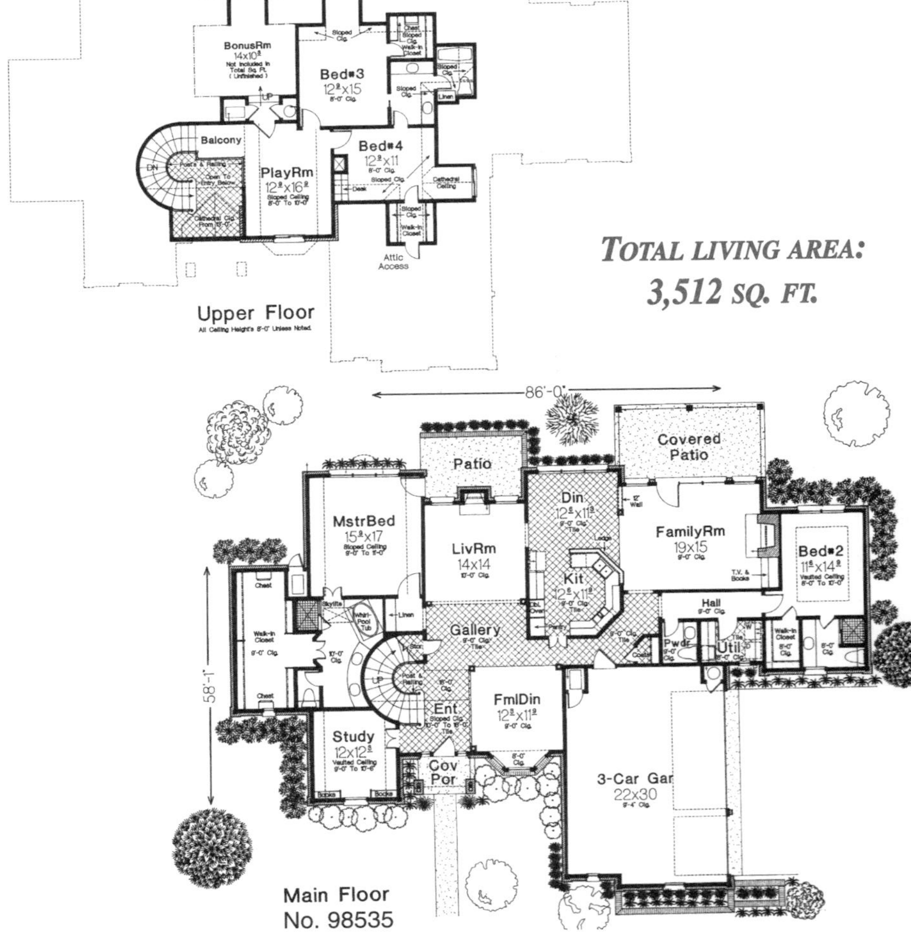

BonusRm
$14x10^{8}$
Bed#3
$12^{8}x15$
Balcony
PlayRm
$12^{8}x16^{8}$
Bed#4
$12^{8}x11$
Attic Access
Upper Floor
All Ceiling Height's 8'-0" Unless Noted.
86'-0"
58'-1"
Covered Patio
Patio
MstrBed
15⁸x17
Sloped Ceiling
LivRm
14x14
Din
$12^{8}x11^{8}$
Kit
FamilyRm
19x15
Bed#2
Hall
Gallery
Pwdr
Util
Ent
FmlDin
$12^{8}x11^{8}$
Study
$12x12^{8}$
Vaulted Ceiling
Cov Por
3-Car Gar
22x30
Main Floor
No. 98535

TOTAL LIVING AREA:
3,512 SQ. FT.

To order your Blueprints, call 1-800-235-5700

Refer to **Pricing Schedule F** on the order form for pricing information

Design by
Donald A. Gardner Architects, Inc.

PLAN NO. 98041

S. NATHAN

TOTAL LIVING AREA:
2,807 SQ. FT.

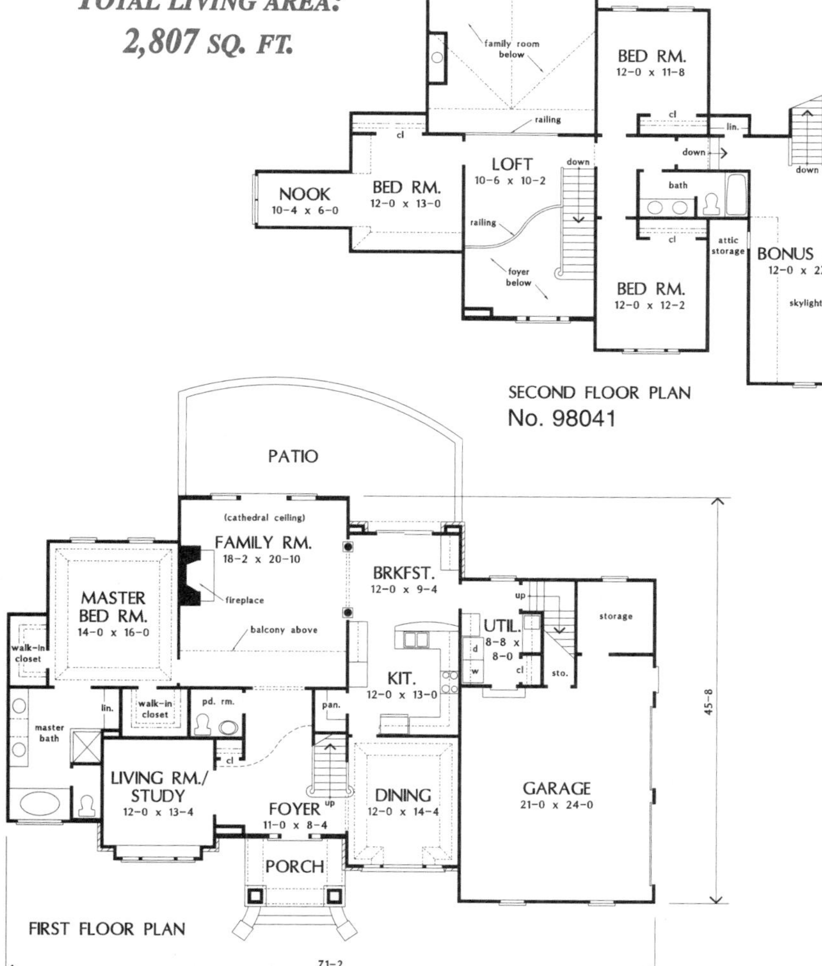

family room below
BED RM.
12-0 x 11-8
railing
cl
lin.
attic storage
LOFT
10-6 x 10-2
down
NOOK
10-4 x 6-0
BED RM.
12-0 x 13-0
bath
railing
foyer below
attic storage
BONUS RM.
12-0 x 27-8
skylights
BED RM.
12-0 x 12-2
SECOND FLOOR PLAN
No. 98041
PATIO
(cathedral ceiling)
FAMILY RM.
18-2 x 20-10
fireplace
balcony above
MASTER BED RM.
14-0 x 16-0
walk-in closet
BRKFST.
12-0 x 9-4
UTIL.
8-8 x 8-0
storage
KIT.
12-0 x 13-0
sto.
master bath
lin.
walk-in closet
pd. rm.
pan.
45-8
LIVING RM./ STUDY
12-0 x 13-4
FOYER
11-0 x 8-4
DINING
12-0 x 14-4
GARAGE
21-0 x 24-0
PORCH
FIRST FLOOR PLAN
71-2
© 1997 Donald A Gardner Architects, Inc.

Graceful in Appearance

- This plan features:
- — Four bedrooms
- — Two full and one half baths
- With a stone and stucco exterior and arched windows, this home has a graceful appearance
- The two-story Foyer creates a formal invitation into the Living Room/Study
- The Dining Room has an elegant tray ceiling
- The generous Family Room has a fireplace and a cathedral ceiling
- Columns mark the entrance to the Breakfast Area
- The spacious Kitchen has a walk-in Pantry
- The Master Suite has a private location on the first floor and includes a tray ceiling

FIRST FLOOR — 1,904 SQ. FT.
SECOND FLOOR — 903 SQ. FT.
BONUS — 434 SQ. FT.
GARAGE — 646 SQ. FT.

PLAN NO. 93319

Design by
Patrick Morabito A.I.A.

Refer to **Pricing Schedule D** on the order form for pricing information

Family Room with a Fireplace

- This plan features:
- — Four bedrooms
- — Two full and one half baths
- An island Kitchen with a built-in Pantry, double sink and a convenient Dinette Area
- A cozy fireplace enhances the Family Room
- A formal Living Room and Dining Room
- A luxurious Master Suite with an ultra Bath and walk-in closet
- Three additional Bedrooms share a full hall Bath
- No materials list is available for this plan

FIRST FLOOR — 1,228 SQ. FT.
SECOND FLOOR — 1,191 SQ. FT.
BASEMENT — 1,228 SQ. FT.
GARAGE — 528 SQ. FT.

TOTAL LIVING AREA:
2,419 SQ. FT.

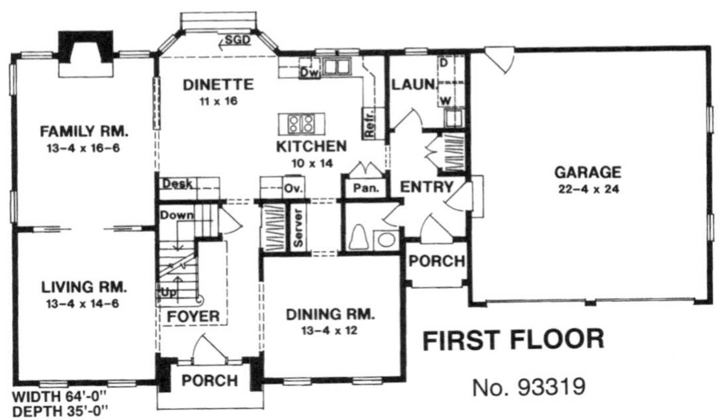
SGD
DINETTE
11 x 16
Dw
LAUN.
D
W
FAMILY RM.
13-4 x 16-6
Refr.
KITCHEN
10 x 14
GARAGE
22-4 x 24
Desk
Ov.
Pan.
ENTRY
Down
Server
PORCH
Up
LIVING RM.
13-4 x 14-6
FOYER
DINING RM.
13-4 x 12
PORCH
WIDTH 64'-0"
DEPTH 35'-0"

FIRST FLOOR

No. 93319

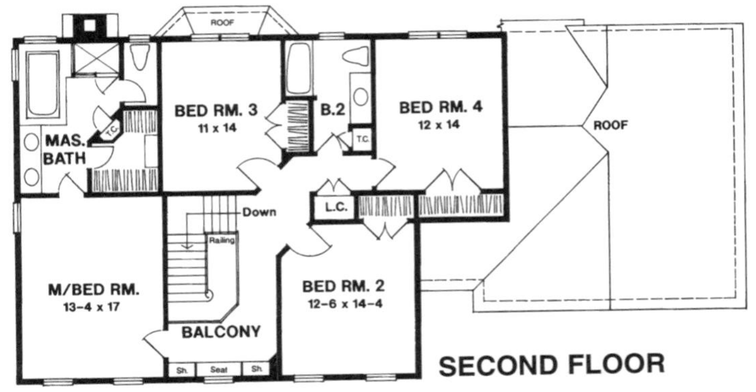
ROOF
BED RM. 3
11 x 14
B.2
BED RM. 4
12 x 14
ROOF
MAS. BATH
T.C.
T.C.
L.C.
Down
Railing
M/BED RM.
13-4 x 17
BED RM. 2
12-6 x 14-4
BALCONY
Sh.
Seat
Sh.

SECOND FLOOR

Refer to **Pricing Schedule F** on the order form for pricing information

Design by
The Garlinghouse Company

PLAN NO. 10735

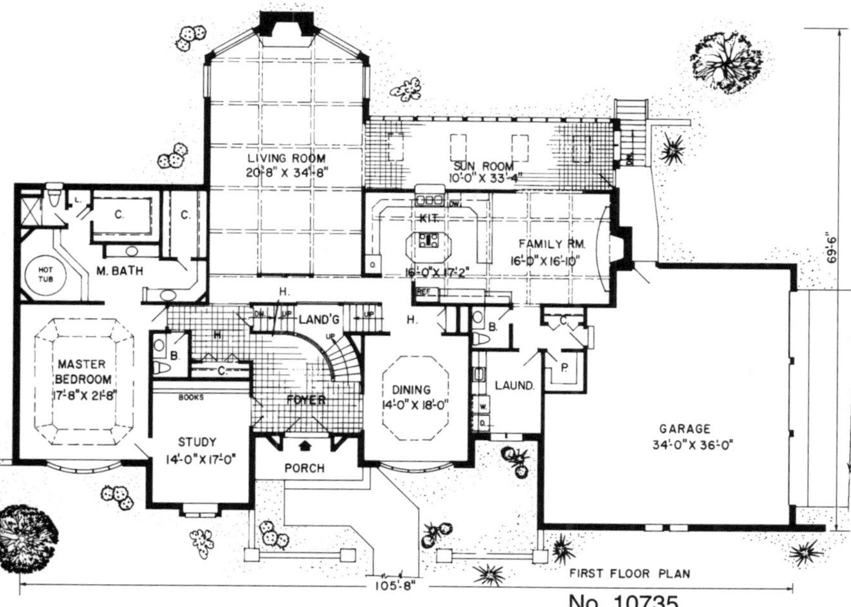

LIVING ROOM
20'-8" X 34'-8"
SUN ROOM
10'-0" X 33'-4"
KIT.
16'-0" X 17'-2"
FAMILY RM.
16'-0" X 16'-10"
HOT TUB
M. BATH
C.
LAND'G
MASTER BEDROOM
17'-8" X 21'-8"
BOOKS
STUDY
14'-0" X 17'-0"
FOYER
PORCH
DINING
14'-0" X 18'-0"
LAUND.
GARAGE
34'-0" X 36'-0"
69'-6"
105'-8"
FIRST FLOOR PLAN

No. 10735

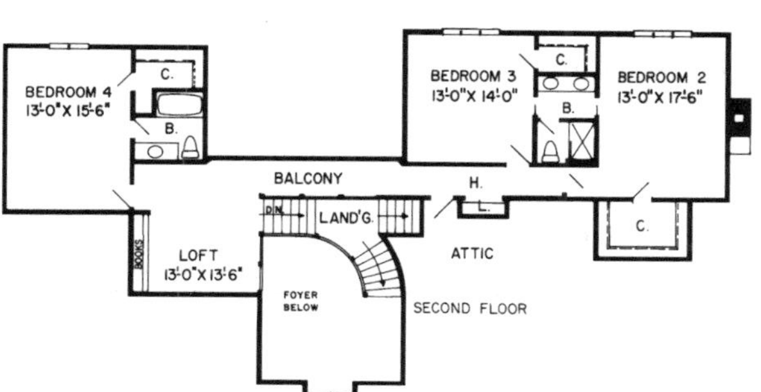

BEDROOM 4
13'-0" X 15'-6"
BEDROOM 3
13'-0" X 14'-0"
BEDROOM 2
13'-0" X 17'-6"
BALCONY
LAND'G.
LOFT
13'-0" X 13'-6"
BOOKS
FOYER BELOW
ATTIC
SECOND FLOOR

Energy-Saving Sunroom Warms Classic Tudor

- This plan features:
- — Four bedrooms
- — Three full and two half baths
- Upstairs Bedrooms with adjoining Baths and built-in bookshelves in the Loft
- A Master Bedroom with a Study and a Bath that is equipped with a hot tub
- An island Kitchen opened to the Family Room which accesses the Sun Room

FIRST FLOOR — 3,332 SQ. FT.
SECOND FLOOR — 1,218 SQ. FT.
SUNROOM — 340 SQ. FT.
BASEMENT — 3,672 SQ. FT.
GARAGE — 1,137 SQ. FT.

TOTAL LIVING AREA:
4,890 SQ. FT.

Everything You Need...
...to Make Your Dream Come True!

You pay only a fraction of the original cost for home designs by respected professionals.

You've Picked Your Dream Home!

You can already see it standing on your lot... you can see yourselves in your new home... enjoying family, entertaining guests, celebrating holidays. All that remains ahead are the details. That's where we can help. Whether you plan to build-it-yourself, be your own contractor, or hand your plans over to an outside contractor, your Garlinghouse blueprints provide the perfect beginning for putting yourself in your dream home right away.

We even make it simple for you to make professional design modifications. We can also provide a materials list for greater economy.

My grandfather, L.F. Garlinghouse, started a tradition of quality when he founded this company in 1907. For over 90 years, homeowners and builders have relied on us for accurate, complete, professional blueprints. Our plans help you get results fast... and save money, too! These pages will give you all the information you need to order. So get started now... I know you'll love your new Garlinghouse home!

Sincerely,

EXTERIOR ELEVATIONS

Elevations are scaled drawings of the front, rear, left and right sides of a home. All of the necessary information pertaining to the exterior finish materials, roof pitches and exterior height dimensions of your home are defined.

CABINET PLANS

These plans, or in some cases elevations, will detail the layout of the kitchen and bathroom cabinets at a larger scale. This gives you an accurate layout for your cabinets or an ideal starting point for a modified custom cabinet design. Available for most plans in our collection. You may also show the floor plan without a cabinet layout. This will allow you to start from scratch and design your own dream kitchen.

TYPICAL WALL SECTION

This section is provided to help your builder understand the structural components and materials used to construct the exterior walls of your home. This section will address insulation, roof components, and interior and exterior wall finishes. Your plans will be designed with either 2x4 or 2x6 exterior walls, but most professional contractors can easily adapt the plans to the wall thickness you require. Available for most plans in our collection.

FIREPLACE DETAILS

If the home you have chosen includes a fireplace, the fireplace detail will show typical methods to construct the firebox, hearth and flue chase for masonry units, or a wood frame chase for a zero-clearance unit. Available for most plans in our collection.

FOUNDATION PLAN

These plans will accurately dimension the footprint of your home including load bearing points and beam placement if applicable. The foundation style will vary from plan to plan. Your local climatic conditions will dictate whether a basement, slab or crawlspace is best suited for your area. In most cases, if your plan comes with one foundation style, a professional contractor can easily adapt the foundation plan to an alternate style.

ROOF PLAN

The information necessary to construct the roof will be included with your home plans. Some plans will reference roof trusses, while many others contain schematic framing plans. These framing plans will indicate the lumber sizes necessary for the rafters and ridgeboards based on the designated roof loads.

TYPICAL CROSS SECTION

A cut-away cross-section through the entire home shows your building contractor the exact correlation of construction components at all levels of the house. It will help to clarify the load bearing points from the roof all the way down to the basement.

DETAILED FLOOR PLANS

The floor plans of your home accurately dimension the positioning of all walls, doors, windows, stairs and permanent fixtures. They will show you the relationship and dimensions of rooms, closets and traffic patterns. The schematic of the electrical layout may be included in the plan. This layout is clearly represented and does not hinder the clarity of other pertinent information shown. All these details will help your builder properly construct your new home.

STAIR DETAILS

If stairs are an element of the design you have chosen, the plans will show the necessary information to build these, either through a stair cross section, or on the floor plans. Either way, the information provides your builders the essential reference points that they need to build the stairs.

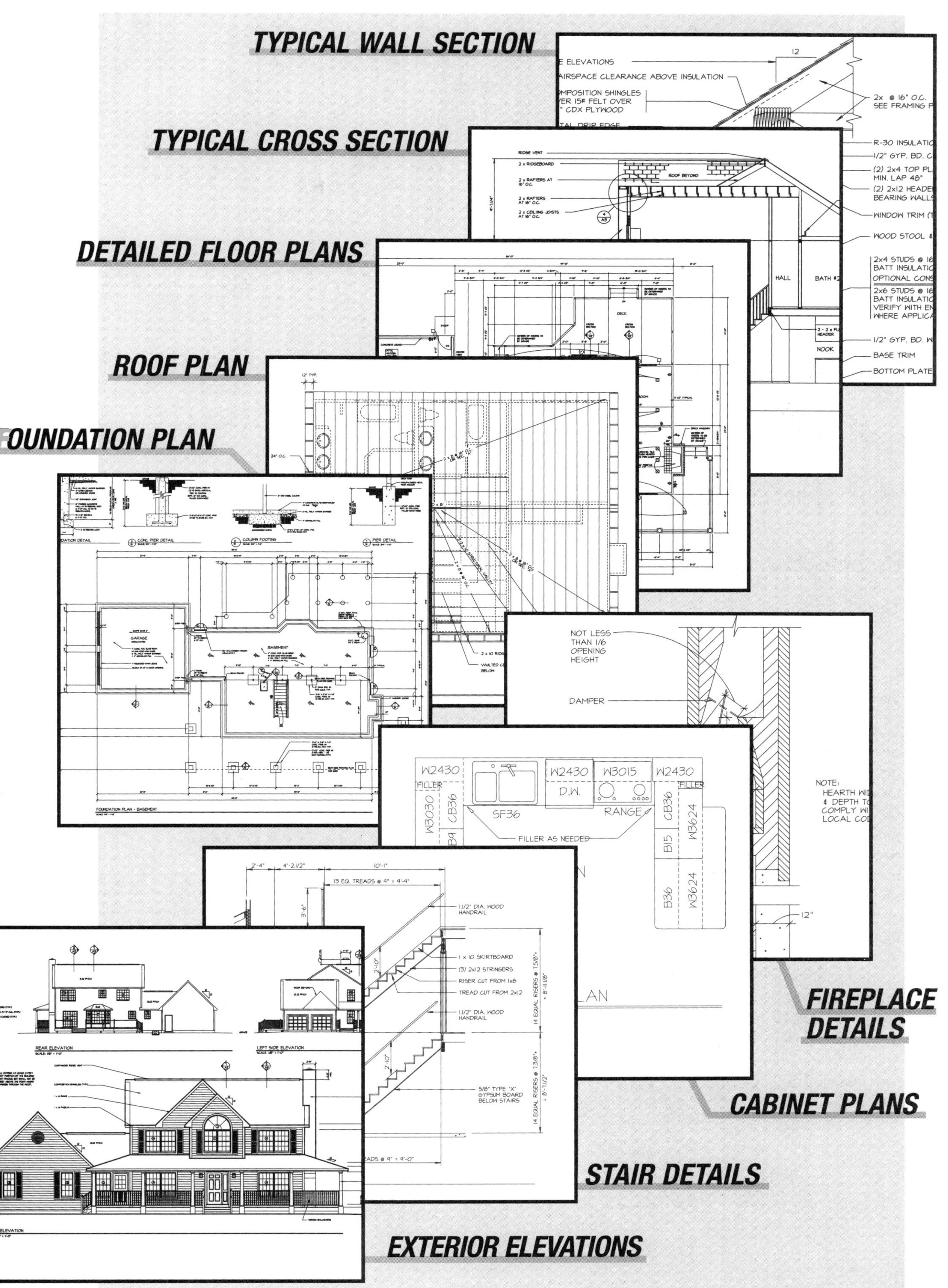
TYPICAL WALL SECTION
TYPICAL CROSS SECTION
DETAILED FLOOR PLANS
ROOF PLAN
FOUNDATION PLAN
FIREPLACE DETAILS
CABINET PLANS
STAIR DETAILS
EXTERIOR ELEVATIONS

Garlinghouse Options & Extras ...Make Your Dream A Home

Reversed Plans Can Make Your Dream Home Just Right!

"That's our dream home...if only the garage were on the other side!"

You could have exactly the home you want by flipping it end-for-end. Check it out by holding your dream home page of this book up to a mirror. Then simply order your plans "reversed." We'll send you one full set of mirror-image plans (with the writing backwards) as a master guide for you and your builder.

The remaining sets of your order will come as shown in this book so the dimensions and specifications are easily read on the job site...but most plans in our collection come stamped "REVERSED" so there is no construction confusion.

As Shown

Reversed

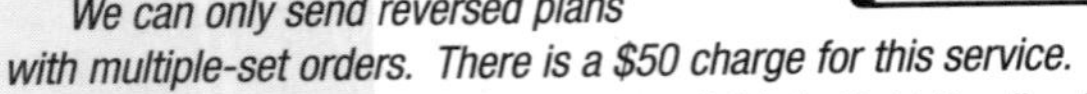

We can only send reversed plans with multiple-set orders. There is a $50 charge for this service.

Some plans in our collection are available in Right Reading Reverse. Right Reading Reverse plans will show your home in reverse, with the writing on the plan being readable. This easy-to-read format will save you valuable time and money. Please contact our Customer Service Department at (860) 343-5977 to check for Right Reading Reverse availability. There is a $165 charge for this service for plan series 998, 964, and 980. The cost is $125 for all other plans.

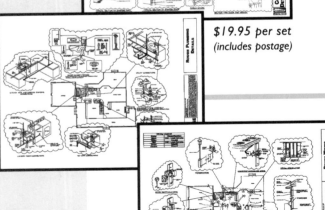

Remember To Order Your Materials List

It'll help you save money. Available at a modest additional charge, the Materials List gives the quantity, dimensions, and specifications for the major materials needed to build your home. You will get faster, more accurate bids from your contractors and building suppliers — and avoid paying for unused materials and waste. Materials Lists are available for all home plans except as otherwise indicated, but can only be ordered with a set of home plans. Due to differences in regional requirements and homeowner or builder preferences... electrical, plumbing and heating/air conditioning equipment specifications are not designed specifically for each plan. However, non-plan specific detailed typical prints of residential electrical, plumbing and construction guidelines can be provided. Please see below for additional information. If you need a detailed materials cost you might need to purchase a Zip Quote. (Details follow)

Specifications & Contract Form

We send this form to you free of charge with your home plan order. The form is designed to be filled in by you or your contractor with the exact materials to use in the construction of your new home. Once signed by you and your contractor it will provide you with peace of mind throughout the construction process.

Detail Plans Provide Valuable Information About Construction Techniques

Because local codes and requirements vary greatly, we recommend that you obtain drawings and bids from licensed contractors to do your mechanical plans. However, if you want to know more about techniques — and deal more confidently with subcontractors — we offer these remarkably useful detail sheets. These detail sheets will aid in your understanding of these technical subjects. ***The detail sheets are not specific to any one home plan and should be used only as a general reference guide.***

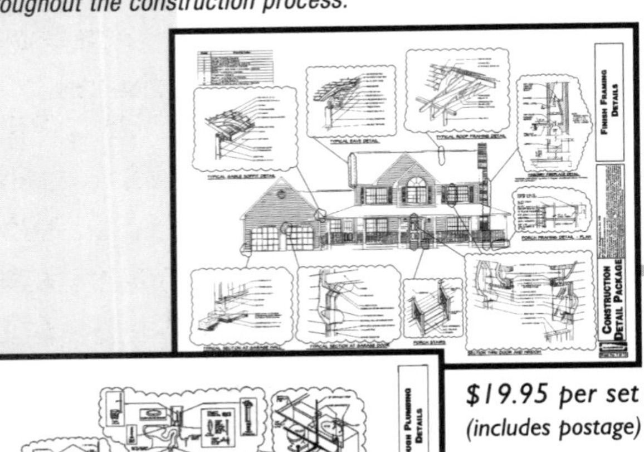

$19.95 per set (includes postage)

RESIDENTIAL CONSTRUCTION DETAILS

Ten sheets that cover the essentials of stick-built residential home construction. Details foundation options — poured concrete basement, concrete block, or monolithic concrete slab. Shows all aspects of floor, wall and roof framing. Provides details for roof dormers, overhangs, chimneys and skylights. Conforms to requirements of Uniform Building code or BOCA code. Includes a quick index and a glossary of terms.

RESIDENTIAL PLUMBING DETAILS

Eight sheets packed with information detailing pipe installation methods, fittings, and sized. Details plumbing hook-ups for toilets, sinks, washers, sump pumps, and septic system construction. Conforms to requirements of National Plumbing code. Color coded with a glossary of terms and quick index.

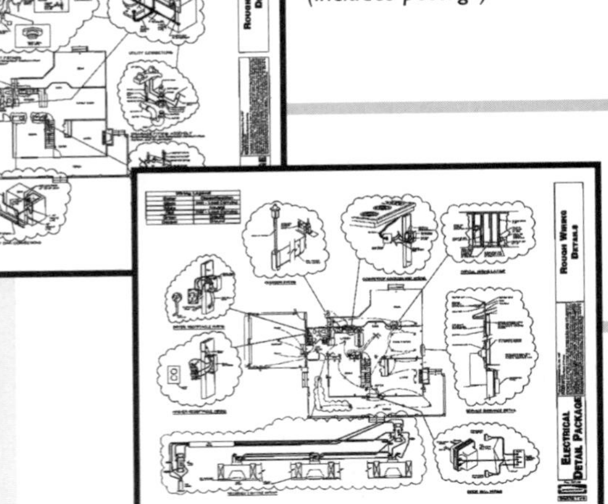

RESIDENTIAL ELECTRICAL DETAILS

Eight sheets that cover all aspects of residential wiring, from simple switch wiring to service entrance connections. Details distribution panel layout with outlet and switch schematics, circuit breaker and wiring installation methods, and ground fault interrupter specifications. Conforms to requirements of National Electrical Code. Color coded with a glossary of terms.

Modifying Your Favorite Design, Made EASY!

OPTION #1

Modifying Your Garlinghouse Home Plan

Simple modifications to your dream home, including minor non-structural changes and material substitutions, can be made between you and your builder by marking the changes directly on your blueprints. However, if you are considering making significant changes to your chosen design, we recommend that you use the services of The Garlinghouse Co. Design Staff. We will help take your ideas and turn them into a reality, just the way you want. Here's our procedure!

*When you place your Vellum order, you may also request a free Garlinghouse Modification Kit. In this kit, you will receive a red marking pencil, furniture cut-out sheet, ruler, a self addressed mailing label and a form for specifying any additional notes or drawings that will help us understand your design ideas. Mark your desired changes directly on the Vellum drawings. NOTE: Please use only a **red pencil** to mark your desired changes on the Vellum. Then, return the redlined Vellum set in the original box to The Garlinghouse Company at, 282 Main Street Extension, Middletown, CT 06457. **IMPORTANT**: Please **roll** the Vellums for shipping, **do not fold** the Vellums for shipping.*

We also offer modification estimates. We will provide you with an estimate to draft your changes based on your specific modifications before you purchase the vellums, for a $50 fee. After you receive your estimate, if you decide to have The Garlinghouse Company Design Staff do the changes, the $50 estimate fee will be deducted from the cost of your modifications. If, however, you choose to use a different service, the $50 estimate fee is non-refundable. (Note: Personal checks cannot be accepted for the estimate.)

Within 5 days of receipt of your plans, you will be contacted by a member of The Garlinghouse Co. Design Staff with an estimate for the design services to draw those changes. A 50% deposit is required before we begin making the actual modifications to your plans.

Once the design changes have been completed to your vellum plan, a representative from The Garlinghouse Co. Design Staff will call to inform you that your modified Vellum plan is complete and will be shipped as soon as the final payment has been made. For additional information call us at 1-860-343-5977. Please refer to the Modification Pricing Guide for estimated modification costs. Please call for Vellum modification availability for plan numbers 85,000 and above.

OPTION #2

Reproducible Vellums for Local Modification Ease

If you decide not to use the Garlinghouse Co. Design Staff for your modifications, we recommend that you follow our same procedure of purchasing our Vellums. You then have the option of using the services of the original designer of the plan, a local professional designer, or architect to make the modifications to your plan.

With a Vellum copy of our plans, a design professional can alter the drawings just the way you want, then you can print as many copies of the modified plans as you need to build your house. And, since you have already started with our complete detailed plans, the cost of those expensive professional services will be significantly less than starting from scratch. Refer to the price schedule for Vellum costs. Again, please call for Vellum availability for plan numbers 85,000 and above.

***IMPORTANT RETURN POLICY:** Upon receipt of your Vellums, if for some reason you decide you do not want a modified plan, then simply return the Kit and the unopened Vellums. Reproducible Vellum copies of our home plans are copyright protected and only sold under the terms of a license agreement that you will receive with your order. Should you not agree to the terms, then the Vellums may be returned, **unopened,** for a full refund less the shipping and handling charges, plus a 15% restocking fee. For any additional information, please call us at 1-860-343-5977.*

MODIFICATION PRICING GUIDE

CATEGORIES	*ESTIMATED COST*
KITCHEN LAYOUT — PLAN AND ELEVATION	$175.00
BATHROOM LAYOUT — PLAN AND ELEVATION	$175.00
FIREPLACE PLAN AND DETAILS	$200.00
INTERIOR ELEVATION	$125.00
EXTERIOR ELEVATION — MATERIAL CHANGE	$140.00
EXTERIOR ELEVATION — ADD BRICK OR STONE	$400.00
EXTERIOR ELEVATION — STYLE CHANGE	$450.00
NON BEARING WALLS (INTERIOR)	$200.00
BEARING AND/OR EXTERIOR WALLS	$325.00
WALL FRAMING CHANGE — 2X4 TO 2X6 OR 2X6 TO 2X4	$240.00
ADD/REDUCE LIVING SPACE — SQUARE FOOTAGE	QUOTE REQUIRED
NEW MATERIALS LIST	QUOTE REQUIRED
CHANGE TRUSSES TO RAFTERS OR CHANGE ROOF PITCH	$300.00
FRAMING PLAN CHANGES	$325.00
GARAGE CHANGES	$325.00
ADD A FOUNDATION OPTION	$300.00
FOUNDATION CHANGES	$250.00
RIGHT READING PLAN REVERSE	$575.00
ARCHITECTS SEAL *(Available for most states)*	$300.00
ENERGY CERTIFICATE	$150.00
LIGHT AND VENTILATION SCHEDULE	$150.00

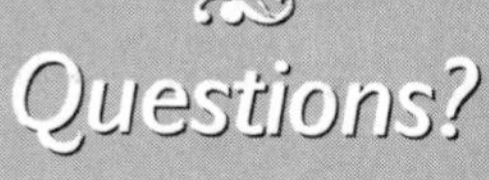
Questions?

Call our customer service department at **1-860-343-5977**

"How to obtain a construction cost calculation based on labor rates and building material costs in your Zip Code area!"

ZIP-QUOTE!

HOME COST CALCULATOR

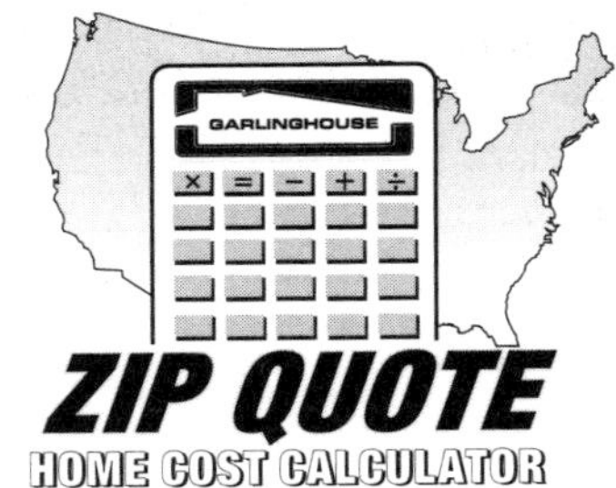
GARLINGHOUSE
ZIP QUOTE
HOME COST CALCULATOR

WHY?

Do you wish you could quickly find out the building cost for your new home without waiting for a contractor to compile hundreds of bids? Would you like to have a benchmark to compare your contractor(s) bids against? ***Well, Now You Can!!,*** with **Zip-Quote** Home Cost Calculator. Zip-Quote is only available for zip code areas within the United States.

HOW?

Our new **Zip-Quote** Home Cost Calculator will enable you to obtain the calculated building cost to construct your new home, based on labor rates and building material costs within your zip code area, without the normal delays or hassles usually associated with the bidding process. Zip-Quote can be purchased in two separate formats, an itemized or a bottom line format.

"How does **Zip-Quote** actually work?" When you call to order, you must choose from the options available, for your specific home, in order for us to process your order. Once we receive your **Zip-Quote** order, we process your specific home plan building materials list through our Home Cost Calculator which contains up-to-date rates for all residential labor trades and building material costs in your zip code area. "The result?" A calculated cost to build your dream home in your zip code area. This calculation will help you (as a consumer or a builder) evaluate your building budget. This is a valuable tool for anyone considering building a new home.

All database information for our calculations is furnished by Marshall & Swift, L.P. For over 60 years, Marshall & Swift L.P. has been a leading provider of cost data to professionals in all aspects of the construction and remodeling industries.

OPTION 1

The **Itemized Zip-Quote** is a detailed building material list. Each building material list line item will separately state the labor cost, material cost and equipment cost (if applicable) for the use of that building material in the construction process. Each category within the building material list will be subtotaled and the entire Itemized cost calculation totaled at the end. This building materials list will be summarized by the individual building categories and will have additional columns where you can enter data from your contractor's estimates for a cost comparison between the different suppliers and contractors who will actually quote you their products and services.

OPTION 2

The **Bottom Line Zip-Quote** is a one line summarized total cost for the home plan of your choice. This cost calculation is also based on the labor cost, material cost and equipment cost (if applicable) within your local zip code area.

COST

The price of your **Itemized Zip-Quote** is based upon the pricing schedule of the plan you have selected, in addition to th price of the materials list. Please refer to the pricing schedule on our order form. The price of your initial **Bottom Line Zip-Quote** is $29.95. Each additional **Bottom Line Zip-Quote** ordered in conjunction with the initial order is only $14.95. **Bottom Line Zip-Quote** may be purchased separately and does NOT have to be purchased in conjunction with a home plan order.

FYI

An **Itemized Zip-Quote** Home Cost Calculation can ONLY be purchased in conjunction with a Home Plan order. The **Itemized Zip-Quote** can not be purchased separately. The **Bottom Line Zip-Quote** can be purchased separately and doesn't have to be purchased in conjunction with a home plan order. Please consult with a sales representative for current availability. If you find within 60 days of your order date that you will be unable to build this home, then you may exchange the plans and the materials list towards the price of a new set of plans (see order info pages for plan exchange policy The **Itemized Zip-Quote** and the **Bottom Line Zip-Quote** are NOT returnable. The price of the initial **Bottom Line Zip-Quote** order can be credited towards the purchase of an **Itemized Zip-Quote** order only. Additional **Bottom Line Zip-Quote** orders, within the same order can not be credited Please call our Customer Service Department for more information.

Zip-Quote is available for plans where you see this symbol. Please call for current availability.

SOME MORE INFORMATION

The Itemized and Bottom Line Zip-Quotes give you approximate costs for constructing the particular house in your area. These costs are not exact and are only intended to be used as a preliminary estimate to help determine the affordability of a new home and/or a guide to evaluate the general competitiveness of actual price quotes obtained through local suppliers and contractors. However, Zip-Quote cost figures should never be relied upon as the only sourc of information in either case. Land, sewer systems, site work, landscaping and other expenses are not included in our building cos figures. The Garlinghouse Company and Marshall & Swift L.P. can n guarantee any level of data accuracy or correctness in a Zip-Quote and disclaim all liability for loss with respect to the same, in excess the original purchase price of the Zip-Quote product. All Zip-Quote calculations are based upon the actual blueprint materials list with options as selected by customer and do not reflect any differences that may be shown on the published house renderings, floor plans, o photographs.

Ignoring Copyright Laws Can Be A $1,000,000 Mistake

*Recent changes in the US copyright laws allow for statutory penalties of up to **$100,000** per incident for copyright infringement involving any of the copyrighted plans found in this publication. The law can be confusing. So, for your own protection, take the time to understand what you can and cannot do when it comes to home plans.*

•••WHAT YOU CANNOT DO•••

You Cannot Duplicate Home Plans

*Purchasing a set of blueprints and making additional sets by reproducing the original is **illegal**. If you need multiple sets of a particular home plan, then you must purchase them.*

You Cannot Copy Any Part of a Home Plan to Create Another

*Creating your own plan by copying even part of a home design found in this publication is called "creating a derivative work" and is **illegal** unless you have permission to do so.*

You Cannot Build a Home Without a License

*You must have specific permission or license to build a home from a copyrighted design, even if the finished home has been changed from the original plan. It is **illegal** to build one of the homes found in this publication without a license.*

What Garlinghouse Offers

Home Plan Blueprint Package

By purchasing a multiple set package of blueprints or a vellum from Garlinghouse, you not only receive the physical blueprint documents necessary for construction, but you are also granted a license to build one, and only one, home. You can also make simple modifications, including minor non-structural changes and material substitutions, to our design, as long as these changes are made directly on the blueprints purchased from Garlinghouse and no additional copies are made.

Home Plan Vellums

By purchasing vellums for one of our home plans, you receive the same construction drawings found in the blueprints, but printed on vellum paper. Vellums can be erased and are perfect for making design changes. They are also semi-transparent making them easy to duplicate. But most importantly, the purchase of home plan vellums comes with a broader license that allows you to make changes to the design (ie, create a hand drawn or CAD derivative work), to make copies of the plan, and to build one home from the plan.

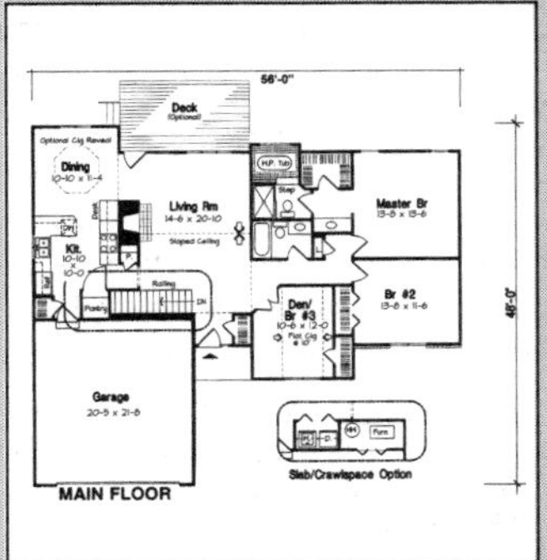
56'-0"
Deck
Living Rm
Master Br
Br #2
Garage
MAIN FLOOR
Slab/Crawlspace Option

License To Build Additional Homes

With the purchase of a blueprint package or vellums you automatically receive a license to build one home and only one home, respectively. If you want to build more homes than you are licensed to build through your purchase of a plan, then additional licenses may be purchased at reasonable costs from Garlinghouse. Inquire for more information.

GARLINGHOUSE

Order Code No. **H9LX5**

Order Form

Plan prices guaranteed until 6/1/00 — After this date call for updated pricing

___ set(s) of blueprints for plan #________ $______

___ Vellum & Modification kit for plan #________ $______

___ Additional set(s) @ $35 each for plan #________ $______

___ Mirror Image Reverse @ $50 each $______

___ Right Reading Reverse (see page 250 for cost) $______

___ Materials list for plan #________ $______

___ Detail Plans @ $19.95 each

❑ Construction ❑ Plumbing ❑ Electrical $______

___ Bottom line ZIP Quote@$29.95 for plan #________ $______

___ Additional Bottom Line Zip Quote

@ $14.95 for plan(s) #________

________ $______

___ Itemized ZIP Quote for plan(s) #________ $______

Shipping (see charts on opposite page) $______

Subtotal $______

Sales Tax (CT residents add 6% sales tax, KS residents add 6.15% sales tax) (Not required for other states) $______

TOTAL AMOUNT ENCLOSED $______

Send your check, money order or credit card information to:
(No C.O.D.'s Please)

Please submit all United States & Other Nations orders to:
Garlinghouse Company
P.O. Box 1717
Middletown, CT. 06457

Please Submit all Canadian plan orders to:
Garlinghouse Company
60 Baffin Place, Unit #5
Waterloo, Ontario N2V 1Z7

ADDRESS INFORMATION:

NAME: ________

STREET: ________

CITY: ________

STATE: ________ **ZIP:** ________

DAYTIME PHONE: ________

Credit Card Information

Charge To: ❑ Visa ❑ Mastercard

Card # |_|_|_|_|_|_|_|_|_|_|_|_|_|_|_|_|

Signature ________ Exp. ___/___

Payment must be made in U.S. funds. Foreign Mail Orders: Certified bank checks in U.S. funds only

IMPORTANT INFORMATION TO READ BEFORE YOU PLACE YOUR ORDER

How Many Sets Of Plans Will You Need?

The Standard 8-Set Construction Package

*Our experience shows that you'll speed every step of construction and avoid costly building errors by ordering enough sets to go around. Each tradesperson wants a set — the general contractor and all subcontractors; foundation, electrical, plumbing, heating/air conditioning and framers. Don't forget your lending institution, building department and, of course, a set for yourself. * Recommended For Construction **

The Minimum 4-Set Construction Package

If you're comfortable with arduous follow-up, this package can save you a few dollars by giving you the option of passing down plan sets as work progresses. You might have enough copies to go around if work goes exactly as scheduled and no plans are lost or damaged by subcontrators. But for only $50 more, the 8-set package eliminates these worries.
** Recommended For Bidding **

The Single Study Set

We offer this set so you can study the blueprints to plan your dream home in detail. They are stamped "study set only-not for construction", and you cannot build a home from them. In pursuant to copyright laws, it is illegal to reproduce any blueprint.

Our Reorder and Exchange Policies:

If you find after your initial purchase that you require additional sets of plans you may purchase them from us at special reorder prices (please call for pricing details) provided that you reorder within 6 months of your original order date. There is a $28 reorder processing fee that is charged on all reorders. For more information on reordering plans please contact our Customer Service Department at (860) 343-5977.

We want you to find your dream home from our wide selection of home plans. However, if for some reason you find that the plan you have purchased from us does not meet your needs, then you may exchange that plan for any other plan in our collection. We allow you sixty days from your original invoice date to make an exchange. At the time of the exchange you will be charged a processing fee of 15% of the total amount of your original order plus the difference in price between the plans (if applicable) plus the cost to ship the new plans to you. Call our Customer Service Department at (860) 343-5977 for more information. Please Note: Reproducible vellums can only be exchanged if they are unopened.

Important Shipping Information

Please refer to the shipping charts on the order form for service availability for your specific plan number. Our delivery service must have a street address or Rural Route Box number — never a post office box. (PLEASE NOTE: Supplying a P.O. Box number only will delay the shipping of your order.) Use a work address if no one is home during the day.

Orders being shipped to APO or FPO must go via First Class Mail. Please include the proper postage.

For our International Customers, only Certified bank checks and money orders are accepted and must be payable in U.S. currency. For speed, we ship international orders Air Parcel Post. Please refer to the chart for the correct shipping cost.

Important Canadian Shipping Information

To our friends in Canada, we have a plan design affiliate in Kitchener, Ontario. This relationship will help you avoid the delays and charges associated with shipments from the United States. Moreover, our affiliate is familiar with the building requirements in your community and country. We prefer payments in U.S. Currency. If you, however, are sending Canadian funds please add 40% to the prices of the plans and shipping fees.

An Important Note About Building Code Requirements:

All plans are drawn to conform to one or more of the industry's major national building standards. However, due to the variety of local building regulations, your plan may need to be modified to comply with local requirements — snow loads, energy loads, seismic zones, etc. Do check them fully and consult your local building officials.

A few states require that all building plans used be drawn by an architect registered in that state. While having your plans reviewed and stamped by such an architect may be prudent, laws requiring non-conforming plans like ours to be completely redrawn forces you to unnecessarily pay very large fees. If your state has such a law, we strongly recommend you contact your state representative to protest.

The rendering, floor plans, and technical information contained within this publication are not guaranteed to be totally accurate. Consequently, no information from this publication should be used either as a guide to constructing a home or for estimating the cost of building a home. Complete blueprints must be purchased for such purposes.

BEFORE ORDERING PLEASE READ ALL ORDERING INFORMATION

MasterCard

Please submit all Canadian plan orders to:
Garlinghouse Company
60 Baffin Place, Unit #5, Waterloo, Ontario N2V 1Z7
Canadian Customers Only: 1-800-561-4169/Fax #: 1-800-719-3291
Customer Service #: 1-519-746-4169

ORDER TOLL FREE — 1-800-235-5700
Monday-Friday 8:00 a.m. to 8:00 p.m. Eastern Time
or FAX your Credit Card order to 1-860-343-5984
All foreign residents call 1-800-343-5977

Please have ready: 1. Your credit card number 2. The plan number 3. The order code number ⇨ H9LX5

Garlinghouse 1999 Blueprint Price Code Schedule

Additional sets with original order $35

PRICE CODE	A	B	C	D	E	F	G	H
SETS OF SAME PLAN	$405	$445	$490	$530	$570	$615	$655	$695
4 SETS OF SAME PLAN	$355	$395	$440	$480	$520	$565	$605	$645
1 SINGLE SET OF PLANS	$305	$345	$390	$430	$470	$515	$555	$595
VELLUMS	$515	$560	$610	$655	$700	$750	$795	$840
MATERIALS LIST	$60	$60	$65	$65	$70	$70	$75	$75
ITEMIZED ZIP QUOTE	$75	$80	$85	$85	$90	$90	$95	$95

Shipping — (Plans 1-84999)

	1-3 Sets	4-6 Sets	7+ & Vellums
Standard Delivery (UPS 2-Day)	$25.00	$30.00	$35.00
Overnight Delivery	$35.00	$40.00	$45.00

Shipping — (Plans 85000-99999)

	1-3 Sets	4-6 Sets	7+ & Vellums
Ground Delivery (7-10 Days)	$15.00	$20.00	$25.00
Express Delivery (3-5 Days)	$20.00	$25.00	$30.00

International Shipping & Handling

	1-3 Sets	4-6 Sets	7+ & Vellums
Regular Delivery Canada (7-10 Days)	$25.00	$30.00	$35.00
Express Delivery Canada (5-6 Days)	$40.00	$45.00	$50.00
Overseas Delivery Airmail (2-3 Weeks)	$50.00	$60.00	$65.00

Option Key

ZIP = Zip Quote Available
RR = Right Reading Reverse
Duplex Plan
ML = Materials List Available

Index

PLAN NO. 99485

Design by
Design Basics, Inc.

Refer to **Pricing Schedule F** on the order form for pricing information

Southern Mansion

- This plan features:
  - — Four bedrooms
  - — Two full and one half baths
- Covered Porches, intricate detailing and illuminating transom windows enhance this home
- The prominent Entry opens to the formal Dining and Living rooms
- The grand Family Room is warmed by a fireplace
- French doors open to the Master Suite, which is topped by a decorative ceiling and includes his-n-her walk-in closets, a large dressing area, two vanities, an oval whirlpool bath
- The secondary Bedrooms have private access to a full Bath

FIRST FLOOR — 1,598 SQ. FT.
SECOND FLOOR — 1,675 SQ. FT.

TOTAL LIVING AREA:
3,273 SQ. FT.

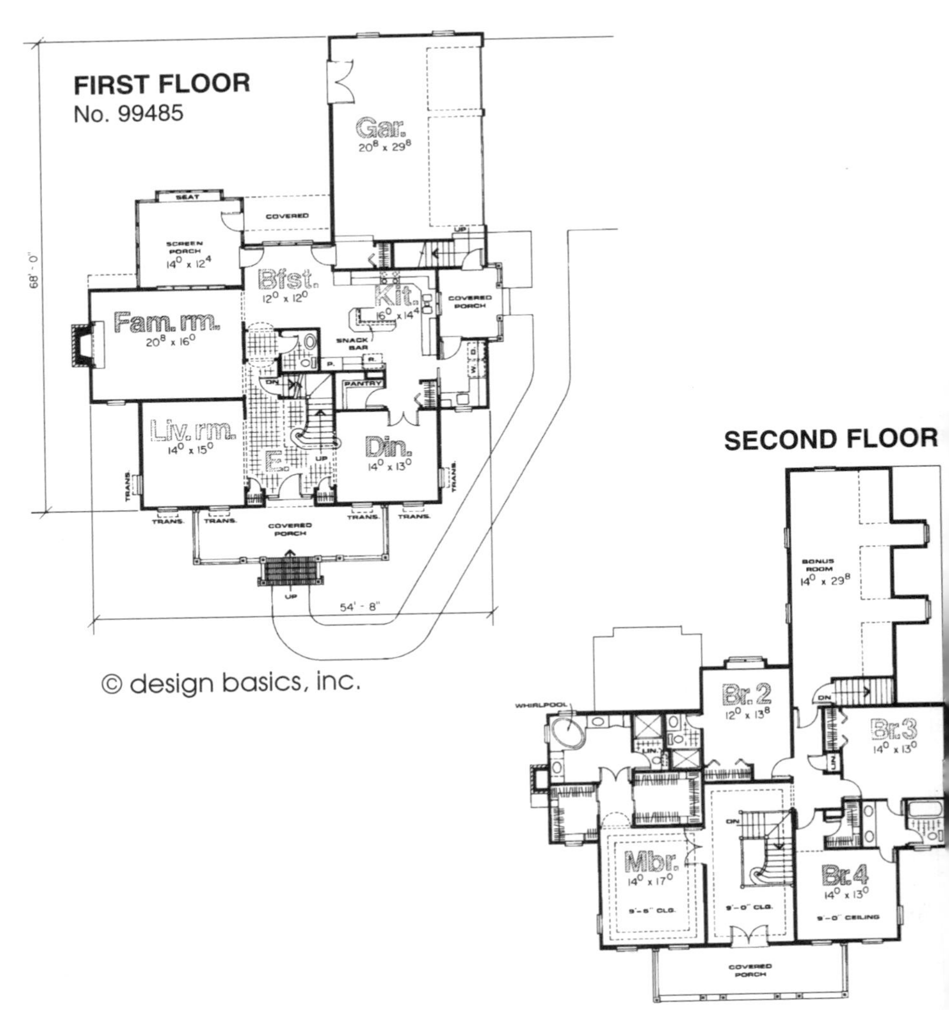
FIRST FLOOR
No. 99485
Gar. 20⁸ x 29⁸
SCREEN PORCH 14⁰ x 12⁴
COVERED
Bfst. 12⁰ x 12⁰
Kit. 16⁰ x 14⁴
COVERED PORCH
Fam. rm. 20⁸ x 16⁰
SNACK BAR
PANTRY
Liv. rm. 14⁰ x 15⁰
E.
Din. 14⁰ x 13⁰
COVERED PORCH
68'-0"
54'-8"
© design basics, inc.
SECOND FLOOR
BONUS ROOM 14⁰ x 29⁸
WHIRLPOOL
Br. 2 12⁰ x 13⁸
Br. 3 14⁰ x 13⁰
Mbr. 14⁰ x 17⁰
Br. 4 14⁰ x 13⁰
9'-0" CEILING
COVERED PORCH